FUNDAMENTALS OF
Derivatives Markets

The Prentice Hall Series in Finance

Alexander/Sharpe/Bailey
Fundamentals of Investments

Andersen
Global Derivatives: A Strategic Risk Management Perspective

Bear/Moldonado-Bear
Free Markets, Finance, Ethics, and Law

Berk/DeMarzo
*Corporate Finance**
*Corporate Finance: The Core**

Bierman/Smidt
The Capital Budgeting Decision: Economic Analysis of Investment Projects

Bodie/Merton/Cleeton
Financial Economics

Click/Coval
The Theory and Practice of International Financial Management

Copeland/Weston/Shastri
Financial Theory and Corporate Policy

Cornwall/Vang/Hartman
Entrepreneurial Financial Management

Cox/Rubinstein
Options Markets

Dorfman
Introduction to Risk Management and Insurance

Dietrich
Financial Services and Financial Institutions: Value Creation in Theory and Practice

Dufey/Giddy
Cases in International Finance

Eakins
Finance in .learn

Eiteman/Stonehill/Moffett
Multinational Business Finance

Emery/Finnerty/Stowe
Corporate Financial Management

Fabozzi
Bond Markets, Analysis and Strategies

Fabozzi/Modigliani
Capital Markets: Institutions and Instruments

Fabozzi/Modigliani/Jones/Ferri
Foundations of Financial Markets and Institutions

Finkler
Financial Management for Public, Health, and Not-for-Profit Organizations

Francis/Ibbotson
Investments: A Global Perspective

Fraser/Ormiston
Understanding Financial Statements

Geisst
Investment Banking in the Financial System

Gitman
*Principles of Managerial Finance**
*Principles of Managerial Finance–Brief Edition**

Gitman/Joehnk
*Fundamentals of Investing**

Gitman/Madura
Introduction to Finance

Guthrie/Lemon
Mathematics of Interest Rates and Finance

Haugen
The Inefficient Stock Market: What Pays Off and Why
Modern Investment Theory
The New Finance: Overreaction, Complexity, and Uniqueness

Holden
Excel Modeling in the Fundamentals of Corporate Finance
Excel Modeling in the Fundamentals of Investments
Excel Modeling in Investments
Excel Modeling in Corporate Finance

Hughes/MacDonald
International Banking: Text and Cases

Hull
Fundamentals of Futures and Options Markets
Options, Futures, and Other Derivatives
Risk Management and Financial Institutions

Keown
Personal Finance: Turning Money into Wealth

Keown/Martin/Petty/Scott
Financial Management: Principles and Applications
Foundations of Finance: The Logic and Practice of Financial Management

Kim/Nofsinger
Corporate Governance

Levy/Post
Investments

May/May/Andrew
Effective Writing: A Handbook for Finance People

Madura
Personal Finance

Marthinsen
Risk Takers: Uses and Abuses of Financial Derivatives

McDonald
Derivatives Markets
Fundamentals of Derivatives Markets

Megginson
Corporate Finance Theory

Melvin
International Money and Finance

Mishkin/Eakins
Financial Markets and Institutions

Moffett
Cases in International Finance

Moffett/Stonehill/Eiteman
Fundamentals of Multinational Finance

Nofsinger
Psychology of Investing

Ogden/Jen/O'Connor
Advanced Corporate Finance

Pennacchi
Theory of Asset Pricing

Rejda
Principles of Risk Management and Insurance

Schoenebeck
Interpreting and Analyzing Financial Statements

Scott/Martin/Petty/Keown/Thatcher
Cases in Finance

Seiler
Performing Financial Studies: A Methodological Cookbook

Shapiro
Capital Budgeting and Investment Analysis

Sharpe/Alexander/Bailey
Investments

Solnik/McLeavey
Global Investments

Stretcher/Michael
Cases in Financial Management

Titman/Martin
Valuation: The Art and Science of Corporate Investment Decisions

Trivoli
Personal Portfolio Management: Fundamentals and Strategies

Van Horne
Financial Management and Policy
Financial Market Rates and Flows

Van Horne/Wachowicz
Fundamentals of Financial Management

Vaughn
Financial Planning for the Entrepreneur

Weston/Mitchel/Mulherin
Takeovers, Restructuring, and Corporate Governance

Winger/Frasca
Personal Finance

* denotes myfinancelab titles
Log onto www.myfinancelab.com to learn more

FUNDAMENTALS OF Derivatives Markets

Robert L. McDonald
Northwestern University
Kellogg School of Management

PEARSON
Addison
Wesley

Boston San Francisco New York
London Toronto Sydney Tokyo Singapore Madrid
Mexico City Munich Paris Cape Town Hong Kong Montreal

Editor-in-Chief: Denise Clinton
Executive Editor: Donna Battista
Assistant Editor: Kerri McQueen
Assistant Development Editor: Sara Holliday
Managing Editor: Nancy Fenton
Senior Marketing Manager: Andrew Watts
Senior Media Producer: Bethany Tidd
Supplements Editor: Heather McNally
Project Management and Composition: Windfall Software, using ZzTEX
Copyeditor: Richard Camp
Proofreader: Jennifer McClain
Indexer: Steve Rath
Cover Designer: Barbara Atkinson
Cover and Interior Image: Private Collection/Art for After Hours/SuperStock
Senior Media Buyer: Ginny Michaud
Senior Manufacturing Buyer: Carol Melville

Many of the designations used by manufacturers and sellers to distinguish their products are claimed as trademarks. Where those designations appear in this book, and Prentice Hall was aware of a trademark claim, the designations have been printed in initial caps or all caps.

Library of Congress Cataloging-in-Publication Data

McDonald, Robert L. (Robert Lynch), 1954–
  Fundamentals of derivatives markets / Robert L. McDonald.
    p. cm.
  Includes bibliographical references and index.
  ISBN-13: 978-0-321-35717-5 (alk. paper)
  ISBN-10: 0-321-35717-5 (alk. paper)
  1. Derivative securities. I. Title.
  HG6024.A3M395 2009
  332.64′57—dc22
                                                       2008003937

Copyright © 2009 by Pearson Education, Inc.

For information on obtaining permission for use of material in this work, please submit a written request to Pearson Education, Inc., Rights and Contract Department, 75 Arlington Street, Suite 300, Boston, MA 02116 or fax your request to (617) 848-7047.

All rights reserved. No part of this publication may be reproduced, stored in a retrieval system, or transmitted, in any form or by any means, electronic, mechanical, photocopying, recording, or any toher media embodiments now known or hereafter to become known, without the prior written permission of the publisher. Printed in the United States of America.

ISBN-13: 9780321357175
ISBN-10: 0321357175

1 2 3 4 5 6 7 8 9 10—CRW—12 11 10 09 08

For Irene, Claire, David, and Henry

Brief Contents

Preface xix

1 **Introduction to Derivatives** 1

PART ONE Insurance, Hedging, and Simple Strategies 27

2 **An Introduction to Forwards and Options** 29

3 **Insurance, Collars, and Other Strategies** 61

4 **Introduction to Risk Management** 93

PART TWO Forwards, Futures, and Swaps 123

5 **Financial Forwards and Futures** 125

6 **The Wide World of Futures Contracts** 157

7 **Interest Rate Forwards and Futures** 183

8 **Swaps** 219

PART THREE Options 247

9 **Parity and Other Option Relationships** 249

10 **Binomial Option Pricing** 277

11 **The Black-Scholes Formula** 309

PART FOUR Financial Engineering and Applications 347

12 Financial Engineering and Security Design 349

13 Corporate Applications 383

14 Real Options 423

APPENDIX A The Greek Alphabet 453

APPENDIX B Continuous Compounding 455

Glossary 461

References 473

Index 481

Contents

Preface xix

Chapter 1
Introduction to Derivatives 1

1.1 What Is a Derivative? 2
1.2 An Overview of Financial Markets 2
    Trading of Financial Assets 3
    Measures of Market Size and Activity 4
    Stock and Bond Markets 5
    Derivatives Markets 6
1.3 The Role of Financial Markets 11
    Financial Markets and the Averages 11
    Risk Sharing 12
1.4 Ways to Think about Derivatives 14
    Uses of Derivatives 15
    Perspectives on Derivatives 16
    Financial Engineering and Security Design 16
1.5 Buying and Short-Selling Financial Assets 17
    Transaction Costs and the Bid-Ask Spread 17
    Ways to Buy or Sell 18
    Short-Selling 19
    The Lease Rate of an Asset 21
Chapter Summary 22
Further Reading 23
Problems 23

PART ONE
Insurance, Hedging, and Simple Strategies 27

Chapter 2
An Introduction to Forwards and Options 29

- 2.1 Forward Contracts 29
  - The Payoff on a Forward Contract 31
  - Graphing the Payoff on a Forward Contract 33
  - Comparing a Forward and Outright Purchase 34
  - Zero-Coupon Bonds in Payoff and Profit Diagrams 36
  - Cash Settlement Versus Delivery 38
  - Credit Risk 38
- 2.2 Call Options 39
  - Option Terminology 40
  - Payoff and Profit for a Purchased Call Option 42
  - Payoff and Profit for a Written Call Option 44
- 2.3 Put Options 46
  - Payoff and Profit for a Purchased Put Option 47
  - Payoff and Profit for a Written Put Option 48
  - The "Moneyness" of an Option 50
- 2.4 Summary of Forward and Option Positions 51
  - Long Positions 51
  - Short Positions 52
- 2.5 Options Are Insurance 54
  - Homeowner's Insurance Is a Put Option 54
  - But I Thought Insurance Was Prudent and Put Options Were Risky . . . 55
  - Call Options Are Also Insurance 56

Chapter Summary 56
Further Reading 57
Problems 58

Chapter 3
Insurance, Collars, and Other Strategies 61

- 3.1 Basic Insurance Strategies 61
  - Insuring a Long Position: Floors 61
  - Insuring a Short Position: Caps 65
  - Selling Insurance 66
- 3.2 Using Options to Create Synthetic Forwards 68
  - Put-Call Parity 70

   3.3 **Spreads and Collars** 72
      Bull and Bear Spreads 73
      Box Spreads 74
      Ratio Spreads 75
      Collars 76
   3.4 **Speculating on Volatility** 79
      Straddles 79
      Butterfly Spreads 82
   3.5 **Application: Equity-Linked CDs** 84
      Graphing the Payoff on the CD 85
      Economics of the CD 85
      Why Equity-Linked CDs? 86
Chapter Summary 87
Further Reading 89
Problems 89

Chapter 4
Introduction to Risk Management 93

   4.1 **Basic Risk Management: The Producer's Perspective** 93
      Hedging with a Forward Contract 94
      Insurance: Guaranteeing a Minimum Price with a Put Option 96
      Insuring by Selling a Call 97
      Adjusting the Amount of Insurance 99
   4.2 **Basic Risk Management: The Buyer's Perspective** 100
      Hedging with a Forward Contract 101
      Insurance: Guaranteeing a Maximum Price with a Call Option 101
   4.3 **Why Do Firms Manage Risk?** 103
      Reasons to Hedge 104
      Reasons *Not* to Hedge 106
      Empirical Evidence on Hedging 107
   4.4 **Golddiggers Revisited** 108
      Selling the Gain: Collars 109
      Other Collar Strategies 113
      Paylater Strategies 113
   4.5 **Basis Risk** 114
      Hedging Jet Fuel with Crude Oil 115
      Stack and Strip Hedges 115
Chapter Summary 117
Further Reading 118
Problems 119

PART TWO
Forwards, Futures, and Swaps 123

Chapter 5
Financial Forwards and Futures 125

   5.1 Alternative Ways to Buy a Stock 125
   5.2 Prepaid Forward Contracts on Stock 127
      Pricing the Prepaid Forward by Analogy 127
      Pricing the Prepaid Forward by Discounted Present Value 127
      Pricing the Prepaid Forward by Arbitrage 128
      Pricing Prepaid Forwards with Dividends 129
   5.3 Forward Contracts on Stock 132
      Creating a Synthetic Forward Contract 133
      Synthetic Forwards in Market-Making and Arbitrage 135
      No-Arbitrage Bounds with Transaction Costs 136
      Quasi-Arbitrage 137
      Does the Forward Price Predict the Future Price? 137
      An Interpretation of the Forward Pricing Formula 139
   5.4 Futures Contracts 139
      The S&P 500 Futures Contract 140
      Margins and Marking-to-Market 142
      Comparing Futures and Forward Prices 145
   5.5 Uses of Index Futures 145
      Asset Allocation 146
      Cross-Hedging with Index Futures 147
   Chapter Summary 150
   Further Reading 151
   Problems 152

Chapter 6
The Wide World of Futures Contracts 157

   6.1 Currency Contracts 157
      Currency Prepaid Forward 157
      Currency Forward 159
      Covered Interest Arbitrage 159
   6.2 Eurodollar Futures 160
   6.3 An Introduction to Commodity Futures 164
      Seasonality and Storage Costs 164
      The Forward Price and the Expected Commodity Price 166
      The Commodity Lease Rate 166

6.4 Energy Futures   168
    Electricity   168
    Natural Gas   169
    Crude Oil   171
6.5 Weather and Housing Futures   173
    Weather Derivatives   174
    Housing Futures   175
Chapter Summary   177
Further Reading   178
Problems   179

Chapter 7
Interest Rate Forwards and Futures   183

7.1 Bond Basics   183
    Zero-Coupon Bonds   185
    Implied Forward Rates   186
    Coupon Bonds   188
    Zeros from Coupons   189
    Interpreting the Coupon Rate   190
    Continuously Compounded Yields   191
7.2 Forward Rate Agreements, Eurodollars, and Hedging   192
    Forward Rate Agreements   193
    Synthetic FRAs   194
    Eurodollar Futures versus FRAs   196
    Interest Rate Strips and Stacks   197
7.3 Duration and Convexity   198
    Duration   198
    Duration Matching   201
    Convexity   202
7.4 Treasury-Bond and Treasury-Note Futures   204
7.5 Repurchase Agreements   207
Chapter Summary   209
Further Reading   210
Problems   210
7.A Interest Rate and Bond Price Conventions   214
    Bonds   215
    Bills   216

Chapter 8
Swaps   219

8.1 An Example of a Commodity Swap   220
    Physical Versus Financial Settlement   221
    Why Is the Swap Price Not $20.50?   222

   The Swap Counterparty 223
   The Market Value of a Swap 225
 8.2 Interest Rate Swaps 227
   A Simple Interest Rate Swap 227
   Pricing and the Swap Counterparty 229
   Computing the Swap Rate in General 230
   Deferred Swaps 232
   The Swap Curve 233
   Amortizing and Accreting Swaps 234
 8.3 Currency Swaps 235
   Currency Swap Formulas 238
   Other Currency Swaps 239
 8.4 Swaptions 240
 8.5 Total Return Swaps 241
Chapter Summary 244
Further Reading 244
Problems 245

PART THREE
Options 247

Chapter 9
Parity and Other Option Relationships 249

 9.1 Put-Call Parity 250
   Options on Stocks 251
   Options on Currencies 254
   Options on Bonds 254
 9.2 Generalized Parity and Exchange Options 255
   Options to Exchange Stock 256
   What Are Calls and Puts? 257
   Currency Options 258
 9.3 Comparing Options with Respect to Style, Maturity, and Strike 260
   European Versus American Options 260
   Maximum and Minimum Option Prices 261
   Early Exercise for American Options 262
   Time to Expiration 264
   Different Strike Prices 265
Chapter Summary 270
Further Reading 271
Problems 272

Chapter 10
Binomial Option Pricing 277

- 10.1 A One-Period Binomial Tree 277
  - Computing the Option Price 278
  - The Binomial Solution 280
  - Arbitraging a Mispriced Option 282
  - A Graphical Interpretation of the Binomial Formula 283
  - Pricing with Dividends 283
  - Risk-Neutral Pricing 285
  - Constructing a Binomial Tree 286
  - Another One-Period Example 287
  - Summary 288
- 10.2 Two or More Binomial Periods 288
  - A Two-Period European Call 289
  - Many Binomial Periods 291
- 10.3 Put Options 293
  - European Put 293
  - American Put 294
- 10.4 American Options 294
- 10.5 Options on Other Assets 295
  - Option on a Stock Index 295
  - Options on Currencies 297
  - Options on Futures Contracts 297
  - Summary 299

Chapter Summary 301
Further Reading 301
Problems 301

- 10.A Lognormality and the Binomial Model 304
- 10.B Alternative Binomial Pricing Models 307
  - The Cox-Ross-Rubinstein Binomial Tree 307
  - The Jarrow-Rudd Tree 308

Chapter 11
The Black-Scholes Formula 309

- 11.1 Introduction to the Black-Scholes Formula 309
  - Call Options 310
  - Put Options 313
  - What Assumptions Underlie the Black-Scholes Formula? 314
- 11.2 Applying the Formula to Other Assets 314
  - Options on Stocks with Discrete Dividends 315
  - Options on Currencies 316
  - Options on Futures 316

11.3 Option Greeks 317
  Definition of the Greeks 317
  Greek Measures for Portfolios 324
  Option Elasticity 325
11.4 Delta-Hedging 330
  Option Risk in the Absence of Hedging 330
  An Example of Delta-Hedging 331
  Interpreting Market-Maker Profit 333
11.5 Volatility 335
  Historical Volatility 335
  Implied Volatility 336
  Trading Volatility 339
Chapter Summary 341
Further Reading 342
Problems 342

PART FOUR
Financial Engineering and Applications 347

Chapter 12
Financial Engineering and Security Design 349

12.1 The Modigliani-Miller Theorem 349
12.2 Structured Notes Without Options 350
  Zero-Coupon Bonds Paying Cash 351
  Coupon Bonds Paying Cash 351
  Equity-Linked Bonds 352
  Commodity-Linked Bonds 355
  Currency-Linked Bonds 357
12.3 Structured Notes with Options 358
  Coupon Bonds with Options 358
  Equity-Linked Notes with Options 359
  Valuing and Structuring an Equity-Linked CD 361
  Alternative Structures 363
  Application: Variable Prepaid Forwards 364
12.4 Engineered Solutions for Golddiggers 366
  Gold-Linked Notes 366
  Notes with Embedded Options 367

12.5 **Credit Structures** 369
   Collateralized Debt Obligations 370
   Credit Default Swaps 373
   CDS Indexes 376
Chapter Summary 378
Further Reading 379
Problems 379

Chapter 13
Corporate Applications 383

13.1 **Equity, Debt, and Warrants** 383
   Debt and Equity as Options 383
   Valuing Credit Guarantees 386
   Leverage and the Expected Return on Debt and Equity 388
   Multiple Debt Issues 392
   Warrants 393
   Convertible Bonds 394
   Callable Bonds 397
   Bond Valuation Based on the Stock Price 401
   Put Warrants 402
13.2 **Compensation Options** 403
   Whose Valuation? 406
   Valuation Inputs 406
   Level 3 Communications 409
13.3 **The Use of Collars in Acquisitions** 412
   The Northrop Grumman–TRW Merger 413
Chapter Summary 417
Further Reading 417
Problems 418

Chapter 14
Real Options 423

14.1 **DCF and Option Valuation for a Single Cash Flow** 424
   Project 1 424
   Project 2 428
   Project 3 431
   Summary 432
14.2 **Multiperiod Valuations** 433
   Project 1 434
   Project 2 436

Project 3   437
Summary   437
14.3 Examples of Real Options in Practice   438
Commodity Extraction   438
Peak-Load Electricity Generation   442
Pharmaceutical Research and Development   446

Chapter Summary   448
Further Reading   448
Problems   449
14.A The Relationship Between DCF and Risk-Neutral Valuation   451

Appendix A
The Greek Alphabet   453

Appendix B
Continuous Compounding   455
B.1 The Language of Interest Rates   455
B.2 The Logarithmic and Exponential Functions   456
Changing Interest Rates   457
Symmetry for Increases and Decreases   458

Problems   459

Glossary   461

References   473

Index   481

Preface

Thirty years ago derivatives was an esoteric and specialized subject. Today, a basic knowledge of derivatives is necessary to understand modern finance. For example, corporations routinely hedge and insure using derivatives, finance activities with structured products, and use derivatives models in capital budgeting. I wrote this book to help you to understand the derivative instruments that exist, how they are used, who sells them, how they are priced, and how the tools and concepts are useful more broadly in finance.

I published the first edition of my book, *Derivatives Markets*, six years ago. Now in its second edition, *Derivatives Markets* was based on my teaching notes for two MBA courses at Northwestern University's Kellogg School of Management. A number of readers requested a briefer book that would be suitable for a one-semester course for either undergraduates or MBAs. *Fundamentals of Derivatives Markets* is the answer to that request. It provides a general introduction to derivative products (principally futures, options, swaps, and structured products), the markets in which they trade, and applications.

Derivatives is necessarily an analytical subject, but I have tried throughout to emphasize intuition and to provide a common sense way to think about the various formulas that are essential in a derivatives course. I also supply a number of concrete examples and illustrations of derivatives in practice. If you understand basic financial concepts such as present value and elementary statistical concepts such as mean and standard deviation, this book should be accessible to you.

PLAN OF THE BOOK

The book has four parts plus appendixes. **Part 1** introduces the basic building blocks of derivatives: forward contracts and call and put options. Chapters 2 and 3 examine these basic instruments and some common hedging and investment strategies. Chapter 4 illustrates the use of derivatives as risk management tools and discusses why firms might care about risk management. These chapters focus on understanding the contracts and strategies, but not on pricing.

Part 2 considers the pricing of forward, futures, and swaps contracts. In these contracts, you are obligated to buy an asset at a pre-specified price, at a future date. The main question is: What is the pre-specified price, and how is it determined? Chapter 5 examines forwards and futures on financial assets, Chapter 6 discusses commodities, and Chapter 7 looks at bond and interest rate forward contracts. Chapter 8 shows how swap prices can be deduced from forward prices.

Part 3 studies option pricing. Chapter 9 develops intuition about options prior to delving into the mechanics of option pricing. Chapter 10 covers binomial option pricing and Chapter 11, the Black-Scholes formula, option Greeks, delta-hedging, and volatility.

Part 4 examines applications. Chapter 12 covers financial engineering, which is the creation of new financial products from the derivatives building blocks in earlier chapters. This chapter includes a discussion of credit derivatives. Debt and equity pricing, compensation options, and mergers are covered in Chapter 13. Chapter 14 studies real options—the application of derivatives models to the valuation and management of physical investments.

Throughout all four parts there are boxes that provide examples related to the material.

EXAMPLES AND CALCULATIONS

The calculations in this book can be replicated using either Excel® or OpenOffice. Spreadsheets for both programs that contain pricing functions are included on the CD-ROM that comes with the book. (Since OpenOffice runs on Windows,® OS X, and Linux,® the option pricing functions will run on all three operating systems.) These spreadsheets will allow you to experiment with the pricing models and build your own spreadsheets. Since you may not be familiar with OpenOffice, I will say more about it below. In both Excel and OpenOffice you can easily incorporate the option pricing functions into your own spreadsheets, and you can examine and modify the code. Standard built-in spreadsheet functions are also mentioned throughout the book.

Reproducing the Calculations in the Book

Many of the numerical examples in the text display intermediate steps to assist you in following the calculations. In most cases it will also be possible for you to create a spreadsheet and compute the same answers starting from the basic assumptions. However, numbers displayed in the text are generally rounded to three or four decimal points, while spreadsheet calculations have many more significant digits. In cases where the displayed result differs from what you would obtain in a spreadsheet, I have used the answer you would obtain by mimicking the calculations in a spreadsheet. The displayed calculations should help you follow the logic of a calculation, but you will not necessarily match the final result by mimicking the displayed calculations. A spreadsheet will be helpful in reproducing the final result.

Spreadsheets

The basic option pricing spreadsheet accompanying this book has a version for Excel (.xls) and a version for OpenOffice (.ods). The option pricing functions in Excel are written in Visual Basic® for Applications, and those in OpenOffice are written in StarBasic. The two macro languages are largely compatible. The significant differences occur when you want to access spreadsheet features from within macros. It is possible that a future version of OpenOffice will support VBA directly.

For those readers who are unfamiliar with OpenOffice, I will say a little more about the program and why I have included spreadsheets for it. Microsoft® Excel is by far the most commonly used spreadsheet, but Microsoft Office for Mac 2008 no longer supports VBA macros. The Excel spreadsheets that accompany this book therefore will not work on an Apple computer running the latest version of Microsoft Office. Less surprisingly, Microsoft has never supported users who wish to run Linux. OpenOffice, by contrast, is a free, open source office suite that runs on Windows, OS X, and Linux, and the same macros run on all three operating systems. I have found the latest version of OpenOffice to be a reliable, high-quality application.

If you are going to use OpenOffice, there are two things you need to know. First, OpenOffice can generally read Excel spreadsheets (except for macros and some other advanced features), but Excel cannot read OpenOffice spreadsheets (which are in Open Document Format (ODF)) unless you obtain the Sun™ ODF plugin from Sun's website. Second, when you enter a function, OpenOffice uses a semicolon rather than a comma as a delimiter. Whereas in Excel you would write "=Max(a1,b1)", in OpenOffice you write "=Max(a1;b1)".

SUPPLEMENTS

A robust package of ancillary materials for both instructors and students accompanies the text.

Instructor's Resources

For instructors, an extensive set of online tools is available for download from the catalog page for *Derivatives Markets* at www.pearsonhighered.com/finance:

- An online **Instructor's Solutions Manual**, adapted and updated for this edition by Mark Cassano, contains complete, detailed solutions to all end-of-chapter problems in the text and spreadsheet solutions to selected problems. The Instructor's Solutions Manual is available as Microsoft Word and Adobe PDF files.

- The online **Test Bank** by Matthew Will, University of Indianapolis, is available in various electronic formats, including Windows or Macintosh TestGen files, Microsoft Word files, and Adobe PDF files.

- Online **PowerPoint slides,** developed by Charles Cao, reviewed and updated for this edition by Matthew Will, provide lecture outlines and selected art from the book. Copies of the slides can be downsized and distributed to students to facilitate note taking during class.
- The **Instructor's Resource CD-ROM** contains the Test Bank files (TestGen, Word, and PDF), the Instructor's Solutions Manual files (Word and PDF), and PowerPoint files.

Student Resources

A printed **Student Solutions Manual**, by Mark Cassano, provides answers to all the even-numbered problems in the textbook.

The printed **Practice Problems and Solutions**, by Mark Cassano, contains additional problems and step-by-step worked-out solutions for each chapter of the textbook.

Spreadsheets with user-defined option pricing functions in Excel and OpenOffice are included on a CD-ROM packaged with the book. The code for both are accessible and modifiable using the editors built into Microsoft Office and OpenOffice. These spreadsheets and any updates are also posted on www.pearsonhighered.com/finance.

Acknowledgments

In the course of writing two editions of *Derivatives Markets*, I received comments, suggestions, and help from numerous individuals, who I thank in *Derivatives Markets*. Many of those comments have indirectly improved this book as well.

In preparing this new version, I received invaluable assistance from Mark Cassano, who carefully read through the material and end-of-chapter problems. Kellogg PhD students Vineet Bhagwat and especially Jonathan Brogaard provided very helpful research assistance. Numerous other students, colleagues, and readers provided helpful comments and feedback on *Derivatives Markets,* and many of these are reflected in this book.

Reviewers who contributed specifically to this book include R. Brian Balyeat (Xavier University), Tom Barkley (Syracuse University), Larry Belcher (Stetson University), Charles Cao (Pennsylvania State University), Carl Chen (University of Dayton), Michael Gallmeyer (Texas A&M University), James Greenleaf (Lehigh University), John Kensinger (University of North Texas), Gary Koppenhaver (Iowa State University), Raman Kumar (Virginia Tech University), Robert Losey (American University), Vivian Okere (Providence College), Brian Prucyk (Marquette University), Adam Schwartz (Washington and Lee University), Helen Simon (Florida International University), Damir Tokic (University of Houston), Michael J. Tomas III (University of Vermont), Alan Tucker (Pace University), Gautam Vora (University of New Mexico), Peihwang Wei (University of New Orleans), and Alice Xie (University of Michigan-Dearborn).

For conversations and helpful suggestions, special thanks are due to Deborah Lucas and Alan Marcus.

Thanks to David Hait, president of OptionMetrics, for permission to include options data on the CD-ROM.

The editorial and production team at Pearson has always made it clear that a high-quality book was their principal goal. I remain fortunate in having had the project overseen by Pearson's talented and tireless Finance Editor, Donna Battista. Project Manager Sara Holliday offered a helpful sounding board. Production Supervisor Nancy Fenton marshalled forces to turn manuscript into a physical book. Among those forces were Paul C. Anagnostopoulos of Windfall Software, and Richard Camp, Jennifer McClain, Laurel Muller, Steve Rath, and Jacqui Scarlott. The design team of Regina Hagen Kolenda and Barbara Atkinson did an excellent job.

The Pearson team and I have tried hard to minimize errors. Nevertheless, of course, I alone bear responsibility for remaining errors. Errata and software updates will be available at www.prenhall.com/mcdonald. Please let us know if you do find errors so we can update the errata list.

As always, my deepest and most heartfelt thanks go to my family for their tolerance, love, and support. This book is dedicated to my wife, Irene Freeman, and children Claire, David, and Henry.

RLM

Robert L. McDonald is Erwin P. Nemmers Distinguished Professor of Finance at Northwestern University's Kellogg School of Management, where he has taught since 1984. He has been co-Editor of the Review of Financial Studies *and has been Associate Editor of the* Journal of Finance, Journal of Financial and Quantitative Analysis, Management Science, *and other journals. He has a BA in Economics from the University of North Carolina at Chapel Hill and a PhD in Economics from MIT.*

FUNDAMENTALS OF
Derivatives Markets

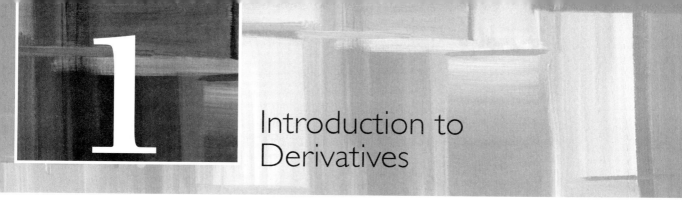

1 Introduction to Derivatives

Risk is the central element that influences financial behavior.
—*Robert C. Merton (1999)*

The world of finance has changed dramatically in recent decades. Electronic processing, globalization, and deregulation have all affected what is traded and how trading occurs. The set of financial claims traded today is quite different than it was in 1970. In addition to ordinary stocks and bonds, there is now a wide array of products collectively referred to as financial derivatives: futures, options, swaps, and other, more exotic, financial products. These products trade in enormous volumes. You have undoubtedly read stories where derivatives figure prominently: Procter & Gamble lost $150 million in 1994, Barings Bank lost $1.3 billion in 1995, Long-Term Capital Management lost $3.5 billion in 1998 (according to some press accounts, almost creating a global financial crisis), and the hedge fund Amaranth lost $6 billion in 2006.[1] At the time of this writing in 2007, derivatives created from risky mortgages were roiling financial markets.

What is *not* in the headlines is the fact that, most of the time, for most companies and most users, these financial products are an everyday part of business. Just as companies routinely issue debt and equity, they also routinely use swaps to fix the cost of production inputs, futures contracts to hedge foreign exchange risk, and options to compensate employees, to mention just a few examples.

In addition to their widespread use, another important reason to understand derivatives is that the language and theory of financial derivatives now pervade finance and financial markets. It is now almost impossible to discuss or perform asset management, risk management, credit evaluation, and capital budgeting without at least a minimal understanding of options and option pricing. Derivatives theory provides a language and a set of analytical techniques that is fundamental for thinking about risk and valuation.

This book provides an introduction to the products and concepts underlying derivatives. In this first chapter, we begin by defining a derivative. We then provide background on financial markets and place derivatives in context. We then briefly examine important financial markets and see that derivatives markets have become increasingly important in

---

[1] A readable summary of derivatives-related losses is in Jorion (2001).

1

recent years. The size of these markets may leave you wondering exactly what functions they serve. We next discuss the role of financial markets in our lives and the importance of risk sharing. We also discuss different perspectives on derivatives. Finally, we discuss how trading occurs, providing some basic concepts and language that will be useful in later chapters.

1.1 WHAT IS A DERIVATIVE?

A **derivative** is a financial instrument (or more simply, an agreement between two people) that has a value determined by the price of something else. Options, futures, and swaps are all examples of derivatives. A bushel of corn is not a derivative; it is a commodity with a value determined in the corn market. However, you could enter into an agreement with a friend that says: If the price of a bushel of corn in one year is greater than $3, you will pay the friend $1. If the price is less than $3, the friend will pay you $1. This is a derivative in the sense that you have an agreement with a value depending on the price of something else (corn, in this case).

You might think: "That doesn't sound like it's a derivative; that's just a bet on the price of corn." Derivatives can in fact be thought of as bets on the price of something. But don't think the term "bet" is necessarily pejorative. Suppose your family grows corn and your friend's family buys corn to mill into cornmeal. The bet provides insurance: You earn $1 if your family's corn sells for a low price; this supplements your income. Your friend earns $1 if the corn his family buys is expensive; this offsets the high cost of corn. Viewed in this light, the bet hedges you both against unfavorable outcomes. The contract has reduced risk for both of you.

Investors who do not make a living growing or processing corn could also use this kind of contract simply to speculate on the price of corn. In this case the contract does not serve as insurance; it is simply a bet. This example illustrates a key point: *It is not the contract itself, but how it is used, and who uses it, that determines whether or not it is risk reducing.* Context is everything.

Although we've just defined a derivative, if you are new to the subject the implications of the definition will probably not be obvious right away. You will come to a deeper understanding of derivatives as we progress through the book, studying different products and their underlying economics.

1.2 AN OVERVIEW OF FINANCIAL MARKETS

In this section we discuss the variety of markets and financial instruments that exist. You should bear in mind that financial markets are rapidly evolving and that any specific description today may soon be out-of-date. Nevertheless, though the specific details may change, the basic economic functions associated with trading will continue to be necessary.

Trading of Financial Assets

The trading of a financial asset—i.e., the process by which an asset acquires a new owner—is more complicated than you might guess and involves at least four discrete steps. To understand the steps, consider the trade of a stock:

- The buyer and seller must locate one another and agree on a price. This process is what most people mean by "trading" and is the most visible step. Stock exchanges, derivatives exchanges, and dealers all facilitate trading, assisting buyers and sellers in finding one another.

- Once the buyer and seller agree on a price, the trade must be *cleared*. In clearing, the obligations of each party are specified. In the case of a stock transaction, the buyer must deliver cash and the seller must deliver the stock. In the case of some derivatives transactions, both parties must post collateral.[2]

- The trade must be *settled*, that is, the buyer and seller must deliver in the required period of time the cash or securities necessary to satisfy their obligations.

- Once the trade is complete, ownership records are updated.

As you would imagine, electronic systems now play an important role in all of these steps. For publicly traded securities, there are organizations you may never have heard of, such as the Depository Trust and Clearing Corporation (DTCC) and its subsidiary, the National Securities Clearing Corporation (NSCC), which play key roles in clearing and settling virtually every stock and bond trade that occurs in the United States. Other countries have similar institutions. Many derivatives trades must also be cleared and settled, so derivatives exchanges are always associated with a clearing organization.

Much trading of financial claims takes place on organized exchanges. An exchange is an organization that provides a venue for trading and that sets rules governing what is traded and how trading occurs. A given exchange will trade a particular set of financial instruments. The New York Stock Exchange, for example, lists approximately 3000 U.S. and 450 non-U.S. firms for which it provides a trading venue. Once upon a time, the exchange was solely a physical location where traders would stand in groups, buying and selling by talking, shouting, and gesturing. However, such in-person trading venues are vanishing, being replaced by electronic networks that provide a virtual trading venue.[3]

It is also possible for large traders to trade many financial claims directly with a dealer, bypassing organized exchanges. Such trading is said to occur in the **over-the-counter** (OTC) market. There are several reasons why buyers and sellers might transact

---

[2] A party "posting collateral" is turning assets over to someone else to ensure that they will be able to meet their obligations. The posting of collateral is a common practice in financial markets.

[3] When trading occurs in person, it is valuable for a trader to be physically close to other traders. With certain kinds of automated electronic trading, it is valuable for a trader's *computer* to be physically close to the computers of the exchange. Amazingly, the delays from transmitting an order over a network can put a trader at a disadvantage.

directly with dealers rather than on an exchange. First, it can be easier to trade a large quantity directly with another party. A seller of one million shares of IBM may negotiate a single price with a dealer, avoiding exchange fees as well as the market tumult and uncertainty about price that might result from simply announcing a million-share sale. Second, we might wish to trade a custom financial claim that is not available on an exchange. Third, we might wish to trade a number of different financial claims at once. A dealer could execute the entire trade as a single transaction, compared to the alternative of executing individual orders on a variety of different markets.

Most of the trading volume numbers you see reported in the newspaper pertain to exchange-based trading. Exchange activity is public and highly regulated. Over-the-counter trading is not easy to observe or measure and is generally less regulated. For many categories of financial claims, the value of OTC trading is greater than the value traded on exchanges.

Financial institutions are rapidly evolving and consolidating, so that any description is at best a snapshot. For example, at the time this was written in July 2007, there had recently been two large exchange mergers. In April 2007, the New York Stock Exchange merged with Euronext, a group of European exchanges, to form NYSE Euronext. After the merger, this group included six equity exchanges and six derivatives exchanges. In July 2007, the Chicago Mercantile Exchange merged with the Chicago Board of Trade. There may have been additional mergers by the time you read this.

Measures of Market Size and Activity

Before we discuss specific markets, it will be helpful to explain some ways in which the size of a market and its activity can be measured. There are at least four different measures that you will see mentioned in the press and on financial Web sites. No one measure is "correct" or best, but some are more applicable to stock and bond markets, others to derivatives markets. The different measures count the number of transactions that occur daily (trading volume), the number of positions that exist at the end of a day (open interest), and the value (market value) and size (notional value) of these positions. Here are more detailed definitions:

Trading volume   This measure counts the number of financial claims that change hands daily or annually. Trading volume is the number commonly emphasized in press coverage, but it is a somewhat arbitrary measure because it is possible to redefine the meaning of a financial claim. For example, on a stock exchange, trading volume refers to the number of shares traded. On an options exchange, trading volume refers to the number of options traded, but each option on an individual stock covers 100 shares of stock.[4]

---

[4] When there are stock splits or mergers, individual stock options will sometimes cover a different number of shares.

Open interest Open interest measures the total number of contracts that are "open," i.e., in which someone has a position where they may have an obligation to pay or to deliver a security. Open interest is an important statistic in derivatives markets.

Market value The market value of the listed financial claims on an exchange is the sum of the market value of the claims that *could* be traded, without regard to whether they have traded. For example, IBM stock is listed on the NYSE. In July 2007, the market value of IBM shares (also called the "market capitalization" or "market cap") was about $172 billion.[5] Some derivative claims can have a zero market value; for such claims, this measure tells us nothing about activity at an exchange.

Notional value Notional value measures the *scale* of a position, usually with reference to some underlying asset. Suppose the price of IBM is $100 and that you have a derivative contract giving you the right to buy 100 shares of IBM at a future date. We would then say that the notional value of one such contract is 100 shares of IBM, or $10,000. The concept of notional value is especially important in derivatives markets. Derivatives exchanges frequently report the notional value of contracts traded during a period of time.

Stock and Bond Markets

Companies often raise funds for purposes such as financing investments. Typically they do so either by selling ownership claims on the company (common stock) or by borrowing money (obtaining a bank loan or issuing a bond). Such financing activity is a routine part of operating a business. Virtually every developed country has a market in which investors can trade with each other the stocks that firms have issued. Bonds are usually traded by dealers, rather than on an exchange.

Table 1.1 shows the market capitalization of stocks traded on the five largest stock exchanges in the world in 2006. To provide some perspective, the aggregate value of publicly traded common stock in the United States was about $20 trillion at the end of 2006. Corporate borrowing was about $9.4 trillion, and federal, state, and local governments borrowed about $6.5 trillion. By way of comparison, the gross domestic product (GDP) of the United States in 2006 was $13.2 trillion.[6]

As its name suggests, an exchange facilitates the exchange of ownership of stock from one party to another. Some exchanges, such as the NYSE, designate individuals to assist in the trading process, buying or selling themselves if appropriate. Other

---

[5] IBM had a share price of about $115 and about 1.5 billion shares outstanding. The market value was thus about $115 × 1.5 billion = $172.5 billion. Market value changes with the price of the underlying shares.

[6] To be clear about the comparison: The values of securities represent the outstanding amount at the end of the year, irrespective of the year in which the securities were first issued. GDP, by contrast, represents output produced in the United States during the year. The market value and GDP numbers are measured in different units—dollars and dollars per year—and are therefore not directly comparable. The comparison is nonetheless frequently made.

TABLE 1.1 The five largest stock exchanges in the world, by market capitalization (in billions of U.S. dollars).

Rank	Exchange	Market Cap (billions of U.S. $)
1	NYSE Group	15,421.2
2	Tokyo Stock Exchange	4614.1
3	NASDAQ Stock Market	3865.0
4	London Stock Exchange	3794.3
5	Euronext	3708.2

Source: http://www.world-exchanges.org/

exchanges, such as NASDAQ, rely on a competitive market among many traders to provide fair prices. In practice, most investors will not notice these distinctions.

The bond market is similar in size to the stock market, but bonds generally trade through dealers rather than on an exchange. Most bonds also trade much less frequently than stocks.

Derivatives Markets

Since a derivative is a financial instrument with a value determined by the price of something else, there is potentially an unlimited variety of derivatives products. Derivatives exchanges trade products based on stock indexes, bond prices, interest rates, commodities, currencies, and other categories (for example, there are futures on weather and real estate). A given exchange may trade futures, options, or both. The distinction between exchanges that trade the physical stocks and bonds, as opposed to derivatives, has largely been due to regulation and custom, and is eroding.

Futures contracts have existed for thousands of years, most often for agricultural products. In Box 1.1, Aristotle tells the story of Thales of Miletus, who rented olive presses in advance of the harvest—this was essentially a forward contract on olive presses—and made money renting them out again at market rates when the olive harvest was large.

The modern market in financial derivatives began in 1972, when the Chicago Mercantile Exchange (CME) started trading futures on seven currencies. The introduction of derivatives in a market often coincides with an increase in price risk in that market. Currencies were permitted to float in 1971 when the gold standard was officially abandoned. OPEC's 1973 reduction in the supply of oil was followed by high and variable oil prices. U.S. interest rates became more volatile following inflation and recessions in the 1970s. The market for natural gas has been deregulated gradually since 1978, resulting in a volatile market in recent years. The deregulation of electricity began during the 1990s.

Box 1.1: An Aristotelian Forward Contract

There is, for example, the story which is told of Thales of Miletus. It is a story about a scheme for making money, which is fathered on Thales owing to his reputation for wisdom; but it involves a principle of general application. He was reproached for his poverty, which was supposed to show the uselessness of philosophy; but observing from his knowledge of meteorology (so the story goes) that there was likely to be a heavy crop of olives [next summer], and having a small sum at his command, he paid down earnest-money, early in the year, for the hire of all the olive presses in Miletus and Chios; and he managed, in the absence of any higher offer, to secure them at a low rate. When the season came, and there was a sudden and simultaneous demand for a number of presses, he let out the stock he had collected at any rate he chose to fix; and making a considerable fortune he succeeded in proving that it is easy for philosophers to become rich if they so desire, though it is not the business which they are really about.

Aristotle (1948, *The Politics*, p. 31)

To illustrate the increase in variability since the early 1970s, Figures 1.1, 1.2, and 1.3 show monthly changes for oil prices, an exchange rate, and an interest rate, respectively. The link between price variability and the development of derivatives markets is natural—there is no need to manage risk when there is no risk.[7] When risk does exist, we would expect that markets would develop to permit efficient risk sharing. Investors who have the most tolerance for risk would bear more of it, and risk bearing would be widely spread among investors.

Table 1.2 provides examples of some of the specific futures contracts that trade on three exchanges.[8] Some of the descriptions are self-explanatory, while others will likely be less familiar to you. Eurodollar and Euribor contracts have a value depending on dollar-denominated and euro-denominated interbank interest rates. The DAX is a German stock index. Heating and cooling degree-day contracts have a value depending upon the average temperature in a specified city. The iTraxx index has a value that depends on the perceived creditworthiness of a basket of companies. Government bonds

---

[7] It is sometimes argued that the existence of derivatives markets can increase the price variability of the underlying asset or commodity. However, the introduction of derivatives can be a response to increased price variability.

[8] The table lists only a fraction of the contracts traded at these exchanges. For example, the Chicago Mercantile Exchange trades futures contracts on dozens of other underlying assets, ranging from butter to weather in Amsterdam.

Chapter 1: Introduction to Derivatives

FIGURE 1.1

Monthly percentage change in the producer price index for oil, 1947–2006.

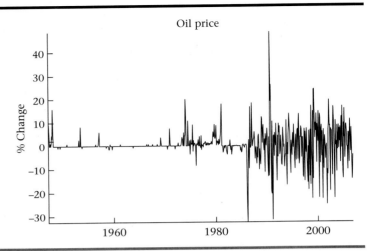

Source: DRI

FIGURE 1.2

Monthly percentage change in the dollar/pound ($/£) exchange rate, 1947–2006.

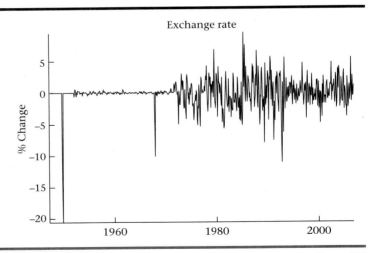

Source: DRI

1.2 An Overview of Financial Markets

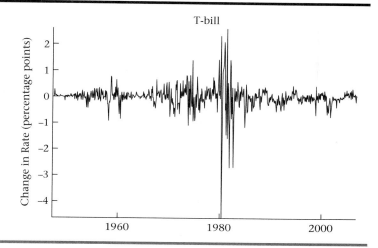

FIGURE 1.3

Monthly change in 3-month Treasury bill rate, 1947–2006.

Source: DRI

TABLE 1.2 Examples of futures contracts traded on the Chicago Mercantile Exchange (CME)/Chicago Board of Trade (CBT), Eurex, and the New York Mercantile Exchange (NYMEX).

CME/CBT	Eurex	NYMEX
S&P 500 index	DJ Euro Stoxx 50 index	Crude oil
10-year U.S. Treasury bonds	Euro-bund (10-year German government bonds)	Natural gas
Eurodollar	Euribor	Heating oil
Japanese yen	DAX stock index	Gasoline
Corn	DAX index volatility	Gold
Soybeans	iTraxx 5-year index	Copper
Heating and cooling degree-days	Individual stocks	Electricity

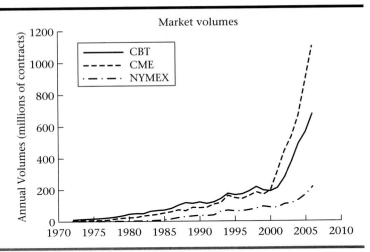

FIGURE 1.4

Millions of futures contracts traded annually at the Chicago Board of Trade (CBT), Chicago Mercantile Exchange (CME), and the New York Mercantile Exchange (NYMEX), 1970–2006. The CME and CBT merged in 2007.

Source: CRB Yearbook

are important financial assets, and on these exchanges there are active futures contracts for government bonds of different maturities for both Germany and the United States.[9]

Figure 1.4 depicts futures contract trading volume for the three largest U.S. futures exchanges over the last 30 years. The point of this graph is that trading activity in futures contracts has grown enormously over this period. Exchanges in other countries have generally experienced similar growth. For example, in 2006 Eurex, an electronic exchange headquartered in Frankfurt, Germany, traded over 1.5 billion contracts, the largest trading volume of any futures exchange in the world at that time. Subsequently, the merger of the Chicago Board of Trade with the Chicago Mercantile Exchange created an exchange with even greater trading volume. There are many other important derivatives exchanges, including the Chicago Board Options Exchange, the International Securities Exchange (an electronic exchange headquartered in the United States), the London International Financial Futures Exchange, and exchanges headquartered in Australia, Brazil, China, Korea, and Singapore, among many others.

The OTC markets have also grown rapidly over this period. Table 1.3 presents an estimated annual notional value of swaps in three important categories. The estimated year-end outstanding notional value of interest rate and currency swaps is an eye-popping

---

[9] German government bonds are known as "Bubills" (bonds with maturity of less than 1 year), "Schaetze" (maturity of 2 years), "Bobls" (5 years), and "Bunds" (10 and 30 years). Futures contracts also trade on Japanese and U.K. government bonds ("gilt").

TABLE 1.3 Estimated year-end notional value of outstanding derivatives contracts, by category, in billions of dollars.

	Interest Rate and Currency	Credit Default Swap	Equity Derivative
1997	29,035.00		
1998	50,997.00		
1999	58,265.00		
2000	63,009.00		
2001	69,207.30	918.87	
2002	101,318.49	2191.57	2455.29
2003	142,306.92	3779.40	3444.08
2004	183,583.27	8422.26	4151.29
2005	213,194.58	17,096.14	5553.97
2006	285,728.14	34,422.80	7178.48

Source: International Swap Dealer's Association

$285 trillion. For a variety of reasons the notional value number can be difficult to interpret, but the enormous growth in these contracts in recent years is unmistakable.

1.3 THE ROLE OF FINANCIAL MARKETS

Stock, bond, and derivatives markets are large and active, but what role do financial markets play in the economy and in our lives? We routinely see headlines stating that the Dow Jones Industrial Average has gone up 100 points, the dollar has fallen against the euro, and interest rates have risen. But why do we care about these things? In this section we examine how financial markets affect our lives.

Financial Markets and the Averages

To understand how financial markets affect us, consider the Average family, living in Anytown. Joe and Sarah Average have 2.3 children and both work for the XYZ Co., the dominant employer in Anytown. Their income pays for their mortgage, transportation, food, clothing, and medical care. Remaining income goes into savings earmarked for their children's college tuition and their own retirement.

The Averages are largely unaware of the ways in which global financial markets affect their lives. Here are a few:

- The Averages invest their savings in mutual funds that own stocks and bonds from companies around the world. The transaction cost of buying stocks and bonds in this way is low. Moreover, the Averages selected mutual funds that provide diversified investments. As a result, the Averages are not heavily exposed to any one company.[10]

- The Averages live in an area susceptible to tornadoes and insure their home. A completely local insurance company could not offer tornado insurance, because one disaster would leave the company unable to pay claims. However, by reinsuring tornado risk in global markets, the insurance company can pool Anytown tornado risk with Japan earthquake risk and Florida hurricane risk. This pooling makes insurance available at lower rates and protects the Anytown insurance company.

- The Averages borrowed money from Anytown bank to buy their house. The bank turned around and sold the mortgage to other investors, freeing itself from interest rate and default risk associated with the mortgage. Because the risks of their mortgage is borne by those willing to pay the highest price for it, the Averages get the lowest possible mortgage rate.

- The Average's employer, XYZ Co., must raise funds to finance operations and investments. It can raise the money it needs by issuing stocks and bonds in global markets. Investors in Asia may thereby finance an improvement to the Anytown factory.

- XYZ Co. insures itself against certain risks. In addition to having property and casualty insurance for its buildings, it uses global derivatives markets to protect itself against adverse currency, interest rate, and commodity price changes. By being able to manage these risks, XYZ is less likely to go into bankruptcy, and the Averages are less likely to become unemployed.

In all of these examples, particular financial functions and risks have been split up and parceled out to others. A bank that sells a mortgage does not have to bear the risk of the mortgage. A single insurance company does not bear the entire risk of a disaster. Risk sharing is one of the most important functions of financial markets.

Risk Sharing

Risk is an inevitable part of our lives and all economic activity. As we've seen in the example of the Averages, financial markets enable at least some of these risks to be shared. Risk arises from natural events, such as earthquakes, floods, and hurricanes, and

---

[10] There is one important risk that the Averages cannot easily avoid. Since both Averages work at XYZ, they run the risk that if XYZ falls on hard times they will lose their jobs.

from unnatural events such as wars and political conflicts. Drought and pestilence destroy agriculture every year in some part of the world. Some economies boom as others falter. On a more personal scale, people are born, die, retire, find jobs, lose jobs, marry, divorce, and become ill.

Given that risk exists, it is natural to have arrangements where the lucky share with the unlucky. There are both formal and informal risk-sharing arrangements. On the formal level, the insurance market is a way to share risk. Buyers pay a premium to obtain various kinds of insurance, such as homeowner's insurance. Total collected premiums are then available to help those whose houses burn down. The lucky, meanwhile, did not need insurance and have lost their premium. This market makes it possible for the lucky to help the unlucky. On the informal level, risk sharing also occurs in families and communities, where those encountering misfortune are helped by others.

In the business world, changes in commodity prices, exchange rates, and interest rates can be the financial equivalent of a house burning down. If the dollar becomes expensive relative to the yen, some companies are helped and others are hurt. It makes sense for there to be a mechanism enabling companies to exchange this risk, so that the lucky can, in effect, help the unlucky.

Even insurers need to share risk. Consider an insurance company that provides earthquake insurance for California residents. A large earthquake could generate claims sufficient to bankrupt a stand-alone insurance company. Thus, insurance companies often use the *reinsurance market* to buy, from reinsurers, insurance against large claims. Reinsurers pool different kinds of risks, thereby enabling insurance risks to become more widely held.

In some cases, reinsurers further share risks by issuing **catastrophe bonds**—bonds that the issuer need not repay if there is a specified event, such as a large earthquake, causing large insurance claims. Bondholders willing to accept earthquake risk can buy these bonds, in exchange for greater interest payments on the bond if there is no earthquake. An earthquake bond allows earthquake risk to be borne by exactly those investors who wish to bear it.

You might be wondering what this discussion has to do with the notions of diversifiable and nondiversifiable risk familiar from portfolio theory. Risk is **diversifiable risk** if it is unrelated to other risks. The risk that a lightning strike will cause a factory to burn down, for example, is idiosyncratic and hence diversifiable. If many investors share a small piece of this risk, it has no significant effect on anyone. Risk that does not vanish when spread across many investors is **nondiversifiable risk**. The risk of a stock market crash, for example, is nondiversifiable.

Financial markets in theory serve two purposes. Markets permit diversifiable risk to be widely shared. This is efficient: By definition, diversifiable risk vanishes when it is widely shared. At the same time, financial markets permit nondiversifiable risk, which does not vanish when shared, to be held by those most willing to hold it. Thus, *the fundamental economic idea underlying the concepts and markets discussed in this book is that the existence of risk-sharing mechanisms benefits everyone.*

Derivatives markets continue to evolve. A recent development has been the growth in **prediction markets**, discussed in Box 1.2.

> **Box 1.2: Prediction Markets**
>
> Prediction markets are derivative markets in which the value of traded claims depends on the outcome of events. With one common contract, an investor can own a claim that receives $1 if the event occurs, or sell a claim that requires the investor to pay $1 if the event occurs. Such markets can be used to speculate on presidential elections, the winner of an Olympic event, the occurrence of a natural disaster, or the value of a government statistic such as employment or the consumer price index.
>
> Much of the interest in prediction markets stems from the idea that the price of a contract will aggregate individual information that could not otherwise be observed. For example, the Hollywood Stock Exchange is a prediction market that uses prices and trading volume to gauge public interest in movies and movie stars. (Speculators in this market earn prizes rather than money.)
>
> In summer 2007, the Iowa Electronic Markets (http://www.biz.uiowa.edu/iem/markets/) permitted speculation on the outcome of the 2008 U.S. presidential election. The "vote share" contracts pay in cents the percentage of the popular vote received by the official candidate of a party. For example, if the Republican were to receive 48% of the vote, the Republican vote share contract on election day would be worth $0.48. The Democratic and Republican "winner-take-all" contracts pay $1 if that party wins the election, and zero otherwise. There are also party nomination contracts, which allow an investor to bet that a specific candidate will win the party nomination. (See Box 1.3.)
>
> Intrade.com allows political bets along with a wide variety of others. One contract states its event as "Bird flu (H5N1) to be confirmed in the USA ON/BEFORE 31th Mar 2008," while another states, "The next independent publicized study of adult talkativeness will find Women talk 10% more than Men."
>
> Prediction markets face significant regulatory hurdles in the United States. As of this writing, a 2006 law prohibiting unauthorized internet gambling made it illegal for U.S. investors to use any prediction market not authorized by the Commodity Futures Trading Commission. David Carruthers, the CEO of BetOnSports, a British Web-based betting site, was arrested in July 2006 by U.S. authorities while changing planes in the United States. The charge was "racketeering conspiracy for participating in an illegal gambling enterprise."

1.4 WAYS TO THINK ABOUT DERIVATIVES

We can think about derivatives and other financial claims in different ways. One is a functional perspective: Who uses them and why? Another is an analytical perspective: When we look at financial markets, how do we interpret the activity that we see? In this section, we discuss these different perspectives.

Uses of Derivatives

What are reasons someone might use derivatives? Here are some motives.

Risk management Derivatives are a tool for companies and other users to reduce risks. The earlier corn example illustrates this in a simple way: The farmer—a seller of corn—enters into a contract that makes a payment when the price of corn is low. This contract reduces the risk of loss for the farmer, who we therefore say is **hedging**. It is common to think of derivatives as forbiddingly complex, but many derivatives are simple and familiar. Every form of insurance is a derivative, for example. Automobile insurance is a bet on whether you will have an accident, which is a bet on the value of your car. If you wrap your car around a tree, your insurance is valuable; if the car remains undamaged, it is not.

Speculation Derivatives can serve as investment vehicles. As you will see later in the book, derivatives can provide a way to make bets that are highly leveraged (that is, the potential gain or loss on the bet can be large relative to the initial cost of making the bet) and tailored to a specific view. For example, if you want to bet that the S&P 500 stock index will be between 1300 and 1400 one year from today, derivatives can be constructed to let you do that.

Reduced transaction costs Sometimes derivatives provide a lower-cost way to undertake a particular financial transaction. For example, the manager of a mutual fund may wish to sell stocks and buy bonds. Doing this entails paying fees to brokers and paying other trading costs, such as the bid-ask spread, which we will discuss later. It is possible to trade derivatives instead and achieve the same economic effect as if stocks had actually been sold and replaced by bonds. Using the derivative might result in lower transaction costs than actually selling stocks and buying bonds.

Regulatory arbitrage It is sometimes possible to circumvent regulatory restrictions, taxes, and accounting rules by trading derivatives. Derivatives are often used, for example, to achieve the economic sale of stock (receive cash and eliminate the risk of holding the stock) while still maintaining physical possession of the stock. This transaction may allow the owner to defer taxes on the sale of the stock, or retain voting rights, without the risk of holding the stock.

These are common reasons for using derivatives. The general point is that derivatives provide an alternative to a simple sale or purchase and thus increase the range of possibilities for an investor or manager seeking to accomplish some goal.

In recent years the U.S. Securities and Exchange Commission (SEC), Financial Accounting Standards Board (FASB), and the International Accounting Standard Board (IASB) have increased the requirements for corporations to report on their use of derivatives. Nevertheless, surprisingly little is known about how companies actually use derivatives to manage risk. The basic strategies companies use are well understood—and will be described in this book—but it is not known, for example, what fraction of perceived risk is hedged by a given company, or by all companies in the aggregate. We frequently do not know a company's specific rationale for hedging or not hedging.

We would expect the use of derivatives to vary by type of firm. For example, financial firms, such as banks, are highly regulated and have capital requirements. They may have assets and liabilities in different currencies, with different maturities, and with different credit risks. Hence, banks could be expected to use interest rate derivatives, currency derivatives, and credit derivatives to manage risks in those areas. Manufacturing firms that buy raw materials and sell in global markets might use commodity and currency derivatives, but their incentives to manage risk are less clear-cut because they are not regulated in the same ways as financial firms.

Perspectives on Derivatives

How you think about derivatives depends on who you are. In this book we will think about three distinct perspectives on derivatives:

The end user perspective   End users are the corporations, investment managers, and investors who enter into derivatives contracts for the reasons listed in the previous section: to manage risk, speculate, reduce costs, or avoid a rule or regulation. End users have a goal (for example, risk reduction) and care about how a derivative helps to meet that goal.

The market-maker perspective   Market-makers are intermediaries, traders who will buy derivatives from customers who wish to sell, and sell derivatives to customers who wish to buy. In order to make money, market-makers charge a spread: They buy at a low price and sell at a high price. In this respect market-makers are like grocers who buy at the low wholesale price and sell at the higher retail price. Market-makers are also like grocers in that their inventory reflects customer demands rather than their own preferences: As long as shoppers buy paper towels, the grocer doesn't care whether they buy the decorative or super-absorbent style. After dealing with customers, market-makers are left with whatever position results from accommodating customer demands. Market-makers typically hedge this risk and thus are deeply concerned about the mathematical details of pricing and hedging.

The economic observer   Finally, we can look at the use of derivatives, the activities of the market-makers, the organization of the markets, the logic of the pricing models, and try to make sense of everything. This is the activity of the economic observer. Regulators must often don their economic-observer hats when deciding whether and how to regulate a certain activity or market participant.

These three perspectives are intertwined throughout the book, with different degrees of emphasis.

Financial Engineering and Security Design

One of the major ideas in derivatives—perhaps *the* major idea—is that it is generally possible to create a given payoff in multiple ways. The construction of a given financial product from other products is sometimes called **financial engineering**. The fact that this is possible has several implications. First, since market-makers need to hedge their positions, this idea is central in understanding how market-making works. The market-maker sells a contract to an end user and then creates an offsetting position that pays him if it is necessary to pay the customer. This creates a hedged position.

Second, the idea that a given contract can be replicated often suggests how it can be customized. The market-maker can, in effect, turn dials to change the risk, initial premium, and payment characteristics of a derivative. These changes permit the creation of a product that is more appropriate for a given situation.

Third, it is often possible to improve intuition about a given derivative by realizing that it is equivalent to something we already understand.

Finally, because there are multiple ways to create a payoff, the regulatory arbitrage discussed above can be difficult to stop. Distinctions existing in the tax code, or in regulations, may not be enforceable, since a particular security or derivative that is regulated or taxed may be easily replaced by one that is treated differently but has the same economic profile.

A theme running throughout the book is that derivative products can generally be constructed from other products.

1.5 BUYING AND SHORT-SELLING FINANCIAL ASSETS

Throughout this book we will talk about buying and selling—and short-selling—assets such as stocks. These basic transactions are so important that it is worth describing the details. First, it is important to understand the costs associated with buying and selling. Second, it is helpful to understand the mechanisms one can use to buy or sell. Third, a very important idea used throughout the book is that of short-sales. The concept of short-selling seems as if it should be intuitive—a short-sale is just the opposite of a purchase—but for almost everyone it is hard to grasp at first. Even if you are familiar with short-sales, you should spend a few minutes reading this section.

Although we will use shares of stock to illustrate the mechanics of buying and selling, there are similar issues associated with buying any asset.

Transaction Costs and the Bid-Ask Spread

Suppose you want to buy 100 shares of XYZ stock. Calculating the cost seems simple: If the price to buy the stock is $50, 100 shares will cost $50 \times 100 = 5000. However, this calculation ignores transaction costs.

First, there is a commission, which is a transaction fee you pay your broker. A commission for the above order could be $15, or 0.3% of the purchase price.

Second, the term "stock price" is, surprisingly, imprecise. There are in fact two prices, a price at which you can buy and a price at which you can sell. The price at which you can buy is called the **offer price** or **ask price**, and the price at which you can sell is called the **bid price**. Where do these terms come from?

To buy stock, you can pick up the phone and call a broker. Suppose that you say you want to buy immediately at the best available price. If the stock is not too obscure and your order is not too large, your purchase will probably be completed in a matter of seconds. Where does the stock come from that you have just bought? It is possible that at the exact same moment, another customer called the broker and put in an order to sell. More likely, however, a market-maker sold you the stock. Market-makers do what their name implies: They make markets. If you want to buy, they sell, and if you want to sell, they buy. In order to earn a living, market-makers sell for a high price and buy for a low price. If you deal with a market-maker, therefore, you buy for a high price and sell for a low price. This difference between the price at which you can buy and the price at which you can sell is called the **bid-ask spread**.[11] In practice the bid-ask spread on the stock you are buying may be $49.75 to $50. This means that you can buy for $50/share and sell for $49.75/share. If you were to buy immediately and then sell, you would pay the commission twice, and you would pay the bid-ask spread.

Example 1.1 Suppose XYZ is bid at $49.75 and offered at $50, and the commission is $15. If you buy 100 shares of the stock, you pay ($50 × 100) + $15 = $5015. If you immediately sell them again, you receive ($49.75 × 100) − $15 = $4960. Your round-trip transaction cost—the difference between what you pay and what you receive from a sale, not counting changes in the bid and ask prices—is $5015 − $4960 = $55.

This discussion reveals where the terms "bid" and "ask" come from. You might at first think that the terminology is backward. The bid price sounds like it should be what you pay. It is in fact what the *market-maker* pays; hence, it is the price at which you sell. The offer price is what the market-maker will sell for—hence, it is what you have to pay. The terminology reflects the perspective of the market-maker.

What happens to your shares after you buy them? Unless you make other arrangements, shares are typically held in a central depository (in the United States, at the DTCC) in the name of your broker. Such securities are said to be held in *street name*.

Ways to Buy or Sell

A buyer or seller of an asset can employ different strategies in trading the asset. You implement these different strategies by telling the broker (or the electronic trading system) what kind of order you are submitting.

A **market order** is an instruction to trade a specific quantity of the asset immediately, at the best price that is currently available. The advantage of a market order is that the trade is executed as soon as possible. The disadvantage of a market order is that you might have been able to get a better price had you been more patient.

---

[11] If you think a bid-ask spread is unreasonable, ask what a world without dealers would be like. Every buyer would have to find a seller, and vice versa. The search would be costly and take time. Dealers, because they maintain inventory, offer an immediate transaction, a service called *immediacy*.

A **limit order** is an instruction to trade a specific quantity of the asset at a specified price, or a better price. A limit order to buy 100 shares at $47.50 can be filled at $47.50 or below. A limit order to sell at $50.25 can be filled at $50.25 or above. Having your limit order filled depends upon whether or not anyone else is willing to trade at that price. As time passes, your order may or may not be filled. Thus, the advantage of a limit order is obtaining a better price. The disadvantage is the possibility that the order is never filled.

There are other kinds of orders. For example, suppose you own 100 shares of XYZ. If you enter a *stop-loss order* at $45, then your order becomes a market order to sell once the price falls to $45. Because your order is a market order, you may end up selling for less than $45.

In the earlier example, we supposed that the bid and ask prices for XYZ were $49.75 and $50, respectively. You can think of those prices as limit orders—someone has offered to buy at $49.75 and (possibly someone different) to sell at $50.

Box 1.3 illustrates bid and offer prices for one prediction market.

Short-Selling

The sale of a stock you do not already own is called a **short-sale**. In order to understand short-sales, we first need to understand the terms "long" and "short."

When we buy something, we are said to have a *long* position in that thing. For example, if we buy the stock of XYZ, we pay cash and receive the stock. Sometime later, we sell the stock and receive cash. This transaction is *lending*, in the sense that we pay money today and receive money back in the future. The rate of return we receive may not be known in advance (if the stock price goes up a lot, we get a high return; if the stock price goes down, we get a negative return), but it is a kind of loan nonetheless.

The opposite of a long position is a short position. A short-sale of XYZ entails borrowing shares of XYZ from an owner and then selling them, receiving the cash.[12] Sometime later, we buy back the XYZ stock, paying cash for it, and return it to the lender. A short-sale can be viewed, then, as just a way of borrowing money. When you borrow money from a bank, you receive money today and repay it later, paying a rate of interest set in advance. This is also what happens with a short-sale, except that you don't necessarily know the rate you pay to borrow.

There are at least three reasons to short-sell:

1. **Speculation:** A short-sale, considered by itself, makes money if the price of the stock goes down. The idea is to first sell high and then buy low. (With a long position, the idea is to first buy low and then sell high.)

2. **Financing:** A short-sale is a way to borrow money, and it is frequently used as a form of financing. This is very common in the bond market, for example.

---

[12] If you read the fine print on your brokerage contract carefully, your broker typically has the right to lend your shares to another investor. The broker earns fees from doing this. You generally do not know that your shares have been loaned.

Box 1.3: Bid and Ask Prices in a Prediction Market

We discussed prediction markets in Box 1.2. Bid-ask spreads appear in these markets, as you would expect. Here is a table showing the bid-ask spreads in the nomination market for Democratic presidential candidates, from the Iowa Presidential Nomination Market, on August 8, 2007 ("low," "high," and "average" are for the day):

Name	Bid	Ask	Last	Low	High	Avg
Clinton	0.582	0.594	0.594	0.575	0.599	0.585
Edwards	0.067	0.077	0.066	0.066	0.068	0.066
Obama	0.277	0.289	0.284	0.275	0.29	0.286
Other	0.065	0.077	0.065	0.065	0.065	0.065
Sum	0.991	1.037				1.002

If you wished to immediately buy the Hillary Clinton contract, you would pay $0.594 per contract. (You can see that the last trade for Clinton was probably a buy order.) An immediate sale would earn you $0.582. If you bought all four contracts, you would be guaranteed to earn $1 by the end of the convention, but the cost would be $1.037. Similarly, if you sold all four, you would have to pay $1 at the end of the convention, but you would receive only $0.991 today.

The prices in the table are limit orders placed by other traders. What you cannot see in the table is how many contracts you can trade at those prices (this is called *market depth*). You also cannot see any additional buy limit orders below the bid price and additional sell limit orders above the ask price.

3. **Hedging:** You can undertake a short-sale to offset the risk of owning the stock or a derivative on the stock. This is frequently done by market-makers and traders.

These reasons are not mutually exclusive. For example, a market-maker might use a short-sale to simultaneously hedge and finance a position.

Example: Short-selling wine Because short-sales can seem confusing, here is a detailed example that illustrates how short-sales work.

There are markets for many collectible items, such as fine wines. Suppose there is a wine from a particular vintage and producer that you believe to be overpriced. Perhaps you expect a forthcoming review of the wine to be negative, or you believe that wines soon to be released will be of extraordinary quality, driving down prices of existing wines. Whatever the reason, you think the price will fall. How could you speculate based on this belief?

If you believe prices will rise, you would buy the wine on the market and plan to sell after the price rises. However, if you believe prices will fall, you would do the opposite: Sell today (at the high price) and buy sometime later (at the low price). How can you accomplish this?

In order to sell today, you must first obtain wine to sell. You can do this by borrowing a case from a collector. The collector, of course, will want a promise that you will return the wine at some point; suppose you agree to return it one week later. Having reached agreement, you borrow the wine and then sell it at the market price. After one week, you acquire a replacement case on the market, then return it to the collector from whom you originally borrowed the wine. If the price has fallen, you will have bought the replacement wine for less than the price at which you sold the original, so you make money. If the price has risen, you have lost money. Either way, you have just completed a *short-sale* of wine. The act of buying replacement wine and returning it to the lender is said to be *closing* or *covering* the short position.

Note that short-selling is a way to borrow money. Initially, you received money from selling the wine. A week later you paid the money back (you had to buy a replacement case to return to the lender). The rate of interest you paid was low if the price of the replacement case was low, and high if the price of the replacement case was high.

This example is obviously simplified. We have assumed several points:

- It is easy to find a lender of wine.
- It is easy to buy, at a fair price, satisfactory wine to return to the lender: The wine you buy after one week is a perfect substitute for the wine you borrowed.
- The collector from whom you borrowed is not concerned that you will fail to return the borrowed wine.

Example: Short-selling stock Now consider a short-sale of stock. As with the previous example, when you short-sell stock you borrow the stock and sell it, receiving cash today. At some future date, you buy the stock in the market and return it to the original owner. You have cash coming in today, equal to the market value of the stock you short-sell. In the future, you repay the borrowing by buying the asset at its then-current market price and returning the asset—this is like the repayment of a loan. Thus, short-selling a stock is equivalent to borrowing money, except that the interest rate you pay is not known in advance. Rather, it is determined by the change in the stock price. The rate of interest is high if the security rises in price and low if the security falls in price. In effect, the rate of return on the security is the rate at which you borrow. With a short-sale, you are like the *issuer* of a security rather than the buyer of a security.

Suppose you want to short-sell IBM stock for 90 days. Table 1.4 depicts the cash flows. Observe in particular that if the share pays dividends, the short-seller must in turn make dividend payments to the share lender. This issue did not arise with wine! This dividend payment is taxed to the recipient, just like an ordinary dividend payment, and it is tax-deductible to the short-seller.

Notice that the cash flows in Table 1.4 are exactly the opposite of the cash flows from purchasing the stock. Thus, *short-selling is literally the opposite of buying.*

The Lease Rate of an Asset

We have seen that when you borrow an asset it may be necessary to make payments to the lender. Dividends on short-sold stock are an example of this. We will refer to the

TABLE 1.4

Cash flows associated with short-selling a share of IBM for 90 days. S_0 and S_{90} are the share prices on days 0 and 90. Note that the short-seller must pay the dividend, D, to the share lender.

	Day 0	Dividend Ex-Day	Day 90
Action	Borrow shares	—	Return shares
Security	Sell shares	—	Purchase shares
Cash	$+S_0$	$-D$	$-S_{90}$

payment required by the lender as the **lease rate** of the asset. This concept will arise frequently, and, as we will see, provides a unifying concept for our later discussions of derivatives.

The wine example did not have a lease payment. But under some circumstances, it might be necessary to make a payment to borrow wine. Wine does not pay an explicit dividend but does pay an implicit dividend if the owner enjoys seeing bottles in the cellar. The owner might thus require a payment in order to lend a bottle. This would be a lease rate for wine.

CHAPTER SUMMARY

Derivatives are financial instruments with a payoff determined by the price of something else. They can be used as a tool for risk management and speculation, and to reduce transaction costs or avoid taxes and regulation.

One important function of financial markets is to facilitate optimal risk sharing. There are different ways to measure the size and activity of stock, bond, and derivatives markets, but these markets are by any measure large and growing. The growth of derivatives markets over the last 50 years has coincided with an increase in the risks evident in various markets. Events such as the 1973 oil shock, the abandonment of fixed exchange rates, and the deregulation of energy markets have created a new role for derivatives.

There are costs to trading an asset, one of which is the bid-ask spread. The bid-ask spread is a key means by which those traders who make markets are compensated for doing so. In markets without explicit market-makers, limit orders create a bid-ask spread.

An important transaction is a short-sale, which entails borrowing a security, selling it, making dividend (or other cash) payments to the security lender, and then returning it. A short-sale is conceptually the opposite of a purchase. Short-sales can be used for speculation, as a form of financing, or as a way to hedge.

FURTHER READING

The derivatives exchanges have Web sites that list their contracts and provide further details. Because the Web addresses can change (e.g., due to mergers), the easiest way to find them is with a Web search.

Jorion (1995) examines in detail one famous "derivatives disaster": Orange County in California. Bernstein (1992) presents a history of the development of financial markets, and Bernstein (1996) discusses the concept of risk measurement and how it evolved over the last 800 years. Miller (1986) discusses origins of past financial innovation, while Merton (1999) and Shiller (2003) provide a stimulating look at possible *future* developments in financial markets. Finally, Lewis (1989) is a classic, funny, insider's account of investment banking, offering a different (to say the least) perspective on the mechanics of global risk sharing.

PROBLEMS

1.1 Pick a derivatives exchange such as CME Group, Eurex, or the Chicago Board Options Exchange. Go to that exchange's Web site and try to determine the following:

    a. What products the exchange trades

    b. The trading volume in the various products

    c. The notional value traded

What do you predict would happen to these measures if the notional value of a popular contract were cut in half? (For example, instead of an option being based on 100 shares of stock, suppose it were based on 50 shares of stock.)

1.2 Consider the widget exchange. Suppose that each widget contract has a market value of $0 and a notional value of $100. There are three traders, A, B, and C. Over one day, the following trades occur:

- A long, B short, 5 contracts
- A long, C short, 15 contract
- B long, C short, 10 contracts
- C long, A short, 20 contracts

    a. What is each trader's net position in the contract at the end of the day? (Calculate long positions minus short positions.)

    b. What are trading volume, open interest, and the notional values of trading volume and open interest? (Calculate open interest as the sum of the net *long positions*, from your previous answer.)

    c. How would your answers have been different if there were an additional trade: C long, B short, 5 contracts?

d. How would you expect the measures in part (b) to be different if each contract had a notional value of $20?

1.3 Heating degree-day and cooling degree-day futures contracts make payments based on whether the temperature is abnormally hot or cold. Explain why the following businesses might be interested in such a contract:

    a. Soft drink manufacturers.

    b. Ski resort operators.

    c. Electric utilities.

    d. Amusement park operators.

1.4 Suppose the businesses in the previous problem use futures contracts to hedge their temperature-related risk. Who do you think might accept the opposite risk?

1.5 ABC stock has a bid price of $40.95 and an ask price of $41.05. Assume there is a $20 brokerage commission.

    a. What amount will you pay to buy 100 shares?

    b. What amount will you receive for selling 100 shares?

    c. Suppose you buy 100 shares, then immediately sell 100 shares with the bid and ask prices being the same in both cases. What is your round-trip transaction cost?

1.6 Repeat the previous problem supposing that the brokerage fee is quoted as 0.3% of the bid or ask price.

1.7 Suppose a security has a bid price of $100 and an ask price of $100.12. At what price can the market-maker purchase a security? At what price can a market-maker sell a security? What is the spread in dollar terms when 100 shares are traded?

1.8 Suppose you short-sell 300 shares of XYZ stock at $30.19 with a commission charge of 0.5%. Supposing you pay commission charges for purchasing the security to cover the short-sale, how much profit have you made if you close the short-sale at a price of $29.87?

1.9 Suppose you desire to short-sell 400 shares of JKI stock, which has a bid price of $25.12 and an ask price of $25.31. You cover the short position 180 days later when the bid price is $22.87 and the ask price is $23.06.

    a. Taking into account only the bid and ask prices (ignoring commissions and interest), what profit did you earn?

    b. Suppose that there is a 0.3% commission to engage in the short-sale (this is the commission to sell the stock) and a 0.3% commission to close the short-sale (this is the commission to buy the stock back). How do these commissions change the profit in the previous answer?

c. Suppose the 6-month interest rate is 3% and that you are paid nothing on the short-sale proceeds. How much interest do you lose during the 6 months in which you have the short position?

1.10 When you open a brokerage account, you typically sign an agreement giving the broker the right to lend your shares without notifying or compensating you. Why do brokers want you to sign this agreement?

1.11 Suppose a stock pays a quarterly dividend of $3. You plan to hold a short position in the stock across the dividend ex-date. What is your obligation on that date? If you are a taxable investor, what would you guess is the tax consequence of the payment? (In particular, would you expect the dividend to be tax deductible?) Suppose the company announces instead that the dividend is $5. Should you care that the dividend is different from what you expected?

1.12 Short interest is a measure of the aggregate short positions on a stock. Check an online brokerage or other financial service for the short interest on several stocks of your choice. Can you guess which stocks have high short interest and which have low? Is it theoretically possible for short interest to exceed 100% of shares outstanding?

1.13 Suppose that you go to a bank and borrow $100. You promise to repay the loan in 90 days for $102. Explain this transaction using the terminology of short-sales.

1.14 Suppose your bank's loan officer tells you that if you take out a mortgage (i.e., you borrow money to buy a house) you will be permitted to borrow no more than 80% of the value of the house. Describe this transaction using the terminology of short-sales.

part 1

Insurance, Hedging, and Simple Strategies

In this part of the book, Chapters 2–4, we examine the basic derivatives contracts: forward contracts, futures contracts, call options, and put options. All of these are contracts between two parties, with a payoff at some future date based on the price of an underlying asset (this is why they are called derivatives).

There are a number of things we want to understand about these instruments. What are they? How do they work and what do they cost? If you enter into a forward contract, futures contract, or option, what obligations or rights have you acquired?

Payoff and profit diagrams provide an important graphical tool to summarize the risk of these contracts.

Once we understand what the basic derivatives contracts are, what can we do with them? We will see that, among other things, they can be used to provide insurance, to convert a stock investment into a risk-free investment and vice versa, and to speculate in a variety of ways. Derivatives can often be customized for a particular purpose. We will see how corporate risk managers can use derivatives, and some reasons for doing so.

In this part of the book, we take the prices of derivatives as given; the underlying pricing models will be covered in much of the rest of the book. The main mathematical tool is present and future value calculations. We do, however, develop one key pricing idea: put-call parity. Put-call parity is important because it demonstrates a link among the different contracts we examine in these chapters, telling us how the prices of forward contracts, call options, and put options are related to one another.

An Introduction to Forwards and Options

This chapter introduces the basic derivatives contracts: forward contracts, call options, and put options. These fundamental contracts are widely used and serve as building blocks for more complicated derivatives that we discuss in later chapters. We explain here how the contracts work and how to think about their risk. We also introduce an extremely important tool for analyzing derivatives positions—namely, payoff and profit diagrams. The terminology and concepts introduced in this chapter are fundamental and will be used throughout this book.

2.1 FORWARD CONTRACTS

A **forward contract** sets today the terms at which you buy or sell an asset or commodity at a specific time in the future. Specifically, a forward contract does the following:

- It specifies the quantity and exact type of the asset or commodity the seller must deliver.
- It specifies delivery logistics, such as time, date, and place.
- It specifies the price the buyer will pay at the time of delivery.
- It obligates the seller to sell and the buyer to buy, subject to the above specifications.

The time at which the contract settles is called the **expiration date.** The asset or commodity on which the forward contract is based is called the **underlying asset.** Apart from commissions and bid-ask spreads (see Section 1.5), a forward contract requires no initial payment or premium. The contractual forward price simply represents the price at which consenting adults agree today to transact in the future, at which time the buyer pays the seller the forward price and the seller delivers the asset.

To better understand forward contracts, it is helpful to compare a forward contract with an outright purchase of stock. Buying a share of stock entails at least three separate steps: (1) setting the price to be paid, (2) transferring cash from the buyer to the seller,

FIGURE 2.1

Index futures price listings.

	Open	High	Contract hi lo	Low	Settle	Chg	Open interest
Index Futures							
DJ Industrial Average (CBT)-$10 x index							
Sept	13275	13380		13250	**13255**	18	37,703
Dec	13427	13465		13346	**13346**	16	218
Mini DJ Industrial Average (CBT)-$5 x index							
Sept	13275	13383		13250	**13255**	18	101,837
Dec	13400	13480		13353	**13346**	16	246
S&P 500 Index (CME)-$250 x index							
Sept	1454.40	1472.50		1453.80	**1455.10**	4.10	577,561
Dec	1481.50	1483.00		1468.00	**1466.90**	4.10	60,487
Mini S&P 500 (CME)-$50 x index							
Sept	1454.50	1472.50		1453.50	**1455.00**	4.00	2,083,824
Dec	1468.50	1484.00		1466.00	**1467.00**	4.25	29,904
Nasdaq 100 (CME)-$100 x index							
Sept	1934.00	1957.00		1932.25	**1942.50**	13.50	68,640
Mini Nasdaq 100 (CME)-$20 x index							
Sept	1933.3	1957.3		1932.0	**1942.5**	13.5	429,354
Dec	1968.3	1979.0		1964.3	**1965.3**	13.5	483
Russell 1000 (NYBOT)-$500 x index							
Sept	798.40	798.50		798.40	**791.25**	2.50	7,367
U.S. Dollar Index (NYBOT)-$1,000 x index							
Sept	80.63	81.04		80.65	**80.97**	.38	34,234
Dec	80.42	80.81		80.52	**80.77**	.38	3,300

Source: Wall Street Journal, August 14, 2007, p. C-6.

and (3) transferring the share from the seller to the buyer. With an outright purchase of stock, all three occur simultaneously. However, as a logical matter, we could set a price today and the transfer of shares and cash would occur at a specified date in the future. This is how a forward contract works.

Futures contracts are similar to forward contracts in that they create an obligation to buy or sell at a predetermined price at a future date. We will discuss the institutional and pricing differences between forwards and futures in Chapter 5. For the time being, think of them as interchangeable.

Figure 2.1 shows futures price listings from the *Wall Street Journal* for futures contracts on several stock indices, including the Dow Jones Industrial Average (DJ 30) and the Standard & Poor's 500 (S&P 500). The indices are the underlying assets for the contracts. (A **stock index** is the average price of a group of stocks. In these examples we work with this group price rather than the price of just one stock.) The first column of the listing gives the expiration month. The columns that follow show the price at the beginning of the day (the open), the high and low during the day, and the settlement price, which reflects the last transactions of the day.

The head of the listing tells us where the contracts trade (the Chicago Board of Trade [CBT] and Chicago Mercantile Exchange [CME]), and the size of the contract, which for the S&P 500 is $250 times the index value. We will discuss such futures contracts in more detail in Chapter 5. There are many more exchange-traded stock index futures contracts than those in Figure 2.1, both in the United States and around the world.

The price quotes in Figure 2.1 are from August. The September and December prices for the two contracts are therefore prices set in August for purchase of the index in later months. For example, the September S&P 500 futures price is $1455.10 and the December price is $1466.90.[1] By contrast, the current S&P index price that day—not shown in the listing—is $1452.56. This is the **spot price** for the index—the market price for immediate delivery of the index.

There are many more exchange-traded futures contracts than just those listed in Figure 2.1. As we will see in Chapters 5, 6, and 7, there are also futures contracts on interest rates and commodities. Futures are widely used in risk management and as an alternative way to invest in the underlying asset. Agricultural futures (such as corn and soybeans) can be used by farmers and others to hedge crop prices. New contracts are frequently discussed and proposed by exchanges, traders, and others. Box 2.1 discusses an unsuccessful proposal for a new futures contract that was in the news in 2003.

We will discuss in Chapter 5 how forward and futures prices are determined and more details about how futures contracts work. In this chapter we take prices as given and examine profit and loss on a forward contract. We will also see how a position in a forward contract is similar to and different from alternative investments, such as a direct investment in the underlying index.

The Payoff on a Forward Contract

Every forward contract has both a buyer and a seller. The term **long** is used to describe the buyer and **short** is used to describe the seller. Generally, a long position is one that makes money when the price goes up and a short is one that makes money when the price goes down. Because the long has agreed to buy at the fixed forward price, a long position profits if prices rise.

The **payoff** to a contract is the value of the position at expiration. The payoff to a long forward contract is

$$\text{Payoff to long forward} = \text{Spot price at expiration} - \text{forward price} \quad (2.1)$$

Because the short has agreed to sell at the fixed forward price, the short profits if prices fall. The payoff to a short forward contract is

$$\text{Payoff to short forward} = \text{Forward price} - \text{spot price at expiration} \quad (2.2)$$

---

[1] The use and nonuse of dollar signs for futures prices can be confusing. Many futures prices, in particular those for index futures, are in practice quoted without dollar signs, and multiplied by a dollar amount to determine the value of the contract. In this and the next several chapters, we will depart from this convention and use dollar signs for index futures prices. When we discuss the S&P 500 index futures contract in Chapter 5, however, we will follow practice and omit the dollar sign.

Box 2.1: Terrorism Futures?

Prediction markets made the news in July 2003, when newspaper readers were undoubtedly startled to see the front-page headline "Pentagon Prepares a Futures Market on Terror Attacks" (*New York Times*, July 29, 2003, p. A1). The article continued:

> Traders bullish on a biological attack on Israel or bearish on the chances of a North Korean missile strike would have the opportunity to bet on the likelihood of such events on a new Internet site established by the Defense Advanced Research Projects Agency.
>
> The Pentagon called its latest idea a new way of predicting events and part of its search for the "broadest possible set of new ways to prevent terrorist attacks."

Critics immediately attacked the plan:

> Two Democratic senators who reported the plan called it morally repugnant and grotesque. . . . One of the two senators, Byron L. Dorgan of North Dakota, said the idea seemed so preposterous that he had trouble persuading people it was not a hoax. "Can you imagine," Mr. Dorgan asked, 'if another country set up a betting parlor so that people could go in . . . and bet on the assassination of an American political figure?

The other critic, Senator Ron Wyden of Oregon, described the plan:

You may think early on that Prime Minister X is going to be assassinated. So you buy the futures contracts for 5 cents each. As more people begin to think the person's going to be assassinated, the cost of the contract could go up, to 50 cents. The payoff if he's assassinated is $1 per future. So if it comes to pass, and those who bought at 5 cents make 95 cents. Those who bought at 50 cents make 50 cents.

Later the same day (July 29), this headline appeared on the *New York Times* Web site: "Pentagon Abandons Plan for Futures Market on Terror."

Before dropping the plan, Defense Department officials defended it: "Research indicates that markets are extremely efficient, effective, and timely aggregators of dispersed and even hidden information. Futures markets have proven themselves to be good at predicting such things as elections results; they are often better than expert opinions."

A common concern about futures markets is the possibility that markets can be manipulated by better informed traders. The possibility of manipulation in this case was described as a "technical challenge and uncertainty." The natural worry was that terrorists would use the futures market to make money from attacks or to mislead authorities about where they would attack.

TABLE 2.1

Payoff after 6 months from a long S&R forward contract and a short S&R forward contract at a forward price of $1020. If the index price in 6 months is $1020, both the long and short have a 0 payoff. If the index price is greater than $1020, the long makes money and the short loses money. If the index price is less than $1020, the long loses money and the short makes money.

S&R Index in 6 Months	S&R Forward Long	Short
900	−$120	$120
950	−70	70
1000	−20	20
1020	0	0
1050	30	−30
1100	80	−80

To illustrate these calculations, consider a forward contract on a hypothetical stock index. Suppose the non-dividend-paying S&R ("Special and Rich") 500 index has a current price of $1000 and the 6-month forward price is $1020.[2] The holder of a long position in the S&R forward contract is obligated to pay $1020 in 6 months for one unit of the index. The holder of the short position is obligated to sell one unit of the index for $1020. Table 2.1 lists the payoff on the position for various possible future values of the index.

Example 2.1 Suppose the index price is $1050 in 6 months. A holder who entered a long position at a forward price of $1020 is obligated to pay $1020 to acquire the index and hence earns $1050 − $1020 = $30 per unit of the index. The short is likewise obligated to sell for $1020 and thus loses $30.

This example illustrates the mechanics of a forward contract, showing why the long makes money when the price rises and the short makes money when the price falls.

Graphing the Payoff on a Forward Contract

We can graph the information in Table 2.1 to show the payoff in 6 months on the forward contract as a function of the index. Figure 2.2 graphs the long and short positions, with

---

[2] We use a hypothetical stock index—the S&R—in order to avoid complications associated with dividends. We discuss dividends—and real stock indices—in Chapter 5.

FIGURE 2.2

Long and short forward positions on the S&R 500 index.

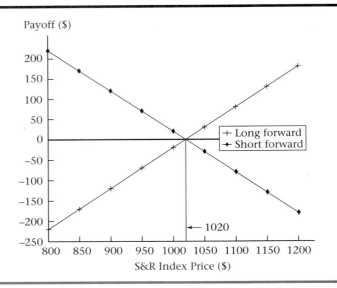

the index price at the expiration of the forward contract on the horizontal axis and payoff on the vertical axis. As you would expect, the two positions have a zero payoff when the index price in 6 months equals the forward price of $1020. The graph for the short forward is a mirror image (about the x-axis) of the graph for the long forward. For a given value of the index, the payoff to the short is exactly the opposite of the payoff to the long. In other words, the gain to one party is the loss to the other.

This kind of graph is widely used because it summarizes the risk of the position at a glance.

Comparing a Forward and Outright Purchase

The S&R forward contract is a way to acquire the index by paying $1020 after 6 months. An alternative way to acquire the index is to purchase it outright at time 0, paying $1000. Is there any advantage to using the forward contract to buy the index, as opposed to purchasing it outright?

If we buy the S&R index today, it costs us $1000. The value of the position in 6 months is the value of the S&R index. The payoff to a long position in the physical S&R index is graphed in Figure 2.3. For comparison, the payoff to the long forward position is graphed as well. Note that the axes have different scales in Figures 2.3 and 2.2.

To see how Figure 2.3 is constructed, suppose the S&R index price is $0 after 6 months. If the index price is $0, the physical index will be worth $0; hence, we plot a 0 on the y-axis against 0 on the x-axis. For all other prices of the S&R index, the payoff equals the value of the S&R index. For example, if we own the index and the price in 6 months is $750, the value of the position is $750.

FIGURE 2.3

Comparison of payoff after 6 months of a long position in the S&R index versus a forward contract in the S&R index.

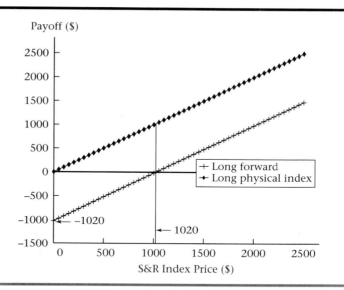

If the index price in 6 months is $0, the payoff to the forward contract, using equation (2.1), is

$$\text{Payoff to long forward} = 0 - \$1020 = -\$1020$$

If instead the index price is $1020, the long index position will be worth $1020 and the forward contract will be worth $0.

With both the physical index and the forward, we own the index after 6 months. What the figure does not reflect, however, is the different *initial* investments required for the two positions. With the cash index, we invest $1000 initially and then we own the index. With the forward contract, we invest $0 initially and $1020 after 6 months; then we own the index. The financing of the two positions is different. The payoff graph tells us how much money we end up with after 6 months but does not account for the initial $1000 investment with the outright purchase. Figure 2.3 is accurate, but it does not answer our question—namely, whether there is an advantage to either a forward purchase or an outright purchase.

Both positions give us ownership of the S&R index after 6 months. We can compare them fairly if we equate the amounts initially invested and then account for interest earned over the 6 months. We can do this in either of two equivalent ways:

1. Invest $1000 in zero-coupon bonds (for example, Treasury bills) along with the forward contract, in which case each position initially costs $1000 at time 0.

2. Borrow to buy the physical S&R index, in which case each position initially costs $0 at time 0.

Suppose the 6-month interest rate is 2%. With alternative 1, we pay $1000 today. After 6 months the zero-coupon bond is worth $1000 × 1.02 = $1020. At that point, we use the bond proceeds to pay the forward price of $1020. We then own the index. The net effect is that we pay $1000 initially and own the index after 6 months, just as if we bought the index outright. Investing $1000 and at the same time entering a long forward contract mimics the effect of buying the index outright.

With alternative 2, we borrow $1000 to buy the index, which costs $1000. Hence, we make no net cash payment at time 0. After 6 months we owe $1000 plus interest. At that time, we repay $1000 × 1.02 = $1020 for the borrowed money. The net effect is that we invest nothing initially and after 6 months pay $1020. We also own the index. Borrowing to buy the stock therefore mimics the effect of entering into a long forward contract.[3]

We conclude that when the index pays no dividends, the only difference between the forward contract and the cash index investment is the timing of a payment that will be made for certain. Therefore, we can compare the two positions by using the interest rate to shift the timing of payments. In the above example, the forward contract and the cash index are equivalent investments, differing only in the timing of the cash flows. Neither form of investing has an advantage over the other.

This analysis suggests a way to systematically compare positions that require different initial investments. We can assume that we borrow any required initial payment. At expiration, we receive the payoff from the contract and repay any borrowed amounts. We will call this the **net payoff** or **profit**. Because this calculation accounts for differing initial investments in a simple fashion, we will primarily use profit rather than payoff diagrams throughout the book.[4] Note that the payoff and profit diagrams are the same for a forward contract because it requires no initial investment.

To summarize, a **payoff diagram** graphs the cash value of a position at a point in time. A **profit diagram** subtracts from the payoff the future value of the investment in the position.

This discussion raises a question: Given our assumptions, should we really expect the forward price to equal $1020, which is the future value of the index? The answer is yes, but we defer a detailed explanation until Chapter 5.

Zero-Coupon Bonds in Payoff and Profit Diagrams

The preceding discussion showed that the long forward contract and outright purchase of the physical S&R index are essentially the same once we take time value of money into account. Buying the physical index is like entering into the forward contract and

---

[3] If the index paid a dividend in this example, then we would receive the dividend by holding the physical index, but not when we entered into the forward contract. We will see in Chapter 5 how to take dividends into account in this comparison.

[4] The term "profit" is defined variously by accountants and economists. All of our profit calculations are for the purpose of *comparing* one position with another, not computing profit in any absolute sense.

simultaneously investing $1000 in a zero-coupon bond. We can see this same point graphically by using a payoff diagram where we include a zero-coupon bond.

Suppose we enter into a long S&R index forward position and at the same time purchase a $1000 zero-coupon bond, which will pay $1020 after 6 months. (This was alternative 1 in the previous section.) Algebraically, the payoff to the forward plus the bond is

$$\text{Forward} + \text{bond} = \underbrace{\text{Spot price at expiration} - \$1020}_{\text{Forward payoff}} + \underbrace{\$1020}_{\text{Bond payoff}}$$

$$= \text{Spot price at expiration}$$

This is the same as the payoff to investing in the physical index.

The payoff diagram for this position is an easy modification of Figure 2.3. We simply add a line representing the value of the bond after 6 months ($1000 × 1.02 = $1020) and then add the bond payoff to the forward payoff. This is graphed in Figure 2.4. The forward plus bond looks exactly like the physical index in Figure 2.3.

What is the profit diagram corresponding to this payoff diagram? For the forward contract, profit is the same as the payoff because there is no initial investment. Profit for the forward plus bond is obtained by subtracting the future value of the initial investment. The initial investment was the cost of the bond, $1000. Its future value is, by definition, $1020, the value of the bond after 6 months. Thus, the profit diagram for a forward contract plus a bond is obtained by *ignoring* the bond! Put differently, adding a bond to a position leaves a profit diagram unaffected.

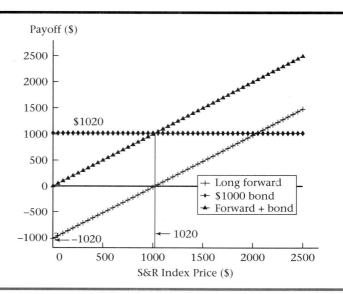

FIGURE 2.4

Payoff diagram for a long S&R forward contract, together with a zero-coupon bond that pays $1020 at maturity. Summing the value of the long forward plus the bond at each S&R index price gives the line labeled "Forward + bond."

Depending on the context, it can be helpful to draw either payoff or profit diagrams. Bonds can be used to shift payoff diagrams vertically, but they do not change the profit calculation.

Cash Settlement Versus Delivery

The foregoing discussion assumed that at expiration of the forward contract, the contract called for the seller (the party short the forward contract) to deliver the cash S&R index to the buyer (the party long the forward contract). However, a physical transaction in a broad stock index will likely have significant transaction costs. An alternative settlement procedure that is widely used is **cash settlement.** Instead of requiring delivery of the actual index, the forward contract settles financially. The two parties make a net cash payment, which yields the same cash flow as if delivery had occurred and both parties had then closed out their positions. We can illustrate this with an example.

Example 2.2 Suppose that the S&R index at expiration is $1040. Because the forward price is $1020, the long position has a payoff of $20. Similarly, the short position loses $20. With cash settlement, the short simply pays $20 to the long, with no transfer of the physical asset and hence no transaction costs. It is as if the long paid $1020, acquired the index worth $1040, and then immediately sold it with no transaction costs.

If the S&R index price at expiration had instead been $960, the long position would have a payoff of −$60 and the short would have a payoff of $60. Cash settlement in this case entails the long paying $60 to the short.

Cash settlement is feasible only when there is an accepted reference price upon which the settlement can be based. Cash settlement is not limited to forward contracts—virtually any financial contract can be settled using cash rather than delivery.

Credit Risk

Any forward or futures contract—indeed, any derivatives contract—has **credit risk,** which means there is a possibility that the counterparty who owes money fails to make a payment. If you agree to sell the index in 1 year at a fixed price and the spot price turns out to be lower than the forward price, the counterparty is obligated to buy the index for more than it is worth. You face the risk that the counterparty will for some reason fail to pay the forward price. Similarly, the counterparty faces the risk that you will not fulfill the contract if the spot price in 1 year turns out to be higher than the forward price.

With exchange-traded contracts, the exchange goes to great lengths to minimize this risk by requiring collateral of all participants and being the ultimate counterparty in all transactions. We will discuss credit risk and collateral in more detail when we discuss futures contracts in Chapter 5. With over-the-counter contracts, the fact that the contracts are transacted directly between two parties means that each counterparty bears the credit risk of the other.[5]

Credit risk is an important problem with all derivatives, but it is also quite complicated. Credit checks of counterparties and credit protections such as collateral and bank letters of credit are commonly employed to guard against losses from counterparty default. Recently, there has been a rapidly growing market in credit derivatives (see Table 1.3 on page 11); these can be used to protect against the credit problems of a counterparty.

2.2 CALL OPTIONS

We have seen that a forward contract obligates the buyer (the holder of the long position) to pay the forward price at expiration, even if the value of the underlying asset at expiration is less than the forward price. Because losses are possible with a forward contract, it is natural to wonder: Could there be a contract where the buyer has the right to walk away from the deal?

The answer is yes; a **call option** is a contract where the buyer has the right to buy, but not the obligation to buy. Here is an example illustrating how a call option works at expiration.

Example 2.3 Suppose that an investor has purchased a 6-month call option, i.e., the investor has agreed to pay $1020 for the S&R index in 6 months but is not obligated to do so. If in 6 months the S&R price is $1100, the buyer will pay $1020 and receive the index. This is a payoff of $80 per unit of the index. If the S&R price is $900, the buyer walks away.

Now think about this transaction from the seller's point of view. The buyer is in control of the option, deciding when to buy the index by paying $1020. Thus, the rights of the option buyer are obligations for the option seller.

Example 2.4 Suppose that in 6 months the S&R price is $1100. The seller of the option will receive $1020 and give to the buyer an index worth $1100, for a loss of $80 per unit of the index. If the S&R price is less than $1020, the buyer will walk away (as in the previous example), so the seller has no obligation. Thus, at expiration, the seller will have a payoff that is zero (if the S&R price is less than $1020) or negative (if the S&R price is greater than $1020).

Does it seem as if something is wrong here? Because the buyer can decide whether to buy, the seller *cannot* make money at expiration. This situation suggests that the seller

---

[5] Of course, credit risk also exists in exchange-traded contracts. The specific details of how exchanges are structured to minimize credit risk is a complicated and fascinating subject (see Edwards and Ma (1992), ch. 3, for details). In practice, exchanges are regarded by participants as good credit risks.

must, in effect, be "bribed" to enter into the contract in the first place. At the time the buyer and seller agree to the contract, the buyer must pay the seller an initial price, or **premium.** This initial payment compensates the seller for being at a disadvantage at expiration. Contrast this with a forward contract, for which the initial premium is zero.

Option Terminology

Here are some key terms used to describe options:

Strike price: The **strike price,** or **exercise price,** of a call option is what the buyer pays for the asset. In the example above, the strike price was $1020. The strike price can be set at any value.

Exercise: The **exercise** of a call option is the act of paying the strike price to receive the asset. In Example 2.3, the buyer decided after 6 months whether to exercise the option—i.e., whether to pay $1020 (the strike price) to receive the S&R index.

Expiration: The **expiration** of the option is the date by which the option must be exercised or it becomes worthless. The option in Example 2.3 had an expiration of 6 months.

Exercise style: The **exercise style** of the option governs the time at which exercise can occur. In the above example, exercise could occur only at expiration. Such an option is said to be a **European-style option.** If the buyer has the right to exercise at any time during the life of the option, it is an **American-style option.** If the buyer can only exercise during specified periods, but not for the entire life of the option, the option is a **Bermudan-style option.** (The terms "European" and "American," by the way, have nothing to do with geography. European, American, and Bermudan options are bought and sold worldwide.)

To summarize, a European call option gives the owner of the call the right, but not the obligation, to buy the underlying asset on the expiration date by paying the strike price. The option described in Examples 2.3 and 2.4 is a *6-month European-style S&R call with a strike price of $1020*. The buyer of the call can also be described as having a *long position* in the call.

Table 2.2 presents a small portion of the option-price listings for the S&P 500 index option traded at the Chicago Board Options Exchange. Each row presents call and put prices, volume, and open interest for a particular expiration date and strike price pair. Almost 500 different combinations of strikes and expirations were available for the S&P 500 index on that date. As with futures, every option trade requires a buyer and a seller, so open interest measures the number of buyer-seller pairs. Box 2.2 discusses some of the mechanics of buying an option.

For the time being, we will discuss European-style options exclusively. We do this because European options are the simplest to discuss and are also quite common in practice. While most exchange-traded options are American, the options in Table 2.2 are European. Later in the book we discuss American options in more detail.

TABLE 2.2 Closing prices, daily volume, and open interest for S&P 500 options, listed on the Chicago Board Options Exchange, on August 14, 2007. The S&P 500 index closed that day at 1426.54.

Expiration	Strike	Bid	Ask	Call Vol.	Open Int.	Bid	Ask	Put Vol.	Open Int.
Sept 2007	1400	65.30	69.30	67	36960	31.40	35.40	30734	152255
Sept 2007	1425	48.60	52.60	12923	31527	39.60	41.50	11014	117580
Sept 2007	1435	33.90	37.90	36280	101618	49.70	52.00	48544	169252
Oct 2007	1400	78.50	82.50	0	7	40.80	44.80	604	43513
Oct 2007	1425	62.00	66.00	14	600	48.90	52.90	4995	50739
Oct 2007	1450	47.20	51.20	8820	22722	59.00	63.00	9364	42057

Source: www.cboe.com

Box 2.2: How Do You Buy an Option?

How would you actually buy an option? The quick answer is that buying an option is just like buying a stock. Option premiums are quoted just like stock prices. Figure 2.2 provides an example. (For current quotes see, for example, http://www.cboe.com; this shows bid and ask prices at the Chicago Board Options Exchange.) Using either an online or flesh-and-blood broker, you can enter an order to buy an option. As with stocks, in addition to the option premium, you pay a commission, and there is a bid-ask spread. Also, an option buyer, like a stock buyer, has to decide whether to use a market order or a limit order to trade the option.

Options on numerous stocks are traded on exchanges, and for any given stock or index, there can be over a hundred options available, differing in strike price and expiration date. (As an experiment, you can see how many different options are listed for the S&P 500 index at the Chicago Board Options Exchange Web site.) Options may be either American or European. If you buy an American option, you have to be aware that exercising the option prior to expiration may be optimal. Thus, you need to have some understanding of why and when exercise might make sense.

You can also sell, or write, options. In this case, you have to post collateral (called *margin*) to protect others against the possibility you will default.

Payoff and Profit for a Purchased Call Option

We can graph call options as we did forward contracts. The buyer is not obligated to buy the index, and hence will only exercise the option if the payoff is greater than zero. The algebraic expression for the *payoff* to a purchased call is therefore

$$\text{Purchased call payoff} = \max[0, \text{spot price at expiration} - \text{strike price}] \quad (2.3)$$

The expression $\max[a, b]$ means "take the greater of the two values a and b." (Spreadsheets contain a max function, so it is easy to compute option payoffs in a spreadsheet.)

Example 2.5 Consider a call option on the S&R index with 6 months to expiration and a strike price of $1000. Suppose the index in 6 months is $1100. Clearly, it is worthwhile to pay the $1000 strike price to acquire the index worth $1100. Using equation (2.3), the call payoff is

$$\max[0, \$1100 - \$1000] = \$100$$

If the index is $900 at expiration, it is not worthwhile paying the $1000 strike price to buy the index worth $900. The payoff is then

$$\max[0, \$900 - \$1000] = \$0$$

As discussed before, the payoff does not take account of the initial cost of acquiring the position. For a purchased option, the premium is paid at the time the option is acquired. In computing profit at expiration, suppose we defer the premium payment; then by the time of expiration we accrue 6 months' interest on the premium. The option *profit* is computed as

$$\text{Purchased call profit} = \max[0, \text{spot price at expiration} - \text{strike price}]$$
$$- \text{future value of option premium} \quad (2.4)$$

The following example illustrates the computation of the profit.

Example 2.6 Use the same option as in Example 2.5, and suppose that the risk-free rate is 2% over 6 months. Assume that the premium for this call is $93.81.[6] Hence, the future value of the call premium is $93.81 × 1.02 = $95.68. If the S&R index price at expiration is $1100, the owner will exercise the option. Using equation (2.4), the call profit is

$$\max[0, \$1100 - \$1000] - \$95.68 = \$4.32$$

---

[6] It is not important at this point how we compute this price, but if you wish to replicate the option premiums, they are computed using the Black-Scholes formula, which we discuss in Chapter 11. Using the BSCall spreadsheet function accompanying this book, the call price is computed as BSCall(1000, 1000, 0.3, 2 × ln(1.02), 0.5, 0) = 93.81.

TABLE 2.3

Payoff and profit after 6 months from a purchased 1,000-strike S&R call option with a future value of premium of $95.68. The option premium is assumed to be $93.81 and the effective interest rate is 2% over 6 months. The payoff is computed using equation (2.3) and the profit using equation (2.4).

S&R Index in 6 Months	Call Payoff	Future Value of Premium	Call Profit
800	$0	−$95.68	−$95.68
850	0	−95.68	−95.68
900	0	−95.68	−95.68
950	0	−95.68	−95.68
1000	0	−95.68	−95.68
1050	50	−95.68	−45.68
1100	100	−95.68	4.32
1150	150	−95.68	54.32
1200	200	−95.68	104.32

If the index is $900 at expiration, the owner does not exercise the option. It is not worthwhile paying the $1000 strike price to buy the index worth $900. Profit is then

$$\max[0, \$900 - \$1000] - \$95.68 = -\$95.68$$

reflecting the loss of the premium.

We graph the call *payoff* by computing, for any index price at expiration, the payoff on the option position as a function of the price. We graph the call *profit* by subtracting from this the future value of the option premium. Table 2.3 computes the payoff and profit at different index values, computed as in Examples 2.5 and 2.6. Note that because the strike price is fixed, a higher market price at expiration of the S&R index benefits the call buyer.

Figure 2.5 graphs the call payoff that is computed in Table 2.3. The graph clearly shows the "optionality" of the option: Below the strike price of $1000, the payoff is zero, whereas above $1000, the payoff is positive and increasing.

The last column in Table 2.3 computes the call profit at different index values. Because a purchased call and a forward contract are both ways to buy the index, it is interesting to contrast the two. Thus, Figure 2.6 plots the profit on both a purchased call and a long forward contract. Note that profit and payoff diagrams for an option differ by the future value of the premium, whereas for a forward contract they are the same.

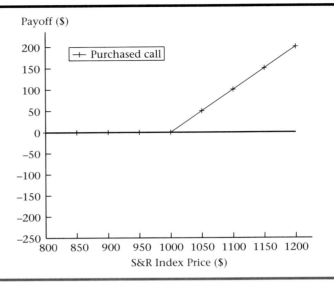

FIGURE 2.5

The payoff at expiration of a purchased S&R call with a $1000 strike price.

If the index rises, the forward contract is more profitable than the option because it does not entail paying a premium. If the index falls sufficiently, however, the option is more profitable because the most the option buyer loses is the future value of the premium. This difference suggests that we can think of the call option as an *insured* position in the index. Insurance protects against losses, and the call option does the same. Carrying the analogy a bit further, we can think of the option premium as, in part, reflecting the cost of that insurance. The forward, which is free, has no such insurance, and potentially has losses larger than those on the call.

This discussion highlights the important point that there are always trade-offs in selecting a position. The forward contract outperforms the call if the index rises, and underperforms the call if the index falls sufficiently. When all contracts are fairly priced, you will not find a contract that has higher profits for all possible index market prices.

Payoff and Profit for a Written Call Option

Now let's look at the option from the point of view of the seller. The seller is said to be the **option writer,** or to have a short position in a call option. The option writer is the counterparty to the option buyer. The writer receives the premium for the option and then has an obligation to sell the underlying security in exchange for the strike price if the option buyer exercises the option.

The payoff and profit to a written call are just the opposite of those for a purchased call:

$$\text{Written call payoff} = -\max[0, \text{spot price at expiration} - \text{strike price}] \quad (2.5)$$

FIGURE 2.6

Profit at expiration for purchase of 6-month S&R index call with strike price of $1000 versus profit on long S&R index forward position.

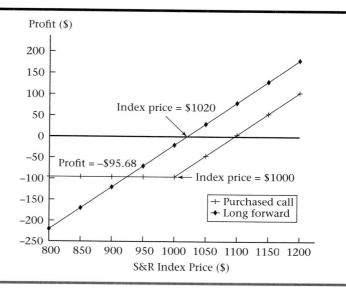

$$\text{Written call profit} = -\max[0, \text{spot price at expiration} - \text{strike price}]$$
$$+ \text{future value of option premium} \qquad (2.6)$$

This example illustrates the option writer's payoff and profit. Just as a call buyer is long in the call, the call seller has a short position in the call.

Example 2.7 Consider a 1000-strike call option on the S&R index with 6 months to expiration. At the time the option is written, the option seller receives the premium of $93.81.

Suppose the index in 6 months is $1100. It is worthwhile for the option buyer to pay the $1000 strike price to acquire the index worth $1100. Thus, the option writer will have to sell the index, worth $1100, for the strike price of $1000. Using equation (2.5), the written call payoff is

$$-\max[0, \$1100 - \$1000] = -\$100$$

The premium has earned 2% interest for 6 months and is now worth $95.68. Profit for the written call is

$$-\$100 + \$95.68 = -\$4.32$$

If the index is $900 at expiration, it is not worthwhile for the option buyer to pay the $1000 strike price to buy the index worth $900. The payoff is then

$$-\max[0, \$900 - \$1000] = \$0$$

The option writer keeps the premium, for a profit after 6 months of $95.68.

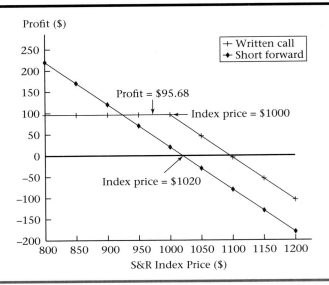

FIGURE 2.7

Profit for writer of 6-month S&R call with strike of $1000 versus profit for short S&R forward.

Figure 2.7 depicts a graph of the option writer's profit, graphed against a short forward contract. Note that it is the mirror image of the call buyer's profit in Figure 2.6.

2.3 PUT OPTIONS

We introduced a call option by comparing it to a forward contract in which the buyer need not buy the underlying asset if it is worth less than the agreed-to purchase price. Perhaps you wondered if there could also be a contract in which the *seller* could walk away if it is not in his or her interest to sell. The answer is yes. A **put option** is a contract where the seller has the right to sell, but not the obligation. Here is an example to illustrate how a put option works.

Example 2.8 Suppose that an investor has purchased a 6-month put option, i.e., the investor has agreed to sell the S&R index for $1020 in 6 months, but is not obligated to do so. If in 6 months the S&R price is $1100, the seller will not sell for $1020 and will walk away. If the S&R price is $900, the seller *will* sell for $1020 and will earn $120 at that time.

A put must have a premium for the same reason a call has a premium. The buyer of the put controls exercise; hence, the seller of the put will never have a positive payoff at expiration. The put buyer pays a premium when purchasing the option in order to compensate the put seller for this no-win position.

It is important to be crystal clear about the use of the terms "buyer" and "seller" in the above example, because there is potential for confusion. The buyer of the put owns a contract giving the right to sell the index at a set price. Thus, *the buyer of the put is a seller of the index*. Similarly, the seller of the put is obligated to *buy* the index, should the put buyer decide to sell. Thus, the buyer of the put is potentially a seller of the index, and the seller of the put is potentially a buyer of the index. (If thinking through these transactions isn't automatic for you now, don't worry. It will become second nature as you continue to think about options.)

Other terminology for a put option is the same as for a call option, with the obvious change that "buy" becomes "sell." In particular, the strike price is the agreed-upon selling price ($1020 in Example 2.8), exercising the option means selling the underlying asset in exchange for the strike price, and the expiration date is that on which you must exercise the option or it is valueless. As with call options, there are European, American, and Bermudan put options.

Payoff and Profit for a Purchased Put Option

We now see how to compute payoff and profit for a purchased put option. The put option gives the put buyer the right to sell the underlying asset for the strike price. The buyer does this only if the asset is less valuable than the strike price. Thus, the payoff on the put option is

$$\text{Put option payoff} = \max[0, \text{strike price} - \text{spot price at expiration}] \quad (2.7)$$

The put buyer owns the put and therefore has a long position in the put.[7] Here is an example.

Example 2.9 Consider a put option on the S&R index with 6 months to expiration and a strike price of $1000.

Suppose the index in 6 months is $1100. You would not sell the index worth $1100 for the $1000 strike price. Using equation (2.7), the put payoff is

$$\max[0, \$1000 - \$1100] = \$0$$

If the index were $900 at expiration, you *would* sell the index for $1000. The payoff is then

$$\max[0, \$1000 - \$900] = \$100$$

---

[7] To elaborate on this statement: If the price of the put increases, the put buyer benefits. Thus, the put buyer has a long position in the put. However, the put gives the right to sell the stock for a fixed price; hence, the put buyer benefits if the stock price goes down. Thus, the put buyer has a *short* position with respect to the underlying stock. The different perspectives on long and short are summarized in Table 2.5.

As with the call, the payoff does not take account of the initial cost of acquiring the position. At the time the option is acquired, the put buyer pays the option premium to the put seller; we need to account for this in computing profit. If we borrow the premium amount, we must pay 6 months' interest. The option *profit* is computed as

$$\text{Purchased put profit} = \max[0, \text{strike price} - \text{spot price at expiration}]$$
$$- \text{future value of option premium} \quad (2.8)$$

The following example illustrates the computation of profit on the put.

Example 2.10 Use the same option as in Example 2.9, and suppose that the risk-free rate is 2% over 6 months. Assume that the premium for this put is $74.20.[8] The future value of the put premium is $74.20 × 1.02 = $75.68.

If the S&R index price at expiration is $1100, the put buyer will not exercise the option. Using equation (2.8), profit is

$$\max[0, \$1000 - \$1100] - \$75.68 = -\$75.68$$

reflecting the loss of the premium.

If the index is $900 at expiration, the put buyer exercises the put, selling the index for $1000. Profit is then

$$\max[0, \$1000 - \$900] - \$75.68 = \$24.32$$

reflecting the payment of premium.

Table 2.4 computes the payoff and profit on a purchased put for a range of index values at expiration. Whereas call profit increases as the value of the underlying asset *increases*, put profit increases as the value of the underlying asset *decreases*.

Because a put is a way to sell an asset, we can compare it to a short forward position, which is a mandatory sale. Figure 2.8 graphs profit from the purchased put described in Table 2.4 against the profit on a short forward.

We can see from the graph that if the S&R index goes down, the short forward, which has no premium, has a higher profit than the purchased put. If the index goes up sufficiently, the put outperforms the short forward. As with the call, the put is like an insured forward contract. With the put, losses are limited should the index go up. With the short forward, losses are potentially unlimited.

Payoff and Profit for a Written Put Option

Now we examine the put from the perspective of the put writer. The put writer is the counterparty to the buyer. Thus, when the contract is written, the put writer receives the

---

[8] This price is computed using the Black-Scholes formula for the price of a put: BSPut(1000, 1000, 0.3, 2 × ln(1.02), 0.5, 0) = 74.20. We discuss this formula in Chapter 11, but you do not need to understand at this point how to compute the price.

2.3 Put Options

TABLE 2.4 Profit after 6 months from a purchased 1000-strike S&R put option with a future value of premium of $75.68.

S&R Index in 6 Months	Put Payoff	Future Value of Premium	Put Profit
$800	$200	−$75.68	$124.32
850	150	−75.68	74.32
900	100	−75.68	24.32
950	50	−75.68	−25.68
1000	0	−75.68	−75.68
1050	0	−75.68	−75.68
1100	0	−75.68	−75.68
1150	0	−75.68	−75.68
1200	0	−75.68	−75.68

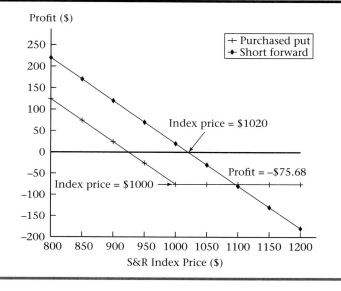

FIGURE 2.8

Profit on a purchased S&R index put with strike price of $1000 versus a short S&R index forward.

premium. At expiration, if the put buyer elects to sell the underlying asset, the put writer must buy it.

The payoff and profit for a written put are the opposite of those for the purchased put:

$$\text{Written put payoff} = - \max[0, \text{strike price} - \text{spot price at expiration}] \quad (2.9)$$

$$\text{Written put profit} = - \max[0, \text{strike price} - \text{spot price at expiration}] \\ + \text{future value of option premium} \quad (2.10)$$

The put seller has sold the put and therefore has a short position in the put.[9]

Example 2.11 Consider a 1000-strike put option on the S&R index with 6 months to expiration. At the time the option is written, the put writer receives the premium of $74.20.

Suppose the index in 6 months is $1100. The put buyer will not exercise the put. Thus, the put writer keeps the premium, plus 6 months' interest, for a payoff of 0 and profit of $75.68.

If the index is $900 in 6 months, the put owner will exercise, selling the index for $1000. Thus, the option writer will have to pay $1000 for an index worth $900. Using equation (2.9), the written put payoff is

$$- \max[0, \$1000 - \$900] = -\$100$$

The premium has earned 2% interest for 6 months and is now worth $75.68. Profit for the written put is therefore

$$-\$100 + \$75.68 = -\$24.32$$

Figure 2.9 graphs the profit diagram for a written put. As you would expect, it is the mirror image of the purchased put.

The "Moneyness" of an Option

Options are often described by their degree of *moneyness*. This term describes whether the option payoff would be positive if the option were exercised immediately. (The term is used to describe both American and European options even though European options cannot be exercised until expiration.) An **in-the-money option** is one that would have a positive payoff (but not necessarily positive profit) if exercised immediately. A call with a strike price less than the asset price and a put with a strike price greater than the asset price are both in-the-money.

---

[9] The put seller benefits if the price of the put falls, and therefore has a short position in the put. However, the put price will fall when the stock price increases, so the put seller is long with respect to the underlying stock. See Table 2.5.

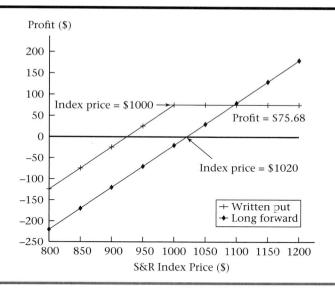

FIGURE 2.9

Written S&R index put option with strike of $1000 versus a long S&R index forward contract.

An **out-of-the-money option** is one that would have a negative payoff if exercised immediately. A call with a strike price greater than the asset price and a put with a strike price less than the asset price are both out-of-the-money.

An **at-the-money option** is one for which the strike price is approximately equal to the asset price.

2.4 SUMMARY OF FORWARD AND OPTION POSITIONS

We have now examined six different positions: Short and long forwards, and purchased and written calls and puts. We can categorize these positions in at least two ways. One way is their potential for gain and loss. Table 2.5 summarizes the maximum possible gain and loss at maturity for forwards and European options.

Another way to categorize the positions is by whether the positions represent buying or selling the underlying asset. Those that represent buying are fundamentally *long* with respect to the underlying asset, while those that represent selling are fundamentally *short* with respect to the underlying asset.

Long Positions

The following positions are long in the sense that there are circumstances in which they represent either a right or an obligation to *buy* the underlying asset:

TABLE 2.5

Maximum possible profit and loss at maturity for long and short forwards and purchased and written calls and puts. FV(premium) denotes the future value of the option premium.

Position	Maximum Loss	Maximum Gain
Positions long with respect to the underlying asset		
Long forward	−Forward price	Unlimited
Purchased call	−FV(premium)	Unlimited
Written put	FV(premium) − Strike price	FV(premium)
Positions short with respect to the underlying asset		
Short forward	Unlimited	Forward price
Written call	Unlimited	FV(premium)
Purchased put	−FV(premium)	Strike price −FV(premium)

Long forward: An *obligation* to buy at a fixed price.

Purchased call: The *right* to buy at a fixed price if it is advantageous to do so.

Written put: An obligation of the put writer to buy the underlying asset at a fixed price if it is advantageous to the option buyer to sell at that price. (Recall that the option *buyer* decides whether or not to exercise.)

Figure 2.10 compares these three positions. Note that the purchased call is long when the asset price is greater than the strike price, and the written put is long when the asset price is less than the strike price. *All three of these positions benefit from rising prices.*

Short Positions

The following positions are short in the sense that there are circumstances in which they represent either a right or an obligation to *sell* the underlying asset:

Short forward: An *obligation* to sell at a fixed price.

Written call: An obligation of the call writer to sell the underlying asset at a fixed price if it is advantageous to the option holder to buy at that price. (Recall that the option *buyer* decides whether to exercise.)

Purchased put: The *right* to sell at a fixed price if it is advantageous to do so.

Figure 2.11 compares these three positions. Note that the written call is short when the asset price is greater than the strike price, and the purchased put is short when the asset price is less than the strike price. *All three of these positions benefit from falling prices.*

2.4 Summary of Forward and Option Positions

FIGURE 2.10

Profit diagrams for the three basic long positions: long forward, purchased call, and written put.

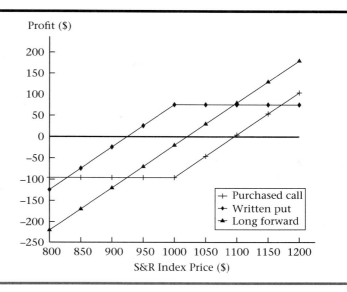

FIGURE 2.11

Profit diagrams for the three basic short positions: short forward, written call, and purchased put.

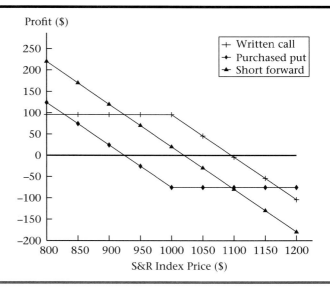

2.5 OPTIONS ARE INSURANCE

In many investment strategies using options, we will see that options serve as insurance against a loss. In what sense are options the same as insurance? In this section we answer this question by considering homeowner's insurance. You will see that options are literally insurance, and insurance is an option.

A homeowner's insurance policy promises that in the event of damage to your house, the insurance company will compensate you for at least part of the damage. The greater the damage, the more the insurance company will pay. Your insurance policy thus derives its value from the value of your house: It is a derivative.

Homeowner's Insurance Is a Put Option

To demonstrate how homeowner's insurance acts as a put option, suppose that you own a house that costs $200,000 to build. To make this example as simple as possible, we assume that physical damage is the only thing that can affect the market value of the house.

Let's say you buy a $15,000 insurance policy to compensate you for damage to the house. Like most policies, this has a deductible, meaning that there is an amount of damage for which you are obligated to pay before the insurance company pays anything. Suppose the deductible is $25,000. If the house suffers $4000 damage from a storm, you pay for all repairs yourself. If the house suffers $45,000 in damage from a storm, you pay $25,000 and the insurance company pays the remaining $20,000. Once damage occurs beyond the amount of the deductible, the insurance company pays for all further damage, up to $175,000. (Why $175,000? Because the house can be rebuilt for $200,000, and you pay $25,000 of that—the deductible—yourself.)

We can graph the profit to you for this insurance policy. Put on the vertical axis the profit on the insurance policy—the payoff less the insurance premium—and on the horizontal axis the value of the house. If the house is undamaged (the house value is $200,000), the payoff is zero, and profit is the loss from the unused insurance premium, $15,000. If the house suffers $50,000 damage, the insurance payoff is $50,000 less the $25,000 deductible, or $25,000. The profit is $25,000 − $15,000 = $10,000. If the house is completely destroyed, the policy pays $175,000, and your profit is $160,000.

Figure 2.12 graphs the profit on the insurance policy. Remarkably, the insurance policy in Figure 2.12 has the same shape as the put option in Figure 2.8. An S&R put is insurance against a fall in the price of the S&R index, just as homeowner's insurance insures against a fall in the price of the house. *Insurance companies are in the business of writing put options!* The $15,000 insurance premium is like the premium of a put, and the $175,000 level at which insurance begins to make payments is like the strike price on a put.

The idea that a put option is insurance also helps us understand what makes a put option cheap or expensive. Two important factors are the riskiness of the underlying asset and the amount of the deductible. Just as with insurance, options will be more expensive when the underlying asset is riskier. Also, the option, like insurance, will be

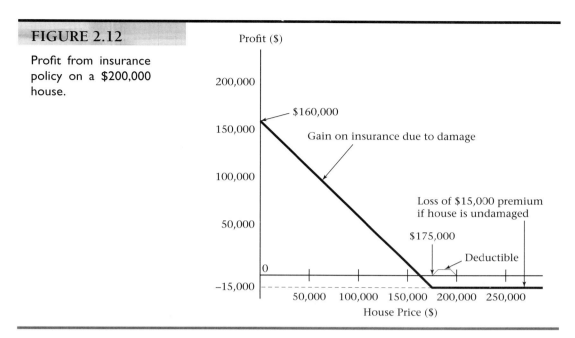

FIGURE 2.12

Profit from insurance policy on a $200,000 house.

less expensive as the deductible gets larger (for the put option, this means lowering the strike price).

You have probably recognized that there are some practical differences between a financial put option and homeowner's insurance. One important difference is that the S&R put pays off no matter why the index price declines. Homeowner's insurance, on the other hand, pays off only if the house declines in value for specified reasons. In particular, a simple decline in real estate prices is not covered by typical homeowner's insurance policies. We avoided this complication by assuming at the outset that only damage could affect the value of the house.

But I Thought Insurance Was Prudent and Put Options Were Risky . . .

If we accept that insurance and put options are the same thing, how do we reconcile this with the common idea that buying insurance is prudent and buying put options is risky?

The risk of a derivative or any other asset or security can only be evaluated in context. Figure 2.12 depicts the risk of an insurance contract *without considering the risk of the insured asset*. This would be like owning insurance on your neighbor's house. It would be "risky" because you would buy the insurance policy, and you would lose your entire investment if there were no insurance claim.[10] We do not normally think of insurance like this, but it illustrates the point that an insurance policy is a put option on the insured asset.

In the same way, Figure 2.8 depicts the risk of a put option without considering the risk of any other positions an investor might be holding. In contrast to homeowner's insurance, many investors *do* own put options without owning the underlying asset. This is why options have a reputation for being risky whereas homeowner's insurance does not. With stock options it is possible to own the insurance without the asset. Of course, many investors who own put options also own the stock. For these investors, the risk is like that of insurance, which we normally think of as risk reducing rather than risk increasing.

Call Options Are Also Insurance

Call options can also be insurance. Whereas a put option is insurance for an asset we already own, a call option is insurance for an asset we plan to own in the future. Put differently, a put option is insurance for a *long* position, while a call option is insurance for a *short* position.

Return to the earlier example of the S&R index. Suppose that the current price of the S&R index is $1000 and that we plan to buy the index in the future. If we buy an S&R call option with a strike price of $1000, this gives us the right to buy S&R for a maximum cost of $1000/share. By buying a call, we have bought insurance against an *increase* in the price.

CHAPTER SUMMARY

Forward contracts and put and call options are the basic derivative instruments that can be used directly and that serve as building blocks for other instruments. A long forward contract represents an obligation to buy the underlying asset at a fixed price, a call option gives its owner the right (but not the obligation) to buy the underlying asset at a fixed price, and a put option gives its owner the right (but not the obligation) to sell the underlying asset at a fixed price. Payoff and profit diagrams are commonly used tools for evaluating the risk of these contracts. Payoff diagrams show the gross value of a position at expiration, and profit diagrams subtract from the payoff the future value of the cost of the position.

Table 2.6 summarizes the characteristics of forwards, calls, and puts, showing which are long or short with respect to the underlying asset. The table describes the strategy associated with each: Forward contracts guarantee a price, purchased options

---

[10] Of course, in real life no insurance company will sell you insurance on your neighbor's house. The reason is that you will then be tempted to cause damage in order to make your policy valuable. Insurance companies call this "moral hazard."

TABLE 2.6 Forwards, calls, and puts at a glance: a summary of forward and option positions.

Derivative Position	Position with Respect to Underlying Asset	Asset Price Contingency	Strategy
Long forward	Long (buy)	Always	Guaranteed price
Short forward	Short (sell)	Always	Guaranteed price
Long call	Long (buy)	> Strike	Insures against high price
Short call	Short (sell)	> Strike	Sells insurance against high price
Long put	Short (sell)	< Strike	Insures against low price
Short put	Long (buy)	< Strike	Sells insurance against low price

are insurance, and written options are selling insurance. Figure 2.13 provides a graphical summary of these positions.

Options can also be viewed as insurance. A put option gives the owner the right to sell if the price declines, just as insurance gives the insured the right to sell (put) a damaged asset to the insurance company.

FURTHER READING

We use the concepts introduced in this chapter throughout the rest of this book. Chapter 3 presents a number of basic option strategies that are widely used in practice, including caps, collars, and floors. Chapter 4 presents the use of options in risk management.

A more general question raised implicitly in this chapter is how the prices of forwards and options are determined. Chapter 5 covers financial forwards and futures in detail, and Chapter 10 introduces the basic ideas underlying option pricing.

Brokerages routinely supply options customers with an introductory pamphlet about options entitled *Characteristics and Risks of Standardized Options*. This is available online from http://www.cboe.com. You can also obtain current option prices from Web sites such as the CBOE's and various brokerage sites.

The notion that options are insurance has been applied in practice. Sharpe (1976), for example, analyzed optimal pension funding policy taking into account pension insurance provided by the Pension Benefit Guaranty Corporation. Merton (1977a) observed that bank deposit insurance, and in fact any loan guarantee, can be modeled as a put option.

FIGURE 2.13

The basic profit diagrams: long and short forward, long and short call, and long and short put.

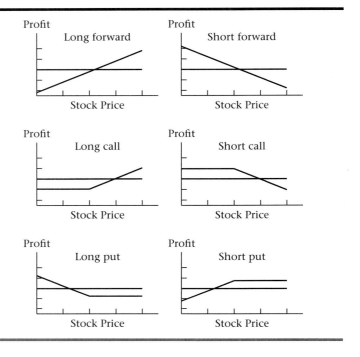

PROBLEMS

In the following problems, if the "effective annual interest rate" is r, a $1 investment yields $1 + r$ after 1 year.

2.1 Suppose XYZ stock has a price of $50 and pays no dividends. The effective annual interest rate is 10%. Draw payoff and profit diagrams for a long position in the stock. Verify that profit is 0 at a price in 1 year of $55.

2.2 Using the same information as the previous question, draw payoff and profit diagrams for a short position in the stock. Verify that profit is 0 at a price in 1 year of $55.

2.3 What position is the opposite of a purchased call? The opposite of a purchased put?

2.4   **a.** Suppose you enter into a long 6-month forward position at a forward price of $50. What is the payoff in 6 months for prices of $40, $45, $50, $55, and $60?

    b. Suppose you buy a 6-month call option with a strike price of $50. What is the payoff in 6 months at the same prices for the underlying asset?

c. Comparing the payoffs of parts (a) and (b), which contract should be more expensive (i.e., the long call or long forward)? Why?

2.5 **a.** Suppose you enter into a short 6-month forward position at a forward price of $50. What is the payoff in 6 months for prices of $40, $45, $50, $55, and $60?

b. Suppose you buy a 6-month put option with a strike price of $50. What is the payoff in 6 months at the same prices for the underlying asset?

c. Comparing the payoffs of parts (a) and (b), which contract should be more expensive (i.e., the long put or short forward)? Why?

2.6 A default-free zero-coupon bond costs $91 and will pay $100 at maturity in 1 year. What is the effective annual interest rate? What is the payoff diagram for the bond? The profit diagram?

2.7 Suppose XYZ stock pays no dividends and has a current price of $50. The forward price for delivery in 1 year is $55. Suppose the 1-year effective annual interest rate is 10%.

a. Graph the payoff and profit diagrams for a forward contract on XYZ stock with a forward price of $55.

b. Is there any advantage to investing in the stock or the forward contract? Why?

c. Suppose XYZ paid a dividend of $2 per year and everything else stayed the same. Now is there any advantage to investing in the stock or the forward contract? Why?

2.8 Suppose XYZ stock pays no dividends and has a current price of $50. The forward price for delivery in 1 year is $53. *If* there is no advantage to buying either the stock or the forward contract, what is the 1-year effective interest rate?

2.9 An *off-market* forward contract is a forward where either you have to pay a premium or you receive a premium for entering into the contract. (With a standard forward contract, the premium is zero.) Suppose the effective annual interest rate is 10% and the S&R index is $1000. Consider 1-year forward contracts.

a. Verify that if the forward price is $1100, the profit diagrams for the index and the 1-year forward are the same.

b. Suppose you are offered a long forward contract at a forward price of $1200. How much would you need to be paid to enter into this contract?

c. Suppose you are offered a long forward contract at $1000. What would you be willing to pay to enter into this forward contract?

2.10 For Figure 2.6, verify the following:

    a. The S&R index price at which the call option diagram intersects the x-axis is $1095.68.

    b. The S&R index price at which the call option and forward contract have the same profit is $924.32.

2.11 For Figure 2.8, verify the following:

    a. The S&R index price at which the put option diagram intersects the x-axis is $924.32.

    b. The S&R index price at which the put option and forward contract have the same profit is $1095.68.

2.12 For each entry in Table 2.5, explain the circumstances in which the maximum gain or loss occurs.

2.13 Suppose the stock price is $40 and the effective annual interest rate is 8%.

    a. Draw on a single graph payoff and profit diagrams for the following options:

        (i) 35-strike call with a premium of $9.12.

        (ii) 40-strike call with a premium of $6.22.

        (iii) 45-strike call with a premium of $4.08.

    b. Consider your payoff diagram with all three options graphed together. Intuitively, why should the option premium decrease with the strike price?

2.14 Suppose the stock price is $40 and the effective annual interest rate is 8%. Draw payoff and profit diagrams for the following options:

    a. 35-strike put with a premium of $1.53.

    b. 40-strike put with a premium of $3.26.

    c. 45-strike put with a premium of $5.75.

Consider your payoff diagram with all three options graphed together. Intuitively, why should the option premium increase with the strike price?

2.15 The profit calculation in the chapter assumes that you borrow at a fixed interest rate to finance investments. An alternative way to borrow is to short-sell stock. What complications would arise in calculating profit if you financed a $1000 S&R index investment by shorting IBM stock rather than by borrowing $1000?

2.16 Construct a spreadsheet that permits you to compute payoff and profit for a short and long stock, a short and long forward, and purchased and written puts and calls. The spreadsheet should let you specify the stock price, forward price, interest rate, option strikes, and option premiums. Use the spreadsheet's max function to compute option payoffs.

3 Insurance, Collars, and Other Strategies

In the last chapter we introduced forwards, calls, and puts; showed that options are insurance; and looked at an example of how options can be building blocks. In this chapter we continue these themes, showing how the use of options can be interpreted as buying or selling insurance. We also continue the building block approach, examining the link between forward prices and option prices, and looking at some common option strategies, including spreads, straddles, and collars. Among your goals in this chapter should be to understand the reasons for using one strategy instead of another and to become facile with drawing and interpreting profit and loss diagrams.

3.1 BASIC INSURANCE STRATEGIES

There are infinite ways to combine options to create different payoffs. In this section we examine two important kinds of strategies in which the option is combined with a position in the underlying asset. First, options can be used to insure long or short asset positions. Second, options can be written against an asset position, in which case the option writer is selling insurance. We will examine four positions: being long the asset coupled with a purchased put or written call, and being short the asset coupled with a purchased call or written put.

In this section we continue to use the S&R index examples presented in Sections 2.2 and 2.3. We assumed a 2% effective 6-month interest rate, and premiums of $93.809 for the 1000-strike 6-month call and $74.201 for the 1000-strike 6-month put.

Insuring a Long Position: Floors

The analysis in Section 2.5 demonstrated that put options are insurance against a fall in the price of an asset. Thus, if we own the S&R index, we can insure the position by buying an S&R put option. The purchase of a put option is also called a **floor**, because we are guaranteeing a minimum sale price for the value of the index.

TABLE 3.1

Payoff and profit at expiration from purchasing the S&R index and a 1000-strike put option. Payoff is the sum of the first two columns. Cost plus interest for the position is ($1000 + $74.201) × 1.02 = $1095.68. Profit is payoff less $1095.68.

Payoff at Expiration		Payoff	−(Cost + Interest)	Profit
S&R Index	S&R Put			
$900	$100	$1000	−$1095.68	−$95.68
950	50	1000	−1095.68	−95.68
1000	0	1000	−1095.68	−95.68
1050	0	1050	−1095.68	−45.68
1100	0	1100	−1095.68	4.32
1150	0	1150	−1095.68	54.32
1200	0	1200	−1095.68	104.32

To examine this strategy, we want to look at the *combined* payoff of the index position and put. In the last chapter we graphed them separately; now we add them together to see the net effect of holding both positions at the same time.

Table 3.1 summarizes the result of buying a 1000-strike put with 6 months to expiration and also buying the index with a price of $1000. The table computes the payoff after 6 months for each position and sums them to obtain the total payoff. The final column takes account of financing cost by subtracting cost plus interest from the payoff to obtain profit. "Cost" here means the initial cash required to establish the position. This is positive when payment is required and negative when cash is received. We also could have computed profit separately for the put and index. For example, if the index is $900 at expiration, we have

$$\underbrace{\$900 - (\$1000 \times 1.02)}_{\text{Profit on S\&R Index}} + \underbrace{\$100 - (\$74.201 \times 1.02)}_{\text{Profit on Put}} = -\$95.68$$

This gives the same result as the calculation performed in Table 3.1. The level of the floor is −$95.68, which is the lowest possible profit.

Figure 3.1 graphs the components of Table 3.1. Panels (c) and (d) show the payoff and profit for the combined index and put positions. The combined payoff graph in panel (c) is created by adding at each index price the value of the index and put positions; this is just like summing columns 1 and 2 in Table 3.1.

Notice in Figure 3.1 that the combined position created by adding the index and the put looks like a call. Intuitively, this equivalence makes sense. A call has a limited loss—the premium—and benefits from gains in the index above the strike price. Similarly, when

FIGURE 3.1

Panel (a) shows the payoff diagram for a long position in the index (column 1 in Table 3.1). Panel (b) shows the payoff diagram for a purchased index put with a strike price of $1000 (column 2 in Table 3.1). Panel (c) shows the combined payoff diagram for the index and put (column 3 in Table 3.1). Panel (d) shows the combined profit diagram for the index and put, obtained by subtracting $1095.68 from the payoff diagram in panel (c)(column 5 in Table 3.1).

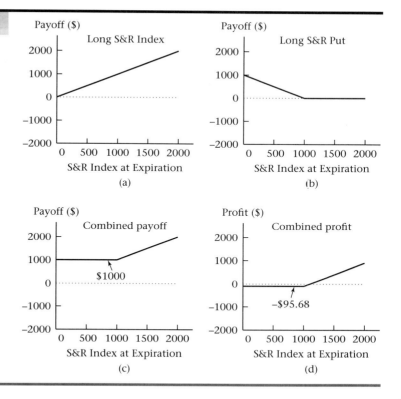

we own the index and buy a put, the put limits losses, but it permits us to benefit from gains in the index. Thus, at a casual level, the call on the one hand and the insured index position on the other seem to have similar characteristics.

Panel (c), however, illustrates that the payoff to the combined position is *not* identical to the payoff from buying a call (compare panel (c) to Figure 2.5). The difference stems from the fact that buying a call entails paying only the option premium, while buying the index and put entails paying for *both* the index and the put option, which together are more expensive than buying a call. The profit diagram in panel (d), however, does look like a call. We discussed in Section 2.1 that adding a bond to a payoff diagram shifts it vertically but leaves a profit diagram unaffected. The combined position of index plus put in panel (c) is actually equivalent to buying a 1000-strike call and buying a zero-coupon bond that pays $1000 at expiration of the option.

The profit diagram in panel (d) of Figure 3.1 is *identical* to the profit diagram for buying an S&R index call with a strike price of $1000, graphed in Figure 2.6. We can see this by comparing Table 2.3 with Table 3.1. The profit of −$95.68 for prices below $1000 is exactly the future value of the 1000-strike 6-month call premium above.

The zero-coupon bond thus affects the payoff in panel (c), but leaves profit in panel (d) unaffected. The cash flows in purchasing a call are different from the cash flows in buying an asset and insuring it, but the profit for the two positions is the same. If we had explicitly borrowed the present value of $1000 ($1000/1.02 = $980.39) to offset the cost of the index and put, then the payoff and profit diagrams, panels (c) and (d) in Figure 3.1, would be identical.

The point that buying an asset and a put generates a position that looks like a call can also be seen using the homeowner's insurance example from Section 2.5. There, we examined the insurance policy in isolation. However, in practice, a buyer of homeowner's insurance also owns the insured asset (the house). Owning a home is analogous to owning the stock index, and insuring the house is like owning a put. Thus, owning a home plus insurance is like owning the index and owning a put. Figure 3.2 depicts the insurance policy from Figure 2.12 together with the uninsured house and the combined position. Interpreting the house as the S&R index and insurance as the put, Figure 3.2 looks exactly like Figure 3.1. *An insured house has a profit diagram that looks like a call option.*

FIGURE 3.2

Payoff to owning a house and owning insurance. We assume a $25,000 deductible and a $200,000 house, with the policy costing $15,000.

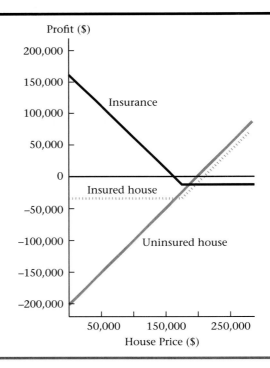

TABLE 3.2

Payoff and profit at expiration from short-selling the S&R index and buying a 1000-strike call option at a premium of $93.809. The payoff is the sum of the first two columns. Cost plus interest for the position is $(-\$1000 + \$93.809) \times 1.02 = -\$924.32$. Profit is payoff plus $924.32.

Payoff at Expiration				
Short S&R Index	S&R Call	Payoff	−(Cost + Interest)	Profit
−$900	$0	−$900	$924.32	$24.32
−950	0	−950	924.32	−25.68
−1000	0	−1000	924.32	−75.68
−1050	50	−1000	924.32	−75.68
−1100	100	−1000	924.32	−75.68
−1150	150	−1000	924.32	−75.68
−1200	200	−1000	924.32	−75.68

Insuring a Short Position: Caps

If we have a short position in the S&R index, we experience a loss when the index rises. We can insure a short position by purchasing a call option to protect against a higher price of repurchasing the index.[1] Buying a call option is also called a **cap.**

Table 3.2 presents the payoff and profit for a short position in the index coupled with a purchased call option. Because we short the index, we earn interest on the short proceeds less the cost of the call option, giving −$924.32 as the future value of the cost.

Figure 3.3 graphs the columns of Table 3.2. The payoff and profit diagrams resemble those of a purchased put. As with the insured index position in Figure 3.1, we have to be careful in dealing with cash flows. The *payoff* in panel (c) of Figure 3.3 is like that of a purchased put coupled with borrowing. In this case, the payoff diagram for shorting the index and buying a call is equivalent to that from buying a put and borrowing the present value of $1000 ($980.39). Since profit diagrams are unaffected by borrowing, however, the profit diagram in panel (d) is exactly the same as that for a purchased S&R index put. You can see this by comparing panel (d) with Figure 2.8. Not only does the insured short position look like a put, it has the same loss as a purchased put if the price is above $1000: $75.68, which is the future value of the $74.201 put premium.

---

[1] Keep in mind that if you have an obligation to buy the index in the future but the price is not fixed, then you have an *implicit* short position (if the price goes up, you will have to pay more). A call is insurance for both explicit and implicit short-sellers.

FIGURE 3.3

Panel (a) shows the payoff diagram for a short position in the index (column 1 in Table 3.2). Panel (b) shows the payoff diagram for a purchased index call with a strike price of $1000 (column 2 in Table 3.2). Panel (c) shows the combined payoff diagram for the short index and long call (column 3 in Table 3.2). Panel (d) shows the combined profit diagram for the short index and long call, obtained by adding $924.32 to the payoff diagram in panel (c) (column 5 in Table 3.2).

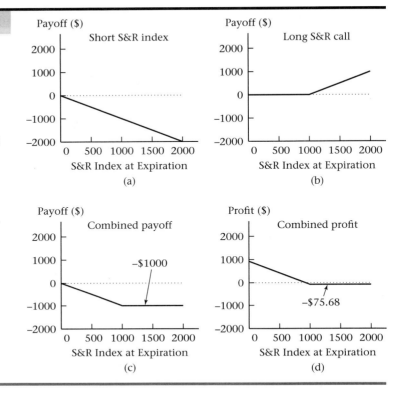

Selling Insurance

We can expect that some investors want to purchase insurance. However, for every insurance buyer there must be an insurance seller. In this section we examine strategies in which investors *sell* insurance.

It is possible, of course, for an investor to simply sell calls and puts. Often, however, investors also have a position in the asset when they sell insurance. Writing an option when there is a corresponding long position in the underlying asset is called **covered writing, option overwriting,** or selling a covered call. All three terms mean essentially the same thing.[2] In contrast, **naked writing** occurs when the writer of an option does not have a position in the asset.

---

[2] Technically, "option overwriting" refers to selling a call on stock you already own, while a "covered write" entails simultaneously buying the stock and selling a call. The distinction is irrelevant for our purposes.

3.1 Basic Insurance Strategies

Covered call writing If we own the S&R index and simultaneously sell a call option, we have written a **covered call**. A covered call will have limited profitability if the index increases, because an option writer is obligated to sell the index for the strike price. Should the index decrease, the loss on the index is offset by the premium earned from selling the call. A payoff with limited profit for price increases and potentially large losses for price decreases sounds like a written put.

Because the covered call looks like a written put, the maximum profit will be the same as with a written put. Suppose the index is $1100 at expiration. The profit is

$$\underbrace{\$1100 - (\$1000 \times 1.02)}_{\text{Profit on S\&R Index}} + \underbrace{(\$93.809 \times 1.02) - \$100}_{\text{Profit on Written Call}} = \$75.68$$

which is the future value of the premium received from writing a 1000-strike put.

The profit from writing the 1000-strike call is computed in Table 3.3 and graphed in Figure 3.4. If the index falls, we lose money on the index, but the option premium partially offsets the loss. If the index rises above the strike price, the written option loses money, negating gains on the index.

Comparing Table 3.3 with Table 2.4, we can see that writing the covered call generates *exactly* the same profit as selling a put.

Why would anyone write a covered call? Suppose you have the view that the index is unlikely to move either up or down. (This is sometimes called a "neutral" market view.) If in fact the index does not move and you have written a call, then you keep the premium. If you are wrong and the stock appreciates, you forgo gains you would have had if you did not write the call.

TABLE 3.3 Payoff and profit at expiration from purchasing the S&R index and selling a 1000-strike call option. The payoff column is the sum of the first two columns. Cost plus interest for the position is ($1000 − $93.809) × 1.02 = $924.32. Profit is payoff less $924.32.

Payoff at Expiration				
S&R Index	Short S&R Call	Payoff	−(Cost + Interest)	Profit
$900	$0	$900	−$924.32	−$24.32
950	0	950	−924.32	25.68
1000	0	1000	−924.32	75.68
1050	−50	1000	−924.32	75.68
1100	−100	1000	−924.32	75.68
1150	−150	1000	−924.32	75.68
1200	−200	1000	−924.32	75.68

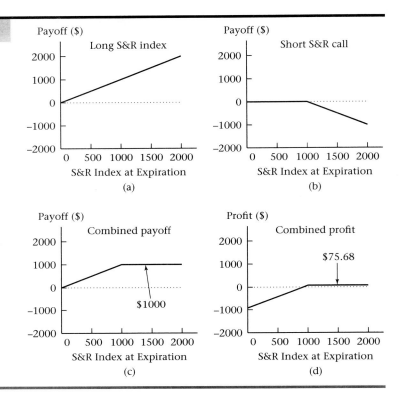

FIGURE 3.4

Payoff and profit diagrams for writing a covered S&R call. Panel (a) is the payoff to a long S&R position. Panel (b) is the payoff to a short S&R call with strike price of $1000. Panel (c) is the combined payoff for the S&R index and written call. Panel (d) is the combined profit, obtained by subtracting ($1000 − $93.809) × 1.02 = $924.32 from the payoff in panel (c).

Covered puts A covered put is achieved by writing a put against a short position on the index. The written put obligates you to buy the index—for a loss—if it goes down in price. Thus, for index prices below the strike price, the loss on the written put offsets the short stock. For index prices above the strike price, you lose on the short stock.

A position where you have a constant payoff below the strike and increasing losses above the strike sounds like a written call. In fact, shorting the index and writing a put produces a profit diagram that is exactly the same as for a written call. Figure 3.5 shows this graphically, and Problem 3.2 asks you to verify this by constructing a payoff table.

3.2 USING OPTIONS TO CREATE SYNTHETIC FORWARDS

It is possible to mimic a long forward position on an asset by buying a call and selling a put, with each option having the same strike price and time to expiration. For example, we could buy the 1000-strike S&R call and sell the 1000-strike S&R put, each with 6 months to expiration. In 6 months we will be obliged to pay $1000 to buy the index, just as if we had entered into a forward contract.

3.2 Using Options to Create Synthetic Forwards

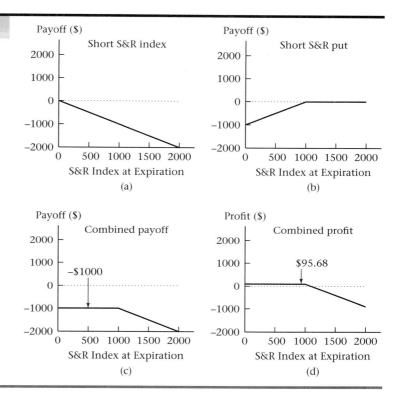

FIGURE 3.5

Payoff and profit diagrams for writing a covered S&R put. Panel (a) is the payoff to a short S&R position. Panel (b) is the payoff to a short S&R put with a strike price of $1000. Panel (c) is the combined payoff for the short S&R index and written put. Panel (d) is the combined profit, obtained by adding ($1000 + $74.201) × 1.02 = $1095.68 to the payoff in panel (c).

To see that buying the 1000-strike call and selling the 1000-strike put mimics the forward, consider what happens at expiration. Suppose the index in 6 months is at $900. We will not exercise the call, but we have written a put. The put buyer will exercise the right to sell the index for $1000; therefore, we are obligated to buy the index at $1000. If instead the index is at $1100, the put is not exercised, but we exercise the call, buying the index for $1000. Thus, whether the index rises or falls, when the options expire we buy the index for the strike price of the options, $1000.

The purchased call, written put, and combined positions are shown in Figure 3.6. The purchase of a call and sale of a put creates a *synthetic* long forward contract, which has two minor differences from the actual forward:

1. The forward contract has a zero premium, while the synthetic forward requires that we pay the net option premium.
2. With the forward contract we pay the forward price, while with the synthetic forward we pay the strike price.

FIGURE 3.6

Purchase of a 1000-strike S&R call, sale of a 1000-strike S&R put, and the combined position. The combined position resembles the profit on a long forward contract.

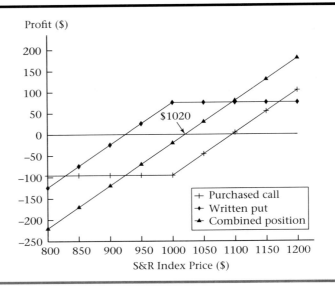

If you think about it, these two considerations must be related. If we set the strike price below the forward price, we are obligated to buy the index at a discount relative to the forward price. Buying at a lower price than the forward price is a benefit. In order to obtain this benefit we have to pay the positive net option premium, which stems from the call being more expensive than the put. In fact, in Figure 3.6, the implicit cost of the synthetic forward—the price at which the profit on the combined call-put position is zero—is $1020, which is the S&R forward price.

Similarly, if we set the strike price above the forward price, we are obligated to buy the index at a high price relative to the forward price. To offset the extra cost of acquiring the index using the high strike options, it makes sense that we would receive payment initially. This would occur if the put that we sell is more expensive than the call we buy.

Finally, if we set the strike price equal to the forward price, then to mimic the forward the initial premium must equal zero. In this case, put and call premiums must be equal.

Put-Call Parity

We can summarize this argument by saying that *the net cost of buying the index using options must equal the net cost of buying the index using a forward contract*. If at time 0 we enter into a long forward position expiring at time T, we obligate ourselves to buying the index at the forward price, $F_{0,T}$. The present value of buying the index in the future is just the present value of the forward price, $\text{PV}(F_{0,T})$.

If instead we buy a call and sell a put today to guarantee the purchase price for the index in the future, the present value of the cost is the net option premium for buying the call and selling the put, Call(K, T) − Put(K, T), plus the present value of the strike price, PV(K). (The notations "Call(K, T)" and "Put(K, T)" denote the premiums of options with strike price K and with T periods until expiration.)

Equating the costs of the alternative ways to buy the index at time t gives us

$$PV(F_{0,T}) = [\text{Call}(K, T) - \text{Put}(K, T)] + PV(K)$$

We can rewrite this as

$$\boxed{\text{Call}(K, T) - \text{Put}(K, T) = PV(F_{0,T} - K)} \tag{3.1}$$

In words, the present value of the bargain element from buying the index at the strike price (the right-hand side of equation (3.1)) must be offset by the initial net option premium (the left-hand side of equation (3.1)). Equation (3.1) is known as **put-call parity**. It is one of the most important relations in options.

Example 3.1 As an example of equation (3.1), consider buying the 6-month 1000-strike S&R call for a premium of $93.809 and selling the 6-month 1000-strike put for a premium of $74.201. These transactions create a synthetic forward permitting us to buy the index in 6 months for $1000. Because the actual forward price is $1020, this synthetic forward permits us to buy the index at a bargain of $20, the present value of which is $20/1.02 = $19.61. The difference in option premiums must therefore be $19.61. In fact, $93.809 − $74.201 = $19.61. This result is exactly what we would get with equation (3.1):

$$\$93.809 - \$74.201 = PV(\$1020 - \$1000)$$

A forward contract for which the premium is not zero is sometimes called an **off-market forward**. This terminology arises because a true forward by definition has a zero premium. Therefore, a forward contract with a nonzero premium must have a forward price that is "off the market (forward) price." Unless the strike price equals the forward price, buying a call and selling a put creates an off-market forward.

Equivalence of different positions We have seen earlier that buying the index and buying a put generates the same profit as buying a call. Similarly, selling a covered call (buying the index and selling a call) generates the same profit as selling a put. Equation (3.1) explains why this happens.

Consider buying the index and buying a put, as in Section 3.1. Recall that, in this example, we have the forward price equal to $1020 and the index price equal to $1000. Thus, the present value of the forward price equals the index price. Rewriting equation (3.1) gives

$$PV(F_{0,T}) + \text{Put}(K, T) = \text{Call}(K, T) + PV(K)$$
$$\$1000 + \$74.201 = \$93.809 + \$980.39$$

That is, buying the index and buying the put costs the same, and generates the same payoff, as does buying the call and buying a zero-coupon bond costing PV(K). (Recall from Section 2.1 that a bond does not affect profit.)

Similarly, in the case of writing a covered call, we have

$$\text{PV}(F_{0,T}) - \text{Call}(K, T) = \text{PV}(K) - \text{Put}(K, T)$$

That is, writing a covered call has the same profit as lending PV(K) and selling a put. Equation (3.1) provides a tool for constructing equivalent positions.

No arbitrage In deriving equation (3.1), and in some earlier discussions, we relied on the idea that if two different investments generate the same payoff, they must have the same cost. This commonsensical idea is one of the most important in this book. If equation (3.1) did not hold, there would be both low-cost and high-cost ways to acquire the index at time T. We could simultaneously buy the index at low cost and sell the index at high cost. This transaction would have no risk (since we both buy and sell the index) and would generate a positive cash flow (because of the difference in costs). Taking advantage of such an opportunity is called arbitrage, and the idea that prices should not permit arbitrage is called "no-arbitrage pricing." We implicitly illustrated this idea earlier in showing how owning the index and buying a put has the same profit as a call, etc. No-arbitrage pricing will be a major theme in Chapter 5 and later chapters.[3]

3.3 SPREADS AND COLLARS

There are many well-known, commonly used strategies that combine two or more options. In this section we discuss some of these strategies and explain the motivation for using them. The underlying theme in this section is that there are always trade-offs in designing a position: It is always possible to lower the cost of a position by reducing its payoff. Thus, there are many variations on each particular strategy.

All the examples in this section will use the set of option prices in Table 3.4. We will assume that the continuously compounded interest rate is 8%; this is equivalent to an effective annual interest rate of 8.33%.[4]

---

[3] Another way to express the principle of no arbitrage is using profit diagrams. Given two profit diagrams, there is an arbitrage opportunity if one diagram is everywhere above the other. This statement is not true for payoff diagrams, because payoff diagrams do not take into account the initial cost of the position.

[4] You should be comfortable quoting interest rates either as effective annual rates or as continuously compounded rates. Appendix B reviews these conventions for quoting interest rates.

TABLE 3.4

Black-Scholes option prices assuming stock price = $40, volatility = 30%, effective annual risk-free rate = 8.33% (8%, continuously compounded), dividend yield = $0, and 91 days to expiration.

Strike	Call	Put
35	6.13	0.44
40	2.78	1.99
45	0.97	5.08

Bull and Bear Spreads

An option **spread** is a position consisting of only calls or only puts, in which some options are purchased and some written. Spreads are a common strategy. In this section we define some typical spread strategies and explain why you might use a spread.

Suppose you believe a stock will appreciate. Let's compare two ways to speculate on this belief: entering into a long forward contract or buying a call option with the strike price equal to the forward price. The forward contract has a zero premium and the call has a positive premium. A difference in payoffs explains the difference in premiums. If the stock price at expiration is greater than the forward price, the forward contract and call have the same payoff. If the stock price is less than the forward price, however, the forward contract has a loss and the call is worth zero. Put-call parity tells us that the call is equivalent to the forward contract plus a put option. Thus, the call premium equals the cost of the put, which is insurance against the stock price being less than the forward price.

You might ask: Is there a lower-cost way to speculate that the stock price will rise that still has the insurance implicit in the call? The answer is yes: You can lower the cost of your strategy if you are willing to reduce your profit should the stock appreciate. You can do this by selling a call at a higher strike price. The owner of this second call buys appreciation above the higher strike price and pays you a premium. You achieve a lower cost by giving up some portion of profit. A position in which you buy a call and sell an otherwise identical call with a higher strike price is an example of a **bull spread**.

Bull spreads can also be constructed using puts. Perhaps surprisingly, you can achieve the same result either by buying a low-strike call and selling a high-strike call or by buying a low-strike put and selling a high-strike put.

Spreads constructed with either calls or puts are sometimes called **vertical spreads**. The terminology stems from the way option prices are typically presented, with strikes arrayed vertically (as in Table 3.4).

TABLE 3.5
Profit at expiration from purchase of 40-strike call and sale of 45-strike call.

Stock Price at Expiration	Purchased 40-Call	Written 45-Call	Premium Plus Interest	Total
$35.0	$0.0	$0.0	−$1.85	−$1.85
37.5	0.0	0.0	−1.85	−1.85
40.0	0.0	0.0	−1.85	−1.85
42.5	2.5	0.0	−1.85	0.65
45.0	5.0	0.0	−1.85	3.15
47.5	7.5	−2.5	−1.85	3.15
50.0	10.0	−5.0	−1.85	3.15

Example 3.2 To see how a bull spread arises, suppose we want to speculate on the stock price increasing. Consider buying a 40-strike call with 3 months to expiration. From Table 3.4, the premium for this call is $2.78. We can reduce the cost of the position—and also the potential profit—by selling the 45-strike call.

An easy way to construct the graph for this position is to emulate a spreadsheet: For each price, compute the profit of each option position and add up the profits for the individual positions. It is worth working through one example in detail to see how this is done.

The initial net cost of the two options is $2.78 − $0.97 = $1.81. With 3 months' interest, the total cost at expiration is $1.81 \times (1.0833)^{0.25} = \$1.85$. Table 3.5 computes the cash flow at expiration for both options and computes profit on the position by subtracting the future value of the net premium.

Figure 3.7 graphs the position in Table 3.5. You should verify that if you buy the 40-strike put and sell the 45-strike put, you obtain exactly the same graph.

The opposite of a bull spread is a **bear spread.** Using the options from the above example, we could create a bear spread by selling the 40-strike call and buying the 45-strike call. The profit diagram would be exactly the opposite of Figure 3.7.

Box Spreads

A **box spread** is accomplished by using options to create a synthetic long forward at one price and a synthetic short forward at a different price. This strategy guarantees a cash flow in the future. Hence, it is an option spread that is purely a means of borrowing or lending money: It is costly but has no stock price risk.

3.3 Spreads and Collars

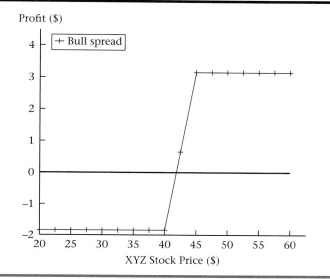

FIGURE 3.7

Profit diagram for a 40–45 bull spread: buying a 40-strike call and selling a 45-strike call.

Example 3.3 Suppose we simultaneously enter into the following two transactions:

1. Buy a 40-strike call and sell a 40-strike put
2. Sell a 45-strike call and buy a 45-strike put

The first transaction is a synthetic forward purchase of a stock for $40, while the second transaction is the synthetic forward sale of the stock for $45. Clearly, the payoff at expiration will be $5; hence, the transaction has no stock price risk. Using the assumptions in Table 3.4, the cost of the strategy should be

$$5 \times (1.0833)^{-0.25} = \$4.90$$

In fact, using the premiums in Table 3.4, the initial cash flow is

$$(\$1.99 - \$2.78) + (\$0.97 - \$5.08) = -\$4.90$$

Another way to view this transaction is that we have bought a 40–45 bull spread using calls (buy 40 call, sell 45 call) and bought a 40–45 bear spread using puts (sell 40 put, buy 45 put).

Ratio Spreads

A **ratio spread** is constructed by buying m calls at one strike and selling n calls at a different strike, with all options having the same time to maturity and same underlying asset. Ratio spreads can also be constructed with puts. You are asked to construct ratio spreads in Problem 3.15. Also, a ratio spread constructed by buying a low-strike call and selling two higher-strike calls is one of the positions depicted in the chapter summary in Figure 3.16.

Since ratio spreads involve buying and selling unequal numbers of options, it is possible to construct ratio spreads with zero premium. The significance of this may not be obvious to you now, but we will see in Chapter 4 that by using ratio spreads we can construct paylater strategies: insurance that costs nothing if the insurance is not needed. The trade-off to this, as you might guess, is that the insurance is *more* costly if it *is* needed.

Collars

A **collar** is the purchase of a put option and the sale of a call option with a higher strike price, with both options having the same underlying asset and having the same expiration date. If the position is reversed (sale of a put and purchase of a call), the collar is written. The **collar width** is the difference between the call and put strikes.

Example 3.4 Suppose we sell a 45-strike call with a $0.97 premium and buy a 40-strike put with a $1.99 premium. This collar is shown in Figure 3.8. Because the purchased put has a higher premium than the written call, the position requires investment of $1.02.

If you hold this book at a distance and squint at Figure 3.8, the collar resembles a short forward contract. Economically, it *is* like a short forward contract in that it is fundamentally a short position: The position benefits from price decreases in the underlying asset and suffers losses from price increases. A collar differs from a short forward contract in having a range between the strikes in which the expiration payoff is unaffected by changes in the value of the underlying asset.

In practice, collars are frequently used to implement insurance strategies—for example, by buying a collar when we own the stock. This position, which we will call a *collared stock*, entails buying the stock, buying a put, and selling a call. It is an insured position because we own the asset and buy a put. The sale of a call helps to pay for the purchase of the put. The collared stock looks like a bull spread; however, it arises from a different set of transactions. The bull spread is created by buying one option and selling another. The collared stock begins with a position in the underlying asset that is coupled with a collar.

Example 3.5 Suppose that you own shares of XYZ for which the current price is $40, and you wish to buy insurance. You do this by purchasing put options. A way to reduce the cost of the insurance is to sell an out-of-the-money call. The profit calculations for this set of transactions—buy the stock, buy a 40-strike put, sell a 45-strike call—are shown in Table 3.6. Comparing this table to Table 3.5 demonstrates that profit on the collared stock position is identical to profit on the bull spread. Note that it is essential to account for interest as a cost of holding the stock.

FIGURE 3.8

Profit diagram of a purchased collar constructed by selling a 45-strike call and buying a 40-strike put.

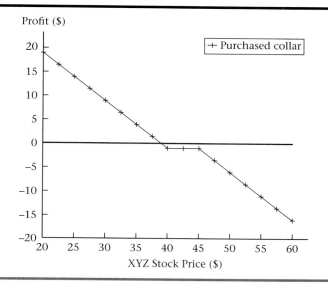

TABLE 3.6

Profit at expiration from purchase of 40-strike put and sale of 45-strike call.

Stock Price at Expiration	Purchased 40-Put	Written 45-Call	Premium Plus Interest	Profit on Stock	Total
$35.00	$5.00	$0.00	−$1.04	−$5.81	−$1.85
37.50	2.50	0.00	−1.04	−3.31	−1.85
40.00	0.00	0.00	−1.04	−0.81	−1.85
42.50	0.00	0.00	−1.04	1.69	0.65
45.00	0.00	0.00	−1.04	4.19	3.15
47.50	0.00	−2.50	−1.04	6.69	3.15
50.00	0.00	−5.00	−1.04	9.19	3.15

If you have a short position in the stock, you can collar the position by buying a call for insurance and selling an out-of-the-money put to partially fund the call purchase. The result looks like a bear spread.

Zero-cost collars The collar depicted in Table 3.6 entails paying a net premium of $1.02: $1.99 for the purchased put, against $0.97 for the written call. It is possible to find

FIGURE 3.9

Zero-cost collar on XYZ, created by buying XYZ at $40, buying a 40-strike put with a premium of $1.99, and selling a 41.72-strike call with a premium of $1.99.

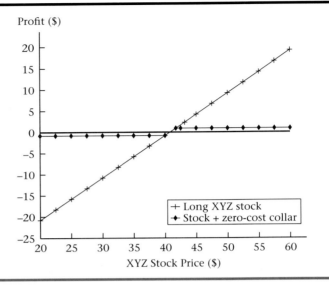

strike prices for the put and call such that the two premiums exactly offset one another. This position is called a **zero-cost collar.**

To illustrate a zero-cost collar, suppose you buy the stock and buy the 40-strike put that has a premium of $1.99. Trial and error reveals that a call with a strike of $41.72 also has a premium of $1.99. Thus, you can buy a 40-strike put and sell a 41.72-strike call without paying any premium. The result is depicted in Figure 3.9. At expiration, the collar exposes you to stock price movements between $40 and $41.72, coupled with downside protection below $40. You pay for this protection by giving up gains should the stock move above $41.72.

For any given stock there are an infinite number of zero-cost collars. One way to see this is to first pick the desired put strike below the forward price. It is then possible to find a strike above the forward price such that a call has the same premium.

Understanding collars One aspect of the zero-cost collar that may seem puzzling is that you can finance the purchase of an at-the-money put by selling an out-of-the-money call. In the above example, with the stock at $40, you were able to costlessly buy a 40-strike put by also selling a 41.72-strike call. This makes it seem as if you have free insurance with some possibility of gain. Even if you are puzzled by this, you probably realize that "free" insurance is not possible and that something must be wrong with this way of thinking about the position.

This puzzle is resolved by taking into account financing cost. Recall that if you pay $40 for stock and sell it for $40 in 91 days, *you have not broken even.* You have lost money, because you have forgone $40 $\times ((1.0833)^{0.25} - 1) = \$0.808$ in interest. Thus, the true break-even stock price in this example is $40.808, about halfway between $40 and $41.72. If you buy the 40-strike put, you are not insuring against all loss; you are instead insuring against an economic loss in excess of $0.808.

To illustrate the use and pricing of collars, consider an executive who owns a large position in company stock. Such executives frequently hedge their stock positions, using zero-cost collars with several years to maturity. Suppose, for example, that Microsoft has a price of $30/share and that an executive wishes to hedge 1 million shares. If the executive buys a 30-strike put with 3 years to maturity, what 3-year call will have the same premium? Assuming an effective annual risk-free rate of 6%, a zero dividend yield, and a 40% volatility, the Black-Scholes price is $5.298 for a 30-strike put with 3 years to maturity.[5] Using trial and error (or a numerical solver), a call option with a strike of $47.39 has the same premium. Once again, the zero-cost collar seems highly asymmetric. However, this comparison does not take into account financing cost. The executive selling stock in 3 years for $30/share will in fact have lost 3 years' worth of interest: $30 \times [(1.06)^3 - 1] = 5.73.

The cost of the collar and the forward price Suppose you try to construct a zero-cost collar in which you set the strike of the put option at the stock price plus financing cost—i.e., the future value of the stock price. In the 91-day example above, this would require that you set the put strike equal to $40.808, which gives a premium of $2.39. The call premium at this strike is also $2.39! *If you try to insure against all losses on the stock, including interest, then a zero-cost collar has zero width.*

This is an implication of put-call parity, equation (3.1). It turns out that $40.808 is also the theoretical forward price. If we set the strike equal to the forward price, the call premium equals the put premium.

3.4 SPECULATING ON VOLATILITY

The positions we have just considered are all directional: A bull spread or a collar is a bet that the price of the underlying asset will increase. Options can also be used to create positions that are nondirectional with respect to the underlying asset. With a nondirectional position, the holder does not care whether the stock goes up or down, but only how much it moves. We now examine straddles, strangles, and butterfly spreads, which are examples of nondirectional speculations.

Straddles

Consider the strategy of buying a call and a put with the same strike price and time to expiration. This strategy is called a **straddle.** The general idea of a straddle is simple: If the stock price rises there will be a profit on the purchased call, and if the stock price

---

[5] Using the spreadsheet accompanying the book, you can compute the Black-Scholes put price as BSPut(30, 30, 0.4, $ln(1 + 0.06)$, 3, 0) = 5.298.

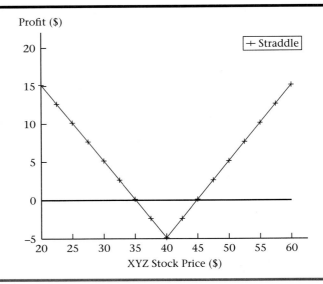

FIGURE 3.10

Combined profit diagram for a purchased 40-strike straddle—i.e., purchase of one 40-strike call option and one 40-strike put option.

declines there will be a profit on the purchased put. Thus, the advantage of a straddle is that it can profit from stock price moves in both directions. The disadvantage to a straddle is that it has a high premium because it requires purchasing two options. If the stock price at expiration is near the strike price, the two premiums are lost. The profit diagram for a 40-strike straddle is graphed in Figure 3.10. The initial cost of the straddle at a stock price of $40 is $4.77: $2.78 for the call and $1.99 for the put.

Figure 3.10 demonstrates that a straddle is a bet that volatility will be high: The buyer of an at-the-money straddle is hoping that the stock price will move but does not care about the direction of the move. Because option prices reflect the market's estimate of volatility, the cost of a straddle will be greater when the market's perception is that volatility is greater. If at a given set of option prices all investors found it desirable to buy straddles, then option prices would increase. Thus, purchasing a straddle is really a bet that volatility is greater than the market's assessment of volatility, as reflected in option prices.

Strangle The disadvantage of a straddle is the high premium cost. To reduce the premium, you can buy out-of-the-money options rather than at-the-money options. Such a position is called a **strangle.** For example, consider buying a 35-strike put and a 45-strike call, for a total premium of $1.41, with a future value of $1.44. These transactions reduce your maximum loss if the options expire with the stock near $40, but they also increase the stock-price move required for a profit.

Figure 3.11 shows the 40-strike straddle graphed against the 35–45 strangle. This comparison illustrates a key point: In comparing any two fairly priced option positions,

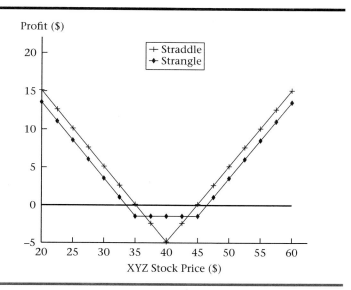

FIGURE 3.11

40-strike straddle and strangle composed of 35-strike put and 45-strike call.

there will always be a region where each outperforms the other. Indeed, this is necessary to have a fairly priced position.

In Figure 3.11, the strangle outperforms the straddle roughly when the stock price at expiration is between $36.57 and $43.43. Obviously, there is a much broader range in which the straddle outperforms the strangle. How can you decide which is the better investment? The answer is that unless you have a particular view on the stock's performance, you cannot say that one position is preferable to the other. An option-pricing model implicitly evaluates the likelihood that one strategy will outperform the other, and it computes option prices so that the two strategies are equivalently fair deals. An investor might have a preference for one strategy over the other due to subjective probabilities that differ from the market's.

Written straddle What if an investor believes that volatility is *lower* than the market's assessment? Because a purchased straddle is a bet that volatility is high (relative to the market's assessment), a **written straddle**—selling a call and put with the same strike price and time to expiration—is a bet that volatility is low (relative to the market's assessment).

Figure 3.12 depicts a written straddle, which is exactly the opposite of Figure 3.10, the purchased straddle. The written straddle is most profitable if the stock price is $40 at expiration, and in this sense it is a bet on low volatility. What is striking about Figure 3.12, however, is the potential for loss. A large change in the stock price in either direction leads to a large, potentially unlimited, loss.

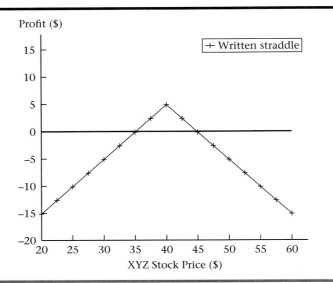

FIGURE 3.12

Profit at expiration from a written straddle—i.e., selling a 40-strike call and a 40-strike put.

It might occur to you that an investor wishing to bet that volatility will be low could write a straddle and acquire insurance against extreme negative outcomes. That intuition is correct and leads to our next strategy.

Butterfly Spreads

The straddle writer can insure against large losses on the straddle by buying options to protect against losses on both the upside and downside. Buying an out-of-the-money put provides insurance on the downside, protecting against losses on the at-the-money written put. Buying an out-of-the-money call provides insurance on the upside, protecting against losses on the written at-the-money call.

Figure 3.13 displays the straddle written at a strike price of $40, along with the options to safeguard the position: A 35-strike put and a 45-strike call. The net result of combining these three strategies is an insured written straddle, which is called a **butterfly spread,** graphed in Figure 3.14. It can be thought of as a written straddle for the timid (or for the prudent!).

Comparing the butterfly spread to the written straddle (Figure 3.14), we see that the butterfly spread has a lower maximum profit (due to the cost of insurance) if the stock at expiration is close to $40, and a higher profit if there is a large move in the stock price, in which case the insurance becomes valuable.

3.4 Speculating on Volatility

FIGURE 3.13

Written 40-strike straddle, purchased 45-strike call, and purchased 35-strike put. These positions combined generate the butterfly spread graphed in Figure 3.14.

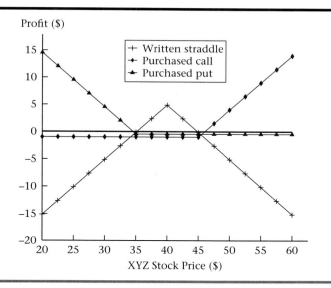

FIGURE 3.14

Comparison of the 35–40–45 butterfly spread—obtained by adding the profit diagrams in Figure 3.13—with the written 40-strike straddle.

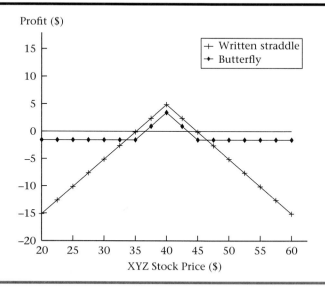

The butterfly spread can be created in a variety of ways: solely with calls, solely with puts, or by using the stock and a combination of calls and puts.[6] You are asked to verify this in Problem 3.18. The spread in Figure 3.14 can also be created by simultaneously buying a 35–40 bull spread and a 40–45 bear spread.

3.5 APPLICATION: EQUITY-LINKED CDS

Although options and forwards are important in and of themselves, they are also commonly used as building blocks in the construction of new financial instruments. For example, banks and insurance companies offer investment products that allow investors to benefit from a rise in a stock index and that provide a guaranteed return if the market declines. As an application of the tools in this chapter, we can "reverse-engineer" such equity-linked CDs and notes using the tools we have developed thus far.[7]

A simple $5\frac{1}{2}$-year CD with a return linked to the S&P 500 might have the following structure: At maturity, the CD is guaranteed to repay the invested amount, plus 70% of the simple appreciation in the S&P 500 over that time.[8]

We can ask several questions about the CD:

- Is the CD fairly priced?
- How can we decompose the product in terms of options and bonds?
- How does the issuing bank hedge the risk associated with issuing the product?
- How does the issuing bank make a profit?

To understand this product, suppose the S&P index is 1300 initially and an investor invests $10,000. If the index is below 1300 after 5.5 years, the CD returns to the investor the original $10,000 investment. If the index is above 1300 after 5.5 years, the investor receives $10,000 plus 70% of the percentage gain on the index. For example, if the index is 2200, the investor receives

$$\$10{,}000 \times [1 + (2200/1300 - 1) \times 70\%] = \$14{,}846$$

At first glance this product *appears* to permit gains but no losses. However, by now you are probably skeptical of a phrase like "gains but no losses"; the investor *must* pay something for an investment like this.

---

[6] Technically, a true butterfly spread is created solely with calls or solely with puts. A butterfly spread created by selling a straddle and buying a strangle is called an "iron butterfly."

[7] A CD (certificate of deposit) is a kind of interest-bearing bank account. You can think of a CD as being the same as a note or a bond.

[8] This is the structure of a CD issued in 1999 by First Union National Bank.

FIGURE 3.15

Payoff at expiration to $10,000 investment in an equity-linked CD that repays the initial investment at expiration plus 70% of the rate of appreciation of the market above 1300.

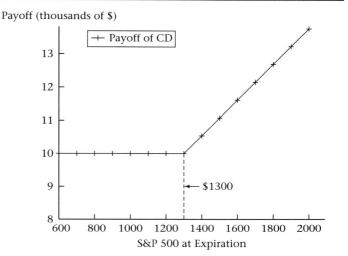

Graphing the Payoff on the CD

As a first step in analyzing the CD, we will draw a payoff diagram. If we invest $10,000, we receive at least $10,000. If the index rises to $S_{\text{final}} > 1300$, we also receive on our investment 70% of the rate of return,

$$\frac{S_{\text{final}}}{1300} - 1$$

Thus, the CD pays

$$\$10{,}000 \times \left(1 + 0.7 \times \max\left[0, \frac{S_{\text{final}}}{1300} - 1\right]\right) \tag{3.2}$$

Figure 3.15 graphs the payoff at expiration to this investment in the CD.

Recall the discussion in Section 2.1 of incorporating a zero-coupon bond into a payoff diagram. Per unit of the index (there are $10{,}000/1300 = 7.69$ units of the index in a $10,000 investment), the CD buyer receives 0.7 of an index call option, plus a zero-coupon bond paying $1300 at expiration.

Table 3.7 computes the payoff to the equity-linked CD for different values of the index.

Economics of the CD

Now we are in a position to understand the economics of this product. Think about what happens if the index is below 1300 at expiration. We pay $10,000 and we receive $10,000 back, plus an option. Thus, we have forgone interest on $10,000 in exchange for the

	TABLE 3.7	Payoff of equity-linked CD at expiration.
	S&P Index After 5.5 Years	**CD Payoff**
	500	$10,000.00
	1000	10,000.00
	1500	11,076.92
	2000	13,769.23
	2500	16,461.54
	3000	19,153.85

possibility of receiving 70% of the gains on the S&P. Suppose that the effective annual interest rate is 6%; after 5.5 years, the buyer has lost interest with a present value of

$$\$10{,}000 \times (1.06)^{-5.5} - \$10{,}000 = -\$2{,}742$$

Essentially, the buyer forgoes interest in exchange for a call option on the index.

With this description we have reverse-engineered the CD, decomposing it in terms of an option and a bond. The question of whether the CD is fairly priced turns on whether the $2742 is a fair price for the index option implicit in the CD. Given information about the interest rate, the volatility of the index, and the dividend yield on the index, it is possible to price the option to determine whether the CD is fairly priced. We perform that analysis for this example in Chapter 12.

Why Equity-Linked CDs?

With reverse-engineering, we see that an investor could create the equivalent of an equity-linked CD by buying a zero-coupon bond and 0.7 call options. Why, then, do products like this exist?

Consider what must be done to replicate the payoff. If a retail investor were to insure an index investment using options, the investor would have to learn about options, decide what maturity, strike price, and quantity to buy, and pay transaction costs. Exchange-traded options have at most 3 years to maturity, so obtaining longer-term protection requires rolling over the position at some point.

An equity-linked CD provides a prepackaged solution. It may provide a pattern of market exposure that many investors could not otherwise obtain at such low transaction costs.

The idea that a prepackaged deal may be attractive should be familiar to you. Supermarkets sell whole heads of lettuce—salad building blocks, as it were—and they also sell, at a premium price, lettuce already washed, torn into bite-sized pieces, and mixed as a salad. The transaction cost of salad preparation leads some consumers to prefer the prepackaged salads.

What does the financial institution get out of this? Just as the supermarket earns profit on prepackaged salads, the issuing bank wants to earn a transaction fee on the CD. When it sells a CD, the issuing bank borrows money (the zero-coupon bond portion of the CD) and receives the premium for writing a call option. The cost of the CD to the bank is the cost of the zero-coupon bond plus the cost of the call option. Obviously, the bank would not issue the equity-linked CD in the first place unless it was less expensive than alternative ways to attract deposits, such as standard CDs. The equity-linked CD is risky because the bank has written a call, but the bank can manage this risk in several ways, one of which is to purchase call options from a dealer to offset the risk of having written calls.[9]

In this discussion we have viewed the equity-linked CD from several perspectives. The end user is interested in the product and whether it meets a financial need at a fair cost. The market-maker (the bank in this case) is interested in making a profit without bearing risk from having issued the CD. And the economic observer is interested in knowing why equity-linked CDs exist. The three perspectives overlap, and a full explanation of the product touches on all of them.

CHAPTER SUMMARY

Puts are insurance against a price decline and calls are insurance against a price increase. Combining a long or short position in the asset with an offsetting position in options (for example, a long position in the asset is coupled with either a purchased put or written call) leads to the various possible positions and their equivalents in Table 3.8.

Buying a call and selling a put with the same strike price and time to expiration creates an obligation to buy the asset at expiration by paying the strike price. This is a synthetic forward. A synthetic forward must have the same cost in present value terms as a true forward. This observation leads to equation (3.1):

$$\text{Call}(K, T) - \text{Put}(K, T) = \text{PV}(F_{0,T} - K) \qquad (3.1)$$

This relationship, called *put-call parity*, explains the difference in call and put premiums for otherwise identical options. It is one of the most important relationships in derivatives.

There are numerous strategies that permit speculating on the direction of the stock or on the size of stock-price moves (volatility). Some of these positions are summarized

---

[9] Using data from the early 1990s, Baubonis et al. (1993) estimated that issuers of equity-linked CDs earned about 3.5% of the value of the CD as a fee, with about 1% as the transaction cost of hedging the written call. A back-of-the-envelope calculation in Chapter 12 suggests the issuer fees for this product are in the neighborhood of 4% to 5%.

Position	Is Equivalent To	And Is Called
Index + put	Zero-coupon bond + call	Insured asset (floor)
Index − call	Zero-coupon bond − put	Covered written call
−Index + call	−Zero-coupon bond + put	Insured short (cap)
−Index − put	−Zero-coupon bond − call	Covered written put

TABLE 3.8 Summary of equivalent positions from Section 3.1.

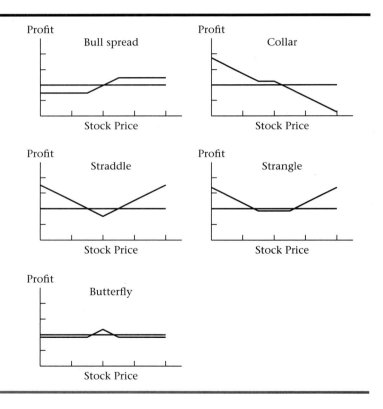

FIGURE 3.16 Profit diagrams for positions discussed in the chapter: bull spread, collar, straddle, strangle, butterfly, and 2:1 ratio spread.

TABLE 3.9 Positions consistent with different views on the stock price and volatility direction.

	Volatility Will Increase	No Volatility View	Volatility Will Fall
Price will fall	Buy puts	Sell underlying	Sell calls
No price view	Buy straddle	Do nothing	Sell straddle
Price will increase	Buy calls	Buy underlying	Sell puts

graphically in Figure 3.16. We also categorize in Table 3.9 various strategies according to whether they reflect bullish or bearish views on the stock-price direction or volatility.[10]

FURTHER READING

In Chapter 4 we will see how firms can use these strategies to manage risk. We further explore put-call parity in Chapter 9.

Put-call parity was first demonstrated in Stoll (1969). Merton (1973a) corrected the original analysis for the case of American options, for which, because of early exercise, parity need not hold. Ronn and Ronn (1989) provide a detailed examination of price bounds and returns on box spreads.

There are numerous practitioner books on option trading strategies. A classic practitioner reference is McMillan (1992).

PROBLEMS

3.1 Suppose that you buy the S&R index for $1000, buy a 1000-strike put, and borrow $980.39. Perform a payoff and profit calculation mimicking Table 3.1. Graph the resulting payoff and profit diagrams for the combined position.

3.2 Suppose that you short the S&R index for $1000 and sell a 1000-strike put. Construct a table mimicking Table 3.1 that summarizes the payoff and profit of this position. Verify that your table matches Figure 3.5.

For the following problems assume the effective 6-month interest rate is 2% and the S&R 6-month forward price is $1020, and use these premiums for S&R options with 6 months to expiration:

---

[10] Table 3.9 was suggested by David Shimko.

Strike	Call	Put
$950	$120.405	$51.777
1000	93.809	74.201
1020	84.470	84.470
1050	71.802	101.214
1107	51.873	137.167

3.3 Suppose you buy the S&R index for $1000 and buy a 950-strike put. Construct payoff and profit diagrams for this position. Verify that you obtain the same payoff and profit diagram by investing $931.37 in zero-coupon bonds and buying a 950-strike call.

3.4 Suppose you short the S&R index for $1000 and buy a 950-strike call. Construct payoff and profit diagrams for this position. Verify that you obtain the same payoff and profit diagram by borrowing $931.37 and buying a 950-strike put.

3.5 Suppose you short the S&R index for $1000 and buy a 1050-strike call. Construct payoff and profit diagrams for this position. Verify that you obtain the same payoff and profit diagram by borrowing $1029.41 and buying a 1050-strike put.

3.6 Verify that you earn the same profit and payoff by (a) buying the S&R index for $1000 and (b) buying a 950-strike S&R call, selling a 950-strike S&R put, and lending $931.37.

3.7 Verify that you earn the same profit and payoff by (a) shorting the S&R index for $1000 and (b) selling a 1050-strike S&R call, buying a 1050-strike put, and borrowing $1029.41.

3.8 Suppose the premium on a 6-month S&R call is $109.20 and the premium on a put with the same strike price is $60.18. What is the strike price?

3.9 Construct payoff and profit diagrams for the purchase of a 950-strike S&R call and sale of a 1000-strike S&R call. Verify that you obtain exactly the same *profit* diagram for the purchase of a 950-strike S&R put and sale of a 1000-strike S&R put. What is the difference in the payoff diagrams for the call and put spreads? Why is there a difference?

3.10 Construct payoff and profit diagrams for the purchase of a 1050-strike S&R call and sale of a 950-strike S&R call. Verify that you obtain exactly the same *profit* diagram for the purchase of a 1050-strike S&R put and sale of a 950-strike S&R put. What is the difference in the initial cost of these positions?

3.11 Suppose you invest in the S&R index for $1000, buy a 950-strike put, and sell a 1050-strike call. Draw a profit diagram for this position. What is the net option premium? If you wanted to construct a zero-cost collar keeping the put strike equal to $950, in what direction would you have to change the call strike?

3.12 Suppose you invest in the S&R index for $1000, buy a 950-strike put, and sell a 1107-strike call. Draw a profit diagram for this position. How close is this to a zero-cost collar?

3.13 Draw profit diagrams for the following positions:

    a. 1050-strike S&R straddle.

    b. Written 950-strike S&R straddle.

    c. Simultaneous purchase of a 1050-strike straddle and sale of a 950-strike S&R straddle.

3.14 Suppose you buy a 950-strike S&R call, sell a 1000-strike S&R call, sell a 950-strike S&R put, and buy a 1000-strike S&R put.

    a. Verify that there is no S&R price risk in this transaction.

    b. What is the initial cost of the position?

    c. What is the value of the position after 6 months?

    d. Verify that the implicit interest rate in these cash flows is 2% over 6 months.

3.15 Compute profit diagrams for the following ratio spreads:

    a. Buy 950-strike call, sell two 1050-strike calls.

    b. Buy two 950-strike calls, sell three 1050-strike calls.

    c. Consider buying n 950-strike calls and selling m 1050-strike calls so that the premium of the position is zero. Considering your analysis in (a) and (b), what can you say about n/m? What exact ratio gives you a zero premium?

3.16 In the previous problem we saw that a ratio spread can have zero initial premium. Can a bull spread or bear spread have zero initial premium? A butterfly spread? Why or why not?

3.17 Here is a quote from an investment Web site about an investment strategy using options:

> One strategy investors are applying to the XYZ options is using "synthetic stock." A synthetic stock is created when an investor simultaneously purchases a call option and sells a put option on the same stock. The end result is that the synthetic stock has the same value, in terms of capital gain potential, as the underlying stock itself. Provided the premiums on the options are the same, they cancel each other out so the transaction fees are a wash.

Suppose, to be concrete, that the premium on the call you buy is the same as the premium on the put you sell, and both have the same strikes and times to expiration.

a. What can you say about the strike price?

b. What term best describes the position you have created?

c. Suppose the options have a bid-ask spread. If you are creating a synthetic purchased stock and the net premium is zero *inclusive of the bid-ask spread*, where will the strike price be relative to the forward price?

d. If you create a synthetic short stock with zero premium inclusive of the bid-ask spread, where will the strike price be relative to the forward price?

e. Do you consider the "transaction fees" to really be "a wash"? Why or why not?

3.18 Verify that the butterfly spread in Figure 3.14 can be duplicated by the following transactions (use the option prices in Table 3.4):

a. Buy 35 call, sell two 40 calls, buy 45 call.

b. Buy 35 put, sell two 40 puts, buy 45 put.

c. Buy stock, buy 35 put, sell two 40 calls, buy 45 call.

3.19 Construct a spreadsheet for which you can input up to five strike prices and quantities of put and call options bought or sold at those strikes, and that will automatically construct the total expiration payoff diagram for that position. Modify the spreadsheet to permit you to choose whether to graph a payoff or profit function.

4 Introduction to Risk Management

Firms convert inputs such as labor, raw materials, and machines into goods and services. The future profitability of this activity is unpredictable. A firm is profitable if the cost of what it produces exceeds the cost of the inputs. Prices can change, however, and what appears to be a profitable activity today may not be profitable tomorrow. Derivatives provide a way to manage some of these risks.

A firm that actively uses derivatives and other techniques to alter its risk and protect its profitability is engaging in **risk management.** In this chapter we take a look at how derivatives—such as forwards, calls, and puts—are used in practice to manage risk.

We first examine two hypothetical firms: Golddiggers, a gold-mining firm, and Auric Enterprises, a manufacturer using gold as an input. Using profit diagrams, we can see what risks they face and demonstrate the use of derivatives strategies to manage those risks. After looking at these examples, we explore the reasons firms seek to manage risk in the first place. We also look at collars, paylater strategies, and cross-hedging as examples of more sophisticated hedging strategies. Throughout the discussion, you will probably recognize that the hedging strategies we discuss in this chapter are the same strategies we discussed in Chapters 2 and 3. Finally, we look at basis risk, which can create hedging problems.

4.1 BASIC RISK MANAGEMENT: THE PRODUCER'S PERSPECTIVE

Golddiggers is a gold-mining firm planning to mine and sell 100,000 ounces of gold over the next year. For simplicity, we will assume that they sell all of the next year's production precisely 1 year from today, receiving whatever the gold price is that day. We will ignore production beyond the next year.

Obviously, Golddiggers—like any producer—hopes that the gold price will rise over the next year. However, Golddiggers' management computes estimated net income for a range of possible prices of gold in 1 year (Table 4.1). The net income calculation shows how Golddiggers' profit is affected by gold prices.

TABLE 4.1   Golddiggers' estimated net income 1 year from today, unhedged.

Gold Price in 1 Year	Fixed Cost	Variable Cost	Net Income
$350	−$330	−$50	−$30
400	−330	−50	20
450	−330	−50	70
500	−330	−50	120

Should Golddiggers simply shut the mine if gold prices fall enough to make net income negative? The answer depends on the extent to which costs are fixed. The firm incurs the fixed cost whether or not it produces gold. Variable costs are incurred only if the mine operates. Thus, for any gold price above the variable cost of $50/oz., it will make sense to produce gold.[1]

Hedging with a Forward Contract

Golddiggers can lock in a price for gold in 1 year by entering into a short forward contract, agreeing today to sell its gold for delivery in 1 year. Suppose that the price of gold today is $405/oz. and that gold to be delivered in 1 year can be sold today for $420/oz. and that Golddiggers agrees to sell forward all of its gold production in 1 year. We will assume in all examples that the forward contract settles financially. As noted earlier, the payoff to a forward is the same with physical or financial settlement.

Profit calculations when Golddiggers is hedged are summarized in Table 4.2. This table adds the profit on the forward contract to net income from Table 4.1. Figure 4.1 contains three curves showing the following:

- **Unhedged profit:** Since cost is $380/oz., the line labeled "unhedged seller" shows zero profit at $380, a loss at lower prices, and profit at higher prices. For example, at $420, profit is $40/oz. Since it has gold in the ground, Golddiggers has a long position in gold.

- **Profit on the short forward position:** The "short gold forward" line represents the profit from going short the gold forward contract at a forward price of $420/oz.

---

[1] Suppose the gold price is $350/oz. If Golddiggers produces no gold, the firm loses its fixed cost, $330/oz. If Golddiggers produces gold, the firm has fixed cost of $330/oz. and variable cost of $50/oz., and so loses $350 − ($330 + $50) = −$30/oz. It is better to lose only $30, so Golddiggers will produce even when they have negative net income. If the gold price were to fall below the variable cost of $50, then it would make sense to stop producing.

4.1 Basic Risk Management: The Producer's Perspective

TABLE 4.2 Golddiggers' net income 1 year from today, hedged with a forward sale of gold.

Gold Price in 1 Year	Fixed Cost	Variable Cost	Profit on Short Forward	Net Income on Hedged Position
$350	−$330	−$50	$70	$40
400	−330	−50	20	40
450	−330	−50	−30	40
500	−330	−50	−80	40

FIGURE 4.1

Producer profit in 1 year, assuming hedging with a short forward contract at a forward price of $420/oz.

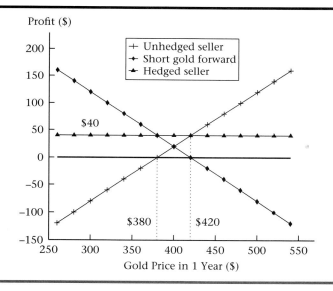

We profit from locking in the price if prices are lower than $420, and we lose if prices are higher.

- **Hedged profit:** The line labeled "hedged seller" is the sum of the other two lines, adding them vertically at every gold price. It is flat at $40/oz., as we would expect from Table 4.2. A quick way to add the lines together is to notice that the "unhedged seller" graph has a positive slope of 1, and the "short gold forward" graph has a slope of −1. Added together vertically, the two graphs will have a slope of 0, so the only question is the height of the line. A profit calculation at a single point tells us that it must be at $40/oz.

TABLE 4.3			Golddiggers' net income 1 year from today, hedged with a 420-strike put option.		
	Gold Price in 1 Year	Fixed Cost	Variable Cost	Profit on Put Option	Net Income
	$350	−$330	−$50	$60.79	$30.79
	400	−330	−50	10.79	30.79
	450	−330	−50	−9.21	60.79
	500	−330	−50	−9.21	110.79

Insurance: Guaranteeing a Minimum Price with a Put Option

A possible objection to hedging with a forward contract is that if gold prices do rise, Golddiggers will still receive only $420/oz.; there is no prospect for greater profit. Gold insurance—i.e., a put option—provides a way to have higher profits at high gold prices while still being protected against low prices. Suppose that the market price for a 420-strike put is $8.77/oz.[2] This put provides a *floor* on the price.

Since the put premium is paid 1 year prior to the option payoff, we must take into account interest cost when we compute profit in 1 year. The future value of the premium is $8.77 × 1.05 = $9.21. As with the forward contract, we assume financial settlement, although physical settlement would yield the same net income.

Table 4.3 shows the result of buying this put. If the price is less than $420, Golddiggers exercises the put, thereby selling gold for $420/oz. Golddiggers also paid for the put, giving a net income of $30.79. If the price is greater than $420, Golddiggers sells gold at the market price.

The insurance strategy—buying the put—performs better than shorting the forward if the price of gold in 1 year is more than $429.21. Otherwise, the short forward outperforms insurance. Figure 4.2 shows the unhedged position, profit from the put by itself, and the result of hedging with the put.

What this analysis does not address is the *probability* that the gold price in 1 year will be in different regions; that is, how likely is it that the gold price will exceed $429.21? The price of the put option implicitly contains information about the likelihood that the gold price will exceed $420, and by how much. The *probability distribution* of the gold price is a key factor determining the pricing of the put. We will see in later chapters how

---

[2] This uses the Black-Scholes formula for the put price with inputs $S = 420$, $K = 420$, $r = 4.879\%$, $\sigma = 5.5\%$, $\delta = 4.879\%$, and $t = 1$ (year).

FIGURE 4.2

Comparison of unhedged position, 420-strike put option, and unhedged position plus 420-strike put.

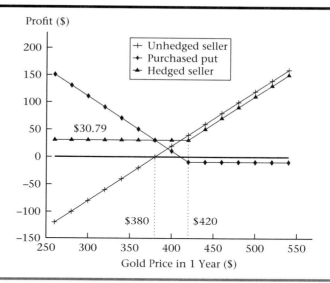

the distribution affects the put price and how to use information about the probability distribution to help us assess risk.

Figure 4.3 compares the profit from the two protective strategies we have examined: selling a forward contract and buying a put. As you would expect, neither strategy is clearly preferable; rather, there are trade-offs, with each contract outperforming the other for some range of prices.

The fact that no hedging strategy always outperforms the other will be true of all fairly priced strategies. In practice, considerations such as transaction costs and market views are likely to govern the choice of a strategy.

Insuring by Selling a Call

With the sale of a call, Golddiggers receives a premium, which reduces losses, but the written call limits possible profits. One can debate whether this really constitutes insurance, but our goal is to see how the sale of a call affects the potential profit and loss for Golddiggers.

Suppose that instead of buying a put, Golddiggers sells a 420-strike call and receives an $8.77 premium. Golddiggers in this case would be said to have sold a *cap*.

Figure 4.4 shows the payoff to this strategy. If we compute the actual profit 1 year from today, we see that if the gold price in 1 year exceeds $420, Golddiggers will show profits of

$$\$420 + \$9.21 - \$380 = \$49.21$$

FIGURE 4.3

Comparison of payoffs for Golddiggers hedged with a forward contract and hedged with a put option.

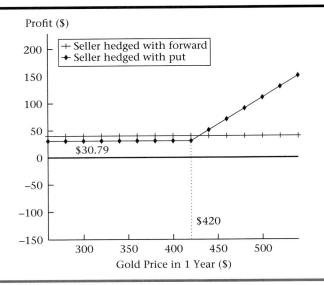

FIGURE 4.4

Comparison of Golddiggers hedging with sale of 420-strike call versus unhedged.

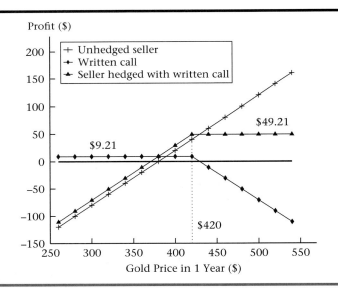

That is, Golddiggers sells gold for $420 (since the written call is exercised by the holder), receives the future value of the premium, and has a cost of $380. If the price of gold is less than $420, Golddiggers will make

$$P_{gold} + \$9.21 - \$380$$

On the downside, Golddiggers has exposure to gold but keeps the option premium.

By writing the call, Golddiggers keeps the $8.77 call premium and 1 year later makes $9.21 more than an unhedged gold seller. On the other hand, if the gold price exceeds $420, the call is exercised and the price Golddiggers receives is thus capped at $420. Therefore, for gold prices above $429.21, an unhedged strategy has a higher payoff than that of writing a 420-strike call. Also, for prices below $410.79, being fully hedged is preferable to having sold the call.

Adjusting the Amount of Insurance

Consider again Golddiggers' strategy of obtaining insurance against a price decline by purchasing a put option. A common objection to the purchase of insurance is that it is expensive. Insurance has a premium because it eliminates the risk of a large loss, while allowing a profit if prices increase. The cost of insurance reflects this asymmetry.

There are at least two ways to reduce the cost of insurance:

- Reduce the insured amount by lowering the strike price of the put option.
- Sell some of the gain received if the gold price is high.

Both of these strategies reduce the asymmetry between gains and losses, and hence lower the cost of insurance. The first strategy, lowering the strike price, permits some additional loss, while the second, selling some of the gain, puts a cap on the potential gain.

Reducing the strike price lowers the amount of insurance; therefore, the put option will have a lower premium. Figure 4.5 compares profit diagrams for Golddiggers' hedging using put options with strikes of $400 (premium = $2.21), $420 (premium = $8.77), and $440 (premium = $21.54). The 400-strike, low-premium option yields the highest profit if insurance is not needed (the price is high), and the lowest profit if insurance is needed (the price is low). The 440-strike, high-premium option yields the lowest profit if insurance is not needed, and the highest profit if insurance is needed.

The manager's view of the market and willingness to absorb risk will undoubtedly influence the choice among these alternatives. Managers relatively more optimistic about the price of gold will opt for low-strike-price puts, whereas pessimistic managers will more likely choose high-strike puts. While corporations per se may not be risk averse, managers may be. Also, some managers may perceive losses to be costly in terms of the public's perception of the firm or the boss's perception of them.

This problem of choosing the appropriate strike price is not unique to corporate risk management. Safe drivers and more careful homeowners often reduce premiums by purchasing auto and homeowner's insurance with larger deductibles. This reflects their proprietary view of the likelihood that the insurance will be used. One important difference between gold insurance and property insurance, however, is that poor drivers

FIGURE 4.5

Comparison of profit for Golddiggers using three different put strikes.

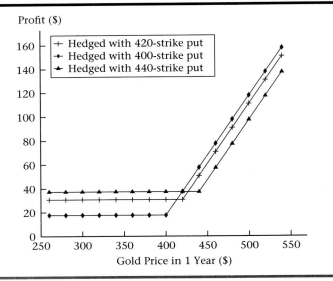

would like smaller deductibles for their auto insurance; this differential demand by the quality of the insured is called *adverse selection* and is reflected in the premiums for different deductibles. A driver known to be good would face a lower premium for any deductible than a driver known to be bad. With gold, however, the price of the put is independent of who is doing the buying.[3]

4.2 BASIC RISK MANAGEMENT: THE BUYER'S PERSPECTIVE

Auric Enterprises is a manufacturer of widgets, a product that uses gold as an input. We will suppose for simplicity that the price of gold is the only uncertainty Auric faces. In particular, we assume that

- Auric sells each widget for a fixed price of $800, a price known in advance.
- The fixed cost per widget is $340.
- The manufacture of each widget requires 1 oz. of gold as an input.

---

[3] You might think that a dealer would charge a higher price for a purchased option if the dealer knew that an option buyer had superior information about the market for gold. However, in general the dealer will quickly hedge the risk from the option and therefore has less concern than an ordinary investor about future movements in the price of gold.

TABLE 4.4		Auric estimated net income, unhedged, 1 year from today.		
Revenue per Widget	Gold Price in 1 Year	Fixed Cost	Variable Cost	Net Income
$800	$350	$340	$0	$110
800	400	340	0	60
800	450	340	0	10
800	500	340	0	−40

- The nongold variable cost per widget is zero.
- The quantity of widgets to be sold is known in advance.

Because Auric makes a greater profit if the price of gold falls, Auric's gold position is implicitly short. As with Golddiggers, we will examine various risk-management strategies for Auric. The pro forma net income calculation for Auric is shown in Table 4.4.

Hedging with a Forward Contract

The forward price is $420 as before. Auric can lock in a profit by entering into a long forward contract. Auric thereby guarantees a profit of

$$\text{Profit} = \$800 - \$340 - \$420 = \$40$$

Note that whereas Golddiggers was *selling* in the forward market, Auric is *buying* in the forward market. Thus, Golddiggers and Auric are natural *counterparties* in an economic sense. In practice they need not be direct counterparties since they can enter into forward contracts through dealers or on exchanges. But in an economic sense, one firm's desire to sell forward has a counterpart in the other's desire to buy forward.

Figure 4.6 compares the profit diagrams for the unhedged buyer and a long forward position in gold. It also shows the profit for the hedged buyer, which is generated by summing up the forward position and the unhedged payoff. We see graphically that the buyer can lock in a profit of $40/oz.

Insurance: Guaranteeing a Maximum Price with a Call Option

Rather than lock in a price unconditionally, Auric might like to pay $420/oz. if the gold price is greater than $420/oz. but pay the market price if it is less. Auric can accomplish this by buying a call option. As a future buyer, Auric is naturally short; hence, a call is insurance. Suppose the call has a premium of $8.77/oz. (recall that this is the same as

FIGURE 4.6

Profit diagrams for unhedged buyer, long forward, and buyer hedged with long forward.

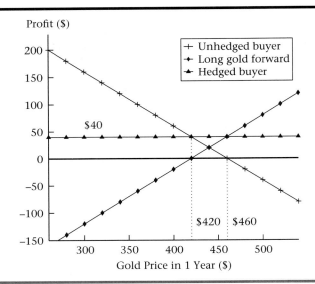

TABLE 4.5

Auric net income 1 year from today, hedged with 420-strike call option.

Gold Price in 1 Year	Unhedged Net Income from Table 4.4	Profit on Call Option	Net Income
$350	$110	−$9.21	$100.79
400	60	−9.21	50.79
450	10	20.79	30.79
500	−40	70.79	30.79

the premium on the put with the same strike price). The future value of the premium is $8.77 \times 1.05 = 9.21.

If Auric buys the insurance contract, net income on the hedged position will be as shown in Table 4.5. If the price is less than $420, the call is worthless at expiration and Auric buys gold at the market price. If the price is greater than $420, the call is exercised and Auric buys gold for $420/oz., less the cost of the call. This gives a profit of $30.79.

If the price of gold in 1 year is less than $410.79, insuring the price by buying the call performs better than locking in a price of $420. At low prices, the option permits us to take advantage of lower gold prices. If the price of gold in 1 year is greater than

FIGURE 4.7

Comparison of profit for unhedged gold buyer, gold buyer hedged with call, and stand-alone call.

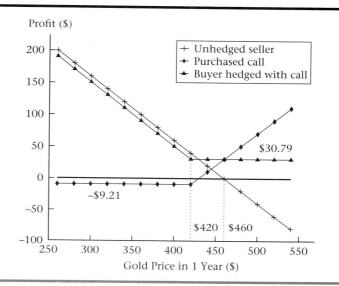

$410.79, insuring the price by buying the call performs worse than locking in a price of $420 since we have paid the call premium.

Figure 4.7 shows the profit from the call by itself, along with the results of hedging with the call. As before, the graph does not show the *probability* that the gold price in 1 year will be in different regions; hence, we cannot evaluate the likelihood of different outcomes.

4.3 WHY DO FIRMS MANAGE RISK?

The Golddiggers and Auric examples illustrate how the two companies can use forwards, calls, and puts to reduce losses in case of an adverse gold price move, essentially insuring their future cash flows. Why would a firm use these strategies?

In Chapter 1 we listed four reasons that firms might use derivatives: to hedge, to speculate, to reduce transaction costs, and to effect regulatory arbitrage. In practice, more than one of these considerations may be important. We have already discussed the fact that market views—for example, opinions about the future price of gold—can affect the choice of a hedging strategy. Thus, the choice of a hedging strategy can have a speculative component. Managers often cite the accounting treatment of a transaction as important, and transaction costs are obviously a consideration.

In this section we discuss why firms might hedge, ignoring speculation, transaction costs, and regulation (but we do consider taxes). It seems obvious that managers would want to reduce risk. However, in a world with fairly priced derivatives, no transaction costs, and no other market imperfections such as taxes, derivatives change the *distribution* of cash flows but do not increase the value of cash flows. Moreover, large publicly held firms are owned by diverse shareholders. These shareholders can, in theory, configure their own portfolios to bear risk optimally, suiting their own taste. In order to hedge, the firm must pay commissions and bid-ask spreads, and bear counterparty credit risk. Why incur these costs?

There are several reasons that firms might seek to manage risk. Before discussing them, let's think about what derivatives accomplish. To be concrete, suppose that Golddiggers sells gold forward at $420/oz. As we saw, this guarantees a net income of $40/oz.

When hedged with the forward, Golddiggers will have a profit of $40 whatever the price in 1 year. In effect, the value of the reduced profits, should the gold price rise, subsidizes the payment to Golddiggers should the gold price fall. If we use the term "state" to denote a particular gold price in 1 year, we can describe the hedging strategy as shifting dollars from more profitable states (when gold prices are high) to less profitable states (when gold prices are low).

This shifting of dollars from high gold price states to low gold price states will have value for the firm *if the firm values the dollar more in a low gold price state than in a high gold price state,* i.e., if losses hurt the firm more than profits help the firm. Why might a firm value a dollar differently in different states?

Reasons to Hedge

There are in fact a number of reasons why losses might be more harmful than profits are beneficial. We now discuss some of those reasons.[4]

Bankruptcy and distress costs An unusually large loss can threaten the survival of a firm. The most obvious reason is that a money-losing firm may be unable to meet fixed obligations, such as debt payments and wages. If a firm appears to be in distress, customers may be less willing to purchase its goods. (Would you buy a car or computer—both of which come with long-term warranties—from a company that appears likely to go out of business and would then be unable to honor its warranties?)

Actual or threatened bankruptcy can be costly; a dollar of loss can cost the company more than a dollar. As with taxes, this is a reason for firms to enter derivatives contracts that transfer income from profit states to loss states, thereby reducing the probability of bankruptcy or distress.

Costly external financing Even if a loss is not large enough to threaten the survival of a firm, the firm must pay for the loss, either by using cash reserves or by raising funds externally (for example, by borrowing or issuing new securities).

Raising funds externally can be costly. There are explicit costs, such as bank and underwriting fees. There can also be implicit costs. If you borrow money, the lender may

---

[4] The following are discussed in Smith and Stulz (1985) and Froot et al. (1994).

worry that you need to borrow because you are in decline, which increases the probability that you will not repay the loan. The lender's thinking this way raises the interest rate on the loan. The same problem arises even more severely with equity issues.

At the same time, cash reserves are valuable because they reduce a firm's need to raise funds externally in the future. So if the firm uses cash to pay for a loss, the reduction in cash increases the probability that the firm will need costly external financing in the future.

The fact that external financing is costly can even lead the firm to forgo investment projects it would have taken had cash been available to use for financing.

Thus, however the firm pays for the loss, a dollar of loss may actually cost the firm more than a dollar. Hedging can safeguard cash reserves and reduce the probability of costly external financing.

Taxes It is typically the case that governments tax business profits but do not give full credits for losses. For example, tax rules may permit a loss to be offset against a profit from a different year. However, in present-value terms, the loss will have a lower effective tax rate than that applied to profits, which still generates a motive to hedge.

There are other aspects of the tax code that can encourage firms to shift income using derivatives; such uses may or may not appear to be hedging and may or may not be approved of by tax authorities. Tax rules that may entice firms to use derivatives include the separate taxation of capital and ordinary income (derivatives can be used to convert one form of income to another), capital gains taxation (derivatives can be used to defer taxation of capital gains income as with collars), and differential taxation across countries (derivatives can be used to shift income from one country to another).

Increased debt capacity Because of the deductibility of interest expense for tax purposes, firms may find debt to be a tax-advantaged way to raise funds.[5] However, lenders, fearful of bankruptcy, may be unwilling to lend to firms with risky cash flows. The amount that a firm can borrow is its **debt capacity**.

A firm that credibly reduces the riskiness of its cash flows should be able to borrow more, since for any given level of debt, bankruptcy is less likely. Such a firm is said to have raised its debt capacity. To the extent debt has a tax advantage, such a firm will also be more valuable.

Managerial risk aversion While large, public firms are owned by well-diversified investors, firm managers are typically *not* well diversified. Salary, bonus, and compensation options are all tied to the performance of the firm.

An individual who is unwilling to take a fair bet (i.e., one with an expected payoff equal to the money at stake) is said to be **risk averse**. Risk-averse persons are harmed by a dollar of loss more than they are helped by a dollar of gain. Thus, they benefit from reducing uncertainty.

---

[5] For a discussion of this issue, see Berk and DeMarzo (2007, ch. 15) or Brealey and Myers (2000, ch. 17).

If managers are risk averse and have wealth that is tied to the company, we might expect that they will try to reduce uncertainty. However, matters are not this simple: Managers are often compensated in ways that encourage them to take more risk. For example, options given to managers as compensation, which we discuss in Chapter 13, are more valuable, other things equal, when the firm's stock price is riskier. Thus, a manager's risk aversion may be offset by compensation that is more valuable if the firm is riskier.

Nonfinancial risk management Firms make risk-management decisions when they organize and design a business. For example, suppose you plan to sell widgets in Europe. You can construct a plant in the United States and export to Europe, or you can construct the plant in Europe, in which case costs of construction, labor, interest rates, and other inputs will be denominated in the same currency as the widgets you sell. Exchange rate hedging, to take one example, would be unnecessary.

Of course, if you build in a foreign country, you will encounter the costs of doing business abroad, including dealing with different tax codes and regulatory regimes.

Risk can also be affected by such decisions as leasing versus buying equipment, which determines the extent to which costs are fixed. Firms can choose flexible production technologies that may be more expensive at the outset but that can be reconfigured at low cost. Risk is also affected by the decision to enter a particular line of business in the first place. Firms making computer mice and keyboards, for example, have to consider the possibility of lawsuits for repetitive stress injuries.

The point is that risk management is not a simple matter of hedging or not hedging using financial derivatives, but rather a series of decisions that start when the business is first conceived.

Reasons *Not* to Hedge

There are also reasons why firms might elect not to hedge:

- Transacting in derivatives entails paying transaction costs, such as commissions and the bid-ask spread.
- The firm must assess costs and benefits of a given strategy; this can require costly expertise.
- The firm must monitor transactions and have managerial controls in place to prevent unauthorized trading.
- The firm must be prepared for the tax and accounting consequences of their transactions. In particular, this may complicate reporting.

Thus, while there are reasons to hedge, there are also costs. When thinking about costs and benefits, keep in mind that some of what firms do could be called risk management but may not obviously involve derivatives. For example, suppose Auric enters into a 2-year agreement with a supplier to buy gold at a fixed price. Will management think of this as a derivative? In fact, this is a derivative under current accounting standards (it is a swap, which we discuss in Chapter 8), but it is exempt from derivatives accounting.[6] Finally, firms can face collateral requirements (the need to post extra cash with their counterparty) if their derivatives position loses money.

Boxes 4.1 (page 108) and 4.2 (page 116)discuss two cases of risk management—one unsuccessful, one successful.

Empirical Evidence on Hedging

We know surprisingly little about the risk-management practice and derivatives use of firms in real life. It is difficult to tell, from publicly available information, the extent to which firms use derivatives. Beginning in 2000, Statement of Financial Accounting Standards (SFAS) 133 required firms to recognize derivatives as assets or liabilities on the balance sheet, to measure them at fair value, and to report changes in their market value.[7] This reporting does not necessarily reveal a firm's hedging position (forward contracts have zero value, for example). Prior to 2000, firms had to report notional exposure; hence, much existing evidence relies on data from the 1990s.

Research tries to address two questions: How much do firms use derivatives and why? *Financial* firms—commercial banks, investment banks, broker-dealers, and other financial institutions—transact in derivatives frequently. Risks are identifiable, and regulators encourage risk management. The more open question is the extent to which *nonfinancial* firms use derivatives. We can summarize research findings as follows:

- Roughly half of nonfinancial firms report using derivatives, with usage greater among large firms (Bodnar et al. (1998); Bartram et al. (forthcoming)).
- Among firms that do use derivatives, less than 25% of perceived risk is hedged, with firms likelier to hedge short-term risks (Bodnar et al. (1998)).
- Firms with more investment opportunities are likelier to hedge (Géczy et al. (1997)).
- Firms that use derivatives have a higher market value (Allayannis and Weston (2001); Allayannis et al. (2004); Bartram et al. (forthcoming)) and more leverage (Graham and Rogers (2002); Haushalter (2000)).

Guay and Kothari (2003) verify many of these findings but conclude that for most firms, derivatives use is of minor economic significance. In their sample of large firms, slightly more than half report derivatives usage. Among derivatives users, the authors estimate that the *median* firm hedges only about 3% to 6% of exposure to interest rates and exchange rates.

---

[6] Current derivatives accounting rules contain a "normal purchases and sales" exemption. Firms need not use derivatives accounting for forward contracts with physical delivery, for quantities likely to be used or sold over a reasonable period in the normal course of business.

[7] See Gastineau et al. (2001) for a discussion of SFAS 133 and previous accounting rules.

Box 4.1: A Hedge Too Far

Ford Motor Co. stunned investors in January 2002 when it announced a $1 billion write-off on stockpiles of palladium, a precious metal Ford used in catalytic converters (devices that reduce polluting emissions from cars and trucks). Ironically, Ford sustained the loss while attempting to actively manage palladium risk.

According to the *Wall Street Journal* (see Gregory L. White, "A Mismanaged Palladium Stockpile Was Catalyst for Ford's Write-Off," February 6, 2002, p. A1), Ford in the late 1980s had begun to use palladium as a replacement for platinum. Palladium prices were steady until 1997, when Russia, a major supplier with a large stockpile of palladium, withheld supply from the market. Prices more than doubled to $350/oz. at a time when Ford was planning to increase its use of the metal. By early 2000, prices had doubled again, to $700. While GM had begun work several years earlier to reduce reliance on palladium, Ford continued to rely heavily on the metal.

In 2000, Ford management agreed to allow the purchasing staff to stockpile palladium. The purchasing staff evidently did not communicate with Ford's treasury department, which had hedging experience. Thus, for example, Ford did not buy puts to protect against a drop in palladium prices. The purchasing staff also did not communicate with Ford's research department, which was working to reduce reliance on palladium. Ford continued to buy palladium in 2001 as prices exceeded $1000. However, by the middle of the year, palladium prices had fallen to $350.

By the end of 2001, Ford had developed technology that would eventually reduce the need for palladium by 50%. The year-end price of palladium was $440/oz.

As a result of this experience, "Ford has instituted new procedures to ensure that treasury-department staffers with experience in hedging are involved in any major commodities purchases in the future, [Ford Chief Financial Officer Martin] Inglis says."

The varied evidence suggests that some use of derivatives is common, especially at large firms, but the evidence is weak that economic theories explain hedging. Practitioners often emphasize the accounting treatment of derivatives as critical, so it would be natural to expect the extent of hedging and the form it takes to change with accounting regulations.

4.4 GOLDDIGGERS REVISITED

We have looked at simple hedging and insurance strategies for buyers and sellers. We now examine some additional strategies that permit tailoring the amount and cost of insurance. For simplicity we will focus primarily on Golddiggers; however, in every case there are analogous strategies for Auric.

TABLE 4.6   Call and put premiums for gold options.

Strike Price	Put Premium	Call Premium
$440	$21.54	$2.49
420	8.77	8.77
400	2.21	21.26

Note: These prices are computed using the Black formula (to be discussed in Chapter 11) for options on futures, with a futures price of $420, effective annual interest rate of 5%, volatility of 5.5%, and 1 year to expiration.

Table 4.6 lists premiums for three calls and puts on gold with 1 year to expiration and three different strikes. The examples use these values.

Selling the Gain: Collars

As discussed earlier, we can reduce the cost of insurance by reducing potential profit, i.e., by selling our right to profit from high gold prices. We can do this by selling a call. If the gold price is above the strike on the call, we are contractually obligated to sell at the strike. This caps our profits, in exchange for an initial premium payment.

A 420–440 collar Suppose that Golddiggers buys a 420-strike put option for $8.77 and sells a 440-strike call option for a premium of $2.49. If the price of gold in 1 year is $450/oz., the call owner will exercise and Golddiggers is obligated to sell gold at the strike price of $440, rather than the market price of $450. The $2.49 premium Golddiggers received initially compensates them for the possibility that this will happen.

Figure 4.8 depicts the combination of the purchased put and written call, while Figure 4.9 shows the two profit diagrams for Golddiggers hedged with a 420-strike put, as opposed to hedged with a 420-strike put plus writing a 440-strike call.

Note that the 420–440 collar still entails paying a premium. The 420 put costs $8.77, and the 440 call yields a premium of only $2.49. Thus, there is a net expenditure of $6.28. It is probably apparent, though, that we can tinker with the strike prices and pay a still lower net premium, including zero premium, if we wish. The trade-off is that the payoff on the collar becomes less attractive as we lower the required premium.

A zero-cost collar To construct a zero-cost collar, we could argue as follows: A 400-strike put and a 440-strike call are equally distant from the forward price of $420. This equivalence suggests that the options should have approximately the same premium. As we can see from the table of premiums for different strike options (Table 4.6), the 400-strike put has a premium of $2.21, while the 440-strike call has a premium of $2.49. The net premium we would *receive* from buying this collar is thus $0.28. We can construct a true zero-cost collar by slightly changing the strike prices, making the put more expensive

FIGURE 4.8

Net profit at expiration resulting from buying a 420-strike put with premium of $8.77 and selling a 440-strike call with premium of $2.49. The profit for gold prices between $420 and $440 is ($2.49 − $8.77) × 1.05 = −$6.60.

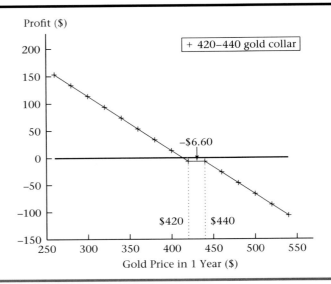

FIGURE 4.9

Comparison of Golddiggers hedged with 420-strike put versus hedged with 420-strike put and written 440-strike call (420–440 collar).

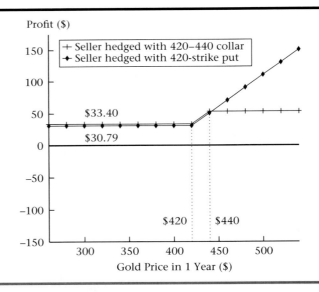

(raising the strike) and the call less expensive (also raising the strike). With strikes of $400.78 for the put and $440.78 for the call, we obtain a premium of $2.355 for both options.

In reality this zero-cost collar of width 40 would be sold at lower strike prices than $400.78 and $440.78. The reason is that there is a bid-ask spread: Dealers are willing to buy a given option at a low price and sell it at a high price.

The purchased put will be bought at the dealer's offer price and the call will be sold at the bid. The dealer can earn this spread in either of two ways: selling the 400.78–440.78 collar and charging an explicit transaction fee, or lowering the strike prices appropriately and charging a zero transaction fee. Either way, the dealer earns the fee. One of the tricky aspects of the more complicated derivatives is that it is relatively easy for dealers to embed fees that are invisible to the buyer. Of course a buyer can mitigate this problem by always seeking quotes from different dealers.

We can examine the payoffs by considering separately the three interesting regions of gold prices:

Price of gold < $400.78: In this region, Golddiggers can sell gold for $400.78 by exercising the put option.

Price of gold between $400.78 and $440.78: In this region, Golddiggers can sell gold at the market price.

Price of gold > $440.78: In this region, Golddiggers sells gold at $440.78. It has sold a call, so the owner of the call will exercise. This forces Golddiggers to sell gold to the call owner for the strike price of $440.78.

Figure 4.10 graphs the zero-cost collar against the unhedged position. Notice that between $400.78 and $440.78, the zero-cost collar graph is coincident with the unhedged profit. Above the 440.78-strike the collar provides profit of $60.78, and below the 400.78-strike the collar provides profit of $20.78.

The forward contract as a zero-cost collar Because the put and call with strike prices of $420 have the same premiums, we could also construct a zero-cost collar by buying the $420-strike put and selling the $420-strike call. If we do this, here is what happens:

Price of gold < $420: Golddiggers will exercise the put option, selling gold at the price of $420.

Price of gold > $420: Golddiggers has sold a 420-strike call. The owner of that call will exercise, obligating Golddiggers to sell gold for $420.

In either case, Golddiggers sells gold at $420. Thus, the "420–420 collar" is exactly like a forward contract. By buying the put and selling the call at the same strike price, Golddiggers has synthetically created a short position in a forward contract. Since a short forward and 420–420 collar have the same payoff, they must cost the same. *This*

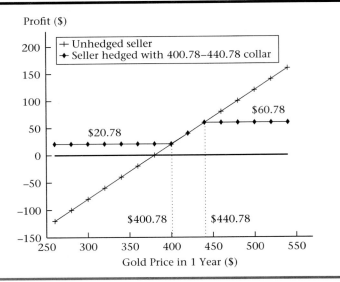

FIGURE 4.10

Comparison of unhedged profit for Golddiggers versus zero-cost collar obtained by buying 400.78-strike put and selling 440.78-strike call.

is why the premiums on the 420-strike options are the same. This example is really just an illustration of equation (3.1).

Synthetic forwards at prices other than $420 We can easily extend this example to understand the relationship between option premiums at other strike prices. In the previous example, Golddiggers created a synthetic forward sale at $420. You might think that you could benefit by creating a synthetic forward contract at a higher price such as $440. Other things being equal, you would rather sell at $440 than $420. To accomplish this you buy the 440 put and sell the 440 call. However, there is a catch: The 440-strike put is in-the-money and the 440-strike call is out-of-the-money. Since we would be buying the expensive option and selling the inexpensive option, we have to pay a premium.

How much is it worth to Golddiggers to be able to lock in a selling price of $440 instead of $420? Obviously, it is worth $20 1 year from today, or $20 ÷ (1.05) = $19.05 in present-value terms. Since locking in a $420 price is free, it should therefore be the case that we pay $19.05 in net premium in order to lock in a $440 price. In fact, looking at the prices of the 440-strike put and call in Table 4.6, we have premiums of $21.54 for the put and $2.49 for the call. This gives us

$$\text{Net premium} = \$21.54 - \$2.49 = \$19.05$$

Similarly, suppose Golddiggers explored the possibility of locking in a $400 price for gold in 1 year. Obviously, Golddiggers would require compensation to accept a lower price. In fact, they would need to be paid $19.05—the present value of $20—today.

Again we compute the option premiums and we see that the 400-strike call sells for $21.26 while the 400-strike put sells for $2.21. Again we have

$$\text{Net premium} = \$2.21 - \$21.26 = -\$19.05$$

Golddiggers in this case receives the net premium for accepting a lower price.

Other Collar Strategies

Collar-type strategies are quite flexible. We have focused on the case where the firm buys one put and sells one call. However, it is also possible to deal with fractional options. For example, consider the 400.78–440.78 collar above. We could buy one put to obtain full downside protection, and we could vary the strike price of the call by selling fractional calls at strike prices other than $440.78. For example, we could lower the call strike price below $440.78, in which case we would obtain a higher premium per call. To offset the higher premium, we could buy less than one call. The trade-off is that we cap the gold price on part of production at a lower level, but we maintain some participation at any price above the strike.

Alternatively, we could raise the cap level (the strike price on the call) and sell more than one call. This would increase participation in gold price increases up to the cap level, but also have the effect of generating a net short position in gold if prices rose above the cap.

Paylater Strategies

A disadvantage to buying a put option is that Golddiggers pays the premium even when the gold price is high and insurance was, after the fact, unnecessary. One strategy to avoid this problem is a **paylater** strategy, where the premium is paid only when the insurance is needed. While it is possible to construct exotic options in which the premium is paid only at expiration and only if the option is in-the-money, the strategy we discuss here is a ratio spread using ordinary put options. The goal is to find a strategy where if the gold price is high, there is no net option premium. If the gold price is low, there is insurance, but the effective premium is greater than with an ordinary insurance strategy.

If there is no premium when the gold price is high, we must have no initial premium. This means that we must sell at least one option. Consider the following strategy for Golddiggers: Sell a 434.6-strike put and buy two 420-strike puts. Using our assumptions, the premium on the 434.6-strike put is $17.55, while the premium on the 420-strike put is $8.77. Thus, the net option premium from this strategy is $17.55 - (2 \times \$8.775) = 0$.

Figure 4.11 depicts the result of Golddiggers' hedging with a paylater strategy. When the price of gold is greater than $434.60, neither put is exercised, and Golddiggers' profit is the same as if it were unhedged. When the price of gold is between $420 and $434.60, because of the written $434.60 put, the firm loses $2 of profit for every $1 decline in the price of gold. Below $420 the purchased 420-strike puts are exercised and profit becomes constant. The net result is an insurance policy that is not paid for unless it is needed.

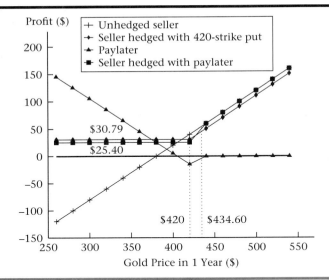

FIGURE 4.11

Depiction of paylater strategy, in which Golddiggers sells a 434.6-strike put and buys two 420-strike puts, compared to the conventional insurance strategy of buying a 420-strike put.

Also depicted in Figure 4.11 is the familiar result from a conventional insurance strategy of hedging by purchasing a single 420-strike put. When the gold price is high, the paylater strategy with a zero premium outperforms the single put. When the gold price is low, the paylater strategy does worse because it offers less insurance. Thus, the premium is paid later, if insurance is needed.

4.5 BASIS RISK

The examples in this chapter have assumed that derivatives were available for the exact commodity being bought or sold—gold in the case of Golddiggers and Auric. In practice, it is often necessary to hedge one thing with another. For example, exchange-traded commodity futures contracts call for delivery of the underlying commodity at specific locations and specific dates. The actual commodity to be bought or sold may reside at a different location, and the desired delivery date may not match that of the futures contract. Additionally, the *grade* of the deliverable under the futures contract may not match the grade that is being delivered.

This general problem of the futures or forward contract not representing exactly what is being hedged is called *basis risk*. Basis risk is a generic problem with commodities because of storage and transportation costs and quality differences. Basis risk can also arise with financial futures, as, for example, when a company hedges its own borrowing cost with the Eurodollar contract.

In this section we examine two examples of basis risk: hedging jet fuel, and hedging long-term commitments with short-term futures.

Hedging Jet Fuel with Crude Oil

Jet fuel futures do not exist in the United States, but airlines sometimes hedge jet fuel with crude oil futures along with futures for related petroleum products.[8] In order to perform this hedge, it is necessary to understand the relationship between crude oil and jet fuel prices. If we own a quantity of jet fuel and hedge by holding H crude oil futures contracts, our mark-to-market profit depends on the change in the jet fuel price and the change in the futures price:

$$(P_t - P_{t-1}) + H(F_t - F_{t-1}) \tag{4.1}$$

where P_t is the price of jet fuel and F_t the crude oil futures price. We can estimate H by regressing the change in the jet fuel price (denominated in cents per gallon) on the change in the crude futures price (denominated in dollars per barrel). Doing so using daily data for January 2000–June 2004 gives (standard errors are in parentheses)

$$P_t - P_{t-1} = \underset{(0.069)}{0.009} + \underset{(0.094)}{2.037}(F_t - F_{t-1}) \qquad R^2 = 0.287 \tag{4.2}$$

The futures price used in this regression is the price of the current near-term contract. The coefficient on the futures price change tells us that, on average, when the crude futures price increases by \$1, a gallon of jet fuel increases by \$0.02. Suppose that 1 gallon of crude oil is used to produce 1 gallon of jet fuel. Then, other things equal, since there are 42 gallons in a barrel, a \$1 increase in the price of a barrel of oil will generate a \$1/42 = \$0.0238 increase in the price of jet fuel. This is approximately the regression coefficient.[9]

The R^2 in equation (4.1) is 0.287, which implies a correlation coefficient of about 0.50. The hedge would therefore have considerable residual risk.

Box 4.2 discusses Southwest Airlines, which has received a great deal of largely favorable publicity for its jet fuel hedging.

Stack and Strip Hedges

Another example of basis risk occurs when hedgers decide to hedge distant obligations with near-term futures. For example, an oil producer might have an obligation to deliver 100,000 barrels per month at a fixed price for a year. The natural way to hedge this obligation would be to buy 100,000 barrels per month, locking in the price and supply

---

[8] For example, Southwest Airlines reportedly used a combination of crude oil and heating oil futures to hedge jet fuel. See Melanie Trottman, "Southwest Airlines' Big Fuel-Hedging Call Is Paying Off," *Wall Street Journal*, January 16, 2004, p. B4.

[9] In Section 5.5 we will estimate a hedge ratio for stock with a regression based on percentage changes. In that case, there is an economic reason (an asset pricing model) to believe that there is a stable relationship based upon rates of return. With crude and jet fuel, crude is used to produce jet fuel, so it makes sense that dollar changes in the price of crude would be related to dollar changes in the price of jet fuel.

> ### Box 4.2: Hedging Jet Fuel: Southwest Airlines
>
> Southwest Airlines is well known for systematically hedging the cost of jet fuel. In the 1990s, fuel on average accounted for 10%–15% of Southwest's operating costs (Carter et al. (2004)). In recent years, fuel costs have been as much as 25% of operating expenses. Since fuel costs have risen over the last decade, Southwest has benefited from hedging. In its 2005 quarterly financial reports, for example, Southwest reported savings from its hedge program of $155, $196, $295, and $258 million, against net income of $75, $159, $227, and $86 million. Fuel hedging has been important for Southwest's profitability.
>
> There is no exchange-traded jet fuel contract, so Southwest uses cross-hedges to hedge jet fuel, and hedges a significant portion of its future projected fuel needs. Here is what Southwest said about its hedging program in its 3rd quarter 2006 financial statement:
>
>> the Company has found commodities for hedging of jet fuel costs, primarily crude oil and refined products such as heating oil and unleaded gasoline. The Company utilizes financial derivative instruments to decrease its exposure to jet fuel price increases. The Company does not purchase or hold any derivative financial instruments for trading purposes. . . .
>>
>> The Company currently has a mixture of purchased call options, collar structures, and fixed price swap agreements in place to protect against over 85 percent of its remaining 2006 total anticipated jet fuel requirements at average crude oil equivalent prices of approximately $43 per barrel, and has also added refinery margins on most of those positions. Based on current growth plans, the Company is also approximately 85 percent protected for 2007 at approximately $49 per barrel, over 43 percent protected for 2008 at approximately $44 per barrel, over 38 percent protected for 2009 at approximately $47 per barrel, approximately 17 percent protected for 2010 at $63 per barrel, and has modest positions in 2011 and 2012.
>
> In the popular discussion of Southwest's hedging, almost nobody asks this question: How would Southwest have fared if oil prices had declined?

on a month-by-month basis. This is called a **strip hedge.** We engage in a strip hedge when we hedge a stream of obligations by offsetting each individual obligation with a futures contract matching the maturity and quantity of the obligation. For the oil producer obligated to deliver every month at a fixed price, the hedge would entail buying the appropriate quantity each month, in effect taking a long position in the strip.

An alternative to a strip hedge is a **stack hedge.** With a stack hedge, we enter into futures contracts with a *single* maturity, with the number of contracts selected so that changes in the *present value* of the future obligations are offset by changes in the value of this "stack" of futures contracts. In the context of the oil producer with a monthly delivery obligation, a stack hedge would entail going long 1.2 million barrels using the near-term contract.[10] When the near-term contract matures, we reestablish the stack hedge by going long contracts in the new near month. This process of stacking futures contracts in the near-term contract and rolling over into the new near-term contract is called a **stack and roll.** If the new near-term futures price is below the expiring near-term price (i.e., there is backwardation), rolling is profitable.

Why would anyone use a stack hedge? There are at least two reasons. First, there is often more trading volume and liquidity in near-term contracts. With many commodities, bid-ask spreads widen with maturity. Thus, a stack hedge may have lower transaction costs than a strip hedge. Second, the manager may wish to speculate on the shape of the forward curve. You might decide that the forward curve looks unusually steep in the early months. If you undertake a stack hedge and the forward curve then flattens, you will have locked in all your oil at the relatively cheap near-term price and implicitly made gains from not having locked in the relatively high strip prices. However, if the curve becomes steeper, it is possible to lose.

Box 4.3 recounts the story of Metallgesellschaft A.G. (MG), in which MG's large losses on a hedged position might have been caused, at least in part, by the use of a stock hedge.

CHAPTER SUMMARY

A producer selling a risky commodity, such as gold, has an inherent long position in the commodity. Assuming costs are fixed, the firm's profit increases when the price of the commodity increases. Such a firm can hedge profit with a variety of strategies, including selling forward, buying puts, and buying collars. A firm that faces price risk on inputs has an inherent short position in the commodity, with profit that decreases when the price of the input increases. Hedging strategies for such a firm include buying forward, buying calls, and selling collars. All of the strategies involving options can be customized by changing the option strike prices. Strategies such as a paylater can provide insurance with no initial premium, but on which the company has greater losses should the insurance be needed.

Hedging can be optimal for a company when an extra dollar of income received in times of high profits is worth less than an extra dollar of income received in times of low profits. Profits for such a firm are concave, in which case hedging can increase expected cash flow. Concave profits can arise from taxes, bankruptcy costs, costly external finance, preservation of debt capacity, and managerial risk aversion. Such a firm can increase expected cash flow by hedging. Nevertheless, firms may elect not to hedge for reasons including transaction costs of dealing in derivatives, the requirement

---

[10] Futures in the near term are being used to offset more distant cash flows, so because of interest we would short less than 1.2 million contracts. This reduction in the position is called "tailing." We discuss tailing in Chapter 5.

Box 4.3: Metallgesellschaft A.G.

In 1992, a U.S. subsidiary of the German industrial firm Metallgesellschaft A.G. (MG) had offered customers fixed prices on over 150 million barrels of petroleum products, including gasoline, heating oil, and diesel fuel, over periods as long as 10 years. To hedge the resulting short exposure, MG entered into futures and swaps.

Much of MG's hedging was done using short-dated NYMEX crude oil and heating oil futures. Thus, MG was using stack hedging, rolling over the hedge each month.

During much of 1993, the near-term oil market was in contango (the forward curve was upward sloping). As a result of the market remaining in contango, MG systematically lost money when rolling its hedges and had to meet substantial margin calls. In December 1993, the supervisory board of MG decided to liquidate both its supply contracts and the futures positions used to hedge those contracts. In the end, MG sustained losses estimated at between $200 million and $1.3 billion.

The MG case was extremely complicated and has been the subject of pointed exchanges among academics—see in particular Culp and Miller (1995), Edwards and Canter (1995), and Mello and Parsons (1995). While the case is complicated, several issues stand out. First, was the stack and roll a reasonable strategy for MG to have undertaken? Second, should the position have been liquidated when it was and in the manner it was liquidated (as it turned out, oil prices increased—which would have worked in MG's favor—following the liquidation). Third, did MG encounter liquidity problems from having to finance losses on its hedging strategy? While the MG case has receded into history, hedgers still confront the issues raised by this case.

---

for expertise, the need to monitor and control the hedging process, and complications from tax and accounting considerations.

Basis risk occurs when the risk being hedged is not exactly offset by the derivative used for hedging. Prominent derivatives success stories (Southwest) and failures (Metallgesellschaft A.G.) illustrate the importance of controlling basis risk.

FURTHER READING

In this and earlier chapters we have examined uses of forwards and options, taking for granted the pricing of those contracts. Two big unanswered questions are: How are those prices determined? How does the market for them work? We discuss these questions in subsequent chapters.

Wharton and CIBC regularly survey nonfinancial firms to assess their hedging. A recent survey is summarized in Bodnar et al. (1998). Bartram et al. (forthcoming) examine hedging behavior in an international sample of over 7000 firms. Tufano (1996, 1998), Petersen and Thiagarajan (2000), and Brown et al. (2006) have studied hedging practices in the gold-mining industry. Other papers examining hedging include Géczy et al. (1997), Allayannis and Weston (2001), Allayannis et al. (2003), and Allayannis et al. (2004). Guay and Kothari (2003) attempt to quantify derivatives usage using information in firm annual reports from 1997. Brown (2001) provides an interesting and detailed description of the hedging decisions by one (anonymous) firm, and Faulkender (2005) examines interest rate hedging in the chemical industry.

Gastineau et al. (2001) discuss Statement of Financial Accounting Standards 133, which currently governs accounting for derivatives.

Southwest is the subject of a case by Carter et al. (2004). Metallgesellschaft A.G. engendered a spirited debate. Papers written about that episode include Culp and Miller (1995), Edwards and Canter (1995), and Mello and Parsons (1995).

Finally, Fleming (1997) relates some of the history of (the fictitious) Auric Enterprises.

PROBLEMS

For the following problems consider these three firms:

- *XYZ* mines copper, with fixed costs of $0.50/lb and variable costs of $0.40/lb.
- *Wirco* produces wire. It buys copper and manufactures wire. One pound of copper can be used to produce one unit of wire, which sells for the price of copper plus $5. Fixed cost per unit is $3 and noncopper variable cost is $1.50.
- *Telco* installs telecommunications equipment and uses copper wire from Wirco as an input. For planning purposes, Telco assigns a fixed revenue of $6.20 for each unit of wire it uses.

The 1-year forward price of copper is $1/lb. The 1-year continuously compounded interest rate is 6%. The table below shows 1-year option prices for copper.[11]

Strike	Call	Put
0.9500	$0.0649	$0.0178
0.9750	0.0500	0.0265
1.0000	0.0376	0.0376
1.0250	0.0274	0.0509
1.0340	0.0243	0.0563
1.0500	0.0194	0.0665

In your answers, at a minimum consider copper prices in 1 year of $0.80, $0.90, $1.00, $1.10, and $1.20.

---

[11] These are option prices from the Black formula assuming that the risk-free rate is 0.06, volatility is 0.1, and time to expiration is 1 year.

4.1 If XYZ does nothing to manage copper price risk, what is its profit 1 year from now, per pound of copper? If, on the other hand, XYZ sells forward its expected copper production, what is its estimated profit 1 year from now? Construct graphs illustrating both unhedged and hedged profit.

4.2 Suppose the 1-year copper forward price were $0.80 instead of $1. If XYZ were to sell forward its expected copper production, what is its estimated profit 1 year from now? Should XYZ produce copper? What if the forward copper price is $0.45?

4.3 Compute estimated profit in 1 year if XYZ buys a put option with a strike of $0.95, $1.00, or $1.05. Draw a graph of profit in each case.

4.4 Compute estimated profit in 1 year if XYZ sells a call option with a strike of $0.95, $1.00, or $1.05. Draw a graph of profit in each case.

4.5 Compute estimated profit in 1 year if XYZ buys collars with the following strikes:

   a. $0.95 for the put and $1.00 for the call.

   b. $0.975 for the put and $1.025 for the call.

   c. $1.05 for the put and $1.05 for the call.

Draw a graph of profit in each case.

4.6 Compute estimated profit in 1 year if XYZ buys paylater *puts* as follows (the net premium may not be exactly zero):

   a. Sell one 1.025-strike put and buy two 0.975-strike puts.

   b. Sell two 1.034-strike puts and buy three 1.00-strike puts.

Draw a graph of profit in each case.

4.7 If Telco does nothing to manage copper price risk, what is its profit 1 year from now, per pound of copper that it buys? If it hedges the price of wire by buying copper forward, what is its estimated profit 1 year from now? Construct graphs illustrating both unhedged and hedged profit.

4.8 Compute estimated profit in 1 year if Telco buys a call option with a strike of $0.95, $1.00, or $1.05. Draw a graph of profit in each case.

4.9 Compute estimated profit in 1 year if Telco sells a put option with a strike of $0.95, $1.00, or $1.05. Draw a graph of profit in each case.

4.10 Compute estimated profit in 1 year if Telco sells collars with the following strikes:

   a. $0.95 for the put and $1.00 for the call.

   b. $0.975 for the put and $1.025 for the call.

   c. $0.95 for the put and $0.95 for the call.

Draw a graph of profit in each case.

4.11 Compute estimated profit in 1 year if Telco buys paylater *calls* as follows (the net premium may not be exactly zero):

   a. Sell one 0.975-strike call and buy two 1.034-strike calls.

   b. Sell two 1.00-strike calls and buy three 1.034-strike calls.

Draw a graph of profit in each case.

4.12 Suppose that Wirco does nothing to manage the risk of copper price changes. What is its profit 1 year from now, per pound of copper? Suppose that Wirco buys copper forward at $1. What is its profit 1 year from now?

4.13 What happens to the variability of Wirco's profit if Wirco undertakes any strategy (buying calls, selling puts, collars, etc.) to lock in the price of copper next year? You can use your answer to the previous question to illustrate your response.

4.14 Golddiggers has zero net income if it sells gold for a price of $380. However, by shorting a forward contract it is possible to guarantee a profit of $40/oz. Suppose a manager decides not to hedge and the gold price in 1 year is $390/oz. Did the firm earn $10 in profit (relative to accounting break-even) or lose $30 in profit (relative to the profit that could be obtained by hedging)? Would your answer be different if the manager did hedge and the gold price had been $450?

For the following problems use the BSCall option pricing function with a stock price of $420 (the forward price), volatility of 5.5%, continuously compounded interest rate of 4.879%, dividend yield of 4.879%, and time to expiration of 1 year. The problems require you to vary the strike prices.

4.15 Consider the example of Auric.

   a. Suppose that Auric insures against a price increase by purchasing a 440-strike call. Verify by drawing a profit diagram that simultaneously selling a 400-strike put will generate a collar. What is the cost of this collar to Auric?

   b. Find the strike prices for a zero-cost collar (buy high-strike call, sell low-strike put) for which the strikes differ by $30.

4.16 Suppose that LMN Investment Bank wishes to sell Auric a zero-cost collar of width 30 without explicit premium (i.e., there will be no cash payment from Auric to LMN). Also suppose that on every option the bid price is $0.25 below the Black-Scholes price and the offer price is $0.25 above the Black-Scholes price. LMN wishes to earn their spread ($0.25 per option) without any explicit charge to Auric. What should the strike prices on the collar be? (*Note:* Since the collar involves two options, LMN is looking to make $0.50 on the deal. You need to find strike prices that differ by 30 such that LMN makes $0.50.)

4.17 Use the same assumptions as in the preceding problem, without the bid-ask spread. Suppose that we want to construct a paylater strategy using a ratio spread. Instead of buying a 440-strike call, Auric will sell one 440-strike call and use the premium to buy two higher-strike calls, such that the net option premium is zero.

   a. What higher strike for the purchased calls will generate a zero net option premium?

   b. Graph the profit for Auric resulting from this strategy.

part 2

Forwards, Futures, and Swaps

Forward contracts permit the purchase of an asset in the future at terms that are set today. In earlier chapters we took forward prices as given. In this part—Chapters 5–8—we explore the pricing of forward and futures contracts on a wide variety of underlying assets: financial assets and commodities. We also examine swaps, which have multiple future settlement dates, as opposed to forward contracts, which settle on a single date. Swaps are in effect a bundle of forward contracts combined with borrowing and lending. As such, swaps are a natural generalization of forward contracts.

Forward contracts involve deferring receipt of, and payment for, the underlying asset. Thus, computing the forward price requires you to determine the costs and benefits of this deferral. As in Part 1, present- and future-value calculations are the primary pricing tool.

5 Financial Forwards and Futures

Forward contracts—which permit firms and investors to guarantee a price for a future purchase or sale—are a basic financial risk management tool. In this chapter we continue to explore these contracts, studying in detail forward and futures contracts on stocks and stock indexes. In the next chapter we consider additional financial futures contracts, including currencies and Eurodollar futures. We also discuss commodities, energy futures, and contracts on weather and housing. Our objectives are to understand how these contracts are priced, how they are used, and how market-makers hedge them.

Questions to keep in mind throughout the chapter include: Who might buy or sell specific contracts? What kinds of firms might use the contract for risk management? Why is the contract designed as it is?

5.1 ALTERNATIVE WAYS TO BUY A STOCK

The purchase of a share of XYZ stock has three components: (1) fixing the price, (2) the buyer making payment to the seller, and (3) the seller transferring share ownership to the buyer. If we allow for the possibility that payment and physical receipt can occur at different times, say, time 0 and time T, then once the price is fixed there are four logically possible purchasing arrangements: Payment can occur at time 0 or T, and physical receipt can occur at time 0 or T. Table 5.1 depicts these four possibilities, along with their customary names. Let's discuss these different arrangements.[1]

> **Outright purchase:** This is the typical way to think about buying stock. You simultaneously pay the stock price in cash and receive ownership of the stock.
>
> **Fully leveraged purchase:** This is a purchase in which you borrow the entire purchase price of the security. Suppose you borrow the share price, S_0, and agree

---

[1] All of these arrangements can be reversed in the case of the seller. Problem 5.1 asks you to describe them from that perspective.

TABLE 5.1

Four different ways to buy a share of stock that has price S_0 at time 0. At time 0 you agree to a price, which is paid either today or at time T. The shares are received either at 0 or T. The interest rate is r.

Description	Pay at Time	Receive Security at Time	Payment
Outright purchase	0	0	S_0 at time 0
Fully leveraged purchase	T	0	$S_0 e^{rT}$ at time T
Prepaid forward contract	0	T	?
Forward contract	T	T	$? \times e^{rT}$

to repay the borrowed amount at time T. If the continuously compounded interest rate is r, at time T you would owe e^{rT} per dollar borrowed, or $S_0 e^{rT}$.[2]

Prepaid forward contract: An arrangement in which you pay for the stock today and receive the stock at an agreed-upon future date.[3] The difference between a prepaid forward contract and an outright purchase is that with the former, you receive the stock at time T. We will see that the price you pay is not necessarily the stock price.

Forward contract: An arrangement in which you both pay for the stock and receive it at time T, with the time T price specified at time 0.

From Table 5.1 it is clear that you pay interest when you defer payment. The interesting question is how deferring the *physical receipt* of the stock affects the price; this deferral occurs with both the forward and prepaid forward contracts. What should you pay for the stock in those cases?[4]

---

[2] From this point on, we will frequently use continuously compounded interest rates and dividend yields. You may at this point wish to consult Appendix B, which reviews continuous interest calculations.

[3] The term *prepaid forward contract*, or *prepay*, is widely used in practice and such contracts are common. The Enron transaction discussed in Chapter 8 and a hedging transaction by Roy Disney, discussed in Chapter 12, used prepaid swaps and forwards.

[4] The arrangements also differ with respect to credit risk, which arises from the possibilility that the person on the other side of the transaction will not fulfill his or her end of the deal. (And of course the person on the other side of the deal may be worried about *you* fulfilling your obligation.)

5.2 PREPAID FORWARD CONTRACTS ON STOCK

A prepaid forward contract entails paying today to receive something—stocks, a foreign currency, bonds—in the future. The sale of a prepaid forward contract permits the owner to sell an asset while retaining physical possession for a period of time.

We will derive the prepaid forward price using three different methods: pricing by analogy, pricing by present value, and pricing by arbitrage.

Pricing the Prepaid Forward by Analogy

Suppose you buy a prepaid forward contract on XYZ. By delaying physical possession of the stock, you do not receive dividends and have no voting or control rights. (We ignore here the value of voting and control.)

In the absence of dividends, whether you receive physical possession today or at time T is irrelevant: In either case you own the stock, and at time T it will be exactly as if you had owned the stock the whole time.[5] *Therefore, when there are no dividends, the price of the prepaid forward contract is the stock price today.* Denoting the prepaid forward price for an asset bought at time 0 and delivered at time T as $F^P_{0,T}$, the prepaid forward price for delivery at time T is

$$F^P_{0,T} = S_0 \qquad (5.1)$$

Pricing the Prepaid Forward by Discounted Present Value

We can also derive the price of the prepaid forward using present value: We calculate the expected value of the stock at time T and then discount that value at an appropriate rate of return. The stock price at time T, S_T, is uncertain. Thus, in computing the present value of the stock price, we need to use an appropriate risk-adjusted rate.

If the expected stock price at time T based on information we have at time 0 is $E_0(S_T)$, then the prepaid forward price is given by

$$F^P_{0,T} = E_0(S_T)e^{-\alpha T} \qquad (5.2)$$

where α, the expected return on the stock, is determined using the CAPM or some other model of expected returns.

How do we compute the expected stock price? By definition of the expected return, on average in T years the stock will be worth

$$E_0(S_T) = S_0 e^{\alpha T}$$

---

[5] Suppose that someone secretly removed shares of stock from your safe and returned them 1 year later. From a purely financial point of view, you would never notice the stock to be missing.

Thus, equation (5.2) gives

$$F_{0,T}^P = E_0(S_T)e^{-\alpha T} = S_0 e^{\alpha T} e^{-\alpha T} = S_0$$

For a non-dividend-paying stock, the prepaid forward price is the stock price.

Pricing the Prepaid Forward by Arbitrage

Classical **arbitrage** describes a situation in which we can generate a positive cash flow either today or in the future by simultaneously buying and selling related assets, with no net investment of funds and with no risk. Arbitrage, in other words, is free money. An extremely important pricing principle, which we will use often, is that *the price of a derivative should be such that no arbitrage is possible.*

Here is an example of arbitrage. Suppose that the prepaid forward price exceeds the stock price—i.e., $F_{0,T}^P > S_0$. The arbitrageur will buy low and sell high by buying the stock for S_0 and selling the prepaid forward for $F_{0,T}^P$. This transaction makes money and it is also risk free: Selling the prepaid forward requires that we deliver the stock at time T, and buying the stock today ensures that we have the stock to deliver. Thus, we earn $F_{0,T}^P - S_0$ today and at expiration we supply the stock to the buyer of the prepaid forward. We have earned positive profits today and offset all future risk. Table 5.2 summarizes this situation.

Now suppose on the other hand that $F_{0,T}^P < S_0$. Then we can engage in arbitrage by buying the prepaid forward and shorting the stock, earning $S_0 - F_{0,T}^P$. One year from now we acquire the stock via the prepaid forward and we use that stock to close the short position. The cash flows in Table 5.2 are simply reversed.

Throughout the book we will assume that prices are at levels that preclude arbitrage. This raises the question: If prices are such that arbitrage is not profitable, who can afford to become an arbitrageur, watching out for arbitrage opportunities? We can resolve this paradox with the insight that in order for arbitrageurs to earn a living, arbitrage opportunities must occur from time to time; there must be "an equilibrium degree

TABLE 5.2 Cash flows and transactions to undertake arbitrage when the prepaid forward price, $F_{0,T}^P$, exceeds the stock price, S_0.

	Cash Flows	
Transaction	Time 0	Time T (expiration)
Buy stock @ S_0	$-S_0$	$+S_T$
Sell prepaid forward @ $F_{0,T}^P$	$+F_{0,T}^P$	$-S_T$
Total	$F_{0,T}^P - S_0$	0

Box 5.1: Low Exercise Price Options

In some countries, including Australia and Switzerland, it is possible to buy stock options with very low strike prices—so low that it is virtually certain the option will expire in-the-money. For example, in Australia, the strike price is a penny. Such an option is called a *low exercise price option* (LEPO). These often exist in order to avoid taxes or transaction fees associated with directly trading the stock. LEPOs do not pay dividends and do not carry voting rights. As with any call option, a LEPO is purchased outright and entitles the option holder to acquire the stock at expiration by paying the (low) strike price. The payoff of a LEPO expiring at time T is

$$\max(0, S_T - K)$$

However, if the strike price, K, is so low that the option is certain to be exercised, this is just

$$S_T - K$$

This option has a value at time 0 of

$$F^P_{0,T} - \text{PV}(K)$$

Since the strike price of the option is close to zero, a LEPO is essentially a prepaid forward contract.

---

of disequilibrium."[6] However, you would not expect arbitrage to be obvious or easy to undertake.

The transactions in Table 5.2 are the same as those of a market-maker who is hedging a position. A market-maker would sell a prepaid forward if a customer wished to buy it. The market-maker then has an obligation to deliver the stock at a fixed price and, in order to offset this risk, can buy the stock. The market-maker thus engages in the same transactions as an arbitrageur, except the purpose is risk management, not arbitrage. Thus, *the transaction described in Table 5.2—selling the prepaid forward and buying the stock—also describes the actions of a market-maker.*

The no-arbitrage arguments we will make thus serve two functions: They tell us how to take advantage of mispricings, and they describe the behavior of market-makers managing risk.

Pricing Prepaid Forwards with Dividends

When a stock pays a dividend, the prepaid forward price is less than the stock price. The owner of stock receives dividends, but the owner of a prepaid forward contract does not. This difference creates a financial distinction between owning the stock and holding the

---

[6] The phrase is from Grossman and Stiglitz (1980), in which this idea was first proposed.

prepaid forward. It is necessary to adjust the prepaid forward price to reflect dividends that are received by the shareholder, but not by the holder of the prepaid forward contract.

Discrete dividends To understand the effects of dividends, we will compare prepaid forwards on two stocks: Stock A pays no dividend, and otherwise identical stock B pays a $5 dividend 364 days from today, just before the expiration of the prepaid forwards. We know that the prepaid forward price for stock A is the current stock price. What is the prepaid forward price for stock B?

Since the $5 dividend is paid just before the delivery date for the stock 1 year from today, on the delivery date stock B will be priced $5 less than stock A. Thus, the price we pay today for stock B should be lower than that for stock A by the present value of $5.

In general, the price for a prepaid forward contract will be the stock price less the present value of dividends to be paid over the life of the contract. Suppose there are multiple dividend payments made throughout the life of the forward contract: A stock is expected to make dividend payments of D_{t_i} at times t_i, $i = 1, \ldots, n$. A prepaid forward contract will entitle you to receive the stock at time T but without receiving the interim dividends. Thus, the prepaid forward price is

$$F_{0,T}^P = S_0 - \sum_{i=1}^{n} \text{PV}_{0,t_i}(D_{t_i}) \tag{5.3}$$

where PV_{0,t_i} denotes the time 0 present value of a time t_i payment.

Example 5.1 Suppose XYZ stock costs $100 today and is expected to pay a $1.25 quarterly dividend, with the first coming 3 months from today and the last just prior to the delivery of the stock. Suppose the annual continuously compounded risk-free rate is 10%. The quarterly continuously compounded rate is therefore 2.5%. A 1-year prepaid forward contract for the stock would cost

$$F_{0,1}^P = \$100 - \sum_{i=1}^{4} \$1.25 e^{-0.025i} = \$95.30$$

The calculation in this example implicitly assumes that the dividends are certain. Over a short horizon this might be reasonable. Over a long horizon we would expect dividend risk to be greater, and we would need to account for this in computing the present value of dividends.

Continuous dividends For stock indexes containing many stocks, it is common to model the dividend as being paid continuously at a rate that is proportional to the level of the index; i.e., the dividend *yield* (the annualized dividend payment divided by the stock price) is constant. This is an approximation, but in a large stock index there can be dividend payments on a large proportion of days.[7] The dividend yield is not likely to be fixed in the short run: When stock prices rise, the dividend yield falls, at least temporarily. Nevertheless, we will assume a constant proportional dividend yield for purposes of this discussion.

To model a continuous dividend, suppose that the index price is S_0 and the annualized daily compounded dividend yield is δ. Then the dollar dividend over 1 day is

$$\text{Daily dividend} = \frac{\delta}{365} \times S_0$$

Now suppose that we reinvest dividends in the index. Because of reinvestment, after T years we will have more shares than we started with. Using continuous compounding to approximate daily compounding, we get

$$\text{Number of shares} = \left(1 + \frac{\delta}{365}\right)^{365 \times T} \approx e^{\delta T}$$

At the end of T years we have approximately $e^{\delta T}$ more shares than initially.

Now suppose we wish to invest today in order to have one share at time T. We can buy $e^{-\delta T}$ shares today. Because of dividend reinvestment, at time T we will have $e^{\delta T}$ more shares than we started with, so we end up with exactly one share. Adjusting the initial quantity in this way in order to offset the effect of income from the asset is called **tailing** the position. Tailing enables us to offset the effect of continuous dividends. We will frequently encounter the concept of tailing.

Since an investment of $e^{-\delta T} S_0$ gives us one share at time T, this is the time 0 prepaid forward price for delivery at time T:

$$\boxed{F^P_{0,T} = S_0 e^{-\delta T}} \qquad (5.4)$$

where δ is the dividend yield and T the time to maturity of the prepaid forward contract.

Example 5.2 Suppose that the index is \$125 and the annualized daily compounded dividend yield is 3%. The daily dollar dividend is

$$\text{Dividend} = (0.03 \div 365) \times \$125 = \$0.01027$$

or a little more than 1 penny per unit of the index. If we start by holding one unit of the index, at the end of 1 year we will have

$$e^{0.03} = 1.030455$$

---

[7] There is significant seasonality in dividend payments, which can be important in practice. A large number of U.S. firms pay quarterly dividends in February, May, August, and November. German firms, by contrast, pay annual dividends concentrated in May, June, and July.

shares. Thus, if we wish to end the year holding one share, we must invest in

$$e^{-0.03} = 0.970446$$

shares. The prepaid forward price is

$$\$125 e^{-0.03} = \$121.306$$

5.3 FORWARD CONTRACTS ON STOCK

Now that we have analyzed prepaid forward contracts, it is easy to derive forward prices. The only difference between the prepaid forward and the forward is the timing of the payment for the stock. Thus, *the forward price is just the future value of the prepaid forward*. Here are forward prices for the cases we have considered:

No dividends: Taking the future value of equation (5.1), for the time 0 forward price of a stock that is delivered at time T, we have

$$F_{0,T} = \text{FV}(F_{0,T}^P) = S_0 e^{rT} \tag{5.5}$$

This formula shows that the forward contract is a purchase of the stock, with deferred payment. The interest adjustment compensates for that deferral.

Discrete dividends: To obtain the forward price for a stock that pays discrete dividends, we take the future value of equation (5.3). The forward price is the future value of the prepaid forward:

$$\boxed{F_{0,T} = S_0 e^{rT} - \sum_{i=1}^{n} e^{r(T-t_i)} D_{t_i}} \tag{5.6}$$

Whereas for the prepaid forward we subtract the present value of dividends from the current stock price, for the forward we subtract the future value of dividends from the future value of the stock price.

Continuous dividends: When the stock pays continuous dividends, we take the future value of equation (5.4):

$$F_{0,T} = e^{rT} S_0 e^{-\delta T}$$

or

$$\boxed{F_{0,T} = S_0 e^{(r-\delta)T}} \tag{5.7}$$

It is important to distinguish between the *forward price* and the *premium* for a forward contract. Because the forward contract has deferred payment, *its initial premium is zero*; it is initially costless. The forward *price*, however, is what the buyer pays at time

T: It is the future value of the prepaid forward price. This difference between the forward price and the premium is in contrast to the prepaid forward, for which the price and the premium are the same: The prepaid forward price is the amount you pay today to acquire the asset in the future.

Occasionally, it is possible to observe the forward price but not the price of the underlying stock or index. For example, the futures contract for the S&P 500 index trades at times when the NYSE is not open, so it is possible to observe the futures price but not the stock price. The asset price implied by the forward pricing formulas above is said to define **fair value** for the underlying stock or index. Equation (5.7) is used in this case to infer the value of the index.

The **forward premium** is the ratio of the forward price to the spot price, defined as

$$\text{Forward premium} = \frac{F_{0,T}}{S_0} \tag{5.8}$$

We can annualize the forward premium and express it as a percentage, in which case we have

$$\text{Annualized forward premium} = \frac{1}{T} \ln\left(\frac{F_{0,T}}{S_0}\right)$$

For the case of continuous dividends, equation (5.7), the annualized forward premium is simply the difference between the risk-free rate and the dividend yield.

Creating a Synthetic Forward Contract

A market-maker or arbitrageur must be able to offset the risk of a forward contract. It is possible to do this by creating a *synthetic* forward contract to offset a position in the actual forward contract.

In this discussion we will assume that dividends are continuous and paid at the rate δ, and hence that equation (5.7) is the appropriate forward price. We can then create a synthetic long forward contract by buying the stock and borrowing to fund the position. To see how the synthetic position works, recall that the payoff at expiration for a long forward position on the index is

$$\text{Payoff at expiration} = S_T - F_{0,T}$$

In order to obtain this same payoff, we buy a tailed position in the stock, investing $S_0 e^{-\delta T}$. This gives us one share at time T. We borrow this amount so that we are not required to pay anything additional at time 0. At time T we must repay $S_0 e^{(r-\delta)T}$ and we sell the stock for S_T. Table 5.3 demonstrates that borrowing to buy the stock replicates the expiration payoff to a forward contract.

Just as we can use the stock and borrowing to synthetically create a forward, we can also use the forward to create synthetic stocks and bonds. Table 5.4 demonstrates that we can go long a forward contract and lend the present value of the forward price to synthetically create the stock. The expiration payoff in this table assumes that equation

TABLE 5.3 Demonstration that borrowing $S_0 e^{-\delta T}$ to buy $e^{-\delta T}$ shares of the index replicates the payoff to a forward contract, $S_T - F_{0,T}$.

	Cash Flows	
Transaction	Time 0	Time T (expiration)
Buy $e^{-\delta T}$ units of the index	$-S_0 e^{-\delta T}$	$+S_T$
Borrow $S_0 e^{-\delta T}$	$+S_0 e^{-\delta T}$	$-S_0 e^{(r-\delta)T}$
Total	0	$S_T - S_0 e^{(r-\delta)T}$

TABLE 5.4 Demonstration that going long a forward contract at the price $F_{0,T} = S_0 e^{(r-\delta)T}$ and lending the present value of the forward price creates a synthetic share of the index at time T.

	Cash Flows	
Transaction	Time 0	Time T (expiration)
Long one forward	0	$S_T - F_{0,T}$
Lend $S_0 e^{-\delta T}$	$-S_0 e^{-\delta T}$	$+S_0 e^{(r-\delta)T}$
Total	$-S_0 e^{-\delta T}$	S_T

(5.7) holds. Table 5.5 demonstrates that if we buy the stock and short the forward, we create cash flows like those of a risk-free bond. The rate of return on this synthetic bond—the construction of which is summarized in Table 5.5—is called the **implied repo rate**.

To summarize, we have shown that

$$\text{Forward} = \text{Stock} - \text{zero-coupon bond} \tag{5.9}$$

We can rearrange this equation to derive other synthetic equivalents:

$$\text{Stock} = \text{Forward} + \text{zero-coupon bond}$$

$$\text{Zero-coupon bond} = \text{Stock} - \text{forward}$$

All of these synthetic positions can be reversed to create synthetic short positions.

TABLE 5.5
Demonstration that buying $e^{-\delta T}$ shares of the index and shorting a forward creates a synthetic bond.

Transaction	Cash Flows	
	Time 0	Time T (expiration)
Buy $e^{-\delta T}$ units of the index	$-S_0 e^{-\delta T}$	$+S_T$
Short one forward	0	$F_{0,T} - S_T$
Total	$-S_0 e^{-\delta T}$	$F_{0,T}$

TABLE 5.6
Transactions and cash flows for a cash-and-carry: A market-maker is short a forward contract and long a synthetic forward contract.

Transaction	Cash Flows	
	Time 0	Time T (expiration)
Buy tailed position in stock, paying $S_0 e^{-\delta T}$	$-S_0 e^{-\delta T}$	$+S_T$
Borrow $S_0 e^{-\delta T}$	$+S_0 e^{-\delta T}$	$-S_0 e^{(r-\delta)T}$
Short forward	0	$F_{0,T} - S_T$
Total	0	$F_{0,T} - S_0 e^{(r-\delta)T}$

Synthetic Forwards in Market-Making and Arbitrage

Now we will see how market-makers and arbitrageurs use these strategies. Suppose a customer wishes to enter into a long forward position. The market-maker, as the counterparty, is left holding a short forward position. He can offset this risk by creating a synthetic long forward position, constructed as in Table 5.6. There is no risk because the total cash flow at time T is $F_{0,T} - S_0 e^{(r-\delta)T}$. All of the components of this cash flow—the forward price, the stock price, the interest rate, and the dividend yield—are known at time 0. The result is a risk-free position.

Similarly, suppose the market-maker wishes to hedge a long forward position. Then it is possible to reverse the positions in Table 5.6. The result is in Table 5.7.

A transaction in which you buy the underlying asset and short the offsetting forward contract is called a **cash-and-carry**. A cash-and-carry has no risk: You have an obligation to deliver the asset but also own the asset. The market-maker offsets the short forward position with a cash-and-carry. An arbitrage that involves buying the underlying asset and

TABLE 5.7

Transactions and cash flows for a reverse cash-and-carry: A market-maker is long a forward contract and short a synthetic forward contract.

Transaction	Cash Flows	
	Time 0	Time T (expiration)
Short tailed position in stock, receiving $S_0 e^{-\delta T}$	$+S_0 e^{-\delta T}$	$-S_T$
Lend $S_0 e^{-\delta T}$	$-S_0 e^{-\delta T}$	$+S_0 e^{(r-\delta)T}$
Long forward	0	$S_T - F_{0,T}$
Total	0	$S_0 e^{(r-\delta)T} - F_{0,T}$

selling it forward is called a **cash-and-carry arbitrage.** As you might guess, a **reverse cash-and-carry** entails short-selling the index and entering into a long forward position.

If the forward contract is priced according to equation (5.7), then profits on a cash-and-carry are zero. We motivated the cash-and-carry in Table 5.6 as risk management by a market-maker. However, an arbitrageur might also engage in a cash-and-carry. If the forward price is too high relative to the stock price—i.e., if $F_{0,T} > S_0 e^{(r-\delta)T}$—then an arbitrageur or market-maker can use the strategy in Table 5.6 to make a risk-free profit.

An arbitrageur would make the transactions in Table 5.7 if the forward were underpriced relative to the stock—i.e., if $S_0 e^{(r-\delta)T} > F_{0,T}$.

As a final point, you may be wondering about the role of borrowing and lending in Tables 5.6 and 5.7. When you explicitly account for borrowing, you account for the opportunity cost of investing funds. For example, if we omitted borrowing from Table 5.6, we would invest $S_0 e^{-\delta T}$ today and receive $F_{0,T}$ at time T. In order to know if there is an arbitrage opportunity, we would need to perform a present-value calculation to compare the time 0 cash flow with the time T cash flow. By explicitly including borrowing in the calculations, this time-value-of-money comparison is automatic.[8]

Similarly, by comparing the implied repo rate with our borrowing rate, we have a simple measure of whether there is an arbitrage opportunity. For example, if we could borrow at 7%, then there is an arbitrage opportunity if the implied repo rate exceeds 7%. On the other hand, if our borrowing rate exceeds the implied repo rate, there is no arbitrage opportunity.

No-Arbitrage Bounds with Transaction Costs

Tables 5.6 and 5.7 demonstrate that an arbitrageur can make a costless profit if $F_{0,T} \neq S_0 e^{(r-\delta)T}$. This analysis ignores transaction costs. In practice, an arbitrageur will face

---

[8] In general, arbitrageurs can borrow and lend at different rates. A pro forma arbitrage calculation needs to account for the appropriate cost of capital for any particular transaction.

trading fees, bid-ask spreads, different interest rates for borrowing and lending, and the possibility that buying or selling in large quantities will cause prices to change. The effect of such costs will be that, rather than there being a single no-arbitrage price, there will be a no-arbitrage *bound*: a lower price and an upper price such that arbitrage will not be profitable when the forward price is between these bounds.

It is likely that the no-arbitrage region will be different for different arbitrageurs at a point in time, and different across time for a given arbitrageur. For example, a large investment bank sees stock order flow from a variety of sources and may have inventory of either long or short positions in stocks. The bank may be able to buy or sell shares at low cost by serving as a market-maker for a customer order. It may be inexpensive for a bank to short if it already owns the stocks, or it may be inexpensive to buy if the bank already has a short position.

Borrowing and lending rates can also vary. For a transaction that is explicitly financed by borrowing, the relevant interest rates are the arbitrageur's marginal borrowing rate (if that is the source of funds to buy stocks) or lending rate (if stocks are to be shorted). However, at other times, it may be possible to borrow at a lower rate or lend at a higher rate. For example, it may be possible to sell T-bills being held for some other purpose as a source of short-term funds. This may effectively permit borrowing at a low rate. Finally, in order to borrow money or securities arbitrageurs must have available capital. Undertaking one arbitrage may prevent undertaking another.

The overall conclusion is not surprising: Arbitrage may be difficult, risky, and costly. Large deviations from the theoretical price may be arbitraged, but small deviations may or may not represent genuine arbitrage opportunities.

Quasi-Arbitrage

The previous section focused on explicit arbitrage. However, it can also be possible to undertake *implicit* arbitrage by substituting a low-yield position for one with a higher return. We call this **quasi-arbitrage.**

Consider, for example, a corporation that can borrow at 8.5% and lend at 7.5%. Suppose there is a cash-and-carry transaction with an implied repo rate of 8%. There is no pure arbitrage opportunity for the corporation, but it would make sense to divert lending from the 7.5% assets to the 8% cash-and-carry. If we attempt explicit arbitrage by borrowing at 8.5% in order to earn 8% on the cash-and-carry, the transaction becomes unprofitable. We can arbitrage only to the extent that we are already lending; this is why it is *quasi*-arbitrage.

Does the Forward Price Predict the Future Price?

It is common to think that the forward price reflects an expectation of the asset's future price. However, from the formula for the forward price, equation (5.7), once we know the current asset price, risk-free rate, and dividend yield, the forward price conveys no additional information about the expected future stock price. Moreover, the forward price *systematically* errs in predicting the future stock price.

The reason is straightforward. When you buy a stock, you invest money that has an opportunity cost (it could otherwise have been invested in an interest-earning asset), and you are acquiring the risk of the stock. On average you expect to earn interest as compensation for the time value of money. You also expect an additional return as compensation for the risk of the stock—this is the risk premium. Algebraically, the expected return on a stock is

$$\alpha = \underbrace{r}_{\text{Compensation for time}} + \underbrace{\alpha - r}_{\text{Compensation for risk}} \quad (5.10)$$

When you enter into a forward contract, there is no investment; hence, you are not compensated for the time value of money. However, the forward contract retains the risk of the stock, so you must be compensated for risk. *This means that the forward contract must earn the risk premium.* If the risk premium is positive, then on average you must expect a positive return from the forward contract. The only way this can happen is if the forward price predicts too low a stock price. In other words, *the forward contract is a biased predictor of the future stock price.*

We can see this algebraically. Let α be the expected return on a non-dividend-paying stock and let r be the effective annual interest rate. Consider a 1-year forward contract. The forward price is

$$F_0 = S_0(1+r)$$

The expected future spot price is

$$E_0(S_1) = S_0(1+\alpha)$$

where E_0 denotes "expectation as of time 0." Thus, the difference between the forward price and the expected future spot price is

$$E_0(S_1) - F_0 = S_0(1+\alpha) - S_0(1+r) = S_0(\alpha - r)$$

The expression $\alpha - r$ is the *risk premium* on the asset—i.e., the amount by which the asset is expected to outperform the risk-free asset. This equation verifies that, as a predictor of the future stock price, *the forward price is biased by the amount of the risk premium on the underlying asset.*

For example, suppose that a stock index has an expected return of 15%, while the risk-free rate is 5%. If the current index price is 100, then on average we expect that the index will be 115 in 1 year. The forward price for delivery in 1 year will be only 105, however. This means that a holder of the forward contract will on average earn positive profits, albeit at the cost of bearing the risk of the index.[9]

This bias does not imply that a forward contract is a good investment. Rather, it tells us that *the risk premium on an asset can be created at zero cost and hence has*

---

[9] Accounting for dividends in this example would not change the magnitude of the bias since dividends would lower the expected future price of the index and the forward price by equal amounts.

a zero value. Though this seems surprising, it is a result from elementary finance that if we buy any asset and borrow the full amount of its cost—a transaction that requires no investment—then we earn the risk premium on the asset. Since a forward contract has the risk of a fully leveraged investment in the asset, it earns the risk premium. This proposition is true in general, not just for the example of a forward on a non-dividend-paying stock.

An Interpretation of the Forward Pricing Formula

The forward pricing formula for a stock index, equation (5.7), depends on $r - \delta$, the difference between the risk-free rate and the dividend yield. This difference is called the **cost of carry.**

Suppose you buy a unit of the index that costs S and fund the position by borrowing at the risk-free rate. You will pay rS on the borrowed amount, but the dividend yield will provide offsetting income of δS. You will have to pay the difference, $(r - \delta)S$, on an ongoing basis. This difference is the net cost of carrying a long position in the asset; hence, it is called the "cost of carry."

Now suppose you were to short the index and invest the proceeds at the risk-free rate. You would receive S for shorting the asset and earn rS on the invested proceeds, but you would have to pay δS to the index lender. We will call δ the **lease rate** of the index; it is what you would have to pay to a lender of the asset. The rate of an asset is the annualized cash payment that the borrower must make to the lender. For a non-dividend-paying stock the lease rate is zero, while for a dividend-paying stock the lease rate is the dividend.

Here is an interpretation of the forward pricing formula:

$$\text{Forward price} = \text{Spot price} + \underbrace{\text{Interest to carry the asset} - \text{Asset lease rate}}_{\text{Cost of carry}} \quad (5.11)$$

The forward contract, unlike the stock, requires no investment and makes no payouts and therefore has a zero cost of carry. One way to interpret the forward pricing formula is that, to the extent the forward contract saves our having to pay the cost of carry, we are willing to pay a higher price. This is what equation (5.11) says.

5.4 FUTURES CONTRACTS

Futures contracts are essentially exchange-traded forward contracts. As with forwards, futures contracts represent a commitment to buy or sell an underlying asset at some future date. Because futures are exchange-traded, they are standardized and have specified delivery dates, locations, and procedures. Futures may be traded either electronically or in trading pits, with buyers and sellers shouting orders to one another (this is called **open outcry**). Each exchange has an associated **clearinghouse.** The role of the clearinghouse is to match the buys and sells that take place during the day and to keep track of the obligations and payments required of the members of the clearinghouse, who are called *clearing members*. After matching trades, the clearinghouse typically becomes the counterparty for each clearing member.

Although forwards and futures are similar in many respects, there are differences:

- Whereas forward contracts are settled at expiration, futures contracts are settled daily. The use of market prices to determine who owes what to whom is called **marking-to-market.** Frequent marking-to-market and settlement of a futures contract can lead to pricing differences between the futures and an otherwise identical forward.

- As a result of daily settlement, futures contracts are liquid—it is possible to offset an obligation on a given date by entering into the opposite position. For example, if you are long the September S&P 500 futures contract, you can cancel your obligation to buy by entering into an offsetting obligation to sell the September S&P 500 contract. If you use the same broker to buy and to sell, your obligation is officially cancelled.[10]

- Over-the-counter forward contracts can be customized to suit the buyer or seller, whereas futures contracts are standardized. For example, available futures contracts may permit delivery of 250 units of a particular index in March or June. A forward contract could specify April delivery of 300 units of the index.

- Because of daily settlement, the nature of credit risk is different with the futures contract. In fact, futures contracts are structured so as to minimize the effects of credit risk.

- There are typically daily price limits in futures markets (and on some stock exchanges as well). A **price limit** is a move in the futures price that triggers a temporary halt in trading. For example, there is an initial 5% limit on *down* moves in the S&P 500 futures contract. An offer to sell exceeding this limit can trigger a temporary trading halt, after which time a 10% price limit is in effect. If that is exceeded, there are subsequent 15% and 20% limits. The rules can be complicated, but it is important to be aware that such rules exist.

We will illustrate futures contracts with the S&P 500 index futures contract as a specific example.

The S&P 500 Futures Contract

The S&P 500 futures contract has the S&P 500 stock index as the underlying asset. There are futures contracts on other stock indexes, including, in the United States, the Dow Jones Industrial Average, the NASDAQ 100, and the Russell 1000, as well as many foreign indexes. The basic idea behind stock index futures contracts is generally the same, regardless of the underlying index, so we will discuss only the S&P contract in detail. One index contract that is different is the Nikkei 225 index futures contract, which we

---

[10] Although forward contracts may not be explicitly marketable, it is generally possible to enter into an offsetting position to cancel the obligation to buy or sell.

Box 5.2: Single Stock Futures

Futures contracts on individual stocks in the United States began trading in November 2002 on OneChicago, an electronic exchange owned jointly by the Chicago Board Options Exchange, the Chicago Board of Trade, and the Chicago Mercantile Exchange. Earlier, the trading of single stock futures had been stalled by disagreements among exchanges and by a regulatory turf battle between the Securities and Exchange Commission, which regulates stocks and stock options, and the Commodity Futures Trading Commission, which regulates commodity and equity index futures.

Single stock futures were controversial even before trading began, with disagreement about how successful the product would be. What need would single stock futures serve? There was already a well-established market for buying and short-selling stocks, and we saw in Chapter 3 that investors could create synthetic stock forwards using options. Would differences in margin requirements, transaction costs, or contract characteristics make the new product successful?

Since 2002, at least one competitor to OneChicago (NQLX) has entered and then exited the market for single stock futures in the United States. Trading volume has been low.

At the same time, there has been an active *over-the-counter* market in swaps based on individual stocks. At least some of these transactions are believed to have been tax-motivated, and the U.S. Senate in fall 2007 was looking into the possibility of tax law changes. (For example, see "How Lehman Sold Plan to Sidestep Tax Man," by Anita Raghavan, *Wall Street Journal*, Sept 17, 2007, p. A.1.)

---

will discuss in Chapter 6. In addition to index futures, futures on individual stocks have recently begun trading in the United States; see Box 5.2.

Figure 2.1 (page 30) shows a newspaper quotation for the S&P 500 index futures contract along with other stock index futures contracts. Figure 5.1 contains the specifications for this contract. The notional value, or size, of the contract is the dollar value of the assets underlying one contract. If the S&P index is 1450, the notional value is $250 \times 1450 = \$362,500$.[11]

The S&P 500 is an example of a cash-settled contract: Instead of settling by actual delivery of the underlying stocks, the contract calls for a cash payment that equals the profit or loss *as if* the contract were settled by delivery of the underlying asset. On the expiration day, the S&P 500 futures contract is marked-to-market against the actual cash index. This final settlement against the cash index guarantees that the futures price equals the index value at contract expiration.

---

[11] Because the S&P 500 index is a fabricated number—a value-weighted average of individual stock prices—the S&P 500 index is treated as a pure number rather than a price and the contract is defined at maturity to have a size of $250 \times$ S&P 500 index.

FIGURE 5.1	Underlying	S&P 500 index
Specifications for the S&P 500 index futures contract.	Where traded	Chicago Mercantile Exchange
	Size	$250 \times$ S&P 500 index
	Months	Mar, Jun, Sep, Dec
	Trading ends	Business day prior to determination of settlement price
	Settlement	Cash-settled, based upon opening price of S&P 500 on third Friday of expiration month

It is easy to see why the S&P 500 is cash-settled. A physical settlement process would call for delivery of 500 shares (or some large subset thereof) in the precise percentage they make up the S&P 500 index. This basket of stocks would be expensive to buy and sell. Cash settlement is an inexpensive alternative.

Margins and Marking-to-Market

Let's explore the logistics of holding a futures position. Suppose the futures price is 1100 and you wish to acquire a $2.2 million position in the S&P 500 index. The notional value of one contract is $250 \times 1100 = \$275,000$; this represents the amount you are agreeing to pay at expiration per futures contract. To go long $2.2 million of the index, you would enter into $2.2 million/$0.275 million = 8 long futures contracts. The notional value of 8 contracts is $8 \times \$250 \times 1100 = \$2000 \times 1100 = \$2.2$ million.

A broker executes your buy order. For every buyer there is a seller, which means that one or more investors must be found who simultaneously agree to sell forward the same number of units of the index. The total number of open positions (buy/sell pairs) is called the **open interest** of the contract.

Both buyers and sellers are required to post a performance bond with the broker to ensure that they can cover a specified loss on the position.[12] This deposit, which can earn interest, is called **margin** and is intended to protect the counterparty against your failure to meet your obligations. The margin is a performance bond, not a premium. Hence, futures contracts are costless (not counting, of course, commissions and the bid-ask spread).

To understand the role of margin, suppose that there is 10% margin and weekly settlement (in practice, settlement is daily). The margin on futures contracts with a notional value of $2.2 million is $220,000.

---

[12] The exchange's clearinghouse determines a minimum margin, but individual brokers can and do demand higher margins from individual customers. The reason is that the broker is liable to the clearing corporation for a customer's failure to pay.

If the S&P 500 futures price drops by 1 to 1099, we lose $2000 on our futures position. The reason is that 8 long contracts obligate us to pay $2000 × 1100 to buy 2000 units of the index that we could now sell for only $2000 × 1099. Thus, we lose $(1099 - 1100) \times \$2000 = -\$2000$. Suppose that over the first week the futures price drops 72.01 points to 1027.99, a decline of about 6.5%. On a mark-to-market basis, we have lost

$$\$2000 \times -72.01 = -\$144{,}020$$

We have a choice of either paying this loss directly or allowing it to be taken out of the margin balance. It doesn't matter which we do, since we can recover the unused margin balance plus interest at any time by selling our position.

If the loss is subtracted from the margin balance, we have earned 1 week's interest and have lost $144,020. Thus, if the continuously compounded interest rate is 6%, our margin balance after 1 week is

$$\$220{,}000 \times e^{0.06 \times 1/52} - \$144{,}020 = \$76{,}233.99$$

Because we have a 10% margin, a 6.5% decline in the futures price results in a 65% decline in margin. Were we to close out our position by entering into 8 short index futures contracts, we would receive the remaining margin balance of $76,233.99.

The decline in the margin balance means the broker has significantly less protection should we default. For this reason, participants are required to maintain the margin at a minimum level, called the **maintenance margin.** This is often set at 70% to 80% of the initial margin level. In this example, where the margin balance declines 65%, we would have to post additional margin. The broker would make a **margin call,** requesting additional margin. If we failed to post additional margin, the broker would close the position by selling 2000 units of the index and return to us the remaining margin. In practice, marking-to-market and settling up are performed at least daily.

The margin you post is the broker's protection against your default. Therefore, a major determinant of margin levels is the volatility of the underlying asset. The minimum margin on the S&P 500 contract has generally been less than the 10% we assume in this example. In August 2007, for example, the minimum margin on the S&P 500 futures contract was about 6% of the notional value of the contract.

To illustrate the effect of periodic settlement, Table 5.8 reports hypothetical futures price moves and tracks the margin position over a period of 10 weeks, assuming weekly marking-to-market and a continuously compounded risk-free rate of 6%. As the party agreeing to buy at a fixed price, we make money when the price goes up and lose when the price goes down. The opposite would occur for the seller.

The 10-week profit on the position is obtained by subtracting from the final margin balance the future value of the original margin investment. Week 10 profit on the position in Table 5.8 is therefore

$$\$44{,}990.57 - \$220{,}000 e^{0.06 \times 10/52} = -\$177{,}562.60$$

TABLE 5.8 Mark-to-market proceeds and margin balance over 10 weeks from long position in 8 S&P 500 futures contracts. The last column does not include additional margin payments. The final row represents expiration of the contract.

Week	Multiplier	Futures Price	Price Change	Margin Balance
0	$2000.00	1100.00	—	$220,000.00
1	2000.00	1027.99	−72.01	76,233.99
2	2000.00	1037.88	9.89	96,102.01
3	2000.00	1073.23	35.35	166,912.96
4	2000.00	1048.78	−24.45	118,205.66
5	2000.00	1090.32	41.54	201,422.13
6	2000.00	1106.94	16.62	234,894.67
7	2000.00	1110.98	4.04	243,245.86
8	2000.00	1024.74	−86.24	71,046.69
9	2000.00	1007.30	−17.44	36,248.72
10	2000.00	1011.65	4.35	44,990.57

What if the position had been a forward rather than a futures position, but with prices the same? In that case, after 10 weeks our profit would have been

$$(1011.65 - 1100) \times \$2000 = -\$176,700$$

Why do the futures and forward profits differ? The reason is that with the futures contract, interest is earned on the mark-to-market proceeds. Given the prices in Table 5.8, the loss is larger for futures than forwards because prices on average are below the initial price and we have to fund losses as they occur. With a forward, by contrast, losses are not funded until expiration. Earning interest on the daily settlement magnifies the gain or loss compared to that on a forward contract. Had there been consistent gains on the position in this example, the futures profit would have exceeded the forward profit.[13]

---

[13] The ultimate value of the two positions differs because the futures price represents a week 10 price, whereas marking-to-market occurs at times prior to week 10, while still using the week 10 price. If marking-to-market occurred using the *present value* of the change in the futures price, the two payoffs would be the same. This can also be accomplished by tailing the position—holding e^{-rT} contracts.

Comparing Futures and Forward Prices

Are futures and forward prices the same? If the interest rate is random, then they can be different. Suppose, for example, that on average the interest rate increases unexpectedly when the futures price increases; i.e., the two are positively correlated. Then the margin balance would grow (due to an increased futures price) just as the interest rate was higher. The margin balance would shrink as the interest rate was lower. On average in this case, a long futures position would outperform a long forward contract.

Conversely, suppose that the interest rate declined as the futures price rose. Then as the margin balance on a long position grew, the proceeds would be invested at a lower rate. Similarly, as the balance declined and required additional financing, this financing would occur at a higher rate. Here a long futures contract would on average perform worse than a long forward contract.

This comparison of the forward and futures payoffs suggests that when the interest rate is positively correlated with the futures price, the futures price will exceed the price on an otherwise identical forward contract: The investor who is long futures buys at a higher price to offset the advantage of marking-to-market. Similarly, when the interest rate is negatively correlated with the forward price, the futures price will be less than an otherwise identical forward price: The investor who is long futures buys at a lower price to offset the disadvantage of marking-to-market.

As an empirical matter, forward and futures prices are very similar.[14] The theoretical difference arises from uncertainty about the interest on mark-to-market proceeds. For short-lived contracts, the effect is generally small. However, for long-lived contracts, the difference can be significant, especially for long-lived interest rate futures, for which there is sure to be a correlation between the interest rate and the price of the underlying asset. For the rest of this chapter we will ignore the difference between forwards and futures.

5.5 USES OF INDEX FUTURES

An index futures contract is economically like borrowing to buy the index. Why use an index futures contract if you can synthesize one? One answer is that index futures can permit trading the index at a lower transaction cost than actually trading a basket of the stocks that make up the index. If you are taking a temporary position in the index, either for investing or hedging, the transaction cost savings could be significant.

In this section we provide two examples of the use of index futures: asset allocation and cross-hedging a related portfolio.

---

[14] See French (1983) for a comparison of forward and futures prices on a variety of underlying assets.

Asset Allocation

Asset allocation strategies involve switching investments among asset classes, such as stocks, money market instruments, and bonds. Trading the individual securities, such as the stocks in an index, can be expensive. Our earlier discussion of arbitrage demonstrated that we can use forwards to create synthetic stocks and bonds. The practical implication is that a portfolio manager can invest in a stock index without holding stocks, commodities without holding physical commodities, and so on.

Switching from stocks to T-bills As an example of asset allocation, suppose that we have an investment in the S&P 500 index and we wish to temporarily invest in T-bills instead of the index. Instead of selling all 500 stocks and investing in T-bills, we can simply keep our stock portfolio and take a short forward position in the S&P 500 index. This converts our cash investment in the index into a cash-and-carry, creating a synthetic T-bill. When we wish to revert to investing in stocks, we simply offset the forward position.

To illustrate this, suppose that the current index price, S_0, is $100 and the effective 1-year risk-free rate is 10%. The forward price is therefore $110. Suppose that in 1 year the index price could be either $80 or $130. If we sell the index and invest in T-bills, we will have $110 in 1 year.

Table 5.9 shows that if, instead of selling, we keep the stock and short the forward contract, we earn a 10% return no matter what happens to the value of the stock. In this example, 10% is the rate of return implied by the forward premium. If there is no arbitrage, this return will be equal to the risk-free rate.

General asset allocation We can use forwards and futures to perform even more sophisticated asset allocation. Suppose we wish to invest our portfolio in Treasury bonds (long-term Treasury obligations) instead of stocks. We can accomplish this reallocation with two forward positions: shorting the forward S&P 500 index and going long the forward T-bond. The first transaction converts our portfolio from an index investment to a T-bill investment. The second transaction converts the portfolio from a T-bill investment

TABLE 5.9 Effect of owning the stock and selling forward, assuming that $S_0 = \$100$ and $F_{0,1} = \$110$.

	Cash Flows		
Transaction	Today	1 year, $S_1=\$80$	1 year, $S_1=\$130$
Own stock @ $100	−$100	$80	$130
Short forward @ $110	0	$110 − $80	$110 − $130
Total	−$100	$110	$110

to a T-bond investment. This use of futures to convert a position from one asset category (stocks) to another (bonds) is called a **futures overlay**.

Futures overlays can have benefits beyond reducing transaction costs. Suppose an investment management company has portfolio managers who successfully invest in stocks they believe to be mispriced. The managers are judged on their performance relative to the S&P 500 stock index and consistently outperform the index by 2% per year (in the language of portfolio theory, their "alpha" is 2%). Now suppose that new clients of the company like the performance record but want to invest in bonds rather than stocks. The investment management company could fire its stock managers and hire bond managers, but its existing investment managers are the reason for the company's success. The company can use a futures overlay to continue to invest in stocks, but to provide a bond return instead of a stock return to investors. By investing in stocks, shorting index futures, and going long bond futures, the managers continue to invest in stocks, but the client receives a bond return plus 2% rather than a stock return plus 2%. This use of futures to transform an outperforming portfolio on one asset class into an outperforming portfolio on a different asset class is called **alpha-porting.**

Cross-Hedging with Index Futures

Index futures are often used to hedge portfolios that are not exactly the same as the index. This is called *cross-hedging*: using a derivative on one asset to hedge a different asset.

Cross-hedging with perfect correlation Suppose that we have a portfolio that is not the S&P 500, and we wish to shift the portfolio into T-bills. Can we use the S&P 500 futures contract to do this? The answer depends on the correlation of the portfolio with the S&P 500. To the extent the two are not perfectly correlated, there will be residual risk.

Suppose that we own $100 million of stocks with a beta relative to the S&P 500 of 1.4. Assume for the moment that the two indexes are perfectly correlated. Perfect correlation means that there is a perfectly predictable relationship between the two indexes, not necessarily that they move by exactly the same amount. Using the Capital Asset Pricing Model (CAPM), the return on our portfolio, r_p, is related to its beta, β_p, by

$$r_p = r + \beta_p(r_{S\&P} - r)$$

Assume also that the S&P 500 is 1100 with a 0 dividend yield and the effective annual risk-free rate is 6%. Hence, the futures price is $1100 \times 1.06 = 1166$.

If we wish to allocate from the index into Treasury bills using futures, we need to short some quantity of the S&P 500. There are two steps to calculating the short futures quantity:

1. *Adjust for the difference in the dollar amounts of our portfolio and the S&P 500 contract.* In this case, one futures contract has a value in dollars today of

TABLE 5.10
Results from shorting 509.09 S&P 500 index futures against a $100 million portfolio with a beta of 1.4.

S&P 500 Index	Gain on 509 Futures	Portfolio Value	Total
900	33.855	72.145	106.000
950	27.491	78.509	106.000
1000	21.127	84.873	106.000
1050	14.764	91.236	106.000
1100	8.400	97.600	106.000
1150	2.036	103.964	106.000
1200	−4.327	110.327	106.000

$250 \times 1166/1.06 = \$275{,}000$.[15] Thus, the number of contracts needed to cover $100 million of stock is

$$\frac{\$100 \text{ million}}{\$0.275 \text{ million}} = 363.636$$

2. *Adjust for the difference in beta*. Since the beta of our portfolio exceeds 1, it moves more than the S&P 500 in either direction. Thus, we need to further increase our S&P 500 position to account for the greater magnitude moves in our portfolio relative to the S&P 500. This gives us

$$\text{Final hedge quantity} = \frac{\$100 \text{ million}}{\$0.275 \text{ million}} \times 1.4 = 509.09$$

Table 5.10 shows the performance of the hedged position. The result, as you would expect, is that the hedged position earns the risk-free rate, 6%.

Cross-hedging with imperfect correlation The preceding example assumes that the portfolio and the S&P 500 index are perfectly correlated. In practice, correlations between two portfolios can be substantially less than 1. Using the S&P 500 to hedge such a portfolio would introduce basis risk, creating a hedge with residual risk.[16]

---

[15] The S&P 500 index is a value in terms of present dollars, while the futures price is expressed in terms of dollars 1 year hence. To make them comparable, it is necessary to take the future value of the S&P cash price or the present value of the futures price.

[16] There is additional basis risk in such a hedge because, for reasons discussed in Section 5.4, the S&P 500 futures contract and the cash price of the S&P 500 index may not move perfectly together.

Denote the return and invested dollars on the portfolio as r_p and I_p. Assume that we short H futures contracts, each with a notional value N. The futures position earns the risk premium, $r_{S\&P} - r$. Thus, the return on the hedged position is

$$\text{Hedged return} = r_p I_p + H \times N \times (r_{S\&P} - r)$$

The variance of the hedged position is

$$\text{Variance} = \sigma_p^2 I_p^2 + H^2 N^2 \sigma_{S\&P}^2 + 2 I_p H \text{Cov}(r_p, r_{S\&P}) \qquad (5.12)$$

The variance-minimizing hedge position, H^*, is

$$H^* = -\frac{I_p}{N} \frac{\text{Cov}(r_p, r_{S\&P})}{\sigma_{S\&P}^2} \qquad (5.13)$$

$$= -\frac{I_p}{N} \beta_p$$

The hedge quantity is denominated in terms of a quantity of futures contracts. The second equality follows because $\text{Cov}(r_p, r_{S\&P})/\sigma_{S\&P}^2$ is the slope coefficient when we regress the portfolio return on the S&P 500 return; i.e., it is the portfolio beta with respect to the S&P 500 index. Equation (5.13) is also the formula we used in concluding that, with perfect correlation, we should short 509.09 contracts.

Notice that the hedge ratio in equation (5.13) depends on the ratio of the market value of the portfolio, I_p, to the notional value of the S&P 500 contract, N. Thus, as the portfolio changes value relative to the S&P 500 index, it is necessary to change the hedge ratio. This rebalancing is necessary when we calculate hedge ratios using a relationship based on returns, which are percentage changes.

When we add H^* futures to the portfolio, the variance of the hedged portfolio, σ_{hedged}^2, is

$$\sigma_{\text{hedged}}^2 = \sigma_p^2 I_p^2 \left(1 - \rho^2\right) \qquad (5.14)$$

where ρ is the correlation coefficient between the portfolio and the S&P 500 index. The correlation coefficient, ρ, can be computed directly from r_p and $r_{S\&P}$, but it is also the square root of the regression r-squared (R^2) when we regress r_P on $r_{S\&P}$ in order to estimate β.

Example 5.3 Suppose we are optimistic about the performance of the NASDAQ index relative to the S&P 500 index. We can go long the NASDAQ index and short the S&P 500 futures. We obtain the variance-minimizing position in the S&P 500 by using equation (5.13). A 5-year regression (from June 1999 to June 2004) of the daily NASDAQ return on the S&P 500 return gives

$$r_{\text{NASD}} = \underset{(0.0003)}{-0.0001} + \underset{(0.0262)}{1.4784} \times (r_{S\&P} - r) \qquad R^2 = 0.7188$$

The regression beta tells us to short a dollar value of the S&P that is 1.4784 times greater than the NASDAQ position we hold. The correlation coefficient between the two returns, ρ, is $\sqrt{0.7188} = 0.8478$.[17] The daily standard deviation of the return on the NASDAQ over this period is 2.24%. Hence, using equation (5.14), for a \$1 million investment, the variance of the hedged position is

$$\sigma_{\text{NASD}}^2 I_p^2 \left(1 - \rho^2\right) = 0.0224^2 \times (\$1m)^2 \times (1 - 0.7188) = (\$11{,}878)^2$$

Thus, the daily standard deviation of the hedged dollar return is \$11,878.

Risk management for stock-pickers An asset manager who picks stocks is often making a bet about the relative, but not the absolute, performance of a stock. For example, XYZ might be expected to outperform a broad range of stocks on a risk-adjusted basis. If the economy suffers a recession, however, XYZ will decline in value even if it outperforms other stocks. Index futures can be used in this case to help isolate the *relative* performance of XYZ.

Suppose the return of XYZ is given by the CAPM:

$$r_{\text{XYZ}} = \alpha_{\text{XYZ}} + r + \beta_{\text{XYZ}}(r_m - r) \tag{5.15}$$

The term α_{XYZ} in this context represents the expected abnormal return on XYZ. If we use the S&P 500 as a proxy for the market, then we can select H according to equation (5.13). The result for the hedged position will be that, on average, we earn $\alpha_{\text{XYZ}} + r$. The risk of the position will be given by equation (5.14). Since the correlation of an individual stock and the index will not be close to 1, there will be considerable remaining risk. However, the portfolio will not have market risk.

CHAPTER SUMMARY

The purchase of a stock or other asset entails agreeing to a price, making payment, and taking delivery of the asset. A forward contract fixes the price today, but payment and delivery are deferred. The pricing of forward contracts reflects the costs and benefits of this deferred payment and delivery. The seller receives payment later, so the price is higher to reflect interest owed the seller, and the buyer receives possession later, so the price is lower to reflect dividends not received by the buyer. A prepaid forward contract requires payment today; hence, it separates these two effects. The price of a prepaid forward is

$$\text{Prepaid forward price} = S_0 e^{-\delta T}$$

---

[17] You can, of course, also compute the correlation coefficient directly from the time series of returns.

TABLE 5.11 Synthetic equivalents assuming the asset pays continuous dividends at the rate δ.

Position		Synthetic Equivalent		
Long forward	+	Buy $e^{-\delta T}$ shares of stock	+	Borrow $S_0 e^{-\delta T}$
Bond paying $F_{0,T}$	+	Buy $e^{-\delta T}$ shares of stock	+	Short forward
Synthetic stock	+	Long forward	+	Lend $e^{-rT} F_{0,T}$

The prepaid forward price is below the asset spot price, S_0, due to dividends forgone by deferring delivery. The forward price also reflects deferral of payment, so it is the future value of the prepaid forward price:

$$\text{Forward price} = S_0 e^{(r-\delta)T}$$

A forward contract is equivalent to a leveraged position in an asset—borrowing to buy the asset. By combining the forward contract with other assets, it is possible to create synthetic stocks and bonds. These equivalents are summarized in Table 5.11. Since a forward contract is risky but requires no investment, it earns the risk premium. The forward price is therefore a biased predictor of the future spot price of the asset, with the bias equal to the risk premium.

The fact that it is possible to create a synthetic forward has two important implications. First, if the forward contract is mispriced, arbitrageurs can take offsetting positions in the forward contract and the synthetic forward contract—in effect buying low and selling high—and make a risk-free profit. Second, dealers who make markets in the forward or in the underlying asset can hedge the risk of their position with a synthetic offsetting position. With transaction costs there is a no-arbitrage *region* rather than a single no-arbitrage price.

Futures contracts are similar to forward contracts, except that with futures there are margin requirements and daily settlement of the gain or loss on the position. The contractual differences between forwards and futures can lead to pricing differences, but in most cases forward prices and futures prices are very close.

In addition to hedging, forward and futures contracts can be used to synthetically switch a portfolio invested in stocks into bonds. A portfolio invested in Asset A can remain invested in Asset A but earn the returns associated with Asset B, as long as there are forward or futures contracts on A and B. This is called a futures overlay.

FURTHER READING

Chapter 6 continues our exploration of forward markets by considering commodity forwards, which are different from financial forwards in important ways. Chapter 7 then examines interest rate forwards. Whereas forward contracts provide a price for delivery at one point in time, swaps, discussed in Chapter 8, provide a price for a series of deliveries over time. Swaps are a natural generalization of forward contracts.

The pricing principles discussed in this chapter will also play important roles when we discuss option pricing in Chapters 10 and 11 and financial engineering in Chapter 12.

To get a sense of the range of traded contracts, look at the futures page of the *Wall Street Journal* and explore the Web sites of futures exchanges: the Chicago Mercantile Exchange Group (www.cme.com), the New York Mercantile Exchange (www.nymex.com), and the London International Financial Futures Exchange (www.liffe.com), among others. These sites typically provide current prices, along with information about the contracts: what the underlying asset is, how the contracts are settled, and so forth. The site for OneChicago (www.onechicago.com) provides information about single stock futures in the United States.

It is well accepted that forward prices are determined by the models and considerations in this chapter. Siegel and Siegel (1990) is a standard reference book on futures. Early papers that examined futures pricing include Modest and Sundaresan (1983), Cornell and French (1983), which emphasized tax effects in futures pricing, and French (1983), which compares forwards and futures when both exist on the same underlying asset. Brennan and Schwartz (1990) explore optimal arbitrage when there are transaction costs, and Reinganum (1986) explores the arbitrage possibilities inherent in time travel. There is a more technical academic literature focusing on the difference between forward and futures contracts, including Black (1976), Cox et al. (1981), Richard and Sundaresan (1981), and Jarrow and Oldfield (1981).

PROBLEMS

5.1 Construct Table 5.1 from the perspective of a seller, providing a descriptive name for each of the transactions.

5.2 A $50 stock pays a $1 dividend every 3 months, with the first dividend coming 3 months from today. The continuously compounded risk-free rate is 6%.

  a. What is the price of a prepaid forward contract that expires 1 year from today, immediately after the fourth-quarter dividend?

  b. What is the price of a forward contract that expires at the same time?

5.3 A $50 stock pays an 8% continuous dividend. The continuously compounded risk-free rate is 6%.

  a. What is the price of a prepaid forward contract that expires 1 year from today?

  b. What is the price of a forward contract that expires at the same time?

5.4 Suppose the stock price is $35 and the continuously compounded interest rate is 5%.

a. What is the 6-month forward price, assuming dividends are zero?

b. If the 6-month forward price is $35.50, what is the annualized forward premium?

c. If the forward price is $35.50, what is the annualized continuous dividend yield?

5.5 Suppose you are a market-maker in S&R index forward contracts. The S&R index spot price is 1100, the risk-free rate is 5%, and the dividend yield on the index is 0.

a. What is the no-arbitrage forward price for delivery in 9 months?

b. Suppose a customer wishes to enter a short index futures position. If you take the opposite position, demonstrate how you would hedge your resulting long position using the index and borrowing or lending.

c. Suppose a customer wishes to enter a long index futures position. If you take the opposite position, demonstrate how you would hedge your resulting short position using the index and borrowing or lending.

5.6 Repeat the previous problem, assuming that the dividend yield is 1.5%.

5.7 The S&R index spot price is 1100, the risk-free rate is 5%, and the dividend yield on the index is 0.

a. Suppose you observe a 6-month forward price of 1135. What arbitrage would you undertake?

b. Suppose you observe a 6-month forward price of 1115. What arbitrage would you undertake?

5.8 The S&R index spot price is 1100, the risk-free rate is 5%, and the continuous dividend yield on the index is 2%.

a. Suppose you observe a 6-month forward price of 1120. What arbitrage would you undertake?

b. Suppose you observe a 6-month forward price of 1110. What arbitrage would you undertake?

5.9 Suppose that 10 years from now it becomes possible for money managers to engage in time travel. In particular, suppose that a money manager could travel to January 1981, when the 1-year Treasury bill rate was 12.5%.

a. If time travel were costless, what riskless arbitrage strategy could a money manager undertake by traveling back and forth between January 1981 and January 1982?

b. If many money managers undertook this strategy, what would you expect to happen to interest rates in 1981?

c. Since interest rates *were* 12.5% in January 1981, what can you conclude about whether costless time travel will ever be possible?

5.10 The S&R index spot price is 1100 and the continuously compounded risk-free rate is 5%. You observe a 9-month forward price of 1129.257.

a. What dividend yield is implied by this forward price?

b. Suppose you believe the dividend yield over the next 9 months will be only 0.5%. What arbitrage would you undertake?

c. Suppose you believe the dividend yield will be 3% over the next 9 months. What arbitrage would you undertake?

5.11 Suppose the S&P 500 index futures price is currently 1200. You wish to purchase four futures contracts on margin.

a. What is the notional value of your position?

b. Assuming a 10% initial margin, what is the value of the initial margin?

5.12 Suppose the S&P 500 index is currently 950 and the initial margin is 10%. You wish to enter into 10 S&P 500 futures contracts.

a. What is the notional value of your position? What is the margin?

b. Suppose you earn a continuously compounded rate of 6% on your margin balance, your position is marked-to-market *weekly*, and the maintenance margin is 80% of the initial margin. What is the greatest S&P 500 index futures price 1 week from today at which will you receive a margin call?

5.13 Verify that going long a forward contract and lending the present value of the forward price creates a payoff of one share of stock when

a. The stock pays no dividends.

b. The stock pays discrete dividends.

c. The stock pays continuous dividends.

5.14 Suppose the S&P index is 1200 and that it is possible to lend at 6% and borrow at 7%. Consider times to maturity of 1 month, 3 months, 6 months, and 1 year.

a. Above what futures price is there arbitrage?

b. Below what futures price is there arbitrage?

5.15 Suppose the S&R index is 800 and that the dividend yield is 0. You are an arbitrageur with a continuously compounded borrowing rate of 5.5% and a continuously compounded lending rate of 5%.

a. Supposing that there are no transaction fees, show that a cash-and-carry arbitrage is not profitable if the forward price is less than 845.23, and that a reverse cash-and-carry arbitrage is not profitable if the forward price is greater than 841.02.

b. Now suppose that there is a $1 transaction fee, paid at time 0, for going either long or short the forward contract. Show that the upper and lower no-arbitrage bounds now become 846.29 and 839.97.

c. Now suppose that in addition to the fee for the forward contract, there is also a $2.40 fee for buying or selling the index. Suppose the contract is settled by delivery of the index, so that this fee is paid only at time 0. What are the new upper and lower no-arbitrage bounds?

d. Make the same assumptions as in the previous part, except assume that the contract is cash-settled. This means that it is necessary to pay the stock index transaction fee (but not the forward fee) at both times 0 and 1. What are the new no-arbitrage bounds?

e. Now suppose that transactions in the index have a fee of 0.3% of the value of the index (this is for both purchases and sales). Transactions in the forward contract still have a fixed fee of $1 per unit of the index at time 0. Suppose the contract is cash-settled so that when you do a cash-and-carry or reverse cash-and-carry you pay the index transaction fee both at time 1 and time 0. What are the new upper and lower no-arbitrage bounds? Compare your answer to that in the previous part. (*Hint:* To handle the time 1 transaction fee, you may want to consider tailing the stock position.)

5.16 Suppose the S&P 500 currently has a level of 875. The continuously compounded return on a 1-year T-bill is 4.75%. You wish to hedge an $800,000 portfolio that has a beta of 1.1 and a correlation of 1.0 with the S&P 500.

a. What is the 1-year futures price for the S&P 500 assuming no dividends?

b. How many S&P 500 futures contracts should you short to hedge your portfolio? What return do you expect on the hedged portfolio?

5.17 Suppose you are selecting a futures contract with which to hedge a portfolio. You have a choice of six contracts, each of which has the same variability, but with correlations of -0.95, -0.75, -0.50, 0, 0.25, and 0.85. Rank the futures contracts with respect to basis risk, from highest to lowest basis risk.

6

The Wide World of Futures Contracts

Futures contracts exist on a great variety of assets, indexes, and commodities. In the last chapter we discussed stock and index futures. In this chapter we discuss some other important financial futures contracts, including currency and Eurodollar futures. We also discuss commodity futures, with a focus on energy futures, including electricity, natural gas, and oil. These contracts illustrate some of the idiosyncracies of commodity futures. Finally, we discuss two relatively new contracts, weather and real estate futures.

6.1 CURRENCY CONTRACTS

Currency futures and forwards are widely used to hedge against changes in exchange rates. The pricing of currency contracts is a straightforward application of the principles we have already discussed. Newspaper listings for exchange-traded currency contracts are shown in Figure 6.1.

Many corporations use currency futures and forwards for short-term hedging. An importer of consumer electronics, for example, may have an obligation to pay the manufacturer ¥150 million 90 days in the future. The dollar revenues from selling these products are likely known in the short run, so the importer bears pure exchange risk due to the payable being fixed in yen. By buying ¥150 million forward 90 days, the importer locks in a dollar price to pay for the yen, which will then be delivered to the manufacturer.

Currency Prepaid Forward

Suppose that 1 year from today you want to have ¥1. A prepaid forward allows you to pay dollars today to acquire ¥1 in 1 year. What is the prepaid forward price? Suppose the yen-denominated interest rate is r_y and the exchange rate today ($/¥) is x_0. We can work backward. If we want ¥1 in 1 year, we must have e^{-r_y} in yen today. To obtain that many yen today, we must exchange $x_0 e^{-r_y}$ dollars into yen.

FIGURE 6.1

Listings for various currency futures contracts from the *Wall Street Journal*, August 10, 2007.

	Open	I High	Contract hi lo	Low	Settle	Chg	Open interest
Currency Futures							
Japanese Yen (CME)-¥12,500,000; $ per 100¥							
Sept	.8401	.8507		.8389	**.8495**	.0098	231,569
Dec	.8489	.8600		.8487	**.8589**	.0098	15,714
Canadian Dollar (CME)-CAD 100,000; $ per CAD							
Sept	.9545	.9559		.9403	**.9476**	-.0070	132,248
Dec	.9556	.9569		.9420	**.9489**	-.0070	4,434
British Pound (CME)-£62,500; $ per £							
Sept	2.0352	2.0385		2.0198	**2.0227**	-.0124	131,981
Dec	2.0329	2.0345		2.0156	**2.0187**	-.0125	893
Swiss Franc (CME)-CHF 125,000; $ per CHF							
Sept	.8378	.8414		.8360	**.8381**	-.0007	124,956
Dec	.8433	.8466		.8419	**.8434**	-.0006	303
Australian Dollar (CME)-AUD 100,000; $ per AUD							
Sept	.8612	.8653		.8470	**.8506**	-.0117	109,973
Dec	.8600	.8622		.8450	**.8478**	-.0117	1,043
Mexican Peso (CME)-MXN 500,000; $ per 10MXN							
Aug	...	...		...	**.90925**	-.00600	3
Sept	.91050	.91300		.90125	**.90725**	-.00600	73,861
Euro (CME)-€125,000; $ per €							
Sept	1.3813	1.3835		1.3672	**1.3703**	-.0113	226,836
Dec	1.3853	1.3864		1.3704	**1.3733**	-.0113	2,806

Thus, the prepaid forward price for a yen is

$$F_{0,T}^P = x_0 e^{-r_y T} \tag{6.1}$$

where T is time to maturity of the forward.

The economic principle governing the pricing of a prepaid forward on currency is the same as that for a prepaid forward on stock. By deferring delivery of the underlying asset, you lose income. In the case of currency, if you received the currency immediately, you could buy a bond denominated in that currency and earn interest. The prepaid forward price reflects the loss of interest from deferring delivery, just as the prepaid forward price for stock reflects the loss of dividend income. This is why equation (6.1) is the same as that for a stock paying a continuous dividend, equation (5.4).

Example 6.1 Suppose that the yen-denominated interest rate is 2% and that the current exchange rate is 0.009 dollars per yen. Then in order to have 1 yen in 1 year, we would invest today

$$0.009\$/\text{¥} \times \text{¥}1 \times e^{-0.02} = \$0.008822$$

Currency Forward

The prepaid forward price is the *dollar* cost of obtaining 1 yen in the future. Thus, to obtain the forward price, compute the future value using the dollar-denominated interest rate, r:

$$F_{0,T} = x_0 e^{(r-r_y)T} \tag{6.2}$$

The forward currency rate will exceed the current exchange rate when the domestic risk-free rate is higher than the foreign risk-free rate.[1]

Example 6.2 Suppose that the yen-denominated interest rate is 2% and the dollar-denominated rate is 6%. The current exchange rate is 0.009 dollars per yen. The 1-year forward rate is

$$0.009 e^{0.06-0.02} = 0.009367$$

Notice that equation (6.2) is just like equation (5.7), for stock index futures, with the foreign interest rate equal to the dividend yield. The interest rate difference $r - r_y$ is the cost of carry for a foreign currency (we borrow at the domestic rate r and invest the proceeds in a foreign money market instrument, earning the foreign rate r_y as an offset to our cost). If we wish to borrow foreign currency, r_y is the lease rate.

Covered Interest Arbitrage

We can synthetically create a forward contract by borrowing in one currency and lending in the other. If we want to have 1 yen in the future, with the dollar price fixed today, we can pay today for the yen and borrow in dollars to do so. To have 1 yen at time T, we need to invest

$$x_0 e^{-r_y T}$$

in dollars, and we obtain this amount by borrowing. At time T we receive 1 yen, and the required dollar repayment is

$$x_0 e^{(r-r_y)T}$$

which is the forward exchange rate.

Example 6.3 Suppose that $x_0 = 0.009$, $r_y = 2\%$, and $r = 6\%$. The dollar cost of buying 1 yen today is $0.009 \times e^{-0.02} = 0.008822$. We defer the dollar payment by borrowing at 6%, for a cost 1 year from today of $0.008822 e^{0.06} = 0.009367$. This transaction is summarized in Table 6.1.

---

[1] Of course if you think about it, every currency transaction can be expressed in terms of either currency, for example, as yen/dollar or dollar/yen. If the forward price exceeds the current exchange rate viewed from the perspective of one currency, it must be less from the perspective of the other.

TABLE 6.1 Synthetically creating a yen forward contract by borrowing in dollars and lending in yen. The payoff at time 1 is ¥1 − $0.009367.

	Cash Flows			
	Year 0		Year 1	
Transaction	$	¥	$	¥
Borrow $x_0 e^{-r_y}$ dollar at 6% ($)	+0.008822	—	−0.009367	—
Convert to yen @ 0.009 $/¥	−0.008822	+0.9802	—	—
Invest in yen-denominated bill (¥)	—	−0.9802	—	1
Total	0	0	−0.009367	1

The example shows that borrowing in one currency and lending in another creates the same cash flow as a forward contract. If we offset this borrowing and lending position with an actual forward contract, the resulting transaction is called **covered interest arbitrage**.

If you undertake this transaction without hedging the exchange rate risk, you are engaged in "uncovered" interest arbitrage. This is sometimes also referred to as a carry trade, discussed in Box 6.1.

To summarize, a forward exchange rate reflects the difference in interest rates denominated in different currencies. Imagine that you want to invest $1 for 1 year. You can do so by buying a dollar-denominated bond, or you can exchange the dollar into another currency and buy a bond denominated in that other currency. You can then use currency forwards to guarantee the exchange rate at which you will convert the foreign currency back into dollars. The principle behind the pricing of currency forwards is that a position in foreign risk-free bonds, with the currency risk hedged, pays the same return as domestic risk-free bonds.

6.2 EURODOLLAR FUTURES

Businesses and individuals face uncertainty about future interest rates. A manager may plan to borrow money 3 months from today but doesn't know today what the interest rate will be at that time. There are forward and futures contracts that permit hedging interest rate risk by allowing the manager to lock in now a borrowing rate for 3 months in the future.

The principles underlying interest rate contracts are exactly those we have been discussing, but interest rates seem more complicated because there are so many of them, depending upon whether you invest for 1 day, 1 month, 1 year, or 30 years. There are

Box 6.1: Carry Trades

Suppose that the yen interest rate is 2% and the dollar interest rate is 6%. On the surface, it might seem to you that it would be profitable to borrow at 2% in yen and lend at 6% in dollars. This strategy of borrowing at a low rate and lending at a high rate is often undertaken in practice and is called a **carry trade**.

If you borrow yen and invest in dollars, you face the risk that the dollars will become less valuable (the dollar will depreciate), or to say the same thing differently, that the yen will appreciate (the dollar price of a yen will increase). Thus, while a carry trade may superficially sound like a money machine, the trade has risk.

To illustrate the risk in a currency carry trade, we will use the assumptions in Example 6.3. Suppose that the yen/dollar exchange rate today is 0.009 and that the rate in 1 year can be 0.0091, 0.009367, or 0.0096. If we plan to invest ¥100,000, the trade entails borrowing $900/0.009 = ¥100,000$ at 2% and lending $900 at 6%. Your dollar profit at the three exchange rates is

- $x_1 = 0.0091$—The yen depreciates relative to the forward price, so the trade is profitable:

$$\text{Profit} = \$900 \times e^{0.06} - ¥100{,}000 \times e^{0.02}$$
$$\times 0.0091 = \$27.2697$$

- $x_1 = 0.009367$—The yen equals the forward price, so the trade breaks even:

$$\text{Profit} = \$900 \times e^{0.06} - ¥100{,}000 \times e^{0.02}$$
$$\times 0.009367 = 0$$

- $x_1 = 0.0096$—The yen appreciates relative to the forward price, so the trade loses money:

$$\text{Profit} = \$900 \times e^{0.06} - ¥100{,}000 \times e^{0.02}$$
$$\times 0.0096 = -\$23.7404$$

This example illustrates what we already knew from studying covered interest arbitrage: The carry trade breaks even when the future exchange rate equals the forward rate. (Covered interest arbitrage adds currency futures to the carry trade, insuring that we can buy yen at the forward price.) The behavior of the exchange rate determines the profitability of the investment.

There are different kinds of carry trades (e.g., borrowing short term and lending long term in the same currency), but all entail some kind of price risk.

---

also implied forward interest rates between any two points in the future.[2] Because of this complexity, Chapter 7 is devoted to interest rates. However, the Eurodollar contract is so important that we discuss it briefly here. The Eurodollar strip (the set of futures prices with different maturities at one point in time) provides basic interest rate information that

---

[2] In addition, there are different rates faced by different classes of borrowers: government, private, and municipal. And of course there are different currencies of denomination.

FIGURE 6.2

Listing for interest rate futures contracts, including the 1-month LIBOR and 3-month Eurodollar contracts, from the *Wall Street Journal*, August 10, 2007.

	Open	High	Contract hi lo	Low	Settle	Chg	Open interest
Interest Rate Futures							
Treasury Bonds (CBT)-$100,000; pts 32nds of 100%							
Sept	108-23	109-27		108-21	**109-04**	6	987,799
Dec	108-26	109-22		108-24	**109-00**	5	9,921
Treasury Notes (CBT)-$100,000; pts 32nds of 100%							
Sept	106-220	107-230		106-215	**107-120**	16.5	2,894,486
Dec	106-120	107-155		106-120	**107-060**	16.5	168,465
5 Yr. Treasury Notes (CBT)-$100,000; pts 32nds of 100%							
Sept	104-280	105-215		104-270	**105-150**	15.0	1,605,940
Dec	105-065	105-170		105-065	**105-150**	15.0	70,015
2 Yr. Treasury Notes (CBT)-$200,000; pts 32nds of 100%							
Sept	102-062	102-192		102-060	**102-170**	9.0	1,013,990
Dec	102-120	102-120		102-110	**102-217**	9.2	11,353
30 Day Federal Funds (CBT)-$5,000,000; 100 - daily avg.							
Aug	94.755	94.835		94.750	**94.795**	.040	131,182
Sept	94.770	94.900		94.770	**94.875**	.100	133,382
1 Month Libor (CME)-$3,000,000; pts of 100%							
Aug	94.6100	94.6100	▼94.5000		**94.5000**	-.1300	38,818
Sept	94.6750	94.7900	▼94.6350		**94.7700**	.0900	28,077
Eurodollar (CME)-$1,000,000; pts of 100%							
Aug	94.6000	94.6175	▼94.5400		**94.6000**	-.0100	44,280
Sept	94.6650	94.7800		94.6400	**94.7600**	.0900	1,804,005
Dec	94.8550	95.0700		94.8300	**95.0400**	.1650	1,594,404
March'08	95.0250	95.2450		95.0000	**95.2250**	.1850	1,837,279

is commonly used to price other futures contracts and to price swaps. Figure 6.2 shows a newspaper listing for the Eurodollar futures contract and the companion 1-month LIBOR contract along with other interest rate futures.

The Eurodollar contract, described in Figure 6.3, is based on a $1 million 3-month deposit earning LIBOR (the London Interbank Offer Rate), which is the average borrowing rate faced by large international banks in London. The 1-month LIBOR contract is similar. Suppose that current LIBOR is 1.5% over 3 months. By convention, this is annualized by multiplying by 4, so the quoted LIBOR rate is 6%. Assuming a bank borrows $1 million for 3 months, a change in annualized LIBOR of 0.01% (one basis point) would raise its borrowing cost by $0.0001/4 \times \$1$ million $= \$25$.

The Eurodollar futures price at expiration of the contract is

$$100 - \text{Annualized 3-month LIBOR}$$

Thus, if LIBOR is 6% at maturity of the Eurodollar futures contract, the final futures price will be $100 - 6 = 94$. It is important to understand that the Eurodollar contract settles based on current LIBOR, which is the interest rate quoted for the *next* 3 months. Thus, for example, the price of the contract that expires in June reflects the 3-month interest rate between June and September. With the futures contract, as with a $1 million LIBOR deposit, a change of 0.01% in the rate is worth $25.

FIGURE 6.3	Where traded	Chicago Mercantile Exchange
Specifications for the Eurodollar futures contract.	Size	3-month Eurodollar time deposit, $1 million principal
	Months	Mar, Jun, Sep, Dec, out 10 years, plus 2 serial months and spot month
	Trading ends	5 A.M. (11 A.M. London) on the second London bank business day immediately preceding the third Wednesday of the contract month.
	Delivery	Cash settlement
	Settlement	100 − British Banker's Association Futures Interest Settlement Rate for 3-Month Eurodollar Interbank Time Deposits. (This is a 3-month rate annualized by multiplying by 360/90.)

Like most money market interest rates, LIBOR is quoted assuming a 360-day year. Thus, the annualized 91-day rate, r_{91}, can be extracted from the futures price, F, by computing the 90-day rate and multiplying by 91/90. The quarterly effective rate is then computed by dividing the result by 4:

$$r_{91} = (100 - F) \times \frac{1}{100} \times \frac{1}{4} \times \frac{91}{90} \qquad (6.3)$$

Three-month Eurodollar contracts have maturities out to 10 years, which means that it is possible to use the contract to lock in a 3-month rate as far as 10 years in the future. The September 2007 futures price in Figure 6.2 is 94.76. A position in this contract can be used to lock in an annualized rate of 5.24% from September 2007 to December 2007.

The Eurodollar contract can be used to hedge interest rate risk. For a borrower, for example, a short position in the contract is a hedge since it pays when the interest rate rises and requires payment when the interest rate falls. To see this, suppose that 7 months from today we plan to borrow $1 million for 90 days, and that our borrowing rate is the same as LIBOR. The Eurodollar futures price for 7 months from today is 94; this implies a 90-day rate of $(100 - 94) \times 90/360 \times 1/100 = 1.5\%$. Now suppose that 7 months hence, 3-month LIBOR is 8%, which implies a Eurodollar futures price of 92. The implied 90-day rate is 2%. Our extra borrowing expense over 90 days on $1 million will therefore be $(0.02 - 0.015) \times \$1$ million $= \$5{,}000$.

This extra borrowing expense is offset by gains on the short Eurodollar contract. The Eurodollar futures price has gone down, giving us a gain of $25 per basis point, or $\$25 \times 100 \times (94 - 92) = \$5{,}000$. The short position in the futures contract compensates us for the increase in our borrowing cost.[3] In the same way, a long position can be used to lock in a lending rate.

The Eurodollar futures price is a construct ($100 - r_{\text{LIBOR}}$), not the price of an asset ($100/(1 + r_{\text{LIBOR}})$). In this sense Eurodollar futures are different from the futures contracts we have already discussed. Although Eurodollar LIBOR is closely related to a number of other interest rates, there is no one specific identifiable asset that underlies the Eurodollar futures contract.

LIBOR is quoted in currencies other than dollars, and comparable rates are quoted in different locations. In addition to LIBOR, there are PIBOR (Paris), TIBOR (Tokyo), SIBOR (Singapore), and Euribor (the European Banking Federation).

Finally, you might be wondering why we are discussing LIBOR rather than rates on Treasury bills. Business and bank borrowing rates move more in tandem with LIBOR than with the government's borrowing rate. Thus, these borrowers use the Eurodollar futures contract to hedge. LIBOR is also a better measure of the cost of funds for a market-maker, so LIBOR is typically used to price forward contracts.

6.3 AN INTRODUCTION TO COMMODITY FUTURES

There are many futures contracts (and other derivatives) based on commodity prices. In this section we discuss at a general level some of the issues that make commodity futures different from financial futures.

Commodities differ from financial assets in several important ways. Commodities can be costly or impossible to store, and demand and supply can be seasonal. Moreover, different commodities have different characteristics, giving rise to pricing differences. Our goal is to understand some of the considerations that arise in pricing commodities. To do this, we will use the example of a farmer who grows corn. While oversimplified, this example will illustrate similarities and differences between commodity futures and financial futures. We will also see that commodity futures prices are generally a biased predictor of the future spot price, and define the lease rate of a commodity.

Seasonality and Storage Costs

Corn in the United States is harvested primarily in the fall, from September through November. The United States is a leading corn producer, generally exporting rather than importing corn. (For simplicity, in this discussion we will ignore imports.)

The seasonality in production is important, because corn is produced at one time of the year but consumed throughout the year. In order to be consumed when it is not being produced, corn must be stored, which is costly.

---

[3] It might occur to you that the Eurodollar contract pays us at the time we borrow, but we do not pay interest until the loan matures, 91 days hence. Since we have time to earn interest on the change in the value of the contract, the hedge ratio should be less than 1 contract per $1 million borrowing. We discuss this complication in Chapter 7.

6.3 An Introduction to Commodity Futures

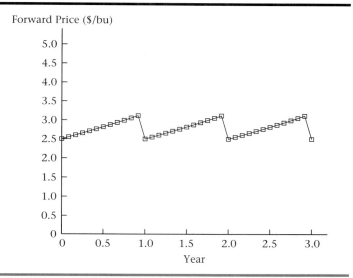

FIGURE 6.4

A hypothetical forward curve for corn, assuming the harvest occurs at years 0, 1, 2, etc.

Storage is an economic decision in which there is a choice between selling today and selling in the future. Suppose, for example, that corn today sells for $2/bu, that each month of storage costs $0.05/bu, and that the interest rate is 1%/month. The farmer storing for 1 month thus incurs $0.02 in interest and $0.05 in storage cost. If the forward price for delivery in 1 month is $2.07 or greater, storage makes sense. Otherwise, the farmer should sell today.

The important point is that since corn is consumed throughout the year but harvested at only one time, for most of the year corn must be stored. The only way that corn can be stored and consumed over the year is if farmers are *indifferent* between selling today and in the future. This can only happen if the forward price rises at the rate of interest plus the cost of storage. In other words, while corn is being stored,

$$F_{0,T} = S_0 e^{rT} + FV_{0,T}(\text{Storage costs}) \tag{6.4}$$

Once the harvest begins, storage is no longer necessary.[4] Thus, the forward price can fall across the harvest due to the expected new supply. Storage cost and interest do not affect the forward price across the harvest, because there is no storage. Instead, the forward price depends on expectations about future demand and supply. The market conditions we have described are graphed in Figure 6.4, which depicts a hypothetical forward curve as seen from time 0. Between harvests, the forward price of corn rises to reward storage, and it falls at each harvest.

---

[4] However, if there has been an exceptionally large harvest, corn may be stored across the harvest.

It should be apparent at this point that there is no simple mechanical formula to price commodity futures. Sometimes there is storage, sometimes there is not, and the equilibrium futures price will differ depending upon which situation we are in. Some commodities cannot be stored for any appreciable time (fresh raspberries and electricity, for example), whereas metals such as gold can be stored indefinitely at low cost.

The Forward Price and the Expected Commodity Price

There is one consistent interpretation of any forward price: The forward price is the expected future spot price, discounted at the risk premium on the underlying asset. If you enter into a prepaid forward contract on any asset or commodity, you pay today $F_{0,T}^P$ in order to receive the asset or commodity at time T. Let $E_0(S_T)$ denote the expected time-T price as of time 0, and let α denote the appropriate discount rate for a time-T cash flow of S_T. Then the present value is

$$E_0(S_T)e^{-\alpha T} \tag{6.5}$$

The forward price is then the future value of the prepaid forward price, or

$$F_{0,T} = e^{rT}\left[E_0(S_T)e^{-\alpha T}\right] \tag{6.6}$$
$$= E_0(S_T)e^{(r-\alpha)T}$$

Equation (6.6) demonstrates the link between the expected commodity price, $E_0(S_T)$, and the forward price. As with financial forwards (see Chapter 5), the forward price is a biased estimate of the expected spot price, $E_0(S_T)$, with the bias due to the risk premium on the commodity, $\alpha - r$.[5]

The Commodity Lease Rate

Chapter 5 introduced a different formula than equation (6.6) for the forward price on a financial asset:

$$F_{0,T} = S_0 e^{(r-\delta)T} \tag{6.7}$$

where S_0 is the spot price of the asset, r is the continuously compounded interest rate, and δ is the continuous dividend yield on the asset.

---

[5] Historical commodity and futures data, necessary to estimate expected commodity returns, are relatively hard to obtain. Bodie and Rosansky (1980) examine quarterly futures returns from 1950 to 1976, while Gorton and Rouwenhorst (2004) examine monthly futures returns from 1959 to 2004. Both studies construct portfolios of synthetic commodities—T-bills plus commodity futures—and find that these portfolios earn the same average return as stocks, are on average negatively correlated with stocks, and are positively correlated with inflation. These findings imply that a portfolio of stocks and synthetic commodities would have the same expected return and less risk than a diversified stock portfolio alone.

6.3 An Introduction to Commodity Futures

In order for equations (6.6) and (6.7) to give the same answer, it must be that the price today, S_0, is the present value of the asset received in the future:

$$S_0 = E_0(S_T)e^{-(\alpha-\delta)T}$$

This relation will hold for a stock or other financial asset (as we discussed in Section 5.2, the price today is the present value of the future price), but it does *not* hold—at least not without some definitional contortions—for a commodity.

What "definitional contortions" allow equation (6.7) to hold for a commodity? We can observe the spot price of a commodity, the forward price, and the interest rate. Only δ is unobservable (in fact, the average investor does not earn a dividend from holding a commodity.) Suppose we *define* δ^* as the value for which equation (6.7) holds. That is, if we set

$$\delta^* = r - \frac{1}{T}\ln(F_{0,T}/S_0) \qquad (6.8)$$

then equation (6.7) will hold with $\delta = \delta^*$. We call δ^* the **convenience yield** or the **lease rate**. Whichever term you use, δ^* is the value that makes equation (6.7) hold with equality. Ownership of a commodity can be valuable; in this case there is "convenience." However, the convenience yield is defined even when there is no storage—for example, when considering corn futures across a harvest. Thus, it can be misleading (although it is common) to always refer to δ^* as a convenience yield.

If you were to short-sell a commodity, you would have to pay the lease rate to the commodity lender. Consider the following example using gold:

Example 6.4 Suppose the current price of gold is $400/oz., the continuously compounded interest rate is 5%, and the forward price for delivery in 2 years is $430. Using equation (6.8), the lease rate is

$$\delta^* = 0.05 - \frac{1}{2}\ln(430/400) = 0.01384$$

If you were to borrow physical gold, in addition to returning the gold, you would pay the gold lender 1.384% (quoted as a continuously compounded rate) of the value of the borrowed gold.

To see that the payment of 1.384% is necessary, suppose we do a reverse cash-and-carry with gold:

1. Borrow $e^{-0.1384 \times 2} = 0.9727$ ounces and promise to return one ounce in 2 years.
2. Sell this gold for $400 \times 0.9727 = \$389.08$. Invest these proceeds for 2 years at 5%.
3. Enter into a long forward contract to buy gold for $430 in 2 years.

We have zero cash flow initially. The result in 2 years is

$$\underbrace{P_2 - \$430}_{\text{Long forward}} - \underbrace{P_2}_{\text{Buy gold}} + \underbrace{389.08 e^{0.05 \times 2}}_{\text{Risk-free investment}} = 0$$

where P_2 is the price of gold.

Two commonly used terms are related to the lease rate. If forward prices at a point in time increase with maturity (longer-dated forward prices are greater than shorter-dated forward prices), then the forward curve for that commodity or asset is said to be in **contango**. In this case the lease rate is less than the interest rate. If forward prices decrease with time to maturity, the forward curve is said to be in **backwardation**. In this case the lease rate exceeds the interest rate.

6.4 ENERGY FUTURES

In this section we consider energy futures, a particular kind of commodity futures. We examine electricity, which cannot be stored; natural gas, for which storage is possible but quite costly; and oil, which can be stored and which is traded in a global market. These different characteristics give rise to different forward price characteristics.

Electricity

Electricity is produced in different ways: from fuels such as coal and natural gas, or from nuclear power, hydroelectric power, wind power, or solar power. Once it is produced, electricity is transmitted over the power grid to end users. Electricity has characteristics that distinguish it not only from financial assets but from other commodities as well. What is special about electricity?

First, electricity is difficult to store. Generally, it must be consumed when it is produced or else it is wasted.[6] Second, at any point in time the maximum supply of electricity is fixed. It is possible to produce less but not more. Third, demand for electricity varies substantially by season, by day of week, and by time of day.

To illustrate the effects of nonstorability, Table 6.2 displays 1-day-ahead hourly prices for 1 megawatt-hour of electricity in New York City. The 1-day-ahead forward price is $27.40 at 3 A.M. and $83.24 at 3 P.M. Since you have learned about arbitrage, you are possibly thinking that you would like to buy electricity at the 3 A.M. price and sell it at the 3 P.M. price. However, there is no way to do so. Because electricity cannot be stored, its price is set by demand and supply at a point in time. In North America electricity is generally less expensive in the winter than in the summer, but nonstorability means

---

[6] Sometimes it is possible to store electricity. For example, *pumped storage hydroelectricity* entails using inexpensive electricity to pump water uphill and then, at a later time when electricity is expensive, releasing it to generate hydroelectricity. Such storage is relatively uncommon, however, and entails losses.

TABLE 6.2 Day-ahead price, by hour, for 1 megawatt-hour of electricity in New York City, October 1, 2007.

Time	Price	Time	Price	Time	Price	Time	Price
0000	$40.72	0600	$55.73	1200	$76.75	1800	$78.69
0100	36.68	0700	57.71	1300	79.94	1900	79.30
0200	28.19	0800	66.81	1400	79.46	2000	75.92
0300	27.40	0900	72.59	1500	83.24	2100	65.86
0400	28.21	1000	74.63	1600	83.99	2200	53.36
0500	37.45	1100	74.90	1700	80.72	2300	45.11

Source: Bloomberg.

that there is also no way to arbitrage this difference. so there are seasonal variations as well as intraday variations. Power producers do use peak-load plants that operate only when prices are high, so power suppliers are able to temporarily increase the supply of electricity. However, expectations about supply are already reflected in the forward price.

There are also location-specific forward markets for electricity. The price is highly dependent on the location because electricity is costly to transport.

Since electricity is nonstorable, the prices in Table 6.2 are best interpreted using equation (6.6). The large price swings over the day primarily reflect changes in the expected spot price, which in turn reflects changes in demand over the day.

Notice two things. First, the swings in Table 6.2 could not occur with financial assets, which are stored. (It is so obvious that financial assets are stored that we usually don't mention it.) The 3 A.M. and 3 P.M. forward prices for a stock will be almost identical. If they were not, it would be possible to engage in arbitrage, buying low at 3 A.M. and selling high at 3 P.M. Second, the forward price for a stock provides information about the current stock price, the interest rate, and the dividend yield. By contrast, the forward prices in Table 6.2 provide information we could not otherwise obtain, revealing information about the future price of the commodity. The forward market in this case provides **price discovery,** with forward prices revealing information, not otherwise obtainable, about the future price of the commodity.

Natural Gas

The natural gas futures contract, introduced in 1990, is one of the most heavily traded futures contracts in the United States. The asset underlying one contract is 1 month's worth of gas, delivered at a specific location (different gas contracts call for delivery at different locations). Figure 6.5 shows a newspaper listing for energy futures, including natural gas futures, and Figure 6.6 details the specifications for the Henry Hub contract.

FIGURE 6.5

Listing for the NYMEX crude oil, heating oil, gasoline, and natural gas futures contracts from the *Wall Street Journal*, August 10, 2007.

Metal & Petroleum Futures

	Open	High hi lo	Low	Settle	Chg	Open interest
Crude Oil, Light Sweet (NYM)-1,000 bbls.; $ per bbl.						
Sept	72.27	72.40	70.50	**71.59**	−0.56	256,749
Oct	71.94	72.17	70.37	**71.40**	−0.54	201,964
Nov	71.71	71.90	70.19	**71.20**	−0.49	87,280
Dec	71.41	71.55	69.97	**70.90**	−0.46	190,412
Jan'08	71.34	71.34	69.85	**70.69**	−0.42	65,751
Dec	70.23	70.23	69.10	**69.72**	−0.35	161,808
Heating Oil No. 2 (NYM)-42,000 gal.; $ per gal.						
Sept	1.9685	1.9926	1.9428	**1.9892**	.0224	62,657
Oct	1.9935	2.0138	1.9640	**2.0102**	.0204	38,966
Gasoline-NY RBOB (NYM)-42,000 gal.; $ per gal.						
Sept	1.9365	1.9474	1.8957	**1.9340**	−.0037	71,422
Oct	1.8870	1.8899	1.8460	**1.8818**	−.0054	40,932
Natural Gas (NYM)-10,000 MMBtu.; $ per MMBtu.						
Sept	6.265	6.650	6.244	**6.586**	.366	103,181
Oct	6.500	6.837	6.465	**6.801**	.349	89,953
Nov	7.387	7.675	7.383	**7.656**	.277	47,347
Dec	8.204	8.430	8.204	**8.424**	.218	49,485
Jan'08	8.650	8.802	8.575	**8.794**	.210	41,303
March	8.480	8.611	8.409	**8.594**	.171	48,484

FIGURE 6.6

Specifications for the NYMEX Henry Hub natural gas contract.

Underlying	Natural gas delivered at Sabine Pipe Lines Co.'s Henry Hub, Louisiana
Where traded	New York Mercantile Exchange
Size	10,000 million British thermal units (MMBtu)
Months	72 consecutive months
Trading ends	Third-to-last business day of month prior to maturity month
Delivery	As uniformly as possible over the delivery month

The seasonal behavior of prices in Figure 6.5 is typical for natural gas in the United States and reflects particular seasonal usage patterns and storage costs.

Natural gas has several interesting characteristics. First, gas is costly to transport internationally, so prices and forward curves vary regionally. Second, it is possible to store gas, but costly to do so. Third, demand for gas in the United States is highly seasonal, with peak demand arising from heating in winter months. Thus, there is a relatively steady stream of production with variable demand, which leads to large and predictable price swings.

The prices in Figure 6.5 tell us something about the economics of natural gas. First, examine the price increase from October to November. You could buy gas in October for $6.370, store it for 1 month, and sell it for $7.168. Assuming an interest rate of 1/2% per month, the profit from doing this is

$$\text{Profit} = F_{\text{November}} - F_{\text{October}} - \text{Interest} - \text{Storage cost} \qquad (6.9)$$
$$= \$7.168 - \$6.370 - 0.005 \times 6.370 - \text{Storage cost}$$
$$= \$0.766 - \text{Storage cost}$$

The forward prices in Figure 6.5 present an arbitrage opportunity unless the marginal cost of storage is about $0.76/month per MMBtu. Since natural gas is an important and active market, it is reasonable to take $0.76 as the expected marginal cost of storage for October 2007.

Storage costs vary with the amount of storage. At the relatively inexpensive end of the storage spectrum, it is possible to pump gas into underground reservoirs. At the high end, it is possible to liquify gas, freezing it for storage. Figure 6.5 illustrates varying expected storage costs, as the implied storage cost remains high from November to December and then declines from December to January. As colder weather is anticipated, the expected amount of storage declines.

Finally, note that the price drops from January to March. This reflects the decline in expected gas usage and hence the decline in storage as winter wanes. Speculators sometimes use natural gas futures to make bets about the weather. One such failed bet, by Amaranth Advisors, is discussed in Box 6.2.

Because of the expense in transporting gas internationally, the seasonal behavior of the forward curve can vary in different parts of the world. In tropical areas where gas is used for cooking and electricity generation, the forward curve is relatively flat because demand is relatively flat. In the Southern Hemisphere, where seasons are reversed from the Northern Hemisphere, the forward curve will peak in June and July rather than December and January.

Recent developments in energy markets have altered the behavior of the natural gas forward curve in the United States. Power producers have made greater use of gas-fired peak-load electricity plants. These plants have increased summer demand for natural gas and may permanently affect seasonal patterns.

Crude Oil

Both oil and natural gas produce energy and are extracted from wells, but the different physical characteristics and uses of oil lead to very different forward prices than for gas. Unlike with gas, seasonalities in the price of crude oil are relatively unimportant. One reason is that oil is easier to store and to transport than gas. Thus, the effect of demand variation over time can be smoothed by storage, and the effect of differing demand in different parts of the world can be smoothed by transportation. Also, oil is refined to create heating oil (for which there is high demand when it is cold) and gasoline (for which there is high demand when it is warm), among other products. It is possible to

Box 6.2: Amaranth Advisors

Natural gas futures contracts made front page news in September 2006 when Amaranth Advisors, a hedge fund, revealed that it had lost $6 billion in 1 week as a result of losses from trading natural gas futures. Among other bets, according to the *New York Times* ("Betting on the Weather and Taking an Ice-Cold Bath," Sept 29, 2006, by Jenny Anderson), natural gas trader Brian Hunter bet that the spread between March and April gas futures would widen, presumably due to high winter demand for gas. Instead the spread narrowed, as the winter was mild and hurricanes that could have disrupted natural gas supplies never materialized.

A Senate subcommittee headed by Carl Levin (D-Mich) and Norm Coleman (R-Mich) concluded that the Amaranth positions were large enough to have affected market prices, and that Amaranth had evaded position limits on NYMEX by trading on the Intercontinental Exchange (ICE), on which there were no position limits (natural gas trading on ICE was not regulated by the CFTC).

Despite the headlines and congressional concern, the Amaranth loss was borne by investors in the hedge fund, the position was liquidated, and the after-effects were minimal.

FIGURE 6.7

Specifications for the NYMEX light sweet crude oil contract.

Underlying	Specific domestic crudes delivered at Cushing, Oklahoma
Where traded	New York Mercantile Exchange
Size	1000 U.S. barrels (42,000 gallons)
Months	30 consecutive months plus long-dated futures out 7 years
Trading ends	Third-to-last business day preceding the 25th calendar day of month prior to maturity month
Delivery	As uniformly as possible over the delivery month

alter the relative amounts of heating oil and gasoline produced to respond to changes in demand. Specifications for the NYMEX light oil contract are shown in Figure 6.7.

Figure 6.5 includes a newspaper listing for oil futures. This shows an expected decline in oil prices from $71.59/barrel in September 2007 to $69.72 in December 2008. The price reflects expectations about future demand and supply. Historically, there have also been many times when the forward curve was upward sloping (when oil was plentiful relative to demand).

Crude oil is refined to make petroleum products, in particular heating oil and gasoline. The refining process entails distillation, which separates crude oil into different components, including gasoline, kerosene, and heating oil. The split of oil into these different components can be complemented by a process known as "cracking"; hence, the difference in price between crude oil and equivalent amounts of heating oil and gasoline is called the **crack spread.**

Oil can be processed in different ways, producing different mixes of outputs. The spread terminology identifies the number of gallons of oil as input and the number of gallons of gasoline and heating oil as outputs. Traders will speak of "5-3-2," "3-2-1," and "2-1-1" crack spreads. The 5-3-2 spread, for example, reflects the profit from taking 5 gallons of oil as input and producing 3 gallons of gasoline and 2 gallons of heating oil. A petroleum refiner producing gasoline and heating oil could use a futures crack spread to lock in both the cost of oil and output prices. This strategy would entail going long oil futures and short the appropriate quantities of gasoline and heating oil futures. Of course there are other inputs to production and it is possible to produce other outputs, such as jet fuel, so the crack spread is not a perfect hedge.

Example 6.5 Suppose we consider buying oil in September and selling gasoline and heating oil in October. On August 10, 2007, the September futures price for oil was \$71.59/barrel, or \$1.7045/gallon (there are 42 gallons per barrel). The October futures prices for unleaded gasoline and heating oil were \$1.8818/gallon and \$2.0102/gallon, respectively. The 3-2-1 crack spread tells us the gross margin we can lock in by buying 3 gallons of oil and producing 2 gallons of gasoline and 1 of heating oil. Using these prices, the spread is

$$(2 \times \$1.8818) + \$2.0102 - (3 \times \$1.7045) = \$0.6602$$

or $\$0.6602/3 = \$0.2201$/gallon. In this calculation we made no interest adjustment for the different expiration months of the futures contract.

The 5-3-2 spread would have a gross margin of

$$(3 \times \$1.8818) + (2 \times \$2.0102) - (5 \times \$1.7045) = \$1.1432$$

or \$0.2286/gallon. Since gasoline usage peaks in the summer and heating oil use in the winter, we would expect spreads producing more heating oil to be more profitable in the fall and winter.

There are crack spread options trading on NYMEX. Two of these options pay based on the difference between the price of heating oil and crude oil, and the price of gasoline and heating oil, both in a 1:1 ratio.

6.5 WEATHER AND HOUSING FUTURES

Exchanges and dealers continue to offer new products. In this section we talk about two recently developed exchange-traded contracts, weather futures and real estate futures, both traded at the Chicago Mercantile Exchange (CME). The contracts illustrate the possibilities and the challenges of developing new financial products. When you read about a new contract, you should ask yourself how such a contract would work mechanically (how the underlying index could be computed, for example) and who might be interested in such a contract.

Weather Derivatives

Weather pervasively affects many businesses. As examples, think of soft drink sales, tourism, recreational activities, agricultural production, and sales of lawn sprinklers. In recent years, it has become possible for businesses to hedge weather risk. In some cases, derivatives dealers offer contracts to hedge specific risks. For example, one investment bank sold a contract hedging a U.K. lawn sprinkler manufacturer against wet weather. Similar deals have been done to hedge ski resorts against warm weather and soft drink manufacturers against cool summers.

The payoffs for weather derivatives are based on weather-related measurements. An example of a weather contract is the degree-day index futures contract traded at the CME. These contracts make payments if it is unusually warm or cool in specific cities. To understand the potential appeal of such contracts, consider that temperature can affect both the prices of energy products and the amount of energy consumed. If a winter is colder than average, homeowners and businesses will consume extra electricity, heating oil, and natural gas, and the prices of these products will tend to be high as well. Conversely, during a warm winter, energy prices and quantities will be low. While it is possible to use futures markets to hedge prices of commodities, there is also the problem that consumers use different quantities of energy at different temperatures. Hedging the price of a known quantity is straightforward with contracts such as natural gas futures. Hedging the quantity is more difficult.

The contracts are based on temperature differences from 65°F, which is a moderate temperature. At higher temperatures, air conditioners may be used, while at lower temperatures, heating may be used. A **heating degree-day** is the maximum of zero and the difference between 65°F and the average daily temperature. A **cooling degree-day** is the maximum of zero and the difference between the average daily temperature and 65°F. A monthly heating degree-day index is constructed by adding the daily heating degree-days over the month. (Cooling degree-days are computed analogously.) The futures contract then settles based on the cumulative heating or cooling degree-days (the two are separate contracts) over the course of a month. The size of the contract is $100 times the degree-day index. As of September 2004, degree-day index contracts were available for over 20 cities in the United States, Europe, and Japan. There are also puts and calls on these futures.

Table 6.3 displays heating degree-day futures price quotes for seven months for three cities. Consider the quote of 594.00 for Atlanta in December. If the average of max(65 − daily temp, 0) during December were 19, an investor in the futures contract would break even ($31 \times 19.16 = 594$). In Minneapolis, an investor would break even if the average were 41.4. In all three cities, the period December through February is expected to be the coldest, and the futures price rises with latitude.

TABLE 6.3			Heating degree-day futures prices, October 1, 2007. *Source:* Chicago Mercantile Exchange	

Month	Atlanta	Chicago	Minneapolis
Oct 2007	83.00	330.00	433.00
Nov 2007	304.00	677.00	862.00
Dec 2007	594.00	1112.00	1284.00
Jan 2008	592.00	1205.00	1444.00
Feb 2008	490.00	1038.00	1227.00
Mar 2008	315.00	843.00	983.00
Apr 2008	135.00	463.00	483.00

With city-specific degree-day index contracts, it is possible to create and hedge payoffs based on average temperatures, or using options, based on ranges of average temperatures. If Minneapolis is unusually cold but the rest of the country is normal, the cooling degree-day contract for Minneapolis will make a large payment that will compensate the holder for the increased consumption of energy. Notice that in this scenario a natural gas price contract (for example) would not provide a sufficient hedge, since unusual cold in Minneapolis alone might not have much effect on national energy prices.

Housing Futures

Residential real estate futures, introduced by the CME in May 2006, are futures contracts that settle based on city-specific indexes of real estate prices. These contracts settle quarterly and are based on indexes constructed by S&P/Case-Shiller for 20 metropolitan areas in the United States.

Before you read further, you might want to stop and think about how you would construct a housing price index. One common purpose of such an index is to measure the change in value of an "average" house. But what does average mean in this context? Houses vary tremendously in size, amenities, quality, and the desirability of their location. They are frequently improved with modifications and additions, but sometimes allowed to deteriorate. The only way to measure the value of houses is by observing transaction prices, but it is extremely difficult to infer the price of one or more houses from the price of one that is sold. Even on a conceptual level, the construction of an index is tricky.

The S&P/Case-Shiller home price index is an attempt to deal with these thorny issues. The index is computed based on repeat sales: Whenever there is a sale, the history of sales is scanned to find an earlier sale of the same house. If there are special circumstances such as substantial modifications to the house, non-arms-length transactions

FIGURE 6.8

Specifications for the CME housing futures index contract.

Underlying	The S&P/Case-Shiller Metro Area Home Price Indices
Where traded	Chicago Mercantile Exchange
Size	$250 times the S&P/Case-Shiller index (one index point is worth $250)
Months	February, May, August, November, out five years
Trading ends	Business day preceding the final Tuesday of the second month following each quarter end.
Settlement	Cash-settled

TABLE 6.4 Real estate futures prices for several cities, October 1, 2007.
Source: Chicago Mercantile Exchange

Expiration	Chicago	New York	Los Angeles	Boston	Miami
November 2007	164.20	203.00	256.20	169.20	251.80
May 2008	161.60	196.00	245.20	162.40	238.40
November 2008	159.40	190.80	237.20	160.00	228.00
November 2009	154.40	180.00	228.40	151.00	214.20
November 2010	152.00	180.20	225.60	146.00	202.60
November 2011	155.20	182.00	221.80	148.00	187.80
Open Interest	8	120	94	134	112

(such as a sale to a family member), or a repeat sale within 6 months, the transaction is excluded. You might object that homes selling frequently could be different than homes that sell infrequently. The point of the index, however, is to track the *change* in housing prices. As long as the prices of frequently traded and infrequently traded homes change together, the index will measure changes in housing prices. The monthly index is computed based on the previous 3 months of data and released 2 months after the end of the third month. Thus, the contract expiring in November settles based on the index covering July to September.

Table 6.4 reports housing futures prices for five major U.S. cities. Note that in every case, futures prices are declining with maturity, consistent with the widely held view (in 2007) that housing prices were likely to decline. Note also, however, that open interest is very small. Trading volume is often zero. Thus, prices may not be reliable.

Who would use a housing price futures contract? It is critical to recognize that everyone requires shelter, and thus everyone is exposed to changes in the pricing of housing. (Renters are exposed to housing prices since rents will increase if real estate becomes more expensive.) This suggests that renters who expect to own (such as young workers) would like to hedge the risk of prices going up by entering into a long position. Owners who expect to become renters (such as workers nearing retirement) would like to hedge against housing price declines, and thus would like to enter a short position. Homeowners who are midcareer have no need to transact and thus need not hedge.[7]

This analysis suggests that the young should go long the contracts and the elderly should go short. For a variety of reasons, however, this is problematic. Both groups would need to be educated about the contract. The young are unlikely to have the resources to post margin. Moreover, there is substantial basis risk: Young workers and retirees might move unexpectedly to a different city, and in any event the housing price index tracks average changes in a large metropolitan area. There is no way to hedge the risk of highly local price changes (such as a neighborhood becoming more or less desirable). Commercial developers might want to short the contract to hedge the value of a new development, but the buyers who would be their natural counterparties are unlikely to participate. One could imagine insurance companies or banks offering insurance policies for houses in specific neighborhoods. These insurance sellers could then hedge their real estate exposure in a region by using housing index futures. Such contracts may yet arise.

To summarize, economic theory suggests that a real estate contract is potentially valuable to many consumers, but this is not necessarily enough to make an exchange-traded real estate futures contract viable. Commercial real estate futures were under development in 2007 and may have different prospects, since potential participants are large and sophisticated.

CHAPTER SUMMARY

Currency forward contracts are priced using the same formula as index forwards, equation (5.7), except that the dividend yield forgone by holding the forward contract instead of the underlying asset, δ, is the interest rate you could earn by investing in foreign-currency-denominated assets. Thus, for currencies, $\delta = r_f$, where r_f is the foreign interest rate.

---

[7] You might object that such owners are nonetheless subject to the risk of housing price fluctuations—they might wish to use housing wealth to retire—and would like to hedge housing prices. This is true, but it is important to realize that housing price risk is nondiversifiable, and therefore it is not possible for everyone to hedge it. Housing price risk, like stock market risk, must be borne in the aggregate by investors. This discussion is really about who should hedge on a *relative* basis. Those most exposed are those who own no housing or who will soon own no housing. Also important, of course, is an investor's willingess to bear risk.

The Eurodollar futures contract, based on LIBOR (London Interbank Offer Rate), is widely used for hedging interest rate risk. Because the Eurodollar futures contract does not represent the price of an asset (at settlement it is 100 − LIBOR), it cannot be priced using the formulas in this chapter.

At a general level, commodity forward prices can be described by the same formula as financial forward prices:

$$F_{0,T} = S_0 e^{(r-\delta)T} \tag{6.10}$$

For financial assets, δ is the dividend yield. For commodities, δ is the commodity *lease rate*—the return that makes an investor willing to buy and then lend a commodity. Thus, for the commodity owner who lends the commodity, it is like a dividend. From the commodity borrower's perspective, it is the cost of borrowing the commodity. As with financial forwards, commodity forward prices are biased predictors of the future spot price when the commodity return contains a risk premium.

While the dividend yield for a financial asset can typically be observed directly, the lease rate for a commodity can typically be estimated only by observing the forward price. The forward curve provides important information about the commodity.

Commodities are complex because every commodity market differs in the details. Forward curves for different commodities reflect different properties of storability, storage costs, production, and demand. Corn, electricity, natural gas, and oil all have distinct forward curves, reflecting the different characteristics of their physical markets. When there are seasonalities in either the demand or supply of a commodity, the commodity will be stored (assuming this is physically feasible), and the forward curve for the commodity will reflect storage costs. Some holders of a commodity receive benefits from physical ownership. This benefit is called the commodity's *convenience yield*.

New contracts are always being introduced. Recent contracts include weather derivatives (based on average daily temperatures) and housing price futures.

FURTHER READING

A useful resource for learning more about commodities is the Chicago Board of Trade (1998). The Web sites of the various exchanges (e.g., NYMEX and the CBOT) are also useful resources, with information about particular commodities and trading and hedging strategies.

Siegel and Siegel (1990) provide a detailed discussion of many commodity futures. There are numerous papers on commodities. Bodie and Rosansky (1980) and Gorton and Rouwenhorst (2004) examine the risk and return of commodities as an investment. Brennan (1991), Pindyck (1993b), and Pindyck (1994) examine the behavior of commodity prices. Schwartz (1997) compares the performance of different models of commodity price behavior. Jarrow and Oldfield (1981) discuss the effect of storage costs on pricing, and Routledge et al. (2000) present a theoretical model of commodity forward curves.

A detailed description of the S&P/Case-Shiller methodology can be found on the S&P Web site.

PROBLEMS

6.1 Suppose the current exchange rate between Germany and Japan is 0.02 €/¥. The euro-denominated annual continuously compounded risk-free rate is 4% and the yen-denominated annual continuously compounded risk-free rate is 1%. What are the 6-month euro/yen and yen/euro forward prices?

6.2 Suppose the spot $/¥ exchange rate is 0.008, the 1-year continuously compounded dollar-denominated rate is 5%, and the 1-year continuously compounded yen-denominated rate is 1%. Suppose the 1-year forward exchange rate is 0.0084. Explain precisely the transactions you could use (being careful about currency of denomination) to make money with zero initial investment and no risk. How much do you make per yen? Repeat for a forward exchange rate of 0.0083.

6.3 The euro exchange rate is $1.25/euro. The continuously compounded dollar interest rate is 5% and the continuously compounded euro interest rate is 4%. Suppose that you borrow euros and lend dollars for 1 year, without using futures to hedge.

a. At what exchange rate will you break even on this position?

b. If the exchange rate in 1 year is $1.30, what is your profit?

c. If the exchange rate in 1 year is $1.22, what is your profit?

6.4 Suppose we wish to borrow $10 million for 91 days beginning next June, and that the quoted Eurodollar futures price is 93.23.

a. What 3-month LIBOR rate is implied by this futures price?

b. What position in Eurodollar contracts will guarantee a borrowing rate?

c. How much will be needed to repay the loan?

6.5 Suppose we plan to lend $10 million for 91 days beginning in March. The March Eurodollar futures price is 94.65.

a. What 3-month LIBOR rate is implied by this futures price?

b. What Eurodollar futures position can we use to hedge the lending interest rate?

c. How much will we have after having invested for 91 days?

6.6 Suppose we plan to borrow $10 million for 182 days beginning in June. The June Eurodollar futures price is 94.45 and the September Eurodollar futures price is 94.80. The loan will be repaid with a single payment.

a. What futures position can we use to hedge our borrowing rate? (*Hint:* By September, we will have borrowed more than $10 million.)

b. If we repay the loan with a single payment after 182 days, how much will we repay?

6.7 The corn spot price in December is $3/bu. The cost of storing corn is $0.04/bu per month and the effective monthly interest rate is 1%. Assuming that corn is stored, what will be the forward price for delivery in January, February, and March?

6.8 Repeat Example 6.4, only assuming that you undertake a cash-and-carry, rather than a reverse cash-and-carry. Verify that the gold owner breaks even only by lending the gold and earning the lease rate.

6.9 Suppose the gold spot price is $300/oz., the 1-year forward price is 310.686, and the continuously compounded risk-free rate is 5%.

  a. What is the lease rate?

  b. What is the return on a cash-and-carry in which gold is not loaned? (You borrow to buy gold and sell the gold forward.)

  c. What is the return on a cash-and-carry in which gold is loaned, earning the lease rate? (You borrow to buy gold, sell the gold forward, and lend the gold, earning the lease rate.)

6.10 The spot price of a widget is $70.00 per unit. Forward prices for 3, 6, 9, and 12 months are $70.70, $71.41, $72.13, and $72.86, respectively. Assuming a 5% continuously compounded annual risk-free rate, what are the annualized lease rates for each maturity? Is this an example of contango or backwardation?

6.11 Natural gas futures prices are $6.85 (Oct), $7.50 (Nov), $8.15 (Dec), $8.20 (Jan), $8.25 (Feb), $8.20 (Mar), and $7.45 (Apr). The effective monthly interest rate is 1%.

  a. During which months is storage expected to occur?

  b. What is your estimate of the expected monthly storage cost during those months?

6.12 Suppose it is October and the price of gas is $6.50/MMBtu. The November forward price is $7.25. If you borrow 1 MMBtu of gas today and promise to return it in 1 month, what additional cash flows must occur for the short-sale to be fairly priced? The effective monthly interest rate is 1%.

6.13 Answer the previous question only supposing it is March and the price of gas is $8/MMBtu. The April forward price is $7.25.

6.14 The current price of oil is $32.00 per barrel. Forward prices for 3, 6, 9, and 12 months are $31.37, $30.75, $30.14, and $29.54, respectively. Assuming a 2% continuously compounded annual risk-free rate, what is the annualized lease rate for each maturity? Is this an example of contango or backwardation?

6.15 The average daily temperatures over one week are 60, 55, 68, 72, 60, 50, 45. What is the average temperature? What are the heating degree-days for this week? What are the cooling degree-days?

6.16 A natural gas company offers a contract where residential customers pay a monthly amount fixed in advance of the heating season, which does not vary with temperature. That is, customers pay the same whether it is warm (in which case they use little gas) or cold.

    a. Explain the risks if the gas company were to use natural gas futures alone to hedge this contract.

    b. How could the gas company use heating degree-day futures to help hedge?

Interest Rate Forwards and Futures

Suppose you have the opportunity to spend $1 one year from today to receive $2 two years from today. What is the value of this opportunity? To answer this question, you need to know the appropriate interest rates for discounting the two cash flows. This comparison is an example of the most basic concept in finance: using interest rates to compute present values. Once we find a present value for one or more assets, we can compare the values of cash flows from those assets even if the cash inflows and cash outflows occur at different times. In order to perform these calculations, we need information about the set of interest rates prevailing between different points in time.

We begin the chapter by reviewing basic bond concepts—coupon bonds, yields to maturity, and implied forward rates. Any reader of this book should understand these basic concepts. We then look at interest rate forwards and forward rate agreements, which permit hedging interest rate risk. Finally, we look at bond futures and the repo market.

7.1 BOND BASICS

Table 7.1 presents information about current interest rates for bonds maturing in from 1 to 3 years. *Identical information is presented in five different ways in the table.* Although the information appears differently across columns, it is possible to take the information in any one column of Table 7.1 and reproduce the other four columns.[1]

Table 7.2 reproduces bond price and yield information from the online *Wall Street Journal*. This listing reports yields for only a few of the many government bonds that exist. The table reports a coupon rate for bonds and notes and a yield to maturity for each bond. A wide range of maturities exists at any point in time, but the U.S. government

---

[1] Depending upon how you do the computation, you may arrive at numbers slightly different from those in Table 7.1. The reason is that all of the entries except those in column 1 are rounded in the last digit, and there are multiple ways to compute the number in any given column. Rounding error will therefore generate small differences among computations performed in different ways.

TABLE 7.1

Five ways to present equivalent information about default-free interest rates. All rates but those in the last column are effective annual rates.

Years to Maturity	(1) Zero-Coupon Bond Yield	(2) Zero-Coupon Bond Price	(3) One-Year Implied Forward Rate	(4) Par Coupon	(5) Continuously Compounded Zero Yield
1	6.00%	0.943396	6.00000%	6.00000%	5.82689%
2	6.50	0.881659	7.00236 $_1F_1$	6.48423	6.29748
3	7.00	0.816298	8.00705 $_2F_1$	6.95485	6.76586

TABLE 7.2

Yields and prices on bills, notes, and bonds issued by the U.S. government, October 12, 2007. Bid and asked yields are reported for bills. Prices for notes, bonds, and strips are ask prices. Note and bond prices are quoted in 32nds (e.g., 100:14 is 100 and 14/32, or 100.4375.) Source: *Wall Street Journal* Online.

	Bills		Notes and Bonds			STRIPS	
Maturity Date	Asked	Bid	Price	Coupon	Yield	Price	Yield
Oct 18, 2007	3.54	3.59					
Oct 25, 2007	3.71	3.76					
Nov 01, 2007	3.88	3.88					
Nov 08, 2007	3.96	3.96					
⋮							
Nov 15, 2008			100:14	4.750	4.28	95.523	4.27
Nov 15, 2009			98:18	3.500	4.22	91.598	4.26
Nov 15, 2010			100:20	4.500	4.27	87.885	4.23
⋮							
May 15, 2017			130:23	8.875	4.72	63.141	4.86
May 15, 2018			135:24	9.125	4.78	59.803	4.92
⋮							
Feb 15, 2036			93:30	4.500	4.88	25.265	4.91
Feb 15, 2037			97:16	4.750	4.91	24.133	4.91

issues Treasury securities only at specific maturities—typically 3 months, 6 months, and 1, 2, 5, 10, and 30 years.[2] Government securities that are issued with less than 1 year to maturity and that make only a single payment, at maturity, are called Treasury *bills*. *Notes* and *bonds* pay coupons and are issued at a price close to their maturity value (i.e., they are issued at par). Notes have 10 or fewer years to maturity and bonds have more than 10 years to maturity. The distinctions between bills, notes, and bonds are not important for our purposes; we will refer to all three as bonds. The government also issues Treasury inflation-protected securities (TIPS). These are bonds for which payments are adjusted for inflation. The most recently issued government bonds are called **on-the-run;** other bonds are called **off-the-run.** These terms are used frequently in talking about government bonds since on-the-run bonds generally have lower yields and greater trading volume than off-the-run bonds. Appendix 7.A discusses some of the conventions used in bond price and yield quotations.

In addition to government bond information, there are also prices for STRIPS. A **STRIPS**—Separate Trading of Registered Interest and Principal of Securities—is a claim to a single interest payment or the principal portion of a government bond. These claims trade separately from the bond. STRIPS are zero-coupon bonds, since they make only a single payment at maturity. "STRIPS" should not be confused with the forward strip, which is the set of forward prices available at a point in time.

We need a way to represent bond prices and interest rates. Interest rate notation is, unfortunately and inevitably, cumbersome, because for any rate we must keep track of three dates: the date on which the rate is quoted, and the period of time (this has beginning and ending dates) over which the rate prevails. We will let $r_t(t_1, t_2)$ represent the interest rate from time t_1 to time t_2, prevailing on date t. If the interest rate is current—i.e., if $t = t_1$—and if there is no risk of confusion, we will drop the subscript.

Zero-Coupon Bonds

We begin by showing that the zero-coupon bond yield and zero-coupon bond price, columns (1) and (2) in Table 7.1, provide the same information. A **zero-coupon bond** is a bond that makes only a single payment at its maturity date. Our notation for zero-coupon bond prices will mimic that for interest rates. The price of a bond quoted at time t_0, with the bond to be purchased at t_1 and maturing at t_2, is $P_{t_0}(t_1, t_2)$. As with interest rates, we will drop the subscript when $t_0 = t_1$.

The 1-year zero-coupon bond price of $P(0, 1) = 0.943396$ means that you would pay $0.943396 today to receive $1 in 1 year. You could also pay $P(0, 2) = 0.881659$ today to receive $1 in 2 years, and $P(0, 3) = 0.816298$ to receive $1 in 3 years.

The **yield to maturity** (or *internal rate of return*) on a zero-coupon bond is simply the percentage increase in dollars earned from the bond. For the 1-year bond, we end

---

[2] Treasury securities are issued using an auction. In the past, the government also issued bonds with maturities of 3 and 7 years. Between 2002 and 2005, the government issued no 30-year bonds.

up with $1/0.943396 - 1 = 0.06$ more dollars per \$1 invested. If we are quoting interest rates as effective annual rates, this is a 6% yield.

For the zero-coupon 2-year bond, we end up with $1/0.881659 - 1 = 0.134225$ more dollars per \$1 invested. We could call this a 2-year effective interest rate of 13.4225%, but it is conventional to quote rates on an annual basis. If we want this yield to be comparable to the 6% yield on the 1-year bond, we could assume annual compounding and get $(1 + r(0, 2))^2 = 1.134225$, which implies that $r(0, 2) = 0.065$. In general,

$$P(0, n) = \frac{1}{[1 + r(0, n)]^n} \tag{7.1}$$

Note from equation (7.1) that *a zero-coupon bond price is a discount factor*: A zero-coupon bond price is what you would pay today to receive \$1 in the future. If you have a future cash flow at time t, C_t, you can multiply it by the price of a zero-coupon bond, $P(0, t)$, to obtain the present value of the cash flow. Because of equation (7.1), multiplying by $P(0, t)$ is the same as discounting at the rate $r(0, t)$, i.e.,

$$C_t \times P(0, t) = \frac{C_t}{[1 + r(0, t)]^t}$$

The inverse of the zero-coupon bond price, $1/P(0, t)$, provides a future-value factor.

In contrast to zero-coupon bond prices, interest rates such as those in Figure 7.1 are subject to quoting conventions that can make their interpretation difficult (if you doubt this, see Appendix 7.A). Because of their simple interpretation, we can consider zero-coupon bond prices as the building block for all of fixed income.

A graph of annualized zero-coupon yields to maturity against time to maturity is called the zero-coupon **yield curve**. A yield curve shows us how yields to maturity vary with time to maturity. In practice, it is common to present the yield curve based on coupon bonds, not zero-coupon bonds.

Implied Forward Rates

We now see how column (3) in Table 7.1 can be computed from either column (1) or (2). The 1-year and 2-year zero-coupon yields are the rates you can earn from year 0 to year 1 and from year 0 to year 2. There is also an *implicit* rate that can be earned from year 1 to year 2 that must be consistent with the other two rates. This rate is called the **implied forward rate.**

Suppose we could today guarantee a rate we could earn from year 1 to year 2. We know that \$1 invested for 1 year earns $[1 + r_0(0, 1)]$ and \$1 invested for 2 years earns $[1 + r_0(0, 2)]^2$. Thus, the time 0 forward rate from year 1 to year 2, $r_0(1, 2)$, should satisfy

$$[1 + r_0(0, 1)][1 + r_0(1, 2)] = [1 + r_0(0, 2)]^2$$

or

FIGURE 7.1

An investor investing for 2 years has a choice of buying a 2-year zero-coupon bond paying $[1 + r_0(0, 2)]^2$ or buying a 1-year bond paying $1 + r_0(0, 1)$ for 1 year, and reinvesting the proceeds at the implied forward rate, $r_0(1, 2)$ between years 1 and 2. The implied forward rate makes the investor indifferent between these alternatives.

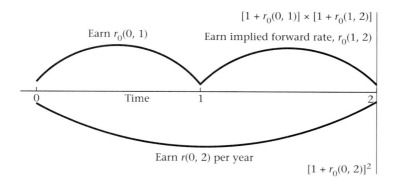

$$1 + r_0(1, 2) = \frac{[1 + r_0(0, 2)]^2}{1 + r_0(0, 1)} \qquad (7.2)$$

Figure 7.1 shows graphically how the implied forward rate is related to 1- and 2-year yields. If $r_0(1, 2)$ did not satisfy equation (7.2), then there would be an arbitrage opportunity. Problem 7.15 asks you to work through the arbitrage. In general, we have

$$\boxed{[1 + r_0(t_1, t_2)]^{t_2 - t_1} = \frac{[1 + r_0(0, t_2)]^{t_2}}{[1 + r_0(0, t_1)]^{t_1}} = \frac{P(0, t_1)}{P(0, t_2)}} \qquad (7.3)$$

Corresponding to 1-year and 2-year interest rates, $r_0(0, 1)$ and $r_0(0, 2)$, we have prices of 1-year and 2-year zero-coupon bonds, $P_0(0, 1)$ and $P_0(0, 2)$. Just as the interest rates imply a forward 1-year interest rate, the bond prices imply a 1-year forward zero-coupon bond price. The implied forward zero-coupon bond price must be consistent with the implied forward interest rate. Rewriting equation (7.3), we have

$$P_0(t_1, t_2) = \frac{1}{[1 + r_0(t_1, t_2)]^{t_2 - t_1}} = \frac{[1 + r_0(0, t_1)]^{t_1}}{[1 + r_0(0, t_2)]^{t_2}} = \frac{P(0, t_2)}{P(0, t_1)} \qquad (7.4)$$

The implied forward zero-coupon bond price from t_1 to t_2 is simply the ratio of the zero-coupon bond prices maturing at t_2 and t_1.

Example 7.1 Using information in Table 7.1, we want to compute the implied forward interest rate from year 2 to year 3 and the implied forward price for a 1-year zero-coupon bond purchased in year 2.

The implied forward interest rate, $r_0(2, 3)$, can be computed as

$$1 + r_0(2, 3) = \frac{[1 + r_0(0, 3)]^3}{[1 + r_0(0, 2)]^2} = \frac{(1 + 0.07)^3}{(1 + 0.065)^2} = 1.0800705$$

or equivalently as

$$1 + r_0(2, 3) = \frac{P_0(0, 2)}{P_0(0, 3)} = \frac{0.881659}{0.816298} = 1.0800705$$

The implied forward 1-year zero-coupon bond price is

$$\frac{P_0(0, 3)}{P_0(0, 2)} = \frac{1}{1 + r_0(2, 3)} = 0.925865$$

Coupon Bonds

Given the prices of zero-coupon bonds—column (1) in Table 7.1—we can price coupon bonds. We can also compute the **par coupon**—column (4) in Table 7.1—the coupon rate at which a bond will be priced at par. To describe a coupon bond, we need to know the date at which the bond is being priced, the start and end date of the bond payments, the number and amount of the payments, and the amount of principal. Some practical complexities associated with coupon bonds, not essential for our purposes, are discussed in Appendix 7.A.

We will let $B_t(t_1, t_2, c, n)$ denote the time t price of a bond that is issued at t_1, matures at t_2, pays a coupon of c per dollar of maturity payment, and makes n evenly spaced payments over the life of the bond, beginning at time $t_1 + (t_2 - t_1)/n$. We will assume the maturity payment is $1. If the maturity payment is different than $1, we can just multiply all payments by that amount.

Since the price of a bond is the present value of its payments, at issuance time t the price of a bond maturing at T must satisfy

$$B_t(t, T, c, n) = \sum_{i=1}^{n} c P_t(t, t_i) + P_t(t, T) \tag{7.5}$$

where $t_i = t + i(T - t)/n$, with i being the index in the summation. Using equation (7.5), we can solve for the coupon as

$$c = \frac{B_t(t, T, c, n) - P_t(t, T)}{\sum_{i=1}^{n} P_t(t, t_i)}$$

A par bond has $B_t = 1$, so the coupon on a par bond is given by

7.1 Bond Basics

$$c = \frac{1 - P_t(t, T)}{\sum_{i=1}^{n} P_t(t, t_i)} \qquad (7.6)$$

Example 7.2 Using the information in Table 7.1, the coupon on a 3-year coupon bond that sells at par is

$$c = \frac{1 - 0.816298}{0.943396 + 0.881659 + 0.816298}$$
$$= 6.95485\%$$

Equation (7.5) computes the bond price by discounting each bond payment at the rate appropriate for a cash flow with that particular maturity. For example, in equation (7.5) the coupon occurring at time t_i is discounted using the zero-coupon bond price $P_t(t, t_i)$. An alternative way to write the bond price is using the yield to maturity to discount all payments. Suppose the bond makes m payments per year. Denoting the per-period yield to maturity as y_m, we have

$$B_t(t, T, c, n) = \sum_{i=1}^{n} \frac{c}{(1 + y_m)^i} + \frac{1}{(1 + y_m)^n} \qquad (7.7)$$

It is common to compute the quoted annualized yield to maturity, y, as $y = m \times y_m$. Government bonds, for example, make two coupon payments per year, so the annualized yield to maturity is twice the semiannual yield to maturity.

The difference between equation (7.5) and equation (7.7) is that in equation (7.5), each coupon payment is discounted at the appropriate rate for a cash flow occurring at that time. In equation (7.7), one rate is used to discount all cash flows. By definition, the two expressions give the same price. However, equation (7.7) can be misleading, since the yield to maturity, y_m, is generally not the return an investor earns by buying and holding a bond (we will explain why shortly). Moreover, equation (7.7) provides no insight into how the cash flows from a bond can be replicated with zero-coupon bonds.

Zeros from Coupons

We have started with zero-coupon bond prices and deduced the prices of coupon bonds. In practice, the situation is often the reverse: We observe prices of coupon bonds and must infer prices of zero-coupon bonds. This procedure in which zero-coupon bond prices are deduced from a set of coupon bond prices is called **bootstrapping.**

Suppose we observe the par coupons in Table 7.1. We can then infer the first zero-coupon bond price from the first coupon bond as follows:

$$1 = (1 + 0.06) P(0, 1)$$

This implies that $P(0, 1) = 1/1.06 = 0.943396$. Using the second par coupon bond with a coupon rate of 6.48423% gives us

$$1 = 0.0648423 P(0, 1) + 1.0648423 P(0, 2)$$

Since we know $P(0, 1) = 0.943396$, we can solve for $P(0, 2)$:

$$P(0, 2) = \frac{1 - 0.0648423 \times 0.943396}{1.0648423}$$
$$= 0.881659$$

Finally, knowing $P(0, 1)$ and $P(0, 2)$, we can solve for $P(0, 3)$ using the 3-year par coupon bond with a coupon of 6.95485%:

$$1 = (0.0695485 \times P(0, 1)) + (0.0695485 \times P(0, 2)) + (1.0695485 \times P(0, 3))$$

which gives us

$$P(0, 3) = \frac{1 - (0.0695485 \times 0.943396) - (0.0695485 \times 0.881659)}{1.0695485}$$
$$= 0.816298$$

There is nothing about the procedure that requires the bonds to trade at par. In fact, we do not even need the bonds to all have different maturities. For example, if we had a 1-year bond and two different 3-year bonds, we could still solve for the three zero-coupon bond prices by solving simultaneous equations.

Interpreting the Coupon Rate

A coupon rate—for example, the 6.95485% coupon on the 3-year bond—determines the cash flows the bondholder receives. However, except in special cases, it does not correspond to the rate of return that an investor actually earns by holding the bond.

Suppose for a moment that interest rates are certain; i.e., the implied forward rates in Table 7.1 are the rates that will actually occur in years 1 and 2. Imagine that we buy the 3-year bond and hold it to maturity, reinvesting all coupons as they are paid. What rate of return do we earn? Before going through the calculations, let's stop and discuss the intuition. We are going to invest an amount at time 0 and reinvest all coupons by buying more bonds. We will not withdraw any cash until time 3. *In effect, we are constructing a 3-year zero-coupon bond.* Thus, we should earn the same return as on a 3-year zero: 7%. This buy-and-hold return is different than the yield to maturity of 6.95485%. The coupon payment is set to make a par bond fairly priced, but it is not actually the return we earn on the bond except in the special case when the interest rate is constant over time.

Consider first what would happen if interest rates were certain, we bought the 3-year bond with a $100 principal and a coupon of 6.95485%, and we held it for 1 year. The price at the end of the year would be

$$B_1 = \frac{6.95485}{1.0700237} + \frac{106.95485}{(1.0700237)(1 + 0.0800705)}$$
$$= 99.04515$$

The 1-period return is thus

$$\text{1-period return} = \frac{6.95485 + 99.04515}{100} - 1$$
$$= 0.06$$

We earn 6%, since that is the 1-year interest rate. Problem 7.13 asks you to compute your 2-year return on this investment.

By year 3, we have received three coupons, two of which have been reinvested at the implied forward rate. The total value of reinvested bond holdings at year 3 is

$$6.95485 \times [(1.0700237)(1.0800705) + (1.0800705) + 1] + 100 = 122.5043$$

The 3-year yield on the bond is thus

$$\left(\frac{122.5043}{100}\right)^{1/3} - 1 = 0.07$$

As we expected, this is equal to the 7% yield on the 3-year zero and different from the coupon rate.

This discussion assumed that interest rates are certain and that coupon payments could be reinvested at the implied forward rate. Suppose that we buy and hold the bond, reinvesting the coupons, and that interest rates are not certain. Can we still expect to earn a return of 7%? The answer is yes if we use interest rate forward contracts to guarantee the rate at which we can reinvest coupon proceeds. Otherwise, the answer in general is no.

The belief that the implied forward interest rate equals the expected future spot interest rate is a version of the **expectations hypothesis.** We saw in Chapters 5 and 6 that forward prices are biased predictors of future spot prices when the underlying asset has a risk premium; the same is true for forward interest rates. When you own a coupon bond, the rate at which you will be able to reinvest coupons is uncertain. If the resulting risk carries a risk premium, then the expected return to holding the bond will not equal the 7% return calculated by assuming interest rates are certain. The expectations hypothesis will generally not hold, and you should not expect implied forward interest rates to be unbiased predictors of future interest rates.

In practice, you can guarantee the 7% return by using forward rate agreements to lock in the interest rate for each of the reinvested coupons. We discuss forward rate agreements in Section 7.2.

Continuously Compounded Yields

Any interest rate can be quoted as either an effective annual rate or a continuously compounded rate. (Or in a variety of other ways, such as a semiannually compounded rate, which is common with bonds. See Appendix 7.A.) Column (5) in Table 7.1 presents the continuously compounded equivalents of the rates in the "zero yield" column.

In general, if we have a zero-coupon bond paying $1 at maturity, we can write its price in terms of an annualized continuously compounded yield, $r^{cc}(0, T)$, as[3]

$$P(0, T) = e^{-r^{cc}(0,T)T}$$

Thus, if we observe the price, we can solve for the yield as

$$r^{cc}(0, T) = \frac{1}{T} \ln[1/P(0, T)]$$

We can compute the continuously compounded 3-year zero yield, for example, as

$$\frac{1}{3} \ln(1/0.816298) = 0.0676586$$

Alternatively, we can obtain the same answer using the 3-year zero yield of 7%:

$$\ln(1 + 0.07) = 0.0676586$$

Any of the zero yields or implied forward yields in Table 7.1 can be computed as effective annual or continuously compounded. The choice hinges on convention and ease of calculation.

7.2 FORWARD RATE AGREEMENTS, EURODOLLARS, AND HEDGING

We now consider the problem of a borrower who wishes to hedge against increases in the cost of borrowing. We consider a firm expecting to borrow $100m for 91 days, beginning 120 days from today, in June. This is the borrowing date. The loan will be repaid in September on the loan repayment date. In the examples we will suppose that the effective quarterly interest rate at that time can be either 1.5% or 2%, and that the implied June 91-day forward rate (the rate from June to September) is 1.8%. Here is the risk faced by the borrower, assuming no hedging:

	120 days	**211 days**	
		$r_{\text{quarterly}} = 1.5\%$	$r_{\text{quarterly}} = 2\%$
Borrow $100m	+100m	−101.5m	−102.0m

Depending upon the interest rate, there is a variation of $0.5m in the borrowing cost. How can we hedge this uncertainty?

---

[3] In future chapters we will denote continuously compounded interest rates simply as r, without the cc superscript.

Forward Rate Agreements

A **forward rate agreement** (FRA) is an over-the-counter contract that guarantees a borrowing or lending rate on a given notional principal amount. FRAs can be settled either at the initiation or maturity of the borrowing or lending transaction. If settled at maturity, we will say the FRA is settled in arrears. In the example above, the FRA could be settled on day 120, the point at which the borrowing rate becomes known and the borrowing takes place, or settled in arrears on day 211, when the loan is repaid.

FRAs are a forward contract based on the interest rate, and as such do not entail the actual lending of money. Rather, the borrower who enters an FRA is paid if a reference rate is above the FRA rate, and the borrower pays if the reference rate is below the FRA rate. The actual borrowing is conducted by the borrower independently of the FRA. We will suppose that the reference rate used in the FRA is the same as the actual borrowing cost of the borrower.

FRA settlement in arrears First consider what happens if the FRA is settled in September, on day 211, the loan repayment date. In that case, the payment to the borrower should be

$$\left(r_{\text{quarterly}} - r_{\text{FRA}}\right) \times \text{notional principal}$$

Thus, if the borrowing rate is 1.5%, the payment under the FRA should be

$$(0.015 - 0.018) \times \$100\text{m} = -\$300{,}000$$

Since the rate is lower than the FRA rate, the borrower pays the FRA counterparty.

Similarly, if the borrowing rate turns out to be 2.0%, the payment under the FRA should be

$$(0.02 - 0.018) \times \$100\text{m} = \$200{,}000$$

Settling the FRA in arrears is simple and seems like the obvious way for the contract to work. However, settlement can also occur at the time of borrowing.

FRA settlement at the time of borrowing If the FRA is settled in June, at the time the money is borrowed, payments will be less than when settled in arrears because the borrower has time to earn interest on the FRA settlement. In practice, therefore, the FRA settlement is tailed by the reference rate prevailing on the settlement (borrowing) date. (Tailing in this context means that we reduce the payment to reflect the interest earned between June and September.) Thus, the payment for a borrower is

$$\text{Notional principal} \times \frac{\left(r_{\text{quarterly}} - r_{\text{FRA}}\right)}{1 + r_{\text{quarterly}}} \qquad (7.8)$$

If $r_{\text{quarterly}} = 1.5\%$, the payment in June is

$$\frac{-\$300{,}000}{1 + 0.015} = -\$295{,}566.50$$

By definition, the future value of this is $-\$300{,}000$. In order to make this payment, the borrower can borrow an extra \$295,566.50, which results in an extra \$300,000 loan payment in September. If on the other hand $r_{\text{quarterly}} = 2.0\%$, the payment is

$$\frac{\$200{,}000}{1 + 0.02} = \$196{,}078.43$$

The borrower can invest this amount, which gives \$200,000 in September, an amount that offsets the extra borrowing cost.

If the forward rate agreement covers a borrowing period other than 91 days, we simply use the appropriate rate instead of the 91-day rate in the above calculations.

Synthetic FRAs

Suppose that today is day 0 and we plan to lend money 120 days hence. By using a forward rate agreement, we can guarantee the lending rate we will receive on day 120. In particular, we will be able to invest \$1 on day 120 and be guaranteed a 91-day return of 1.8%.

We can synthetically create the same effect as with an FRA by trading zero-coupon bonds. In order to accomplish this, we need to guarantee cash flows of \$0 on day 0, $-\$1$ on day 120, and $+\$1.018$ on day 211.[4]

First, let's get a general sense of the transaction. To match the FRA cash flows, we want cash going out on day 120 and coming in on day 211. To accomplish this, on day 0 we will need to borrow with a 120-day maturity (to generate a cash outflow on day 120) and lend with a 211-day maturity (to generate a cash inflow on day 211). Moreover, we want the day 0 value of the borrowing and lending to be equal so that there is no initial cash flow. This description tells us what we need to do.

In general, suppose that today is day 0, and that at time t we want to lend \$1 for the period s, earning the implied forward rate $r_0(t, t + s)$ over the interval from t to $t + s$. To simplify the notation in this section, $r_0(t, t + s)$ will denote the *nonannualized* percent return from time t to time s. Recall first that

$$1 + r_0(t, t + s) = \frac{P(0, t)}{P(0, t + s)}$$

---

[4] The example in the previous section considered locking in a borrowing rate, but in this section we lock in a lending rate; the transactions can be reversed for borrowing.

7.2 Forward Rate Agreements, Eurodollars, and Hedging

The strategy we use is to:

1. Buy $1 + r_0(t, t+s)$ zero-coupon bonds maturing at time $t+s$.
2. Short-sell 1 zero-coupon bond maturing at time t.

The resulting cash flows are illustrated in Table 7.3, which shows that transactions made on day 0 synthetically create a loan commencing on day t and paying the implied forward rate, $r_0(t, t+s)$, on day $t+s$.

This example can be modified slightly to synthetically create the cash flows from a forward rate agreement that settles on the borrowing date, day t. To make this modification, we sell at time t the bond maturing at time $t+s$. The result is presented in Table 7.4. Note that if we reinvested the FRA proceeds at the market rate prevailing on day t, $r_t(t, t+s)$, we would receive $r_0(t, t+s) - r_t(t, t+s)$ on day $t+s$.

Example 7.3 Consider the example above and suppose that $P(0, 211) = 0.95836$ and $P(0, 120) = 0.97561$, which implies a 120-day interest rate of 2.5%. In order to receive $1.018 on day 211, we buy 1.018 211-day zero-coupon bonds. The cost of this is

$$1.018 \times P(0, 211) = \$0.97561$$

In order to have zero cash flow initially and a cash outflow on day 120, we borrow 0.97561, with a 120-day maturity. This entails borrowing one 120-day bond, since

$$\frac{0.97561}{P(0, 120)} = 1$$

The result on day 120 is that we pay $1 to close the short position on the 120-day bond, and on day 211 we receive $1.018 since we bought that many 211-day bonds.

TABLE 7.3 Investment strategy undertaken at time 0, resulting in net cash flows of $-\$1$ on day t, and receiving the implied forward rate, $1 + r(t, t+s)$ at $t+s$. This synthetically creates the cash flows from entering into a forward rate agreement on day 0 to lend at day t.

	Cash Flows		
Transaction	0	t	t + s
Buy $1 + r_0(t, t+s)$ zeros maturing at $t+s$	$-P(0, t+s) \times (1 + r_0(t, t+s))$	—	$1 + r_0(t, t+s)$
Short 1 zero maturing at t	$+P(0, t)$	-1	—
Total	0	-1	$1 + r_0(t, t+s)$

TABLE 7.4 Example of synthetic FRA. The transactions in this table are exactly those in Table 7.3, except that all bonds are sold at time t.

	Cash Flows	
Transaction	0	t
Buy $1 + r_0(t, t+s)$ zeros maturing at $t+s$	$-P(0, t+s) \times \left[1 + r_0(t, t+s)\right]$	$\frac{1+r_0(t,t+s)}{1+r_t(t,t+s)}$
Short 1 zero maturing at t	$+P(0, t)$	-1
Total	0	$\frac{r_0(t,t+s) - r_t(t,t+s)}{1+r_t(t,t+s)}$

To summarize, we have shown that an FRA is just like the stock and currency forwards we have considered, both with respect to pricing and synthesizing. If at time 0 we want to lock in a borrowing rate from time t to time $t+s$, we can create a rate forward synthetically by buying the underlying asset (the bond maturing at $t+s$) and borrowing (shorting) the bond maturing at day t.

In general, we have the following conclusions concerning a rate forward covering the period t_1 to t_2:

- The forward rate we can obtain is the implied forward rate—i.e., $r_{t_0}(t_1, t_2) = P_{t_0}(t_0, t_1)/P_{t_0}(t_0, t_2) - 1$.
- We can synthetically create the payoff to an FRA, $\frac{r_{t_0}(t_1,t_2) - r_{t_1}(t_1,t_2)}{1+r_{t_1}(t_1,t_2)}$, by borrowing to buy the prepaid forward, i.e., by
  1. Buying $1 + r_{t_0}(t_1, t_2)$ of the zero-coupon bond maturing on day t_2, and
  2. Shorting 1 zero-coupon bond maturing on day t_1.

Eurodollar Futures versus FRAs

Eurodollar futures contracts, which we discussed in Chapter 6, are similar to FRAs in that they can be used to guarantee a borrowing rate. Although FRAs and Eurodollar futures seem interchangeable, there are subtle differences between the two. These differences imply that the Eurodollar rate will exceed the comparable FRA rate (though the difference will generally be small).

Suppose as before that we plan to borrow $10 million on day 120 for repayment on day 211. The interest rate we pay will be known in June, and our payment of interest and principal is due in September. If the forward rate in April for a 91-day loan made in June is 1.8%, we can obtain an FRA that will pay us in September the difference between the interest rate and 1.8%. This precisely hedges the payment we must make.

A Eurodollar contract, by contrast, will pay us *in June* the difference between the interest rate and the Eurodollar forward rate. This means that once we receive a payment on the contract (if the interest rate has increased), we have 91 days to earn interest on the payment we received. If we have to make a payment (if the interest rate has decreased), we have will have 91 days to pay interest on the payment we made. This timing difference has two implications.

1. We should short less than $10 million in Eurodollar futures. Whether we are paid or make a payment in June, in order to match the required cash flow in September we want a smaller cash flow in June. This means that we must tail the position.

2. A more subtle implication is that the Eurodollar interest rate will be greater than the FRA rate. To understand this, suppose that interest rates are high. We will receive payment in June, and we can reinvest this payment at a high rate. If interest rates are low, we will make a payment in June, and we can fund this payment at a low rate. Thus, by hedging with short Eurodollar futures, we will either invest at a high rate or borrow at a short rate. This provides a systematic benefit to hedging with Eurodollar futures rather than FRAs. Since in equilibrium, investors must be indifferent between Eurodollar futures and FRAs, the Eurodollar rate must be greater than the FRA rate. This effect is generally small, especially at short horizons, but it is real.

Interest Rate Strips and Stacks

Suppose a borrower plans to borrow $100m by rolling over 3-month debt for a period of 2 years, beginning in 6 months. Thus, the borrowing will take place in month 6, month 9, month 12, etc. The borrower in this situation faces 8 unknown quarterly borrowing rates. We saw in Section 4.5 that an oil hedger could hedge each commitment individually (a strip) or could hedge the entire commitment using one near-dated contract (a stack). The same alternatives are available with interest rates.

One way to hedge is to enter into separate $100m FRAs for each future 3-month period. Thus, we would enter into one FRA for months 6–9, another for months 9–12, etc. This strip hedge should provide a perfect hedge for future borrowing costs.

Depending on market conditions, using a strip is not always feasible. For example, forward prices may not be available with distant maturities, or liquidity may be poor at distant maturities. Rather than individually hedging the borrowing cost of each quarter, an alternative in the context of this example is to use a "stack" of short-term FRAs or Eurodollar contracts to hedge the present value of future borrowing costs.

In the above example, we will be borrowing $100 million per quarter for 8 quarters. To effect a stack, we would enter into forward agreements on the 3-month rate, maturing in 6 months, for slightly less than $800 million. (We enter into less than $800 million of forward rate agreements due to tailing for quarters 2 through 8.)

The obvious problem with a stacking strategy is basis risk: Quarterly borrowing costs in distant quarters may not move perfectly with borrowing costs in near quarters.

Once we reach the first quarter of borrowing, all of the forward agreements mature and we need to renew our hedge. We now face 7 quarters with unknown borrowing costs and therefore enter into forward agreements for slightly less than $700 million. The constant renewal of the hedging position necessary to effect a stack and roll is exactly like that in the oil example.

7.3 DURATION AND CONVEXITY

An important characteristic of a bond is the sensitivity of its price to interest rate changes, which we measure using **duration.** Duration tells us approximately how much the bond's price will change for a given change in the bond's yield. Duration is thus a summary measure of the risk of a bond, permitting a comparison of bonds with different coupons, times to maturity, and discounts or premiums relative to principal. In this section we also discuss **convexity,** which is another measure related to bond price risk.

Duration

Suppose a bond makes m coupon payments per year for T years in the amount C/m, paying M at maturity. Let y/m be the per-period yield to maturity (by convention, y is the annualized yield to maturity) and $n = m \times T$ the number of periods until maturity. The price of the bond, $B(y)$, is given by

$$B(y) = \sum_{i=1}^{n} \frac{C/m}{(1+y/m)^i} + \frac{M}{(1+y/m)^n}$$

The change in the bond price for a unit change in the yield, y, is[5]

$$\begin{aligned}\frac{\text{Change in bond price}}{\text{Unit change in yield}} &= -\sum_{i=1}^{n} \frac{i}{m}\frac{C/m}{(1+y/m)^{i+1}} - \frac{n}{m}\frac{M}{(1+y/m)^{n+1}} \\ &= -\frac{1}{1+y/m}\left[\sum_{i=1}^{n} \frac{i}{m}\frac{C/m}{(1+y/m)^i} + \frac{n}{m}\frac{M}{(1+y/m)^n}\right]\end{aligned} \quad (7.9)$$

Equation (7.9) tells us the *dollar* change in the bond price for a change of 1.0 in y. It is natural to scale this either to reflect a change per percentage point (in which case we divide equation (7.9) by 100) or per basis point (divide equation (7.9) by 10,000). Equation (7.9) divided by 10,000 is also known as the **price value of a basis point** (PVBP). To interpret PVBP for a bond, we need to know the par value of the bond.

Example 7.4 Consider the 3-year zero-coupon bond in Table 7.1 with a yield to maturity of 7%. The bond price per \$100 of maturity value is $\$100/1.07^3 = \$81.62979$. At a yield of 7.01%, 1 basis point higher, the bond price is $\$100/1.0701^3 = \$81.60691$, a change of $-\$0.02288$ per \$100 of maturity value.

---

[5] This is obtained by computing the derivative of the bond price with respect to the yield, $dB(y)/dy$.

As an alternative way to derive the price change, we can compute equation (7.9) with $C = 0$, $M = \$100$, $n = 3$, and $m = 1$ to obtain

$$-\frac{1}{1.07} \times 3 \times \frac{\$100}{1.07^3} = -\$228.87$$

In order for this to reflect a change of 1 basis point, we divide by 10,000 to obtain $-\$228.87/10{,}000 = -\$0.02289$, almost equal to the actual bond price change. This illustrates the importance of scaling equation (7.9) appropriately.

When comparing bonds with different prices and par values, it is helpful to have a measure of price sensitivity expressed *per dollar of bond price*. We obtain this by dividing equation (7.9) by the bond price, $B(y)$, and multiplying by -1. This gives us a measure known as **modified duration**, which is the *percentage* change in the bond price for a unit change in the yield:

$$\text{Modified duration} = -\frac{\text{Change in bond price}}{\text{Unit change in yield}} \times \frac{1}{B(y)}$$

$$= \boxed{\frac{1}{B(y)} \frac{1}{1+y/m} \left[\sum_{i=1}^{n} \frac{i}{m} \frac{C/m}{(1+y/m)^i} + \frac{n}{m} \frac{M}{(1+y/m)^n} \right]} \quad (7.10)$$

We obtain another measure of bond price risk—**Macaulay duration**[6]—by multiplying equation (7.10) by $1 + y/m$. This puts both bond price and yield changes in percentage terms and gives us an expression with a clear interpretation:

$$\text{Macaulay duration} = -\frac{\text{Change in bond price}}{\text{Unit change in yield}} \times \frac{1+y/m}{B(y)}$$

$$= \boxed{\frac{1}{B(y)} \left[\sum_{i=1}^{n} \frac{i}{m} \frac{C/m}{(1+y/m)^i} + \frac{n}{m} \frac{M}{(1+y/m)^n} \right]} \quad (7.11)$$

To interpret this expression, note that $(C/m)/(1 + y/m)^i$ is the present value of the ith bond payment, which occurs in i/m years. The quantity $C/m/[(1 + y/m)^i B(y)]$ is therefore the fraction of the bond value that is due to the ith payment. Macaulay duration is a *weighted average of the time (number of periods) until the bond payments occur*, with the weights being the percentage of the bond price accounted for by each payment. This interpretation of Macaulay duration as a time-to-payment measure explains why

---

[6] This measure of duration is named after Frederick Macaulay, who wrote a classic history of interest rates (Macaulay (1938)).

these measures of bond price sensitivity are called "duration."[7] For a zero-coupon bond, equation (7.11) implies that Macaulay duration equals time to maturity.

Macaulay duration illustrates why maturity alone is not a satisfactory risk measure for a coupon bond. A coupon bond makes a series of payments, each with a different maturity. Macaulay duration summarizes bond price risk as a weighted average of these different maturities.

Example 7.5 Returning to Example 7.4, using equation (7.11), Macaulay duration for the 7% bond is

$$-\frac{-\$228.87}{1} \times \frac{1.07}{\$81.62979} = 3.000$$

Example 7.6 Consider the 3-year coupon bond in Table 7.1. For a par bond, the yield to maturity is the coupon, 6.95485% in this case. For each payment we have

$$\%\text{Payment 1} = \frac{0.0695485}{1.0695485} = 0.065026$$

$$\%\text{Payment 2} = \frac{0.0695485}{(1.0695485)^2} = 0.060798$$

$$\%\text{Payment 3} = \frac{1.0695485}{(1.0695485)^3} = 0.874176$$

Thus, with $n = 3$ and $m = 1$, Macaulay duration is

$$(1 \times 0.065026) + (2 \times 0.060798) + (3 \times 0.874176) = 2.80915$$

The interpretation of the duration of 2.81 is that the bond responds to interest rate changes as if it were a pure discount bond with 2.81 years to maturity. Modified duration is $2.80915/1.0695485 = 2.626482$.

Since duration tells us the sensitivity of the bond price to a change in the interest rate, it can be used to compute the approximate bond price change for a given change in interest rates. Suppose the bond price is $B(y)$ and the yield on the bond changes from y to $y + \epsilon$, where ϵ is a small change in the yield. The formula for modified duration, D, can be written as

$$D = -\frac{[B(y+\epsilon) - B(y)]}{\epsilon} \frac{1}{B(y)}$$

Letting Macaulay duration be denoted by D_{Mac}, we have $D_{\text{Mac}} = D(1+y)$. We can therefore rewrite this equation to obtain the new bond price in terms of the old bond

---

[7] The Excel duration functions are *Duration* for Macaulay duration and *MDuration* for modified duration.

price and either duration measure:

$$B(y+\epsilon) = B(y) - [D \times B(y)\epsilon] = B(y) - [D_{\text{Mac}}/(1+y) \times B(y)\epsilon] \quad (7.12)$$

Example 7.7 Consider the 3-year zero-coupon bond with a price of $81.63 per $100 maturity value. The yield is 7% and the bond's Macaulay duration is 3.0. If the yield were to increase to 7.25%, the predicted price would be

$$B(7.25\%) = \$81.63 - (3/1.07) \times \$81.63 \times 0.0025 = \$81.058$$

The actual new bond price is $\$100/(1.0725)^3 = \$81.060$. The prediction error is about 0.02% of the bond price.

Although duration is an important concept and is frequently used in practice, it has a conceptual problem. We emphasized in the previous section that a coupon bond is a collection of zero-coupon bonds, and therefore each cash flow has its own discount rate. Yet both duration formulas are computed assuming that all cash flows are discounted by a single artificial number, the yield to maturity.

Duration Matching

Suppose we own a bond with time to maturity t_1, price B_1, and Macaulay duration D_1. We are considering a short position in a bond with maturity t_2, price B_2, and Macaulay duration D_2. We can ask the following question: How much of the second bond should we short-sell in order that the resulting portfolio—long the bond with duration D_1 and short the bond with duration D_2—is insensitive to interest rate changes?

Equation (7.12) gives us a formula for the change in price of each bond. Let N denote the quantity of the second bond. The value of the portfolio is

$$B_1 + NB_2$$

and, using equation (7.12), the change in price due to an interest rate change of ϵ is

$$[B_1(y_1+\epsilon) - B_1(y_1)] + N[B_2(y_2+\epsilon) - B_2(y_2)]$$
$$= -D_1 B_1(y_1)\epsilon/(1+y_1) - ND_2 B_2(y_2)\epsilon/(1+y_2)$$

where D_1 and D_2 are Macaulay durations. If we want the net change to be zero, we choose N to set the right-hand side equal to zero. This gives

$$\boxed{N = -\frac{D_1 B_1(y_1)/(1+y_1)}{D_2 B_2(y_2)/(1+y_2)}} \quad (7.13)$$

When a portfolio is duration-matched in this fashion, the net investment in the portfolio will typically not be zero. That is, either the value of the short bond is less than the value of the long bond, in which case additional financing is required, or vice versa, in which case there is cash to invest. This residual can be financed or invested in very short-term bonds, with duration approximately zero, in order to leave the portfolio duration-matched.

Example 7.8 Suppose we own a 7-year, 6% coupon bond with a yield of 7%, and want to find the duration-matched short position in a 10-year, 8% coupon bond yielding 7.5%. Assuming annual coupon payments, the Macaulay duration and price of the two bonds is 5.882 years and $94.611, and 7.297 years and $103.432, respectively. Thus, if we own one of the 7-year bonds, we must hold

$$-\frac{5.882 \times 94.611/(1.07)}{7.297 \times 103.432/(1.075)} = -0.7408$$

units of the 10-year bond. The short position in the 10-year bond is not enough to pay for the 7-year bond; hence, investment in the portfolio is $1 \times 94.611 - 0.7408 \times 103.432 = 17.99$. If the yield on both bonds increases 25 basis points, the price change of the portfolio is

$$-1.289 + (-0.7408) \times -1.735 = -0.004$$

Convexity

The hedge in Example 7.8 is not perfect because duration changes as the interest rate changes.[8] *Convexity* measures the extent to which duration changes as the bond's yield changes. The formula for convexity is[9]

$$\text{Convexity} = \frac{1}{B(y)} \left[\sum_{i=1}^{n} \frac{i(i+1)}{m^2} \frac{C/m}{(1+y/m)^{i+2}} + \frac{n(n+1)}{m^2} \frac{M}{(1+y/m)^{n+2}} \right] \quad (7.14)$$

We can use convexity in addition to duration to obtain a more accurate prediction of the new bond price. When we include convexity, the price prediction formula, equation (7.12), becomes[10]

$$B(y + \epsilon) = B(y) - [D \times B(y) \times \epsilon] + 0.5 \times \text{Convexity} \times B(y) \times \epsilon^2 \quad (7.15)$$

where D is modified duration. Here is an example of computing a bond price at a new yield using both duration and convexity.

---

[8] At the original yields, we computed a hedge ratio of 0.7408. Problem 7.19 asks you to compute the hedge ratio that would have exactly hedged the portfolio had both interest rates increased 25 basis points and decreased 25 basis points. The two hedge ratios are different, which means that one hedge ratio would not have worked perfectly.

[9] This is obtained by taking the second derivative of the bond price with respect to the yield to maturity, $d^2 B(y)/dy^2$, and normalizing the result by dividing by the bond price.

[10] If you recall calculus, you may recognize equation (7.12) as a Taylor series expansion of the bond price.

FIGURE 7.2

Comparison of the value of three bond positions as a function of the yield to maturity: 2.718 10-year zero-coupon bonds, one 10-year bond paying a 10% annual coupon, and one 25-year bond paying a 10% coupon. The duration (D) and convexity (C) of each bond at a yield of 10% are in the legend.

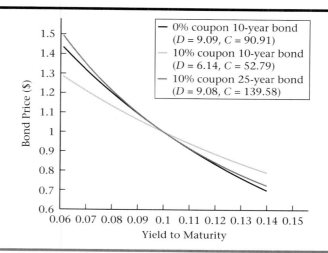

Example 7.9 Consider again Example 7.7. We want to predict the new price of a 3-year zero-coupon bond when the interest rate changes from 7% to 7.25%. Using equation (7.14) with $C = 0$, $m = 1$, and $M = \$100$, convexity of the bond is

$$\text{Convexity} = 3 \times 4 \times \frac{100}{1.07^{(3+2)}} \times \frac{1}{81.63} = 10.4812$$

Using equation (7.15), the price at a yield of 7.25% is

$$B(7.25\%) = \$81.63 - (3/1.07) \times \$81.63 \times 0.0025 + 0.5 \times 10.4812 \times \$81.63 \times 0.0025^2$$
$$= \$81.060$$

The predicted price of $81.060 is the same as the actual price at a yield of 7.25%, to an accuracy of three decimal points. In Example 7.7, the predicted price was slightly lower ($81.058) than the actual new price. The difference without a convexity correction occurs because the bond's sensitivity to the interest rate changes as the interest rate changes.[11] Convexity measures this effect and can be used to correct for it.

Figure 7.2 illustrates duration and convexity by comparing three bond positions that have identical prices at a yield of 10%. Duration is the slope of the bond price graph

---

[11] You might wonder about this statement since the bond in Example 7.7 is a zero-coupon bond, for which Macaulay duration is constant. Notice, however, that the bond price prediction formula, equation (7.12), depends on *modified* duration, which is $D_{\text{Mac}}/(1 + y)$. Modified duration does change with the yield on the bond.

at a given yield, and convexity is the curvature of the graph. The 10%, 10-year bond has the lowest duration and is the shallowest bond price curve. The other two bonds have almost equal durations at a yield of 10%, and their slopes are equal in the figure. However, the 25-year bond exhibits greater curvature: Its price is above the 10-year bond at both lower and higher yields. This greater curvature is what it means for the 25-year bond to have greater convexity.

7.4 TREASURY-BOND AND TREASURY-NOTE FUTURES

Treasury-note and Treasury-bond futures contracts are important instruments for hedging interest rate risk.[12] Figure 6.2 (page 162) includes newspaper listings for these futures. The specifications for the T-note contract are listed in Figure 7.3. The bond contract is similar except that the deliverable bond has a maturity of at least 15 years, or if the bond is callable, has 15 years to first call. The two contracts are similar; we will focus here on the T-note contract. In this discussion we will use the terms "bond" and "note" interchangeably.

The basic idea of the T-note contract is that a long position is an obligation to buy a 6% bond with between 6.5 and 10 years to maturity. To a first approximation we can think of the underlying as being like a stock with a dividend yield of 6%. The futures price would then be computed as with a stock index: the future value of the current bond price, less the future value of coupons payable over the life of the futures contract.

This description masks a complication that may already have occurred to you. The delivery procedure permits the short to deliver any note maturing in 6.5 to 10 years. Hence, the delivered note can be one of many outstanding notes, with a range of coupons and maturities. Which bond does the futures price represent?

Of all bonds that *could* be delivered, there will generally be one that is the most advantageous for the short to deliver. This bond is called the **cheapest to deliver.** A description of the delivery procedure will demonstrate the importance of the cheapest-to-deliver bond.

In fulfilling the note futures contract, the short delivers the bond in exchange for payment. The payment to the short—the *invoice price* for the delivered bond—is the futures price times the conversion factor. The conversion factor is the price of the bond if it were priced to yield 6%. Thus, the short delivering a bond is paid

$$\text{Invoice price} = (\text{Futures price} \times \text{conversion factor}) + \text{accrued interest}$$[13]

---

[12] The interest rate on the 10-year Treasury note is a commonly used benchmark interest rate, hence the 10-year note futures are important.

FIGURE 7.3

Specifications for the Treasury-note futures contract.

Where traded	CBOT
Underlying	6% 10-year Treasury note
Size	$100,000 Treasury note
Months	Mar, Jun, Sep, Dec, out 15 months
Trading ends	Seventh business day preceding last business day of month. Delivery until last business day of month.
Delivery	Physical T-note with at least 6.5 years to maturity and not more than 10 years to maturity. Price paid to the short for notes with other than 6% coupon is determined by multiplying futures price by a conversion factor. The conversion factor is the price of the delivered note ($1 par value) to yield 6%. Settlement until last business day of the month.

Example 7.10 Consider two bonds making semiannual coupon payments. Bond A is a 7% coupon bond with exactly 8 years to maturity, a price of 103.71, and a yield of 6.4%. This bond would have a price of 106.28 if its yield were 6%. Thus, its conversion factor is 1.0628.

Bond B has 7 years to maturity and a 5% coupon. Its current price and yield are 92.73 and 6.3%. It would have a conversion factor of 0.9435, since that is its price at a 6% yield.

Now suppose that the futures contract is close to expiration, the observed futures price is 97.583, and the only two deliverable bonds are Bonds A and B. The short can decide which bond to deliver by comparing the market value of the bond to its invoice price if delivered. For Bond A we have

$$\text{Invoice price} - \text{market price} = (97.583 \times 1.0628) - 103.71 = 0.00$$

For Bond B we have

$$\text{Invoice price} - \text{market price} = (97.583 \times 0.9435) - 92.73 = -0.66$$

These calculations are summarized in Table 7.5.

Based on the yields for the two bonds, the short breaks even delivering the 8-year 7% bond and would lose money delivering the 7-year 5% coupon bond (the invoice price

TABLE 7.5

Prices, yields, and the conversion factor for two bonds. The futures price is 97.583. The short would break even delivering the 8-year 7% bond and lose money delivering the 7-year 5% bond. Both bonds make semiannual coupon payments.

Description	8-Year 7% Coupon, 6.4% Yield	7-Year 5% Coupon, 6.3% Yield
Market price	103.71	92.73
Price at 6% (conversion factor)	106.28	94.35
Invoice price (futures × conversion factor)	103.71	92.09
Invoice − market	0	−0.66

is less than the market price). In this example, the 8-year 7% bond is thus the cheapest to deliver.

In general there will be a single cheapest-to-deliver bond. You might be wondering why both bonds are not equally cheap to deliver. The reason is that the conversion factor is set by a mechanical procedure (the price at which the bond yields 6%), taking no account of the current relative market prices of bonds. Except by coincidence, two bonds will not be equally cheap to deliver.

Also, all but one of the bonds must have a negative delivery value. The only no-arbitrage configuration in general has one bond worth zero to deliver (Bond A in Example 7.10), and the rest lose money if delivered. To avoid arbitrage, the futures price is

$$\text{Futures price} = \frac{\text{Price of cheapest to deliver}}{\text{Conversion factor for cheapest to deliver}} \quad (7.16)$$

This discussion glosses over subtleties involving transaction costs (whether you already own a bond may affect your delivery profit calculation) and uncertainty before the delivery period about which bond will be cheapest to deliver. Also, the T-note is deliverable at any time during the expiration month, but trading ceases with 7 business days remaining. Consequently, if there are any remaining open contracts during the last week of the month, the short has the option to deliver any bond at a price that might be a week out-of-date. This provides a delivery option for the short that is also priced into the contract. There are other complications, but suffice it to say that the T-bond and T-note contracts are complex.

The T-bond and T-note futures contracts have been extremely successful. The contracts illustrate some important design considerations for a futures contract. Consider first how the contract is settled. If the contract designated a particular T-bond as the underlying asset, that T-bond could be in short supply, and in fact it might be possible for someone to corner the available supply. (A **market corner** occurs when someone buys most or all of the deliverable asset or commodity.) A short would then be unable to obtain the bond to deliver. In addition, the deliverable T-bond would change from year to year, and the contract would become more complicated, since traders would have to price the futures differently to reflect different underlying bonds for different maturity dates.

An alternative scheme could have had the contract cash-settle against a T-bond index, much like the S&P 500. This arrangement, however, introduces basis risk, as the T-bond futures contract might then track the index but fail to track any particular bond.

In the end, settlement procedures for the T-bond and T-note contracts permitted a range of bonds and notes to be delivered. Since a high-coupon bond is worth more than an otherwise identical low-coupon bond, there had to be a conversion factor, in order that the short is paid more for delivering the high-coupon bond.

The idea that there is a cheapest to deliver is not exclusive to Treasury bonds. The same issue arises with commodities, where a futures contract may permit delivery of commodities at different locations or of different qualities.

7.5 REPURCHASE AGREEMENTS

An extremely important kind of forward contract is a repurchase agreement, or **repo**.[14] A repo entails selling a security with an agreement to buy it back at a fixed price. It is effectively a reverse cash-and-carry—a sale coupled with a long forward contract. Like any reverse cash-and-carry, it is equivalent to borrowing. The particular twist with a repo is that the underlying security is held as collateral by the counterparty, who has bought the security and agreed to sell it at a fixed price. Thus, a repo is collateralized borrowing. Repos are common in bond markets, but in principle a repurchase agreement can be used for any asset.

Example 7.11 Suppose you enter into a 1-week repurchase agreement for a 9-month $1m Treasury bill. The current price of the T-bill is $956,938, and you agree to repurchase it in 1 week for $958,042. You have borrowed money at a 1-week rate of $958,042/956,938 - 1 = 0.115\%$, receiving cash today and promising to repay cash plus interest in a week. The security provides collateral for the loan.

The party who initiates the repo owns the asset when the transaction is completed and is therefore the financial owner of the security. During the repo, however, the counterparty owns the bond. Most repos are overnight. A longer-term repurchase agreement is called a **term repo**.

---

[14] For a detailed treatment of repurchase agreements, see Steiner (1997).

The counterparty is said to have entered into a reverse repurchase agreement, or **reverse repo,** and is short the forward contract. This is a loan of cash for the duration of the agreement with a security held as collateral. It can also be described as a cash-and-carry.

If the borrower does not repay the loan, the lender keeps the security. Thus, the counterparty's view of the risk of the transaction differs according to the quality of the collateral. Collateral with a more variable price and a less liquid market is lower quality from the perspective of the lender. Because collateral quality varies, every security can have its own market-determined repo rate.

Repurchase agreements are most common for government securities, and they can be negotiated to require a specific security as collateral—called a *special collateral repurchase agreement*—or with any of a variety of government securities as collateral—called a *general collateral repurchase agreement*. General collateral repos have greater flexibility and hence lower transaction costs.

In addition to a repo rate that reflects collateral quality, dealers can also charge a **haircut,** which is the amount by which the value of the collateral exceeds the amount of the loan. The haircut reflects the credit risk of the borrower. A 2% haircut would mean that the borrower receives only 98% of the market value of the security, providing an additional margin of protection for the counterparty.

Repurchase agreements are frequently used by dealers to finance inventory. In the ordinary course of business, a dealer buys and sells securities. The purchase of a security requires funds. A dealer can buy a bond from a customer and then repo it overnight. The money raised with the repo provides the cash needed to pay the seller. The dealer then has a cost of carrying the bond equal to the repo rate.[15] The counterparty on this transaction is an investor with cash to invest short term, such as a corporation. The investor buys the bond, promising to sell it back. This is lending.

The same techniques can be used to finance speculative positions. Hedge funds, for example, use repurchase agreements. A hedge fund speculating on the price difference between two Treasury bonds can finance the transaction with repos. An example of this is discussed in Box 7.1.

In practice, haircuts on both bond positions are a transaction cost. Haircuts are a capital requirement imposed by the counterparty, which means that an arbitrageur must have capital to undertake an otherwise self-financing arbitrage transaction. Differences in repo rates on the assets can be an additional transaction cost. Even if the price gap between the two bonds does not close, the arbitrage can be prohibitively costly if the difference in repo rates on the two bonds is sufficiently great. Cornell and Shapiro (1989) document that in one well-known episode of on-the-run/off-the-run arbitrage (see Box 7.1), the repo rate on an on-the-run (short-sold) bond went to zero, making arbitrage costly even though the price gap remained when the on-the-run bond became off-the-run.

---

[15] The repurchase agreement in this example provides financing. The dealer still is the ultimate owner of the bond and thus has price risk that could be hedged with futures contracts.

Box 7.1: Long-Term Capital Management

Repurchase agreements are a common financing strategy, but they achieved particular notoriety during the Long-Term Capital Management (LTCM) crisis in 1998. LTCM was a hedge fund with a luminous roster of partners, including star bond trader John Meriwether, former Federal Reserve Vice Chairman David Mullins, and academics Robert Merton and Myron Scholes, who won the Nobel Prize in Economics while associated with LTCM.

Many of LTCM's strategies involved so-called convergence trades, meaning that they were a bet that the prices of two assets would grow closer together. One well-known convergence trade involved newly issued on-the-run 30-year Treasury bonds, which typically sold at a lower yield than the almost identical off-the-run 29½-year Treasury bond. One might bet that the yields of the 30-year and 29½-year bonds would converge as the 30-year bond aged and became off-the-run. Traders made this bet by short-selling the on-the-run bond and buying the off-the-run bond. When the on-the-run bond became off-the-run, its yield should (in theory) have equaled that of the other off-the-run bond, and the price of the two bonds should have converged. The trader would profit from the convergence in price, buying back the former on-the-run bond at its new, cheaper price.

In his book about LTCM, Lowenstein (2000, p. 45) described the trade like this: "No sooner did Long-Term buy the off-the-run bonds than it loaned them to some other Wall Street firm, which then wired cash to Long-Term as collateral. Then Long-Term turned around and used this cash as collateral on the bonds that *it* borrowed. The collateral it paid equaled the collateral it collected. In other words, Long-Term pulled off the entire $2 billion trade *without using a dime of its own cash*." (Emphasis in original.) Many forward contracts, of course, are entered into without a party "using a dime of its own cash." LTCM also reportedly paid small or no haircuts.

When LTCM failed in the fall of 1998, it had many such transactions and thus potentially many creditors. The difficulty of unwinding all of these intertwined positions was one of the reasons the Fed brokered a buyout of LTCM by other banks, rather than have LTCM explicitly declare bankruptcy.

CHAPTER SUMMARY

The price of a zero-coupon bond with T years to maturity tells us the value today of $1 to be received at time T. The set of these bond prices for different maturities is the zero-coupon yield curve and is the basic input for present-value calculations. There are equivalent ways to express the same information about interest rates, including the par coupon rate and implied forward rates.

Forward rate agreements (FRAs) permit borrowers and lenders to hedge the interest rate by locking in the implied forward rate. If the interest rate changes, FRAs require a payment reflecting the change in the value of the interest rate as of the loan's maturity day. Eurodollar contracts are an alternative to FRAs as a hedging mechanism. However, Eurodollar contracts make payment on the initiation date for the loan rather than the maturity date, so there is a timing mismatch between the Eurodollar payment and the interest payment date. This gives rise to convexity bias, which causes the rate implied by the Eurodollar contract to be greater than that for an otherwise equivalent FRA.

Duration is a measure of a bond's risk. Modified duration is the percentage change in the bond price for a unit change in the interest rate. Macaulay duration is the percentage change in the bond price for a percentage change in the discount factor. Duration is not a perfect measure of bond price risk. A portfolio is said to be duration-matched if it consists of short and long bond positions with equal value-weighted durations. Convexity is a measure of the change in duration as the bond's yield to maturity changes.

Treasury-note and Treasury-bond futures contracts have Treasury notes and bonds as underlying assets. A complication with these contracts is that a range of bonds are deliverable, and there is a cheapest to deliver. The futures price will reflect expectations about which bond is cheapest to deliver.

Repurchase agreements and reverse repurchase agreements are synthetic short-term borrowing and lending transactions, the equivalent of reverse cash-and-carry and cash-and-carry transactions.

FURTHER READING

Basic interest rate concepts are fundamental in finance and are used throughout this book. Some of the formulas in this chapter will appear again as swap rate calculations in Chapter 8. Chapter 12 shows how to price bonds that make payments denominated in foreign currencies or commodities and how to price bonds containing options.

Useful references for bond and money market calculations are Stigum (1990) and Stigum and Robinson (1996). Sundaresan (2002) and Tuckman (1995) are fixed-income texts that go into topics in this chapter in more depth. Grinblatt and Longstaff (2000) discuss the market for STRIPS and study the pricing relationships between Treasury bonds and STRIPS. The repo market is discussed in Fleming and Garbade (2002, 2003, 2004).

PROBLEMS

7.1 Suppose you observe the following zero-coupon bond prices per $1 of maturity payment: 0.96154 (1-year), 0.91573 (2-year), 0.87630 (3-year), 0.82270 (4-year), 0.77611 (5-year). For each maturity year, compute the zero-coupon bond yields (effective annual and continuously compounded), the par coupon rate, and the 1-year implied forward rate.

7.2 Using the information in the previous problem, find the price of a 5-year coupon bond that has a par payment of $1,000.00 and annual coupon payments of $60.00.

Problems

7.3 Suppose you observe the following effective annual zero-coupon bond yields: 0.030 (1-year), 0.035 (2-year), 0.040 (3-year), 0.045 (4-year), 0.050 (5-year). For each maturity year, compute the zero-coupon bond prices, continuously compounded zero-coupon bond yields, the par coupon rate, and the 1-year implied forward rate.

7.4 Suppose you observe the following 1-year implied forward rates: 0.050000 (1-year), 0.034061 (2-year), 0.036012 (3-year), 0.024092 (4-year), 0.001470 (5-year). For each maturity year, compute the zero-coupon bond prices, effective annual and continuously compounded zero-coupon bond yields, and the par coupon rate.

7.5 Suppose you observe the following continuously compounded zero-coupon bond yields: 0.06766 (1-year), 0.05827 (2-year), 0.04879 (3-year), 0.04402 (4-year), 0.03922 (5-year). For each maturity year, compute the zero-coupon bond prices, effective annual zero-coupon bond yields, the par coupon rate, and the 1-year implied forward rate.

7.6 Suppose you observe the following par coupon bond yields: 0.03000 (1-year), 0.03491 (2-year), 0.03974 (3-year), 0.04629 (4-year), 0.05174 (5-year). For each maturity year, compute the zero-coupon bond prices, effective annual and continuously compounded zero-coupon bond yields, and the 1-year implied forward rate.

7.7 Using the information in Table 7.1, complete the following:

   a. Compute the implied forward rate from time 1 to time 3.

   b. Compute the implied forward price of a par 2-year coupon bond that will be issued at time 1.

7.8 Suppose that in order to hedge interest rate risk on your borrowing, you enter into an FRA that will guarantee a 6% effective annual interest rate for 1 year on $500,000.00. On the date you borrow the $500,000.00, the actual interest rate is 5%. Determine the dollar settlement of the FRA assuming the following:

   a. Settlement occurs on the date the loan is initiated.

   b. Settlement occurs on the date the loan is repaid.

7.9 Using the same information as the previous problem, suppose the interest rate on the borrowing date is 7.5%. Determine the dollar settlement of the FRA assuming the following:

   a. Settlement occurs on the date the loan is initiated.

   b. Settlement occurs on the date the loan is repaid.

Use the following zero-coupon bond prices to answer the next three questions.

Days to Maturity	Zero-Coupon Bond Price
90	0.99009
180	0.97943
270	0.96525
360	0.95238

7.10 What is the rate on a synthetic FRA for a 90-day loan commencing on day 90? A 180-day loan commencing on day 90? A 270-day loan commencing on day 90?

7.11 What is the rate on a synthetic FRA for a 180-day loan commencing on day 180? Suppose you are the counterparty for a borrower who uses the FRA to hedge the interest rate on a $10m loan. What positions in zero-coupon bonds would you use to hedge the risk on the FRA?

7.12 Suppose you are the counterparty for a lender who enters into an FRA to hedge the lending rate on $10m for a 90-day loan commencing on day 270. What positions in zero-coupon bonds would you use to hedge the risk on the FRA?

7.13 Using the information in Table 7.1, suppose you buy a 3-year par coupon bond and hold it for 2 years, after which time you sell it. Assume that interest rates are certain not to change and that you reinvest the coupon received in year 1 at the 1-year rate prevailing at the time you receive the coupon. Verify that the 2-year return on this investment is 6.5%.

7.14 As in the previous problem, consider holding a 3-year bond for 2 years. Now suppose that interest rates can change, but that at time 0 the rates in Table 7.1 prevail. What transactions could you undertake using forward rate agreements to guarantee that your 2-year return is 6.5%?

7.15 Consider the implied forward rate between year 1 and year 2, based on Table 7.1.

  a. Suppose that $r_0(1, 2) = 6.8\%$. Show how buying the 2-year zero-coupon bond and borrowing at the 1-year rate and implied forward rate of 6.8% would earn you an arbitrage profit.

  b. Suppose that $r_0(1, 2) = 7.2\%$. Show how borrowing the 2-year zero-coupon bond and lending at the 1-year rate and implied forward rate of 7.2% would earn you an arbitrage profit.

7.16 Suppose the September Eurodollar futures contract has a price of 96.4. You plan to borrow $50m for 3 months in September at LIBOR, and you intend to use the Eurodollar contract to hedge your borrowing rate.

  a. What rate can you secure?

  b. Will you be long or short the Eurodollar contract?

c. How many contracts will you enter into?

d. Assuming the true 3-month LIBOR is 1% in September, what is the settlement in dollars at expiration of the futures contract? (For purposes of this question, ignore daily marking-to-market on the futures contract.)

7.17 A lender plans to invest $100m for 150 days, 60 days from today. (That is, if today is day 0, the loan will be initiated on day 60 and will mature on day 210.) The implied forward rate over 150 days, and hence the rate on a 150-day FRA, is 2.5%. The actual interest rate over that period could be either 2.2% or 2.8%.

a. If the interest rate on day 60 is 2.8%, how much will the lender have to pay if the FRA is settled on day 60? How much if it is settled on day 210?

b. If the interest rate on day 60 is 2.2%, how much will the lender have to pay if the FRA is settled on day 60? How much if it is settled on day 210?

7.18 Consider the same facts as the previous problem, only now consider hedging with the 3-month Eurodollar futures. Suppose the Eurodollar futures contract that matures 60 days from today has a price on day 0 of 94.

a. What issues arise in using the 3-month Eurodollar contract to hedge a 150-day loan?

b. If you wish to hedge a lending position, should you go long or short the contract?

c. What 3-month LIBOR is implied by the Eurodollar futures price? Approximately what lending rate should you be able to lock in?

d. What position in Eurodollar futures would you use to lock in a lending rate? In doing this, what assumptions are you making about the relationship between 90-day LIBOR and the 150-day lending rate?

7.19 Consider the bonds in Example 7.8. What hedge ratio would have exactly hedged the portfolio if interest rates had decreased by 25 basis points? Increased by 25 basis points? Repeat assuming a 50-basis-point change.

7.20 Compute Macaulay and modified durations for the following bonds:

a. A 5-year bond paying annual coupons of 4.432% and selling at par

b. An 8-year bond paying semiannual coupons with a coupon rate of 8% and a yield of 7%

c. A 10-year bond paying annual coupons of 6% with a price of $92 and maturity value of $100

7.21 Consider the following two bonds, which make semiannual coupon payments: a 20-year bond with a 6% coupon and 20% yield, and a 30-year bond with a 6% coupon and a 20% yield.

a. For each bond, compute the price value of a basis point.

b. For each bond, compute Macaulay duration.

c. "For otherwise identical bonds, Macaulay duration is increasing in time to maturity." Is this statement always true? Discuss.

7.22 An 8-year bond with 6% annual coupons and a 5.004% yield sells for $106.44 with a Macaulay duration of 6.631864. A 9-year bond has 7% annual coupons with a 5.252% yield and sells for $112.29 with a Macaulay duration of 7.098302. You wish to duration-hedge the 8-year bond using a 9-year bond. How many 9-year bonds must we short for every 8-year bond?

7.23 A 6-year bond with a 4% coupon sells for $102.46 with a 3.5384% yield. The conversion factor for the bond is 0.90046. An 8-year bond with 5.5% coupons sells for $113.564 with a conversion factor of 0.9686. (All coupon payments are semiannual.) Which bond is cheaper to deliver given a T-note futures price of 113.81?

7.24 a. Compute the convexity of a 3-year bond paying annual coupons of 4.5% and selling at par.

b. Compute the convexity of a 3-year 4.5% coupon bond that makes semiannual coupon payments and that currently sells at par.

c. Is the convexity different in the two cases? Why?

7.25 Suppose a 10-year zero-coupon bond with a face value of $100 trades at $69.20205.

a. What is the yield to maturity and modified duration of the zero-coupon bond?

b. Calculate the approximate bond price change for a 50-basis-point increase in the yield, based on the modified duration you calculated in part (a). Also calculate the exact new bond price based on the new yield to maturity.

c. Calculate the convexity of the 10-year zero-coupon bond.

d. Now use the formula (equation 7.15) that takes into account both duration and convexity to approximate the new bond price. Compare your result to that in part (b).

Appendix 7.A INTEREST RATE AND BOND PRICE CONVENTIONS

This appendix will focus on conventions for computing yields to maturity for different kinds of bonds, as well as the conventions for quoting bond prices. When discussing yields to maturity, it is necessary to distinguish on the one hand between notes and bonds, which make coupon payments and are issued with more than 1 year to maturity, and on the other hand bills, which have no coupons and are issued with 1 year or less to maturity. The quotation conventions are different for notes and bonds than for bills. For a full treatment of bond pricing and quoting conventions, see Stigum and Robinson (1996).

Bonds

We first consider notes and bonds, which we will refer to as just "bonds." Bond coupons and yields are annualized. If a bond is described as paying a 6% semiannual coupon, this means that the bond pays $6\%/2 = 3\%$ every 6 months. Further, if the bond yield is 7%, this means that the bond's 6-month yield to maturity is $7\%/2 = 3.5\%$. Bond coupons and yields are annualized by multiplying by 2 rather than by compounding.

Suppose a bond makes semiannual coupon payments of $C/2$ and has a semiannual yield of $y/2$. The quoted coupon and yield are C and y.[16] Let d be the actual number of days until the next coupon and d' the number of days between the previous and next coupon. We take into account a fractional period until the next coupon by discounting the cash flows for that fractional period. The price of the bond is

$$B(y) = \sum_{i=1}^{n} \frac{C/2}{(1+y/2)^{i-1+d/d'}} + \frac{M}{(1+y/2)^{n-1+d/d'}} \quad (7.17)$$

This can be rewritten as

$$B(y) = \left(\frac{1}{1+y/2}\right)^{d/d'} \left(C/2 + \frac{C/2}{y/2}\left[1 - \frac{1}{(1+y/2)^{n-1}}\right] + \frac{M}{(1+y/2)^{n-1}}\right) \quad (7.18)$$

In the special case when the bond has just paid a coupon, then $d = d'$, and equation (7.17) becomes

$$B(y) = \sum_{i=1}^{n} \frac{C/2}{(1+y/2)^{i}} + \frac{M}{(1+y/2)^{n}} \quad (7.19)$$

This formula assumes there is one full period until the next coupon.

Example 7.12 Consider a 7% $100 maturity coupon bond that makes semiannual coupon payments on February 15 and August 15, and matures on August 15, 2012. Suppose it is August 15, 2004, and the August coupon has been paid. There are 16 remaining payments. If the semiannual yield, y, is 3.2%, then using equation (7.19), the price of the bond is

$$\frac{\$3.5}{0.032}\left[1 - \frac{1}{(1+0.032)^{16}}\right] + \frac{\$100}{(1+0.032)^{16}} = \$103.71$$

---

[16] If a bond makes coupon payments m times a year, the convention is to quote the coupon rate as m times the per-period payment. The yield to maturity is computed per payment period and multiplied by m to obtain the annual quoted yield.

Example 7.13 Consider the same bond as in Example 7.12. Suppose that on November 11, 2004, the semiannual yield is still 3.2%. There are 96 days until the February coupon payment and 184 days between the August and February payments. Using equation (7.18), the price for the bond at a 6.4% yield (3.2% semiannual) is

$$\left(\frac{1}{1.032}\right)^{96/184} \left(\$3.5 + \frac{\$3.5}{0.032}\left[1 - \frac{1}{(1.032)^{15}}\right] + \frac{\$100}{(1.032)^{15}}\right) = \$105.286$$

The bond-pricing formulas in Examples 7.12 and 7.13 illustrate that even with a constant yield to maturity, the bond price will vary with the time until the next coupon payment. This occurs because equation (7.17) computes a bond price that fully reflects the coming coupon payment. Using this formula, the bond price rises over time as a coupon payment approaches, then falls on the coupon payment date, and so forth. The bond price quoted in this fashion is called the **dirty price.**

Intuitively, if you buy a bond three-fourths of the way from one coupon payment to the next, the price you pay should reflect three-fourths of the coming coupon payment. This prorated amount is **accrued interest,** which is included in the price in equation (7.17). Accrued interest is calculated as the prorated portion of the coupon since the last coupon date. With $d' - d$ days since the last coupon, accrued interest is $C \times (d' - d)/d'$.

In practice, bond prices are quoted net of accrued interest. The dirty price less accrued interest is the **clean price,** which does not exhibit the predictable rise and fall in price due to the coming coupon payment.[17]

Example 7.14 Consider the bond in Example 7.13. Accrued interest as of November 11 would be $3.5 \times (184 - 96)/184 = 1.674$. Thus, the clean price for the bond would be

$$\text{Clean price} = \text{Dirty price} - \text{accrued interest}$$
$$= \$105.286 - \$1.674 = \$103.612$$

Bills

Table 7.6 presents typical Treasury-bill quotations. Suppose today is January 1. A bond maturing February 13 has 43 days to maturity, and one maturing December 18 has 351 days to maturity (assuing it is not a leap year).

The "ask yields" in this table are "bond-equivalent yields" (Stigum and Robinson (1996)), intended to make Treasury-bill yields comparable to Treasury-bond yields. To obtain the yields, we first find the market prices of the T-bills. A T-bill price is quoted on an annualized discount basis. The discount is the number subtracted from 100 to obtain

---

[17] Because accrued interest is amortized linearly rather than geometrically, this statement is not precisely true; see Smith (2002).

TABLE 7.6 Treasury-bill quotations.

Maturity	Days to Maturity	Ask Discount	Ask Yield
February 13	43	3.65	3.72
December 18	351	3.87	4.04

the invoice price for the T-bill, P. The formula, normalizing the face value of the T-bill to be 100, is

$$P = 100 - \frac{\text{discount} \times \text{days}}{360}$$

The T-bills in Table 7.6 have invoice prices of

$$100 - 3.65 \times 43/360 = 99.5640$$
$$100 - 3.87 \times 351/360 = 96.2268$$

Thus, an investor pays 0.995640 per dollar of maturity value for the 43-day bill and 0.962268 for the 351-day bill. Note that these prices give us "true" 43-day and 351-day discount factors. Given the prices, what are the yields?

A 43-day bill yields $\frac{100}{99.5640} = 1.004379$ or 0.4379% over 43 days, while the 351-day bill yields 3.9212% over 351 days. The bond-equivalent yield calculations annualize these yields in a way that makes them more comparable to bond yields. This necessarily involves making arbitrary assumptions.

For bills less than 182 days from maturity, a bill is directly comparable to a maturing bond since neither makes a coupon payment over that period. In this case we need only to adjust for the fact that bonds are quoted using the actual number of days (i.e., a 365-day basis) and bills are quoted on a 360-day basis:

$$r_{be} = \frac{365 \times \text{discount}/100}{360 - \text{discount}/100 \times \text{days}}$$

where r_{be} stands for "bond-equivalent yield." Applying this formula to the 43-day T-bill, we see that

$$\frac{365 \times 0.0365}{360 - 0.0365 \times 43} = 0.0372$$

If you use this formula for the 351-day bill, however, you obtain a yield of 4.078 rather than the 4.04 listed in Table 7.6. The bond-equivalent yield calculation for this bill takes into account that a bond with more than 182 days to maturity would make a coupon payment. Hence, to make the bill yield comparable to that for a bond, we need to account for the imaginary coupon. The formula from Stigum and Robinson (1996) is

$$r_{be} = \frac{-\frac{2\times\text{days}}{365} + 2\sqrt{\left(\frac{\text{days}}{365}\right)^2 - \left(\frac{2\times\text{days}}{365} - 1\right)\left(1 - \frac{100}{P}\right)}}{\frac{2\times\text{days}}{365} - 1} \tag{7.20}$$

Applying this to the 351-day bond gives

$$\frac{-\frac{2\times 351}{365} + 2\sqrt{\left(\frac{351}{365}\right)^2 - \left(\frac{2\times 351}{365} - 1\right)\left(1 - \frac{1}{0.962268}\right)}}{\frac{2\times 351}{365} - 1} = 0.040384$$

This matches the quoted yield in Table 7.6. In Excel, the function **TBILLEQ** provides the bond-equivalent yield for a T-bill.

8 Swaps

Thus far we have talked about derivatives contracts that settle on a single date. A forward contract, for example, fixes a price for a transaction that will occur on a specific date in the future. However, many financial transactions generate a series of payments. Firms that issue bonds make periodic coupon payments. Multinational firms frequently exchange currencies. Firms that buy commodities as production inputs make payments linked to commodity prices on an ongoing basis.

These examples raise the question: If a manager seeking to reduce risk confronts a risky payment *stream*—as opposed to a single risky payment—what is the easiest way to hedge this risk? One obvious answer to this question is that we can enter into a separate forward contract for each payment we wish to hedge. However, it might be more convenient, and entail lower transaction costs, if there were a single transaction that we could use to hedge a stream of payments.

A **swap** is a contract calling for an exchange of payments over time. One party makes a payment to the other depending upon whether a price turns out to be greater or less than a reference price that is specified in the swap contract. A swap thus provides a means to hedge a stream of risky payments. By entering into an oil swap, for example, an oil buyer confronting a stream of uncertain oil payments can lock in a fixed price for oil over a period of time. The swap payments would be based on the difference between a fixed price for oil and a market price that varies over time.

From this description, you can see that there is a relationship between swaps and forward contracts. In fact, a forward contract is a single-payment swap. It is possible to determine the fixed price in a swap (for example, the oil swap just mentioned) by using information from the set of forward prices with different maturities (i.e., the strip). We will see that swaps are nothing more than forward contracts coupled with borrowing and lending money.

8.1 AN EXAMPLE OF A COMMODITY SWAP

We begin our study of swaps by presenting an example of a simple commodity swap. Our purpose here is to understand the economics of swaps. In particular, we wish to understand how a swap is related to forwards, why someone might use a swap, and how market-makers hedge the risk of swaps. In later sections we present swap-price formulas and examine interest rate swaps, total return swaps, and more complicated commodity swap examples.

An industrial producer, IP Inc., is going to buy 100,000 barrels of oil 1 year from today and 2 years from today. Suppose that the forward price for delivery in 1 year is $20/barrel and in 2 years is $21/barrel. We need interest rates in this discussion, so suppose that annual interest rates are as in Table 7.1 (see page 184): The 1- and 2-year zero-coupon bond yields are 6% and 6.5%.

IP can use forward contracts to guarantee the cost of buying oil for the next 2 years. Specifically, IP could enter into long forward contracts for 100,000 barrels in each of the next 2 years, committing to pay $20/barrel in 1 year and $21/barrel in 2 years. The present value of this cost is

$$\frac{\$20}{1.06} + \frac{\$21}{1.065^2} = \$37.383$$

IP could invest this amount today and ensure that it had the funds to buy oil in 1 and 2 years. Alternatively, IP could pay an oil supplier $37.383, and the supplier would commit to delivering 1 barrel in each of the next 2 years. A single payment today for a single delivery of oil in the future is a prepaid forward. A single payment today to obtain *multiple* deliveries in the future is a **prepaid swap**.

Although it is possible to enter into a prepaid swap, buyers might worry about the resulting credit risk: They have fully paid for oil that will not be delivered for up to 2 years. (The prepaid forward has the same problem.) For the same reason, the swap counterparty would worry about a postpaid swap, where the oil is delivered and full payment is made after 2 years. A more attractive solution for both parties is to defer payment until the oil is delivered, while still fixing the total price.

Note that there are many feasible ways to have the buyer pay; any payment stream with a present value of $37.383 is acceptable. Typically, however, a swap will call for equal payments in each year. The payment per year per barrel, x, will then have to be such that

$$\frac{x}{1.06} + \frac{x}{1.065^2} = \$37.383$$

To satisfy this equation, the payments must be $20.483 in each year. We then say that the 2-year swap price is $20.483. *However, any payments that have a present value of $37.383 are acceptable.*

FIGURE 8.1

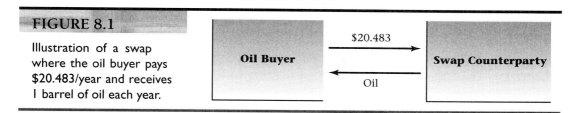

Illustration of a swap where the oil buyer pays $20.483/year and receives 1 barrel of oil each year.

Physical Versus Financial Settlement

Thus far we have described the swap as if the swap counterparty supplied physical oil to the buyer. Figure 8.1 shows a swap that calls for physical settlement. In this case $20.483 is the per-barrel cost of oil.

However, we could also arrange for *financial settlement* of the swap. With financial settlement, the oil buyer, IP, pays the swap counterparty the difference between $20.483 and the spot price (if the difference is negative, the counterparty pays the buyer), and the oil buyer then buys oil at the spot price. For example, if the market price is $25, the swap counterparty pays the buyer

$$\text{Spot price} - \text{swap price} = \$25 - \$20.483 = \$4.517$$

If the market price is $18, the spot price less the swap price is

$$\text{Spot price} - \text{swap price} = \$18 - \$20.483 = -\$2.483$$

In this case, the oil buyer makes a payment to the swap counterparty. Whatever the market price of oil, the net cost to the buyer is the swap price, $20.483:

$$\underbrace{\text{Spot price} - \text{swap price}}_{\text{Swap payment}} - \underbrace{\text{spot price}}_{\text{Spot purchase of oil}} = -\text{Swap price}$$

Figure 8.2 depicts cash flows and transactions when the swap is settled financially. *The results for the buyer are the same whether the swap is settled physically or financially*. In both cases, the net cost to the oil buyer is $20.483.

We have discussed the swap on a per-barrel basis. For a swap on 100,000 barrels, we simply multiply all cash flows by 100,000. In this example, 100,000 is the notional amount of the swap, meaning that 100,000 barrels is used to determine the magnitude of the payments when the swap is settled financially.

To illustrate how a commodity swap would be specified in practice, Figure 8.3 is an abbreviated example of a **term sheet** for an oil swap. Term sheets are commonly used by broker-dealers to succinctly convey the important terms of a financial transaction. The specific example is hypothetical, but the language is from a real term sheet. This particular example is a 3-month oil swap with settlement each month based on the

FIGURE 8.2

Cash flows from a transaction where the oil buyer enters into a financially settled 2-year swap. Each year the buyer pays the spot price for oil and receives spot price − $20.483. The buyer's net cost of oil is $20.483/barrel.

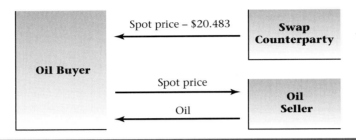

difference between a fixed price and the average over the month of the NYMEX near-month futures price.. As you would expect, the complete documentation for such a deal is lengthy. Transaction confirmations typically make reference to standard documentation supplied by the International Swap Dealers Association (ISDA). The use of standard documentation makes swaps less costly to trade and prices more comparable across dealers.

Why Is the Swap Price Not $20.50?

The swap price, $20.483, is close to the average of the two oil forward prices, $20.50. However, it is not exactly the same. Why?

Suppose that the swap price were $20.50. The oil buyer would then be committing to pay $0.50 more than the forward price the first year and would pay $0.50 less than the forward price the second year. Thus, *relative to the forward curve, the buyer would have made an interest-free loan to the counterparty*. There is implicit lending in the swap.

Now consider the actual swap price of $20.483/barrel. Relative to the forward curve prices of $20 in 1 year and $21 in 2 years, we are overpaying by $0.483 in the first year and we are underpaying by $0.517 in the second year. Therefore, the swap is equivalent to being long the two forward contracts, coupled with an agreement to lend $0.483 to the swap counterparty in 1 year, and receive $0.517 in 2 years. This loan has the effect of equalizing the net cash flow on the two dates.

The interest rate on this loan is $0.517/0.483 - 1 = 7\%$. Where does 7% come from? We assumed that 6% is the 1-year zero yield and 6.5% is the 2-year yield. Given these interest rates, 7% is the 1-year implied forward yield from year 1 to year 2. (See Table 7.1.) By entering into the swap, we are lending the counterparty money for 1 year beginning in 1 year. If the deal is priced fairly, the interest rate on this loan should be the implied forward interest rate.

FIGURE 8.3

Illustrative example of the terms for an oil swap based on West Texas Intermediate (WTI) crude oil.

Sample Commodity Swap Term Sheet

Fixed-rate payer:	Broker-dealer
Floating-rate payer	Counterparty
Notional Amount:	100,000 barrels
Trade Date:	November 8, 2007
Effective Date:	January 1, 2008
Termination Date:	March 31, 2008
Period End Date:	Final Pricing Date of each Calculation Period as defined in the description of the Floating Price.
Fixed Price:	93.87 USD per barrel
Commodity Reference Price:	OIL-WTI-NYMEX
Floating price:	The average of the first nearby NYMEX WTI Crude Oil Futures settlement prices for each successive day of the Calculation Period during which such prices are quoted
Calculation Period:	Each calendar month during the transaction
Method of averaging:	Unweighted
Settlement and payment:	If the Fixed Amount exceeds the Floating Amount for such Calculation Period, the Fixed Price Payor shall pay the Floating Price Payor an amount equal to such excess. If the Floating Amount exceeds the Fixed Amount for such Calculation Period, the Floating Price Payor shall pay the Fixed Price Payor an amount equal to such excess.
Payment Date:	5 business days following each Period End Date

The Swap Counterparty

The swap counterparty in this example is a dealer, who hedges the oil price risk resulting from the swap. The dealer can hedge in several ways. First, imagine that an oil seller would like to lock in a fixed selling price of oil. In this case, the dealer locates the oil buyer and seller and serves as a go-between for the swap, receiving payments from one party and passing them on to the other. In practice, the fixed price paid by the buyer exceeds the fixed price received by the seller. This price difference is a bid-ask spread and is the dealer's fee.

FIGURE 8.4

Cash flows from a transaction where an oil buyer and seller each enters into a financially settled 2-year swap. The buyer pays the spot price for oil and receives spot price − $20.483 each year as a swap payment. The oil seller receives the spot price for oil and receives $20.483 − spot price as a swap payment.

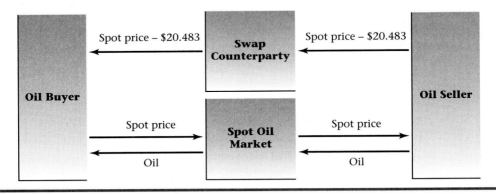

Figure 8.4 illustrates how this transaction would work with financial settlement. The oil seller receives the spot price for oil and receives the swap price less the spot price, on net receiving the swap price. The oil buyer pays the spot price and receives the spot price less the swap price. The situation where the dealer matches the buyer and seller is called a **back-to-back transaction** or "matched book" transaction. The dealer bears the credit risk of both parties but is not exposed to price risk.

A more interesting situation occurs when the dealer serves as counterparty and hedges the transaction using forward markets. Let's see how this would work.

After entering the swap with the oil buyer, the dealer has the obligation to pay the spot price and receive the swap price. If the spot price rises, the dealer can lose money. The dealer has a short position in 1- and 2-year oil.

The natural hedge for the dealer is to enter into long forward or futures contracts to offset this short exposure. Table 8.1 illustrates how this strategy works. As we discussed earlier, there is an implicit loan in the swap and this is apparent in Table 8.1. The net cash flow for the hedged dealer is a loan, where the dealer receives cash in year 1 and repays it in year 2.

This example shows that *hedging the oil price risk in the swap does not fully hedge the position*. The dealer also has interest rate exposure. If interest rates fall, the dealer will not be able to earn a sufficient return from investing $0.483 in year 1 to repay $0.517 in year 2. Thus, in addition to entering oil forwards, it would make sense for the dealer to use Eurodollar contracts or forward rate agreements to hedge the resulting interest rate exposure.

TABLE 8.1
Positions and cash flows for a dealer who has an obligation to receive the fixed price in an oil swap and who hedges the exposure by going long year 1 and year 2 oil forwards.

Year	Payment from Oil Buyer	Long Forward	Net
1	$20.483 − year 1 spot price	Year 1 spot price − $20	$0.483
2	$20.483 − year 2 spot price	Year 2 spot price − $21	−$0.517

The Market Value of a Swap

When the buyer first enters the swap, its market value is zero, meaning that either party could enter or exit the swap without having to pay anything to the other party (apart from commissions and bid-ask spreads). From the oil buyer's perspective, the swap consists of two forward contracts plus an agreement to lend money at the implied forward rate of 7%. The forward contracts and forward rate agreement have zero value, so the swap does as well.

Once the swap is struck, however, its market value will generally no longer be zero, for two reasons. First, the forward prices for oil and interest rates will change over time. New swaps would no longer have a fixed price of $20.483; hence, one party will owe money to the other should one party wish to exit or *unwind* the swap.

Second, even if oil and interest rate forward prices do not change, the value of the swap will remain zero only *until the first swap payment is made*. Once the first swap payment is made, the buyer has overpaid by $0.483 relative to the forward curve, and hence, in order to exit the swap, the counterparty would have to pay the oil buyer $0.483. Thus, even if prices do not change, the market value of swaps can change over time due to the implicit borrowing and lending.

A buyer wishing to exit the swap could negotiate terms with the original counterparty to eliminate the swap obligation. An alternative is to leave the original swap in place and enter into an offsetting swap with whoever offers the best price. The original swap called for the oil buyer to pay the fixed price and receive the floating price; the offsetting swap has the buyer receive the fixed price and pay floating. The original obligation would be cancelled except to the extent that the fixed prices are different. However, the difference is known, so oil price risk is eliminated. (There is still credit risk when the original swap counterparty and the counterparty to the offsetting swap are different. This could be a reason for the buyer to prefer offsetting the swap with the original counterparty.)

To see how a swap can change in value, suppose that immediately after the buyer enters the swap, the forward curve for oil rises by $2 in years 1 and 2. Thus, the year 1 forward price becomes $22 and the year 2 forward price becomes $23. The original swap will no longer have a zero market value.

Assuming interest rates are unchanged, the new swap price is $22.483. (Problem 8.1 asks you to verify this.) The buyer could unwind the swap at this point by agreeing to sell oil at $22.483, while the original swap still calls for buying oil at $20.483. Thus, the net swap payments in each year are

$$\underbrace{(\text{Spot price} - \$20.483)}_{\text{Original swap}} + \underbrace{(\$22.483 - \text{spot price})}_{\text{New swap}} = \$2$$

The present value of this difference is

$$\frac{\$2}{1.06} + \frac{\$2}{1.065^2} = \$3.650$$

The buyer can receive a stream of payments worth $3.65 by offsetting the original swap with a new swap. Thus, $3.65 is the market value of the swap. If interest rates had changed, we would have used the new interest rates in computing the new swap price.

As a practical matter, swaps and other derivatives can cause problems for regulators, accountants, and investors, all of whom would like an accurate depiction of activities within a firm. Box 8.1 shows an extreme example of a hedged transaction—

Box 8.1: Enron's Hidden Debt

When energy giant Enron collapsed in the fall of 2001, there were charges that other companies had helped Enron mislead investors. In July 2003, the Securities and Exchange Commission announced that J. P. Morgan Chase and Citigroup had each agreed to pay more than $100 million to settle allegations that they had helped Enron commit fraud. Specifically, the SEC alleged that both banks had helped Enron characterize loan proceeds as operating income.

The basic outline of the transaction with J. P. Morgan Chase is as follows. Enron entered into "prepaid forward sales contracts" (essentially a prepaid swap) with an entity called Mahonia; Enron received a lump-sum payment and agreed to deliver natural gas in the future. Mahonia in turn received a lump-sum payment from Chase and agreed to deliver natural gas in the future. Chase, which controlled Mahonia, then hedged its Mahonia transaction with Enron. With all transactions netted out, Enron had no commodity exposure, and received its lump-sum initial payment from Mahonia in exchange for making future fixed installment payments to Chase. In other words, Enron in effect had a loan with Chase. Not only did Enron not record debt from these transactions, but the company reported operating income. The transaction is illustrated in Figure 8.5.

The SEC complaint included a revealing excerpt from internal Chase e-mail:

WE ARE MAKING DISGUISED LOANS, USUALLY BURIED IN COMMODITIES OR EQUITIES DERIVATIVES (AND I'M SURE IN OTHER AREAS). WITH A FEW [sic] EXCEPTIONS, THEY ARE UNDERSTOOD TO BE DISGUISED LOANS AND APPROVED AS SUCH. (Capitalization in the original.)

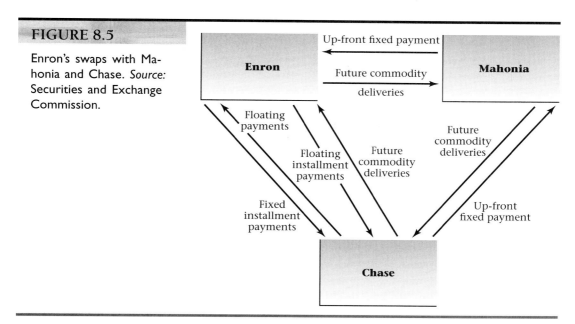

FIGURE 8.5

Enron's swaps with Mahonia and Chase. *Source:* Securities and Exchange Commission.

allegedly used to hide debt and manipulate earnings—involving Enron and J. P. Morgan Chase. Figure 8.5, which was taken from an SEC account of the transaction, illustrates the transactions and flows.

The examples we have analyzed in this section illustrate the fundamental characteristics of swaps and their cash flows. In the rest of the chapter, we will compute more realistic swap prices for interest rates, currencies, and commodities and see some of the ways in which we can modify the terms of a swap.

8.2 INTEREST RATE SWAPS

Companies use interest rate swaps to modify their interest rate exposure. In this section we will begin with a simple example of an interest rate swap, similar to the preceding oil swap example. We will then present general pricing formulas and discuss ways in which the basic swap structure can be altered.

A Simple Interest Rate Swap

Suppose that XYZ Corp. has $200m of floating-rate debt at LIBOR—meaning that every year XYZ pays that year's current LIBOR—but would prefer to have fixed-rate debt with 3 years to maturity. There are several ways XYZ could effect this change.

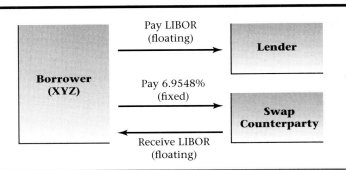

FIGURE 8.6

Illustration of cash flows for a company that borrows at LIBOR and swaps to fixed-rate exposure at 6.9548%.

First, XYZ could change their interest rate exposure by retiring the floating-rate debt and issuing fixed-rate debt in its place. However, an actual purchase and sale of debt has transaction costs.

Second, they could enter into a strip of forward rate agreements (FRAs) in order to guarantee the borrowing rate for the remaining life of the debt. Since the FRA for each year will typically carry a different interest rate, the company will lock in a different rate each year, and hence, the company's borrowing cost will vary over time, even though it will be fixed in advance.

A third alternative is to obtain interest rate exposure equivalent to that of fixed-rate debt by entering into a swap. XYZ is already paying a floating interest rate. They therefore want to enter a swap in which they receive a floating rate and pay the fixed rate, which we will suppose is 6.9548%. This swap is illustrated in Figure 8.6. Notice the conceptual similarity to the oil swap.

In a year when the fixed 6.9548% swap rate exceeds 1-year LIBOR, XYZ pays 6.9548% − LIBOR to the swap counterparty. Conversely, when the 6.9548% swap rate is less than LIBOR, the swap counterparty pays LIBOR − 6.9548% to XYZ. On net, XYZ pays 6.9548%. Algebraically, the net interest payment made by XYZ is

$$\text{XYZ net payment} = -\underbrace{\text{LIBOR}}_{\text{Floating payment}} + \underbrace{\text{LIBOR} - 6.9548\%}_{\text{Swap payment}} = -6.9548\%$$

The notional principal of the swap is $200m: It is the amount on which the interest payments—and, hence, the net swap payment—is based. The life of the swap is the **swap term** or **swap tenor**.

There are timing conventions with a swap similar to those for a forward rate agreement. At the beginning of a year, the borrowing rate for that year is known. However, the interest payment on the loan is due at the end of the year. The interest rate determination date for the floating interest payment would therefore occur at the beginning of the period. As with an FRA, we can think of the swap payment being made at the end of the period (when interest is due).

With the financially settled oil swap, only net swap payments—in this case the difference between LIBOR and 6.9548%—are actually made between XYZ and the counterparty. If one party defaults, they owe to the other party at most the present value of net swap payments they are obligated to make at current market prices. This means that a swap generally has less credit risk than a bond: Whereas principal is at risk with a bond, only net swap payments are at risk in a swap.

The swap in this example is a construct, making payments *as if* there were an exchange of payments between a fixed-rate and floating-rate bond. In practice, a fund manager might own fixed-rate bonds and wish to have floating-rate exposure while continuing to own the bonds. A swap in which a fund manager receives a floating rate in exchange for the payments on bonds the fund continues to hold is called an **asset swap.**

Pricing and the Swap Counterparty

To understand the pricing of the swap, we will examine it from the perspective of both the counterparty and the firm. We first consider the perspective of the counterparty, who we assume is a market-maker.

The market-maker is a counterparty to the swap in order to earn fees, not to take on interest rate risk. Therefore, the market-maker will hedge the transaction. The market-maker receives the fixed rate from the company and pays the floating rate; the danger for the market-maker is that the floating rate will rise. The risk in this transaction can be hedged by entering into forward rate agreements. We express the time 0 implied forward rate between time t_i and t_j as $r_0(t_i, t_j)$ and the realized 1-year rate as $\tilde{r}_{t_i}$. The current 1-year rate, 6%, is known. With the swap rate denoted R, Table 8.2 depicts the risk-free (but time-varying) cash flows faced by the hedged market-maker.

How is R determined? Obviously, a market-maker receiving the fixed rate would like to set a high swap rate, but the swap market is competitive. We expect R to be bid down by competing market-makers until the present value of the hedged cash flows is zero. In computing this present value, we need to use the appropriate rate for each cash flow: The 1-year rate for $R - 6\%$, the 2-year rate for $R - 7.0024\%$, and so forth. Using the rate information from Table 7.1, we compute

$$\frac{R - 6\%}{1.06} + \frac{R - 7.0024\%}{1.065^2} + \frac{R - 8.0071\%}{1.07^3} = 0$$

TABLE 8.2 Cash flows faced by a market-maker who receives fixed and pays floating and hedges the resulting exposure using forward rate agreements.

Year	Payment on Forward	Net Swap Payment	Net
1	—	$R - 6\%$	$R - 6\%$
2	$\tilde{r}_2 - 7.0024\%$	$R - \tilde{r}_2$	$R - 7.0024\%$
3	$\tilde{r}_3 - 8.0071\%$	$R - \tilde{r}_3$	$R - 8.0071\%$

TABLE 8.3 Cash flows faced by a floating-rate borrower who enters into a 3-year swap with a fixed rate of 6.9548%.

Year	Floating-Rate Debt Payment	Net Swap Payment	Net
1	-6%	$6\% - 6.9548\%$	-6.9548%
2	$-\tilde{r}_2$	$\tilde{r}_2 - 6.9548\%$	-6.9548%
3	$-\tilde{r}_3$	$\tilde{r}_3 - 6.9548\%$	-6.9548%

This formula gives us an R of 6.9548%, which from Table 7.1 is the same as the par coupon rate on a 3-year bond! In fact, our swap-rate calculation is a roundabout way to compute a par bond yield. On reflection, this result should be no surprise. Once the borrower has entered into the swap, the net effect is exactly like borrowing at a fixed rate. Thus, the fixed swap rate should be the rate on a coupon bond.

Notice that the unhedged net cash flows in Table 8.2 (the "net swap payment" column) can be replicated by borrowing at a floating rate and lending at a fixed rate. In other words, *an interest rate swap is equivalent to borrowing at a floating rate to buy a fixed-rate bond*.

The borrower's calculations are just the opposite of the market-maker's. The borrower continues to pay the floating rate on its floating-rate debt, and receives floating and pays fixed in the swap. Table 8.3 details the cash flows.

Since the swap rate is the same as the par 3-year coupon rate, the borrower is indifferent between the swap and a coupon bond, ignoring transaction costs. Keep in mind that the borrower could also have used forward rate agreements, locking in an escalating interest rate over time: 6% the first year, 7.0024% the second, and 8.0071% the third. By using interest rate forwards, the borrower would have eliminated uncertainty about future borrowing rates and created an uneven but certain stream of interest payments over time. The swap provides a way to both guarantee the borrowing rate and lock in a constant rate in a single transaction.

A hypothetical interest rate swap term sheet is shown in Figure 8.7. Note that floating payments are made every 3 months and fixed payments every 6 months. This is common practice in swaps denominated is U.S. dollars, and creates cash flows that mimic borrowing in the Eurodollar market to buy a bond making semiannual payments. Different kinds of swaps can be created by changing the terms, for example, by denominating rates in different currencies.

Computing the Swap Rate in General

We now examine more carefully the general calculations for determining the swap rate. We will use the interest rate and bond price notation introduced in Chapter 7. Suppose there are n swap settlements, occurring on dates t_i, $i = 1, \ldots, n$. The implied forward interest rate from date t_{i-1} to date t_i, known at date 0, is $r_0(t_{i-1}, t_i)$. (We will treat

FIGURE 8.7

Example of a term sheet for an interest rate swap.

Sample Interest Rate Swap Term Sheet

Fixed-Rate Payer		**Floating-Rate Payer**	
Payer:	Broker-dealer	Payer:	Counterparty
Fixed Rate:	6.59%	Floating Rate:	3-month USD LIBOR
Notional Principal:	USD 100,000,000	Notional:	USD 100,000,000
Currency:	USD	Currency:	USD
Day Count:	30/360	Day Count:	Actual/360
Payment Dates:	Semiannually on the 15th day of each April and October	Payment Dates:	Quarterly on the 15th day of each January, April, July, and October

$r_0(t_{i-1}, t_i)$ as *not* having been annualized; i.e., it is the return earned from t_{i-1} to t_i.) The price of a zero-coupon bond maturing on date t_i is $P(0, t_i)$.

The market-maker can hedge the floating-rate payments using forward rate agreements. The requirement that the hedged swap have zero net present value is

$$\sum_{i=1}^{n} P(0, t_i)[R - r_0(t_{i-1}, t_i)] = 0 \quad (8.1)$$

where there are n payments on dates $t_1, t_2, \ldots, t_n$. The cash flows $R - r_0(t_{i-1}, t_i)$ can also be obtained by buying a fixed-rate bond paying R and borrowing at the floating rate.

Equation (8.1) can be rewritten as

$$R = \frac{\sum_{i=1}^{n} P(0, t_i) r(t_{i-1}, t_i)}{\sum_{i=1}^{n} P(0, t_i)} \quad (8.2)$$

The expression $\sum_{i=1}^{n} P(0, t_i) r(t_{i-1}, t_i)$ is the present value of interest payments implied by the strip of forward rates. The expression $\sum_{i=1}^{n} P(0, t_i)$ is just the present value of a $1 annuity when interest rates vary over time. Thus, the swap rate annuitizes the interest payments on the floating-rate bond.

We can rewrite equation (8.2) to make it easier to interpret:

$$R = \sum_{i=1}^{n} \left[\frac{P(0, t_i)}{\sum_{j=1}^{n} P(0, t_j)} \right] r(t_{i-1}, t_i)$$

Since the terms in square brackets sum to 1, this form of equation (8.2) emphasizes that the fixed swap rate is a weighted average of the implied forward rates, where zero-coupon bond prices are used to determine the weights.

There is another, equivalent way to express the swap rate. Recall from Chapter 7, equation (7.4), that the implied forward rate between times t_1 and t_2, $r_0(t_1, t_2)$, is given by the ratio of zero-coupon bond prices, i.e.,

$$r_0(t_1, t_2) = P(0, t_1)/P(0, t_2) - 1$$

Therefore, equation (8.1) can be rewritten

$$\sum_{i=1}^{n} P(0, t_i)[R - r(t_{i-1}, t_i)] = \sum_{i=1}^{n} P(0, t_i) \left[R - \frac{P(0, t_{i-1})}{P(0, t_i)} + 1 \right]$$

Setting this equation equal to zero and solving for R gives us

$$R = \frac{1 - P_0(0, t_n)}{\sum_{i=1}^{n} P_0(0, t_i)} \qquad (8.3)$$

You may recognize this as the formula for the coupon on a par coupon bond, equation (7.6), from Chapter 7. This in turn can be rewritten as

$$R \sum_{i=1}^{n} P(0, t_i) + P(0, t_n) = 1$$

This is the valuation equation for a bond priced at par with a coupon rate of R.

The conclusion is that *the swap rate is the coupon rate on a par coupon bond*. This result is intuitive since a firm that swaps from floating-rate to fixed-rate exposure ends up with the economic equivalent of a fixed-rate bond.

Deferred Swaps

We can construct a swap that begins at some date in the future but for which the swap rate is agreed upon today. This type of swap is called a **deferred swap.** To demonstrate this type of swap, we can use the information in Table 7.1 to compute the value of a 2-period swap that begins 1 year from today. The reasoning is exactly as before: The swap rate will be set by the market-maker so that the present value of the fixed and floating payments is the same. This gives us

$$\frac{R - 0.070024}{1.065^2} + \frac{R - 0.080071}{1.07^3} = 0$$

Solving for R, the deferred swap rate is 7.4854%. In general, the fixed rate on a deferred swap beginning in k periods is computed as

$$\boxed{R = \frac{\sum_{i=k}^{n} P_0(0, t_i) r_0(t_{i-1}, t_i)}{\sum_{i=k}^{n} P(0, t_i)}} \qquad (8.4)$$

8.2 Interest Rate Swaps

This can also be written as

$$R = \frac{P(0, t_{k-1}) - P(0, t_n)}{\sum_{i=k}^{n} P(0, t_i)} \quad (8.5)$$

Equation (8.4) is equal to equation (8.2) when $k = 1$.

The Swap Curve

As discussed in Chapter 5, the Eurodollar futures contract provides a set of 3-month forward LIBOR rates extending out 10 years. It is possible to use this set of forward interest rates to compute equation (8.2) or (8.3). As discussed in Chapter 7, zero-coupon bond prices can be constructed from implied forward rates.

The set of swap rates at different maturities implied by LIBOR is called the *swap curve*. There is an over-the-counter market in interest rate swaps, which is widely quoted. The swap curve should be consistent with the interest rate curve implied by the Eurodollar futures contract, which is used to hedge swaps.[1]

Here is how we construct the swap curve using the set of Eurodollar prices.[2] Column 2 of Table 8.4 lists 2 years of Eurodollar futures prices from November 2007. The next column shows the implied 91-day interest rate, beginning in the month in column 1. For example, using equation (6.3), the December price of 95.250 implies a December to March quarterly interest rate of

$$(100 - 95.250)\frac{91}{90}\frac{1}{400} = 0.01201$$

Column 4 reports the corresponding implied zero-coupon bond price, which is the cost in December of $1 paid the following March. The second row gives the December price of $1 paid in June, and so forth. The calculation producing the value in the third row is

$$\frac{1}{1.01201} \times \frac{1}{1.01082} \times \frac{1}{1.01020} = 0.96769$$

The swap rate in the June 2008 row is the fixed quarterly interest rate for a loan initiated in December that matures in September, with swap payments made in March,

---

[1] The Eurodollar contract is a futures contract, while a swap is a set of forward rate agreements. Because of convexity bias, discussed in Chapter 7, the swap curve constructed from Eurodollar futures contracts following the procedure described in this section will be somewhat greater than the observed swap curve. This is discussed by Burghardt and Hoskins (1995) and Gupta and Subrahmanyam (2000).

[2] Collin-Dufresne and Solnik (2001) point out that the credit risk implicit in the LIBOR rate underlying the Eurodollar futures contract is different than the credit risk of an interest rate swap. LIBOR is computed as an average 3-month borrowing rate for international banks with good credit. Banks that experience credit problems are dropped from the sample. Thus, by construction, the pool of banks represented in the Eurodollar contract never experience a credit downgrade. A firm with a swap, by contrast, could be downgraded.

TABLE 8.4

Three-month LIBOR forward rates and swap rates implied by Eurodollar futures prices with maturity dates given in the first column. Prices are from November 8, 2007. *Source: Wall Street Journal online.*

Maturity Date of Eurodollar Futures Contract	Price of Eurodollar Futures	3-Month Forward Rate Implied by Eurodollar Futures Price	Implied Dec 2008 Price of $1 Paid 3 Months after Futures Mat. Date	Swap Rate (%) for Loan Made Dec 2008, Ending 3 Months after Futures Mat. Date
Dec 2007	95.250	0.01201	0.98814	4.8028
Mar 2008	95.720	0.01082	0.97756	4.5664
Jun 2008	95.965	0.01020	0.96769	4.4059
Sep 2008	96.075	0.00992	0.95818	4.2982
Dec 2008	96.080	0.00991	0.94878	4.2326
Mar 2009	96.000	0.01011	0.93928	4.2021
Jun 2009	95.865	0.01045	0.92957	4.1991
Sep 2009	95.735	0.01078	0.91965	4.2128
Dec 2009	95.605	0.01111	0.90955	4.2374

June, and September. We can compute this in two equivalent ways.[3] Using equation (8.2), we have

$$\frac{0.01201 \times 0.98814 + 0.01082 \times 0.97756 + 0.01020 \times 0.96769}{0.98814 + 0.97756 + 0.96769} \times 4 = 0.044059$$

Alternatively, using equation (8.3), we obtain

$$\frac{1 - 0.9851}{0.9964 + 0.9914 + 0.9851} \times 4 = 0.044059$$

In practice, market participants often refer to the **swap spread**, which is the difference between swap rates and Treasury-bond yields for comparable maturities.

Amortizing and Accreting Swaps

We have assumed that the notional value of the swap remains fixed over the life of the swap. However, it is also possible to engage in a swap where the notional value

---

[3] Because of rounding, the two calculations actually give slightly different answers. Without rounding, they give the same result.

is changing over time. For example, consider a floating-rate mortgage, for which every payment contains an interest and principal component. Since the outstanding principal is declining over time, a swap involving a mortgage would need to account for this. Such a swap is called an **amortizing swap** because the notional value is declining over time. It is also possible for the principal in a swap to grow over time. This is called an **accreting swap.**

Let Q_t be the relative notional amount at time t. Then the basic idea in pricing a swap with a time-varying notional amount is the same as with a fixed notional amount: The present value of the fixed payments should equal the present value of the floating payments:

$$\sum_{i=1}^{n} Q_{t_i} P(0, t_i)[R - r(t_{i-1}, t_i)] = 0 \tag{8.6}$$

where, as before, there are n payments on dates $t_1, t_2, \ldots, t_n$. Equation (8.6) can be rewritten as

$$R = \frac{\sum_{i=1}^{n} Q_{t_i} P(0, t_i) r(t_{i-1}, t_i)}{\sum_{i=1}^{n} Q_{t_i} P(0, t_i)} \tag{8.7}$$

The fixed swap rate is still a weighted average of implied forward rates, only now the weights also involve changing notional principal.

Many other structures are possible for swaps based on interest rates or other prices. One notorious swap structure is described in Box 8.2, which recounts the 1993 swap between Procter & Gamble and Bankers Trust.

8.3 CURRENCY SWAPS

Firms sometimes issue debt denominated in a foreign currency. A firm may do this as a hedge against revenues received in that currency, or because perceived borrowing costs in that currency are lower. Whatever the reason, if the firm later wants to change the currency to which they have exposure, there are a variety of ways to do so. The firm can use forward contracts to hedge exchange rate risk, or it can use a **currency swap,** in which payments are based on the difference in debt payments denominated in different currencies.

To understand these alternatives, let's consider the example of a dollar-based firm that has euro-denominated 3-year fixed-rate debt. The annual coupon rate is ρ. The firm is obligated to make a series of payments that are fixed in euro terms but variable in dollar terms.

Since the payments are known, eliminating euro exposure is a straightforward hedging problem using currency forwards. We have cash flows of $-\rho$ each year, and $-(1 + \rho)$ in the maturity year. If currency forward prices are $F_{0,t}$, we can enter into long euro forward contracts to acquire at a known exchange rate the euros we need to pay to the lenders. Hedged cash flows in year t are $-\rho F_{0,t}$.

Box 8.2: The Procter & Gamble Swap

In November 1993, consumer products company Procter & Gamble (P&G) entered into a 5-year $200m notional value swap with Bankers Trust. The contract called for P&G to receive a 5.3% fixed rate from Bankers Trust and pay the 30-day commercial paper rate less 75 basis points, plus a spread. Settlements were to be semiannual. The spread would be zero for the first settlement, and thereafter be fixed at the spread as of May 4, 1994.

The spread was determined by the difference between the 5-year constant maturity Treasury (CMT) rate (the yield on a 5-year Treasury bond, but a constructed rate since there is not always a Treasury bond with exactly 5 years to expiration) and the price per $100 of maturity value of the 6.25% 30-year Treasury bond. The formula for the spread was

$$\text{Spread} = \max\left(\frac{\frac{\text{5-year CMT\%}}{0.0578} \times 98.5 - \text{price of 30-year bond}}{100}, 0\right)$$

At inception in November 1993, the 5-year CMT rate was 5.02% and the 30-year Treasury price was 102.57811. The expression in the max function evaluated to $-.17$ (-17%), so the spread was zero.

If the spread were zero on May 4, 1994, P&G would save 75 basis points per year on $200m for 4.5 years, an interest rate reduction worth approximately $7m. However, notice something important: If interest rates rise before the spread determination date, then the 5-year CMT goes up *and the price of the 30-year bond goes down*. Thus, the swap is really a bet on the *direction* of interest rates, not the difference in rates!

The swap is recounted in Smith (1997) and Srivastava (1999). Interest rates rose after P&G entered the swap. P&G and Bankers Trust renegotiated the swap in January 1994, and P&G liquidated the swap in March, with a loss of about $100m. P&G sued Bankers Trust, complaining in part that the risks of the swap had not been adequately disclosed by Bankers Trust.

In the end, P&G and Bankers Trust settled, with P&G paying Bankers Trust about $35m. (Forster (1996) and Horwitz (1996) debate the implications of the trial and settlement.) The notion that Procter & Gamble might have been uninformed about the risk of the swap, and if so, whether this should have mattered, was controversial. U.S. securities laws are often said to protect "widows and orphans." Nobel Prize–winning economist Merton Miller wryly said of the case, "Procter is the widow and Gamble is the orphan."

As we have seen in other examples, the forward transactions eliminate risk but leave the firm with a variable (but riskless) stream of cash flows. The variability of hedged cash flows is illustrated in the following example.

Example 8.1 Suppose the effective annual euro-denominated interest rate is 3.5% and the dollar-denominated rate is 6%. The spot exchange rate is $0.90/€. A dollar-based firm has a 3-year 3.5% euro-denominated bond with a €100 par value and price of €100.

8.3 Currency Swaps

TABLE 8.5 Unhedged and hedged cash flows for a dollar-based firm with euro-denominated debt.

Year	Unhedged Euro Cash Flow	Forward Exchange Rate	Hedged Dollar Cash Flow
1	−€3.5	0.922	−$3.226
2	−€3.5	0.944	−$3.304
3	−€103.5	0.967	−$100.064

The firm wishes to guarantee the dollar value of the payments. Since the firm will make debt payments in euros, it buys the euro forward to eliminate currency exposure. Table 8.5 summarizes the transaction and reports the currency forward curve and the unhedged and hedged cash flows. The value of the hedged cash flows is

$$\frac{\$3.226}{1.06} + \frac{\$3.304}{1.06^2} + \frac{\$100.064}{1.06^3} = \$90$$

Example 8.1 verifies what we knew had to be true: Hedging does not change the value of the debt. The initial value of the debt in euros is €100. Since the exchange rate is $0.90/€, the debt should have a dollar value of $90, which it has.

As an alternative to hedging each euro-denominated payment with a forward contract, a firm wishing to change its currency exposure can enter into a currency swap, which entails making debt payments in one currency and receiving debt payments in a different currency. There is typically an exchange of principal at both the start and end of the swap. Compared with hedging the cash flows individually, the currency swap generates a different cash flow stream, but with equivalent value. We can examine a currency swap by supposing that the firm in Example 8.1 uses a swap rather than forward contracts to hedge its euro exposure.

Example 8.2 Make the same assumptions as in Example 8.1. The dollar-based firm enters into a swap where it pays dollars (6% on a $90 bond) and receives euros (3.5% on a €100 bond). The firm's euro exposure is eliminated. The market-maker receives dollars and pays euros. The position of the market-maker is summarized in Table 8.6. The present value of the market-maker's net cash flow is

$$\frac{\$2.174}{1.06} + \frac{\$2.096}{1.06^2} - \frac{\$4.664}{1.06^3} = 0$$

The market-maker's net exposure in this transaction is long a dollar-denominated bond and short a euro-denominated bond. Table 8.6 shows that after hedging there is a series of net dollar cash flows with zero present value. As in all the previous examples, the effect of the swap is equivalent to entering into forward contracts, coupled with

TABLE 8.6
Unhedged and hedged cash flows for a dollar-based firm with euro-denominated debt. The effective annual dollar-denominated interest rate is 6%, and the effective annual euro-denominated interest rate is 3.5%.

Year	Forward Exchange Rate ($/€)	Receive Dollar Interest	Pay Hedged Euro Interest	Net Cash Flow
1	0.9217	$5.40	−€3.5 × 0.9217	$2.174
2	0.9440	$5.40	−€3.5 × 0.9440	$2.096
3	0.9668	$95.40	−€103.5 × 0.9668	−$4.664

borrowing or lending. In this case, the firm is lending to the market-maker in the first 2 years, with the implicit loan repaid at maturity.

The fact that a currency swap is equivalent to borrowing in one currency and lending in the other is familiar from our discussion of currency forwards in Chapter 5. There we saw the same is true of currency forwards.

Currency Swap Formulas

Currency swap calculations are the same as those for the other swaps we have discussed. To see this, consider a swap in which a dollar annuity, R, is exchanged for an annuity in another currency, R^*. Given the foreign annuity, R^*, what is R?

We start with the observation that the present value of the two annuities must be the same. There are n payments and the time-0 forward price for a unit of foreign currency delivered at time t_i is F_{0,t_i}. This gives

$$\sum_{i=1}^{n}\left[RP_{0,t_i} - R^*F_{0,t_i}P_{0,t_i}\right] = 0$$

In calculating the present value of the payment R^*, we first convert to dollars by multiplying by F_{0,t_i}. We can then compute the present value using the dollar-denominated zero-coupon bond price, P_{0,t_i}. Solving for R gives

$$R = \frac{\sum_{i=1}^{n} P_{0,t_i} R^* F_{0,t_i}}{\sum_{i=1}^{n} P_{0,t_i}} \tag{8.8}$$

This expression is exactly like equation (8.2), with the implied forward rate, $r_0(t_{i-1}, t_i)$, replaced by the foreign-currency-denominated annuity payment translated into dollars, R^*F_{0,t_i}.

When coupon bonds are swapped, we have to account for the difference in maturity value as well as the coupon payment, which is an annuity. If the dollar bond has a par value of $1, the foreign bond will have a par value of $1/x_0$, where x_0 is the current exchange rate expressed as dollars per unit of the foreign currency. If R^* is the coupon rate on the foreign bond and R is the coupon rate on the dollar bond, the present value of the difference in payments on the two bonds is

$$\sum_{i=1}^{n} \left[R P_{0,t_i} - R^* F_{0,t_i} P_{0,t_i}/x_0 \right] + P_{0,t_n}(1 - F_{0,t_n}/x_0) = 0$$

The division by x_0 accounts for the fact that a \$1 bond is equivalent to $1/x_0$ bonds with a par value of 1 unit of the foreign currency. The dollar coupon in this case is

$$R = \frac{\sum_{i=1}^{n} P_{0,t_i} R^* F_{0,t_i}/x_0 + P_{0,t_n}(F_{0,t_n}/x_0 - 1)}{\sum_{i=1}^{n} P_{0,t_i}} \quad (8.9)$$

The fixed payment, R, is the dollar equivalent of the foreign coupon plus the amortized value of the difference in the maturity payments of the two bonds. Problem 8.14 asks you to verify that equation (8.9) gives 6% using the assumptions in Tables 8.5 and 8.6.

Other Currency Swaps

There are other kinds of currency swaps. The preceding examples assumed that all borrowing was fixed rate. Suppose the dollar-based borrower issues a euro-denominated loan with a *floating* interest rate. In this case there are two future unknowns: the exchange rate at which interest payments are converted and—because the bond is floating rate—the amount of the interest payment. Swapping this loan to a dollar loan is still straightforward, however; we just require one extra hedging transaction.

We first convert the floating interest rate into a fixed interest rate with a *euro* interest rate swap. The resulting fixed-rate euro-denominated exposure can then be hedged with currency forwards and converted into dollar interest rate exposure. Given the assumptions in Table 8.6, the euro-denominated loan would swap to a 3.5% floating-rate loan. From that point on, we are in the same position as in the previous example.

In general, we can swap fixed-to-fixed, fixed-to-floating, floating-to-fixed, and floating-to-floating. The analysis is similar in all cases.

One kind of swap that might on its face seem similar is a **diff swap,** short for differential swap. In this kind of swap, payments are made based on the difference in floating interest rates in two different currencies, with the notional amount in a single currency. For example, we might have a swap with a \$10m notional amount, but the swap would pay in dollars, based on the difference in a euro-denominated interest rate and a dollar-denominated interest rate. If the short-term euro interest rate rises from 3.5% to 3.8% with the dollar rate unchanged, the annual swap payment would be 30 basis points on \$10m, or \$30,000. This is like a standard interest rate swap, only for a diff swap, the reference interest rates are denominated in different currencies.

Standard currency forward contracts cannot be used to hedge a diff swap. The problem is that we can hedge the change in the foreign interest rate, but doing so requires a transaction denominated in the foreign currency. We can't easily hedge the exchange rate at which the value of the interest rate change is converted *because we don't know in advance how much currency will need to be converted.* In effect there is quantity uncertainty regarding the foreign currency to be converted.

8.4 SWAPTIONS

An option to enter into a swap is called a **swaption.** We can see how a swaption works by returning to the two-date oil swap example in Section 8.1. The 2-year oil swap price was $20.483. Suppose we are willing to buy oil at $20.483/barrel, but we would like to speculate on the swap price being even lower over the next 3 months.

Consider the following contract: If in 3 months the fixed price for a swap commencing in 9 months (1 year from today) is $20.483 or above, we enter into the swap, agreeing to pay $20.483 and receive the floating price for 2 years. If, on the other hand, the market swap price is below $20.483, we have no obligation. If the swap price in 3 months is $19.50, for example, we could enter into a swap at that time at the $19.50 price, or we could elect not to enter any swap.

With this contract we are entering into the swap with $20.483 as the swap price only when the market swap price is greater; hence, this contract will have a premium. In this example, we would have purchased a **payer swaption,** since we have the right, but not the obligation, to pay a fixed price of $20.483 for 2 years of oil. The counterparty has sold this swaption.

When exercised, the swaption commits us to transact at multiple times in the future. It is possible to exercise the option and then offset the swap with another swap, converting the stream of swap payments into a certain stream with a fixed present value. Thus, the swaption is analogous to an ordinary option, with the present value of the swap obligations (the price of the prepaid swap) as the underlying asset.

The strike price in this example is $20.483, so we have an at-the-money swaption. We could make the strike price different from $20.483. For example, we could reduce the swaption premium by setting the strike above $20.483.

Swaptions can be American or European, and the terms of the underlying swap—fixed price, floating index, settlement frequency, and tenor—will be precisely specified.

Example 8.3 Suppose we enter into a European payer oil swaption with a strike price of $21. The underlying swap commences in 1 year and has two annual settlements. After 3 months, the fixed price on the underlying swap is $21.50. We exercise the option, obligating us to pay $21/barrel for 2 years. If we wish to offset the swap, we can enter into a swap to receive the $21.50 fixed price. In year 1 and year 2 we will then receive $21.50 and pay $21, for a certain net cash flow each year of $0.50. The floating payments cancel.

A **receiver swaption** gives you the right to pay the floating price and receive the fixed strike price. Thus, the holder of a receiver swaption would exercise when the fixed swap price is below the strike.

Although we have used a commodity swaption in this example, an interest rate or currency swaption would be analogous, with payer and receiver swaptions giving the right to pay or receive the fixed interest rate.

8.5 TOTAL RETURN SWAPS

A **total return swap** is a swap in which one party pays the realized total return (dividends plus capital gains) on a reference asset and the other party pays a floating return such as LIBOR. The two parties exchange only the difference between these rates. The party paying the return on the reference asset is the *total return payer*.

As with other swaps, there are multiple settlement dates over the life of the swap. The cumulative effect for the total return payer is of being short the reference asset and long an asset paying the floating rate.

To see how a total return swap works in practice, Figure 8.8 illustrates the terms of a swap based on the S&P 500 index. While the number of details may seem confusing at first, the basic idea is very simple. Once a month, the broker-dealer pays to the counterparty the total return (capital gains plus dividends) on a hypothetical $100,000,000

FIGURE 8.8

Example of a term sheet for an equity swap based on the S&P 500 total return index. TBD means "To be determined."

Sample Equity Swap Term Sheet

First Leg		Second Leg	
Payer:	Broker-dealer	Payer:	Counterparty
Equity:	S&P Total Return Index	Floating Rate:	1-month USD LIBOR
Notional:	USD 100,000,000	Notional:	Equity notional
Number of Index Units:	TBD	Spread(bps):	+12bps
Initial Price:	TBD	Initial Rate:	TBD
Currency:	USD	Currency:	USD
Valuation Dates:	TBD	Day Count:	Actual/360
Payment Dates:	3 business days following valuation dates	Payment Dates:	Equity
Pay Frequency:	Monthly	Frequency:	Monthly
Return:	Total Return		

FIGURE 8.9

Cash flows for a total return swap. The total return payer pays the per-period total return on the reference asset, receiving the floating rate from the counterparty.

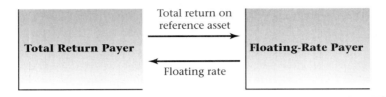

notional investment in the S&P 500 index. In return, the counterparty pays to the dealer interest (1-month LIBOR plus 12 basis points) on $100,000,000. The cash flows on a total return swap are illustrated in Figure 8.9.

Example 8.4 ABC Asset Management has a $2 billion investment in the S&P stock index. However, fund managers have become pessimistic about the market and would like to reduce their exposure to stocks from $2 billion to $1 billion. One way to do this is to sell $1 billion of stocks. However, the fund can retain the stock position but financially transfer the return of the stocks by engaging in a total return swap, obligating the fund to pay the total return (dividends plus capital gains) on the swapped stocks, while receiving a floating-rate return such as LIBOR on the swapped $1 billion notional amount. This avoids the transaction costs of a sale of physical stock.

Table 8.7 illustrates the payments on such a swap. In year 1, ABC earns 6.5% on the S&P index. However, on the portion it has swapped, it must pay the 6.5% in exchange for the 7.2% floating rate. The net payment of 0.7% leaves ABC as well off as if it had sold the index and invested in an asset paying the floating rate. In year 2, ABC receives 18%, compensating it for the difference between the 7.5% floating return and the 10.5% loss on the S&P index. Finally, in year 3 the S&P index does well, and ABC pays 16.5% to the counterparty.

You might wonder about the economics of a swap like this. The stock index on average earns a higher return than LIBOR. So if the fund swaps the stock index in exchange for LIBOR, it will on average make payments to the counterparty.

This observation is correct, but notice that the fund is paying the difference between the index return and a short-term interest rate—this difference is the risk premium on the index. In Section 5.3, we had a similar result for a forward contract: On average a short position in a forward contract on a stock index loses money because the risk premium has zero value.

TABLE 8.7 Illustration of cash flows on a total return swap with annual settlement for 3 years.

Year	S&P Capital Gain	S&P Dividend	Floating Rate	Net Payment to Total Return Payer
1	5%	1.5%	7.2%	0.7%
2	−12%	1.5%	7.5%	18.0%
3	22%	1.5%	7.0%	−16.5%

The average loss associated with swapping a stock index for LIBOR is the same as the average loss associated with selling the stock and buying a floating-rate note paying LIBOR. The swap makes the loss obvious since it requires a payment.

Some investors have used total return swaps to avoid taxes on foreign stocks. In many cases, countries impose withholding taxes on foreign investors, meaning that if, for example, a firm in country A pays a dividend, country A withholds a fraction of that dividend from investors based in country B. A total return swap enables a country B investor to own country A stocks without physically holding them, and thus in many cases without having to pay withholding taxes. For example, a U.S. investor could first swap out of a U.S. stock index and then swap into a European stock index, effectively becoming the counterparty for a European investor wanting to swap out of European stock exposure. Because net swap payments are not always recognized by withholding rules, this transaction can be more tax-efficient than holding the foreign stocks directly. Similarly, total return swaps have been used by investors to hedge a stock position so they could own voting shares without bearing the price risk of the stock (Hu and Black (2006)), a practice called "empty voting."

Another use of total return swaps is the management of credit risk. A fund manager holding corporate debt can swap the return on a particular bond for a floating-rate return. If the company that issued the bond goes bankrupt, the debt holder receives a payment on the swap compensating for the fact that the bond is worth a fraction of its face value.

Total return swaps are a crude tool for managing credit risk specifically. The problem is that bond prices also change due to interest rate changes. A corporate bond holder might wish to retain interest rate risk but not bankruptcy risk. Thus, **default swaps**, or **credit default swaps**, are essentially default options, in which the buyer pays a premium, usually amortized over a series of payments. If the reference asset experiences a "credit event" (for example, a failure to make a scheduled payment on a particular bond or class of bonds), then the seller makes a payment to the buyer. Frequently, these contracts split the return on the bond into the portion due to interest rate changes (with Treasury securities used as a reference) and the portion due to credit quality changes, with the swap making payments based only on the latter. We discuss these swaps in Chapter 12.

CHAPTER SUMMARY

A swap is a contract calling for an exchange of payments, on one or more dates, determined by the difference in two prices. A single-payment swap is the same thing as a cash-settled forward contract. In the simplest swaps, a fixed payment is periodically exchanged for a floating payment. A firm can use a swap to lock in a long-term commodity price, a fixed interest rate, or a fixed exchange rate. Considering only the present value of cash flows, the same result is obtained using a strip of forward contracts and swaps. The difference is that hedging with a strip of forward contracts results in net payments that are time-varying. In contrast, hedging with a swap results in net payments that are constant over time. The value of a swap is zero at inception, though as swap payments are made over time, the value of the swap can change in a predictable way.

The fixed price in a swap is a weighted average of the corresponding forward prices. The swap formulas in different cases all take the same general form. Let $f_0(t_i)$ denote the forward price for the floating payment in the swap. Then the fixed swap payment is

$$R = \frac{\sum_{i=1}^{n} P(0, t_i) f_0(t_i)}{\sum_{i=1}^{n} P(0, t_i)} \qquad (8.10)$$

This formula can be generalized to permit time variation in the notional amount and the swap price, and the swap can start on a deferred basis.

An important characteristic of swaps is that they require only the exchange of net payments, and not the payment of principal. So if a firm enters an interest rate swap, for example, it is required only to make payments based on the difference in interest rates, not on the underlying principal. As a result, swaps have less credit risk than bonds.

Total return swaps involve exchanging the return on an asset for a floating rate such as LIBOR. The term *swap* is also used to describe agreements like credit default swaps, which are insurance against default on a bond, and the Procter & Gamble swap (Box 8.2), which required payments based on the difference in interest rates and bond prices, as well as default swaps.

FURTHER READING

The same formulas used to price swaps will appear again in the context of structured notes, which we will encounter in Chapter 12.

Litzenberger (1992) provides an overview of the swap market. Turnbull (1987) discusses arguments purporting to show that the use of swaps can have a positive net present value. Default swaps are discussed by Tavakoli (1998). Because of convexity bias (Chapter 7), the market interest rate swap curve is not exactly the same as the swap curve constructed from Eurodollar futures. This is discussed in Burghardt and Hoskins (1995) and Gupta and Subrahmanyam (2000). The SEC complaint against J. P. Morgan Chase is at http://www.sec.gov/litigation/complaints/comp18252.htm.

TABLE 8.8

Quarter	1	2	3	4	5	6	7	8
Oil forward price	21	21.1	20.8	20.5	20.2	20	19.9	19.8
Gas swap price	2.2500	2.4236	2.3503	2.2404	2.2326	2.2753	2.2583	2.2044
Zero-coupon bond price	0.9852	0.9701	0.9546	0.9388	0.9231	0.9075	0.8919	0.8763
Euro-denominated zero-coupon bond price	0.9913	0.9825	0.9735	0.9643	0.9551	0.9459	0.9367	0.9274
Euro forward price ($/€)	0.9056	0.9115	0.9178	0.9244	0.9312	0.9381	0.9452	0.9524

PROBLEMS

Some of the problems that follow use Table 8.8. Assume that the current exchange rate is $0.90/€.

8.1 Consider the oil swap example in Section 8.1 with the 1- and 2-year forward prices of $22/barrel and $23/barrel. The 1- and 2-year interest rates are 6% and 6.5%. Verify that the new 2-year swap price is $22.483.

8.2 Suppose that oil forward prices for 1 year, 2 years, and 3 years are $20, $21, and $22. The 1-year effective annual interest rate is 6.0%, the 2-year interest rate is 6.5%, and the 3-year interest rate is 7.0%.

    a. What is the 3-year swap price?

    b. What is the price of a 2-year swap beginning in 1 year? (That is, the first swap settlement will be in 2 years and the second in 3 years.)

8.3 Consider the same 3-year oil swap. Suppose a dealer is paying the fixed price and receiving floating. What position in oil forward contracts will hedge oil price risk in this position? Verify that the present value of the locked-in net cash flows is zero.

8.4 Consider the 3-year swap in the previous example. Suppose you are the fixed-rate payer in the swap. How much have you overpaid relative to the forward price after the first swap settlement? What is the cumulative overpayment after the second swap settlement? Verify that the cumulative overpayment is zero after the third payment. (Be sure to account for interest.)

8.5 Consider the same 3-year swap. Suppose you are a dealer who is paying the fixed oil price and receiving the floating price. Suppose that you enter into the swap and immediately thereafter all interest rates rise 50 basis points (oil forward prices are unchanged). What happens to the value of your swap position? What if interest rates fall 50 basis points? What hedging instrument would have protected you against interest rate risk in this position?

8.6 Supposing the effective quarterly interest rate is 1.5%, what are the per-barrel swap prices for 4-quarter and 8-quarter oil swaps? (Use oil forward prices in Table 8.8.) What is the total cost of prepaid 4- and 8-quarter swaps?

8.7 Using the information about zero-coupon bond prices and oil forward prices in Table 8.8, construct the set of swap prices for oil for 1 through 8 quarters.

8.8 Using the information in Table 8.8, what is the swap price of a 4-quarter oil swap with the first settlement occurring in the third quarter?

8.9 Using the zero-coupon bond prices and oil forward prices in Table 8.8, what is the price of an 8-period swap for which 2 barrels of oil are delivered in even-numbered quarters and 1 barrel of oil in odd-numbered quarters?

8.10 Using the zero-coupon bond prices and natural gas swap prices in Table 8.8, what are gas forward prices for each of the 8 quarters?

8.11 What is the fixed rate in a 5-quarter interest rate swap with the first settlement in quarter 2?

8.12 Using the zero-coupon bond yields in Table 8.8, what is the fixed rate in a 4-quarter interest rate swap? What is the fixed rate in an 8-quarter interest rate swap?

8.13 What 8-quarter dollar annuity is equivalent to an 8-quarter annuity of €1?

8.14 Using the assumptions in Tables 8.5 and 8.6, verify that equation (8.9) equals 6%.

8.15 Using the information in Table 8.8, what are the *euro-denominated* fixed rates for 4- and 8-quarter swaps?

8.16 Using the information in Table 8.8, verify that it is possible to derive the 8-quarter dollar interest swap rate from the 8-quarter euro interest swap rate by using equation (8.9).

part 3

Options

In earlier chapters we have seen how options work and introduced some of the terminology related to options. In this part of the book we return to options, with the goal of understanding how they are priced.

Forward contracts (and futures and swaps) represent a binding commitment to buy or sell the underlying asset in the future. Because the commitment is binding, but deferred, time value of money is the main economic idea used in determining forward prices.

Options, on the other hand, need not be exercised. Intuitively, you would expect the probability distribution of the stock to affect the option price. Consequently, in discussing option pricing we will use some concepts from basic probability. However, it turns out that there is much to say about options without needing to think about the probability distribution of the stock. In Chapter 9 we explore concepts such as parity in more depth and discuss some basic intuition about option prices that can be gleaned using only time value of money arguments.

Chapter 10 introduces the binomial option pricing model. This model assumes that the stock can move only in a very simple way, but provides the intuition underlying more complicated option pricing calculations. Chapter 11 presents the Black-Scholes option pricing formula, which is one of the most important formulas in finance.

Parity and Other Option Relationships

Up to this point we have primarily studied the pricing of contracts entailing *firm commitments*, such as forwards, futures, and swaps. These contracts do not permit either party to back away from the agreement. Optionality occurs when backing away is possible. The principal question in option pricing is: *How do you value the right to back away from a commitment?*

Before we delve into pricing models, we devote this chapter to refining our common sense about options. For example, Table 9.1 contains call and put prices for IBM for three different strikes and three different expiration dates. Based on our earlier discussions of put-call parity, you might be pondering the difference between put and call prices at a given strike. Here are some of the other things you might wonder about when you examine the table:

- It appears that, for a given strike, options prices increase with time to expiration. (For example, the April options are more expensive than the January and November options.)
- Call premiums decrease as the strike price increases and put premiums increase as the strike price increases.
- Both call and put premiums change by less than the change in the strike price. (When strikes change by $10, premiums change by less than $10.)

Are we likely to see the same relationships from examining different options on different underlying assets? Also, these are American options. What would be different if these options were European rather than American?

In this chapter we will discuss these questions, but you should take a minute and think about the answers now, drawing on what you have learned in previous chapters. While doing so, pay attention to *how* you are trying to come up with the answers. What constitutes a persuasive argument? Along with finding the answers, we want to understand how to think about questions like these.

TABLE 9.1 IBM option prices, dollars per share, October 16, 2007. The closing price of IBM on that day was $119.60.

Strike	Expiration	Calls Bid ($)	Calls Ask ($)	Puts Bid ($)	Puts Ask ($)
110	Nov 2007	10.70	11.00	0.95	1.05
120	Nov 2007	3.70	3.90	4.00	4.20
130	Nov 2007	0.65	0.75	10.80	11.20
110	Jan 2008	12.80	13.10	2.30	2.45
120	Jan 2008	6.20	6.40	5.60	5.80
130	Jan 2008	2.20	2.35	11.70	12.00
110	April 2008	14.90	15.30	3.60	3.80
120	April 2008	8.60	8.90	7.10	7.40
130	April 2008	4.20	4.50	12.80	13.10

Source: Chicago Board Options Exchange (www.cboe.com).

9.1 PUT-CALL PARITY

Put-call parity is perhaps the single most important relationship among option prices. In Chapter 2 we argued that synthetic forwards (created by buying the call and selling the put) must be priced consistently with actual forwards. The basic parity relationship for European options with the same strike price and time to expiration is

$$C(K, T) - P(K, T) = \text{PV}_{0,T}(F_{0,T} - K) \qquad (9.1)$$
$$= e^{-rT}(F_{0,T} - K)$$

where $C(K, T)$ is the price of a European call with strike price K and time to expiration T, $P(K, T)$ is the price of a European put, $F_{0,T}$ is the forward price for the underlying asset, K is the strike price, T is the time to expiration of the options, and $\text{PV}_{0,T}$ denotes the present value over the life of the options. Note that $e^{-rT} F_{0,T}$ is the prepaid forward price for the asset and that $e^{-rT} K$ is the prepaid forward price for the strike, so we can also think of parity in terms of prepaid forward prices.

The intuition for equation (9.1) is that buying a call and selling a put with the strike equal to the forward price ($F_{0,T} = K$) creates a synthetic forward contract and hence must have a zero price. If we create a synthetic long forward position at a price other than the forward price, we have to pay $\text{PV}_{0,T}(F_{0,T} - K)$ since this is the benefit of buying the asset at the strike price rather than the forward price. You should be aware that parity generally fails for American-style options, which may be exercised prior to maturity.

We now consider the parity relationship in more detail for different underlying assets.

Options on Stocks

If the underlying asset is a stock and Div is the stream of dividends paid on the stock, then from Chapter 5, $e^{-rT}F_{0,T} = S_0 - \text{PV}_{0,T}(\text{Div})$. Thus, from equation (9.1), the parity relationship for European options on stocks is

$$C(K, T) = P(K, T) + [S_0 - \text{PV}_{0,T}(\text{Div})] - e^{-rT}K \qquad (9.2)$$

where S_0 is the current stock price and $\text{PV}_{0,T}(\text{Div})$ is the present value of dividends payable over the life of the option. For index options, we know that $S_0 - \text{PV}_{0,T}(\text{Div}) = S_0 e^{-\delta T}$. Hence, we can write

$$C(K, T) = P(K, T) + S_0 e^{-\delta T} - \text{PV}_{0,T}(K)$$

Example 9.1 Suppose that the price of a non-dividend-paying stock is $40, the continuously compounded interest rate is 8%, and options have 3 months to expiration. A 40-strike European call sells for $2.78 and a 40-strike European put sells for $1.99. This is consistent with equation (9.2) since

$$\$2.78 = \$1.99 + \$40 - \$40 e^{-0.08 \times 0.25}$$

Why does the price of an at-the-money call exceed the price of an at-the-money put by $0.79? We can answer this question by recognizing that buying a call and selling a put is a synthetic alternative to buying the stock, with different cash flows than an outright purchase.

Figure 9.1 represents the cash flows for a synthetic and outright purchase. Note that the synthetic purchase of the stock entails a cash outflow of $0.79 today and $40 at expiration, compared with an outright purchase that entails spending $40 today.

Both positions result in the ownership of the stock 3 months from today. With the outright purchase of stock, we have possession of the stock for 3 months. With the

FIGURE 9.1

Cash flows for outright purchase of stock and for synthetic stock created by buying a 40-strike call and selling a 40-strike put.

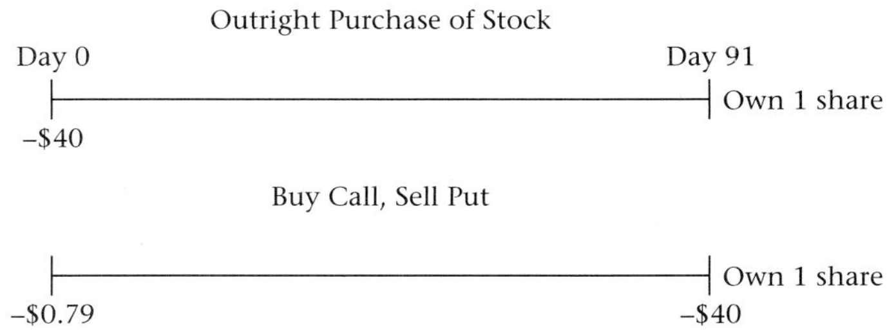

Outright Purchase of Stock

Day 0 ————————————————— Day 91
−$40   Own 1 share

Buy Call, Sell Put

————————————————— Own 1 share
−$0.79   −$40

synthetic purchase, we will own the stock if the price is above $40 because we will exercise the call. We will also own the stock if the price is below $40, because we sold a put that will be exercised; as the put-writer we have to buy the stock. In either case, in 3 months we pay $40 and acquire the stock.

Finally, the dollar risk of the positions is the same. In both cases, a $1 change in the stock price at 3 months will lead to a $1 change in the value of the position. In other words, both positions entail economic ownership of the stock. You can verify that the risk is the same by drawing a profit-and-loss diagram for the two positions.

Thus, by buying the call and selling the put we own the stock, but we have deferred the payment of $40 until expiration. To obtain this deferral we must pay 3 months of interest on the $40, the present value of which is $0.79. *The option premiums differ by interest on the deferral of payment for the stock*. Interest is the reason that at-the-money European calls on non-dividend-paying stock always sell for more than at-the-money European puts with the same expiration.

Note that if we reverse the position by selling the call and buying the put, then we are synthetically short-selling the stock. In 3 months, the options will be exercised and we will receive $40. In this case, the $0.79 compensates us for deferring receipt of the stock price.

There are differences between the outright and synthetic positions. First, the stock pays dividends and the synthetic does not. This example assumed that the stock paid no dividends. If it did, the cost of the actual stock would exceed that of the synthetic by the present value of dividends paid over the life of the options. Second, the actual stock has voting rights, unlike the synthetic position.

Example 9.2 Make the same assumptions as in Example 9.1, except suppose that the stock pays a $5 dividend just before expiration. The price of the European call is $0.74 and the price of the European put is $4.85. These prices satisfy parity with dividends, equation (9.2):

$$\$0.74 - \$4.85 = (\$40 - \$5e^{-0.08 \times 0.25}) - \$40e^{-0.08 \times 0.25}$$

The call price is higher than the put price by interest on the strike ($0.79) and lower by the present value of the dividend ($4.90), for a net difference of $4.11.

In this example, the at-the-money call sells for less than an at-the-money put since dividends on the stock exceed the value of interest on the strike price.

It is worth mentioning a common but erroneous explanation for the higher premium of an at-the-money call compared to an at-the-money put. The profit on a call is potentially unlimited since the stock price can go to infinity, while the profit on a put can be no greater than the strike price. This explanation seems to suggest that the call should be more expensive than the put.[1] However, parity shows that the true reason for the call being more expensive (as in Example 9.1) is time value of money.

Synthetic stock Parity provides a cookbook for the synthetic creation of options, stocks, and T-bills.

The example above shows that buying a call and selling a put is like buying the stock, except that the timing of the payment for the stock differs in the two cases. Rewriting equation (9.2) gives us

$$S_0 = C(K,T) - P(K,T) + \text{PV}_{0,T}(\text{Div}) + e^{-rT}K \tag{9.3}$$

To match the cash flows for an outright purchase of the stock, in addition to buying the call and selling the put, we have to lend the present value of the strike and dividends to be paid over the life of the option. We then receive the stock in 91 days.

Example 9.3 In Example 9.1, $\text{PV}_{0,0.25}(K) = \$40e^{-0.08 \times 0.25} = \$39.21$. Hence, by buying the call for $2.78, selling the put for $1.99, and lending $39.21, we invest a total of $40 today. In 91 days, we have the two options and a T-bill worth $40. We acquire the stock via one of the exercised options, using the $40 T-bill to pay the strike price.

Synthetic T-bills If we buy the stock, sell the call, and buy the put, we have purchased the stock and short-sold the synthetic stock. This transaction gives us a hedged position that has no risk but requires investment. Parity shows us that

$$S_0 + P(K,T) - C(K,T) = \text{PV}_{0,T}(K) + \text{PV}_{0,T}(\text{Div})$$

We have thus created a position that costs $\text{PV}(K) + \text{PV}_{0,T}(\text{Div})$ and that pays $K + FV_{0,T}(\text{Div})$ at expiration. This is a synthetic Treasury bill.

Example 9.4 In Example 9.1, $\text{PV}_{0,0.25}(K) = \$39.21$. Hence, by buying the stock, buying a put, and selling the call, we can create a T-bill that costs $39.21 and pays $40 in 91 days.

Since T-bills are taxed differently than stocks, the ability to create a synthetic Treasury bill with the stock and options creates problems for tax and accounting authorities. How should the return on this transaction be taxed—as a stock transaction or as interest income? Tax rules call for this position to be taxed as interest, but you can imagine taxpayers trying to skirt these rules.

The creation of a synthetic T-bill by buying the stock, buying a put, and selling a call is called a **conversion.** If we short the stock, buy a call, and sell a put, we have created a synthetic short T-bill position and this is called a **reverse conversion.**

---

[1] In fact, the argument also seems to suggest that every stock is worth more than its price!

Synthetic options Parity tells us that

$$C(K, T) = S_0 - \text{PV}_{0,T}(\text{Div}) - \text{PV}_{0,T}(K) + P(K, T)$$

and that

$$P(K, T) = C(K, T) - S_0 + \text{PV}_{0,T}(K) + \text{PV}_{0,T}(\text{Div})$$

The first relation says that a call is equivalent to a leveraged position on the underlying asset $[S_0 - \text{PV}_{0,T}(\text{Div}) - \text{PV}(K)]$, which is insured by the purchase of a put. The second relation says that a put is equivalent to a short position on the stock, insured by the purchase of a call.

Options on Currencies

Suppose we have options to buy euros by paying dollars. From our discussion of currency forward contracts in Chapter 5, we know that the dollar forward price for a euro is $F_{0,T} = x_0 e^{(r - r_{\euro})T}$, where x_0 is the current exchange rate denominated as \$/€, $r_{\euro}$ is the euro-denominated interest rate, and r is the dollar-denominated interest rate. The parity relationship for options to buy 1 euro by paying x_0 is then

$$C(K, T) - P(K, T) = x_0 e^{-r_{\euro} T} - K e^{-rT} \tag{9.4}$$

Buying a euro call and selling a euro put is equivalent to lending euros and borrowing dollars. Equation (9.4) tells us that the difference in the call and put premiums simply reflects the difference in the amount borrowed and loaned, in the currency of the country in which the options are denominated.

Example 9.5 Suppose the current \$/€ exchange rate is 0.9, the dollar-denominated interest rate is 6%, and the euro-denominated interest rate is 4%. By buying a dollar-denominated euro call with a strike of \$0.92 and selling a dollar-denominated euro put with the same strike, we construct a position where in 1 year we will buy €1 by paying \$0.92. We can accomplish the same thing by lending the present value of €1 today (with a dollar cost of $\$0.9 e^{-0.04} = \$0.8647$) and paying for this by borrowing the present value of \$0.92 ($\$0.92 e^{-0.06} = \$0.8664$). The proceeds from borrowing exceed the amount we need to lend by \$0.0017. Equation (9.4) performs exactly this calculation, giving us a difference between the call premium and put premium of

$$\begin{aligned} x_0 e^{-r_{\euro} T} - K e^{-rT} &= 0.9 \$/\euro \times \euro e^{-0.04 \times 1} - \$0.92 \times e^{-0.06 \times 1} \\ &= \$0.8647 - \$0.8664 \\ &= -\$0.0017 \end{aligned}$$

Options on Bonds

Finally, we can construct the parity relationship for options on bonds. The prepaid forward for a bond differs from the bond price due to coupon payments (which are like dividends). Thus, if the bond price is B_0, we have

$$C(K, T) = P(K, T) + [B_0 - \text{PV}_{0,T}(\text{Coupons})] - \text{PV}_{0,T}(K) \qquad (9.5)$$

Note that for a pure-discount bond, the parity relationship is exactly like that for a non-dividend-paying stock.

9.2 GENERALIZED PARITY AND EXCHANGE OPTIONS

The preceding section showed how the parity relationship works for different underlying assets. Now we will generalize parity to apply to the case where the strike asset is not necessarily cash but could be any other asset. This version of parity includes all previous versions as special cases.

Suppose we have an option to exchange one asset for another. Let the underlying asset, asset A, have price S_t, and the strike asset (the asset which, at our discretion, we surrender in exchange for the underlying asset), asset B, have the price Q_t. Let $F^P_{t,T}(S)$ denote the time t price of a prepaid forward on the underlying asset, paying S_T at time T, and let $F^P_{t,T}(Q)$ denote the time t price of a prepaid forward on asset B, paying Q_T at time T. We use the notation $C(S_t, Q_t, T - t)$ to denote the time t price of an option with $T - t$ periods to expiration, which gives us the right to give up asset B in exchange for asset A. $P(S_t, Q_t, T - t)$ is defined similarly as the right to give up asset A in exchange for asset B. Now suppose that the call payoff at time T is

$$C(S_T, Q_T, 0) = \max(0, S_T - Q_T)$$

and the put payoff is

$$P(S_T, Q_T, 0) = \max(0, Q_T - S_T)$$

Then for European options we have this form of the parity equation:

$$\boxed{C(S_t, Q_t, T - t) - P(S_t, Q_t, T - t) = F^P_{t,T}(S) - F^P_{t,T}(Q)} \qquad (9.6)$$

The use of prepaid forward prices in the parity relationship completely takes into account the dividend and time value of money considerations. This version of parity tells us that there is nothing special about an option having the strike amount designated as cash. In general, options can be designed to exchange any asset for any other asset, and the relative put and call premiums are determined by prices of prepaid forwards on the underlying and strike assets.

To prove equation (9.6), we can use a payoff table in which we buy a call, sell a put, sell a prepaid forward on A, and buy a prepaid forward on B. This transaction is illustrated in Table 9.2.

If the strategy in Table 9.2 does not pay zero at expiration, there is an arbitrage opportunity. Thus, we expect equation (9.6) to hold. All European options satisfy this formula, whatever the underlying asset.

TABLE 9.2 Payoff table demonstrating that there is an arbitrage opportunity unless $-C(S_t, Q_t, T-t) + P(S_t, Q_t, T-t) + F^P_{t,T}(S) - F^P_{t,T}(Q) = 0$.

Transaction	Time 0	Expiration $S_T \leq Q_T$	$S_T > Q_T$
Buy call	$-C(S_t, Q_t, T-t)$	0	$S_T - Q_T$
Sell put	$P(S_t, Q_t, T-t)$	$S_T - Q_T$	0
Sell prepaid Forward on A	$F^P_{t,T}(S)$	$-S_T$	$-S_T$
Buy prepaid Forward on B	$-F^P_{t,T}(Q)$	Q_T	Q_T
Total	$-C(S_t, Q_t, T-t)$ $+P(S_t, Q_t, T-t)$ $+F^P_{t,T}(S) - F^P_{t,T}(Q)$	0	0

Example 9.6 Suppose that non-dividend-paying stock A has a price of $20, and non-dividend-paying stock B has a price of $25. Because neither stock pays dividends, their prepaid forward prices equal their prices. If A is the underlying asset and B is the strike asset, then put-call parity implies that

$$\text{Call} - \text{put} = \$20 - \$25 = -\$5$$

The put is $5 more expensive than the call for any time to expiration of the options.

Options to Exchange Stock

Executive stock options are sometimes constructed so that the strike price of the option is the price of an index, rather than a fixed cash amount. The idea is to have an option that pays off only when the company outperforms competitors, rather than one that pays off simply because all stock prices have gone up. As a hypothetical example of this, suppose Bill Gates, chairman of Microsoft, is given compensation options that pay off only if Microsoft outperforms Google. He will exercise these options if and only if the share price of Microsoft, S_{MSFT}, exceeds the share price of Google, S_{GOOG}, i.e., $S_{\text{MSFT}} > S_{\text{GOOG}}$. From Gates's perspective, this is a call option, with the payoff

$$\max(0, S_{\text{MSFT}} - S_{\text{GOOG}})$$

Now consider the compensation option for Eric Schmidt, CEO of Google. He will receive a compensation option that pays off only if Google outperforms Microsoft, i.e.,

$$\max(0, S_{\text{GOOG}} - S_{\text{MSFT}})$$

This is a call from Schmidt's perspective.

Here is the interesting twist: Schmidt's Google call looks to Gates like a Microsoft put! And Gates's Microsoft call looks to Schmidt like a Google put. Either option can be viewed as a put or call; it is simply a matter of perspective. *The distinction between a put and a call in this example depends upon what we label as the underlying asset and what we label as the strike asset.*

What Are Calls and Puts?

The preceding discussion suggests that labeling an option as a call or put is always a matter of convention. It is an important convention because we use it all the time in talking about options. Nevertheless, in general we can interpret calls as being puts and vice versa. We can see why by using an analogy.

When you go to the grocery store to obtain bananas, you typically say that you are *buying* bananas. The actual transaction involves handing cash to the grocer and receiving a banana. This is an exchange of one asset (cash) for another (a banana). We could also describe the transaction by saying that we are *selling cash* (in exchange for bananas). The point is that an exchange occurs, and we can describe it as either buying the thing we receive or selling the thing we surrender.

Any transaction is an exchange of one thing for another. Whether we say we are buying or selling is a matter of convention. This insight may not impress your grocer, but it is important for options since it suggests that the labeling we commonly use to distinguish calls and puts is a matter of convention.

To see how a call could be considered a put, consider a call option on a stock. This is the right to exchange a given number of dollars, the strike price K, for stock worth S, if the stock is worth more than the dollars. For example, suppose that if $S > K$, we earn $S - K$. We can view this as either of two transactions:

- Buying one share of stock by paying K. In this case we exercise when $S > K$. This is a call option on stock.

- Selling K dollars in exchange for one share of stock. Again we exercise when $S > K$—i.e., when the dollars we sell are worth less than the stock. This is a put option on dollars, with a share of stock as the strike asset.

Under either interpretation, if $S < K$ we do not exercise the option. If the dollars are worth more than the stock, we would not sell them for the stock.

Now consider a put option on a stock. The put option confers the right to exchange one share of stock for a given number of dollars. Suppose $S < K$; we earn $K - S$. We can view this in either of two ways:

- Selling one share of stock at the price K.

- Buying K dollars by paying one share of stock. This is a call where we have the right to give up stock to obtain dollars.

If $S > K$, we do not exercise under either interpretation. If the dollars are worth less than the stock, we would not pay the stock to obtain the dollars.

Currency Options

The idea that calls can be relabeled as puts is not just academic; it is used frequently by currency traders. A currency transaction involves the exchange of one kind of currency for another. In this context, it is obvious to market participants that referring to a particular currency as having been bought or sold is a matter of convention. Labeling a particular option a call or a put depends upon which currency you regard as your home currency.

In the following example we will show that a dollar-denominated call option on euros, which gives you the right to pay dollars to receive euros, is equivalent to a euro-denominated put option on dollars, which gives the right to sell a dollar for euros. Obviously, the strike prices and option quantities must be chosen appropriately for there to be an equivalence.

We will say that an option is "dollar-denominated" if the strike price and premium are denominated in dollars. An option is "euro-denominated" if the strike price and premium are in euros.

Suppose the current exchange rate is $x_0 = 0.90\$/€$, and consider the following two options:[2]

1. A 1-year *dollar-denominated call option* on euros with a strike price of $0.92 and premium of $0.0337. In 1 year, the owner of the option has the right to buy €1 for $0.92. The payoff on this option, in dollars, is therefore

$$\max(0, x_1 - 0.92)$$

2. A 1-year *euro-denominated put option* on dollars with a strike of $\frac{1}{0.92} = €1.0870$. The premium of this option is €0.0407. In 1 year the owner of this put has the right to give up $1 and receive €1.0870; the owner will exercise the put when $1 is worth less than €1.0870. The euro value of $1 in 1 year will be $1/x_1$. Hence, the payoff of this option is

$$\max\left(0, \frac{1}{0.92} - \frac{1}{x_1}\right)$$

Since $x_1 > 0.92$ exactly when $\frac{1}{0.92} > \frac{1}{x_1}$, the euro-denominated dollar put will be exercised when, and only when, the dollar-denominated euro call is exercised.

Though they will be exercised under the same circumstances, the dollar-denominated euro call and the euro-denominated dollar put differ in two respects:

- The scale of the two options is different. The dollar-denominated euro call is based on 1 euro (which has a current dollar value of $0.90), and the euro-denominated dollar put is based on 1 dollar.
- The currency of denomination is different.

---

[2] These are Black-Scholes prices with a current exchange rate of 0.90 $/€, a dollar-denominated interest rate of 6%, a euro-denominated interest rate of 4%, and exchange rate volatility of 10%.

9.2 Generalized Parity and Exchange Options

TABLE 9.3   The equivalence of buying a dollar-denominated euro call and a euro-denominated dollar put. In transaction I, we buy $\frac{1}{0.92}$ dollar-denominated call options permitting us to buy €1 for a strike price of $0.92. In transaction II, we buy one euro-denominated put permitting us to sell $1 for a strike price of €$\frac{1}{0.92}$ = €1.0870. The option premium is €0.0407.

	Transaction	Year 0 $	Year 0 €	Year 1 $ ($x_1 < 0.92$)	Year 1 € ($x_1 < 0.92$)	Year 1 $ ($x_1 \geq 0.92$)	Year 1 € ($x_1 \geq 0.92$)
I:	Buy $\frac{1}{0.92}$ euro calls	−0.0366	—	0	0	−1	$\frac{1}{0.92}$
II:	Convert dollars to euros	−0.0366	0.0407				
	Buy dollar put		−0.0407	0	0	−1	$\frac{1}{0.92}$

We can equate the scale of the two options by holding more of the smaller option or less of the larger option: We can either scale up the dollar-denominated euro calls, holding $\frac{1}{0.92}$ of them, or we can scale down the euro-denominated dollar puts, holding 0.92 of them. To see the equivalence of the euro call and the dollar put, consider the following two transactions:

1. Buy $\frac{1}{0.92}$ 1-year dollar-denominated euro call options with a strike of $0.92. If we exercise, we will give up $1 for €$\frac{1}{0.92}$. The cost is $\frac{1}{0.92} \times \$0.0337 = \$0.0366$.

2. Buy one 1-year euro-denominated put option on dollars with a strike of €1.0870. The cost of this in dollars is 0.90$/€ × €0.0407 = $0.0366. When the option expires, convert the proceeds back from euros to dollars.

Table 9.3 compares the payoffs of these two option positions. At exercise, each position results in surrendering $1 for €$\frac{1}{0.92}$ if $x_1 > 0.92$. Thus, the two positions must cost the same, or else there is an arbitrage opportunity.

We can summarize this result algebraically. The price of a dollar-denominated foreign currency call with strike K, when the current exchange rate is x_0, is $C_\$(x_0, K, T)$. The price of a foreign-currency–denominated dollar put with strike $\frac{1}{K}$, when the exchange rate is $\frac{1}{x_0}$, is $P_f(\frac{1}{x_0}, \frac{1}{K}, T)$. Adjusting for currency and scale differences, the prices are related by

$$C_\$(x_0, K, T) = x_0 K P_f\left(\frac{1}{x_0}, \frac{1}{K}, T\right) \tag{9.7}$$

This insight—that calls in one currency are the same as puts in the other—is commonplace among currency traders. While this observation is interesting in and of itself, its generalization to *all* options provides a fresh perspective for thinking about what calls and puts actually are.

9.3 COMPARING OPTIONS WITH RESPECT TO STYLE, MATURITY, AND STRIKE

We now examine how option prices change when there are changes in option characteristics, such as exercise style (American or European), the strike price, and time to expiration. Remarkably, we can say a great deal without a pricing model and without making any assumptions about the distribution of the underlying asset.[3] Thus, *whatever* the particular option model or stock-price distribution used for valuing a given option, we can still expect option prices to behave in certain ways.

Here are the results that we will discuss in this section:

European vs. American options. American options are always at least as expensive as otherwise identical European options.[4]

Early exercise of American options. It is never optimal to early-exercise American options on a non-dividend-paying stock. American put options and American call options on different underlying assets may be early-exercised.

Time to expiration. Longer-lived American options are always at least as valuable as otherwise identical shorter-lived options. Longer-lived European calls and puts may be more or less expensive.

Strike price. If the strike price increases by $1, the price of a call will decrease by less than $1 and the price of a put will increase by less than $1. If the strike price continues to increase, the call price will decrease at a decreasing rate and the put price will increase at an increasing rate.

A word of warning before we begin this discussion: If you examine option-price listings online or in the newspaper, you may find option prices that seemingly give rise to arbitrage opportunities. This can happen if the reported prices are stale, i.e., they do not reflect current market prices. More generally, however, it is important to understand that an apparent arbitrage opportunity only becomes genuine when bid-ask spreads (see Table 9.1), commissions, costs of short-selling, and market impact are taken into account. The results we discuss in this chapter are known to most market participants. Caveat arbitrageur!

European Versus American Options

Since an American option can be exercised at any time, it must always be at least as valuable as an otherwise identical European option. You can always convert an American

---

[3] The "theory of rational option pricing," on which this section is based, was first presented in 1973 by Robert Merton in an astonishing paper (Merton (1973b)). This material is also superbly exposited in Cox and Rubinstein (1985).

[4] "Otherwise identical" is a phrase we will use often in this section. It simply means that two options are the same except for one attribute. For example, European and American options are otherwise identical if they have the same underlying asset, time to expiration, and strike price.

option into a European option by just deciding not to exercise the option. Therefore, the American option cannot be less valuable. Thus, we have

$$C_{\text{Amer}}(S, K, T) \geq C_{\text{Eur}}(S, K, T) \tag{9.8a}$$

$$P_{\text{Amer}}(S, K, T) \geq P_{\text{Eur}}(S, K, T) \tag{9.8b}$$

We will see that there are times when the right to early-exercise is worthless, and, hence, American and European options have the same value.

Maximum and Minimum Option Prices

It is often useful to understand just how expensive or inexpensive an option can be. Here are some basic limits.

Calls The price of a European call option

- cannot be negative, because the call need not be exercised;
- cannot exceed the stock price, because the best that can happen with a call is that you end up owning the stock; and
- must be at least as great as the price implied by parity with a zero put value. That is,

$$C(S, K, T) \geq \text{PV}_{0,T}(F_{0,T}) - \text{PV}_{0,T}(K) \tag{9.9}$$

Puts Similarly, the price of a European put option

- cannot be negative, because the put need not be exercised;
- cannot be worth more than the strike price, since the strike price is the greatest payoff a put can have (if the stock price drops to zero, the put pays K when exercised); and
- must be at least as great as the price implied by parity with a zero call value, i.e.,

$$P(S, K, T) \geq \text{PV}_{0,T}(K) - \text{PV}_{0,T}(F_{0,T}) \tag{9.10}$$

Example 9.7 Suppose a non-dividend-paying stock has a price of $100 and the continuously compounded interest rate is 8%. The forward price of the stock is therefore $100 \times e^{0.08} = \$108.329$. Using equation (9.9), the minimum price of a 105-strike call option is

$$\text{PV}(F_{0,1}) - \text{PV}_{0,1}K = e^{-0.08}[108.329 - 105] = \$3.073$$

The minimum price of the otherwise equivalent put is zero.

Using equation (9.10), the minimum price of a 110-strike put option is

$$\text{PV}_{0,1}K - \text{PV}(F_{0,1}) = e^{-0.08}[110 - 108.329] = \$1.543$$

The minimum price of the otherwise equivalent call is zero.

Early Exercise for American Options

It can be difficult to say when an option *should* be exercised prior to maturity, but there are straightforward conditions under which an option *should not* be exercised prior to expiration. We will now discuss these "no early-exercise" conditions. If you understand the intuition behind these conditions, you will have deepened your understanding of options in general.

We will see that an American call option on a non-dividend-paying stock should never be exercised prior to expiration. You may, however, rationally exercise an American-style put option prior to expiration.

Calls on a non-dividend-paying stock It is never profitable to exercise a call on a non-dividend-paying stock, because the price of the call will always exceed what you would receive from exercise. The proof of this proposition uses put-call parity.

If you exercise a call option at time t, you pay the strike price, K, and receive the stock price, S_t, so your net payoff is $S_t - K$. As an alternative to exercising the option, you could sell it and receive the premium, $C_{\text{Amer}}(S_t, K, T - t)$. To demonstrate that you would never want to exercise the call, we want to show that

$$C_{\text{Amer}}(S_t, K, T - t) > S_t - K$$

If this inequality holds, you would lose money by early-exercising (receiving $S_t - K$) as opposed to selling the option (receiving $C_{\text{Amer}}(S_t, K, T - t)$). We will use put-call parity to demonstrate that this inequality holds.

If the option expires at T, parity implies that for a European option,

$$C_{\text{Eur}}(S_t, K, T - t) = \underbrace{S_t - K}_{\text{Exercise value}} + \underbrace{P_{\text{Eur}}(S_t, K, T - t)}_{\text{Insurance against } S_T < K} + \underbrace{K(1 - e^{-r(T-t)})}_{\text{Time value of money on } K}$$

(9.11)

The put price, $P_{\text{Eur}}(S_t, K, T - t)$, is nonnegative, and the time value of money on the strike, $K(1 - e^{-r(T-t)})$, is positive. If we simply eliminate both terms, this reduces the value of the right-hand side and we can see that the value of the European option is greater than $S_t - K$. We also know that $C_{\text{Amer}} \geq C_{\text{Eur}}$. Thus, we have

$$C_{\text{Amer}} \geq C_{\text{Eur}} > S_t - K$$

Since C_{Amer}, the American option premium, always exceeds $S_t - K$, we would lose money exercising an American call prior to expiration, as opposed to selling the option.

Equation (9.11) is useful because it shows us precisely *why* we would never early-exercise. First, we throw away the implicit put protection should the stock later move below the strike price. Second, we accelerate the payment of the strike price, which has an interest cost. A third effect is the possible loss from deferring receipt of the stock. However, when there are no dividends, we lose nothing by waiting to take physical possession of the stock.

It is important to realize that this proposition does *not* say that you must hold the option until expiration. It says that if you no longer wish to hold the call, you should sell it rather than early-exercising it.[5]

Exercising calls just prior to a dividend If dividends are sufficiently great, early exercise can be optimal. To take an extreme example, consider a 90-strike American call with 1 week to expiration on a stock selling for $100. Suppose that the stock is about to pay a dividend of $99.99. If we exercise—paying $90 to acquire the $100 stock—we have a net position worth $10. If we delay past the ex-dividend date, the option will be worthless. In this case, exercise is optimal.

To see this algebraically, if the stock pays dividends, the parity relationship is

$$C(S_t, K, T - t) = P(S_t, K, T - t) + S_t - \text{PV}_{t,T}(\text{Div}) - \text{PV}_{t,T}(K)$$
$$\geq S_t - K - \text{PV}_{t,T}(\text{Div}) + [K - \text{PV}_{t,T}(K)]$$

We can omit the value of the put as before, leaving us with the expression on the second line. We can see that the value of the call is sure to exceed $S_t - K$ as long as

$$K - \text{PV}_{t,T}(K) > \text{PV}_{t,T}(\text{Div}) \tag{9.12}$$

That is, if interest on the strike price (which induces us to delay exercise) exceeds the present value of dividends (which induces us to exercise), then we will for certain never early-exercise at that time. By the same token, if inequality (9.12) is violated, we cannot rule out the possibility that early exercise will be optimal. This does not tell us that we *will* exercise, only that we cannot rule it out.

If it is optimal to early-exercise a call, it will be optimal to wait to exercise until the last moment before the ex-dividend date. By exercising earlier than that, we pay the strike price prematurely and thus at a minimum lose interest on the strike price.

Early exercise for puts When the underlying stock pays no dividend, a call will not be early-exercised, but a put might be. To see that early exercise for a put can make economic sense, suppose a company is bankrupt and the stock price falls to zero. Then a 100-strike put that would not be exercised until expiration will be worth $\text{PV}_{t,T}(\$100)$. If we could early-exercise, we would receive $100 immediately. Early exercise would be optimal in order to receive the strike price earlier and begin earning interest.

We can also use a parity argument to understand this. The put will never be exercised as long as $P(S, K, T) > K - S$. Supposing that the stock pays no dividends, parity for the put is

$$P(S_t, K, T - t) = C(S_t, K, T - t) - S_t + \text{PV}_{t,T}(K)$$

---

[5] Some options, such as compensation options, cannot be sold. In practice it is common to see executives exercise options prior to expiration and then sell the stock. The discussion in this section demonstrates that such exercise would be irrational if the option could be sold or if the stock could be sold short.

$P > K - S$ then implies

$$C(S_t, K, T - t) - S_t + \text{PV}_{t,T}(K) > K - S_t$$

or

$$C(S_t, K, T - t) > K - \text{PV}_{t,T}(K)$$

If the call is sufficiently valueless (as in the above example of a bankrupt company), parity cannot rule out early exercise. This does not mean that we *will* early-exercise at this point; it simply means that we cannot rule out early exercise.

Early exercise summary There are three issues that arise when we consider early-exercising an option. If we early-exercise,

- we receive the underlying asset (a stock in the case of a call, cash in the case of a put) sooner rather than later;
- we give up the strike asset (cash in the case of a call, stock in the case of a put) sooner rather than later; and
- we eliminate the insurance that is implicit in the option price. (In the case of a call, we have insurance against $S_T < K$; in the case of a put, insurance against $S_T > K$.)

For early exercise to be optimal, we must either prefer to receive the underlying asset sooner or prefer to give up the strike asset sooner, and the insurance must not be too expensive. For calls, dividends on the stock provide a reason to receive the stock earlier. For puts, interest on the strike is a reason to receive the strike price earlier. Thus, dividends and interest play similar roles in the two analyses of early exercise. In fact, if we view interest as the dividend on cash, then dividends (broadly defined) become the sole reason to early-exercise an option.

Similarly, dividends on the strike asset become a reason not to early-exercise. In the case of calls, interest is the dividend on the strike asset, and in the case of puts, dividends on the stock are the dividend on the strike asset.

The point of this section has been to make some general statements about when early exercise will not occur, or under what conditions it *might* occur. In general, figuring out when to exercise requires an option pricing model. We will discuss early exercise further in Chapter 10.

Time to Expiration

How does an option price change as we increase time to expiration? If the options are American, the option price can never decline with an increase in time to expiration. If the options are European, the price can go either up or down as we increase time to expiration.

American options An American call with more time to expiration is at least as valuable as an otherwise identical call with less time to expiration. An American call with 2 years to expiration, for example, can always be turned into an American option with 1 year to expiration by voluntarily exercising it after 1 year. Therefore, the 2-year call is at least as valuable as the 1-year call.

The same is true for puts: A longer-lived American put is always worth at least as much as an otherwise equivalent European put.

European options A European call on a non-dividend-paying stock will be at least as valuable as an otherwise identical call with a shorter time to expiration. We know this because a European call on such a stock has the same price as an otherwise identical American call. With dividends, however, longer-lived European options may be less valuable than shorter-lived European options. Economic forces that make it optimal to exercise an option early can make a short-lived European option worth more than a long-lived European option.

As an example, imagine a stock that will pay a liquidating dividend 2 weeks from today.[6] A European call with 1 week to expiration will have value since it is exercisable prior to the dividend. A European call with 3 weeks to expiration will have no value since the stock will have no value at expiration. This is an example of a longer-lived option being less valuable than a shorter-lived option. Note that if the options were American, we would simply exercise the 3-week option prior to the dividend, so the 1-week and 3-week options would have the same value.

Longer-lived European puts can also be less valuable than shorter-lived European puts. A good example of this is a bankrupt company. The put will be worth the present value of the strike price, with the present value calculated until time to expiration. Longer-lived puts will be worth less than shorter-lived puts. If the options were American, they would all be exercised immediately and hence would be worth the strike price.

Different Strike Prices

Suppose you have three call options, with strikes of $40, $45, and $50. How will the premiums on these options differ? Common sense suggests that, with a call option on any underlying asset, the premium will go up as you lower the strike price: It is more valuable to be able to buy at a lower price. Moreover, the increase in the premium cannot be greater than $5. (The right to buy for a $5 cheaper price cannot be worth more than $5.)

Following this logic, the premium will rise as we decrease the strike from $50 to $45, and rise again when we decrease the strike further from $45 to $40. Here is a more subtle question: In which case will the premium rise more? It turns out that the rise in the premium from $45 to $40 *must* be greater than the rise from $50 to $45, or else there is an arbitrage opportunity. Similar propositions hold for put options.

---

[6] A liquidating dividend occurs when a firm pays its entire value to shareholders. A firm is worthless after paying a liquidating dividend.

Here is a more formal statement of these propositions. Suppose we have three strike prices, $K_1 < K_2 < K_3$, with corresponding call option prices $C(K_1)$, $C(K_2)$, and $C(K_3)$ and put option prices $P(K_1)$, $P(K_2)$, and $P(K_3)$. Here are the propositions we discuss in this section:

1. A call with a low strike price is at least as valuable as an otherwise identical call with a higher strike price:

$$\boxed{C(K_1) \geq C(K_2)} \quad (9.13)$$

A put with a high strike price is at least as valuable as an otherwise identical put with a low strike price:

$$\boxed{P(K_2) \geq P(K_1)} \quad (9.14)$$

2. The premium difference between otherwise identical calls with different strike prices cannot be greater than the difference in strike prices:

$$\boxed{C(K_1) - C(K_2) \leq K_2 - K_1} \quad (9.15)$$

The premium difference for otherwise identical puts also cannot be greater than the difference in strike prices:

$$\boxed{P(K_2) - P(K_1) \leq K_2 - K_1} \quad (9.16)$$

3. Premiums decline at a decreasing rate as we consider calls with progressively higher strike prices. The same is true for puts as strike prices decline. This is called **convexity** of the option price with respect to the strike price:

$$\boxed{\frac{C(K_1) - C(K_2)}{K_2 - K_1} \geq \frac{C(K_2) - C(K_3)}{K_3 - K_2}} \quad (9.17)$$

$$\boxed{\frac{P(K_2) - P(K_1)}{K_2 - K_1} \leq \frac{P(K_3) - P(K_2)}{K_3 - K_2}} \quad (9.18)$$

These statements are all true for both European and American options.[7] It turns out that these three propositions are equivalent to saying that if you enter into an option spread, there must be a possibility for you to lose money. If the options were priced so that the spread could not lose money, you have an arbitrage opportunity. Each of the propositions can be graphically illustrated using option spreads we discussed in

---

[7] In fact, if the options are European, the second statement can be strengthened: The difference in option premiums must be less than the *present value* of the difference in strikes.

Chapter 3. In all cases, the arbitrage involves buying the relatively underpriced option and selling the relatively overpriced option. Specifically:

1. If equation (9.13) were not true, buy the low-strike call and sell the high-strike call (this is a call bull spread). If equation (9.14) were not true, buy the high-strike put and sell the low-strike put (a put bear spread).

2. If equation (9.15) were not true, sell the low-strike call and buy the high-strike call (a call bear spread). If equation (9.16) were not true, buy the low-strike put and sell the high-strike put (a put bull spread).

3. If either of equations (9.17) or (9.18) were not true, there is an asymmetric butterfly spread with positive profits at all prices.

We will illustrate these propositions with numerical examples. In all of these examples we will assume that these are 6-month options and that the 6-month effective interest rate is 4%, but you should persuade yourself that the specific time to maturity and interest rate don't matter given the prices in the examples.

The first example will illustrate the arbitrage when a higher-strike call has a greater premium than a lower-strike call.

Example 9.8 Suppose that $C(50) = \$9$ and $C(55) = \$10$. This violates equation (9.13). The arbitrage is to buy the relatively underpriced call and sell the relatively overpriced call. This is a call bull spread costing us $\$9 - \$10 = -\$1$—in other words, we *receive payment* for entering into a call bull spread. The profit diagram is in Figure 9.2. This is an arbitrage because you cannot lose money.

You should verify that there is also an arbitrage if a higher-strike put has a lower premium than a lower-strike put.

The next two examples illustrate the proposition that the change in premium cannot be greater than the change in the strike price.

Example 9.9 Suppose that $C(50) = \$18$ and $C(55) = \$12$. This violates equation (9.15) because there is a $6 change in premium with a $5 change in the strike price. The arbitrage is to buy the relatively underpriced call (which is the 55-strike call) and sell the relatively overpriced call (the 50-strike). This is a call bear spread costing $\$12 - \$18 = -\$6$. Because we are selling a call spread, it is not a surprise that we receive a premium. However, we are receiving too much premium.[8] The profit diagram illustrating the arbitrage is in Figure 9.3.

We will now demonstrate the same result, only using puts.

---

[8] If the options are European, the difference in premiums must be less than the present value of the difference in strikes if there is to be no arbitrage.

268 Chapter 9: Parity and Other Option Relationships

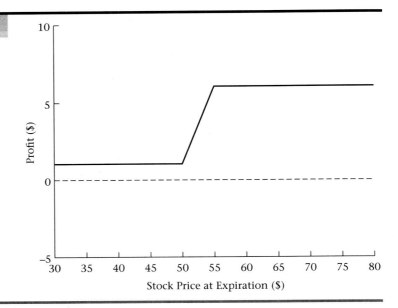

FIGURE 9.2

Profit from purchasing a 50-strike call for $9 and selling a 55-strike call for $10. This is an arbitrage.

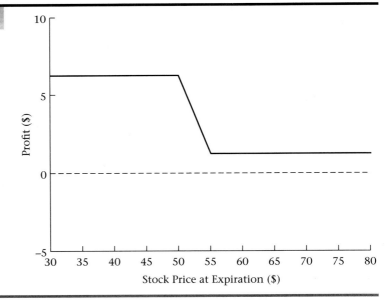

FIGURE 9.3

Profit from selling a 50-strike call for $18 and buying a 55-strike call for $12. This is an arbitrage.

FIGURE 9.4

Profit from purchasing a 50-strike put for $9 and selling a 55-strike put for $15. This is an arbitrage.

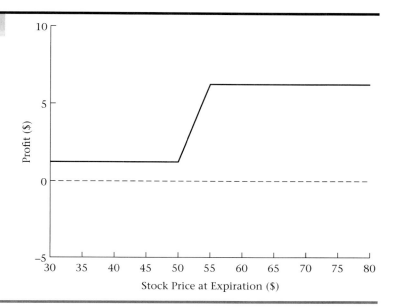

Example 9.10 Suppose that $P(50) = \$9$ and $P(55) = \$15$. This violates equation (9.16): There is a $6 change in premium with a $5 change in the strike price. The arbitrage is to buy the relatively underpriced put and sell the relatively overpriced put. This is a put bull spread costing $\$9 - \$15 = -\$6$. The profit diagram illustrating the arbitrage is in Figure 9.4. Notice that the figure looks very similar to that in Figure 9.2.

Finally, we will illustrate the proposition that option prices decrease at a decreasing rate.

Example 9.11 Suppose that $P(50) = \$4$, $P(55) = \$8$, and $P(60) = \$11$. The premiums decrease as the strike price decreases, and the decrease is always less than the change in the strike price. However the premium decreases at a rate of $\$0.60 \ (= (11 - 8)/(60 - 55))$ per dollar change in strike from 60 to 55, and at a rate of $\$0.80 \ (= (8 - 4)/(55 - 50))$ per dollar change in strike from 55 to 50. The arbitrage is to buy a butterfly spread. That is, we buy the 50- and 60-strike puts, and sell two 55-strike puts. The premium is

$$-\$4 + 2 \times \$8 - \$11 = \$1$$

We receive $1 for buying a butterfly spread. The arbitrage is illustrated in Figure 9.5.

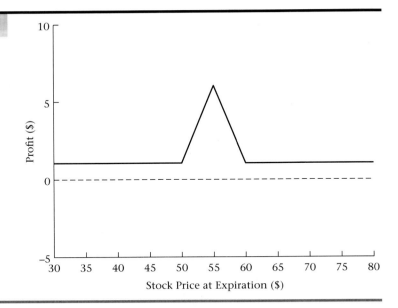

FIGURE 9.5

Profit from purchasing a 50-strike put for $4, selling two 55-strike puts for $8, and buying a 60-strike put for $11. This is an arbitrage.

CHAPTER SUMMARY

Put-call parity is one of the most important relations in option pricing. Parity is the observation that buying a European call and selling a European put with the same strike price and time to expiration is equivalent to making a leveraged investment in the underlying asset, less the value of cash payments to the underlying asset over the life of the option. Different versions of parity for different underlying assets appear in Table 9.4. In every case the value on the left-hand side of the parity equation is the price of the underlying asset less its cash flows over the life of the option. The parity relationship can be algebraically rearranged so that options and the underlying asset create a synthetic bond, options and a bond create a synthetic stock, and one kind of option together with the stock and bond synthetically create the other kind of option.

The idea of an option can be generalized to permit an asset other than cash to be the strike asset. This insight blurs the distinction between a put and a call. The idea that puts and calls are different ways of looking at the same contract is commonplace in currency markets.

Option prices must obey certain restrictions when we vary the strike price, time to maturity, or option exercise style. American options are at least as valuable as European options. American calls and puts become more expensive as time to expiration increases, but European options need not. European options on a non-dividend-paying stock do become more expensive with increasing time to maturity if the strike price grows at the

TABLE 9.4

Versions of put-call parity. Notation in the table includes the spot currency exchange rate, x_0; the risk-free interest rate in the foreign currency, r_f; and the current bond price, B_0.

Underlying Asset	Parity Relationship
Futures contract	$e^{-rT} F_{0,T} = C(K,T) - P(K,T) + e^{-rT} K$
Stock, no dividend	$S_0 = C(K,T) - P(K,T) + e^{-rT} K$
Stock, discrete dividend	$S_0 - PV_{0,T}(\text{Div}) = C(K,T) - P(K,T) + e^{-rT} K$
Stock, continuous dividend	$e^{-\delta T} S_0 = C(K,T) - P(K,T) + e^{-rT} K$
Currency	$e^{-r_f T} x_0 = C(K,T) - P(K,T) + e^{-rT} K$
Bond	$B_0 - PV_{0,T}(\text{Coupons}) = C(K,T) - P(K,T) + e^{-rT} K$

interest rate. Dividends are the reason to exercise an American call early, while interest is the reason to exercise an American put early. A call option on a non-dividend-paying stock will always have a price greater than its value if exercised; hence, it should never be exercised early.

There are a number of pricing relationships related to changing strike prices. In particular, as the strike price increases, calls become less expensive with their price decreasing at a decreasing rate. The absolute value of the change in the call price is less than the change in the strike price. As the strike price decreases, puts become less expensive with their price decreasing at a decreasing rate. The change in the put price is less than the change in the strike price.

FURTHER READING

Two of the ideas in this chapter will prove particularly important in later chapters.

The first key idea is put-call parity, which tells us that if we understand calls we also understand puts. This equivalence makes it easier to understand option pricing since the pricing techniques and intuition about one kind of option are directly applicable to the other.

A second key idea that will prove important is the determination of factors influencing early exercise. As a practical matter, it is more work to price an American than a European option, so it is useful to know when this extra work is not necessary.

Much of the material in this chapter can be traced to Merton (1973b), which contains an exhaustive treatment of option properties that must hold if there is to be no arbitrage. Cox and Rubinstein (1985) also provides an excellent treatment of this material.

PROBLEMS

9.1 A stock currently sells for $32.00. A 6-month call option with a strike of $35.00 has a premium of $2.27. Assuming a 4% continuously compounded risk-free rate and a 6% continuous dividend yield, what is the price of the associated put option?

9.2 A stock currently sells for $32.00. A 6-month call option with a strike of $30.00 has a premium of $4.29, and a 6-month put with the same strike has a premium of $2.64. Assume a 4% continuously compounded risk-free rate. What is the present value of dividends payable over the next 6 months?

9.3 Suppose the S&R index is 800, the continuously compounded risk-free rate is 5%, and the dividend yield is 0%. A 1-year 815-strike European call costs $75 and a 1-year 815-strike European put costs $45. Consider the strategy of buying the stock, selling the 815-strike call, and buying the 815-strike put.

   a. What is the rate of return on this position held until the expiration of the options?

   b. What is the arbitrage implied by your answer to part a?

   c. What difference between the call and put prices would eliminate arbitrage?

   d. What difference between the call and put prices eliminates arbitrage for strike prices of $780, $800, $820, and $840?

9.4 Suppose the exchange rate is 0.95 $/€, the euro-denominated continuously compounded interest rate is 4%, the dollar-denominated continuously compounded interest rate is 6%, and the price of a 1-year 0.93-strike European call on the euro is $0.0571. What is the price of a 0.93-strike European put?

9.5 The premium of a 100-strike yen-denominated put on the euro is ¥8.763. The current exchange rate is 95 ¥/€. What is the strike of the corresponding euro-denominated yen call, and what is its premium?

9.6 The price of a 6-month dollar-denominated call option on the euro with a $0.90 strike is $0.0404. The price of an otherwise equivalent put option is $0.0141. The annual continuously compounded dollar interest rate is 5%.

   a. What is the 6-month dollar-euro forward price?

   b. If the euro-denominated annual continuously compounded interest rate is 3.5%, what is the spot exchange rate?

9.7 Suppose the dollar-denominated interest rate is 5%, the yen-denominated interest rate is 1% (both rates are continuously compounded), the spot exchange rate is 0.009 $/¥, and the price of a dollar-denominated European call to buy one yen with 1 year to expiration and a strike price of $0.009 is $0.0006.

   a. What is the dollar-denominated European yen put price such that there is no arbitrage opportunity?

b. Suppose that a dollar-denominated European yen put with a strike of $0.009 has a premium of $0.0004. Demonstrate the arbitrage.

c. Now suppose that you are in Tokyo, trading options that are denominated in yen rather than dollars. If the price of a dollar-denominated at-the-money yen call in the United States is $0.0006, what is the price of a yen-denominated at-the-money dollar call—an option giving the right to buy one dollar, denominated in yen—in Tokyo? What is the relationship of this answer to your answer to part a? What is the price of the at-the-money dollar put?

9.8 Suppose call and put prices are given by

Strike	50	55
Call premium	9	10
Put premium	7	6

What no-arbitrage property is violated? What spread position would you use to effect arbitrage? Demonstrate that the spread position is an arbitrage.

9.9 Suppose call and put prices are given by

Strike	50	55
Call premium	16	10
Put premium	7	14

What no-arbitrage property is violated? What spread position would you use to effect arbitrage? Demonstrate that the spread position is an arbitrage.

9.10 Suppose call and put prices are given by

Strike	50	55	60
Call premium	18	14	9.50
Put premium	7	10.75	14.45

Find the convexity violations. What spread would you use to effect arbitrage? Demonstrate that the spread position is an arbitrage.

9.11 Suppose call and put prices are given by

Strike	80	100	105
Call premium	22	9	5
Put premium	4	21	24.80

Find the convexity violations by computing the change in premium per dollar change in the strike price. What spread would you use to effect arbitrage? (*Hint:* In this problem, consider buying one 80-strike option, selling five 100-strike options, and buying four 105-strike options.) Demonstrate that the spread position is an arbitrage.

9.12 In each case identify the arbitrage and demonstrate how you would make money by creating a table showing your payoff.

    a. Consider two European options on the same stock with the same time to expiration. The 90-strike call costs $10 and the 95-strike call costs $4.

    b. Now suppose these options have 2 years to expiration and the continuously compounded interest rate is 10%. The 90-strike call costs $10 and the 95-strike call costs $5.25. Show again that there is an arbitrage opportunity. (*Hint:* It is important in this case that the options are European.)

9.13 Suppose the interest rate is 0% and the stock of XYZ has a positive dividend yield. Is there any circumstance in which you would early-exercise an American XYZ call? Is there any circumstance in which you would early-exercise an American XYZ put? Explain.

9.14 In the following, suppose that neither stock pays a dividend.

    a. Suppose you have a call option that permits you to receive one share of Apple by giving up one share of AOL. In what circumstance might you early-exercise this call?

    b. Suppose you have a put option that permits you to give up one share of Apple, receiving one share of AOL. In what circumstance might you early-exercise this put? Would there be a loss from not early-exercising if Apple had a zero stock price?

    c. Now suppose that Apple is expected to pay a dividend. Which of the above answers will change? Why?

9.15 The price of a non-dividend-paying stock is $100 and the continuously compounded risk-free rate is 5%. A 1-year European call option with a strike price of $100 \times e^{0.05 \times 1} = \$105.127$ has a premium of $11.924. A $1\tfrac{1}{2}$ year European call option with a strike price of $100 \times e^{0.05 \times 1.5} = \$107.788$ has a premium of $11.50. Demonstrate an arbitrage.

9.16 Suppose that to buy either a call or a put option you pay the quoted ask price, denoted $C_a(K, T)$ and $P_a(K, T)$, and to sell an option you receive the bid, $C_b(K, T)$ and $P_b(K, T)$. Similarly, the ask and bid prices for the stock are S_a and S_b. Finally, suppose you can borrow at the rate r_H and lend at the rate r_L. The stock pays no dividend. Find the bounds between which you cannot profitably perform a parity arbitrage.

9.17 In this problem we consider whether parity is violated by any of the option prices in Table 9.1. Suppose that you buy at the ask and sell at the bid, and that your continuously compounded lending rate is 4% and your borrowing rate is 6%. Ignore transaction costs on the stock, for which the price is $119.60. Assume that IBM is expected to pay a $0.40 dividend in early November and in early

February. In this problem you can assume that the options are European. For each strike and expiration, what is the cost under the following conditions:

  a. You buy the call, sell the put, short the stock, and lend the present value of the strike price?

  b. You sell the call, buy the put, buy the stock, and borrow the present value of the strike price?

9.18 Consider the April 110, 120, and 130 call option prices in Table 9.1.

  a. Does convexity hold if you buy a butterfly spread, buying at the ask price and selling at the bid?

  b. Does convexity hold if you *sell* a butterfly spread, buying at the ask price and selling at the bid?

  c. Does convexity hold if you are a market-maker either buying or selling a butterfly, paying the bid and receiving the ask?

10

Binomial Option Pricing

In earlier chapters we discussed how the price of one option is related to the price of another, but we did not explain how to determine the price of an option relative to the price of the underlying asset. In this chapter we discuss the binomial option pricing model, with which we can compute the price of an option, given the characteristics of the stock or other underlying asset.

The binomial option pricing model is well known and widely used because it provides a simple solution to the difficult problem of pricing an option. The model assumes that, over a period of time, the price of the underlying asset can move only up or down by a specified amount—that is, the asset price follows a binomial distribution. Given this assumption, it is possible to determine a no-arbitrage price for the option. Surprisingly, this approach, which appears at first glance to be overly simplistic, can be used to price options, and importantly, it conveys much of the intuition underlying more complex (and seemingly more realistic) option pricing models that we will encounter in later chapters. An understanding of binomial pricing provides an excellent foundation for understanding more complicated option pricing models such as the Black-Scholes model. It is hard to overstate the value of thoroughly understanding the binomial approach to pricing options.

In this chapter, we will see how the binomial model works and use it to price both European and American call and put options on stocks, currencies, and futures contracts. As part of the pricing analysis, we will also see how market-makers can create options synthetically using the underlying asset and risk-free bonds.

10.1 A ONE-PERIOD BINOMIAL TREE

Binomial pricing achieves its simplicity by making a very strong assumption about the stock price: At any point in time, the stock price can change to either an up value or a down value. In-between, greater, or lesser values are not permitted. The restriction to two possible prices is why the method is called "binomial." The appeal of binomial pricing

FIGURE 10.1

Binomial tree depicting the movement of XYZ stock over 1 year. The current stock price is $41.

is that it displays the logic of option pricing in a simple setting, using only algebra to price options.

The binomial approach to pricing was first used by Sharpe (1978) as an intuitive way to explain option pricing. Binomial pricing was developed more formally by Cox et al. (1979) and Rendleman and Bartter (1979), who showed how to implement the model, demonstrated the link between the binomial model and the Black-Scholes model, and showed that the method provides a tractable way to price options for which early exercise may be optimal. The binomial model is often referred to as the "Cox-Ross-Rubinstein pricing model."

We begin with a simple example. Consider a European call option on the stock of XYZ, with a $40 strike and 1 year to expiration. XYZ does not pay dividends and its current price is $41. The continuously compounded risk-free interest rate is 8%. We wish to determine the option price.

Since the stock's return over the next year is uncertain, the option could expire either in-the-money or out-of-the-money, depending upon whether the stock price is more or less than $40. Intuitively, the valuation for the option should take into account both possibilities. If the option expires out-of-the-money, its value is zero. If the option expires in-the-money, its value will depend upon how far in-the-money it is. To price the option, then, we need to characterize the uncertainty about the stock price at expiration.

Figure 10.1 represents the evolution of the stock price: Today the price is $41, and in 1 year the price can be either $60 or $30. This depiction of possible stock prices is called a **binomial tree.** For the moment we take the tree as given and price the option. Later we will learn how to construct such a tree.

Computing the Option Price

Now we compute the price of our 40-strike 1-year call. Consider two portfolios:

> **Portfolio A**. Buy one call option. The cost of this is the call premium, which is what we are trying to determine.

Portfolio B. Buy 2/3 of a share of XYZ and borrow $18.462 at the risk-free rate.[1] This position costs

$$2/3 \times \$41 - \$18.462 = \$8.871$$

Now we compare the payoffs to the two portfolios 1 year from now. Since the stock can take on only two values, we can easily compute the value of each portfolio at each possible stock price.

For Portfolio A, the time 1 payoff is max[0, S_1 − $40]:

	Stock Price in 1 Year (S_1)	
	$30	$60
Payoff	0	$20

In computing the payoff for Portfolio B, we assume that we sell the shares at the market price and that we repay the borrowed amount, plus interest ($18.462 × $e^{0.08}$ = $20). Thus, we have

	Stock Price in 1 Year (S_1)	
	$30	$60
2/3 purchased shares	$20	$40
Repay loan of $18.462	−$20	−$20
Total payoff	0	$20

Note that Portfolios A and B have the same payoff: zero if the stock price goes down, in which case the option is out-of-the-money, and $20 if the stock price goes up. Therefore, both portfolios should have the same cost. Since Portfolio B costs $8.871, then given our assumptions, *the price of one option must be $8.871*. Portfolio B is a **synthetic call**, mimicking the payoff to a call by buying shares and borrowing.

The idea that positions that have the same payoff should have the same cost is called the **law of one price**. This example uses the law of one price to determine the option price. We will see shortly that there is an arbitrage opportunity if the law of one price is violated.

The call option in the example is replicated by holding 2/3 shares, which implies that one option has the risk of 2/3 shares. The value 2/3 is the *delta* (Δ) of the option: the number of shares that replicates the option payoff. Delta is a key concept, and we will say much more about it later.

Finally, we can say something about the expected return on the option. Suppose XYZ has a positive risk premium (i.e., the expected return on XYZ is greater than the risk-free rate). Since we create the synthetic call by borrowing to buy the stock, the

---

[1] Of course, it is not possible to buy fractional shares of stock. As an exercise, you can redo this example, multiplying all quantities by 3. You would then compare three call options (Portfolio A) to buying two shares and borrowing $18.462 × 3 = $55.387 (Portfolio B).

call is equivalent to a leveraged position in the stock, and therefore the call will have an expected return greater than that on the stock. The option elasticity, which we will discuss in Chapter 11, measures the amount of leverage implicit in the option.

The Binomial Solution

In the preceding example, how did we know that buying 2/3 of a share of stock and borrowing $18.462 would replicate a call option?

We have two instruments to use in replicating a call option: shares of stock and a position in bonds (i.e., borrowing or lending). To find the replicating portfolio, we need to find a combination of stock and bonds such that the portfolio mimics the option.

To be specific, we wish to find a portfolio consisting of Δ shares of stock and a dollar amount B in lending, such that the portfolio imitates the option whether the stock rises or falls. We will assume in this section that stock does not pay a dividend. Later we will see how dividends affect the analysis.

We can write the stock price as uS_0 when the stock goes up and as dS_0 when the price goes down. We can represent the stock price tree as follows:

In this tree u is interpreted as 1 plus the rate of capital gain on the stock if it goes up, and d is 1 plus the rate of capital loss if it goes down. (If there are dividends, the total return is the capital gain or loss, plus the dividend.)

Let C_u and C_d represent the value of the option when the stock goes up or down, respectively. The tree for the stock implies a corresponding tree for the value of the option:

If the length of a period is h, the interest factor per period is e^{rh}. The problem is to solve for Δ and B such that our portfolio of Δ shares and B in lending duplicates the option payoff. The value of the replicating portfolio at time h, with stock price S_h, is

$$\Delta S_h + e^{rh} B$$

At the prices $S_h = dS$ and $S_h = uS$, a successful replicating portfolio will satisfy

$$(\Delta \times dS) + (B \times e^{rh}) = C_d$$
$$(\Delta \times uS) + (B \times e^{rh}) = C_u$$

10.1 A One-Period Binomial Tree

This is two equations in the two unknowns Δ and B. Solving for Δ and B gives

$$\Delta = \frac{C_u - C_d}{S(u - d)} \tag{10.1}$$

$$B = e^{-rh}\frac{uC_d - dC_u}{u - d} \tag{10.2}$$

Given the expressions for Δ and B, we can derive a simple formula for the value of the option. The cost of creating the option is the net cash required to buy the shares and bonds. Thus, the cost of the option is $\Delta S + B$. Using equations (10.1) and (10.2), we have

$$\Delta S + B = e^{-rh}\left(C_u \frac{e^{rh} - d}{u - d} + C_d \frac{u - e^{rh}}{u - d}\right) \tag{10.3}$$

The assumed stock price movements, u and d, should not give rise to arbitrage opportunities. In particular, we require that

$$u > e^{rh} > d \tag{10.4}$$

Consider the arbitrage opportunities if the condition were violated. If $e^{rh} \geq u$, we would short the stock to hold bonds. Similarly, if $d \geq e^{rh}$, we would borrow to buy the stock. Either way, we would earn an arbitrage profit. Therefore, the assumed process could not be consistent with any possible equilibrium.

Note that because Δ is the number of shares in the replicating portfolio, it can also be interpreted as the sensitivity of the option to a change in the stock price. If the stock price changes by \$1, then the option price, $\Delta S + B$, changes by Δ. This interpretation will be quite important later.

Example 10.1 Here is the solution for Δ, B, and the option price using the stock price tree depicted in Figure 10.1. There we have $u = \$60/\$41 = 1.4634$, $d = \$30/\$41 = 0.7317$, and $\delta = 0$. In addition, the call option had a strike price of \$40 and 1 year to expiration—hence, $h = 1$. Thus, $C_u = \$60 - \$40 = \$20$ and $C_d = 0$. Using equations (10.1) and (10.2), we have

$$\Delta = \frac{\$20 - 0}{\$41 \times (1.4634 - 0.7317)} = 2/3$$

$$B = e^{-0.08}\frac{1.4634 \times \$0 - 0.7317 \times \$20}{1.4634 - 0.7317} = -\$18.462$$

Hence, the option price is given by

$$\Delta S + B = 2/3 \times \$41 - \$18.462 = \$8.871$$

Note that *if we are interested only in the option price, it is not necessary to solve for Δ and B;* that is just an intermediate step. If we want to know only the option price, we can use equation (10.3) directly:

$$\Delta S + B = e^{-0.08}\left(\$20 \times \frac{e^{0.08} - 0.7317}{1.4634 - 0.7317} + \$0 \times \frac{1.4634 - e^{0.08}}{1.4634 - 0.7317}\right)$$
$$= \$8.871$$

Throughout this chapter we will continue to report Δ and B, since we are interested not only in the price but also in the replicating portfolio.

Arbitraging a Mispriced Option

What if the observed option price differs from the theoretical price? Because we have a way to replicate the option using the stock, it is possible to take advantage of the mispricing and fulfill the dream of every trader—namely, to buy low and sell high.

The following examples illustrate that if the option price is anything other than the theoretical price, arbitrage is possible.

The option is overpriced Suppose that the market price for the option is $9.00, instead of $8.871. We can sell the option, but this leaves us with the risk that the stock price at expiration will be $60 and we will be required to deliver the stock.

We can address this risk by buying a synthetic option at the same time we sell the actual option. We have already seen how to create the synthetic option by buying 2/3 shares and borrowing $18.462. If we simultaneously sell the actual option and buy the synthetic, the initial cash flow is

$$\underbrace{\$9.00}_{\text{Receive option premium}} - \underbrace{2/3 \times \$41}_{\text{Cost of shares}} + \underbrace{\$18.462}_{\text{Borrowing}} = \$0.129$$

We earn $0.129, the amount by which the option is mispriced.

Now we verify that there is no risk at expiration. We have

	Stock Price in 1 Year (S_1)	
	$30	**$60**
Written call	$0	−$20
2/3 Purchased shares	$20	$40
Repay loan of $18.462	−$20	−$20
Total payoff	$0	$0

By hedging the written option, we eliminate risk.

The option is underpriced Now suppose that the market price of the option is $8.25. We wish to buy the underpriced option. Of course, if we are unhedged and the stock price falls at expiration, we lose our investment. We can hedge by selling a synthetic option. We accomplish this by reversing the position for a synthetic purchased call: We short

2/3 shares and invest $18.462 of the proceeds in Treasury bills. The cost of this is

$$\underbrace{-\$8.25}_{\text{Option premium}} + \underbrace{2/3 \times \$41}_{\text{Short–sale proceeds}} - \underbrace{\$18.462}_{\text{Invest in T–bills}} = \$0.621$$

At expiration we have

	Stock Price in 1 Year (S_1)	
	$30	$60
Purchased call	$0	$20
2/3 short-sold shares	−$20	−$40
T-bill	$20	$20
Total payoff	$0	$0

We have earned the amount by which the option was mispriced and hedged the risk associated with buying the option.

A Graphical Interpretation of the Binomial Formula

The binomial solution for Δ and B, equations (10.1) and (10.2), is obtained by solving two equations in two unknowns. Letting C_h and S_h be the option and stock value after one binomial period, and supposing $\delta = 0$, the equations for the portfolio describe a line with the formula

$$C_h = \Delta \times S_h + e^{rh} B$$

This is graphed as line AED in Figure 10.2, which shows the option payoff as a function of the stock price at expiration.

We choose Δ and B to yield a portfolio that pays C_d when $S_h = dS$, and C_u when $S_h = uS$. Hence, by construction this line runs through points E and D. We can control the slope of a payoff diagram by varying the number of shares, Δ, and its height by varying the number of bonds, B. It is apparent that a line that runs through both E and D must have slope $\Delta = (C_u - C_d)/(uS - dS)$. Also, the point A is the value of the portfolio when $S_h = 0$, which is the time-h value of the bond position, $e^{rh} B$. Hence, $e^{rh} B$ is the y-axis intercept of the line.

You can see by looking at Figure 10.2 that *any* line replicating a call will have a positive slope ($\Delta > 0$) and a negative intercept ($B < 0$). As an exercise, you can verify graphically that a portfolio replicating a put would have a negative slope ($\Delta < 0$) and a positive intercept ($B > 0$).

Pricing with Dividends

We now consider the case where the stock has a continuous dividend yield of δ, which we reinvest in the stock. As in Section 5.2, if you buy one share at time t, at time $t + h$ you will have $e^{\delta h}$ shares. The up and down movements of the stock price then reflect the *ex-dividend* price.

FIGURE 10.2

The payoff to an expiring call option is the dark heavy line. The payoff to the option at the points dS and uS are C_d and C_u (at point D). The portfolio consisting of Δ shares and B bonds has intercept $e^{rh}B$ and slope Δ, and by construction goes through both points E and D. The slope of the line is calculated as $\frac{\text{Rise}}{\text{Run}}$ between points E and D, which gives the formula for Δ.

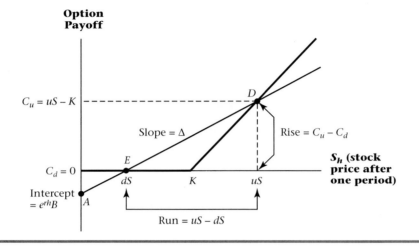

The key to understanding the effect of dividends is to recognize that if we start with one share, reinvestment of dividends gives us more than one share. Thus, we have to tail the stock position: We create our replicating portfolio using $e^{-\delta h}$ as many shares as in the absence of dividends. We can verify this intuition by going again through the algebra, only allowing the firm to pay dividends.

Proceeding as before, the value of the replicating portfolio at time h, with stock price S_h, is

$$\Delta S_h + e^{rh} B$$

At the prices $S_h = dS$ and $S_h = uS$, a successful replicating portfolio will satisfy

$$(\Delta \times dS \times e^{\delta h}) + (B \times e^{rh}) = C_d$$
$$(\Delta \times uS \times e^{\delta h}) + (B \times e^{rh}) = C_u$$

Solving for Δ and B, we obtain

$$\Delta = e^{-\delta h} \frac{C_u - C_d}{S(u - d)}$$

As expected, we tail the position in the stock to offset the effect of dividends. The formula for the bond position is the same as before:

$$B = e^{-rh}\frac{uC_d - dC_u}{u - d}$$

Finally, we compute $\Delta S + B$ to obtain the option price:

$$\Delta S + B = e^{-rh}\left(C_u \frac{e^{(r-\delta)h} - d}{u - d} + C_d \frac{u - e^{(r-\delta)h}}{u - d}\right) \quad (10.5)$$

Risk-Neutral Pricing

So far we have not specified the probabilities of the stock going up or down. In fact, probabilities were not used anywhere in the option price calculations. Since the strategy of holding Δ shares and B bonds replicates the option whichever way the stock moves, the probability of an up or down movement in the stock is irrelevant for pricing the option.

Although probabilities are not needed for pricing the option, there is a probabilistic interpretation of equation (10.5). Notice that in equation (10.5) the terms $(e^{(r-\delta)h} - d)/(u - d)$ and $(u - e^{(r-\delta)h})/(u - d)$ sum to 1 and are both positive (when $\delta = 0$, this follows from inequality 10.4). Thus, we can interpret these terms as probabilities. Let

$$p^* = \frac{e^{(r-\delta)h} - d}{u - d} \quad (10.6)$$

Equation (10.3) can then be written as

$$C = e^{-rh}[p^*C_u + (1 - p^*)C_d] \quad (10.7)$$

This expression has the appearance of a discounted expected value. It is peculiar, though, because we are discounting at the risk-free rate, even though the risk of the option is at least as great as the risk of the stock (a call option is a leveraged position in the stock since $B < 0$). In addition, there is no reason to think that p^* is the true probability that the stock will go up; in general, it is not.

What happens if we use p^* to compute the expected *undiscounted* stock price? Doing this, we obtain

$$p^*uS + (1 - p^*)dS = e^{(r-\delta)h}S = F_{t,t+h} \quad (10.8)$$

When we use p^* as the probability of an up move, the expected stock price equals the forward price, $e^{(r-\delta)h}S$. (We derived this expression for the forward price of the stock in Chapter 5, equation (5.7).) Thus, *we can compute the forward price using the binomial tree*. In fact, one way to think about p^* is that it is the probability for which the expected stock price is the forward price.

We will call p^* the **risk-neutral probability** of an increase in the stock price.

Constructing a Binomial Tree

We now explain the construction of the binomial tree. Recall that the goal of the tree is to characterize future uncertainty about the stock price in an economically reasonable way.

As a starting point, we can ask: What if there were no uncertainty about the future stock price? Without uncertainty, the stock price next period must equal the forward price. Recall from Chapter 5 that the formula for the forward price is

$$F_{t,t+h} = S_t e^{(r-\delta)h} \tag{10.9}$$

Thus, without uncertainty we must have $S_{t+h} = F_{t,t+h}$. To interpret this, under certainty, the rate of return on the stock must be the risk-free rate. Thus, the stock price must rise at the risk-free rate less the dividend yield, $r - \delta$.

Now we incorporate uncertainty, but we first need to define what we mean by uncertainty. A natural measure of uncertainty about the stock return is the *annualized standard deviation of the continuously compounded stock return*, which we will denote by σ. The standard deviation measures how sure we are that the stock return will be close to the expected return. Stocks with a larger σ will have a greater chance of a return far from the expected return.

We want to be able to define binomial moves over arbitrary periods of time. This raises the following question: If σ is the annual standard deviation, what is the standard deviation over a period of time other than a year? The answer is that if σ is the annual standard deviation of the stock return, and h is the fraction of a year, then $\sigma\sqrt{h}$ is the standard deviation of the stock over a period of length h.

A simple calculation will illustrate why we scale σ by the square root of time. Suppose that r_1 is the random stock return over year 1, and r_2 is the random stock return over year 2; that the standard deviation of both r_1 and r_2 is σ; and the two returns are uncorrelated. The variance of the total two-year stock return is then

$$\text{Two-year stock return variance} = \text{Var}(r_1 + r_2) = 2\sigma^2$$

The standard deviation is the square root of the variance, so

$$\text{Two-year stock return standard deviation} = \sqrt{2\sigma^2} = \sqrt{2}\,\sigma$$

Using the same argument, we can see that the monthly standard deviation, for example, is $\sqrt{1/12}\,\sigma$.

We incorporate uncertainty into the binomial tree by modeling the up and down moves of the stock price relative to the forward price, with the difference from the forward price being related to the standard deviation. We thus can model the stock-price evolution as

$$\begin{aligned} uS_t &= F_{t,t+h} e^{+\sigma\sqrt{h}} \\ dS_t &= F_{t,t+h} e^{-\sigma\sqrt{h}} \end{aligned} \tag{10.10}$$

Using equation (10.9), we can rewrite this as

$$u = e^{(r-\delta)h + \sigma\sqrt{h}}$$
$$d = e^{(r-\delta)h - \sigma\sqrt{h}} \qquad (10.11)$$

This is the formula we will use to construct binomial trees. The standard deviation of the continously compounded return, σ, is also called the **volatility**.

Note that if we set volatility equal to zero (i.e., $\sigma = 0$), we will have $uS_t = dS_t = F_{t,t+h}$. Thus, with zero volatility, the price will still rise over time, just as with a Treasury bill. Zero volatility does not mean that prices are *fixed*; it means that prices are *known in advance*.

We will refer to a tree constructed using equation (10.11) as a "forward tree." In Appendix 10.B we will discuss alternative ways to construct a tree, including the Cox-Ross-Rubinstein tree.

Another One-Period Example

We began this section by assuming that the stock price followed the binomial tree in Figure 10.1. The up and down stock prices of $30 and $60 were selected to make the example easy to follow. Now we present an example where everything is the same except that we use equation (10.11) to construct the up and down moves.

Suppose volatility is 30%. Since the period is 1 year, we have $h = 1$, so that $\sigma\sqrt{h} = 0.30$. We also have $S_0 = \$41$, $r = 0.08$, and $\delta = 0$. Using equation (10.11), we get

$$uS = \$41 e^{(0.08-0) \times 1 + 0.3 \times \sqrt{1}} = \$59.954$$
$$dS = \$41 e^{(0.08-0) \times 1 - 0.3 \times \sqrt{1}} = \$32.903 \qquad (10.12)$$

Because the binomial tree is different than in Figure 10.1, the option price will be different as well.

Using the stock prices given in equation (10.12), we have $u = \$59.954/\$41 = 1.4623$ and $d = \$32.903/\$41 = 0.8025$. With $K = \$40$, we have $C_u = \$59.954 - \$40 = \$19.954$ and $C_d = 0$. Using equations (10.1) and (10.2), we obtain

$$\Delta = \frac{\$19.954 - 0}{\$41 \times (1.4623 - 0.8025)} = 0.7376$$

$$B = e^{-0.08} \frac{1.4623 \times \$0 - 0.8025 \times \$19.954}{1.4623 - 0.8025} = -\$22.405$$

Hence, the option price is given by

$$\Delta S + B = 0.7376 \times \$41 - \$22.405 = \$7.839$$

This example is summarized in Figure 10.3.

FIGURE 10.3

Binomial tree for pricing a European call option; assumes $S = \$41.00$, $K = \$40.00$, $\sigma = 0.30$, $r = 0.08$, $T = 1.00$ years, $\delta = 0.00$, and $h = 1.000$. At each node the stock price, option price, Δ, and B are given. Option prices in **bold italic** signify that exercise is optimal at that node.

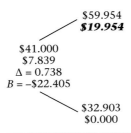

Summary

We have covered a great deal of ground in this section, so we pause for a moment to review the main points:

- In order to price an option, we need to know the stock price, the strike price, the standard deviation of returns on the stock (in order to compute u and d), the dividend yield, and the risk-free rate.
- Using the risk-free rate, dividend yield, and σ, we can approximate the future distribution of the stock by creating a binomial tree using equation (10.11).
- Once we have the binomial tree, it is possible to price the option using equation (10.3). The solution also provides the recipe for synthetically creating the option: Buy Δ shares of stock (equation 10.1) and borrow B (equation 10.2).
- The formula for the option price, equation (10.3), can be written so that it has the appearance of a discounted expected value.

There are still many issues we have to deal with. The simple binomial tree seems too simple to provide an accurate option price. Unanswered questions include how to handle more than one binomial period, how to price put options, how to price American options, etc. With the basic binomial formula in hand, we can now turn to those questions.

10.2 TWO OR MORE BINOMIAL PERIODS

We now see how to extend the binomial tree to more than one period.

FIGURE 10.4

Binomial tree for pricing a European call option; assumes $S = \$41.00$, $K = \$40.00$, $\sigma = 0.30$, $r = 0.08$, $T = 2.00$ years, $\delta = 0.00$, and $h = 1.000$. At each node the stock price, option price, Δ, and B are given. Option prices in **bold italic** signify that exercise is optimal at that node.

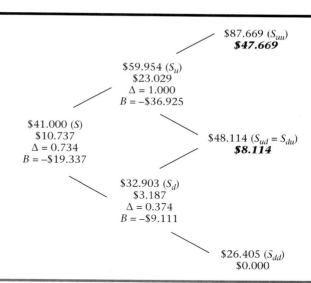

A Two-Period European Call

We begin first by adding a single period to the tree in Figure 10.3; the result is displayed in Figure 10.4. We can use that tree to price a 2-year option with a $40 strike when the current stock price is $41, assuming all inputs are the same as before.

Since we are increasing the time to maturity for a call option on a non-dividend-paying stock, then based on the discussion in Section 9.3 we expect the option premium to increase. In this example the two-period tree will give us a price of $10.737, compared to $7.839 in Figure 10.3.

Constructing the tree To see how to construct the tree, suppose that we move up in year 1, to $S_u = \$59.954$. If we reach this price, then we can move further up or down according to equation (10.10). We get

$$S_{uu} = \$59.954 e^{0.08 + 0.3} = \$87.669$$

and

$$S_{ud} = \$59.954 e^{0.08 - 0.3} = \$48.114$$

The subscript uu means that the stock has gone up twice in a row and the subscript ud means that the stock has gone up once and then down.

Similarly, if the price in 1 year is $S_d = \$32.903$, we have

$$S_{du} = \$32.903 e^{0.08 + 0.3} = \$48.114$$

and

$$S_{dd} = \$32.903 e^{0.08-0.3} = \$26.405$$

Note that an up move followed by a down move (S_{ud}) generates the same stock price as a down move followed by an up move (S_{du}). This is called a **recombining tree**. If an up move followed by a down move led to a different price than a down move followed by an up move, we would have a **nonrecombining tree**.[2] A recombining tree has fewer nodes, which means less computation is required to compute an option price.

We also could have used equation (10.11) directly to compute the year 2 stock prices. Recall that $u = e^{0.08+0.3} = 1.462$ and $d = e^{0.08-0.3} = 0.803$. We have

$$S_{uu} = u^2 \times \$41 = e^{2\times(0.08+0.3)} \times \$41 = \$87.669$$
$$S_{ud} = S_{du} = u \times d \times \$41 = e^{(0.08+0.3)} \times e^{(0.08-0.3)} \times \$41 = \$48.114$$
$$S_{dd} = d^2 \times \$41 = e^{2\times(0.08-0.3)} \times \$41 = \$26.405$$

Pricing the call option How do we price the option when we have two binomial periods? The key insight is that we work *backward* through the binomial tree. In order to use equation (10.3), we need to know the option prices resulting from up and down moves in the subsequent period. At the outset, the only period where we know the option price is at expiration.

Knowing the price at expiration, we can determine the price in period 1. Having determined that price, we can work back to period 0.

Figure 10.4 exhibits the option price at each node as well as the details of the replicating portfolio at each node. Remember, however, when we use equation (10.3), it is not necessary to compute Δ and B in order to derive the option price.[3] Here are details of the solution:

Year 2, Stock Price = $87.669 Since we are at expiration, the option value is $\max(0, S - K) = \$47.669$.

Year 2, Stock Price = $48.114 Again we are at expiration, so the option value is $8.114.

Year 2, Stock Price = $26.405 Since the option is out-of-the-money at expiration, the value is 0.

Year 1, Stock Price = $59.954 At this node we use equation (10.3) to compute the option value. (Note that once we are at this node, the "up" stock price, uS, is $87.669, and the "down" stock price, dS, is $48.114.)

$$e^{-0.08}\left(\$47.669 \times \frac{e^{0.08} - 0.803}{1.462 - 0.803} + \$8.114 \times \frac{1.462 - e^{0.08}}{1.462 - 0.803}\right) = \$23.029$$

---

[2] In cases where the tree recombines, the representation of stock-price movements is also (and, some argue, more properly) called a *lattice*. The term *tree* would then be reserved for nonrecombining stock movements.

[3] As an exercise, you can verify the Δ and B at each node.

Year 1, Stock Price = $32.903 Again we use equation (10.3) to compute the option value:

$$e^{-0.08}\left(\$8.114 \times \frac{e^{0.08} - 0.803}{1.462 - 0.803} + \$0 \times \frac{1.462 - e^{0.08}}{1.462 - 0.803}\right) = \$3.187$$

Year 0, Stock Price = $41 Again using equation (10.3):

$$e^{-0.08}\left(\$23.029 \times \frac{e^{0.08} - 0.803}{1.462 - 0.803} + \$3.187 \times \frac{1.462 - e^{0.08}}{1.462 - 0.803}\right) = \$10.737$$

Notice the following:

- The option price is greater for the 2-year than for the 1-year option, as we would expect.
- We priced the option by working backward through the tree, starting at the end and working back to the first period.
- The option's Δ and B are different at different nodes. In particular, at a given point in time, Δ increases to 1 as we go further into the money.
- We priced a European option, so early exercise was not permitted. However, permitting early exercise would have made no difference. At every node prior to expiration, the option price is greater than $S - K$; hence, we would not have exercised even if the option had been American.
- Once we understand the two-period option, it is straightforward to value an option using more than two binomial periods. The important principle is to work backward through the tree.

Many Binomial Periods

An obvious objection to the binomial calculations thus far is that the stock can only have two or three different values at expiration. It seems unlikely that the option-price calculation will be accurate. The solution to this problem is to divide the time to expiration into more periods, generating a more realistic tree.

The generalization to many binomial periods is straightforward. We can represent only a small number of binomial periods here, but a spreadsheet or computer program can handle a very large number of binomial nodes.

To illustrate how to do this, at the same time illustrating a tree with more than two periods, we will reexamine the 1-year European call option in Figure 10.3, which has a $40 strike and initial stock price of $41. Let there be three binomial periods. Since it is a 1-year call, this means that the length of a period is $h = \frac{1}{3}$. We will assume that other inputs stay the same, so $r = 0.08$ and $\sigma = 0.3$.

Figure 10.5 depicts the stock-price and option-price tree for this option. The option price is $7.074, as opposed to $7.839 in Figure 10.3. The difference occurs because the numerical approximation is different; it is quite common to see large changes in a binomial price when the number of periods, n, is changed, particularly when n is small.

FIGURE 10.5

Binomial tree for pricing a European call option; assumes $S = \$41.00$, $K = \$40.00$, $\sigma = 0.30$, $r = 0.08$, $T = 1.00$ year, $\delta = 0.00$, and $h = 0.333$. At each node the stock price, option price, Δ, and B are given. Option prices in **bold italic** signify that exercise is optimal at that node.

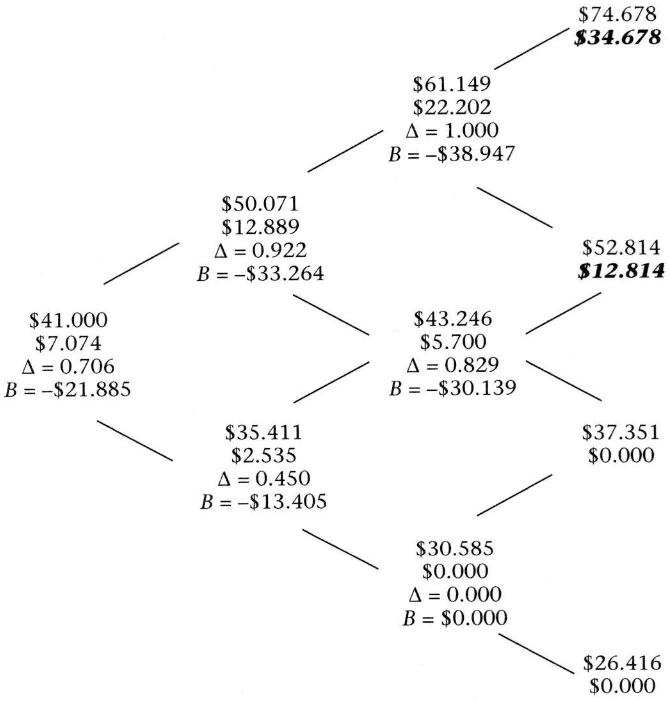

```
                                                          $74.678
                                                          $34.678
                                      $61.149
                                      $22.202
                                      Δ = 1.000
                                      B = -$38.947
                       $50.071
                       $12.889                            $52.814
                       Δ = 0.922                          $12.814
                       B = -$33.264
        $41.000                       $43.246
        $7.074                        $5.700
        Δ = 0.706                     Δ = 0.829
        B = -$21.885                  B = -$30.139
                       $35.411                            $37.351
                       $2.535                             $0.000
                       Δ = 0.450
                       B = -$13.405
                                      $30.585
                                      $0.000
                                      Δ = 0.000
                                      B = $0.000
                                                          $26.416
                                                          $0.000
```

Since the length of the binomial period is shorter, u and d are smaller than before (1.2212 and 0.8637 as opposed to 1.462 and 0.803 with $h = 1$). Just to be clear about the procedure, here is how the second-period nodes are computed:

$$S_u = \$41e^{0.08 \times 1/3 + 0.3\sqrt{1/3}} = \$50.071$$

$$S_d = \$41e^{0.08 \times 1/3 - 0.3\sqrt{1/3}} = \$35.411$$

The remaining nodes are computed similarly.

The option price is computed by working backward. The risk-neutral probability of the stock price going up in a period is

$$\frac{e^{0.08 \times 1/3} - 0.8637}{1.2212 - 0.8637} = 0.4568$$

The option price at the node where $S = \$43.246$, for example, is then given by

$$e^{-0.08 \times 1/3} \left([\$12.814 \times 0.4568] + [\$0 \times (1 - 0.4568)]\right) = \$5.700$$

Option prices at the remaining nodes are priced similarly.

10.3 PUT OPTIONS

Thus far we have priced only call options. The binomial method easily accommodates put options also, as well as other derivatives. We compute put option prices using the same stock-price tree and in almost the same way as call option prices. The only difference with a European put option occurs at expiration: Instead of computing the price as $\max(0, S - K)$, we use $\max(0, K - S)$.

European Put

Figure 10.6 shows the binomial tree for a European put option with 1 year to expiration and a strike of $40 when the stock price is $41. This is the same stock-price tree as in Figure 10.5.

To illustrate the calculations, consider the option price at the node where the stock price is $35.411. The option price at that node is computed as

$$e^{-0.08 \times 1/3} \left(\$1.401 \times \frac{e^{0.08 \times 1/3} - 0.8637}{1.2212 - 0.8637} + \$8.363 \times \frac{1.2212 - e^{0.08 \times 1/3}}{1.2212 - 0.8637} \right) = \$5.046$$

FIGURE 10.6

Binomial tree for pricing a European put option; assumes $S = \$41.00$, $K = \$40.00$, $\sigma = 0.30$, $r = 0.08$, $T = 1.00$ year, $\delta = 0.00$, and $h = 0.333$. At each node the stock price, option price, Δ, and B are given. Option prices in **bold italic** signify that exercise is optimal at that node.

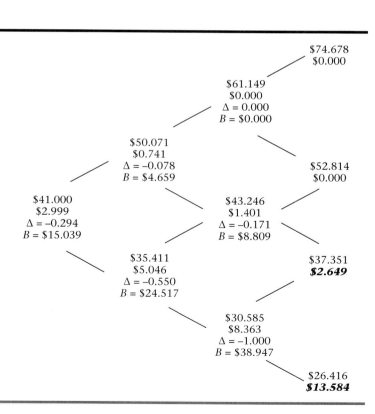

American Put

Figure 10.6 does raise one issue that we have not previously had to consider. Notice that at the node where the stock price is $30.585, the option price is $8.363. If this option were American, it would make sense to exercise at that node. The option is worth $8.363 when held until expiration, but it would be worth $40 − $30.585 = $9.415 if exercised at that node. Thus, in this case the American option should be more valuable than the otherwise equivalent European option. We will now see how to use the binomial approach to value American options.

10.4 AMERICAN OPTIONS

Since it is easy to check at each node whether early exercise is optimal, the binomial method is well suited to valuing American options. The value of the option if it is left "alive" (i.e., unexercised) is given by the value of holding it for another period, equation (10.3). The value of the option if it is exercised is given by $\max(0, S - K)$ if it is a call and $\max(0, K - S)$ if it is a put.

Thus, for an American put, the value of the option at a node is given by

$$P(S, K, t) = \max\left(K - S, e^{-rh}\left[P(uS, K, t+h)p^* + P(dS, K, t+h)(1-p^*)\right]\right) \quad (10.13)$$

where, as in equation (10.6),

$$p^* = \frac{e^{(r-\delta)h} - d}{u - d}$$

Figure 10.7 presents the binomial tree for the American version of the put option valued in Figure 10.6. The only difference in the trees occurs at the node where the stock price is $30.585. The American option at that point is worth $9.415, its early-exercise value. We have just seen in the previous section that the value of the option if unexercised is $8.363.

The greater value of the option at that node ripples back through the tree. When the option price is computed at the node where the stock price is $35.411, the value is greater in Figure 10.7 than in Figure 10.6; the reason is that the price is greater at the subsequent node S_{dd} due to early exercise.

The initial option price is $3.293, greater than the value of $2.999 for the European option. This increase in value is due entirely to early exercise at the S_{dd} node.

In general the valuation of American options proceeds as in this example. At each node we check for early exercise. If the value of the option is greater when exercised, we assign that value to the node. Otherwise, we assign the value of the option unexercised. We work backward through the tree as usual.

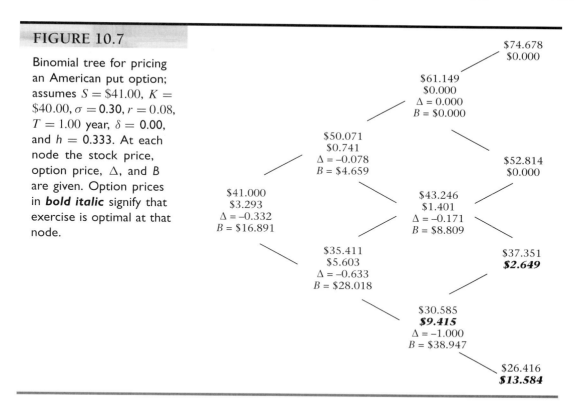

FIGURE 10.7

Binomial tree for pricing an American put option; assumes $S = \$41.00$, $K = \$40.00$, $\sigma = 0.30$, $r = 0.08$, $T = 1.00$ year, $\delta = 0.00$, and $h = 0.333$. At each node the stock price, option price, Δ, and B are given. Option prices in **bold italic** signify that exercise is optimal at that node.

10.5 OPTIONS ON OTHER ASSETS

The model developed thus far can be modified easily to price options on underlying assets other than non-dividend-paying stocks. In this section we present examples of how to do so. We examine options on stock indexes, currencies, and futures contracts. In every case the general procedure is the same: We compute the option price using equation (10.7). The difference for different underlying assets will be the construction of the binomial tree and the risk-neutral probability.

Option on a Stock Index

Suppose a stock index pays continuous dividends at the rate δ. This type of option has in fact already been covered by our derivation in Section 10.1. The up and down index moves are given by equation (10.11), the replicating portfolio by equations (10.1) and

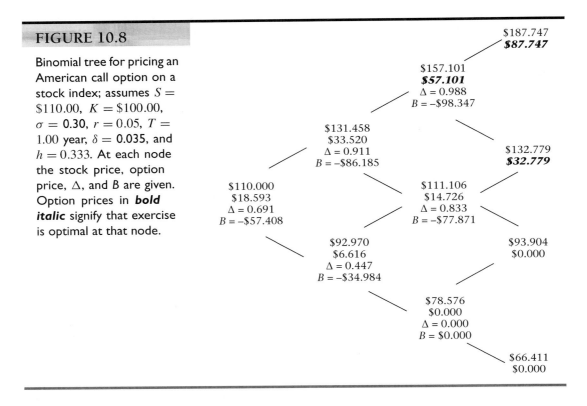

FIGURE 10.8

Binomial tree for pricing an American call option on a stock index; assumes $S = \$110.00$, $K = \$100.00$, $\sigma = 0.30$, $r = 0.05$, $T = 1.00$ year, $\delta = 0.035$, and $h = 0.333$. At each node the stock price, option price, Δ, and B are given. Option prices in **bold italic** signify that exercise is optimal at that node.

(10.2), and the option price by equation (10.3). The risk-neutral probability is given by equation (10.6).[4]

Figure 10.8 displays a binomial tree for an American call option on a stock index. Note that because of dividends, early exercise is optimal at the node where the stock price is $157.101. Given these parameters, we have $p^* = 0.457$; hence, when $S = \$157.101$, the value of the option unexercised is

$$e^{-0.05 \times 1/3} \left[0.457 \times \$87.747 + (1 - 0.457) \times \$32.779\right] = \$56.942$$

Since $57.101 > 56.942$, we exercise the option at that node.

---

[4] Intuitively, dividends can be taken into account either by (1) appropriately lowering the nodes on the tree and leaving risk-neutral probabilities unchanged, or (2) reducing the risk-neutral probability and leaving the tree unchanged. We adopt the first approach.

Options on Currencies

With a currency with spot price x_0, the forward price is $F_{0,h} = x_0 e^{(r-r_f)h}$, where r_f is the foreign interest rate. Thus, we construct the binomial tree using

$$ux = xe^{(r-r_f)h + \sigma\sqrt{h}}$$
$$dx = xe^{(r-r_f)h - \sigma\sqrt{h}}$$

There is one subtlety in creating the replicating portfolio: Investing in a "currency" means investing in a money market fund or fixed-income obligation denominated in that currency. (We encountered this idea previously in Chapter 6.) Taking into account interest on the foreign-currency-denominated obligation, the two equations are

$$\Delta \times dxe^{r_f h} + e^{rh} \times B = C_d$$
$$\Delta \times uxe^{r_f h} + e^{rh} \times B = C_u$$

The risk-neutral probability of an up move in this case is given by

$$p^* = \frac{e^{(r-r_f)h} - d}{u - d} \qquad (10.14)$$

Notice that if we think of r_f as the dividend yield on the foreign currency, these two equations look exactly like those for an index option. In fact, the solution is the same as for an option on an index: Set the dividend yield equal to the foreign risk-free rate and the current value of the index equal to the spot exchange rate.

Figure 10.9 prices a dollar-denominated American put option on the euro. The current exchange rate is assumed to be \$1.05/€ and the strike is \$1.10/€. The euro-denominated interest rate is 3.1%, and the dollar-denominated rate is 5.5%.

Because volatility is low and the option is in-the-money, early exercise is optimal at three nodes prior to expiration.

Options on Futures Contracts

We now consider options on futures contracts. We assume the forward price is the same as the futures price. Since we build the tree based on the forward price, we simply add up and down movements around the current price. Thus, the nodes are constructed as

$$u = e^{\sigma\sqrt{h}}$$
$$d = e^{-\sigma\sqrt{h}}$$

Note that this solution for u and d is exactly what we would get for an option on a stock index if δ, the dividend yield, were equal to the risk-free rate.

In constructing the replicating portfolio, recall that in each period a futures contract pays the change in the futures price, and there is no investment required to enter a futures contract. The problem is to find the number of futures contracts, Δ, and the lending, B,

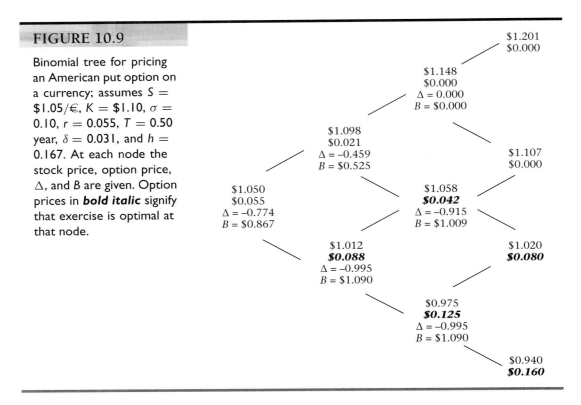

FIGURE 10.9

Binomial tree for pricing an American put option on a currency; assumes $S = \$1.05/€$, $K = \$1.10$, $\sigma = 0.10$, $r = 0.055$, $T = 0.50$ year, $\delta = 0.031$, and $h = 0.167$. At each node the stock price, option price, Δ, and B are given. Option prices in **bold italic** signify that exercise is optimal at that node.

that replicates the option. We have

$$\Delta \times (dF - F) + e^{rh} \times B = C_d$$
$$\Delta \times (uF - F) + e^{rh} \times B = C_u$$

Solving gives[5]

---

[5] The interpretation of Δ here is the number of futures contracts in the replicating portfolio. Another interpretation of Δ is the price sensitivity of the option when the price of the underlying asset changes. These two interpretations usually coincide, but not in the case of options on futures. The reason is that the futures price at time t reflects a price denominated in future dollars. The effect on the option price of a futures price change today is given by $e^{-rh}\Delta$. To see this, consider an option that is one binomial period from expiration and for which $uF > dF > K$. Then

$$\Delta = \frac{uF - K - (dF - K)}{F(u - d)} = 1$$

$$\Delta = \frac{C_u - C_d}{F(u - d)}$$

$$B = e^{-rh}\left(C_u \frac{1-d}{u-d} + C_d \frac{u-1}{u-d}\right)$$

While Δ tells us how many futures contracts to hold to hedge the option, the value of the option in this case is simply B. The reason is that the futures contract requires no investment, so the only investment is that made in the bond. We can again price the option using equation (10.3).

The risk-neutral probability of an up move is given by

$$p^* = \frac{1-d}{u-d} \tag{10.15}$$

Figure 10.10 shows a tree for pricing an American call option on a gold futures contract. Early exercise is optimal when the price is \$336.720. The intuition for early exercise is that when an option on a futures contract is exercised, the option holder pays nothing, is entered into a futures contract, and receives mark-to-market proceeds of the difference between the strike price and the futures price. The motive for exercise is the ability to earn interest on the mark-to-market proceeds.

Summary

Here is the general procedure for pricing options on the assets discussed in this section.

- Construct the binomial tree for the price of the underlying asset using

$$uS_t = F_{t,t+h} e^{+\sigma\sqrt{h}} \quad \text{or} \quad u = \frac{F_{t,t+h}}{S_t} e^{+\sigma\sqrt{h}}$$

$$dS_t = F_{t,t+h} e^{-\sigma\sqrt{h}} \quad \text{or} \quad d = \frac{F_{t,t+h}}{S_t} e^{-\sigma\sqrt{h}} \tag{10.16}$$

Since different underlying assets will have different forward price formulas, the tree will be different for different underlying assets.

- The option price at each node, if the option is unexercised, can then be computed as follows:

But we also have

$$B = e^{-rh}\left[(uF - K)\frac{1-d}{u-d} + (dF - K)\frac{u-1}{u-d}\right]$$

$$= e^{-rh}(F - K)$$

From the second expression, you can see that if the futures price changes by \$1, the option price changes by e^{-rh}.

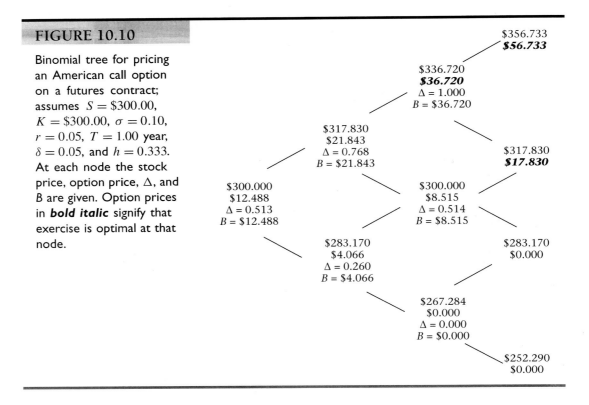

FIGURE 10.10

Binomial tree for pricing an American call option on a futures contract; assumes $S = \$300.00$, $K = \$300.00$, $\sigma = 0.10$, $r = 0.05$, $T = 1.00$ year, $\delta = 0.05$, and $h = 0.333$. At each node the stock price, option price, Δ, and B are given. Option prices in **bold italic** signify that exercise is optimal at that node.

$$p^* = \frac{F_{t,t+h}/S_t - d}{u - d}$$
$$= \frac{e^{(r-\delta)h} - d}{u - d} \tag{10.17}$$

and, as before,

$$C = e^{-rh}\left(p^* C_u + (1 - p^*) C_d\right) \tag{10.18}$$

where C_u and C_d are the up and down nodes relative to the current node. For an American option, at each node take the greater of this value and the value if exercised.

Pricing options with different underlying assets requires adjusting the risk-neutral probability for the borrowing cost or lease rate of the underlying asset. Mechanically, this means that we can use the formula for pricing an option on a stock index with an appropriate substitution for the dividend yield.

CHAPTER SUMMARY

In order to price options, we must make an assumption about the probability distribution of the underlying asset. The binomial distribution provides a particularly simple stock-price distribution: At any point in time, the stock price can go from S up to uS or down to dS, where the movement factors u and d are given by equation (10.11).

Given binomial stock-price movements, the option can be replicated by holding Δ shares of stock and B bonds. The option price is the cost of this replicating portfolio, $\Delta S + B$. For a call option, $\Delta > 0$ and $B < 0$, so the option is replicated by borrowing to buy shares. For a put, $\Delta < 0$ and $B > 0$. If the option price does not equal this theoretical price, arbitrage is possible. The replicating portfolio is dynamic, changing as the stock price moves up or down. Thus, it is unlike the replicating portfolio for a forward contract, which is fixed.

The binomial option pricing formula has an interpretation as a discounted expected value, with the risk-neutral probability (equation 10.6) used to compute the expected payoff to the option and the risk-free rate used to discount the expected payoff. This is known as risk-neutral pricing.

The binomial model can be used to price American and European calls and puts on a variety of underlying assets, including stocks, indexes, futures, currencies, commodities, and bonds.

FURTHER READING

We will see in Chapter 11 that the binomial option pricing formula gives results equivalent to the Black-Scholes formula when h becomes small and there are many binomial periods. Consequently, if you thoroughly understand binomial pricing, you also understand the Black-Scholes formula.

In addition to the original papers by Cox et al. (1979) and Rendleman and Bartter (1979), Cox and Rubinstein (1985) provides an excellent exposition of the binomial model.

PROBLEMS

In these problems, n refers to the number of binomial periods. Assume all rates are continuously compounded unless the problem explicitly states otherwise.

10.1 Let $S = \$100$, $K = \$105$, $r = 8\%$, $T = 0.5$, and $\delta = 0$. Let $u = 1.3$, $d = 0.8$, and $n = 1$.

  a. What are the premium, Δ, and B for a European call?

  b. What are the premium, Δ, and B for a European put?

10.2 Let $S = \$100$, $K = \$95$, $r = 8\%$, $T = 0.5$, and $\delta = 0$. Let $u = 1.3$, $d = 0.8$, and $n = 1$.

    a. Verify that the price of a European call is $16.196.

    b. Suppose you observe a call price of $17. What is the arbitrage?

    c. Suppose you observe a call price of $15.50. What is the arbitrage?

10.3 Let $S = \$100$, $K = \$95$, $r = 8\%$, $T = 0.5$, and $\delta = 0$. Let $u = 1.3$, $d = 0.8$, and $n = 1$.

    a. Verify that the price of a European put is $7.471.

    b. Suppose you observe a put price of $8. What is the arbitrage?

    c. Suppose you observe a put price of $6. What is the arbitrage?

10.4 Let $S = \$100$, $K = \$95$, $\sigma = 30\%$, $r = 8\%$, $T = 1$, and $\delta = 0$. Let $u = 1.3$, $d = 0.8$, and $n = 2$. Construct the binomial tree for a call option. At each node provide the premium, Δ, and B.

10.5 Repeat the option-price calculation in the previous question for stock prices of $80, $90, $110, $120, and $130, keeping everything else fixed. What happens to the initial option Δ as the stock price increases?

10.6 Let $S = \$100$, $K = \$95$, $\sigma = 30\%$, $r = 8\%$, $T = 1$, and $\delta = 0$. Let $u = 1.3$, $d = 0.8$, and $n = 2$. Construct the binomial tree for a European put option. At each node provide the premium, Δ, and B.

10.7 Repeat the option-price calculation in the previous question for stock prices of $80, $90, $110, $120, and $130, keeping everything else fixed. What happens to the inital put Δ as the stock price increases?

10.8 Let $S = \$100$, $K = \$95$, $\sigma = 30\%$, $r = 8\%$, $T = 1$, and $\delta = 0$. Let $u = 1.3$, $d = 0.8$, and $n = 2$. Construct the binomial tree for an American put option. At each node provide the premium, Δ, and B.

10.9 Suppose $S_0 = \$100$, $K = \$50$, $r = 7.696\%$ (continuously compounded), $\delta = 0$, and $T = 1$.

    a. Suppose that for $h = 1$, we have $u = 1.2$ and $d = 1.05$. What is the binomial option price for a call option that lives one period? Is there any problem with having $d > 1$?

    b. Suppose now that $u = 1.4$ and $d = 0.6$. Before computing the option price, what is your guess about how it will change from your previous answer? Does it change? How do you account for the result? Interpret your answer using put-call parity.

    c. Now let $u = 1.4$ and $d = 0.4$. How do you think the call option price will change from (a)? How does it change? How do you account for this? Use put-call parity to explain your answer.

10.10 Let $S = \$100$, $K = \$95$, $r = 8\%$ (continuously compounded), $\sigma = 30\%$, $\delta = 0$, $T = 1$ year, and $n = 3$.

  a. Verify that the binomial option price for an American call option is $18.283. Verify that there is never early exercise; hence, a European call would have the same price.

  b. Show that the binomial option price for a European put option is $5.979. Verify that put-call parity is satisfied.

  c. Verify that the price of an American put is $6.678.

10.11 Repeat the previous problem assuming that the stock pays a continuous dividend of 8% per year (continuously compounded). Calculate the prices of the American and European puts and calls. Which options are early-exercised?

10.12 Let $S = \$40$, $K = \$40$, $r = 8\%$ (continuously compounded), $\sigma = 30\%$, $\delta = 0$, $T = 0.5$ year, and $n = 2$.

  a. Construct the binomial tree for the stock. What are u and d?

  b. Show that the call price is $4.110.

  c. Compute the prices of American and European puts.

10.13 Use the same data as in the previous problem, only suppose that the call price is $5 instead of $4.110.

  a. At time 0, assume you write the option and form the replicating portfolio to offset the written option. What is the replicating portfolio and what are the net cash flows from selling the overpriced call and buying the synthetic equivalent?

  b. What are the cash flows in the next binomial period (3 months later) if the call at that time is fairly priced and you liquidate the position? What would you do if the option continues to be overpriced the next period?

  c. What would you do if the option is underpriced the next period?

10.14 Suppose that the exchange rate is $0.92/€. Let $r_\$ = 4\%$, and $r_€ = 3\%$, $u = 1.2$, $d = 0.9$, $T = 0.75$, $n = 3$, and $K = \$0.85$.

  a. What is the price of a 9-month European call?

  b. What is the price of a 9-month American call?

10.15 Use the same inputs as in the previous problem, except that $K = \$1.00$.

  a. What is the price of a 9-month European put?

  b. What is the price of a 9-month American put?

10.16 Suppose that the exchange rate is 1 dollar for 120 yen. The dollar interest rate is 5% (continuously compounded) and the yen rate is 1% (continuously compounded). Consider an at-the-money American dollar call that is yen-denominated (i.e., the call permits you to buy 1 dollar for 120 yen). The option has 1 year to expiration and the exchange rate volatility is 10%. Let $n = 3$.

    a. What is the price of a European call? An American call?

    b. What is the price of a European put? An American put?

    c. How do you account for the pattern of early exercise across the two options?

10.17 An option has a gold futures contract as the underlying asset. The current 1-year gold futures price is $300/oz., the strike price is $290, the risk-free rate is 6%, volatility is 10%, and time to expiration is 1 year. Suppose $n = 1$. What is the price of a call option on gold? What is the replicating portfolio for the call option? Evaluate the following statement: "Replicating a call option always entails borrowing to buy the underlying asset."

10.18 Suppose the S&P 500 futures price is 1000, $\sigma = 30\%$, $r = 5\%$, $\delta = 5\%$, $T = 1$, and $n = 3$.

    a. What are the prices of European calls and puts for $K = \$1000$? Why do you find the prices to be equal?

    b. What are the prices of American calls and puts for $K = \$1000$?

    c. What are the time-0 replicating portfolios for the European call and put?

10.19 For a stock index, $S = \$100$, $\sigma = 30\%$, $r = 5\%$, $\delta = 3\%$, and $T = 3$. Let $n = 3$.

    a. What is the price of a European call option with a strike of $95?

    b. What is the price of a European put option with a strike of $95?

    c. Now let $S = \$95$, $K = \$100$, $\sigma = 30\%$, $r = 3\%$, and $\delta = 5\%$. (You have exchanged values for the stock price and strike price and for the interest rate and dividend yield.) Value both options again. What do you notice?

10.20 Repeat the previous problem calculating prices for American options instead of European. What happens?

10.21 Suppose that $u < e^{(r-\delta)h}$. Show that there is an arbitrage opportunity. Now suppose that $d > e^{(r-\delta)h}$. Show again that there is an arbitrage opportunity.

Appendix 10.A LOGNORMALITY AND THE BINOMIAL MODEL

The binomial tree approximates a lognormal distribution, which is commonly used to model stock prices.

The lognormal distribution is the probability distribution that arises from the assumption that *continuously compounded returns on the stock are normally distributed*.

FIGURE 10.11

Construction of a binomial tree depicting stock-price paths, along with risk-neutral probabilities of reaching the various terminal prices.

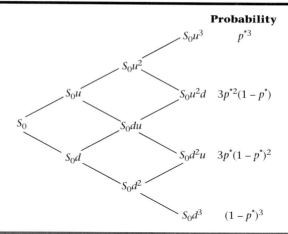

When we traverse the binomial tree, we are implicitly adding up binomial random return components of $(r - \delta)h \pm \sigma\sqrt{h}$. In the limit (as $n \to \infty$ or, the same thing, $h \to 0$), the sum of binomial random variables is normally distributed. Thus, continuously compounded returns in a binomial tree are (approximately) normally distributed, which means that the stock is lognormally distributed.

The binomial model implicitly assigns probabilities to the various nodes. Figure 10.11 depicts the construction of a tree for three binomial periods, along with the risk-neutral probability of reaching each final period node. There is only one path—sequence of up and down moves—reaching the top or bottom node (*uuu* or *ddd*), but there are three paths reaching each intermediate node. For example, the first node below the top ($S_0 u^2 d$) can be reached by the sequences *uud*, *udu*, or *duu*. Thus, there are more paths that reach the intermediate nodes than the extreme nodes.

We can take the probabilities and outcomes from the binomial tree and plot them against a lognormal distribution with the same parameters. Figure 10.12 compares a three-period binomial approximation with a lognormal distribution assuming that the initial stock price is $100, volatility is 30%, the expected return on the stock is 10%, and the time horizon is 1 year. Because we need different scales for the discrete and continuous distributions, lognormal probabilities are graphed on the left vertical axis and binomial probabilities on the right vertical axis.

Suppose that a binomial tree has n periods and the risk-neutral probability of an up move is p^*. To reach the top node, we must go up n times in a row, which occurs with a probability of $(p^*)^n$. The price at the top node is Su^n. There is only one path through the tree by which we can reach the top node. To reach the first node below the top node, we must go up $n-1$ times and down once, for a probability of $(p^*)^{n-1} \times (1 - p^*)$. The price at that node is $Su^{n-1}d$. Since the single down move can occur in any of the

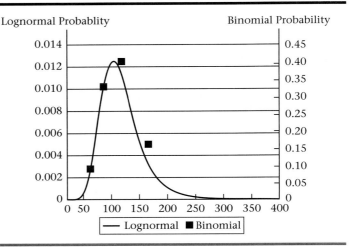

FIGURE 10.12

Comparison of lognormal distribution with three-period binomial approximation.

n periods, there are n ways this can happen. The probability of reaching the ith node below the top is $(p^*)^{n-i} \times (1 - p^*)^i$. The price at this node is $Su^{n-i}d^i$. The number of ways to reach this node is

$$\text{Number of ways to reach } i\text{th node} = \frac{n!}{(n-i)!\,i!} = \binom{n}{i}$$

where $n! = n \times (n-1) \times \cdots \times 1$.[6]

We can construct the implied probability distribution in the binomial tree by plotting the stock price at each final period node, $Su^{n-i}d^i$, against the probability of reaching that node. The probability of reaching any given node is the probability of one path reaching that node times the number of paths reaching that node:

$$\text{Probability of reaching } i\text{th node} = p^{*n-i}(1-p^*)^i \frac{n!}{(n-i)!\,i!} \qquad (10.19)$$

Figure 10.13 compares the probability distribution for a 25-period binomial tree with the corresponding lognormal distribution. The two distributions appear close; as a practical matter, a 25-period approximation works fairly well for an option expiring in a few months.

---

[6] The expression $\binom{n}{i}$ can be computed in Excel or OpenOffice using the combinatorial function, $Combin(n, i)$.

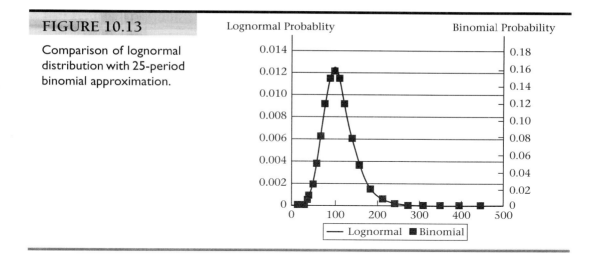

FIGURE 10.13

Comparison of lognormal distribution with 25-period binomial approximation.

Figures 10.12 and 10.13 show you what the lognormal distribution for the stock price looks like. The stock price is positive, and the distribution is skewed to the right; that is, there is a chance that extremely high stock prices will occur.

Appendix 10.B ALTERNATIVE BINOMIAL PRICING MODELS

There are other ways besides equation (10.11) to construct an acceptable binomial tree. A tree must generate a process for the stock that matches the standard deviation of the continuously compounded return on the asset and must generate an appropriate distribution for the stock as the length of the binomial period, h, goes to 0. Different methods of constructing the binomial tree will result in different u and d stock movements. No matter how we construct the tree, however, we use equation (10.6) to determine the risk-neutral probability and equation (10.7) to determine the option value.

The Cox-Ross-Rubinstein Binomial Tree

The best-known way to construct a binomial tree is that in Cox et al. (1979), in which the tree is constructed as

$$u = e^{\sigma\sqrt{h}}$$
$$d = e^{-\sigma\sqrt{h}}$$
(10.20)

The Cox-Ross-Rubinstein approach is often used in practice. A problem with this approach, however, is that if h is large or σ is small, it is possible that $e^{rh} > e^{\sigma\sqrt{h}}$, in which case the binomial tree violates the restriction in equation (10.4). In real applications h would be small, so this problem does not occur. In any event, the tree based on the forward price never violates equation (10.4).

The Jarrow-Rudd Tree

Another alternative is to construct the tree using

$$u = e^{(r-\delta-0.5\sigma^2)h+\sigma\sqrt{h}}$$
$$d = e^{(r-\delta-0.5\sigma^2)h-\sigma\sqrt{h}} \qquad (10.21)$$

This procedure for generating a tree was proposed by Jarrow and Rudd (1983). You will find in computing equation (10.6) that the risk-neutral probability of an up move is generally close to 0.5.

All three methods of constructing a binomial tree yield different option prices for finite n, but approach the same price as $n \to \infty$. Also, while the different binomial trees all have different up and down movements, all have the same ratio of u to d:

$$\frac{u}{d} = e^{2\sigma\sqrt{h}} \qquad \text{or} \qquad \ln(u/d) = 2\sigma\sqrt{h}$$

This is the sense in which, however the tree is constructed, the proportional distance between u and d measures volatility.

The Black-Scholes Formula

In 1973 Fischer Black and Myron Scholes (Black and Scholes (1973)) published a formula—the Black-Scholes formula—for computing the theoretical price of a European call option on a stock. Their paper, coupled with closely related work by Robert Merton, revolutionized both the theory and practice of finance. The history of the Black-Scholes formula is discussed in Box 11.1.

In this chapter we discuss four major topics. First, we present the Black-Scholes formula for pricing European options and explain how it is used for different underlying assets. Second, we discuss the so-called option Greeks—delta, gamma, theta, vega, rho, and psi—which measure the behavior of the option price when inputs to the formula change. Third, we discuss delta-hedging, which is the means by which market-makers hedge the risk of option positions. Finally, we examine volatility, showing the different ways that volatility can be measured (historical and implied), how implied volatility behaves over time and across options at a point in time, and the various ways in which volatility can be traded.

11.1 INTRODUCTION TO THE BLACK-SCHOLES FORMULA

To introduce the Black-Scholes formula, we first return to the binomial model, discussed in Chapter 10. When computing a binomial option price, we can vary the number of binomial steps, holding fixed the time to expiration. Table 11.1 computes binomial call option prices, using the same inputs as in Figure 10.3, and increases the number of steps, n. Changing the number of steps changes the option price, but once the number of steps becomes great enough we appear to approach a limiting value for the price. The last row reports the call option price if we were to use an infinite number of steps. We can't literally have an infinity of steps in a binomial tree, but it is possible to show that as the number of steps approaches infinity, the option price is given by the Black-Scholes formula. Thus, the Black-Scholes formula is a limiting case of the binomial formula for the price of a European option.

> **Box 11.1: The History of the Black-Scholes Formula**
>
> The Black-Scholes formula was first published in the May/June 1973 issue of the *Journal of Political Economy* (*JPE*) (see Black and Scholes (1973)). By coincidence, the Chicago Board Options Exchange (CBOE) opened at almost the same time, on April 26, 1973. Initially, the exchange traded call options on just 16 stocks. Puts did not trade until 1977. In 2000, by contrast, the CBOE traded both calls and puts on over 1200 stocks.
>
> Fischer Black told the story of the formula in Black (1989). He and Myron Scholes started working on the option pricing problem in 1969, when Black was an independent consultant in Boston and Scholes an assistant professor at MIT. While working on the problem, they had extensive discussions with Robert Merton of MIT, who was also working on option pricing.
>
> The first version of their paper was dated October 1970 and was rejected for publication by the *JPE* and subsequently by another prominent journal. However, in 1971, Eugene Fama and Merton Miller of the University of Chicago, recognizing the importance of their work, interceded on their behalf with the editors of the *JPE*. Later in 1973 Robert Merton published an important and wide-ranging follow-up paper (Merton (1973b)), which, among other contributions, established the standard no-arbitrage restrictions on option prices discussed in Chapter 9, significantly generalized the Black-Scholes formula and their derivation of the model, and provided formulas for pricing perpetual American puts and down-and-out calls.
>
> In 1997 Robert Merton and Myron Scholes won the Nobel Prize in Economics for their work on option pricing. Fischer Black was ineligible for the Prize, having died in 1995 at the age of 57.

Call Options

The Black-Scholes formula for a European call option on a stock that pays dividends at the continuous rate δ is

$$C(S, K, \sigma, r, T, \delta) = Se^{-\delta T} N(d_1) - Ke^{-rT} N(d_2) \quad (11.1)$$

where

$$d_1 = \frac{\ln(S/K) + (r - \delta + \frac{1}{2}\sigma^2)T}{\sigma\sqrt{T}} \quad (11.2a)$$

$$d_2 = d_1 - \sigma\sqrt{T} \quad (11.2b)$$

As with the binomial model, there are six inputs to the Black-Scholes formula: S, the current price of the stock; K, the strike price of the option; σ, the volatility of the stock;

TABLE 11.1 Binomial option prices for different numbers of binomial steps. As in Figure 10.2, all calculations assume that the stock price $S = \$41$, the strike price $K = \$40$, volatility $\sigma = 0.30$, risk-free rate $r = 0.08$, time to expiration $T = 1$, and dividend yield $\delta = 0$.

Number of Steps (n)	Binomial Call Price ($)
1	7.839
4	7.160
10	7.065
50	6.969
100	6.966
500	6.960
∞	6.961

r, the continuously compounded risk-free interest rate; T, the time to expiration; and δ, the dividend yield on the stock.

$N(x)$ in the Black-Scholes formula is the cumulative normal distribution function, which is the probability that a number randomly drawn from a standard normal distribution (i.e., a normal distribution with mean 0 and variance 1) will be less than x. Most spreadsheets have a built-in function for computing $N(x)$. In Excel and OpenOffice, the function is "NormSDist." The normal and cumulative normal distributions are illustrated in Figure 11.1.

Two of the inputs (K and T) describe characteristics of the option contract. The others describe the stock (S, σ, and δ) and the discount rate for a risk-free investment (r). All of the inputs are self-explanatory with the exception of volatility, which we will discuss in Section 11.5. Volatility is the standard deviation of the rate of return on the stock—a measure of the uncertainty about the future return on the stock.

It is important to be clear about units in which inputs are expressed. Several of the inputs in equation (11.1) are expressed per unit time: The interest rate, volatility, and dividend yield are typically expressed on an annual basis. In equation (11.1), these inputs are all multiplied by time: The interest rate, dividend, and volatility appear as $r \times T$, $\delta \times T$, and $\sigma^2 \times T$ (or equivalently, $\sigma \times \sqrt{T}$). Thus, when we enter inputs into the formula, the specific time unit we use is arbitrary as long as we are consistent. If time is measured in years, then r, δ, and σ should be annual. If time is measured in days, then we need to use the daily equivalent of r, σ, and δ, and so forth. We will always assume inputs are per year unless we state otherwise.

FIGURE 11.1

Top panel: Area under the normal curve to the left of 0.3. *Bottom panel:* Cumulative normal distribution. The height at $x = 0.3$, given by $N(0.3)$, is 0.6179.

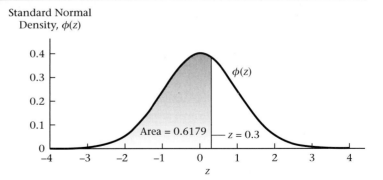

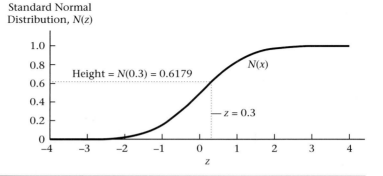

Example 11.1 Let $S = \$41$, $K = \$40$, $\sigma = 0.3$, $r = 8\%$, $T = 0.25$ (3 months), and $\delta = 0$. Computing the Black-Scholes call price, we obtain[1]

$$\$41 \times e^{-0 \times 0.25} \times N\left(\frac{\ln(\frac{41}{40}) + (0.08 - 0 + \frac{0.3^2}{2}) \times 0.25}{0.3\sqrt{0.25}}\right)$$

$$- \$40 \times e^{-0.08 \times 0.25} \times N\left(\frac{\ln(\frac{41}{40}) + (0.08 - 0 - \frac{0.3^2}{2}) \times 0.25}{0.3\sqrt{0.25}}\right) = \$3.399$$

There is one input that does *not* appear in the Black-Scholes formula, namely, the expected return on the stock. You might guess that stocks with a high beta would have a

---

[1] The call price here can be computed using the Black-Scholes formula call spreadsheet formula, BSCall:

$$\text{BSCall}(S, K, \sigma, r, t, \delta) = \text{BSCall}(41, 40, 0.3, 0.08, 0.25, 0) = \$3.399$$

higher expected return; hence, options on these stocks would have a higher probability of settlement in-the-money. The higher expected return would therefore seem to imply a higher option price. However, it turns out that a high stock beta implies a high option beta, so the discount rate for the expected payoff to such an option is correspondingly greater. The net result—one of the key insights from the Black-Scholes analysis—is that beta is irrelevant: The larger average payoff to options on high beta stocks is exactly offset by the larger discount rate.

Put Options

The Black-Scholes formula for a European put option is

$$P(S, K, \sigma, r, T, \delta) = Ke^{-rT}N(-d_2) - Se^{-\delta T}N(-d_1) \qquad (11.3)$$

where d_1 and d_2 are given by equations (11.2a) and (11.2b).

Since the Black-Scholes call and put prices—equations (11.1) and (11.3)—are for European options, put-call parity must hold:

$$P(S, K, \sigma, r, T, \delta) = C(S, K, \sigma, r, T, \delta) + Ke^{-rT} - Se^{-\delta T} \qquad (11.4)$$

This version of the formula follows from equations (11.1) and (11.3), together with the fact that for any x, $1 - N(x) = N(-x)$. (This equation says that the probability of a random draw from the standard normal distribution being above x, $1 - N(x)$, equals the probability of a draw being below $-x$, $N(-x)$.)

Example 11.2 Using the same inputs as in Example 11.1, the put price is $1.607. We can compute the put price in two ways. First, computing it using equation (11.3), we obtain[2]

$$\$40e^{-0.08 \times 0.25} N\left(-\frac{\ln(\frac{41}{40}) + (0.08 - 0 - \frac{0.3^2}{2})0.25}{0.3\sqrt{0.25}}\right)$$

$$- \$41e^{-0 \times 0.25} N\left(-\frac{\ln(\frac{41}{40}) + (0.08 - 0 + \frac{0.3^2}{2})0.25}{0.3\sqrt{0.25}}\right) = \$1.607$$

Computing the price using put-call parity, equation (11.4), we have

$$P(41, 40, 0.3, 0.08, 0.25, 0) = 3.339 + 40e^{-0.08 \times 0.25} - 41$$
$$= \$1.607$$

---

[2] The put price here can be computed using the Black-Scholes put spreadsheet formula, BSPut:

$$\text{BSPut}(S, K, \sigma, r, t, \delta) = \text{BSPut}(41, 40, 0.3, 0.08, 0.25, 0) = \$1.607$$

What Assumptions Underlie the Black-Scholes Formula?

Derivations of the Black-Scholes formula make a number of assumptions that can be sorted into two groups: assumptions about how the stock price is distributed and assumptions about the economic environment. For the version of the formula we have presented, assumptions about the distribution of the stock price include the following:

- Continuously compounded returns on the stock are normally distributed and independent over time. (In particular, we assume there are no "jumps" in the stock price.)
- The volatility of continuously compounded returns is known and constant.
- Future dividends are known, either as a dollar amount or as a fixed dividend yield.

Assumptions about the economic environment include these:

- The risk-free rate is known and constant.
- There are no transaction costs or taxes.
- It is possible to short-sell costlessly and to borrow at the risk-free rate.

Many of these assumptions can easily be relaxed. For example, with a small change in the formula, we can permit the volatility and interest rate to vary over time in a known way.

As a practical matter, the first set of assumptions—those about the stock-price distribution—are the most crucial. Most academic and practitioner research on option pricing concentrates on relaxing these assumptions. You should keep in mind that almost *any* valuation procedure, including ordinary discounted cash flow, is based on assumptions that appear strong; the interesting question is how well the procedure works in practice.

11.2 APPLYING THE FORMULA TO OTHER ASSETS

The Black-Scholes formula is often thought of as a formula for pricing European options on stocks. Specifically, equations (11.1) and (11.3) provide the price of a call and put option, respectively, on a stock paying continuous dividends. In practice, we also want to be able to price European options on stocks paying discrete dividends, options on futures, and options on currencies. As with the binomial model, the Black-Scholes model can be adapted to different underlying assets by adjusting the dividend yield.

We can rewrite d_1 in the Black-Scholes formula, equation (11.2a), as

$$d_1 = \frac{\ln(Se^{-\delta T}/Ke^{-rT}) + \frac{1}{2}\sigma^2 T}{\sigma\sqrt{T}}$$

When d_1 is rewritten in this way, it is apparent that the dividend yield enters the formula *only* to discount the stock price, as $Se^{-\delta T}$, and the interest rate enters the formula *only* to discount the strike price, as Ke^{-rT}. Notice also that volatility enters only as $\sigma^2 T$.

The prepaid forward prices for the stock and strike asset are $F^P_{0,T}(S) = Se^{-\delta T}$ and $F^P_{0,T}(K) = Ke^{-rT}$. Therefore, we can write the Black-Scholes formula, equation (11.1), entirely in terms of prepaid forward prices and $\sigma\sqrt{T}$:[3]

$$C(F^P_{0,T}(S), F^P_{0,T}(K), \sigma, T) = F^P_{0,T}(S)N(d_1) - F^P_{0,T}(K)N(d_2) \quad (11.5)$$

$$d_1 = \frac{\ln[F^P_{0,T}(S)/F^P_{0,T}(K)] + \frac{1}{2}\sigma^2 T}{\sigma\sqrt{T}}$$

$$d_2 = d_1 - \sigma\sqrt{T}$$

This version of the formula is interesting because the dividend yield and the interest rate do not appear explicitly; they are already implicitly incorporated into the prepaid forward prices.

To price options on underlying assets other than stocks, we can use equation (11.5) in conjunction with the forward price formulas from Chapters 5 and 6. For all of the examples in this chapter, we will have a strike price denominated in cash, so that $F^P_{0,T}(K) = Ke^{-rT}$.

Options on Stocks with Discrete Dividends

When a stock makes discrete dividend payments, the prepaid forward price is

$$F^P_{0,T}(S) = S_0 - PV_{0,T}(Div)$$

where $PV_{0,T}(Div)$ is the present value of dividends payable over the life of the option. Thus, using equation (11.5), we can price a European option with discrete dividends by subtracting the present value of dividends from the stock price and entering the result into the formula in place of the stock price.

Example 11.3 Suppose $S = \$41$, $K = \$40$, $\sigma = 0.3$, $r = 8\%$, and $T = 0.25$ (3 months). The stock will pay a $3 dividend in 1 month, but makes no other payouts over the life of the option (hence, $\delta = 0$). The present value of the dividend is

$$PV(Div) = \$3e^{-0.08 \times 1/12} = \$2.98$$

Setting the stock price in the Black-Scholes formula equal to $\$41 - \$2.98 = \$38.02$, the Black-Scholes call price is $1.763.

---

[3] We can also let $V(T) = \sigma\sqrt{T}$ represent total volatility—uncertainty about the relative time T values of the underlying and strike assets—over the life of the option. The option price can then be written solely in terms of $F^P_{0,T}(S)$, $F^P_{0,T}(K)$, and $V(T)$. This gives us a minimalist version of the Black-Scholes formula: To price an option you need to know the prepaid forward prices of the underlying asset and the strike asset, and the relative volatility of the two.

Compared to the $3.399 price computed in Example 11.1, the dividend reduces the option price by about $1.64, or over half the amount of the dividend. Note that this is the price of a *European* option. An American option might be exercised just prior to the dividend and hence would have a greater price.

Options on Currencies

We can price an option on a currency by replacing the dividend yield with the foreign interest rate. If the spot exchange rate is x (expressed as domestic currency per unit of foreign currency), and the foreign currency interest rate is r_f, the prepaid forward price for the currency is

$$F^P_{0,T}(x) = x_0 e^{-r_f T}$$

Using equation (11.5), the Black-Scholes formula becomes

$$C(x, K, \sigma, r, T, r_f) = x e^{-r_f T} N(d_1) - K e^{-rT} N(d_2) \quad (11.6)$$

$$d_1 = \frac{\ln(x/K) + (r - r_f + \frac{1}{2}\sigma^2)T}{\sigma \sqrt{T}}$$

$$d_2 = d_1 - \sigma \sqrt{T}$$

This formula for the price of a European call on currencies is called the Garman-Kohlhagen model, after Garman and Kohlhagen (1983).

The price of a European currency put is obtained using parity:

$$P(x, K, \sigma, r, T, r_f) = C(x, K, \sigma, r, T, r_f) + K e^{-rT} - x e^{-r_f T}$$

Example 11.4 Suppose the spot exchange rate is $x = \$0.92/€$, $K = \$0.9$, $\sigma = 0.10$, $r = 6\%$ (the dollar interest rate), $T = 1$, and $r_f = 3.2\%$ (the euro-denominated interest rate). The price of a dollar-denominated euro call is $0.0606, and the price of a dollar-denominated euro put is $0.0172.

Options on Futures

The prepaid forward price for a futures contract is just the present value of the futures price. Thus, we price a European option on a futures contract by using the futures price as the stock price and setting the dividend yield equal to the risk-free rate. The resulting formula is also known as the **Black formula**:

$$C(F, K, \sigma, r, T, r) = F e^{-rT} N(d_1) - K e^{-rT} N(d_2) \quad (11.7)$$

$$d_1 = \frac{\ln(F/K) + \frac{1}{2}\sigma^2 T}{\sigma \sqrt{T}}$$

$$d_2 = d_1 - \sigma \sqrt{T}$$

The put price is obtained using the parity relationship for options on futures:

$$P(F, K, \sigma, r, T, r) = C(F, K, \sigma, r, T, r) + Ke^{-rT} - Fe^{-rT}$$

Example 11.5 Suppose the 1-year futures price for natural gas is $2.10/MMBtu and the volatility is 0.25. We have $F = \$2.10$, $K = \$2.10$, $\sigma = 0.25$, $r = 0.055$, $T = 1$, and $\delta = 0.055$ (the dividend yield is set to equal the interest rate). The Black-Scholes call price and put price are both $0.197721.

11.3 OPTION GREEKS

Option Greeks are formulas that express the change in the option price when an input to the formula changes, taking as fixed all the other inputs.[4] One important use of Greek measures is to assess the risk exposure of an option or a portfolio of options. For example, a market-making bank with a large portfolio of options would want to understand its exposure to stock-price changes, interest rates, volatility, etc. A portfolio manager wants to know what happens to the value of a portfolio of stock index options if there is a change in the level of the stock index. An options investor would like to know how interest rate changes and volatility changes affect profit and loss.

By assumption, the Greek measures change only *one* input at a time. In real life, we would expect interest rates and stock prices, for example, to change together. However, the Greek measures assume that *one and only one* input changes.

Greek measures can be computed for options on any kind of underlying asset, but we will focus here on stock options.

Definition of the Greeks

The units in which changes are measured are a matter of convention: For example, is the change in the interest rate a 1 percentage point change or a 1 basis point change? When we define a Greek measure, we will also provide the assumed unit of change.

Delta (Δ) measures the option-price change when the stock price increases by $1.

Gamma (Γ) measures the change in delta when the stock price increases by $1.

Vega measures the change in the option price when there is an increase in volatility of one percentage point.[5]

Theta (θ) measures the change in the option price when there is a decrease in the time to maturity of 1 day.

---

[4] Specifically, the Greeks are mathematical derivatives of the option-price formula with respect to the inputs.

[5] "Vega" is not a Greek letter. "Kappa" and "lambda" are also sometimes used to mean the same thing as vega.

Rho (ρ) measures the change in the option price when there is an increase in the interest rate of 1 percentage point (100 basis points).

Psi (Ψ) measures the change in the option price when there is an increase in the continuous dividend yield of 1 percentage point (100 basis points).

A useful mnemonic device for remembering some of these is that "vega" and "volatility" share the same first letter, as do "theta" and "time." Also "r" is often used to denote the interest rate and is the first letter in "rho."

We will discuss each Greek measure in turn, assuming for simplicity that we are talking about the Greek for a purchased option. The Greek for a written option is opposite in sign to that for the same purchased option.

Delta We have already encountered delta in Chapter 10, where we defined it as the number of shares in the portfolio that replicates the option. For a call option, delta is positive: As the stock price increases, the call price increases. Delta is also the sensitivity of the option price to a change in the stock price: If an option is replicated with 50 shares, the option should exhibit the price sensitivity of approximately 50 shares. You can think of delta as the *share-equivalent* of the option.

Figure 11.2 represents the behavior of delta for calls and puts with three different times to expiration. The figure illustrates that an in-the-money option ($S > \$40$ for a call and $S < \$40$ for a put) will be more sensitive to the stock price than an out-of-the-money option. If a call option is deep in-the-money it is likely to be exercised and hence the option should behave much like a leveraged position in a full share. Delta approaches 1 in this case and the share-equivalent of the option is 1. If the option is out-of-the money, it is unlikely to be exercised and the option has a low price, behaving like a position with very few shares. In this case delta is approximately 0 and the share-equivalent is 0. An at-the-money option may or may not be exercised and, hence, behaves like a position with between 0 and 1 share. This behavior of delta for a call can be seen in Figure 11.2. Note that as time to expiration increases, delta is less at high stock prices and greater at low stock prices. This behavior of delta reflects the fact that, for the depicted options that have greater time to expiration, the likelihood is greater that an out-of-the money option will eventually become in-the-money, and the likelihood is greater that an in-the-money option will eventually become out-of-the-money.

We can use the interpretation of delta as a share-equivalent to interpret the Black-Scholes price. The formula both prices the option and also tells us what position in the stock and borrowing is equivalent to the option. The formula for the call delta is

$$\Delta = e^{-\delta T} N(d_1)$$

If we hold $e^{-\delta t} N(d_1)$ shares and borrow $Ke^{-rT} N(d_2)$ dollars, the cost of this portfolio is

$$Se^{-\delta T} N(d_1) - Ke^{-rT} N(d_2)$$

This is the Black-Scholes price. Thus, the pieces of the formula tell us what position in the stock and borrowing synthetically re-creates the call. Figure 11.2 shows

FIGURE 11.2

Deltas for European puts and calls with different times to expiration; assumes $K = \$40$, $\sigma = 30\%$, $r = 8\%$, and $\delta = 0$.

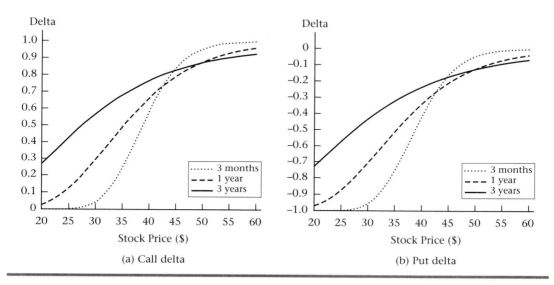

(a) Call delta

(b) Put delta

that delta changes with the stock price, so as the stock price moves, the replicating portfolio changes and must be adjusted dynamically. We also saw this in Chapter 10.

Delta for a put option is negative, so a stock price increase reduces the put price. This relationship can be seen in Figure 11.2(b). Since the put delta is just the call delta minus $e^{-\delta T}$ (from put-call parity), Figure 11.2(b) behaves similarly to Figure 11.2(a).

Gamma Gamma—the change in delta as the stock price changes—is always positive for a purchased call or put. Because of put-call parity, gamma is the same for a European call and put with the same strike price and time to expiration. As the stock price increases, delta increases, tending toward 1 for a call and zero for a put. This behavior can be seen in Figure 11.2.

Figure 11.3 graphs call and put gammas for options with three different expirations. Deep in-the-money options have a delta of about 1 and, hence, a gamma of about zero. (If delta is 1, it cannot change much as the stock price changes.) Similarly, deep out-of-the-money options have a delta of about zero and, hence, a gamma of about zero. The large gamma for the 3-month options in Figure 11.3 corresponds to the steep increase in delta for the same option in Figure 11.2.

FIGURE 11.3

Gammas for European calls and puts with different times to expiration; assumes $K = \$40$, $\sigma = 30\%$, $r = 8\%$, and $\delta = 0$. The figures in the two panels are identical.

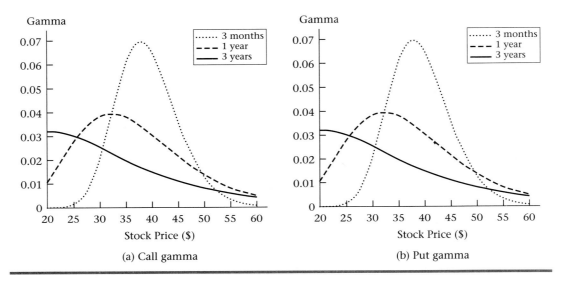

A derivative for which gamma is always positive is said to be *convex*. If gamma is positive, then delta is always increasing, and a graph of the price function will have curvature like that of the cross section of a bowl.

Vega An increase in volatility raises the price of a call or put option. Vega measures the sensitivity of the option price to volatility. Figure 11.4 shows that vega tends to be greater for at-the-money options, and greater for options with moderate than with short times to expiration.[6] Because of put-call parity, vega, like gamma, is the same for calls and puts with the same strike price and time to expiration.

Vega is low for out-of-the-money options because these options are inexpensive. An increase in volatility may raise the price a great deal in percentage terms, but only a small amount absolutely. A deep in-the-money option will have little option value (most of its value comes from intrinsic value). Vega will be small in both absolute and percentage terms for such an option. Here is an example illustrating this point.

---

[6] Be aware that neither result is true for very-long-lived options. With a 20-year option, for example, vega is greatest for out-of-the-money calls and lower than that for a 3-year call for the range of prices in the figure.

FIGURE 11.4

Vega for European calls with different times to expiration; assumes $K = \$40, \sigma = 30\%, r = 8\%$, and $\delta = 0$. The figures in the two panels are identical.

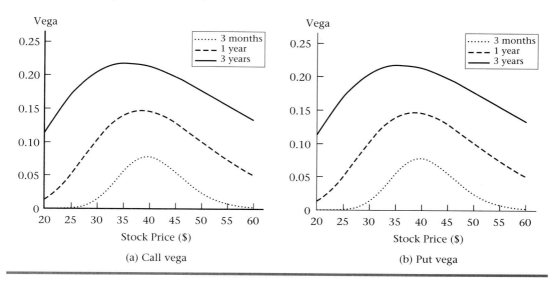

(a) Call vega

(b) Put vega

Example 11.6 Suppose $S = 40$, $\sigma = 0.30$, $r = 0.08$, $T = 1$, and $\delta = 0$. A 20-strike put is deep out-of-the-money and will have the price

$$\text{BSPut}(40, 20, 0.30, 0.08, 1, 0) = \$0.0127$$

If volatility increases to 31%, the price is

$$\text{BSPut}(40, 20, 0.30, 0.08, 1, 0) = \$0.0170$$

This is an increase of only $0.0043. However, the percentage increase is $0.0043/0.0127 = 33.86\%$. For a 40-strike put, the change in price is $3.3556 - 3.2092 = \$0.1464$, but the percentage change is $0.1464/3.2092 = 4.56\%$.

As an example of an in-the-money option, consider a 20-strike one-year call. By put-call parity, its price is

$$40 - 20e^{-0.08} + 0.0127 = \$21.5504$$

A 1 percentage point increase in volatility affects only the value of the put, and thus raises the price to $21.5547, a change of $0.0043. The percentage change is still smaller.

It is important to be clear about the units in which vega is expressed: How large is the assumed change in volatility? It is common to express vega as the change in option price for a *1 percentage point* (0.01) change in volatility.[7] Figure 11.4 follows this convention.

Theta Options generally—but not always—become less valuable as time to expiration decreases. Figure 11.5(a) depicts the call price for out-of-the-money, at-the-money, and in-the-money options as a function of the time to expiration. For the at-the-money (strike = $40) option, time decay is most rapid at expiration. For the others, time decay is more steady. Figure 11.5(c) graphs the call theta explicitly for three different times to expiration, showing that time decay is greatest for the at-the-money short-term option.

Time decay can be positive for European options in some special cases. Deep-in-the-money call options on an asset with a high dividend yield and deep-in-the-money puts are two examples. In both cases we would want to exercise the options early if possible. Since we cannot, the option effectively becomes a T-bill, appreciating as it gets close to expiration. This effect is evident in Figure 11.5(b), in which the in-the-money (50-strike) put becomes more valuable, other things equal, as expiration approaches. Figure 11.5(d) graphs the put theta explicitly, illustrating where it is positive.

When interpreting theta we need to know how long is the assumed change in time. The plots in Figure 11.5(c) and (d) are computed assuming a *1-day* change in time to expiration. It is also common practice to compute theta over longer periods, such as 10 days.

Rho Rho is positive for an ordinary stock call option. Exercising a call entails paying the fixed strike price to receive the stock; a higher interest rate reduces the present value of the strike. Similarly, for a put, rho is negative, since the put entitles the owner to receive cash, and the present value of this is lower with a higher interest rate. Figure 11.6 shows that as the time to expiration increases and as a call option becomes more in-the-money, rho is greater.

Figure 11.6 assumes a 1 percentage point (100 basis point) change in the interest rate.

Psi Psi is negative for an ordinary stock call option. A call entitles the holder to receive stock, but without receiving the dividends paid on the stock prior to exercising the option. Thus, the present value of the stock to be received is lower, the greater the dividend yield. Owning a put entitles an obligation to deliver the stock in the future in exchange for cash. The present value of the stock to be delivered goes down when the dividend yield goes up, so the put is more valuable when the dividend yield is greater. Hence, psi for a put is positive.

Figure 11.7 shows that the absolute value of psi increases with time to expiration. An increase in the dividend yield has little effect with a short time to maturity, but

---

[7] Vega is the derivative of the option price with respect to σ. It is expressed as the result of a percentage point change in volatility by dividing the derivative by 100.

11.3 Option Greeks

FIGURE 11.5

Panels (a) and (b) show the price as a function of time to expiration for in-the-money, at-the-money, and out-of-the-money calls and puts. Panels (c) and (d) show call and put thetas as a function of the stock price for three different times to expiration. Unless otherwise stated, graphs assume $S = \$40$, $K = \$40$, $\sigma = 30\%$, $r = 8\%$, and $\delta = 0$.

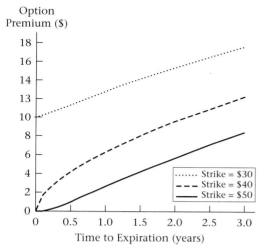

(a) Call price as a function of time to expiration

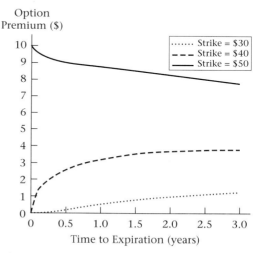

(b) Put price as a function of time to expiration

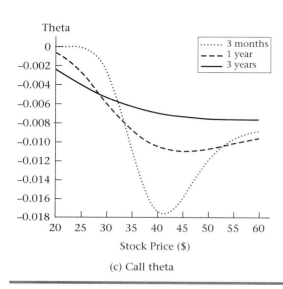

(c) Call theta

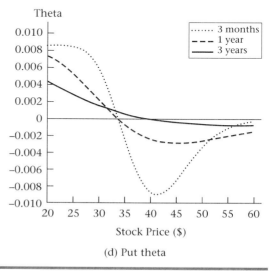

(d) Put theta

FIGURE 11.6

Rho for call options with different maturities at different stock prices; assumes $K = \$40$, $\sigma = 30\%$, $r = 8\%$, and $\delta = 0$.

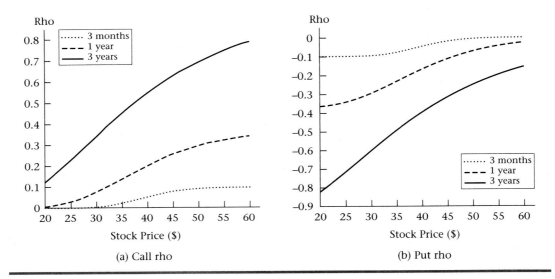

(a) Call rho   (b) Put rho

dividends lost by not owning the stock increase with time to maturity. Note that Figure 11.7(a) is a mirror image of Figure 11.6(a). The effect of an increase in the dividend yield on the underlying asset is the opposite of the effect of an increase in the interest rate, which is the dividend yield on the strike asset.

Greek Measures for Portfolios

The Greek measure of a portfolio is the sum of the Greeks of the individual portfolio components. This relationship is important because it means that the risk of complicated option positions is easy to evaluate. For a portfolio containing n options with a single underlying stock, where the quantity of each option is given by n_i, we have

$$\Delta_{\text{portfolio}} = \sum_{i=1}^{n} n_i \Delta_i$$

The same relation holds true for the other Greeks as well.

Example 11.7 Table 11.2 lists Greek measures for a 40–45 bull spread. Greeks for the spread are Greeks for the 40-strike call less those for the 45-strike call.

FIGURE 11.7

Psi for call options with different maturities at different stock prices; assumes $K = \$40$, $\sigma = 30\%$, $r = 8\%$, and $\delta = 0$.

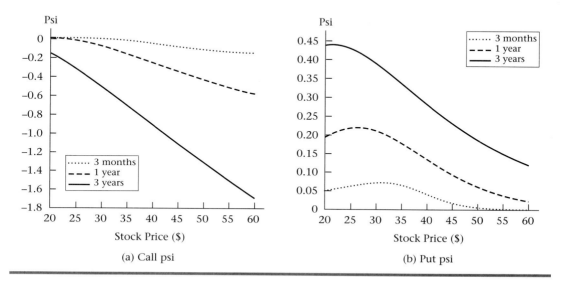

(a) Call psi

(b) Put psi

Option Elasticity

An option is an alternative to investing in the stock. Delta tells us the dollar risk of the option relative to the stock: If the stock price changes by $1, by how much does the option price change? The option elasticity, by comparison, tells us the risk of the option relative to the stock in percentage terms: If the stock price changes by 1%, what is the percentage change in the value of the option?

Dollar risk of the option If the stock price changes by ϵ, the **delta approximation** gives the approximate change in the option price:

$$\text{Change in option price} = \text{Change in stock price} \times \text{option delta}$$
$$= \epsilon \times \Delta \quad (11.8)$$

The **delta-gamma approximation** is an alternate formula that gives a more precise approximation of the change in the option price:

$$\text{Change in option price} = \epsilon \times \Delta + \frac{1}{2}\epsilon^2 \times \Gamma \quad (11.9)$$

TABLE 11.2

Greeks for the bull spread examined in Chapter 3, where $S = \$40$, $\sigma = 0.3$, $r = 0.08$, and $T = 91$ days, with a purchased 40-strike call (option 1) and a written 45-strike call (option 2). The column titled "combined" is the difference between column 1 and column 2.

	Option 1	Option 2	Combined
ω_i	1	-1	—
Price	2.7804	0.9710	1.8094
Delta	0.5824	0.2815	0.3009
Gamma	0.0652	0.0563	0.0088
Vega	0.0780	0.0674	0.0106
Theta	-0.0173	-0.0134	-0.0040
Rho	0.0511	0.0257	0.0255

Example 11.8 Suppose that the stock price is $S = \$41$, the strike price is $K = \$40$, volatility is $\sigma = 0.30$, the risk-free rate is $r = 0.08$, the time to expiration is $T = 1$, and the dividend yield is $\delta = 0$. As we saw earlier in the chapter, the option price is $\$6.961$. Delta is 0.6911 and gamma is 0.0286. If we own options to buy 1000 shares of stock, the delta of the position is

$$1000 \times \Delta = 691.1 \text{ shares of stock}$$

Thus, the option position at this stock price has a "share-equivalent" of 691 shares. If the stock price changes by $\$0.75$, the option price at $\$41.75$ is $\$7.4872$ and the actual change in the option price is $\$0.52620$. The change in value of the position is therefore $\$526.25$. Based on equation (11.8), we expect an option-price change of

$$\Delta \times \$0.75 = 0.6911 \times \$0.75 = \$0.5183$$

The more accurate delta-gamma approximation gives us an option-price change of

$$\Delta \times \$0.75 + \frac{1}{2}\$0.75^2 \times \Gamma = 0.6911 \times \$0.75 + \frac{1}{2}\$0.75^2 \times 0.0286 = \$0.5264$$

The error with the delta approximation is $\$0.0079$; the error with the delta-gamma approximation is $-\$0.0001$.

Percentage risk of the option The **option elasticity** computes the percentage change in the option price relative to the percentage change in the stock price. The percentage change in the stock price is simply ϵ/S. The percentage change in the option price is the dollar change in the option price, $\epsilon \Delta$, divided by the option price, C:

$$\frac{\epsilon \Delta}{C}$$

The option elasticity, denoted by Ω, is the ratio of these two:

$$\Omega \equiv \frac{\% \text{ change in option price}}{\% \text{ change in stock price}} = \frac{\frac{\epsilon \Delta}{C}}{\frac{\epsilon}{S}} = \frac{S\Delta}{C} \qquad (11.10)$$

The elasticity tells us the percentage change in the option for a 1% change in the stock. It is effectively a measure of the leverage implicit in the option.

For a call, $\Omega \geq 1$. We saw in Chapter 10 that a call option is replicated by a levered investment in the stock. A levered position in an asset is always riskier than the underlying asset.[8] Also, the implicit leverage in the option becomes greater as the option is more out-of-the-money. Thus, Ω decreases as the strike price decreases.

For a put, $\Omega \leq 0$. This occurs because the replicating position for a put option involves shorting the stock.

Example 11.9 Suppose $S = \$41$, $K = \$40$, $\sigma = 0.30$, $r = 0.08$, $T = 1$, and $\delta = 0$. The option price is $\$6.961$ and $\Delta = 0.6911$. Hence, the call elasticity is

$$\Omega = \frac{\$41 \times 0.6911}{\$6.961} = 4.071$$

The put has a price of $\$2.886$ and Δ of -0.3089; hence, the elasticity is

$$\Omega = \frac{\$41 \times -0.3089}{\$2.886} = -4.389$$

Figure 11.8 shows the behavior of elasticity for a call and put, varying both the stock price and time to expiration. The 3-month out-of-the-money options have elasticities exceeding 15. For longer time-to-expiration options, elasticity is much less sensitive to the moneyness of the option.

The volatility of an option The volatility of an option is the elasticity times the volatility of the stock:

$$\sigma_{\text{option}} = \sigma_{\text{stock}} \times |\Omega| \qquad (11.11)$$

where $|\Omega|$ is the absolute value of Ω. Since elasticity is a measure of leverage, this calculation is analogous to the computation of the standard deviation of levered equity by multiplying the unlevered beta by the ratio of firm value to equity. Based on Figure 11.8, for a stock with a 30% volatility, an at-the-money option could easily have a volatility of 120% or more.

---

[8] Mathematically, this follows since $S\Delta = Se^{-\delta t}N(d_1) > C(S)$.

FIGURE 11.8

Elasticity for call and put options with different maturities at different stock prices; assumes $K = \$40$, $\sigma = 30\%$, $r = 8\%$, and $\delta = 0$.

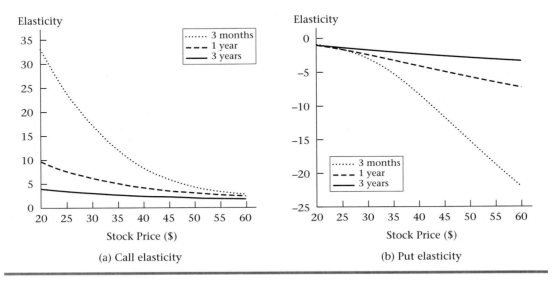

(a) Call elasticity

(b) Put elasticity

The risk premium of an option Since elasticity measures the percentage sensitivity of the option relative to the stock, it tells us how the risk premium of the option compares to that of the stock.

At a point in time, the option is equivalent to a position in the stock and in bonds; hence, the return on the option is a weighted average of the return on the stock and the risk-free rate. Let α denote the expected rate of return on the stock, γ the expected return on the option, and r the risk-free rate. We have

$$\gamma = \frac{\Delta S}{C(S)}\alpha + \left(1 - \frac{\Delta S}{C(S)}\right)r$$

Since $\Delta S/C(S)$ is elasticity, this can also be written as

$$\gamma = \Omega\alpha + (1 - \Omega)r$$

or

$$\gamma - r = (\alpha - r) \times \Omega \tag{11.12}$$

Thus, the risk premium on the option equals the risk premium on the stock times Ω.

Using our earlier facts about elasticity, we conclude that if the stock has a positive risk premium, then a call always has an expected return at least as great as the stock and that, other things equal, the expected return on an option goes down as the stock price goes up. In terms of the capital asset pricing model, we would say that the option beta goes down as the option becomes more in-the-money. For puts, we conclude that the put always has an expected return less than that of the stock.

The Sharpe ratio of an option The Sharpe ratio for any asset is the ratio of the risk premium to volatility:

$$\text{Sharpe ratio} = \frac{\alpha - r}{\sigma} \tag{11.13}$$

Using equations (11.11) and (11.12), the Sharpe ratio for an option is

$$\text{Sharpe ratio for option} = \frac{\Omega(\alpha - r)}{|\Omega|\sigma} = \text{sign}(\Omega)\frac{\alpha - r}{\sigma} \tag{11.14}$$

Thus, the Sharpe ratio for a call equals the Sharpe ratio for the underlying stock. The Sharpe ratio for a put, for which Ω is negative, is the negative of the Sharpe ratio for the stock. This equivalence of the Sharpe ratios is obvious once we realize that the option is always equivalent to a levered position in the stock, and that leverage per se does not change the Sharpe ratio.

The elasticty and risk premium of a portfolio The elasticity of a portfolio is the *weighted average* of the elasticities of the portfolio components. This is in contrast to the Greeks expressed in dollar terms (delta, gamma, etc.), for which the portfolio Greek is the *sum* of the component Greeks.

To understand this, suppose there is a portfolio of n different calls on the same underlying stock. The portfolio contains n_i units of the ith call, which has value C_i and delta Δ_i. The portfolio value is then $\sum_{i=1}^{n} n_i C_i$. Let $\omega_i = n_i C_i / \sum_{j=1}^{n} n_j C_j$ be the fraction of the portfolio invested in the ith call. For a \$1 change in the stock price, the change in the portfolio value is the sum of the deltas

$$\sum_{i=1}^{n} n_i \Delta_i \tag{11.15}$$

The elasticity of the portfolio is the percentage change in the portfolio divided by the percentage change in the stock, or

$$\Omega_{\text{portfolio}} = \frac{\frac{\sum_{i=1}^{n} n_i \Delta_i}{\sum_{j=1}^{n} n_j C_j}}{\frac{1}{S}} = \sum_{i=1}^{n} \left(\frac{n_i C_i}{\sum_{j=1}^{n} n_j C_j}\right) \frac{S \Delta_i}{C_i} = \sum_{i=1}^{n} \omega_i \Omega_i \tag{11.16}$$

Using equation (11.12), the risk premium of the portfolio, $\gamma - r$, is just the portfolio elasticity times the risk premium on the stock, $\alpha - r$:

$$\gamma - r = \Omega_{\text{portfolio}}(\alpha - r) \tag{11.17}$$

11.4 DELTA-HEDGING

When you buy or sell an option, a market-maker typically takes the other side of the transaction, selling if you buy and buying if you sell. Over the course of a day, a market-maker will accumulate a diverse inventory of option positions resulting from customer demand. Some of these positions will naturally offset (different customers might buy and sell similar IBM calls, for example). In general, however, the option positions will give a market-maker exposure to the underlying stock. How can a market-maker measure and hedge this exposure?[9]

We have already seen in Section 11.3 that the Greeks are risk measures. If a market-maker has a portfolio containing 1000 IBM options with a variety of strikes and expirations, it is possible to measure the exposure of the portfolio to IBM's stock price by summing the option deltas. In this section we will see how market-makers can manage exposure to the stock price by delta-hedging, which entails using the stock to offset the risk of the option. We will illustrate delta-hedging in an example where a market-maker has sold a call.

Option Risk in the Absence of Hedging

Suppose a customer wishes to buy a 91-day call option. The market-maker can fill this order by selling a call option. To be specific, suppose that $S = \$40$, $K = \$40$, $\sigma = 0.30$, $r = 0.08$ (continuously compounded), and $\delta = 0$. We will let T denote the expiration time of the option and t the present, so time to expiration is $T - t$. Let $T - t = 91/365$. The price, delta, gamma, and theta for this call are listed in Table 11.3.

Because the market-maker has written the option, the signs of the Greek measures for the position are opposite those of a purchased option. The written option is like shorting shares of stock (negative delta), and gains in value over time if the stock price does not change (positive theta). Because delta is negative, the risk for the market-maker who has written a call is that the stock price will rise.

Figure 11.9 graphs the overnight profit of the unhedged written call option as a function of the stock price, against the profit of the option at expiration. In computing overnight profit, we are varying the stock price, holding fixed all other inputs to the Black-Scholes formula except for time to expiration, which decreases by 1 day. It is apparent from the graph that the risk for the market-maker is a rise in the stock price. Although it is not obvious from the graph, if the stock price does not change, the market-maker will profit because of time decay: It would be possible to liquidate the option position by buying options at a lower price the next day than the price at which they were sold originally.

---

[9] You may be wondering if a market-maker *wants* to hedge the exposure to a basket of options. Think of market-making as a business like selling televisions: The goal is to buy low and sell high while accommodating customer demands, not to speculate on the price of inventory. Market-makers do sometimes take speculative positions, but in this discussion we will focus on pure market-making, ignoring speculation.

11.4 Delta-Hedging

TABLE 11.3 Price and Greek information for a call option with $S = \$40$, $K = \$40$, $\sigma = 0.30$, $r = 0.08$ (continuously compounded), $T - t = 91/365$, and $\delta = 0$.

	Purchased	Written
Call price	2.7804	−2.7804
Delta	0.5824	−0.5824
Gamma	0.0652	−0.0652
Theta	−0.0173	0.0173

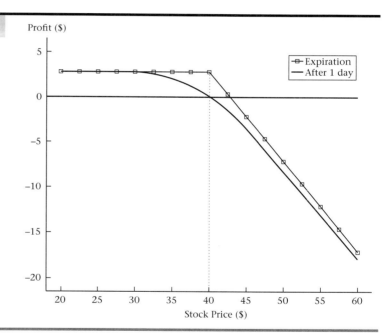

FIGURE 11.9 Depiction of overnight and expiration profit from writing a call option on one share of stock, if the market-maker is unhedged.

An Example of Delta-Hedging

We now see how the market-maker would delta-hedge a written 40-strike option on 100 shares of stock. Upon writing the option, the market-maker receives the premium $278.04. Since $\Delta = -0.5824$ for the written call, the share-equivalent of the option is -58.24 shares. Thus, to delta-hedge, the market-maker will buy 58.24 shares. (We will permit fractional share purchases in this example.) The net investment is

$$(58.24 \times \$40) - \$278.04 = \$2051.58$$

332 ● Chapter 11: The Black-Scholes Formula

We suppose that the market-maker finances this position by borrowing. At an 8% interest rate, there is an overnight financing charge of $\$2051.58 \times \left(e^{0.08/365} - 1\right) = \$0.45$.

Day 1: Marking-to-market The market-maker holds the delta-hedged position overnight. The next day, is there a profit or loss? A standard way to assess profit is by marking-to-market: We ask what the profit would be if we were to liquidate the position. The result is the mark-to-market profit.

Suppose the new stock price is $40.40. The new call option price with 1 day less to expiration and at the new stock price is $3.0010.[10] The overnight mark-to-market profit is a gain of $0.79, computed as follows:

Gain on 58.24 shares	$58.24 \times (\$40.40 - \$40) =$	$\$23.30$
Gain on written call option	$\$278.04 - \$300.10 =$	$-\$22.06$
Interest	$-(e^{0.08/365} - 1) \times \$2051.58 =$	$-\$0.45$
Overnight profit		**$0.79**

Thus, if we simply liquidate the portfolio, the amount left over is the mark-to-market profit. In this example we will suppose that we pay the $0.79 to ourselves. Similarly, if there had been a loss, we would have paid the loss out of pocket.

Day 1: Rebalancing the portfolio At the new stock price of $40.40, delta has increased in magnitude to 0.6078. (Figure 11.2 shows how delta changes with the stock price.) The option is now equivalent to a larger short position in the stock. If we wish to restore a net delta of zero, we must buy $60.784 - 58.240 = 2.544$ additional shares. This transaction requires an additional investment of $\$40.40 \times 2.54 = \$102.76$.[11] We can think about the net cash flows resulting from this activity as follows:

- The net value of the stock we hold and option we sold is now $2155.58. We can borrow this amount.
- We repay our previous borrowing of $2051.58 plus interest of $0.45.
- We buy $102.76 in additional shares.

Summing these amounts, we obtain

$$\$2155.58 - (\$2051.58 + \$0.45) - \$102.76 = \$0.79$$

Thus, another interpretation of the mark-to-market profit is that it is the amount left over after we borrow the maximum amount, repay our former borrowing (including interest), and buy the necessary additional shares.

---

[10] This is the Black-Scholes value calculated with one day less to expiration: BSCall (40.40, 40, 0.30, 0.08, 90/365, 0) = $3.001.

[11] In order to obtain this exact result, you need to compute the change in deltas in a spreadsheet, without rounding.

Day 2: Marking-to-market On day 2, suppose the stock price now rises further to $41.50. The market-maker again loses money on the written option (the price of which has risen to $386.95) and makes money on the 60.78 shares. Interest expense has increased over the previous day because additional investment was required for the extra shares. The net result from marking-to-market is a loss of −$2.46:

Gain on 60.78 shares	$60.78 \times (\$41.50 - \$40.40) =$	$66.86
Gain on written call option	$\$300.10 - \$368.95 =$	−$68.85
Interest	$-(e^{0.08/365} - 1) \times \$2155.58 =$	−$0.47
Overnight profit		**−$2.46**

Interpreting Market-Maker Profit

Why does the market-maker profit on day 1 and lose on day 2? And if the market-maker was hedged, why was there any profit or loss at all?

First, you can see that profit is not determined by the *direction* in which the stock price changes, since the stock price increased on both days, generating a profit and then a loss. This is reasonable: We would not expect the direction of the price change to matter since the market-maker is delta-hedged. What does matter is the *size* of the price change. When it is small, the delta-hedged position makes a profit. When it is large, the delta-hedged position makes a loss. Why?

The important insight is that as soon as the stock price changes, the market-maker is no longer exactly delta-hedged. The delta of the option changes because the option gamma is not zero. Moreover, as the stock price changes, because the gamma of the written call is negative, the net delta of the position changes in a way that systematically works against the market-maker. When the stock price increases, the delta of the written call decreases (becomes more negative), so the market-maker has a net short position (the delta of the written option position at the higher price is greater in magnitude than the fixed number of shares). When the stock price decreases, the delta of the option becomes less negative, so the market-maker has a net long position (the delta of the written option position at the lower price is smaller in magnitude than the fixed number of shares). Thus, the market-maker is short the stock as the stock price increases and long the stock as the stock price decreases. This loss in either direction is characteristic of a negative gamma position. On top of this, the market-maker pays interest on the position.

One factor works in the market-maker's favor: The theta of the written option is positive. Other things equal, the option becomes less expensive, and therefore less of a liability to the market-maker, as the time to expiration grows nearer. If the stock price had not moved at all, the market-maker would have earned profit due to theta.

We can graph market-maker profit to see the net result. To draw the graph, we repeat our overnight profit calculation at different stock prices. The result is in Figure 11.10. You can see that maximum profit occurs if the stock price does not move, and that large moves in either direction result in market-maker losses. A net loss occurs when the loss from gamma and interest expense exceed the gain from theta. Figure 11.10 depicts a typical shape for the profit graph of a delta-hedged negative gamma position.

334 ■ Chapter 11: The Black-Scholes Formula

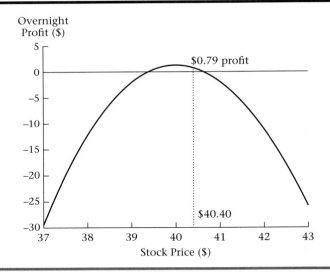

FIGURE 11.10

Overnight profit as a function of the stock price for a delta-hedged market-maker who has written a call.

You will notice that there are two points in Figure 11.10 where the market-maker breaks even. These points occur when the stock price moves approximately 1 standard deviation. One standard deviation in this example is approximately $\$40 \times 0.30/\sqrt{365} = \$0.628$. Thus, at stock prices of \$40.63 and \$39.37, the gain from theta exactly offsets the loss from gamma and interest. This is in fact what happens in the binomial model: We assume that the stock price can *only* move one standard deviation. In such a world, the delta-hedging market-maker always breaks even.

Figure 11.10 may look dire for the market-maker, but you should keep in mind that the probability that a lognormally distributed stock will move 1 standard deviation or less is about 68%. (This is the probability that a standard normal random variable will have a value between -1 and 1.) Thus, the profitable portion of the figure is more likely to occur than the unprofitable portion, and the highly unprofitable portions are relatively unlikely. If the volatility of the stock had been greater, the option price would have been greater and the region within which the market-maker made a profit would also have been greater.

As a final comment, the fact that the market-maker breaks even when the stock moves 1 standard deviation is not an accident or a coincidence. Black and Scholes derived the option pricing formula in an economic setting where 1 standard-deviation moves of the stock are typical (as in the binomial model) and by assuming that competitive market-makers would break even in such a setting.[12]

---

[12] McDonald (2006a, chapter 13) explains the rationale for the Black-Scholes model in more detail.

11.5 VOLATILITY

The volatility we use to price an option can dramatically affect the option price (see Figure 11.4), but volatility is unobservable. In this section we discuss volatility estimation using past returns (historical volatility), and the use of option prices to infer volatility (implied volatility).

Before we discuss volatility measures, it is worth repeating that the Black-Scholes model assumes that volatility is constant. As we discussed in Chapter 10, this means that the variance of continuously compounded returns is proportional to time, and the standard deviation of continuously compounded returns is proportional to the square root of time. This is why, in the Black-Scholes model, volatility always appears as either $\sigma^2 T$ or $\sigma\sqrt{T}$.

Historical Volatility

The annualized standard deviation of historical continuously compounded stock returns is called **historical volatility.** To illustrate the computation of historical volatility, Table 11.4 lists 8 weeks of Wednesday closing prices for the S&P 500 composite index. The third column reports the continuously compounded weekly return. For example, the continuously compounded return from 8/29/2007 to 9/5/2007 is computed as

$$\ln\left(\frac{1472.29}{1463.76}\right) = 0.0058$$

TABLE 11.4 Weekly closing prices and continuously compounded returns for the S&P 500 index.

Date	S&P Closing Price	Continuously Compounded Return
8/29/2007	1463.76	
9/5/2007	1472.29	0.0058
9/12/2007	1471.56	−0.0005
9/19/2007	1529.03	0.0383
9/26/2007	1525.42	−0.0024
10/3/2007	1539.59	0.0093
10/10/2007	1562.47	0.0147
10/17/2007	1541.24	−0.0137
Standard Deviation		**0.0164**

The standard deviation of the continously compounded returns is computed using the *StDev* function in Excel, and then annualized by multiplying by $\sqrt{52}$. Over the 8-week period in the table, the realized weekly standard deviation of returns was 0.0164 for the S&P 500 index. The estimated historical annualized standard deviation is therefore $0.0164 \times \sqrt{52} = 0.1184$. This volatility estimate is meant to illustrate the mechanics of the volatility calculation; it is computed using only seven returns and you would therefore expect it to be measured with error.

This calculation uses weekly data, which avoids some complications of using daily data. In practice, returns over a weekend are not as volatile as theory suggests (the variance over the 3 days from Friday to Monday should be three times greater than over a single weekday; weekend variance is substantially less than this). Holidays are also less volatile than weekdays. Using weekly data avoids this kind of complication and using Wednesdays avoids most holidays. On the other hand, with daily data we have more observations and thus can obtain a more precise estimate of volatility. It is conventional when using daily data to annualize by multiplying by $\sqrt{252}$, which is the number of trading days in a typical year. By instead using daily data from August 1, 2007, to October 18, 2007, we obtain a daily volatility of 0.0116, which gives an annual volatility of $0.0116 \times \sqrt{252} = 0.1851$.

The procedure outlined above is a reasonable way to estimate volatility if continuously compounded returns are independent and identically distributed. However, in some cases returns are not independent. If a high price of oil today leads to decreased demand and increased supply, we would expect prices in the future to be lower. In this case, the volatility over T years will be less than $\sigma\sqrt{T}$, reflecting the tendency of prices to revert from extreme values. Extra care is required with volatility if returns are not independent over time.

Implied Volatility

A problem with historical volatility is that history is not a reliable guide to the future: Markets have quiet and turbulent periods and predictable events (such as government announcements of economic statistics) that can create periods of greater than normal uncertainty. There are sophisticated statistical models designed to provide better volatility estimates, but the fundamental problem is that history cannot provide a reliable estimate of *future* volatility.

If we observe an option price, we can compute the volatility input implied by the price of the option. This is called the **implied volatility** of the option. Assuming that we observe the stock price S, strike price K, interest rate r, dividend yield δ, and time to expiration T, the implied call volatility is the $\hat{\sigma}$ that solves

$$\text{Market option price} = C(S, K, \hat{\sigma}, r, T, \delta) \tag{11.18}$$

By definition, if we use implied volatility to price an option, we obtain the market price of the option. Thus, we cannot use implied volatility to assess whether an option price is correct, but implied volatility does tell us the market's assessment of volatility.

Computing an implied volatility requires that we (1) observe a market price for an option and (2) have an option pricing model with which to infer volatility. Equation (11.18) cannot be solved directly for the implied volatility, $\hat{\sigma}$, so it is necessary to use an iterative procedure to solve the equation. Any pricing model can be used to calculate an implied volatility, but Black-Scholes implied volatilities are frequently used as benchmarks.

Example 11.10 Suppose we observe a 45-strike 6-month European call option with a premium of $8.07. The stock price is $50, the interest rate is 8%, and the dividend yield is zero. We can compute the option price as

$$\$8.07 = \text{BSCall}(50, 45, \sigma, 0.08, 0.5, 0).$$

By trial and error (or by using a tool such as Excel's Goalseek), we find that setting $\sigma = 28.7\%$ gives us a call price of $8.07.[13]

Implied volatility is commonly computed and reported. Just as stock markets provide information about stock prices and permit trading stocks, option markets provide information about volatility, and, in effect, permit the trading of volatility. Market volatility is important since it may affect the willingness of investors to hold stocks, it affects the margins required for derivatives positions, and it often reflects general uncertainty about economic conditions. Viewed from this perspective, we should expect information about volatility to be one of the most important things we can learn from option prices.

Implied volatility provides a quick way to describe the general level of option prices for a given underlying asset. One could describe prices by saying "the 40-strike option has a price of $2.78 when the stock price is $40." It is much simpler to say that the option has a 30% implied volatility. As a result, option prices are sometimes quoted in terms of volatility, rather than as a dollar price. Implied volatility can also be used to compute a price for an option that does not trade, in a manner consistent with prices of options that do trade.

Implied volatility can also be used to assess the performance of the Black-Scholes model. Volatility skew provides a measure of how well option pricing models work. If the Black-Scholes model were literally true, *all options on a given asset would have the same implied volatility*. This is a strong empirical prediction, that is quite obviously violated by the prices we observe. Implied volatility varies over time, and at a point in time, it varies across option strikes. for a given asset.

To illustrate variation over time, Figure 11.11 displays a history of the 30-day implied volatility of the S&P 500 index, known as the VIX index.[14] As a measure of

---

[13] An implied volatility function is available with the spreadsheets accompanying this book.

[14] The VIX index is calculated using a weighted sum of near-term, out-of-the-money call and put prices. If K_i is the ith strike and $F_{0,T}$ is the forward price for the index, the formula is

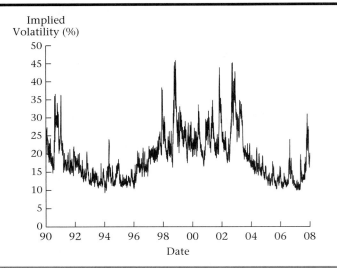

FIGURE 11.11

The VIX index (implied volatility on the S&P 500 index), 1990–2007. *Source:* Chicago Board Options Exchange.

index volatility, you can think of the VIX index as a broad measure of uncertainty. The press sometimes refers to the VIX as the "fear index" for the market, since it is a forward-looking measure of volatility. It is apparent that the VIX has been quite variable over the last two decades, with implied volatility ranging from 10% to 45%.

To illustrate variation in implied volatility across options on a given asset, Table 11.5 reports sample Black-Scholes implied volatilities of calls and puts on the S&P 500 index, computed separately for the bid and ask option prices. These options are European, so the Black-Scholes model is appropriate.

It is apparent that the implied volatilities in the table are not all equal, but there are two patterns that are quite important.

First, notice that the implied volatilities of calls and put, generally move together. When the call volatilities are high, the put volatilities are as well. This is what we would expect from put-call parity: An effect that raises a put price (and thus put implied volatility) would also raise the call price.

Second, the implied volatilities for the out-of-the money puts/in-the-money calls (the 1400 strike options) are systematically greater than for the near-the-money options

$$\hat{\sigma}^2 = \frac{2}{T} \sum_{K_i \leq K_0} \frac{\Delta K_i}{K_i^2} e^{rT} \text{Put}(K_i) + \frac{2}{T} \sum_{K_i > K_0} \frac{\Delta K_i}{K_i^2} e^{rT} \text{Call}(K_i) - \frac{1}{T} \left[\frac{F_{0,T}}{K_0} - 1 \right]^2$$

where K_0 is the first strike below the forward price for the index and $\Delta K_i = (K_{i+1} - K_{i-1})/2$. It is not at all obvious how this equation computes implied volatility. For more details about this calculation, see Chicago Board Options Exchange (2003).

| TABLE 11.5 | | \multicolumn{5}{l}{Black-Scholes implied volatilities for S&P 500 options, October 19, 2007, based on midday option prices from www.cboe.com; assumes $S = 1508.08$, $r = 4.5\%$, and $\delta = 0.02$.} |

		Calls		Puts	
Expiration	Strike	Bid	Ask	Bid	Ask
Nov 2007	1400	0.2558	0.2348	0.2779	0.2592
Nov 2007	1500	0.1940	0.1804	0.2064	0.1929
Nov 2007	1525	0.1798	0.1667	0.1906	0.1769
Nov 2007	1550	0.1657	0.1488	0.1759	0.1618
Dec 2007	1400	0.2506	0.2325	0.2732	0.2510
Dec 2007	1500	0.2008	0.1870	0.2172	0.2035
Dec 2007	1525	0.1890	0.1752	0.2049	0.1868
Dec 2007	1550	0.1840	0.1671	0.1929	0.1789
Mar 2008	1400	0.2365	0.2240	0.2492	0.2370
Mar 2008	1500	0.2050	0.1950	0.2155	0.2014
Mar 2008	1525	0.1971	0.1876	0.2074	0.1979
Mar 2008	1550	0.1901	0.1798	0.1996	0.1901

in the same month. This is quite typical for stocks and stock indices, and is referred to as **volatility skew**.

When you graph implied volatility against the strike price, the resulting line can take different shapes, often described as "smiles," "frowns," and "smirks." Explaining these patterns and modifying pricing models to account for them is an active area of research in option pricing theory.

When examining implied volatilities, it is useful to keep put-call parity in mind. If options are European, then *puts and calls with the same strike and time to expiration must have the same implied volatility*. This is true because prices of European puts and calls must satisfy the parity relationship or else there is an arbitrage opportunity. Thus, skew is not related to whether an option is a put or a call, but rather to differences in the strike price and time to expiration. Although call and put volatilities are not exactly equal in Table 11.5, they are generally close enough that parity arbitrage would not be profitable after transaction costs are taken into account.

Trading Volatility

There are a variety of ways to trade volatility, including option spreads, delta-neutral positions, and futures contracts on volatility. You could trade volatility in order

FIGURE 11.12
Specifications for the CBOE VIX futures contract.

Underlying	The VIX index
Where traded	Chicago Board Options Exchange
Size	$1000 times the VIX index
Months	Up to 6 consecutive near-term months and February, May, August, November to a maximum of 15 months
Trading ends	The Wednesday 30 days prior to the following month's option expiration date
Settlement	Cash-settled

to speculate about whether volatility will change, or you could trade volatility as a hedge (for example, if you are a market-maker).

Trading volatility with option spreads is common. We saw in Chapter 3 that straddles provide a way to bet that volatility will be high. Investors who expect that implied volatility will increase, for example, can buy a straddle. A written straddle or a purchased butterfly spread is a bet that volatility will decrease.

We also saw in the previous section that a delta-neutral hedge position when gamma is not zero is a way to trade volatility. Look again at Figure 11.10. The position depicted in this figure resembles the profit on a written straddle (Figure 3.12 on page 82), and like the written straddle is a bet that the stock will not be volatile. As we discussed, if the stock moves by more than 1 standard deviation, the market-maker loses money; if the stock moves by less than 1 standard deviation, the market maker makes money.

There are also several exchange-traded futures contracts that are based directly on different volatility measures. The two basic approaches permit hedging or speculation based on (1) what implied volatility will be at a future date or (2) what historical volatility will have been at a future date.

The CBOE's VIX futures contract is a contract of the first kind, settling based on the implied volatility of the S&P 500 at a specific future date (there are also volatility contracts for other indexes). Figure 11.13 displays the specifications for the VIX futures contract. The payoff of the contract is

$$1000 \times [\text{VIX}_T - F_{0,T}(V)]$$

where $F_{0,T}(V)$ is the VIX futures price. An investor with a long position in that contract will earn $1000 if the VIX increases by 100 basis points (for example, from 20% to 21%). The expiration date on the VIX is set so that the settlement volatility is determined when the options used to compute the VIX index have exactly 30 days to expiration. Thus, the VIX futures contract settles based on a forward-looking measure of volatility.

The second approach to a volatility futures contract is to settle the contract based on historical variance. A **variance swap** is a contract that has a payoff based on the

FIGURE 11.13

Specifications for the CBOE S&P 500 3-month variance futures contract.

Underlying	The 3-month historical variance on the S&P 500 index
Where traded	Chicago Board Options Exchange
Size	Realized variance $\times$ 10,000 $\times$ \$50
Months	March, June, September, December, out 1 year
Trading ends	The third Friday of the expiration month
Settlement	Cash-settled

difference between the actual variance of an asset over time and a reference variance. The payoff to a variance swap settled at maturity is

$$[\hat{V}^2 - F_{0,T}(V^2)] \times N$$

where V^2 is the actual variance over the life of the contract and N is the notional amount of the contract. The payoff computes the difference between the actual variance and a forward variance, $F_{0,T}(V^2)$. The CBOE variance futures contract is essentially the same, settling based on historical variance. For simplicity, we treat the payoff as if it were a forward contract, settling on one day. Let ϵ_i be the continuously compounded return on day i. The payoff at expiration for the CBOE contract is

$$\$50 \times \left[10,000 \times 252 \times \sum_{i=1}^{n_a-1} \frac{\epsilon_i^2}{n_e - 1} - F_{0,T}(V^2) \right]$$

where the ϵ_i are the continuously compounded daily returns for the S&P 500 index, n_a is the actual number of S&P prices used in constructing the V^2 idea of a variance (hence there are $n_a - 1$ returns), and n_e is the number of expected trading days at the outset of the contract. The payoff is thus based on the annualized sum of squared, continuously compounded daily returns over a 3-month period, $\hat{V}^2$. The measured price is quoted as $\hat{V}^2 \times 10,000$, and by definition a 1-unit change in this number (called a *variance point*) is worth \$50. There is also a 12-month variance contract.

CHAPTER SUMMARY

Under certain assumptions, the Black-Scholes formula provides an exact formula—approximated by the binomial formula—for pricing European options. The inputs to the Black-Scholes formula are the same as for the binomial formula: the stock price, strike price, volatility, interest rate, time to expiration, and dividend yield. As with the binomial formula, the Black-Scholes formula accommodates different underlying assets by changing the dividend yield.

Option Greeks measure the change in the option price (or other option characteristic) for a change in an option input. Delta, gamma, vega, theta, rho, and psi are widely used in practice to assess the risk of an option position. The option elasticity is the percentage change in the option's price for a 1% change in the stock price. The volatility and beta of an option are the volatility and beta of the stock times the option elasticity. Thus, an option and the underlying stock have the same Sharpe ratio.

Market-makers use delta to determine how many shares to hold in order to hedge option positions. This is called "delta-hedging."

Of the inputs to the Black-Scholes formula, volatility is hardest to estimate. In practice, it is common to use the formula in backward fashion to infer the market's estimate of volatility from the option price. This implied volatility is computed by finding the volatility for which the formula matches observed market prices for options. In theory, all options of a given maturity should have the same implied volatility. In practice, they do not, a phenomenon known as volatility skew. There are a variety of ways to trade volatility, including option spreads such as straddles, delta-neutral positions, implied volatility futures, and realized variance futures.

FURTHER READING

In Chapters 12, 13, and 14, we will use option pricing to explore applications of option pricing, including the creation of structured products, issues in compensation options, capital structure, tax management with options, and real options.

The classic early papers on option pricing are Black and Scholes (1973) and Merton (1973b). The details of how the binomial model converges to the Black-Scholes model are in Cox et al. (1979).

PROBLEMS

In answering many of these problems you can use the functions BSCall, BSPut, and the accompanying functions for the Greeks (see the spreadsheets on the CD-ROM accompanying this book).

11.1 Use a spreadsheet to verify the option prices in Examples 11.1 and 11.2.

11.2 Using the BinomCall and BinomPut functions, compute the binomial approximations for the options in Examples 11.1 and 11.2. Be sure to compute prices for $n = 8, 9, 10, 11,$ and 12. What do you observe about the behavior of the binomial approximation?

11.3 Let $S = \$100$, $K = \$120$, $\sigma = 30\%$, $r = 0.08$, and $\delta = 0$.

    a. Compute the Black-Scholes call price for 1 year to maturity and for a variety of very long times to maturity. What happens to the option price as $T \to \infty$?

b. Set $\delta = 0.001$. Repeat (a). Now what happens to the option price? What accounts for the difference?

11.4 Let $S = \$120$, $K = \$100$, $\sigma = 30\%$, $r = 0$, and $\delta = 0.08$.

    a. Compute the Black-Scholes call price for 1 year to maturity and for a variety of very long times to maturity. What happens to the price as $T \to \infty$?

    b. Set $r = 0.001$. Repeat (a). Now what happens? What accounts for the difference?

11.5 The exchange rate is ¥95/€, the yen-denominated interest rate is 1.5%, the euro-denominated interest rate is 3.5%, and the exchange rate volatility is 10%.

    a. What is the price of a 90-strike yen-denominated euro put with 6 months to expiration?

    b. What is the price of a 1/90-strike euro-denominated yen call with 6 months to expiration?

    c. What is the link between your answer to (a) and your answer to (b), converted to yen?

11.6 Suppose XYZ is a non-dividend-paying stock. Suppose $S = \$100$, $\sigma = 40\%$, $\delta = 0$, and $r = 0.06$.

    a. What is the price of a 105-strike call option with 1 year to expiration?

    b. What is the 1-year forward price for the stock?

    c. What is the price of a 1-year 105-strike option, where the underlying asset is a futures contract maturing at the same time as the option?

11.7 Suppose $S = \$100$, $K = \$95$, $\sigma = 30\%$, $r = 0.08$, $\delta = 0.03$, and $T = 0.75$.

    a. Compute the Black-Scholes price of a call.

    b. Compute the Black-Scholes price of a call for which $S = \$100 \times e^{-0.03 \times 0.75}$, $K = \$95 \times e^{-0.08 \times 0.75}$, $\sigma = 0.3$, $T = 0.75$, $\delta = 0$, $r = 0$. How does your answer compare to that for (a)?

11.8 Make the same assumptions as in the previous problem.

    a. What is the 9-month forward price for the stock?

    b. Compute the price of a 95-strike 9-month call option on a futures contract.

    c. What is the relationship between your answer to (b) and the price you computed in the previous problem? Why?

11.9 Assume $K = \$40$, $\sigma = 30\%$, $r = 0.08$, $T = 0.5$, and the stock is to pay a single dividend of $2 tomorrow, with no dividends thereafter.

a. Suppose $S = \$50$. What is the price of a European call option? Consider an otherwise identical American call. What is its price?

b. Repeat, only suppose $S = \$60$.

c. Under what circumstance would you not exercise the option today?

11.10 "Time decay is greatest for an option close to expiration." Use the spreadsheet functions to evaluate this statement. Consider both the dollar change in the option value and the percentage change in the option value, and examine both in-the-money and out-of-the-money options.

11.11 In the absence of an explicit formula, we can estimate the change in the option price due to a change in an input—such as σ—by computing the following for a small value of ϵ:

$$\text{Vega} = \frac{\text{BSCall}(S, K, \sigma + \epsilon, r, t, \delta) - \text{BSCall}(S, K, \sigma - \epsilon, r, t, \delta)}{2\epsilon}$$

a. What is the logic behind this calculation? Why does ϵ need to be small?

b. Compare the results of this calculation with results obtained from BSCallVega.

11.12 Suppose $S = \$100$, $K = \$95$, $\sigma = 30\%$, $r = 0.08$, $\delta = 0.03$, and $T = 0.75$. Using the technique in the previous problem compute the Greek measure corresponding to a change in the dividend yield. What is the predicted effect of a change of 1 percentage point in the dividend yield?

11.13 Consider a bull spread where you buy a 40-strike call and sell a 45-strike call. Suppose $S = \$40$, $\sigma = 0.30$, $r = 0.08$, $\delta = 0$, and $T = 0.5$. Draw a graph with stock prices ranging from $20 to $60 depicting the profit on the bull spread after 1 day, 3 months, and 6 months.

11.14 Consider a bull spread where you buy a 40-strike call and sell a 45-strike call. Suppose $\sigma = 0.30$, $r = 0.08$, $\delta = 0$, and $T = 0.5$.

a. Suppose $S = \$40$. What are delta, gamma, vega, theta, and rho?

b. Suppose $S = \$45$. What are delta, gamma, vega, theta, and rho?

c. Are any of your answers to (a) and (b) different? If so, why?

11.15 Consider a bull spread where you buy a 40-strike put and sell a 45-strike put. Suppose $\sigma = 0.30$, $r = 0.08$, $\delta = 0$, and $T = 0.5$.

a. Suppose $S = \$40$. What are delta, gamma, vega, theta, and rho?

b. Suppose $S = \$45$. What are delta, gamma, vega, theta, and rho?

c. Are any of your answers to (a) and (b) different? If so, why?

d. Are any of your answers different in this problem from those in Problem 11.14? If so, why?

11.16 Assume $r = 8\%$, $\sigma = 30\%$, and $\delta = 0$. In doing the following calculations, use a stock-price range of $60–$140, stock-price increments of $5, and two different times to expiration: 1 year and 1 day. Consider purchasing a 100-strike straddle, i.e., buying one 100-strike put and one 100-strike call.

    a. Compute delta, vega, theta, and rho of the call and put separately, for the different stock prices and times to expiration.

    b. Compute delta, vega, theta, and rho of the purchased straddle (do this by adding the Greeks of the individual options). As best you can, explain intuitively the signs of the straddle Greeks.

    c. Graph delta, vega, theta, and rho of the straddle with 1 year to expiration as a function of the stock price. In each case explain why the graph looks as it does.

11.17 Assume $r = 8\%$, $\sigma = 30\%$, and $\delta = 0$. Using 1-year-to-expiration European options, construct a position where you sell two 80-strike puts, buy one 95-strike put, buy one 105-strike call, and sell two 120-strike calls. For a range of stock prices from $60 to $140, compute delta, vega, theta, and rho of this position. As best you can, explain intuitively the signs of the Greeks.

11.18 Let $S = \$100$, $K = \$90$, $\sigma = 30\%$, $r = 8\%$, $\delta = 5\%$, and $T = 1$.

    a. What is the Black-Scholes call price?

    b. Now price a put where $S = \$90$, $K = \$100$, $\sigma = 30\%$, $r = 5\%$, $\delta = 8\%$, and $T = 1$.

    c. What is the link between your answers to (a) and (b)? Why?

11.19 Suppose you sell a 45-strike call with 91 days to expiration. What is delta? If the option is on 100 shares, what investment is required for a delta-hedged portfolio? What is your overnight profit if the stock tomorrow is $39? What if the stock price is $40.50?

11.20 Suppose you sell a 40-strike put with 91 days to expiration. What is delta? If the option is on 100 shares, what investment is required for a delta-hedged portfolio? What is your overnight profit if the stock price tomorrow is $39? What if it is $40.50?

part 4

Financial Engineering and Applications

In the preceding chapters we have focused on forwards, swaps, and options as stand-alone financial claims. In the next three chapters we will see that these claims can be used as financial building blocks to create new claims, and also see that derivatives pricing theory can help us understand corporate financial policy and the valuation of investment projects.

Specifically, in Chapter 12 we see how it is possible to construct and price bonds that make payments that, instead of being denominated in cash, are denominated in stocks, commodities, and different currencies. Such bonds can be structured to contain embedded options. We also see how such claims can be used for risk management and how their issuance can be motivated by tax and regulatory considerations. Chapter 13 examines some corporate contexts in which derivatives are important, including corporate financial policy, compensation options, and mergers. Chapter 14 examines real options, in which the insights from derivatives pricing are used to value investment projects.

12 Financial Engineering and Security Design

Forwards, calls, puts, and other kinds of derivatives can be added to bonds or otherwise combined to create new securities. For example, many traded securities are effectively bonds with embedded options. Individual derivatives thus become building blocks—ingredients used to construct new kinds of financial products. In this chapter we will see how to assemble the ingredients to create new products. The process of constructing new instruments from these building blocks is called **financial engineering**.

12.1 THE MODIGLIANI-MILLER THEOREM

The starting point for any discussion of modern financial engineering is the analysis of Franco Modigliani and Merton Miller (Modigliani and Miller (1958)). Before their work, financial analysts would puzzle over how to compare the values of firms with similar *operating* characteristics but different *financial* characteristics. Modigliani and Miller realized that different financing decisions (for example, the choice of the firm's debt-to-equity ratio) may carve up the firm's cash flows in different ways, but if the *total* cash flows paid to all claimants is unchanged, the total value of all claims would remain the same. They showed that if firms differing only in financial policy differed in market value, profitable arbitrage would exist. Using their famous analogy, the price of whole milk should equal the total prices of the skim milk and butterfat that can be derived from that milk.[1]

The Modigliani-Miller analysis relies upon numerous assumptions: For example, there are no taxes, no transaction costs, no bankruptcy costs, and no private information. Nevertheless, the basic Modigliani-Miller result provided clarity for a confusing issue, and it created a starting point for thinking about the effects of taxes, transaction costs, and the like, revolutionizing finance.

---

[1] Standard corporate finance texts offer a more detailed discussion of the Modigliani-Miller results. The original paper (Modigliani and Miller (1958)) is a classic.

All of the no-arbitrage pricing arguments we have been using embody the Modigliani-Miller spirit. For example, we saw in Chapter 2 that we could synthetically create a forward contract using options, a call option using a forward contract, bonds, and a put, and so forth. In Chapter 10 we saw that an option could also be synthetically created from a position in the stock and borrowing or lending. If prices of actual claims differ from their synthetic equivalents, arbitrage is possible.

Financial engineering is an application of the Modigliani-Miller idea. We can combine claims such as stocks, bonds, forwards, and options and assemble them to create new claims. The price for this new security is the sum of the pieces combined to create it. When we create a new instrument in this fashion, as in the Modigliani-Miller analysis, value is neither created nor destroyed. Thus, financial engineering has no value in a pure Modigliani-Miller world. However, in real life, the new instrument may have different tax, regulatory, or accounting characteristics, or may provide a way for the issuer or buyer to obtain a particular payoff at lower transaction costs than the alternatives. Financial engineering thus provides a way to create instruments that meet specific needs of investors and issuers.

As a starting point, you can ask the following questions when you confront new financial instruments:

- What is the payoff of the instrument?
- Is it possible to synthetically create the same payoffs using some combination of assets, bonds, and options?
- Who might issue or buy such an instrument?
- What problem does the instrument solve?

12.2 STRUCTURED NOTES WITHOUT OPTIONS

An ordinary note (or bond) has interest and maturity payments that are fixed at the time of issue. A **structured note** has interest or maturity payments that are not fixed in dollars but are contingent in some way. Structured notes can make payments based on stock prices, interest rates, commodities, or currencies, and they can have options embedded in them. The equity-linked CD discussed in Chapter 2 is an example of a structured note, as it has a maturity payment based upon the performance of the S&P 500 index.

In this section we will discuss the pricing of notes making payments in something other than cash: equity, commodities, or currency. In the next section we see how to add options.

Throughout this chapter we will value claims, even relatively complicated claims, using these two steps:

1. Express the payoff to the claim in terms of simple individual claims such as zero-coupon bonds, prepaid forward contracts, and options.
2. Value the claim by summing the values of these individual pieces.

You will see that the general valuation procedure is the same whether the claims have payments denominated in cash, stock, commodities, or a foreign currency.

Zero-Coupon Bonds Paying Cash

The most basic financial instrument is a zero-coupon bond. As in Chapter 7, let $r_s(t_0, t_1)$ represent the annual continuously compounded interest rate prevailing at time $s \leq t_0$, for a loan from time t_0 to time t_1. Similarly, the price of a zero-coupon bond purchased at time t_0, maturing at time t_1, and quoted at time s is $P_s(t_0, t_1)$. Thus, we have

$$P_s(t_0, t_1) = e^{-r_s(t_0, t_1)(t_1 - t_0)}$$

When there is no risk of misunderstanding, we will assume that the interest rate is quoted at time $t_0 = 0$, and the bond is also purchased then. We will denote the rate $r_0(0, t) = r(t)$, and the corresponding bond price P_t. So we will write

$$P_t = e^{-r(t)t}$$

P_t is the current price of a t-period zero-coupon bond.

There are two important, equivalent interpretations of P_t. First, P_t is a discount factor, since it is the price today for \$1 delivered at time t. Second, P_t is the prepaid forward price for \$1 delivered at time t. These are different ways of saying the same thing:

Zero-coupon bond price = Discount factor for \$1 = Prepaid forward price for \$1

Financial valuation entails discounting, which is why zero-coupon bonds are a basic building block. The notion that prepaid forward prices are discount factors will play an important role in this chapter.

Coupon Bonds Paying Cash

Once we have a set of zero-coupon bonds, we can analyze other fixed-payment instruments, such as ordinary coupon bonds. Consider a bond that pays the coupon c, n times over the life of the bond, makes the maturity payment M, and matures at time T. We will denote the price of this bond as $B(0, T, c, n, M)$. The time between coupon payments is T/n, and the ith coupon payment occurs at time $t_i = i \times T/n$.

We can value this bond by discounting its payments at the interest rate appropriate for each payment. This bond has the price

$$\begin{aligned} B(0, T, c, n, M) &= \sum_{i=1}^{n} c e^{-r(t_i)t_i} + M e^{-r(T)T} \\ &= \sum_{i=1}^{n} c P_{t_i} + M P_T \end{aligned} \qquad (12.1)$$

This valuation equation shows us how to price the bond and also how to replicate the bond using zero-coupon bonds. Suppose we buy c zero-coupon bonds maturing in 1 year, c maturing in 2 years, and so on, and $c + M$ zero-coupon bonds maturing in T years. This set of zero-coupon bonds will pay c in 1 year, c in 2 years, and $c + M$ in T years. We can say that the coupon bond is *engineered* from a set of zero-coupon bonds with the same maturities as the cash flows from the bond.

In practice, bonds are usually issued at par, meaning that the bond sells today for its maturity value, M. We can structure the bond to make this happen by setting the coupon so that the price of the bond is M. Using equation (12.1), $B(0, T, c, n, M) = M$ if the coupon is set so that

$$c = M \frac{(1 - P_T)}{\sum_{i=1}^{n} P_{t_i}} \tag{12.2}$$

We have seen this formula before in Chapter 7 and as the formula for the swap rate, equation (8.3) in Chapter 8.

Equity-Linked Bonds

Rather than paying M in cash at maturity, a bond could pay *one share* of XYZ stock at maturity. With this change in terms, the bond has an uncertain maturity value. Moreover, this change raises questions. What does it mean for such a bond to sell at par? If there are coupon payments, should they be paid in cash or in shares of XYZ? For regulatory and tax purposes, is this instrument a stock or a bond?

Zero-coupon equity-linked bond Suppose an equity-linked bond pays the bondholder one share of stock at time T. There are no interim payments. What is a fair price for this bond?

Although the language is now different, this valuation problem is the same as that of valuing a prepaid forward contract, which we analyzed in Chapter 5. In both cases the investor pays today to receive a share of stock at time T. In the context of this chapter, we could also call this instrument a *zero-coupon equity-linked bond*. Recall from Chapter 5 that the prepaid forward price is the present value of the forward price, $F_{0,T}^P = P_T F_{0,T}$. This relationship implies that for a non-dividend-paying stock, $F_{0,T}^P = e^{-rT} S_0 e^{(r-\delta)T} = S_0$ since $\delta = 0$. The prepaid forward price is the stock price.

Example 12.1 Suppose that XYZ stock has a price of $100 and pays no dividends, and that the annual continuously compounded interest rate is 6%. *In the absence of dividends, the prepaid forward price equals the stock price.* Thus, we would pay $100 to receive the stock in 5 years.

This example shows that if we issue a bond promising to pay one share of a non-dividend-paying stock at maturity, and the bond pays no coupon, then the bond will sell for the current stock price. In general, a bond is at par if the bond price equals the maturity payment of the bond. The bond in Example 12.1 is at par since the bond pays one share of stock at maturity and the price of the note equals the price of one share of stock today.

Suppose the stock makes discrete dividend payments of D_{t_i}. Then we saw in Chapter 5 that the prepaid forward price is

$$F_{0,T}^P = S_0 - \sum_{i=1}^{n} P_{t_i} D_{t_i} \qquad (12.3)$$

If the stock pays dividends and the bond makes no coupon payments, the bond will sell at less than par.

Example 12.2 Suppose the price of XYZ stock is \$100, the quarterly dividend is \$1.20, and the annual continuously compounded interest rate is 6% (the quarterly interest rate is therefore 1.5%). From equation (12.3), the 5-year prepaid forward price for XYZ is

$$\$100 - \sum_{i=1}^{20} \$1.20 e^{-0.015 \times i} = \$79.42$$

Thus, a zero-coupon equity-linked bond promising to pay one share of XYZ in 5 years would have a price of \$79.42.

Cash coupon payments We now add cash coupon payments to the bond. Represent the price of a bond paying n coupons of c each and a share at maturity as $B(0, T, c, n, S_T)$. The valuation equation for such a note—the analog of equation (12.1)—is

$$B(0, T, c, n, S_T) = c \sum_{i=1}^{n} P_{t_i} + F_{0,T}^P \qquad (12.4)$$

The value today of the maturity payment, which is one share of stock, is the prepaid forward price, $F_{0,T}^P$.

If the stock pays dividends, then in order for the bond to sell at par—the current price of the stock—it must make coupon payments. In particular, *the note must pay coupons with a present value equal to the present value of dividends over the life of the note*. To see this, use equation (12.3) to rewrite equation (12.4):

$$B(0, T, c, n, S_T) = c \sum_{i=1}^{n} P_{t_i} + S_0 - \sum_{i=1}^{n} P_{t_i} D_{t_i}$$

In words: The price of the bond, B, will equal the stock price, S_0, as long as the present value of the bond's coupons (the first term on the right-hand side) equals the present value of the stock dividends (the third term on the right-hand side).

In general, if we wish to price an equity-linked note at par, from equation (12.4), the bond price, B, will equal the stock price, S_0, if the coupon, c, is set so that

$$c = \frac{S_0 - F_{0,T}^P}{\sum_{i=1}^{n} P_{t_i}} \qquad (12.5)$$

That is, the coupon must amortize the difference between the stock price and the prepaid forward price.

Example 12.3 Consider XYZ stock as in Example 12.2. If the note promised to pay $1.20 quarterly—a coupon equal to the stock dividend—the note would sell for $100.

Notice that equation (12.5) is the same as the equation for a par coupon on a cash bond, equation (12.2). Instead of $1 - P_T$ in the numerator, we have $S_0 - F_{0,T}^P$. The former is the difference between the price of $1 and the prepaid forward price for $1 delivered at time T. The latter is the difference between the price of one share and the prepaid forward price for one share delivered at time T.

In practice, dividends may change unexpectedly over the life of the note. The note issuer must decide: Should the dividend on the note change to match the dividend paid by the stock, or should the dividend on the note be fixed at the outset using equation (12.5)? The price should be the same in either case, but a different party bears dividend risk.

Interest in-kind An alternative to paying interest in cash is to pay interest in fractional shares. For example, the coupon could be the value of 2% of a share at the time of payment, rather than a fixed $2. To price such a bond, we represent the number of fractional shares received at each coupon payment as c^*. The value at time 0 of a share received at time t is $F_{0,t}^P$. Thus, the formula for the value of the note at time t_0, V_0, is

$$V_0 = c^* \sum_{i=1}^{n} F_{0,t_i}^P + F_{0,T}^P$$

The number of fractional shares that must be paid each year for the note to be initially priced at par, i.e., for $V_0 = S_0$, is

$$c^* = \frac{S_0 - F_{0,T}^P}{\sum_{i=1}^{n} F_{0,t_i}^P} \quad (12.6)$$

When we pay coupons as shares rather than cash, the coupons have variable value. Thus, it is appropriate to use the prepaid forward for the stock as a discount factor rather than the prepaid forward for cash.

In the special case of a constant expected continuous dividend yield, δ, this equation becomes

$$c^* = \frac{1 - e^{-\delta T}}{\sum_{i=1}^{n} e^{-\delta t_i}} \quad (12.7)$$

We can compare this expression for c^* with that for the coupon on an ordinary cash bond. In the special case of a constant interest rate and assuming a $1 par value, equation (12.2) becomes

$$c = \frac{1 - e^{-rT}}{\sum_{i=1}^{n} e^{-rt_i}} \qquad (12.8)$$

Comparing the equations for c and c^* makes it apparent that the appropriate discount factor for a coupon is determined from the lease rate on the underlying asset. In the case of a bond denominated in cash, the lease rate is the interest rate, while in the case of a bond completely denominated in shares, the lease rate is the dividend yield.

Commodity-Linked Bonds

Now we repeat the analysis of equity-linked bonds, except that instead of paying a share of *stock* at maturity, we suppose the note pays one unit of a *commodity*. We ask the same questions about how to structure this note. We will see that the commodity lease rate replaces the dividend yield. A commodity-linked note will pay a coupon if the lease rate is positive, and the present value of coupon payments on the note must equal the present value of the lease payments on the commodity.

Zero-coupon commodity-linked bonds Suppose we have a note that pays one unit of a commodity in the future, with no interim cash flows. What is the price of the note? Once again, the answer is, by definition, the present value of the forward price, or the prepaid forward price. As we saw in Chapter 6, the difference between the spot price and the prepaid forward price is summarized by the lease rate. Thus, the discount from the spot price on a zero-coupon note reflects the lease rate.

Example 12.4 Suppose the spot price of gold is \$400/oz., the 3-year forward price is \$455/oz., and the 3-year continuously compounded interest rate is 6.25%. Then a zero-coupon note paying 1 ounce of gold in 3 years would sell for

$$F_{0,T}^P = \$455 e^{-0.0625 \times 3} = \$377.208$$

This amount is less than the spot price of \$400 because the lease rate is positive.

Cash interest Suppose we have a commodity with a current price of S_0 and a forward price of $F_{0,T}$, and we have a commodity-linked note paying a cash coupon. For the note to sell at par, we need to set the coupon so that

$$S_0 = c \sum_{i=1}^{n} P_{t_i} + P_T F_{0,T}$$

Since by definition of the prepaid forward price, $P_T F_{0,T} = F_{0,T}^P$, we have

$$c = \frac{S_0 - F_{0,T}^P}{\sum_{i=1}^{n} P_{t_i}}$$

exactly as with a dividend-paying stock. The coupon serves to amortize the lease rate. Thus, *the lease rate plays the role of a dividend yield in pricing a commodity-linked note*. The present-value calculation treats the lease rate exactly as if it were a dividend yield; what matters is that there is a difference between the prepaid forward price and the current spot price.[2]

Example 12.5 Suppose the spot price of gold is \$400/oz., the 3-year forward price is \$455/oz., the 1-year continuously compounded interest rate is 5.5%, the 2-year rate is 6%, and the 3-year rate is 6.25%. The annual coupon is then determined as

$$c = \frac{\$400 - \$377.208}{e^{-0.055} + e^{-0.06 \times 2} + e^{-0.0625 \times 3}} = \$8.561$$

The annual coupon on a 3-year gold-linked note is therefore about 2% of the spot price.

A 2% yield in this example might seem like cheap financing, but this is illusory and stems from denominating the note in terms of gold. When the yield on gold (the lease rate) is less than the yield on cash (the interest rate), the yield on a gold-denominated note is less than the yield on a dollar-denominated note. This effect is reversed in cases where the interest rate in a particular currency is below the lease rate of gold. In Japan during the late 1990s, the yen-denominated interest rate was close to zero, so the coupon rate on a gold note would have been greater than the interest rate on a yen-denominated note.

Interest in-kind As with stocks, we can pay fractional units of the commodity as a periodic interest payment. The present value of the payment at time t is computed using the prepaid forward price, $F^P_{0,t}$. Thus, the value of a commodity-linked note at par is exactly the same as for an equity-linked note paying interest in-kind:

$$S_0 = c^* \sum_{i=1}^{n} F^P_{0,t_i} + F^P_{0,T}$$

The formula for c^* is given by equation (12.6).

Perpetuities A perpetuity is an infinitely lived coupon bond. We can use equations (12.7) and (12.8) to consider two perpetuities: one that makes annual payments in dollars and another that pays in units of a commodity. Suppose we want the dollar perpetuity to have a price of M and the commodity perpetuity to have a price of S_0. Using standard perpetuity calculations, if we let $T \to \infty$ in equation (12.8) (this also means that $n \to \infty$),

---

[2] As we saw in Chapter 6, a lease rate can be negative if there are storage costs. In this case, the holder of a commodity-linked note benefits by not having to pay storage costs associated with the physical commodity and will therefore pay a price above maturity value (in the case of a zero-coupon note) or else the note must carry a negative dividend, meaning that the holder must make coupon payments to the issuer.

the coupon rate on the dollar bond is

$$c = M \frac{1}{\frac{e^{-r}}{1-e^{-r}}} = M(e^r - 1) = \hat{r} M$$

where $\hat{r}$ is the effective annual interest rate. Similarly, for a perpetuity paying a unit of a commodity, equation (12.7) becomes

$$c^* = S_0 \frac{1}{\frac{e^{-\delta}}{1-e^{-\delta}}} = S_0(e^\delta - 1) = \hat{\delta} S_0$$

where $\hat{\delta}$ is the effective annual lease rate. Thus, in order for a commodity perpetuity to be worth one unit of the commodity, it must pay the lease rate in units of the commodity. (For example, if the lease rate is 2%, the bond pays 0.02 units of the commodity per year.)

What if a bond pays one unit of the commodity per year, forever? We know that if it pays $\hat{\delta} S_t$ in perpetuity it is worth S_0. Thus, if it pays S_t it is worth

$$\frac{S_0}{\hat{\delta}} \qquad (12.9)$$

This is the commodity equivalent of a perpetuity.

Our conclusion is simple: Commodity-linked notes are formally like equity-linked notes, with the lease rate taking the place of the dividend yield.

Currency-Linked Bonds

We now see what happens if we change the currency of denomination of the bond. As you can probably guess by now, the foreign interest rate, being the lease rate on the foreign currency, takes the place of the dividend yield on the stock.

Suppose that we want to compare issuing a par-coupon bond denominated entirely in dollars and a par-coupon bond denominated entirely in another currency. We will let B^F denote zero-coupon bond prices denominated in the foreign currency, $r_F(t)$ the foreign interest rate, and P_t^F the price of a zero-coupon bond denominated in the foreign currency.

As you would expect, a bond completely denominated in a foreign currency will have a coupon given by the formula

$$c^F = M \frac{1 - P_T^F}{\sum_{i=1}^n P_{t_i}^F}$$

In other words, foreign interest rates are used to compute the coupon.

What happens when the principal, M, is in the domestic currency and the interest payments are in the foreign currency? Once again we just solve for the coupon payment that makes the bond sell at par. There are two ways to do this.

First, we can discount the foreign currency coupon payments using the foreign interest rate, and then translate their value into dollars using the current exchange rate, x_0 (denominated as \$/unit of foreign currency). The value of the ith coupon is $x_0 P_i^F c$, and the value of the bond is

$$B(0, T, c^F, n, M) = x_0 c^F \sum_{i=1}^{n} P_{t_i}^F + M P_T$$

Alternatively, we can translate the future coupon payment into dollars using the forward currency rate, $F_{0,t}$, and then discount back at the dollar-denominated interest rate, P_t. The value of the bond in this case is

$$B(0, T, c^F, n, M) = c^F \sum_{i=1}^{n} F_{0,t_i} P_{t_i} + M P_T$$

The two calculations give the same result since the currency forward rate, from equation (6.2), is given by

$$F_{0,t} = x_0 e^{r(t)t} e^{-r_F(t)t} = x_0 \frac{P_t^F}{P_t}$$

The forward price for foreign exchange is set so that it makes no difference whether we convert the currency and then discount, or discount and then convert the currency.

The coupon on a par bond with foreign interest and dollar principal is given by

$$c^F = M \frac{1 - P_T}{\sum_{i=1}^{n} F_{0,t_i} P_{t_i}} \qquad (12.10)$$

The currency formula is the same as that for equities and commodities. If we think of the foreign interest rate as a dividend yield on the foreign currency, equation (12.10) is the same as our previous coupon expressions.

12.3 STRUCTURED NOTES WITH OPTIONS

In this section we see how to add options to bonds denominated in cash or equity. We saw in the last section the similarity between notes that make payments denominated in stock, commodities, and currencies. Thus, if you understand how to price equity-linked notes with options, you can also price commmodity- and currency-linked notes with options.

Coupon Bonds with Options

There are many bonds where the bondholder potentially receives some fraction of the return on a stock or other risky asset but does not suffer a loss of principal if the stock declines. We obtain this structure by embedding call options in the note.[3] Let's see how such bonds are constructed.

Let γ denote the extent to which the bond participates in the appreciation of the underlying stock; we will call γ the **price participation** of the bond. In general, the value V_0 of a bond with fixed maturity payment M, coupon c, maturity T, strike price K, and price participation γ can be written as

$$V_0 = MP_T + c \sum_{i=1}^{n} P_{t_i} + \gamma \, \text{BSCall}(S_0, K, \sigma, r, T, \delta) \quad (12.11)$$

Equation (12.11) assumes that the principal payment is cash. It could just as well be shares. Equation (12.11) also assumes that the note has a single embedded call option.

Given equation (12.11), we could arbitrarily select M, T, c, K, and γ and then value the note, but it is common to structure notes in particular ways. To take one example, suppose that the initial design goals are as follows:

1. The note's initial price should equal the price of a share, i.e., $V_0 = S_0$.
2. The note should guarantee a return of at least zero, i.e., $M = V_0$.
3. The note should pay some fraction of stock appreciation above the initial price, i.e., $K = V_0$.

These conditions imply that $V_0 = S_0 = M = K$, and thus the price of the note satisfies the equation

$$S_0 = c \sum_{i=1}^{n} P_{t_i} + S_0 P_T + \gamma \, \text{BSCall}(S_0, S_0, \sigma, r, T, \delta) \quad (12.12)$$

Given these constraints, equation (12.12) implies a relationship between the coupon, c, and price participation, γ. Given a coupon, c, we can solve for γ and vice versa.

Equity-Linked Notes with Options

There are many equity-linked notes containing options. Some examples of such notes are given in Box 12.1.

The price of a note at par paying one unit of a share at expiration, and with a single embedded option, is

$$S_0 = c \sum_{i=1}^{n} P_{t_i} + F_{0,T}^P + \gamma \, \text{BSCall}(S, K, \sigma, r, T, \delta) \quad (12.13)$$

---

[3] One common example of this kind of bond is a *convertible bond*. These are bonds where the holder has the right to exchange the bond for shares of the issuing firm if the shares are sufficiently valuable. We discuss these bonds in Chapter 13.

Box 12.1: A Plethora of Equity-linked Notes

Investment banks and dealers frequently issue exchange-traded notes with a return that depends on the return on an index or the stock of a third party. These claims may have payoffs resembling the following examples:

- Covered calls. Apple SPARQS, issued in June 2007, mature in 2008, convert into 0.20 shares of Apple, pay a 10% coupon, and beginning in January 2008 can be called by the issuer for a price that gives the holder a 19% return. This cap on the return creates a payment very similar to a covered call.

- A bond plus a call. Dow Jones MITTS, issued in 2002, maturing in 2009, pay $10 plus the percent appreciation on the Dow Jones Industrial Index, less 2.10% per year, amortized daily. Since the MITTS traded for 7 years, this terminal index value is multiplied by approximately $e^{-7 \times 0.021} = 0.863$. Thus, the security pays nothing unless the index appreciates approximately 14%. After that appreciation, it pays 86.3% of the rate of return on the index. Implicitly, the bondholder owns 0.863 out-of-the-money index calls.

- A bond plus a bull spread. Dow Jones EAGLES make a guaranteed cash payment at maturity, plus an incremental return based on the cumulative quarterly performance of the Dow Jones Industrial index. The performance each quarter used to compute the cumulative return is capped at 6.5% with unlimited losses. The guaranteed minimum return over 6 years is 4% total.

This is just a small sampling of the many such products that are available. You can find a listing of structured products on the American Stock Exchange Web site (www.amex.com). Many of these products are issued in relatively small dollar amounts.

Different dealers will issue essentially identical products, but give them unique (and sometimes tortured) names. For example, the covered call structure is a "Stock Participation Accreting Redemption Quarterly-pay Security" (SPARQS) when issued by Morgan Stanley, and "STock Return Income DEbt Securities" (STRIDES) when issued by Merrill Lynch. The third product is "Minimum Return Equity Appreciation Growth LinkEd Securities" (EAGLES) when issued by Bank of America, and "Capped Return Notes" when issued by J. P. Morgan. Other well-known structure names include DECS (Debt Exchangeable for Common Stock), PEPS (Premium Equity Participating Shares), and PERCS (Preferred Equity Redeemable for Common Stock), all of which are effectively bonds plus option positions.

Compare equations (12.12) and (12.13). Instead of paying S_0 dollars at expiration, the equity-linked note pays one share. If the share pays no dividends, then (assuming $\gamma \geq 0$) the equity-linked note can sell at par only if $c = \gamma = 0$. To the extent the share pays dividends, it is necessary for the note to offer either coupons or options.

Valuing and Structuring an Equity-Linked CD

We have already described in Section 3.5 an example of an equity-linked CD, but we did not analyze the pricing. The CD we discussed has a promised minimum cash payment, 5.5 years to maturity, and a return linked to the S&P 500 index.

Pricing the CD Suppose the S&P index at issue is S_0 and is $S_{5.5}$ at maturity. The CD pays no coupons ($c = 0$), and it gives the investor 0.7 at-the-money calls ($\gamma = 0.7$ and $K = S_0$). After 5.5 years the CD pays

$$S_0 + 0.7 \times \max\left(S_{5.5} - S_0, 0\right) \tag{12.14}$$

Using equation (12.11), the value of this payoff at time 0 is

$$S_0 \times P_{5.5} + 0.7 \times \text{BSCall}(S_0, S_0, \sigma, r, 5.5, \delta) \tag{12.15}$$

where $P_{5.5} = e^{-r \times 5.5}$.

To perform this valuation, we need to make assumptions about the interest rate, the volatility, and the dividend yield on the S&P 500 index. Suppose the 5.5-year interest rate is 6%, the 5-year index volatility is 30%, the S&P index is 1300, and the dividend yield is 1.5%. We have two pieces to value. The zero-coupon bond paying $1300 is worth

$$\$1300 e^{-0.06 \times 5.5} = \$934.60$$

The 0.7 call options have a value of

$$0.7 \times \text{BSCall}(\$1300, \$1300, 0.3, 0.06, 5.5, 0.015) = \$309.01$$

The two pieces together, assuming they could be purchased without fees or spreads in the open market, would cost

$$\$934.60 + \$309.01 = \$1243.61$$

This is $56.39 less than the $1300 initial investment. This difference suggests that the sellers earn a 4.3% commission (56.39/1300) for selling the CD. This analysis makes it clear why the CD does not provide 100% of market appreciation. At 100%, the value of the CD would exceed $1300, and the bank would lose money by offering it.

The bank is a retailer, offering the CD to the public in order to make a profit from it. The bank's position is that it has borrowed $934.60 and written 0.7 call options. You can think of equation (12.15) as the *wholesale* cost of the CD—it is the theoretical cost to the bank of this payoff. As a retailer, an issuing bank typically does not accept the market risk of issuing the CD. Banks offering products like this often hedge the option exposure by buying call options from an investment bank or dealer. The bank itself need not have option expertise in order to offer this kind of product.

The CD is offered by a bank that wants to earn commissions. The originating bank will hedge the CD, and must either bear the cost and risks of delta-hedging or else buy the underlying option from another source. Retail customers may have trouble comparing subtly different products offered by different banks. Customers who have not read this book might not understand option pricing, and hence they will be unable to calculate the theoretical value of the CD. On balance, it seems reasonable that we would find the value of the CD to be less than its retail cost by at least several percent. Here are some other considerations:

- It would have been costly for retail customers to duplicate this payoff, particularly since 5-year options were not readily available to public investors at the time of issue.
- Investors buying this product are spared the need to learn as much about options and, for example, taxes on options, as they would were they to replicate this payoff for themselves.[4]
- The price we have just computed is a ballpark approximation: It is not obvious what the appropriate volatility and dividend inputs are for a 5.5-year horizon.

Any specific valuation conclusion obviously depends entirely on the interest rate, volatility, and dividend assumptions. However, Baubonis et al. (1993) suggest that fees in this range are common for equity-linked CD products.

If we allow for issuer profit, α, as a fraction of the issue price, a general expression for the value of a CD issued at par is

$$V(1-\alpha) = MP_T + c \sum_{i=1}^{n} P_{t_i} + \gamma \operatorname{BSCall}(S, K, \sigma, r, T, \delta) \quad (12.16)$$

In the above example, $\alpha = 0.043$ and $V = 1300$.

Structuring the product Many issues arise when designing an equity-linked CD. For example:

- What index should we link the note to? In addition to the S&P, possibilities include the Dow Jones Industrials, the NYSE, the NASDAQ, sector indexes such as high-tech, and foreign indexes, with or without currency exposure.
- How much participation in the market should the note provide? The CD we have been discussing provides 70% of the return (if positive) over the life of the CD.
- Should the note make interest payments? (The example CD does not.)
- How much of the original investment should be insured? (The example CD fully insures the investment.)

---

[4] It turns out that the tax treatment in the United States of an equity-linked CD such as this one is fairly complicated. A bond with a payment linked to a stock index is considered to be "contingent interest debt." The bondholder must pay tax annually on imputed interest, and there is a settling-up procedure at maturity. Issuers of such bonds frequently recommend that they be held in tax-exempt accounts.

Box 12.2: Asian and Barrier Options

Just as it is possible to tweak the structure of bonds, it is also possible to tweak the structure of options to create "nonstandard" or "exotic" options. Two important kinds of nonstandard options are *Asian* options and *barrier* options:

- An **Asian option** has a payoff that depends on the average price over some period of time. For example, a 5-year Asian call on the S&P 500 index could be structured as follows: Each month during the life of the option, record the month-end value of the S&P 500 index. At expiration, the payoff is

$$\max[S_{\text{Avg}} - K, 0]$$

where $S_{\text{Avg}} = \sum_{i=1}^{n} S_i/n$ and S_i is the month-end price in month i. The average index value will be less volatile than the terminal index value, so an Asian call is less valuable than an ordinary call. It is possible to define the average price based on different time intervals (daily, weekly, quarterly), or using different averaging methods (arithmetic or geometric).

- A **barrier option** is an option with a payoff that depends upon whether, over the life of the option, the price of the underlying asset reaches a specified level, called the *barrier*. Barrier puts and calls either come into existence (in which case they are called "knock-ins") or go out of existence ("knock-outs") the first time the asset price reaches the barrier. A barrier option may not exist at expiration (a knock-out may have been knocked out, and a knock-in may not have knocked in), so barrier options are less expensive than otherwise equivalent ordinary options.

Asian and barrier options are very common in practice, but they are by no means the only kinds of nonstandard options. If you dream up a new kind of exotic option, the limiting factors are whether it is possible to hedge it and whether anyone is interested in trading it.

Alternative Structures

Numerous other variations in the structure of the CD are possible. Some examples follow:

- Use Asian options (see Box 12.2) instead of ordinary options.
- Cap the market participation rate, turning the product into a collar.
- Incorporate a put instead of a call.
- Make the promised payment different from the price.

We will consider the first two alternatives in this section. Problems 12.9 and 12.11 cover the other two.

Asian options The payoff discussed in Box 12.2 depends on the simple return over a period of 5.5 years. We could instead compute the return based on the average of year-end prices. An Asian option is worth less than an otherwise equivalent ordinary option.

Therefore, when an Asian option is used, the participation rate will be greater than with an ordinary call.

Suppose we base the option on the geometric average price recorded five times over the 5.5-year life of the option, and set the strike price equal to the current index level. The value of this Asian call is $240.97, as opposed to $441.44 for an ordinary call. Assuming the equity-linked note pays no coupon and keeping the present value the same, the participation rate with this geometric-average Asian option is

$$0.7 \times \frac{441.44}{240.97} = 1.28$$

If instead we base the option on the arithmetic average, the option price is $273.12, giving us a participation rate of

$$0.7 \times \frac{441.44}{273.12} = 1.13$$

The arithmetic Asian option has a higher price than one based on the geometric average, hence we get a lower participation rate.

Increasing the number of prices averaged would lower the price of either option, raising the participation rate.

Capped participation Another way to raise the participation rate is to cap the level of participation. For example, suppose we set a cap of k times the initial price. Then the investor writes to the issuer a call with a strike of kS_0, and the valuation equation for the CD becomes

$$S_0(1 - \alpha) = S_0 e^{-r \times t} + \gamma \times [\text{BSCall}(S_0, S_0, \sigma, r, t, \delta) - \text{BSCall}(S_0, kS_0, \sigma, r, t, \delta)]$$

Example 12.6 Suppose we set a cap of a 100% return and seek profit of $\alpha = 0.043$. Then the investor writes a call with a strike of $2600 to the issuer, and the valuation equation for the CD becomes

$$1300(1 - 0.043) = 1300 e^{-0.06 \times 5.5} + \gamma \times [\text{BSCall}(1300, 1300, 0.3, 0.06, 5.5, 0.015) \\ - \text{BSCall}(1300, 2600, 0.3, 0.06, 5.5, 0.015)]$$

The value of the written 2600-strike call is $162.48. The participation rate implied by this equation is 1.11.

Application: Variable Prepaid Forwards

Stockholders with large appreciated stock positions often seek to reduce the risk of their holdings while continuing to hold the stock. One strategy is to use a zero-cost collar. For example, Paul Allen, a cofounder of Microsoft, entered into collars on 76 million Microsoft shares during October and November of 2000.[5]

---

[5] It is possible to find the details of the collar by using the SEC's Edgar Web site, www.edgar.sec.gov, where the transactions were reported on Form 4.

12.3 Structured Notes with Options

It is also possible to engineer a single instrument that hedges a stock position and pays cash to the owner. In August 2003, Walt Disney Co. vice-chairman Roy Disney sold a 5-year variable prepaid forward (VPF) contract covering a large percentage of his Disney stock holdings. The contract called for Roy Disney to deliver to Credit Suisse First Boston a variable number of shares in 5 years. To quote from the Form 4 filed with the SEC on August 20, (available through the SEC's Edgar Website):

> The VPF Agreement provides that on August 18, 2008 ("Settlement Date"), [Roy Disney] will deliver a number of shares of Common Stock to CSFB LLC (or . . . the cash equivalent of such shares) as follows: (a) if the average VWAP ["Value Weighted Average Price"] of the Common Stock for the 20 trading days preceding and including the Settlement Date ("Settlement Price") is less than $21.751, a delivery of 7,500,000 shares; (b) if the Settlement Price is equal to or greater than $21.751 per share ("Downside Threshold") but less than or equal to $32.6265 per share ("Upside Threshold"), a delivery of shares equal to the Downside Threshold/Settlement Price ×7,500,000; and (c) if the Settlement Price is greater than the Upside Threshold, a delivery of shares equal to (1 − (10.8755/Settlement Price)) × 7,500,000.

Figure 12.1 graphs the dollar value of the payoff of the prepaid forward, along with the net payoff for owning a share and selling the prepaid forward. The net payoff

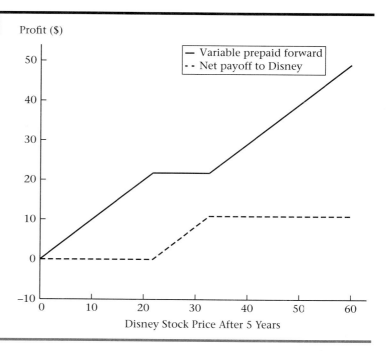

FIGURE 12.1

Maturity payoff in dollars of the Disney variable prepaid forward contract.

is the same as that for a collared stock. You could replicate this transaction by buying shares, buying a put on each share with a strike price of $21.751, and selling a call with a strike of $32.6265. This transaction permitted Roy Disney to retain the voting rights in the shares, receive substantial cash, and presumably defer any capital gains he had on the position. Jagolinzer et al. (2007) document 200 such transactions between 2000 and 2004.

12.4 ENGINEERED SOLUTIONS FOR GOLDDIGGERS

We now return to the Golddiggers example from Chapter 4 in order to show how Golddiggers could have used structured notes in place of forwards and options in the hedging scenarios we discussed.

Gold-Linked Notes

Any hedger using a forward (or futures) contract to hedge faces the risk that the forward contract will suffer a loss prior to expiration of the hedge. That loss generally must be funded when it occurs.[6] This need to fund interim losses arises from the structure of the hedging instrument, in particular the fact that it is a zero-investment contract linked to the price of gold, meant to serve as a hedging instrument and not as a financing instrument.

Instead of shorting a forward contract, Golddiggers could issue a note promising to pay an ounce of gold 1 year from now. Such a note is effectively debt collateralized by future sales of gold. Ordinarily, we would think a risky commodity like gold to be poor collateral for a debt issue. But if a *gold-mining firm* issues gold-linked debt, the risk of the bond and the risk of the collateral are the same. Bondholders provide financing as well as absorbing gold price risk.

We begin with the information from Chapter 4: The current price of gold is $405/oz., the forward price is $420, and the effective annual interest rate is 5%. The effective annual lease rate is therefore $0.05 - (420/405 - 1) = 1.296\%$. We wish to construct a debt contract that raises $405 today (the cost of 1 ounce of gold), pays 1 ounce of gold 1 year from today, and if necessary, pays a coupon, c.

---

[6] As discussed earlier, forward contracts and swaps typically have collateralization requirements. In practice, a company must have capital to cover a large loss on a financial contract, even when there is an offsetting gain. For example, in a well-known incident in 1999, Ashanti Goldfields had sold forward eight times annual production. The company suffered a $500 million loss on its forward gold sales when the gold price rose significantly. Although Ashanti had gold in the ground, it did not have cash to cover this loss. Ultimately, Ashanti was able to keep operating by giving warrants on 15% of its stock to its counterparties on the forward sale. For details, see Cooper (2000) and the *Wall Street Journal* (October 7, 1999, p. C1).

TABLE 12.1
Dollar bond payments and net cash flow to Golddiggers with gold-linked bond paying 1 ounce of gold plus $5.25. The cost of producing 1 ounce of gold is $380.

Price of Gold ($)	Profit Before Bond Flows ($)	FV(Gross Bond Proceeds) ($)	Payment to Bondholders ($)	Net Cash Flow ($)
350	−30	425.25	−355.25	40
400	20	425.25	−405.25	40
450	70	425.25	−455.25	40
500	120	425.25	−505.25	40

We have already seen that the lease rate plays the role of a dividend. Thus, if the bond has a coupon equal to the lease payment on an ounce of gold, it should be priced fairly. A bond with these characteristics should pay a coupon of $1.296\% \times \$405 = \$5.25$.

We can verify that such a bond is fairly priced. The payoff to the bond in 1 year is $5.25 plus 1 ounce of gold. We know we can sell the gold in 1 year for $420 since that is the forward price. The present value of the payoff is therefore the value of the coupon plus the prepaid forward price for gold:

$$\$5.25 \times P_1 + F_{0,1}^P = \frac{\$5.25}{1.05} + \frac{\$420}{1.05} = \$405$$

Because the lease rate is paid as interest, the bond sells at par.

We should verify that the bond serves as an appropriate hedge for Golddiggers. Table 12.1 summarizes the payoffs to Golddiggers and the bondholders at different gold prices in 1 year. The table assumes that Golddiggers invests the $405 at 5%—this yields the $425.25 that is labeled "FV(Gross Bond Proceeds)." The net cash flow is determined by adding profits without consideration of bond payments (column 2) to the difference between the invested bond proceeds (column 3) and the payment to bondholders (column 4). In this case, issuing the bond achieves the same result as selling a forward contract (compare Table 12.1 and Table 4.2), so Golddiggers is completely hedged.

The chief difference between the gold-linked note and the forward contract is that the former provides financing, the latter doesn't. If Golddiggers seeks financing (in order to construct the mine, for example), the issuance of a gold-linked note might be preferable to borrowing and hedging separately.

Notes with Embedded Options

A gold-linked bond leaves bondholders with the risk of a loss should the gold price drop. Golddiggers could instead offer a bond that promises bondholders that they will receive interest plus appreciation of gold above $420.

Such a bond implicitly gives holders a call option on gold with a strike price of $420. From Chapter 2, the cost of this option today is $8.77, with a future value of $8.77 \times 1.05 = 9.21. Let the promised payment on the bond be the $405 issue price plus the coupon, c. In 1 year, the bond is worth

$$\$405 + c + \max(0, S_1 - \$420)$$

The valuation equation for the bond is

$$\frac{\$405 + c}{1.05} + \$8.77 = \$405$$

Solving for c gives $c = \$11.04$, which is a yield of 2.726%. Golddiggers thus issues a bond for $405, with a 2.726% coupon, with additional payments to bondholders if the price of gold exceeds $420. The difference between the 2.726% coupon and 5% is due to the value of the embedded call option.

What is the result for Golddiggers from having issued this bond? If Golddiggers invests at 5% the $405 bond proceeds, then it will have $425.25 cash in 1 year. Recall that costs are $380/oz. If the gold price in 1 year exceeds $420, Golddiggers will show profits of

$$\$420 + \$9.21 - \$380 = \$49.21$$

whereas if gold is less than $420, Golddiggers will make

$$S_1 + \$9.21 - \$380$$

Table 12.2 summarizes the cash flows to bondholders and to Golddiggers from the issuance of this bond. You can verify that this is exactly the same payoff as obtained when Golddiggers hedges by writing a call. The commodity-linked bond achieves the same effect.

Instead of having a low coupon and protection against low gold prices, bondholders might be willing to bear the risk of a decline in the price of gold in exchange for a

TABLE 12.2 Dollar bond payments and net cash flow to Golddiggers with gold-linked bond providing gold appreciation to bondholders.

Price of Gold ($)	Profit Before Bond Flows ($)	FV(Gross Bond Proceeds) ($)	Payment to Bondholders ($)	Net Cash Flow ($)
350	−30	425.25	−416.04	−20.79
400	20	425.25	−416.04	29.21
450	70	425.25	−446.04	49.21
500	120	425.25	−496.04	49.21

TABLE 12.3 Dollar bond payments and net cash flow to Golddiggers with gold-linked bond in which bondholders sell put option to Golddiggers.

Price of Gold ($)	Profit Before Bond Flows ($)	FV(Gross Bond Proceeds) ($)	Payment to Bondholders ($)	Net Cash Flow ($)
350	−30	425.25	−364.46	30.79
400	20	425.25	−414.46	30.79
450	70	425.25	−434.46	60.79
500	120	425.25	−434.46	110.79

higher coupon. For example, Golddiggers could issue a bond in which bondholders sell a 420-strike put to Golddiggers. Golddiggers in turn would have to pay greater interest to compensate bondholders for selling the put. The bond would be structured as follows:

- The initial bond price is $405.
- The promised payment on the bond is $434.46, a 7.274% rate of interest.
- If gold sells for less than $420, the payment is reduced by $420 − S_1$.

The bondholders have written a put option to Golddiggers and hence in 1 year receive the future value of the premium. If the price of gold is above $420, Golddiggers makes

$$\$425.25 - \$434.46 + (S_1 - \$380) = S_1 - \$380 - \$9.21$$

If gold is below $420, Golddiggers makes

$$\$425.25 - \$434.46 + (\$420 - S_1) + (S_1 - \$380) = \$30.79$$

With this bond, Golddiggers in effect buys a 420-strike put. Table 12.3 depicts the net cash flow to Golddiggers from issuing this bond. The cash flows are identical to Table 4.3, where Golddiggers purchased a 420-strike put option as insurance against low gold prices.

12.5 CREDIT STRUCTURES

To this point in the book we have largely ignored credit risk, which is the risk that a counterparty will fail to meet a contractual payment. In practice, of course, credit risk is critically important. You would hesitate to buy an option, enter into a swap, or buy an equity-linked note if you thought the counterparty would fail to pay. In recent years, financial products have been created to deal with credit risk, and it is fair to say that the ability to hedge and trade credit as an asset has been one of the most significant changes in financial markets in the last 30 years. In this section we will discuss several developments in this market:

- Collateralized debt obligations (CDOs): a structure that reconfigures cash flows from a pool of assets
- Credit default swaps (CDSs): insurance (put options) for bonds that default
- CDS indexes: CDOs comprised of CDSs

Collateralized Debt Obligations

A **collateralized debt obligation** (CDO) is a financial structure that repackages the cash flows from a set of assets. You create a CDO by pooling the returns from a set of assets and issuing financial claims on this pool. The CDO claims reapportion the returns on the asset pool. Thus, instead of modifying the payoff of a single bond, a CDO creates a new payoff based on a pool of bonds. The bonds in the pool may be ordinary corporate bonds, loans, mortgages, or other assets. Typically, CDO claims are *tranched*, meaning that the different CDO claims have differing priorities with respect to the cash flows generated by the collateral. With a CDO, it is possible to take a group of risky bonds, for example, and create new claims, some of which are less risky than the original bonds and others that are riskier.

Given this general description, there are many different ways a CDO can be structured. First, the asset pool can be a fixed set of assets, in which case the CDO is *static*. If instead a manager buys and sells assets, the CDO is *managed*. Second, the CDO claims can directly receive the cash flows generated by the pool of assets; this is a *cash flow* CDO. Alternatively, the CDO claims can receive payments based on cash flows and the gain or loss from asset sales; this is a *market value* CDO.

There are at least two reasons for creating CDOs. First, financial institutions will sometimes want to securitize assets, effectively removing them from the institution's balance sheet by selling them to other investors. A CDO can be used to accomplish this, in which case it is a *balance sheet CDO*. Second, a CDO can be created in response to institutional frictions. For example, some investors are permitted to hold only investment-grade bonds. As we will see, CDOs can potentially be used to create investment-grade bonds from a pool of non-investment-grade bonds. This is called an *arbitrage CDO*.

A CDO with independent defaults A simple example can illustrate how CDOs work. Suppose there are three risky bonds that each promise to pay $100 in 1 year. Defaults are independent and occur only at maturity of the bond. Each bond has a 10% risk-neutral probability of default and pays $40 in default (this is a 40% *recovery rate*), and the risk-free rate is 6%. The price of each bond is

$$e^{-0.06} \left[(1 - 0.1) \times \$100 + 0.1 \times \$40 \right] = \$88.526$$

The yield on each bond is $\ln(100/88.526) = 0.1219$.

Now suppose that there are investors wishing to invest in bonds, but some investors are happy to hold a speculative-grade bond, while others seek safer bonds. We can create

FIGURE 12.2

Structure of a CDO.

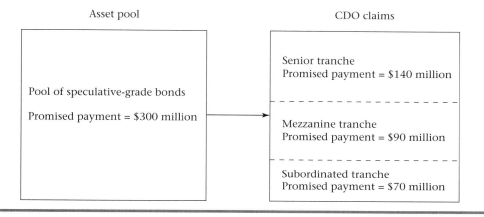

a CDO, reapportioning the cash flows from the pool of bonds, in order to accommodate the different kinds of investors. The structure of the CDO is illustrated in Figure 12.2. The total promised payoff on the three bonds is $300; the CDO apportions this payoff among three tranches of unequal size. The senior tranche ($140) receives first claim to the bond payments, the mezzanine tranche ($90) has the next claim, and the subordinated tranche ($70) receives whatever is left. For the bond that is ith in line, with a promised payment of $\bar{B}_i$, the payoff is

$$\text{Bond } i \text{ maturity payoff} = \min\left[\max\left(A_T - \sum_{j=1}^{i-1} \bar{B}_j, 0\right), \bar{B}_i\right] \quad (12.17)$$

where A_T is the maturity value of the asset pool.

To understand the pricing of the CDO claims, recognize that in our simple example there are four possible outcomes: no defaults ($0.90^3 = 72.9\%$ probability), one bond defaults ($3 \times 0.90^2 \times 0.10 = 24.3\%$ probability), two bonds default ($3 \times 0.90 \times 0.10^2 = 2.71\%$ probability), and three bonds default ($0.10^3 = 0.1\%$ probability). To compute the price of a CDO tranche, we can compute the expected payoff of the tranche using the risk-neutral default probabilities.

The CDO pricing is illustrated in Table 12.4. The senior tranche is almost risk-free. The only time the senior tranche is not fully paid is in the unlikely event (0.1% probability) that all three bonds default. In that case, the senior tranche receives $120, a recovery rate of 85.7%. Since it is almost always paid in full, investors will pay $131.828 for the senior tranche, which is a yield of 6.02%.

TABLE 12.4 Pricing of CDO in Figure 12.2, assuming that bond defaults are uncorrelated. Promised payoffs to the bonds are $140 (senior), $90 (mezzanine), and $70 (subordinated).

Number of Defaults	Probability	Total Payoff	Bond Payoff Senior	Mezzanine	Subordinated
0	0.729	300	140	90	70
1	0.243	240	140	90	10
2	0.027	180	140	40	0
3	0.001	120	120	0	0
		Price	131.828	83.403	50.347
		Yield	0.0601	0.07613	0.3296
	Default probability		0.0010	0.0280	0.2710
	Average recovery rate		0.8571	0.4286	0.1281

The mezzanine tranche is fully paid if there is one default, but it is not fully paid if there are two or three defaults. The yield is 7.61% and the average recovery rate is $40/90 \times 0.027/0.028 = 0.4285$. Finally, the subordinated tranche receives less than full payment if there are any defaults. Consequently, it is priced to yield 32.96%. Note that the sum of the prices of the three tranches is $265.58. As you would expect, this is the same as the price of the three bonds put into the asset pool.

A CDO with correlated defaults In the preceding example we assumed that the bonds were uncorrelated. This is a critical assumption and it is important to understand how correlation affects CDO pricing. Table 12.5 shows how the CDO tranches are priced if the bonds are perfectly correlated—i.e., if at maturity, either all firms default or none do. A comparison of Tables 12.4 and 12.5 shows the effect of default correlation: The senior tranche becomes riskier, and the subordinated tranche less risky.

The senior tranche becomes riskier because the probability of three defaults—the only circumstance in which the senior tranche is not fully paid—is greater with perfect correlation. The mezzanine tranche is also riskier. The subordinated tranche is less risky because there is a greater chance that it will be fully repaid. Given the structure of the CDO and the assumptions about the recovery rate in this example, the mezzanine and subordinated tranches have the same yield when there is perfect correlation of defaults.

By comparing Tables 12.4 and 12.5, you can understand how investors could speculate using CDOs. The pricing of CDOs implies a belief about correlation. If you believe that defaults are more correlated than the market's implied correlation, you would buy the subordinated tranche and sell the senior tranche. If you believe that defaults are less correlated, you would sell the subordinated tranche and buy the senior tranche.

TABLE 12.5			Pricing of CDO in Figure 12.2, assuming that bond defaults are perfectly correlated. Promised payoffs to the bonds are $140 (senior), $90 (mezzanine), and $70 (subordinated).		
Number of Defaults	Probability	Total Payoff	Bond Payoff		
			Senior	Mezzanine	Subordinated
0	0.9	300	140	90	70
1	0	240	140	90	10
2	0	180	140	40	0
3	0.1	120	120	0	0
		Price	129.963	76.283	59.331
		Yield	0.074	0.165	0.165
	Default probability		0.1	0.1	0.1
	Average recovery rate		0.857143	0	0

The subprime crisis of 2007 (discussed in Box 12.3) illustrated the effect on CDOs of unexpectedly correlated defaults. The market value of even the highest-rated tranches plummeted.

Nth to Default Baskets Another CDO variant permits investors to earn the return on the nth bond to default. Consider again the pool of three identical bonds. Over the life of the CDO there can be anywhere between 0 and 3 defaults. It is possible to create tranches where particular bondholders bear the consequences of a particular default.

As you would guess from the name, the first-to-default tranche receives the returns on the first bond to suffer a default. This is the riskiest tranche. The owner of the last-to-default generally bears the least risk, since all bonds must default in order for this claim to bear a loss.

Table 12.6 shows the pricing that results from this structure, assuming that the defaults are uncorrelated and occur only at time T. By comparing Table 12.6 with Table 12.4, you can observe a similarity between the subordinated tranche and the first-to-default on the one hand, and on the other, the senior tranche and the third to default. Table 12.7 illustrates that if defaults are perfectly correlated, the nth to default claims all have the same yield.

Credit Default Swaps

Credit default swaps (CDS) are an important recent innovation, permitting holders of corporate bonds to buy insurance against default. (A CDS is really more an option than a swap, but the "swap" terminology is standard.) The CDS buyer pays a premium, usually amortized over a series of payments. If the reference asset experiences a "credit

> ### Box 12.3: CDOs and the Subprime Crisis
>
> CDOs backed by risky mortgage loans, called "subprime" mortgages, made headlines in the second half of 2007. To qualify for a standard, "prime" mortage, the buyer must have a good credit score, high income relative to the mortgage repayment, and the ratio of the loan amount to the house price (the loan-to-value ratio) should be no more than 80%. Investors who cannot qualify for a prime mortgage can often borrow in the subprime market. Subprime mortgages are clearly riskier than prime mortgages, so the question is who lends money to subprime borrowers? This is where the CDO market enters the story.
>
> A mortgage-lending firm would *originate* a mortgage (i.e., find and certify a borrower and offer initial financing). The subprime mortgages were then packaged and resold via a CDO. Buyers expected that some of the subprime mortgages would default, but many would not, and the senior tranches were highly likely to be repaid. Credit-rating agencies gave their highest ratings to these senior tranches, and they were purchased by financial institutions and other institutional investors. Structures were created in which highly rated subprime CDOs were bought by large financial institutions, which financed their purchase by issuing short-term commercial paper (this is an example of a carry trade—see Box 6.1).
>
> This commercial paper was highly rated and in turn was bought by conservative institutional investors and money market mutual funds. The purpose of all this was to enable investors seeking relatively safe investments to lend money—via the CDO—to risky borrowers. The CDO equity tranche would of course have been extremely risky, but the buyers of those tranches would be those willing to accept the risk. The ultimate collateral for any mortgage is the underlying home, and home prices had been rising for years.
>
> Throughout 2007, mortgage defaults increased and mortgage lenders experienced losses and bankruptcies. The ABX index is a tranched CDS index based on bonds backed by subprime loans. Prices of even the highly rated ABX tranches fell as low as $0.70 on the dollar. As of this writing in November 2007, major financial institutions including Citigroup, Merrill Lynch, and Morgan Stanley had reported total losses in excess of $40 billion, with predictions that losses could exceed $200 billion. Investors and regulators were left asking a number of questions: Which highly rated securities would be the next to experience a credit downgrade? How great were the losses that financial institutions had not yet reported? How far would real estate prices fall? Would the financial turmoil spill over into the real economy and affect employment and growth?

event" (for example, a failure to make a scheduled payment on a particular bond or class of bonds), then the seller makes a payment to the buyer.

A single name CDS makes a payment when a specific company experiences a credit event. The buyer of the swap is the *protection buyer*. An institutional bondholder, for example, could use a CDS to buy protection against the credit risk of a company. The counterparty providing the credit insurance is the *swap writer* or *protection seller*.

TABLE 12.6 Pricing of Nth to default bonds; assumes the bonds owned as assets have uncorrelated defaults.

Default	Probability	Probability N or More	Payoffs Default	Payoffs No Default	Expected Payoff	Price	Yield
First	0.243	0.271	40	100	83.74	78.863	0.237
Second	0.027	0.028	40	100	98.32	92.594	0.077
Third	0.001	0.001	40	100	99.94	94.120	0.061

TABLE 12.7 Pricing of Nth to default bonds; assumes the bonds owned as assets have perfectly correlated defaults.

Default	Probability	Probability N or More	Payoffs Default	Payoffs No Default	Expected Payoff	Price	Yield
First	0.100	0.100	40	100	94.000	88.526	0.122
Second	0.100	0.100	40	100	94.000	88.526	0.122
Third	0.100	0.100	40	100	94.000	88.526	0.122

If a credit event occurs, the protection buyer receives

$$\text{Protection buyer payoff} = \text{Bond par value} - \text{Bond market value} \quad (12.18)$$

The bond market value is generally determined within 30 days of a credit event. The protection buyer pays to the seller a periodic insurance premium over time rather than a single amount initially. The premium payments stop once default occurs.

Figure 12.3 illustrates the cash flows and parties involved in a credit default swap on XYZ. Note in particular that there is no connection between XYZ and the swap writer. A default swap typically specifies a particular XYZ debt issue, called the *reference asset* or *reference obligation*. The reference asset is important because bonds from the same issuer with different seniority levels will have different prices after a default. Generally, the protection buyer can deliver any bond with payment rights equal to that of the reference asset.

If there is an actual default, the default swap could settle either financially or physically. In a financial (cash) settlement, the swap writer would pay the bondholder the value of the loss on the bond. In a physical settlement, the swap writer would buy the defaulted bond at the price it would have in the absence of default.

Financial settlement and physical settlement are economically equivalent in theory. However, the market for a defaulted corporate bond may not be liquid, and it may

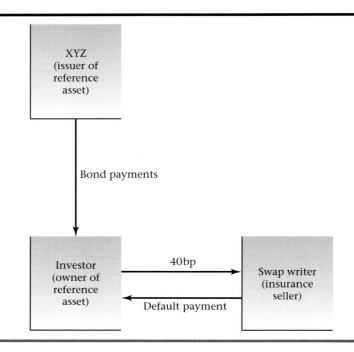

FIGURE 12.3

Depiction of the cash flows in a credit default swap. The investor owns the reference asset, which was issued by XYZ. The investor buys a credit default swap and pays 40 basis points per year in exchange for the swap writer's payment in the event of a default by XYZ.

be difficult to determine a fair price upon which to base financial settlement. To avoid this problem, default swaps often call for, or at least permit, physical settlement. Nevertheless, cash settlement is increasingly common.

For many firms, it is possible to trade CDSs with a variety of different expirations. The set of prices with different maturities generates a *credit spread curve*, where, for example, you may observe that credit spreads are small at short horizons and substantially larger over 5 years. With this array of contracts it is possible to make sophisticated bets. For example, you could buy protection with a 4-year horizon and sell protection with a 5-year horizon; this is a bet that default will not occur in the fifth year.

Finally, recognize that both parties to a default swap face credit risk from the swap itself. The protection buyer may default on premium payments, and the protection seller could go bankrupt at the same time that a default occurs on the reference asset.

CDS Indexes

A CDS index is an average of the premiums on a set of credit default swaps. Thus, a CDS index provides a way to track the overall market for credit. Most trading in the credit market is in CDS indexes.

To a first approximation, it is possible to replicate a CDS index by holding a pool of CDSs.[7] As with a single CDS, one party is a protection seller, receiving premium payments, and the other is a protection buyer, making the payments but receiving a payment from the seller if there is a credit event.

There are numerous ways in which a CDS index product can be structured and traded:

- A CDS index can be funded or unfunded. The unfunded version is like a credit default swap, except that the underlying asset is a basket of firms. The funded index is a note linked to the index with a collateral arrangement in case the note buyer had to make a payment.
- The claims are generally tranched in various ways, for example, simple priority or Nth to default.
- The underlying assets can represent different countries, currencies, maturities, or industries.

A 0–100% tranche on a CDS index can also be described as a *synthetic CDO*. The returns on a CDS index reflect the performance of the bonds in the index, just as the returns on a CDO reflect the performance of the bonds in the asset pool.

Credit indexes have had a relatively brief history.[8] There are a number of potential challenges in trading credit risk. Historically, the corporate bond market has been less liquid than the stock market. Trading volume for bonds is lower than for stocks, and bid-ask spreads have been higher. A large firm can have dozens of different bond issues outstanding.

Single name credit default swaps first traded in the mid-1990s. In 2001 Morgan Stanley introduced TRACERS, a basket of corporate bonds that investors could trade as a unit, much like an exchange-traded fund. There were both funded and nonfunded TRACERS products. J. P. Morgan created a competing product called HYDI. In 2003 Morgan Stanley and J. P. Morgan merged these products to create TRAC-X. Later in 2003 competing banks introduced CDX as an alternative credit index. In 2004 the TRAC-X and CDX products merged into Dow Jones CDX. These indexes could be traded in both funded and nonfunded products.

Firms can drop out of an index due to bankruptcy or illiquidity, but otherwise the makeup of a given CDX offering is set for the life of the offering. A new CDX is currently offered every 6 months with 5- and 10-year maturities, with the most recent offering being the most heavily traded. For North America, there are versions of the index reflecting investment-grade companies, high-volatility companies, and high-yield companies. The CDX North America index is an equally weighted basket of 125 CDSs representing

---

[7] The replication may not be exact since a default index can define a credit event differently than a single name CDS. For example, DJ TRAC-X, discussed below, specifies bankruptcy and failure to pay as credit events. A single name CDS can have a broader definition.

[8] See Duffie and Yurday (2004) for an interesting account of the development of credit index products.

FIGURE 12.4

The structure of tranched CDX.

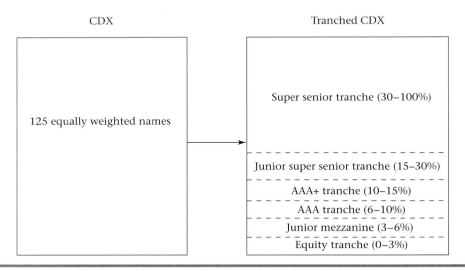

Source: Morgan Stanley.

investment-grade companies. There are also credit indexes for North America, Europe, Asia, Japan, Australia, and emerging markets.

Another notable index is the ABX, an index based on default swaps on bonds backed by risky mortgages. The pricing of ABX tranches was in the news in late 2007 as the subprime mortgage crisis unfolded. (See Box 12.3.)

Tranched CDX has a payoff structure illustrated in Figure 12.4. There are both funded and unfunded products based on this structure. As you would expect from our earlier discussion of CDOs and default correlation, the pricing of the various tranches is sensitive to correlation. In fact, tranche pricing is quoted using implied correlation in much the same way equity option premiums are quoted using implied volatility.

CHAPTER SUMMARY

Zero-coupon bonds, forwards, calls, and puts serve as building blocks that can be used to engineer new financial products. Fair pricing of a product will depend upon volatility, the dividend or lease rate, and the currency of denomination. Ordinary bonds that are simply denominated in something other than cash follow a simple pricing principle: The lease rate of the underlying asset becomes the coupon rate on the bond.

The specific characteristics of a financial product can be varied, though when one characteristic is changed, another must be changed to keep the value the same. The dials that we can turn include the participation in the underlying asset (via embedded calls and puts), the guaranteed minimum, and the coupon. Pricing theory tells us how to make these trade-offs.

Instruments can be designed specifically to take advantage of tax rules and regulations. The Disney prepaid forward is an example of this. A party to a contract may fail to make a required future payment. This possibility, which is called default, gives rise to credit risk. Various financial vehicles permit the trading of credit risk. Collateralized debt obligations (CDOs) are claims to an asset pool. The claims are tranched so as to create new claims, some of which are more and some of which are less sensitive to default than the pool as a whole. The value of these claims depends importantly on the default correlation of the assets in the pool.

Credit default swaps pay to the protection buyer the loss on a corporate bond when there is a default. In exchange, the protection buyer makes a periodic premium payment to the seller. Much trading of credit is done via credit indexes, which are baskets of credit default swaps.

FURTHER READING

In this chapter we focused on the creation of engineered instruments using basic building blocks such as assets, bonds, forward contracts, and options. However, using the Black-Scholes technology based on delta-hedging (discussed in Chapter 11), it is possible to engineer more complicated instruments.

Readings about structured products (including some not discussed in this chapter) include Baubonis et al. (1993), McConnell and Schwartz (1992), Arzac (1997), and Crabbe and Argilagos (1994).

The set of actual traded credit contracts continues to evolve. Books discussing credit from a practitioner perspective include Goodman and Fabozzi (2002) and Tavakoli (2001). Duffie (1999) discusses the pricing of credit default swaps. Frameworks for analyzing credit risk are discussed in Credit Suisse Financial Products (1997), J. P. Morgan (1997), Kealhofer (2003a, b) and white papers on the Moody's KMV Web site, www.moodyskmv.com.

Data on bankruptcies are available from www.bankruptcydata.com. Simple summary data, such as the largest bankruptcies sorted by year, are available without charge.

PROBLEMS

Some of the problems that follow use Table 12.8 and the following assumptions: The spot price of oil is $20.90. Let S_t denote the time price of the S&P 500 index, and assume that the price of the S&P 500 index is $S_0 = \$1200$ and the continuous annual dividend yield on the S&P 500 index is 1.5%.

TABLE 12.8 Data for selected problems.

	\multicolumn{8}{c}{Quarter}							
	1	2	3	4	5	6	7	8
Oil forward price ($)	21.0	21.1	20.8	20.5	20.2	20.0	19.9	19.8
Zero-coupon bond price ($)	0.9852	0.9701	0.9546	0.9388	0.9231	0.9075	0.8919	0.8763

12.1 Consider a 5-year equity-linked note that pays one share of XYZ at maturity. The price of XYZ today is $100, and XYZ is expected to pay its annual dividend of $1 at the end of this year, increasing by $0.50 each year. The fifth dividend will be paid the day before the note matures. The appropriate discount rate for dividends is a continuously compounded risk-free rate of 6%.

Suppose that the day after the note is issued, XYZ announces a permanent dividend increase of $0.25. What happens to the price of the equity-linked note?

12.2 Suppose the effective semiannual interest rate is 3%.

   a. What is the price of a bond that pays one unit of the S&P index in 3 years?

   b. What semiannual dollar coupon is required if the bond is to sell at par?

   c. What semiannual payment of fractional units of the S&P index is required if the bond is to sell at par?

12.3 Use information from Table 12.8.

   a. What is the price of a bond that pays one unit of the S&P index in 2 years?

   b. What quarterly dollar coupon is required if the bond is to sell at par?

   c. What quarterly payment of fractional units of the S&P index is required if the bond is to sell at par?

12.4 Assume that the volatility of the S&P index is 30%.

   a. What is the price of a bond that after 2 years pays $S_2 + \max(0, S_2 - S_0)$?

   b. Suppose the bond pays $S_2 + [\lambda \times \max(0, S_2 - S_0)]$. For what λ will the bond sell at par?

12.5 Assume that the volatility of the S&P index is 30%.

   a. What is the price of a bond that after 2 years pays $S_0 + \max(0, S_2 - S_0)$?

   b. Suppose the bond pays $S_0 + [\lambda \times \max(0, S_2 - S_0)]$ in year 2. For what λ will the bond sell at par?

12.6 Assume that the volatility of the S&P index is 30% and consider a bond with the payoff $S_2 + \lambda \times [\max(0, S_2 - S_0) - \max(0, S_2 - K)]$.

a. If $\lambda = 1$ and $K = \$1500$, what is the price of the bond?

b. Suppose $K = \$1500$. For what λ will the bond sell at par?

c. If $\lambda = 1$, for what K will the bond sell at par?

The next six problems will deal with the CD linked to the S&P 500, discussed on pages 361–364. If necessary, use the assumptions in that section.

12.7 Explain how to synthetically create the equity-linked CD by using a forward contract on the S&P index and a put option instead of a call option. (*Hint:* Use put-call parity. Remember that the S&P index pays dividends.)

12.8 Assuming that profit for the issuing bank is zero, draw a graph showing how the participation rate, γ, varies with the coupon, c. Repeat assuming the issuing bank earns a profit of 5%.

12.9 Compute the required semiannual cash dividend if the expiration payoff to the CD is $\$1300 - \max(0, 1300 - S_{5.5})$ and the initial price is to be $\$1300$.

12.10 Compute λ if the dividend on the CD is 0 and the payoff is $\$1300 - \max(0, 1300 - S_{5.5}) + \lambda \times \max(0, S_{5.5} - 2600)$ and the initial price is to be $\$1300$.

12.11 Compute λ if the dividend on the CD is 0, the initial price is $\$1300$, and the payoff is $\$1200 + \lambda \times \max(0, S_{5.5} - 1300)$.

12.12 In this problem we examine how changes in inputs affect the CD.

a. What happens to the value of the CD as the interest rate, volatility, and dividend yield change? In particular, consider alternative volatilities of 20% and 40%, interest rates of 0.5% and 7%, and dividend yields of 0.5% and 2.5%.

b. For each parameter change in (a), suppose that we want the product to continue to earn a 4.3% commission. What price participation, γ, would the CD need to have in each case to keep the same market value?

12.13 Use the information in Table 12.8.

a. What is the price of a bond that pays one barrel of oil 2 years from now?

b. What annual cash payment would the bond have to make in order to sell for $\$20.90$?

12.14 Using the information in Table 12.8, suppose we have a bond that pays one barrel of oil in 2 years.

a. Suppose the bond pays a fractional barrel of oil as an interest payment after 1 year and after 2 years, in addition to the one barrel after 2 years. What payment would the bond have to make in order to sell for par ($20.90)?

b. Suppose that the oil payments are quarterly instead of annual. How large would they need to be for the bond to sell at par?

12.15 Using the information in Table 12.8, suppose we have a bond that after 2 years pays one barrel of oil plus $\lambda \times \max(0, S_2 - 20.90)$, where S_2 is the year 2 spot price of oil. If the bond is to sell for $20.90 and oil volatility is 15%, what is λ?

12.16 Using the information in Table 12.8, assume that the volatility of oil is 15%.

a. Show that a bond that pays one barrel of oil in 1 year sells today for $19.2454.

b. Consider a bond that in 1 year has the payoff $S_1 + \max(0, K_1 - S_1) - \max(0, S_1 - K_2)$. Find the strike prices K_1 and K_2 such that $K_2 - K_1 = \$2$, and the price of the bond is $19.2454. How would you describe this payoff?

c. Now consider a claim that in 1 year pays $S_1 - \$20.50 + \max(0, K_1 - S_1) - \max(0, S_1 - K_2)$, where K_1 and K_2 are from the previous answer. What is the value of this claim? What have you constructed?

12.17 Swaps often contain caps or floors. In this problem you are to construct an oil contract that has the following characteristics: The initial cost is zero. Then in each period, the buyer pays the market price of oil if it is between K_1 and K_2; otherwise, if $S < K_1$, the buyer pays K_1, and if $S > K_2$, the buyer pays K_2 (there is a floor and a cap). Assume that $K_2 - K_1 = \$2$ and that oil volatility is 15%.

a. If there is a single settlement date in 1 year, what are K_1 and K_2?

b. If the swap settles quarterly for 8 quarters, what are K_1 and K_2?

12.18 You have been asked to construct an oil contract that has the following characteristics: The initial cost is zero. Then in each period, the buyer pays $S - \overline{F}$, with a cap of $\$21.90 - \overline{F}$ and a floor of $\$19.90 - \overline{F}$. Assume oil volatility is 15%. What is $\overline{F}$?

12.19 Suppose that in Table 12.4 the tranches have promised payments of $160 (senior), $50 (mezzanine), and $90 (subordinated). Reproduce the table for this case, assuming zero default correlation.

12.20 Repeat the previous problem, only assuming that defaults are perfectly correlated.

13 Corporate Applications

In this chapter we look at contexts in which firms issue derivatives, either explicitly or implicitly. Black and Scholes (1973) observed that common debt and equity can be viewed as options, with the firm's assets as the underlying asset. First, we show how this insight can be used to price debt subject to default, as well as the implications for determining how leverage affects the expected return on equity. We also examine warrants, convertible debt, and callable debt as examples of securities that explicitly contain options.

Second, many firms grant options as compensation to employees. These options typically cannot be exercised for some period of time and cannot be sold, so they raise interesting valuation issues. In addition, compensation options often have nonstandard features.

Third, merger deals in which firm A offers their own stock to buy firm B sometimes offer price protection to firm B shareholders. This protection can take the form of a collar. We examine one merger—Northrop Grumman–TRW—that used a collar for this purpose.

13.1 EQUITY, DEBT, AND WARRANTS

Firms often issue securities that have derivative components. For example, firms issue options to employees for financing, and convertible debt is a bond coupled with a call option. However, even simple securities, such as ordinary debt and equity, can be viewed as derivatives. In this section we examine both implicit and explicit options issued by firms.

Debt and Equity as Options

Consider a firm with the following very simple capital structure. The firm has non-dividend-paying equity outstanding, along with a single zero-coupon debt issue. Represent the time t values of the assets of the firm, the debt, and the equity as A_t, B_t, and E_t. The debt matures at time T and has maturity value $\overline{B}$. We assume throughout this section that there are no taxes, bankruptcy costs, transaction costs, or other market imperfections.

The value of the debt and equity at time T will depend upon the value of the firm's assets. Equity holders are the legal owners of the firm; in order for them to have unambiguous possession of the firm's assets, they must pay the debt holders $\overline{B}$ at time T. If $A_T > \overline{B}$, equity holders will pay $\overline{B}$ to the bondholders since equity will then be worth the value of the assets less the payment to bondholders, or $A_T - \overline{B} > 0$. However, if $A_T < \overline{B}$, equity holders would have to inject additional funds in order to pay off the debt. In this case equity holders would declare bankruptcy, permitting the bondholders to take possession of the assets. Therefore, the value of the equity at time T, E_T, is

$$E_T = \max(0, A_T - \overline{B}) \tag{13.1}$$

This expression is the payoff to a call option with the assets of the firm as the underlying asset and $\overline{B}$ as the strike price.

Because equity holders control the firm, bondholders receive the *smallest* payment to which they are legally entitled. If the firm is bankrupt—i.e., if $A_T < \overline{B}$—the bondholders receive A_T. If the firm is solvent—i.e., if $A_T \geq \overline{B}$—the bondholders receive $\overline{B}$. Thus, the value of the debt is

$$B_T = \min(A_T, \overline{B}) \tag{13.2}$$

This expression can be written[1]

$$\begin{aligned} B_T &= A_T + \min(0, \overline{B} - A_T) \\ &= A_T - \max(0, A_T - \overline{B}) \end{aligned} \tag{13.3}$$

Equation (13.3) says that the bondholders own the firm, but have written a call option to the equity holders. This way of expressing the debt value explains where the call option in equation (13.1) comes from. Summing equations (13.1) and (13.2) gives the total value of the firm—equity plus debt—as A_T.

A different way to write equation (13.2) is the following:

$$\begin{aligned} B_T &= \overline{B} + \min(0, A_T - \overline{B}) \\ &= \overline{B} - \max(0, \overline{B} - A_T) \end{aligned} \tag{13.4}$$

The interpretation of equation (13.4) is that the bondholders own risk-free debt with a payoff equal to $\overline{B}$, but have written a put option on the assets with strike price $\overline{B}$.[2]

---

[1] To follow these derivations, note that $\min(0, x - y) = -\max(0, y - x)$.

[2] A bond with a payoff specified as in equation (13.2) is a **debenture**—a bond for which payments are secured only by the general credit worthiness of the company. Such a bond is said to be *unsecured*. It is also possible for bonds to be secured by specific collateral. For example, lenders to airlines may have an airplane as collateral for their bond.

13.1 Equity, Debt, and Warrants

FIGURE 13.1

Value of debt and equity at maturity of the debt, as a function of assets, for a firm that has a single issue of zero-coupon debt with a maturity value of $6000.

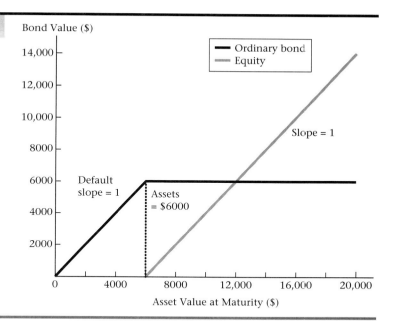

Example 13.1 Suppose a firm has issued zero-coupon debt with a face value of $\overline{B} = \$6000$. The maturity value of the equity is given by equation (13.1), and the maturity value of the debt is given by equation (13.4). The two payoffs are graphed in Figure 13.1 as a function of corporate assets at maturity.

If we assume that the assets of the firm are lognormally distributed, then we can use the Black-Scholes model to value the payoffs to the firm's equity and debt, equations (13.1) and (13.4). For purposes of option pricing, the firm's assets are the underlying asset, the strike price is the promised payment on debt, $\overline{B}$, the volatility of the firm's assets, σ, is volatility, and the payout rate from the firm becomes the dividend yield. If the risk-free rate is r and the debt matures at time T, we have

$$E_t = \text{BSCall}(A_t, \overline{B}, \sigma, r, T-t, \delta) \tag{13.5}$$
$$B_t = A_t - E_t \tag{13.6}$$

Assuming that the debt is zero-coupon, we can compute the yield to maturity on debt, ρ. By definition of the yield to maturity, we have $B_t = \overline{B}e^{-\rho(T-t)}$; hence, we can solve for ρ to obtain

$$\rho = \frac{1}{T-t} \ln(\overline{B}/B_t) \tag{13.7}$$

This model of the firm is very simple, in that there are no coupons or dividends, no refinancings or subsequent debt issues, etc. It is possible to create more complicated models of a firm's capital structure; nevertheless, this model provides a starting point for understanding how leverage affects returns on debt and equity and determines the yield on risky debt.

Example 13.2 Suppose that $\overline{B} = \$100$, $A_0 = \$90$, $r = 6\%$, $\sigma = 25\%$, $\delta = 0$ (the firm makes no payouts), and $T = 5$ years. The value of the equity is

$$E_0 = \text{BSCall}(\$90, \$100, 0.25, 0.06, 5, 0)$$
$$= \$27.07$$

The value of the debt is

$$B_0 = \$90 - \$27.07$$
$$= \$62.93$$

The debt-to-value ratio of this firm is therefore $\$62.93/\$90 = 0.699$. The yield to maturity on debt is

$$\rho = \frac{1}{5}\ln(100/62.93)$$
$$= 0.0926$$

The debt yield of 9.26% is 326 basis points greater than the risk-free rate.

Valuing Credit Guarantees

Viewing debt and equity as options provides a framework for thinking about credit risk. Recall from Section 12.5 that a credit default swap is a contract that pays the difference between the bond's par value and market value if a bond defaults. The analysis we have just performed, in which we viewed debt and equity as options, provides a framework for valuing credit guarantees, such as default swaps.

Equation (13.4) shows that defaultable debt is equivalent to owning default-free debt and writing a put option on the assets of the firm. The strike price on this put option is the promised payment on debt, $\overline{B}$. If there is default ($A_T < \overline{B}$), the put pays $\overline{B} - A_T$. Thus, the value of the put is the cost of insurance that protects bondholders against a loss due to default. If such a put option is traded, then an investor who owned a corporate bond could buy the put option; this would offset the implicit written put in equation (13.4) and transform the corporate bond into a synthetic default-free bond. Conversely, an investor who owned a default-free bond (such as a government bond) could sell a put and transform their bond into a synthetic corporate bond. In practice, investors use credit default swaps as an alternative to corporate bonds as a way to trade corporate credit risk. In addition to the trading of credit guarantees in the default swap market, the U.S. government is a major provider of credit guarantees. Some of these are discussed in Box 13.1.

> **Box 13.1: Government Credit Guarantees**
>
> The U.S. government is a major supplier of credit guarantees in a variety of financial activities. Some of the guarantees are front-page news when they are granted: The government guarantees for the debt of Chrysler in the 1980s and US Airways in 2002 are well-known examples. However, there are also a host of governmental and quasi-governmental insurance programs that many of us take for granted. Here is a partial list:
>
> - The Federal Deposit Insurance Corporation (FDIC) guarantees bank deposits against default of the bank.
> - The Pension Benefit Guarantee Corporation (PBGC) guarantees defined benefit pensioners against the failure of the firm to honor its pension obligations.
> - The Federal National Mortgage Association (Fannie Mae) and the Federal Home Loan and Mortgage Corporation (Freddie Mac) buy mortgages that meet certain characteristics and resell them with a guarantee against default by the borrower. The government does not explicitly guarantee Fannie and Freddie bondholders against the default of the two companies, but it is widely believed by market participants that there is an implicit government guarantee.
> - The federal government assumes the credit risk for most student loans.
>
> The accounting for these various programs is complex and inconsistent; Lucas (forthcoming) examines the intricate details of many of these programs. It is fair to say that government decision makers in many cases do not have an accurate sense of the market value of the insurance they mandate.

In practice, credit default swaps are more complicated than the contract we just described because default can occur at times other than maturity, most corporate bonds pay coupons, and the CDS premium is paid over time until a default, rather than in an inital lump sum. Nevertheless, the underlying idea remains that a credit default swap is effectively a put option on a bond. The following example illustrates the valuation of default insurance.

Example 13.3 As in Example 13.2, suppose that a firm with assets worth $90 issues a 5-year zero-coupon bond promising to pay $100 in 5 years. Using the same assumptions as before, we can use the Black-Scholes put formula to value an insurance contract on the bond. The value of the put in this case is

$$\text{Insurance} = \text{BSPut}(\$90, \$100, 0.25, 0.06, 5, 0)$$
$$= \$11.15$$

A default-free 5-year bond would sell for

$$\text{Default-free bond} = \$100 e^{-0.06 \times 5} = \$74.08$$

The defaultable bond therefore sells for

Defaultable Bond = Default-free bond − Insurance = $74.08 − $11.15 = $62.93

This is the same price we obtained in Example 13.2.

Leverage and the Expected Return on Debt and Equity

Example 13.2 shows that, because of the possibility of bankruptcy, the yield to maturity on debt exceeds the risk-free rate. However, an investor in the bond earns the yield to maturity only if the firm does not go bankrupt. Accounting for the possibility of bankruptcy, the investor on average will earn a return less than the yield to maturity and greater than the risk-free rate. In effect, debt that can default bears some of the risk of the assets, sharing this risk with the equity holders.

We can compute the expected return on both debt and equity using the concept of *option elasticity*, which we discussed in Chapter 11. Recall that the elasticity of an option tells us the relationship between the expected return on the underlying asset and that on the option. Using equation (11.12), we can compute the expected return on equity as

$$r_E = r + (r_A - r) \times \Omega_E \tag{13.8}$$

where r_A is the expected return on assets, r is the risk-free rate, and Ω_E is the elasticity of the equity. The formula for elasticity is

$$\Omega_E = \frac{A_t \Delta_E}{E_t} \tag{13.9}$$

where Δ_E is the option delta.

We can compute the expected return on debt using the debt elasticty, Ω_B:

$$r_B = r + (r_A - r) \times \Omega_B \tag{13.10}$$

The elasticity calculation is slightly more involved for debt than for equity. Since we compute debt value as $B_t = A_t - E_t$, the elasticity of debt is a weighted average of the asset and equity elasticities:

$$\Omega_B = \frac{A_t}{A_t - E_t} \Omega_A - \frac{E_t}{A_t - E_t} \Omega_E \tag{13.11}$$

The elasticity of any asset with respect to itself is one, so we have $\Omega_A = 1$.

Using equations (13.8)–(13.11), you can verify that if you owned a proportional interest in the debt and equity of the firm, the expected return on your portfolio would be the expected return on the assets of the firm:

$$(\%\text{Equity} \times r_E) + (\%\text{Debt} \times r_B) = r_A \tag{13.12}$$

It bears emphasizing that this relationship requires that r_B represent the *expected return* on debt, not the yield to maturity.

Using the option model, we can also see how the dollar values of debt and equity change when there is a change in the value of the assets. In other words, we can ask what the *deltas* of debt and equity are. From equation (13.5), if assets increase in value by $1, equity will increase by the delta of the call option. From equation (13.6), debt will increase by one less the equity delta.

It is instructive to compare the expected return calculation for equity in equation (13.8) with a common alternative calculation. If we assume the debt is risk-free, the expected return on equity is[3]

$$\hat{r}_E = r + (r_A - r)\frac{1}{\%\text{Equity}} \qquad (13.13)$$

This is the familiar Modigliani-Miller expression for the expected return on levered equity. Equation (13.13) can be obtained from equation (13.8) by assuming that the delta of the equity is 1, which implies that the delta of the debt is zero. Viewing debt and equity as options, by contrast, allows us to take into account the effects of possible bankruptcy. Equation (13.8) assumes that debt and equity holders share the risk of the assets, so equation (13.3) will give a higher r_E than equation (13.8).

Example 13.4 Use the same assumptions as in Example 13.2, and suppose that the expected return on assets, r_A, is 10%. The equity delta is

$$\text{BSCallDelta}(90, 100, 0.25, 0.06, 5, 0) = 0.735$$

The debt delta is $1 - 0.735 = 0.265$. Thus, if the asset value increases by $1, the value of the debt increases by $0.735 and the value of the debt increases by $0.265.

Using equation (13.9), the equity elasticity is

$$\frac{90 \times 0.735}{27.07} = 2.443$$

The expected return on equity is therefore

$$r_E = 0.06 + (0.1 - 0.06) \times 2.443$$
$$= 0.1577$$

Using equation (13.11), the debt elasticity is

$$\frac{90}{90 - 27.07} \times 1 - \frac{27.07}{90 - 27.07} \times 2.443 = 0.3793$$

The expected return on debt is therefore

$$r_B = 0.06 + (0.1 - 0.06) \times 0.3793$$
$$= 0.0752$$

---

[3] This expression is also sometimes written as $r_E = r_A + (r_A - r) \times D/E$.

Note that the 7.52% expected return on debt is greater than the risk-free rate (6%) and less than the yield to maturity on debt (9.26%).

If we owned equity and debt in the same proportion in which they were issued by the firm, we would have a return of

$$\frac{27.07}{90} \times 0.1577 + \frac{90 - 27.07}{90} \times 0.0752 = 0.1000$$

Since 10% is the expected return on assets, this illustrates equation (13.12).

Finally, if we were to (erroneously) assume that debt is risk-free and use equation (13.13) to compute the expected return on equity, we would obtain

$$\hat{r}_E = 0.06 + \frac{1}{27.07/90}(0.1 - 0.06)$$
$$= 0.1929$$

This calculation gives an expected return on equity substantially greater than 15.77%.

This example computes expected returns for a particular leverage ratio. As the firm becomes more levered, equity holders bear more asset risk per dollar of equity. If assets have a positive beta, the expected return on equity will increase with leverage. At the same time, debt also becomes riskier as leverage increases and there is increased chance of default on the debt.

Figure 13.2 graphs the debt-to-asset ratio (computed using equation (13.5)) and the expected return on equity (computed using equation (13.8)) as a function of the asset value of the firm, using the assumptions in Example 13.4. For very low asset values, the debt-to-asset ratio is almost 1 and the expected return on equity is almost 40%. As the asset value exceeds $200, the expected return on equity is about 12%.

For purposes of comparison, Figure 13.2 graphs the expected return on equity, computed assuming that the debt is risk-free. For asset values close to $200, the difference is less than 20 basis points. For a very highly levered (low asset value) firm, however, the difference in Figure 13.2 is dramatic.

Conflicts between debt and equity The idea that equity and debt can be modeled using options on corporate assets provides insights into relations between debt and equity holders. Since equity holders control the firm, bondholders may be concerned that equity holders will take actions that would harm them, or may fail to take actions that would help them.

There are two decisions equity holders make that affect the relative value of debt and equity. First, equity holders can affect the volatility of assets. Equity holders can increase asset volatility either by increasing the operating risk of existing assets or by "asset substitution," replacing existing assets with riskier assets. An increase in volatility, other things equal, increases the value of the equity holder's call option and therefore reduces the value of debt. In Example 13.2, the vega of the equity is 0.66, so an increase

FIGURE 13.2

The top panel graphs the debt-to-asset ratio as a function of the asset value of the firm, using the Black-Scholes formula to compute the value of the debt. The bottom panel graphs the expected return on equity as a function of the asset value of the firm, using equations (13.13) and (13.8). Both graphs assume that there is a single zero-coupon debt issue with maturity value $100 and 5 years to maturity, and also assume that $r = 6\%$, $\sigma = 25\%$ (for the assets), and $\delta = 0$.

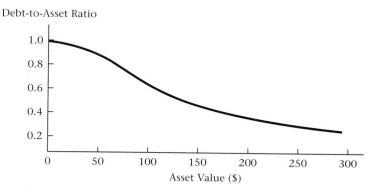

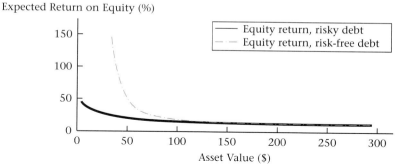

in asset volatility of 0.01 leads to an increase in the market value of equity of $0.66, which is $0.66/27.07 = 2.4\%$ of equity value. Debt value would decline by $0.66.

A second decision that equity holders can make is the size of payouts to shareholders, such as dividends and share repurchases. To see why payouts are a potential problem for bondholders, suppose that the firm makes an unexpected one-time $1 payout to shareholders. This payout reduces assets by $1. The delta of the equity with respect to assets is less than one, so the value of equity declines by less than $1. Since the value of debt plus equity equals assets, *the value of the debt must decline by one less the delta of the equity*. Unanticipated payouts to equity holders therefore can hurt bondholders.

Bondholders are well aware of the potentially harmful effects of asset substitution and dividends. Bond covenants (legal restrictions on the firm) often limit the ability of the firm to change assets or pay dividends. Viewing debt and equity as options makes it clear why such restrictions exist.

Bondholders can also encounter problems from actions that shareholders fail to take. Suppose the firm has a project worth $2 that requires shareholders to make a $1 investment. If shareholders make the investment, they pay $1, the value of the assets increases by $2, and the value of the shares rises by $2 \times \Delta$. The gain to shareholders is less than the increase in the value of assets. The difference of $2 - 2 \times \Delta$ goes to the bondholders. In making a positive NPV investment, shareholders help bondholders.

The shareholders in this example will make the investment only if the value of shares goes up by more than the $1 they invest, which will occur if $\Delta > 0.5$. In order for shareholders to be willing to invest, the NPV must be great enough that shareholders gain after allowing for the value increase that is lost to debt holders.[4] Thus, because of debt, the shareholders may fail to make positive NPV investments. A related problem is asset substitution: Shareholders might make negative NPV investments that increase asset risk, thereby transferring value from bondholders to stockholders.

Multiple Debt Issues

The option-based model of debt accommodates multiple issues of zero-coupon debt with different seniorities, as long as all debt expires on the same date. By definition, more senior debt has priority in the event of bankruptcy. Suppose that there are three debt issues, with maturity values of $30, $30, and $40, ranked in seniority from highest to lowest. We will refer to each distinct level of seniority as a tranche. The value of equity will be the same as in Example 13.2, since it is still necessary for equity holders to pay $100 to receive ownership of the assets. However, the option pricing approach permits us to assign appropriate yields to each level of debt.

Senior debt holders are the first in line to be paid. They own the firm and have written a call option permitting the next set of bondholders to buy the firm from them by paying the maturity value of the senior debt, $30. Intermediate debt holders own a call option permitting them to buy the firm for $30, and have sold a call option permitting the junior bondholders to buy the firm for $60. Junior bondholders in turn own the call option to buy the firm for $60, and have written a call option permitting the equity holders to buy the firm for $100. The values of these options are

$$\text{BSCall}(\$90, \$30, 0.25, 0.06, 5, 0) = \$67.82 \quad (13.14)$$

$$\text{BSCall}(\$90, \$60, 0.25, 0.06, 5, 0) = \$47.25 \quad (13.15)$$

$$\text{BSCall}(\$90, \$100, 0.25, 0.06, 5, 0) = \$27.07 \quad (13.16)$$

---

[4] The idea that the debt may harm investment incentives is developed in Myers (1977).

TABLE 13.1 Market values, yields, and expected returns on three debt tranches.

Claim	Owns	Writes	Value ($)	Yield (%)	Expected Return (%)
Senior bonds	Assets	C(30)	22.18	6.04	6.04
Intermediate bonds	C(30)	C(60)	20.57	7.54	7.03
Junior bonds	C(60)	C(100)	20.18	13.69	9.63
Equity	C(100)		27.07		15.77

Table 13.1 summarizes the value, yield to maturity, and expected return of each tranche of debt. The junior tranche has a yield to maturity of 13.69%, very close to the required return on equity. The senior tranche, according to the model, is almost risk-free.

The expected returns in Table 13.1 are computed using option elasticities. To illustrate the calculation, consider the junior bond, which is created by buying a 60-strike call on the assets of the firm and selling a 100-strike call. The two option elasticities are 1.7875 (60-strike) and 2.4432 (100-strike). Using the fact that the elasticity of a portfolio is a weighted average of the elasticities of the portfolio components, the elasticity of the junior bond is

$$\frac{47.25}{47.25 - 27.07} \times 1.7875 - \frac{27.07}{47.25 - 27.07} \times 2.4432 = 0.9077$$

The expected return on the junior debt is therefore

$$r_{junior} = 0.06 + (0.10 - 0.06) \times 0.9077 = 0.0963$$

Table 13.1 makes it clear why debt cannot be treated as a single homogeneous class when firms with complex capital structures enter bankruptcy. The interests of the most junior debt holders may well resemble the interests of equity holders more than those of senior debt holders.

Warrants

Firms sometimes issue options explicitly. If a firm issues a call option on its own stock, it is known as a **warrant.** (The term "warrant" is used here to denote options on a firm issued by the firm itself, though in practice the term includes traded options issued in fixed supply.) When a warrant is exercised, the warrant holder pays the firm the strike price, K, and receives a share worth more than K (or else the holder would not have exercised the warrant). Thus, the act of exercise is dilutive to other shareholders in the sense that the firm has sold a share for less than it is worth. Of course, existing shareholders are aware of warrants outstanding and can anticipate this potential exercise. The problem is how to value the warrant and how to value the equity given the existence of warrants. This valuation problem does not arise with ordinary options because they are traded by third parties and their exercise has no effect on the firm.

To see how to value a warrant, suppose the firm has n shares outstanding and that the outstanding warrants are European, on m shares, with strike price K. The asset value is A.

At expiration, if warrant holders exercise the warrants, they pay K per share and receive m shares. After the warrants are exercised, the firm has assets worth $A + mK$; hence, exercised warrants are worth

$$\frac{A + mK}{n + m} - K = \frac{n}{n + m}\left(\frac{A}{n} - K\right) \qquad (13.17)$$

The expression A/n is the value of a share of equity in the absence of warrants. Thus, equation (13.17) suggests that we can value a warrant in two steps. First, we compute an option price with A/n as the underlying asset and K as the strike price, ignoring dilution. Second, we multiply the result by a dilution correction factor, $n/(n + m)$. This second step accounts for the fact that warrant exercise changes the number of shares outstanding, with the new shares issued at a "below-market" price of K. The warrant can be valued by using the Black-Scholes formula:

$$\frac{n}{n + m}\,\text{BSCall}\left(\frac{A}{n}, K, \sigma, r, t, \delta\right) \qquad (13.18)$$

Convertible Bonds

In addition to issuing warrants directly, firms can issue warrants embedded in bonds. A **convertible bond** is a bond that, at the option of the bondholder, can be exchanged for shares in the issuing company. A simple convertible bond resembles the equity-linked notes we studied in Chapter 12, except that the bond is convertible into the company's own shares rather than the shares of a third party. The call option in the bond gives the bondholder the right to surrender the bond's maturity payment, M, in exchange for q shares. The valuation of a convertible bond entails valuing both debt subject to default and a warrant.

Suppose there are m bonds with maturity payment M, each of which is convertible into q shares. The value of the firm at time T is A_T. If there are n original shares outstanding, then there will be $n + mq$ shares if the bond is converted. At expiration, the bondholders will convert if the value per share of the assets after conversion, $A_T/(n + mq)$, exceeds the value per share of the maturity payment that bondholders would forgo:

$$\frac{A_T}{n + mq} > \frac{M}{q}$$

or

$$\frac{n}{n + mq}\left(\frac{A_T}{n} - \frac{M}{q}\frac{n + mq}{n}\right) > 0 \qquad (13.19)$$

This expression is different from equation (13.12) for warrants, because rather than injecting new cash into the firm when they convert, the bondholders instead avoid taking cash out of the firm.

Conversion occurs if the assets increase sufficiently in value. If the assets decrease, the firm could default on the promised maturity payment. Assuming the convertible is the only debt issue, bankruptcy occurs if assets are worth less than the promised payment to all convertible holders, or $A_T < mM$. The payoff of the convertible at maturity, time T, is

$$\underbrace{mM}_{\text{Bond}} - \underbrace{\max(0, mM - A_T)}_{\text{Written put}} + \underbrace{mq \times \frac{n}{n + mq} \times \max\left(0, \frac{A_T}{n} - \frac{M}{q}\frac{n + mq}{n}\right)}_{mq \text{ purchased warrants}} \quad (13.20)$$

Thus, owning m convertibles can be valued as owning a risk-free bond with maturity payment mM, selling a put on the firm's assets, and buying mq warrants with strike $M/q \times (n + mq)/n$.

Equation (13.20) can be rewritten as

$$\max\left[\min\left(mM, A_T\right), \frac{mq}{n + mq} A_T\right] \quad (13.21)$$

This version of the convertible payoff can be interpreted as follows: Shareholders give bondholders the least they can ($\min[M, A_T/m]$); if it is optimal to do so, convertible holders can then exchange this amount for the conversion value, which is their proportionate share of the assets ($mq/[n + mq] \times A_T$).

Example 13.5 Suppose a firm has issued $m = 6$ convertible bonds, each with maturity value $M = \$1000$ and convertible into $q = 50$ shares. The firm has $n = 400$ common shares outstanding. Figure 13.3 shows the maturity payoff for the aggregate value of the convertible bonds, comparing it with the maturity payoff of otherwise identical nonconvertible bonds issued by the same firm. The six bonds have a total promised maturity value of $6000, so default occurs when assets are below that level. Equation (13.19) implies that conversion occurs when assets exceed $1000 \times 700/50 = \$14,000$. The slope of the convertible payoff above $14,000 is $mq/(n + mq) = 3/7$, less than the slope in default, because convertible investors share gains with existing shareholders, but once in default, convertible bondholders bear additional losses alone (in default, shares are already worthless).

Just as we valued ordinary zero-coupon bonds with the Black-Scholes formula, we can also use the Black-Scholes formula to value a bond convertible at maturity.

Example 13.6 Suppose a firm has assets of $10,000 with a single debt issue consisting of six zero-coupon bonds, each with a maturity value of $1000 and with $T = 5$ years to maturity. The asset volatility is $\sigma = 30\%$ and the risk-free rate is $r = 6\%$. The firm makes no payouts.

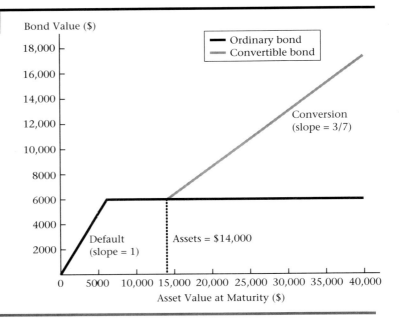

FIGURE 13.3

Maturity payoffs for the aggregate value of an ordinary bond and a convertible bond, using the parameters in Example 13.5.

If the single debt issue is not convertible, the price is

$$\$1000 \times e^{-0.06 \times 5} - \text{BSPut}\left(\frac{\$10,000}{6}, \$1000, 0.30, 0.06, 5, 0\right) = \$701.27$$

The yield on the nonconvertible bond is $\ln(1000/701.27)/5 = 0.0710$, greater than the risk-free rate because of the risk of bankruptcy.

Suppose the debt issue is instead the convertible bond described in Example 13.5. Using equation (13.20), the value of all convertible bonds is

$$6 \times \$1000 \times e^{-0.06 \times 5} - \text{BSPut}\left(\$10,000, 6 \times \$1000, 0.30, 0.06, 5, 0\right)$$
$$+ 6 \times 50 \times \frac{400}{400 + 6 \times 50} \times \text{BSCall}\left(\frac{\$10,000}{400}, \frac{\$1000}{50} \times \frac{400 + 6 \times 50}{400}, 0.30, 0.06, 5, 0\right)$$
$$= \$5276.35$$

Each bond has a price of $879.39. The yield on a bond is $\ln(\$1000/\$879.39)/5 = 0.0257$. This is below the yield on an otherwise equivalent nonconvertible bond because of the conversion option: The bondholders have a call option for which they pay by accepting a lower yield on the debt. The value of a share is $(\$10,000 - \$5276.35)/400 = \$11.809$. Bondholders will convert if at maturity the assets are worth more than

$$M \times (n + mq)/q = \$1000 \times (400 + 6 \times 50)/50 = \$14,000$$

Convertible bonds are typically issued at terms such that a significant increase in the stock price is required for conversion to be worthwhile. In Example 13.6, each bond gives the holder the right to convert into 50 shares, so the strike price is $1000/50 = $20. Since the stock price is $11.809, the ratio of the strike price to the stock price, which is called the **conversion premium,** is $20/$11.809 − 1 = 69.4%. In practice, conversion premiums are most commonly between 20% and 40%.

Why do firms issue convertible bonds? One explanation is that convertible bonds resolve one of the conflicts between equity and debt holders. Shareholders can take value from holders of ordinary bonds by increasing volatility, even if this action has no beneficial effect from the perspective of the firm as a whole. However, convertibles are harmed less than ordinary debt by an increase in volatility, and may even be helped. Financing with convertibles instead of ordinary debt thus reduces the incentive of shareholders to raise volatility.

In practice, valuation of convertible bonds is more complicated than in this example.[5] First, convertible bonds are typically American options, convertible for much of the life of the bond. Second, convertible bonds typically are not zero-coupon. The payment of coupons complicates the analysis because bankruptcy becomes possible at times other than expiration and the reduction in assets stemming from the payment of the coupon (or any other cash payment to the firm's security holders). This coupon reduces assets but is also paid to the bondholders. Third, many companies pay dividends. If the dividends that can be earned by converting the bond into stock exceed the bond coupon, there can be a reason for bondholders to convert before maturity. Finally, interest rates and volatility can change, and the circumstances of default may be more complicated than we have assumed (for example, when there are other debt issues, default could occur prior to maturity). The value of the bond can then change for reasons other than stock price changes.

Callable Bonds

Many bonds are *callable*, meaning that, prior to maturity, the company has the right to give bondholders a predetermined payment in exchange for the bonds. The idea underlying a callable bond is that the bond issuer can buy the bond back at a relatively cheap price, fixed in advance, if it becomes more valuable. A bond can become more valuable because interest rates have fallen, in which case the issuer would like to exchange the existing bonds for new bonds carrying a lower coupon rate. A bond can also become more valuable if the market perceives that the company is less likely to default. Again, in this case the company would like to exchange the existing bond for a newly issued bond with a lower default premium. A firm can always buy bonds back at a market price, but there is generally no advantage to doing so. Callability permits the company to buy bonds back at a prespecified price. Of course the company pays for this right by receiving a lower price when it issues the bond.

---

[5] Ingersoll (1977) and Brennan and Schwartz (1977) discuss the valuation of convertible bonds.

The predetermined price at which a company can call a bond is specified by a **call schedule.** Bonds are typically noncallable for several years after issuance, a period during which the bond is said to have **call protection.** Callability is, in effect, an option that investors sell to the bond issuer. In return, the company issuing the bonds pays a higher yield on the bonds.

Convertible bonds are typically callable. When the issuer calls a convertible bond, the holder of the bond has the choice of surrendering the bond in exchange for the call price or converting. Callability is a way for issuers to shorten the life of the bond, potentially forcing holders to convert prior to maturity. The issuer—acting in the interests of shareholders—follows a call strategy that *minimizes* the value of the bond. Bondholders, by contrast, follow a conversion strategy that *maximizes* the value of the bond.

Since bonds can be called prior to expiration, we cannot value the call provision using Black-Scholes. However, we can value a callable bond binomially. The call strategy for an issuer is like the exercise of an American option: The issuer calls if it is more valuable to do so than to leave the bond outstanding for another period.

Figure 13.4 presents binomial valuation examples for four bonds: an ordinary bond, a callable bond, a convertible bond, and a callable convertible bond. We examine noncallable bonds as benchmarks in order to better understand the effect of callability. We value these bonds using the binomial pricing model outlined in Chapter 10. In each case, the assets of the firm are the underlying asset, and the value of the bonds is determined by the value of the assets. To perform the valuation, we move backward through the tree, as in Chapter 10. The assumptions in Figure 13.4 are the same as those in Example 13.6, so the results in the example and figure are comparable for the ordinary and convertible bonds.

Callable nonconvertible bonds We first consider the binomial valuation of an ordinary noncallable bond (Panel B in Figure 13.4) and its callable counterpart (Panel D in Figure 13.4). The yield on the callable bond (7.57%) exceeds that on the noncallable bond (7.29%) because of the option that bondholders have written to the firm.

How are bond prices in Figure 13.4 computed? For the ordinary bond, the value in year 5 is

$$B_5 = \min(mM, A_5) = \min(\$6000, A_5)$$

There are six $1000 bonds outstanding, and shareholders will pay to these bondholders the value of the firm or $6000, whichever is less. Note that default occurs at the bottom node in year 5 since the value of assets is less than the required bond payment, $6000. Prior to maturity, the value at each node is calculated as in a typical binomial valuation, with

$$B_t = e^{-rh}[pB_{t+h}^+ + (1-p)B_{t+h}^-]$$

For a given node at time t, B_{t+h}^+ is the bond value if assets move up from that node, and B_{t+h}^- is the bond value if assets move down from that node.

FIGURE 13.4

Binomial valuation of a callable nonconvertible and a callable convertible bond. The assumptions are the same as those in Example 13.6. The binomial tree for assets in Panel A is generated using equation (10.10) (a forward tree) with $u = 1.6279$, $d = 0.7503$, $p^* = 0.4044$, $T = 5$, and three binomial time steps (hence, the time between binomial periods is $h = 5/3 = 1.67$). In each case there are six bonds outstanding with a total maturity value of $6000. Convertible bonds convert into 50 shares. The yield for each bond is computed as $\ln(6000/B_0)/5$, where B_0 is the time 0 value of the six bonds. The price is $B_0/6$. The call schedule in Panel C is the price of a zero-coupon bond maturing in year 5 and yielding 6.75%. Callable bonds are call-protected until year 1.67. Prices in *italics* denote calls of the bond; prices in **bold** denote conversions, and prices in ***bold italics*** denote conversions in response to a call.

Panel	Year:	0	1.67	3.33	5
A: Firm assets		10,000.00	16,279.12	26,500.98	43,141.27
			7502.88	12,214.03	19,883.36
				5629.32	9164.04
					4223.61
B: Ordinary bond		4166.82	4912.38	5429.02	6000.00
Price = $694.47			4396.40	5429.02	6000.00
Yield = 7.29%				4471.64	6000.00
					4223.61
C: Call schedule		N/A	4791.10	5361.58	6000.00
D: Callable bond		4109.14	*4791.10*	*5361.58*	6000.00
Price = $684.86			4371.73	*5361.58*	6000.00
Yield = 7.57%				4471.64	6000.00
					4223.61
E: Convertible bond		5324.34	7578.78	11,357.56	**18,489.12**
Price = $887.39			4733.96	6351.59	**8521.44**
Yield = 2.39%				4471.64	6000.00
					4223.61
F: Callable convertible bond		4908.85	***6976.77***	**11,357.56**	**18,489.12**
Price = $818.14			4371.73	*5361.58*	**8521.44**
Yield = 4.01%				4471.64	6000.00
					4223.61

The binomial valuation of the callable bond is straightforward. Let K_t^{call} denote the call schedule. The call price in this example is set to equal the price of a bond yielding 6.75%. At time 1.67, for example, the company could call by paying the bondholders $4791.10, which, for a bond maturing in 3.33 years, is a yield of 6.75%. We assume that the risk-free rate is fixed; thus, the only reason for the company to call the bond is if the company could issue replacement bonds at a lower coupon due to a decrease in default risk.

Shareholders wish to minimize the value of the bonds; hence, their value is

$$B_t = \min \left[\text{Leave the bond outstanding, call} \right]$$
$$= \min \left[e^{-rh}(pB_{t+h}^+ + (1-p)B_{t+h}^-), K_t^{\text{call}} \right] \quad (13.22)$$

If you compare the binomial trees in Panels B and D, it is apparent why the callable bond has a lower price at issue than the ordinary bond. At the top node in year 1.67, the noncallable bonds are worth $4912.38, for a yield of 6%. (If assets reach that node, default will not occur.) The firm calls the callable bond at that node since it is now possible to issue default-free debt. The prospect of this call prevents the bondholders from receiving a capital gain. This in turn lowers the initial price of the bond. Problem 13.15 asks you to compute share prices at each node so that you can see the effect on shareholders of the different bonds.

Callable convertible bonds We now consider noncallable and callable convertible bonds, Panels E and F in Figure 13.4. Note first that, as in Example 13.6, the yield on the convertible noncallable bond (2.39%) is lower than that on the ordinary bond (7.29%) because convertible bondholders receive a call option and pay for this with a lower yield.

Using equation (13.21), the year 5 value for the convertible bond is

$$\max[\min(mM, A_5), \frac{mq}{n+mq} A_5]$$

In Panel E in Figure 13.3, bondholders convert at the top two nodes in year 5, receive the maturity payment in cash at the next node, and the firm defaults at the bottom node.

Prior to maturity, the convertible investor values the bond as the greater of its conversion value and the value of letting the bond live one more period:

$$B_t = \max \left[\text{Continue to hold, convert} \right]$$
$$= \max \left[e^{-rh}(pB_{t+h}^+ + (1-p)B_{t+h}^-), \frac{mq}{n+mq} A_t \right] \quad (13.23)$$

B_t is the total value of the bonds. You may recognize this expression as almost identical to equation (10.11) for valuing an American call option on a stock. The difference is that the payoff is the conversion value instead of $S_t - K$.

When the bond is both convertible and callable, there is a tug-of-war between the firm and the bond investors. We can imagine the bond value being determined as follows: The bondholders decide whether to hold or convert (maximizing the bond value). Given this decision, the firm decides whether to call (minimizing the bond value). If the firm calls, bondholders revisit their decision about whether or not to convert (again maximizing the bond value, conditional upon the behavior of the firm). This chain of reasoning implies the following valuation equation:

$$B_t = \max \{\min [\max(\text{Continue to Hold, Convert), Call}], \text{Convert}\}$$
$$= \max \left\{ \min \left[\max \left(\underbrace{e^{-rh}[pB^+_{t+h} + (1-p)B^-_{t+h}]}_{\text{Hold}}, \underbrace{\frac{mq}{n+mq}A_t}_{\text{Convert}} \right), \underbrace{K^{\text{call}}_t}_{\text{Call}} \right], \underbrace{\frac{mq}{n+mq}A_t}_{\text{Convert}} \right\} \quad (13.24)$$

As you would expect, the ability to call a convertible bond lowers its price, raising its yield from 2.39% to 4.01%. By comparing Panels E and F in Figure 13.4, you can see why this happens. In year 1.67 at the top node, it is optimal to wait to convert if the bond is noncallable. This gives a bond value in Panel E of $7578.78. However, if the bond is callable using the call schedule in Panel C, the firm will call at the top node in year 1.67. In response, the bondholders convert, giving them 50 shares worth $6976.66. The bond is worth less because shareholders cannot delay the conversion. The firm does not call at the lower node in year 1.67 because the credit quality of the bond deteriorates at that node.

Bond Valuation Based on the Stock Price

The binomial examples in Figure 13.4 assume that the assets of the firm follow a binomial process and use the resulting tree to value a convertible bond. This approach becomes complicated when the firm's capital structure contains multiple bonds and convertible securities.

An alternative approach, often used in practice, is to base valuation of a convertible bond on a binomial tree for the stock, rather than on assets. A standard binomial tree for the stock, however, will never reach a zero stock price, and thus a convertible bond valued on this tree will be priced as if it were default-free. This raises the question: How can we incorporate bond default risk into the pricing procedure?

Tsiveriotis and Fernandes (1998) suggest valuing separately the bond income and the stock income from an optimally managed convertible bond. Their procedure accounts for default by discounting bond income at a rate greater than the risk-free rate, while the component of the bond income related to conversion into stock is discounted at the risk-free rate.

Put Warrants

When shares are used to pay employees (as, for example, with compensation options), there is an increase in the number of shares outstanding. Companies making heavy use of share compensation frequently buy shares back from other shareholders (a *share repurchase*) so there is no net increase in the number of shares outstanding.[6]

Many companies that repurchased shares during the 1990s also sold put options on their own stock; a commonly stated rationale for issuing such put warrants is that the put sales are a hedge against the cost of repurchasing shares. Intel, Microsoft, and Dell, for example, all sold significant numbers of puts, with Microsoft alone earning well over $1 billion in put premiums during the 1990s. Here is a quote from Microsoft's 1999 10-K describing the put program:

> Microsoft enhances its repurchase program by selling put warrants. . . . On June 30, 1999, 163 million warrants were outstanding with strike prices ranging from $59 to $65 per share. The put warrants expire between September 1999 and March 2002. The outstanding put warrants permit a net-share settlement at the Company's option and do not result in a put warrant liability on the balance sheet.

How do we think about this transaction? If Microsoft repurchases shares, via a written put or by any other means, nonselling shareholders are in effect buying shares from selling shareholders. It is common to say that managers should maximize shareholder value, but which set of shareholders do they care about? Despite this theoretical ambiguity, we will examine the transaction using a standard profit and loss calculation.

Figure 13.5 is a profit diagram for various alternatives. Suppose that the share price today is $100 and the firm will for certain buy one share back in 3 years. The firm has 3 years to earn interest on the $100 it could have spent today. The profit diagram shows that if the price is still $100 in 3 years, the firm has profited by the amount of this interest. The sale of a put expiring in 3 years generates the curve labeled "Written put."

The third curve in Figure 13.5 shows the combined profit and loss for a short share and written put. (By put-call parity, this position looks like a written call.) Should the share price rise, the firm repurchases shares at a higher price but keeps the put premium. If the share price falls, the firm is obligated to pay the strike price to repurchase shares. This transaction is the mirror image of covered call writing, discussed in Chapter 3.

In practice, dealers have purchased the puts written by firms such as Microsoft, Intel, and Dell. The dealers reportedly hold the puts and delta-hedge the position, as in Chapter 11, thus reducing their risk. Moreover, the transactions, including the dealer's hedging trades, occur without any public announcement. In effect, put-selling firms transact with shareholders using the dealer as a conduit. When the share price rises, the delta of the dealer's purchased put, which is negative, increases toward zero and the dealer sells the shares it had purchased to hedge the put. When the share price falls, delta

---

[6] Corporate finance theory offers no justification for this practice, but firms seem to believe that it is important.

FIGURE 13.5

Profit diagram for being short a share of stock, writing a put, and the combination of the two.

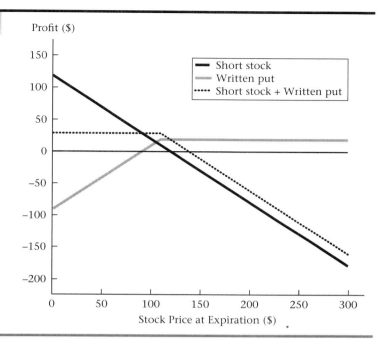

increases to −1 and the dealer buys additional shares to hedge its position. The dealer, acting on behalf of the firm, buys as the share price declines and sells as the share price rises.

Problem 13.17 asks you to examine a binomial example of this transaction, showing first that the firm could accomplish the same end as put writing by transacting directly in its shares. Second, the problem asks you to show how the counterparty dealer delta-hedges the transaction.

13.2 COMPENSATION OPTIONS

Many firms compensate executives and other employees with call options on the company's own stock. The use of such *compensation options* is common and significant in many companies, but has declined since 2002.

Microsoft, for example, estimated in its 1999 annual report (10-K) that its new grants that year of 78 million options were worth about $1.6 billion. This is approximately $52,000 per employee (Microsoft had 31,000 employees). Elsewhere in its 10-K, Microsoft reported that total outstanding options on 766 million shares (against 5 billion shares outstanding) had a market value on June 30, 1999, of $69 billion, or $2 *million* per employee.

> ### Box 13.2: Microsoft and Compensation Options
>
> In July 2003 the *Wall Street Journal* proclaimed: "The golden age of stock options is over." (See "Microsoft Ushers Out the Era of Options," by Robert A. Guth and Joann S. Lublin, *Wall Street Journal*, July 14, 2003.) Microsoft stock had fallen recently and many employees had out-of-the-money options. Employees expressed what CEO Steve Ballmer called "angst" about the low stock price and the effect on option values.
>
> Microsoft's CFO was quoted in the article as saying that employees could no longer expect to become wealthy from stock options:
>
>> If you think what happened in the nineties is going to happen again—it's not," said Microsoft Chief Financial Officer John Connors. In a recent interview he described the PC market boom as a "phenomenon" that "nobody will ever likely repeat."
>
> Microsoft announced that it would eliminate the use of options as compensation, issuing restricted stock instead. (Restricted stock is stock that cannot be sold for a period of time.)
>
> In addition, Microsoft entered into an agreement with JP Morgan Chase whereby the bank would, on a one-time basis, offer to buy employee options. The bank bought the options at modified terms; for example, maturities were reduced to a maximum of 3 years. As a result, employees sold their options for a price that in many cases was significantly less than the unrestricted price for an otherwise equivalent traded option. JP Morgan Chase, which would hold the options it acquired, informed Microsoft employees that it would be short-selling shares in order to delta-hedge the option position. Slightly more than half of employee options were sold in this fashion.
>
> Microsoft's avoidance of options appeared to be part of a general trend. One survey found a 50% reduction in the value of option grants between 2001 and 2003. (See "Stock Option Awards Sharply Cut," by Ruth Simon, *Wall Street Journal*, December 14, 2004, p. D3.)
>
> In 2005 Microsoft chairman Bill Gates even told a group of business writers, "I regret that we ever used stock options." (Reuters, "Gates Regrets Paying with Stock Options," www.cnn.com, May 3, 2005.)

The use of compensation options has declined in recent years. Several developments seem to be responsible for this change. First, the market decline in 2000 left many employees with deep out-of-the-money options and created morale problems for companies heavily dependent upon options. Box 13.2 discusses Microsoft's response to its overhang of out-of-the-money options.

Second, both the Financial Accounting Standards Board (FASB) in the United States and the International Accounting Standards Board (IASB) announced that they would require companies to recognize employee option grants as a compensation expense. Throughout the 1990s most companies had treated compensation options as worthless when computing earnings.[7] An attempt by the FASB to require option expensing in the early 1990s was defeated by companies opposed to expensing. Many of these companies were concerned about the decline in reported earnings that would result from expensing.

The logic behind requiring companies to expense option grants is straightforward. If a company pays cash to an employee, the company deducts the payment as an expense. If an otherwise identical company replaces some of the cash with an option grant, that company will report systematically higher earnings than the first *unless* the value of the option grant is also deducted as an expense. If options are not expensed, companies can use option compensation instead of cash as a way to inflate earnings.

To think about expensing, you can perform the following thought experiment: Imagine that a firm that issues options to employees were to hedge its obligations by buying a contract from a third party. Under the terms of this contract, the third party would pay the firm the value of the option when the employee exercises it. The firm could grant an option and buy the hedging contract, thereby insulating shareholders from the effect of the grant. The cost of this hedging contract is the cost to the firm of the option grant.

If a firm does not buy such a contract, it self-insures, meaning that shareholders bear the cost of the option grant. Either way, the cost of the insurance is the cost to shareholders of the compensation option. The problem of valuing a compensation option amounts to asking how much it would cost the firm to hedge its compensation commitments.

In December 2004 the FASB issued Statement of Financial Accounting Standards (SFAS) 123R, which contained the final rules, effective in June 2005, for companies to follow in expensing options. The statement

> requires a public entity to measure the cost of employee services received in exchange for an award of equity instruments based on the grant-date fair value of the award (with limited exceptions). That cost will be recognized over the period during which an employee is required to provide service in exchange for the award—the requisite service period (usually the vesting period).[8]

A company might grant options that vest after 3 years and expire after 7 years. Under SFAS 123R, the company could value these options using the Black-Scholes or the binomial formula and then expense 1/3 of their value over each year of the vesting period.

The valuation of compensation options is complicated by the fact that there are many special considerations in valuing them:

- Compensation options cannot be sold and typically are not fully vested (i.e., the employee does not own them) for several years.

---

[7] Statement of Financial Accounting Standards (SFAS) 123 did require companies to report the value of options in a footnote. This value—frequently computed using the Black-Scholes formula—did not affect reported earnings.

[8] Statement of Financial Accounting Standards No. 123R, p. ii.

- The executive may resign, be fired, die, or become disabled, or the company may be acquired. Any of these may affect the value of the option grant, either by forcing early exercise (as may happen with a death) or requiring that the options be forfeited (in the event the executive is fired).
- The term of the options can be 10 years or more, which makes volatility and dividend estimates difficult.
- The company may not have a publicly traded stock, in which case the stock price must be estimated.
- There may be unusual contractual features of the compensation option contract. For example, the strike price may be an industry stock-price index.

Such considerations make it harder to value compensation options than short-lived exchange-traded options. We will now discuss some of the issues that arise in option expensing.

Whose Valuation?

Compensation options cannot be freely traded, although at least one company, Google, routinely permits employees to sell options to a dealer prior to their expiration (Box 13.3). An employee who cannot sell options will typically discount their value. As a result, you can expect that firms and employees will value compensation options differently. Such a difference in valuation can occur for any compensation other than immediate cash.

Accounting standards require that companies deduct the *cost to the company*. The goal is to measure cost to nonemployee shareholders, not value to employees. For example, suppose a company grants employees nontradable membership in a golf club costing $15,000 per year. No one would value the membership at more than $15,000, because it can be purchased for that amount. However, someone who does not play golf might value the membership at zero. Thus, while for one executive the membership might displace $15,000 of salary, for another, it might not displace any salary. However, in either case, shareholders bear the $15,000 cost. *The fact that the employee discounts the membership's value does not reduce the cost to the firm.* For shareholders, the key question is the cost to the company: How should shareholders value option grants, given the behavior of employees?

Valuation Inputs

SFAS 123R calls for the valuation to measure fair market value of the option. This requires that companies estimate the likely behavior of employees with respect to exercise and forfeiture of options, and also that the company estimate prospective volatility and dividends.[9] To illustrate several practical issues in measuring cost to the company, we

---

[9] Since dividends reduce the value of an option, it is possible that widespread use of compensation options has resulted in a reduction in corporate dividends.

> ### Box 13.3: Google and Compensation Options
>
> Microsoft renounced compensation options in 2003, but Google continues to use them. If a company is heavily dependent on compensation options, a decline in the stock price can cause morale problems for employees who are hoping their options will be valuable. An out-of-the-money option with years to expiration can have substantial value, but employees who cannot sell the option and who cannot observe a price may not appreciate this. Concern about morale seems to have been part of Microsoft's rationale for abandoning the use of options.
>
> Google addresses this problem with transferable stock options (TSOs), a program introduced in 2007. Google typically grants options with 10 years to expiration, and the options vest after 4 years. Once an option vests, employees using the TSO program can offer to sell their options to investment banks, which bid for the options in an internal market. Any options sold in this way have a maximum maturity of 2 years. As a consequence, an employee whose options have just vested, and which therefore have 6 years to expiration, faces a substantial loss in theoretical value by selling the options, shortening the maturity by 4 years. However, the options will be more valuable than if the employee were to exercise them at that point. Moreover, employees can observe the internal market price for options and can thereby place a lower bound on the value of their vested, unexercised options.
>
> Google's TSO program is similar to the one-time option purchase program Microsoft offered when it eliminated options (see Box 13.2). The ability of employees to accurately assign a value to out-of-the-money options could reduce morale problems should Google's stock price decline.
>
> One ramification of the TSO program for Google is that tradable options will have a longer life than nontradable options—employees who would have exercised options upon vesting will sell them instead, extending the life by 2 years. This increase in the expected life of the options increases their theoretical value when they are granted. Google's reported option compensation expense will therefore be greater as a result of the TSO program.

again consider Microsoft as an example. In accord with SFAS 123, Microsoft in 1999 valued its options using Black-Scholes and disclosed this value in a footnote. The options vested in 4 1/2 years and expired after 7 years. Here is the discussion from Microsoft's 1999 10-K:

> [Option] value was estimated using an expected life of 5 years, no dividends, volatility of 0.32 in 1999 and 1998 and 0.30 in 1997, and risk-free interest rates of 6.5%, 5.7%, and 4.9% in 1997, 1998, and 1999.

Microsoft does not document how it chose volatilities, but these are close to historical volatilities in each year. Using weekly data, historical volatilities for Microsoft for July to June were 32% for 1996–1997, 30% for 1997–1998, and 39% for 1998–1999.

Why did Microsoft use a 5-year expiration to value options expiring in 7 years? We learned in Chapter 9 that it is never optimal to early-exercise a publicly traded call option on a non-dividend-paying stock since it can be sold for more than its intrinsic value. However, compensation options cannot be sold. Thus, the value of the options *to the holder* may be less than intrinsic value. In this case, employees may exercise the options before expiration.[10] This is in fact how employees behave: In practice, executives frequently exercise a large fraction of their in-the-money options as soon as they vest.[11] In addition to exercise by continuing employees, options are often canceled due to death, termination, or retirement of the employee. Taxes can also potentially affect the exercise decision, although a common tax-motivated argument for early exercise is incorrect.[12] Finally, compensation options cannot be exercised until they vest. A realistic valuation would account for the likelihood of these various factors. The assumed 5-year life is intended to account for the *expected* life of an option.[13]

It is possible to modify both the Black-Scholes and binomial models to account for complications due to early exercise. For example, suppose that 4-year options vest after 3 years. The company examines historical data and estimates that 5% of outstanding options will be forfeited each year during the vesting period. Furthermore, the company believes that half of the remaining options will be exercised at vesting, with the other half exercised at expiration. One could then value the option grant as being partially a 3-year option and partially a 4-year option:

$$(1 - 0.05)^3 \left[0.5 \times \text{3-year option} + (1 - 0.05) \times 0.5 \times \text{4-year option}\right] \quad (13.25)$$

In this expression, each option price is weighted by the fraction of employees who historically exercised at that time. A problem with this approach is that it does not recognize that employee behavior depends on the stock price. If the option is deeply in-the-money in the early years, fewer employees are likely to resign before the options vest. If the option is out-of-the-money in year 3, all employees who do not resign will wait before deciding whether to exercise, which lengthens option maturity. Thus, the

---

[10] See Kulatilaka and Marcus (1994) for a discussion of the employee's valuation of options.

[11] Huddart (1998) shows that options are disproportionately exercised on the first through fourth anniversaries of the grant, in blocks of 25% of the grant. Since it is common for grants to vest 25% annually, this finding suggests that many options are being exercised as soon as possible.

[12] An employee is taxed at ordinary income rates on the exercise of a nonqualified option, with subsequent gains on the stock being taxed at capital gains rate. Some have argued that employees optimistic about the share price should exercise compensation options early in order to maximize the percentage of income taxed at the favorable capital gains rate. This argument is incorrect. However, if the ordinary income rate is expected to increase, early exercise can be optimal. For a discussion, see McDonald (2003).

[13] If a company alters its assumption about the exercise behavior of employees, the estimated value of newly issued options will change. Cisco, for example, changed its assumed option life from 5.6 to 3.3 years, reducing the estimated value of its option grants by 23%, from $1.3 to $1.0 billion. See "Cisco May Profit on New Option Assumptions," by Scott Thurm, *Wall Street Journal*, December 7, 2004, p. C1.

assumptions about exercise behavior will generally be incorrect. Bodie et al. (2003) point out that for these reasons, equation (13.25) will undervalue the option. A binomial model permits a more flexible and realistic treatment of early exercise.

Level 3 Communications

Level 3 Communications was one of the first companies to account for the cost of compensation options as a deduction from earnings. However, Level 3 also granted unusually complex and valuable options and did not fully take this complexity and extra value into account when reporting option expense. In a June 1998 proxy statement, Level 3 described its outperform stock options (OSOs), granted to employees. This is how they are described in the proxy:

> Participants in the OSO Program do not realize any value from awards unless the Level 3 Common Stock outperforms the Standard & Poor's 500 Index. When the stock price gain is greater than the corresponding gain on the Standard & Poor's 500 Index, the value received for awards under the OSO Program is based on a formula involving a Multiplier related to how much the Common Stock outperforms the Standard & Poor's 500 Index.

The multiplier is then described as follows:

> The Multiplier shall be based on the "Outperform Percentage" . . . for the Period, determined on the date of exercise. The Outperform Percentage shall be the excess of the annualized percentage change . . . in the Fair Market Value of the Common Stock over the Period . . . over the annualized percentage increase or decrease . . . in the Standard & Poor's 500 Index over the Period. . . .

The multiplier is computed based on the outperform percentage as follows:

Outperform Percentage	Multiplier
$x \leq 0$	0
$0 < x \leq 11\%$	$x \times \frac{8}{11} \times 100$
$x > 11\%$	8.0

Because of the multiplier, if Level 3 outperforms the S&P 500 index by at least an annual average of 11%, the option recipient will have the payoff of eight options. The options have a 4-year maturity and are exercisable and fully vested after 2 years.

Example 13.7 Suppose that at the grant of an option, the price of Level 3 is $100, and the S&P 500 index is at 1300. After 4 years, the price of Level 3 is $185, and the S&P 500 index is at 1950. A "nonmultiplied" outperformance option would have had a payoff of

$$\$185 - \$100 \times \frac{1950}{1300} = \$35$$

The (nonannualized) returns on Level 3 and the S&P 500 index are 85% and 50%. The outperform percentage is

$$1.85^{0.25} - 1.50^{0.25} = 5.957\%$$

The multiplier is therefore

$$0.05957 \times \frac{8}{11} \times 100 = 4.332$$

The payment on the option is

$$\left(\$185 - \$100 \times \frac{1950}{1300}\right) \times 4.332 = \$151.64$$

This option is worth between 0 and 8 times as much as an ordinary option. We will see how Level 3 dealt with the outperformance feature of the option. We will discuss, but not value, the multiplier.

Valuing the outperformance feature First, what would be the value of an ordinary 4-year-to-maturity at-the-money call? Using a volatility of 25% (which Level 3 says in its 1999 Annual Report is the "expected volatility" of its common stock) and a risk-free rate of 6%, we obtain an option price of

$$\text{BSCall}(\$100, \$100, 0.25, 0.06, 4, 0) = \$30.24$$

The Level 3 1999 Annual Report discusses the valuation of the outperformance option as follows:

> The fair value of the options granted was calculated by applying the Black-Scholes method with an S&P 500 expected dividend yield rate of 1.8% and an expected life of 2.5 years. The Company used a blended volatility rate of 24% between the S&P 500 expected volatility rate of 16% and the Level 3 Common Stock expected volatility rate of 25%. The expected correlation factor of 0.4 was used to measure the movement of Level 3 stock relative to the S&P 500.

Box 13.4 explains that, to value the Level 3 outperformance option, we use the Black-Scholes formula but make the following substitutions:

$$\sigma_{\text{Level 3}} \rightarrow \hat{\sigma} = \sqrt{\sigma^2_{\text{Level 3}} + \sigma^2_{\text{S\&P}} - 2\rho\sigma_{\text{Level 3}}\sigma_{\text{S\&P}}}$$

$$r \rightarrow \delta_{\text{S\&P}}$$

where ρ is the correlation between Level 3 and S&P 500 returns and r is the risk-free rate. The net effect on value of granting an outperformance call depends upon the effect of these substitutions. The "blended" volatility, $\hat{\sigma}$, can be greater or less than σ_{Level3}. Typically, $\delta_{\text{S\&P}}$ is less than r. The calculation Level 3 makes for the blended volatility is

$$\hat{\sigma} = \sqrt{0.25^2 + 0.16^2 - 2 \times 0.4 \times 0.25 \times 0.16}$$
$$= 0.2368$$

Box 13.4: Exchange Options

A standard option gives the owner the right to exchange stock (or some other asset) for cash. It is also possible to have an option that gives the owner the right to exchange one stock for another. (We discussed such options in Section 9.2.) Such an option is called an **exchange option** or **outperformance option**, since the option gives the right to exchange asset A for asset B if asset A outperforms asset B.

If the Black-Scholes assumptions hold for both assets, a European exchange option can be valued using the Black-Scholes formula with modifications to two inputs. To see how to price an outperformance option, suppose we have an option giving us the right to receive one IBM call by giving up 3.5 Microsoft shares. This is an IBM call using Microsoft as a strike asset. We need to know the volatilities of both IBM and Microsoft as well as their return correlation. To value the option we use the following inputs:

Stock price. Share price of IBM

Strike price. $3.5 \times$ share price of Microsoft

Volatility.
$$\hat{\sigma} = \sqrt{\sigma_{\text{IBM}}^2 + \sigma_{\text{Microsoft}}^2 - 2\rho\sigma_{\text{IBM}}\sigma_{\text{Microsoft}}},$$
where ρ is the return correlation between the two stocks

Interest rate. Dividend yield on Microsoft

Dividend yield. Dividend yield on IBM

You will note that there are two differences compared to valuing an ordinary option with a cash strike. First, to take account of the riskiness of the strike asset, we use the volatility of the difference in returns between the two assets in place of the volatility of the underlying asset. Computing the volatility of the difference in returns requires that we know the correlation between the two assets, as well as their individual volatilities. Second, we replace the interest rate (the dividend yield on cash) with the dividend yield on the strike asset.

---

which is rounded to 24%. The price of the outperformance option is therefore

$$\text{BSCall}(\$100, \$100, 0.2368, 0.018, 4, 0) = \$21.75$$

This is about $2/3$ of the value of the ordinary option. This reduction in value is primarily due to replacing the 6% interest rate with a 1.8% dividend yield. The volatility reduction by itself lowers the option price only to $29.44.

Taking into account the multiplier The other twist in the valuation for the Level 3 option is the multiplier. The effect of the multiplier is to grant additional options as Level 3 stock outperforms the S&P 500 index. There are several ways to value this multiplier, including the binomial method. We will not discuss the valuation in detail, but taking into account the multiplier produces a value of about $150, or seven times the value of one option.

It is possible to understand at an intuitive level why the multiplier adds significantly to the value of the option. When an option is in-the-money, it is most likely to be in-the-money by a small amount, and least likely to be deep in-the-money. However,

TABLE 13.2 Prices for a call option that pays $S - \$100$ when $S > (1+g)^T$, where g is the outperform percentage; assumes $S = \$100$, $K = \$100$, $\sigma = 0.24$, $r = 0.018$, $\delta = 0$. The option is valued by using the Black-Scholes formula except that within d_1 and d_2, K is multiplied by $(1+g)^T$.

Outperform Percentage (g)	Time to Expiration (T)					
	1	2	3	4	5	6
0.000	10.385	15.079	18.794	21.983	24.825	27.413
0.025	10.335	14.941	18.543	21.604	24.304	26.738
0.050	10.191	14.541	17.823	20.516	22.813	24.816
0.075	9.962	13.913	16.706	18.850	20.557	21.941
0.100	9.658	13.100	15.290	16.781	17.812	18.513
0.125	9.293	12.149	13.681	14.498	14.867	14.938
0.150	8.877	11.106	11.982	12.175	11.979	11.554

much of the value of an option comes from those relatively rare times when it is deep in-the-money. The multiplier is valuable because it gives the option holder extra options precisely when they are most valuable.

Table 13.2 makes this intuition more precise. The table presents prices for options that make payments of $S - K$ only when S exceeds K by a particular amount.[14] For example, with 1 year to expiration, an option that pays $S - \$100$ only when $S > \$115$ is worth $8.877, which is 85% of the value of the ordinary option ($10.385). With 4 years to expiration, as in the case of Level 3, an option that pays $S - \$100$ when $S > \$100 \times (1.1)^4$ is worth $16.781, about 75% of the value of an ordinary 4-year option ($21.983). Looking at the table, you can see that most option value is due to large returns. In light of these results, it is not surprising that the multiplied option is as valuable as a grant of 7 options.

13.3 THE USE OF COLLARS IN ACQUISITIONS

A common financial transaction is for one firm (the *acquirer*) to buy another (the *target*) by buying its common stock. The acquirer can pay for these shares with cash or by exchanging its own shares for target firm shares. Collarlike structures are frequently used in these transactions.

---

[14] To value this option, you can use the Black-Scholes formula with modified d_1 and d_2 terms. Specifically, replace $\ln(S/K)$ with $\ln(S/K_2)$, where K_2 is the threshold above which the option is exercised.

13.3 The Use of Collars in Acquisitions

Suppose that under the purchase agreement, each target share will be exchanged for x shares of the acquirer (x is the *exchange ratio*). Once the target agrees to the purchase, the acquisition will generally take time to complete, often 6 months or more.[15] Target shareholders will be concerned that the acquirer's stock will drop before the merger is completed, in which case the dollar value of x acquirer shares will be lower. To protect against a price drop, it is possible to exchange whatever number of shares have a fixed dollar value. (For example, if the acquirer price is $100, exchange one share for each target share. If the acquirer price is $50, exchange two shares for each target share.) However, target shareholders may also wish to participate in share price gains that the acquirer experiences; this suggests fixing the exchange ratio rather than the dollar value. There are four common offer structures that address considerations such as these:[16]

- **Fixed stock offer:** A offers to pay B a fixed number of A shares per B share.
- **Floating stock offer:** A offers to pay B however many shares have a given dollar value, based on A's share price just before the merger is completed.
- **Fixed collar offer:** There is a range for A's share price within which the offer is a fixed stock offer. Outside this range the deal can become a floating stock offer or may be subject to cancellation.
- **Floating collar offer:** There is a range for A's share price within which the offer is a floating stock offer. Outside this range the deal can become a fixed stock offer or may be subject to cancellation.

Figure 13.6 illustrates these four types of acquisition offers. As this list shows, it is possible to modify the extent to which the target bears the risk of a change in the stock price of the acquirer. More complicated structures are also possible.

The Northrop Grumman–TRW Merger

Northrop Grumman's 2002 bid for TRW is an example of a merger offer with a collar. In July 2002 Northrop Grumman and TRW agreed that Northrop would pay $7.8 billion for TRW. News headlines stated that Northrop offered "$60 per share," but the offer actually resembled a collar. The number of Northrop Grumman shares to be exchanged for each TRW share would be determined by dividing $60 by the average Northrop Grumman price over the 5 days preceding the close of the merger, with the exchange ratio to be no less than 0.4348 ($60/$138) and no more than 0.5357 ($60/$112). Thus, if the price of Northrop Grumman at the merger closing was below $112, TRW shareholders would receive 0.5357 shares. If the price was above $138, TRW shareholders would receive 0.4348 shares. If the price, S, was in between $112 and $138, TRW shareholders would

---

[15] In many cases, for example, regulatory agencies examine the acquisition to see if it is anticompetitive.

[16] Fuller (2003) discusses the kinds of offers and the motives for using alternative kinds of collars.

FIGURE 13.6

Four acquisition offer types: (a) a fixed stock offer of one share for one share; (b) a floating stock offer for $50 worth of acquirer shares; (c) and (d) fixed and floating collar offers with strike prices of $40 and $60.

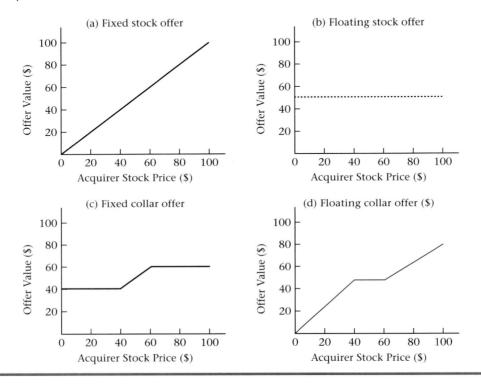

receive $60/S$, which is $60 worth of shares.[17] The deal closed on December 11, 2002, when the closing price of Northrop Grumman was $96.50; TRW shareholders therefore received shares worth

$$0.5357 \times \$96.50 = \$51.69$$

How would TRW shareholders value the Northrop offer? Suppose that TRW shareholders were certain the merger would occur at time T, but uncertain about the future

---

[17] The acquisition terms changed between February and July. Initially, Northrop offered to exchange $47 worth of Northrop Grumman stock for each TRW share: The number of shares to be exchanged was to be no more than 0.4563 ($47/$103) or less than 0.4159 ($47/$113). In May, the value of the bid was increased to $53 (no more than 0.4690 shares ($53/$113) or less than 0.4309 ($53/$123) shares).

13.3 The Use of Collars in Acquisitions

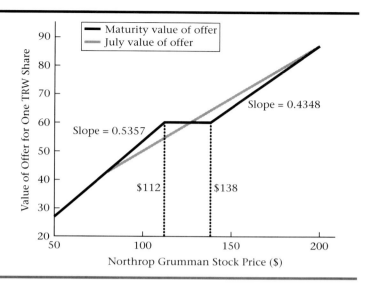

FIGURE 13.7

Value of Northrop Grumman offer for TRW at closing of the merger and with 4 1/2 months until closing.

Northrop Grumman stock price, S. TRW shareholders could then value the offer by noting that the offer is equivalent to buying 0.5357 shares of Northrop Grumman, selling 0.5357 112-strike calls, and buying 0.4348 138-strike calls. In addition, the TRW shareholders would not receive Northrop dividends paid prior to closing and would continue to receive TRW dividends. The time t value of TRW shares would then be

$$0.5357 \times \left[Se^{-\delta(T-t)} - \text{BSCall}(S, 112, \sigma, r, T-t, \delta) \right] \quad (13.26)$$
$$+ 0.4348 \times \text{BSCall}(S, 138, \sigma, r, T-t, \delta) + \text{PV}_{t,T}(\text{TRW dividends})$$

If the exchange ratio had been fixed, then the TRW share would simply be a fractional prepaid forward for Northrop, plus expected TRW dividends over the life of the offer.

Figure 13.7 graphs the value of the Northrop Grumman offer for one TRW share, as a function of the Northrop Grumman share price. The figure depicts the value of the offer both at closing and assuming there are 5 months to expiration.[18] Because of the structure of the offer, the value of a TRW share could either exceed or be less than the expiration value.

Figure 13.8 depicts equation (13.26) using the historical Northrop Grumman stock price from July to December 2002, assuming that the offer would close on December 11.[19] The theoretical value of a TRW share under the terms of the offer is consistently

---

[18] The calculation also assumes a risk-free rate of 1.5%, dividend yield of 1.25%, and volatility of 36%.

[19] It was necessary for Northrop Grumman and TRW to receive regulatory approval from European authorities, the U.S. Department of Defense and the U.S. Department of Justice. Final approval from the Department of Justice was on December 10, and the merger was completed on December 11.

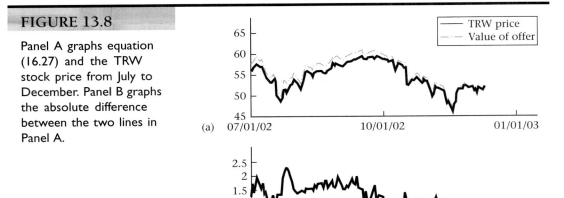

FIGURE 13.8

Panel A graphs equation (16.27) and the TRW stock price from July to December. Panel B graphs the absolute difference between the two lines in Panel A.

greater than the market price of a TRW share. This is what we would expect to see, since in order to induce the target company to accept an offer, the acquirer generally has to offer a price greater than the perceived value of the target as a stand-alone company. Since there is some chance the merger might not occur, the target share price is below the value of the offer. The difference between the value of a TRW share and the theoretical value of the offer declined toward zero as December approached. Had the merger been cancelled for some reason, the value of a TRW share would have diverged from the value under the terms of the offer.

Risk arbitrageurs take positions in the two stocks in order to speculate on the success or failure of the merger.[20] Equation (13.26) tells us that the offer is equivalent to a portfolio of Northrop shares and options. Thus, using delta hedging, we can hold Northrop shares and borrow or lend to synthetically create a position equivalent to the offer. Because the price of TRW is less than the offer value, an arbitrageur speculating that the merger would succeed could then take a long position in TRW shares and a short position in the offer, short-selling delta shares of Northrop. If the offer succeeds, the position earns the difference in price depicted in Figure 13.8; if the offer fails, the difference will likely increase and the arbitrageur would lose money.

---

[20] Mitchell and Pulvino (2001) examine the historical returns earned by risk arbitrageurs.

CHAPTER SUMMARY

Three corporate contexts in which options appear, either explicitly or implicitly, are capital structure (debt, equity, and warrants), compensation, and acquisitions.

If we view the assets of the firm as being like a stock, then debt and equity can be valued as options with the assets of the firm as the underlying asset. Viewing corporate securities as options illuminates conflicts between bondholders and stockholders and provides a natural way to measure bankruptcy risk and to compute the value of a debt guarantee.

Compensation options are an explicit use of options by corporations. They exhibit a variety of complications, some naturally occurring (early exercise decisions by risk-averse employees) and some created by the issuer.

Offers by one firm to purchase another sometimes have embedded collars. The Grumman offer to buy TRW is an example of this.

FURTHER READING

The idea that debt and equity are options was first pointed out by Black and Scholes (1973). Merton (1974, 1977) analyzed the pricing of perpetual debt and demonstrated that the Modigliani-Miller theorem holds even with (costless) bankruptcy. Two principal applications of this idea are the determination of the fair yield on risky debt and the assessment of bankruptcy probabilities. Galai and Masulis (1976) derived the link between the return on assets and the return on the firm's stock.

The discussion of warrants and convertible bonds in this chapter assumes that the options are European. With American warrants the optimal exercise strategy can be more complicated than with European options. The reason is that exercise alters the assets of the firm. The problem of optimal American warrant exercise is studied by Emanuel (1983), Constantinides (1984), and Spatt and Sterbenz (1988). McDonald (2004) examines the tax implications of warrant issues, including put warrants. Complications also arise with convertible bonds, which in practice are almost always callable. Thus, valuing a convertible bond requires understanding the call strategy. Classic papers studying the pricing of convertibles include Brennan and Schwartz (1977) and Ingersoll (1977). Harris and Raviv (1985) discuss how asymmetric information affects the decision to call the bond, and Stein (1992) discusses the decision to issue convertibles in the first place. Finally, there is a large empirical literature on the convertible call decision; for example, see Asquith (1995). Güntay et al. (2004) examine the decision to issue callable bonds.

Papers on compensation options include Acharya et al. (2000), Chance et al. (2000), Saly et al. (1999), and Johnson and Tian (2000a, 2000b). Fuller (2003) examines the use of collars in acquisitions.

PROBLEMS

For all problems, unless otherwise stated assume that the firm has assets worth $A = \$100$, and that $\sigma = 30\%$, $r = 8\%$, and the firm makes no payouts prior to the maturity date of the debt.

13.1 There is a single debt issue with a maturity value of $120. Compute the yield on this debt assuming that it matures in 1 year, 2 years, 5 years, or 10 years. What debt-to-equity ratio do you observe in each case?

13.2 There is a single debt issue. Compute the yield on this debt assuming that it matures in 1 year and has a maturity value of $127.42, 2 years with a maturity value of $135.30, 5 years with a maturity value of $161.98, or 10 years with a maturity value of $218.65. (The maturity value increases with maturity at a 6% rate.) What debt-to-equity ratio do you observe in each case?

13.3 There are four debt issues with different priorities, each promising $30 at maturity.

  a. Compute the yield on each debt issue assuming that all four mature in 1 year, 2 years, 5 years, or 10 years.

  b. Assuming that each debt issue matures in 5 years, what happens to the yield on each when you vary σ? When you vary r?

13.4 Suppose there is a single 5-year zero-coupon debt issue with a maturity value of $120. The expected return on assets is 12%. What is the expected return on equity? The volatility of equity? What happens to the expected return on equity as you vary A, σ, and r?

13.5 Repeat the previous problem for debt instead of equity.

13.6 In this problem we examine the effect of changing the assumptions in Example 13.2.

  a. Compute the yield on debt for asset values of $50, $100, $150, $200, and $500. How does the yield on debt change with the value of assets?

  b. Compute the yield on debt for asset volatilities of 10% through 100%, in increments of 5%.

For the next three problems, assume that a firm has assets of $100 and 5-year-to-maturity zero-coupon debt with a face value of $150. Assume that investment projects have the same volatility as existing assets.

13.7 The firm is considering an investment project costing $1. What is the amount by which the project's value must exceed its cost in order for shareholders to be willing to pay for it? Repeat for project values of $10 and $25.

13.8 Now suppose the firm finances the project by issuing debt that has *lower* priority than existing debt. How much must a $1, $10, or $25 project be worth if the shareholders are willing to fund it?

13.9 Now suppose the firm finances the project by issuing debt that has *higher* priority than existing debt. How much must a $10 or $25 project be worth if the shareholders are willing to fund it?

13.10 Assume there are 20 shares outstanding. Compute the value of the warrant and the share price for each of the following situations.

    a. Warrants for 2 shares expire in 5 years and have a strike price of $15.

    b. Warrants for 15 shares expire in 10 years and have a strike of $20.

13.11 A firm has outstanding a bond with a 5-year maturity and maturity value of $50, convertible into 10 shares. There are also 20 shares outstanding. What is the price of the warrant? The share price? Suppose you were to compute the value of the convertible as a risk-free bond plus an option, valued using the Black-Scholes formula and the share price you computed. How accurate is this?

13.12 Suppose a firm has 20 shares of equity, a 10-year zero-coupon debt with a maturity value of $200, and warrants for 8 shares with a strike price of $25. What is the value of the debt, the share price, and the price of the warrant?

13.13 Suppose a firm has 20 shares of equity and a 10-year zero-coupon convertible bond with a maturity value of $200, convertible into 8 shares. What is the value of the debt and the share price?

13.14 Using the assumptions of Example 13.5 and 13.6, suppose you were to perform a "naive" valuation of the convertible as a risk-free bond plus 50 call options on the stock. Using the stock price with a volatility of 43%, how does the price you compute compare with that computed in Example 13.6?

13.15 Consider Panels B and D in Figure 13.4. Using the information in each panel, compute the share price at each node for each bond issue.

13.16 As discussed in the text, compensation options are prematurely exercised or canceled for a variety of reasons. Suppose that compensation options both vest and expire in 3 years and that the probability is 10% that the executive will die in year 1 and 10% in year 2. Thus, the probability that the executive lives to expiration is 80%. Suppose that the stock price is $100, the interest rate is 8%, the volatility is 30%, and the dividend yield is 0.

    a. Value the option by computing the expected time to exercise and plugging this into the Black-Scholes formula as time to maturity.

    b. Compute the expected value of the option given the different possible times until exercise.

    c. Why are the answers for the two calculations different?

13.17 Suppose that $S = \$100$, $\sigma = 30\%$, $r = 6\%$, $t = 1$, and $\delta = 0$. XYZ writes a European put option on 1 share with strike price $K = \$90$.

a. Construct a two-period binomial tree for the stock and price the put. Compute the replicating portfolio at each node.

b. If the firm were synthetically creating the put (i.e., trading to obtain the same cash flows as if it issued the put), what transactions would it undertake?

c. Consider the bank that buys the put. What transactions does it undertake to hedge the transaction?

d. Why might a firm prefer to issue the put warrant instead of borrowing and repurchasing shares?

13.18 Firm A has a stock price of $40 and has made an offer for firm B where A promises to pay $60/share for B, as long as A's stock price remains between $35 and $45. If the price of A is below $35, A will pay 1.714 shares, and if the price of A is above $45, A will pay 1.333 shares. The deal is expected to close in 9 months. Assume $\sigma = 40\%$, $r = 6\%$, and $\delta = 0$.

a. How are the values 1.714 and 1.333 arrived at?

b. What is the value of the offer?

c. How sensitive is the value of the offer to the volatility of A's stock?

13.19 Firm A has a stock price of $40 and has made an offer for firm B where A promises to pay 1.5 shares for each share of B, as long as A's stock price remains between $35 and $45. If the price of A is below $35, A will pay $52.50/share, and if the price of A is above $45, A will pay $67.50/share. The deal is expected to close in 9 months. Assume $\sigma = 40\%$, $r = 6\%$, and $\delta = 0$.

a. How are the values $52.50 and $67.50 arrived at?

b. What is the value of the offer?

c. How does the value of this offer compare with that in Problem 13.18?

13.20 The strike price of a compensation option is generally set on the day the option is issued. On November 10, 2000, the CEO of Analog Devices, Jerald Fishman, received 600,000 options. The stock price was $44.50. Four days later, the price rose to $63.25 after an earnings release:

> Maria Tagliaferro of Analog said the timing of the two events [option grant and earnings release] is irrelevant because company policy is that no option vests until at least three years from its granting date. "What happens to the stock price in the day, the hour, the year the option is granted is not relevant to that option," she said. "The stock price only becomes relevant after that option has vested."[21]

---

[21] See "SEC Probes Analog Devices' Options," *Wall Street Journal*, December 2, 2004, p. B6.

In its annual report for 2000, Analog Devices reported that the expected life of its options granted that year was 4.9 years, with a 56.6% volatility and 6% risk-free rate. The company paid no dividends until 2003.

    a. Using the inputs from the annual report, and assuming no dividends, estimate the value to the CEO of an at-the-money option grant at a stock price of $44.50.

    b. Estimate the value of an at-the-money grant at a price of $63.25.

    c. Estimate the value of a newly granted option at a strike of $44.50 when the stock price is $63.25.

    d. Do you agree with Maria Tagliaferro? Why or why not?

13.21 Four years after the option grant, the stock price for Analog Devices was about $40. Using the same input as in the previous problem, compute the market value of the options granted in 2000, assuming that they were issued at strikes of $44.50 and $63.25.

14 Real Options

Thus far we have primarily discussed financial assets. Many of the most important decisions that firms make concern *real assets*, a term that broadly encompasses machines, factories, mines, office buildings, research and development, and other nonfinancial firm assets. When you studied basic corporate finance, you undoubtedly learned discounted cash flow (DCF) as a method for valuing assets. However, many real assets have option-like cash flows (for example, the ability to shut down an unprofitable project is a put option on the project cash flows). A natural question is therefore how the option pricing models we have studied can be used to value real assets, and how option pricing methods relate to DCF. It turns out that when properly used, DCF and option pricing methods are consistent and produce identical valuations. However, when valuing real assets, it is often helpful to use *both* methods to perform a valuation.

We will refer to option pricing methodology applied to real assets as "real options valuation." A succinct definition is that "real options" is the analysis of investment decisions taking into account the ability to revise future operating decisions. The term "real options" is common in practice, but you should keep in mind that we will be using the same techniques that we discussed in earlier chapters; the only difference will be that the underlying asset is real instead of financial. We will use the term "real options" to signify that we are performing valuation using option pricing methods.

We will discuss real options using a series of examples, both single- and multi-period, that will illustrate the relationship between DCF and option pricing. In addition, we will discuss some examples of investment projects—peak-load electricity generation, pharmaceutical R&D, and natural resource extraction—in which it is helpful and common in practice to use option pricing methods to value projects.

14.1 DCF AND OPTION VALUATION FOR A SINGLE CASH FLOW

In this section we will compare DCF and option pricing methods in three simple examples where there is a one-period binomial cash flow.[1] The goal here is to illustrate how the two valuation methods provide the same answer, and moreover to show that traditional DCF is an essential component when performing a risk-neutral valuation for real assets. In turn, as projects become more complex, risk-neutral valuation is a valuable adjunct to traditional DCF.

We begin by explaining how the terms "DCF" and "real options valuation" are used. The standard DCF methodology calls for computing an expected future cash flow, and using as a discount rate the expected return on an asset of comparable risk. At this level of description DCF is tautologically correct. It is common in practice to implement DCF by assuming that cash flows grow at a constant rate and that the period-to-period discount rate is constant.

The real options methodology typically entails describing future cash flows from the asset as a function of some randomly evolving state variable, such as sales resulting from a project.[2] When we price financial options, the future cash flows to the option depend on a state variable, such as the stock price. Using the binomial pricing method, we would compute expected cash flows using the risk-neutral probability, and discount the expected cash flow at the risk-free rate. This is the risk-neutral valuation we discussed in Chapter 10. It is common in option pricing to assume that characteristics of the state variable, such as volatility, are constant over time. As we discussed above, traditional DCF and real options valuations give the same answer when implemented correctly and applied to the same problem.

We will now study three related one-period projects to illustrate and compare the use of DCF and option pricing methods.

Project 1

Suppose an analyst is evaluating a project that will generate a single cash flow, X, occurring at time T. As with many investment projects, we will assume that it is not possible to directly observe market characteristics of the project. The analyst considers the economic fundamentals of the project and makes educated inferences about project returns and the covariance of the project with the stock market. The analyst could look for public firms with a business resembling the project and then use information about these public firms to infer characteristics of the project.

After examining all available data, the analyst estimates that the cash flow will be X_u if the economy is doing well—an event with the probability p—and X_d if the

---

[1] The examples in this and the next section are drawn from McDonald (2006b).

[2] If you are unfamiliar with the terminology, a *state variable* is an underlying process that specifies the environment (or the *state* of a system) at a point in time. Given the state variables, we control the system by selecting the values of *control variables*.

14.1 DCF and Option Valuation for a Single Cash Flow

TABLE 14.1 Assumptions used in valuation example. Project 2 cash flows are those of project 1 less $35. Project 3 cash flows are the greater of the project 2 cash flows and zero.

Characteristic	Variable	Project 1	Project 2	Project 3
Cash flow in up state	X_u	$51.361	$16.361	$16.361
Cash flow in down state	X_d	$31.152	−$3.848	$0
Probability of up state	p	0.571		
Beta for discounting cash flows	β	1.25		
Risk-free rate	r	6%		
Expected return on the market	r_M	10%		

economy is doing poorly. The analyst further determines that projects with comparable risk have systematic risk β, and therefore an effective annual expected rate of return of $\alpha = r + \beta(r_M - r)$, where r is the risk-free rate and r_M the expected return on the market.

DCF valuation The standard discounted cash flow method for finding the value of the project, V, calls for computing the expected cash flow, C, and using as a discount rate the expected return on a project of comparable risk:

$$V = \frac{E(X)}{(1+\alpha)^T} = \frac{pX_u + (1-p)X_d}{(1+\alpha)^T} \tag{14.1}$$

For example, suppose that the risk-free rate is $r = 6\%$, the expected return on the market is $r_M = 10\%$, the project beta is $\beta = 1.25$, $p = 0.571$, $T = 1$, $X_u = \$51.361$, and $X_d = \$31.152$. Since we refer to them often, these assumptions are summarized in Table 14.1 under the heading "Project 1." The table also includes the cash flows on two closely related projects that we will discuss later.

The expected return on an asset with the same risk as project 1 is

$$\alpha = 0.06 + 1.25 \times (0.10 - 0.06) = 0.11$$

The expected cash flow is

$$E(X) = 0.571 \times \$51.361 + 0.429 \times \$31.152 = \$42.692$$

Using equation (14.1), the present value of the project cash flow is

$$V = \frac{\$42.692}{1+0.11} = \$38.461$$

This is the price we would pay today to receive the cash flow at time 1.

The forward price Another name for the present value of a cash flow is the *prepaid forward price*. We use this terminology from Chapter 5 to emphasize that we can use the present value to compute the forward price for the cash flow. Discussions of DCF do not typically emphasize the cash flow forward price, but it will provide a helpful link between DCF and risk-neutral valuations.

The relationship between the forward price, $F_{0,1}$, and the prepaid forward price (project value), V, is

$$\frac{F_1}{1+r} = V \quad \text{or} \quad F_1 = V(1+r)$$

Sometimes we can directly observe a forward price for a cash flow (for example, if there is a forward market for what we are producing). In that case, we can compute the present value of the cash flow by discounting the forward price at the risk-free rate. For example, if we will be producing 10,000 barrels of oil per month for 5 years, we can discount the strip of forward prices at this risk-free rate to compute the present value of the oil revenue. If there is no forward market, we can infer the fair forward price by first using α to compute the discounted present value, V, and then using the risk-free rate to compute the future value of V.

In our example, the forward price is

$$\text{Forward price} = F_1 = (1.06) \times \$38.461 = \$40.769 \qquad (14.2)$$

This is the price we would observe if a forward market existed.

Note that *the forward price in equation (14.2) is less than the expected cash flow*. This is due to the result (from Chapter 5) that the forward price is the expected price less the risk premium. The dollar risk premium for the cash flows in this example is the project value, V, times the percentage risk premium for the project, $\beta(r_M - r)$:

$$V\beta(r_M - r) = \$38.461 \times 1.25 \times (0.04) = \$1.923 \qquad (14.3)$$

The forward price is the expected cash flow less the dollar risk premium:

$$F_{0,1} = E(X) - V\beta(r_M - r) = \$42.692 - \$1.923 = \$40.769 \qquad (14.4)$$

As you would hope, equations (14.2) and (14.4) give the same value for the forward price. Another term for the forward price is the *certainty-equivalent cash flow*. An investor is indifferent between accepting the risky cash flow or the certainty-equivalent cash flow without risk.

To summarize this brief one-period example, we used DCF to compute the present value of the cash flow, V. Having computed V, we saw that we can compute the forward price for the cash flow in either of two ways: by computing the future value of V or by subtracting the dollar risk premium from the expected cash flow. Algebraically, the project value is

$$V = \frac{E(X)}{1 + r + \beta(r_M - r)} \qquad (14.5)$$

and the forward price is

$$F_{0,1} = V(1+r) = E(X) - \beta V(r_M - r) \quad (14.6)$$

Risk-neutral valuation The present-value calculation in the preceding section is typical. Of necessity, the analyst specified numerous inputs to the valuation: the cash flows in different states, the probabilities of those states, and—in specifying beta—the comparability of the project to a traded asset.[3] What may not be obvious is that the assumptions required to value the project using DCF also permit us to value the project using risk-neutral valuation. To see this, we will repeat the valuation exercise using the language and apparatus of option pricing.

The cash flows above may have reminded you of a binomial tree. With standard binomial option pricing for a stock option, we measure the stock-price volatility and then construct a stock-price tree based on that volatility. Volatility gives us the up and down moves for the stock. Once we have the stock price tree, we have no further need to consider volatility. In the case of our project, the analyst derived the up and down cash flows by considering the economics of the investment. The analyst thus specified an *implicit* volatility in these cash flows, but need never have used the term "volatility," or thought in terms of volatility.

Given the information in Table 14.1, we now use an option pricing approach to value the same cash flows. With option pricing, we compute expected cash flows using a probability—commonly called the *risk-neutral* probability, which we denote p^*—that is different than the true probability. We then discount these new expected cash flows at the risk-free rate:

$$V = \frac{p^* X_u + (1 - p^*) X_d}{(1+r)^T} \quad (14.7)$$

Compare this to equation (14.1). At first glance, risk-neutral valuation seems odd and perhaps incorrect, since there seems to be no consideration of the systematic risk of the cash flows. However, when you compare equations (14.1) and (14.7), it's apparent that there will be *some* p^* such that equation (14.7) gives the same answer as (14.1).

To better understand the economic meaning of the risk-neutral probability, we can calculate the risk-neutral probability using the forward price. As we discussed in Chapter 10, *the expected cash flow computed using the risk-neutral probability is the forward price*. That is,

$$p^* X_u + (1 - p^*) X_d = F_1 \quad (14.8)$$

---

[3] The last assumption in particular deserves some additional comment. When we specify a beta for the project, we are assuming that the returns of the project are *spanned* by existing traded assets; in other words, the addition of the project to the universe of assets does not materially change the opportunities available to investors. If this were not true, we would have to know more about the preferences of investors in order to evaluate the project.

Thus, if we observe a forward price and the possible cash flow realizations, we can compute the risk-neutral probability from equation (14.8) as

$$p^* = \frac{F_1 - X_d}{X_u - X_d} \qquad (14.9)$$

In our example, the risk-neutral probability is

$$p^* = \frac{40.769 - 31.152}{51.361 - 31.152} = 0.476 \qquad (14.10)$$

Given this p^*, we can compute the value of the project using equation (14.7):

$$V = \frac{0.476 \times 51.361 + (1 - 0.476) \times 31.152}{1.06} = 38.461$$

We used the DCF value of 38.461 to obtain the risk-neutral probability, so this calculation seems circular. However, a constructive way to think about this procedure is that the DCF valuation is a necessary input into the risk-neutral valuation.

If it seems odd to think of a DCF valuation as part of a risk-neutral valuation, recognize that *we implicitly rely upon DCF when pricing a stock option using the Black-Scholes formula*. The Black-Scholes formula requires knowing the current stock price. When we observe the price of a traded stock, we are relying on the market to have already performed a present-value calculation to determine the stock price. In our valuation problem the cash flow is playing the same role as the stock price. In order to use option pricing methods, we need to know the present value of the cash flow.

These examples illustrate the important point that in order to do a real options-style valuation, *we need to know the forward price for the cash flows*, or we need to have enough information to infer the forward price. If there is no explicit forward market, as is frequently the case in capital budgeting calculations, then we must perform a DCF calculation. In that case, we can infer the forward price. The mechanics of DCF, in particular the estimation of risk premia, are in most cases an inevitable part of capital budgeting.

At this point you may be thinking that there is no point in performing a risk-neutral valuation. If we need to perform a DCF valuation in order to do a risk-neutral valuation, why bother with the risk-neutral valuation at all? If we were only considering project 1, this would be correct. However, what we have done with DCF is to provide important summary information about the underlying cash flow, X. In our subsequent examples, cash flows will be functions of X, and option pricing methods will simplify valuation.

Project 2

Now we consider a variant of the project in which the firm pays $35 at time 1 to produce the cash flow, whether or not the resulting cash flow is positive. (Assume that the firm has a binding commmitment to produce.) This generates the cash flows in the "Project 2" column of Table 14.1. This example will illustrate differences between a DCF valuation and a real options valuation.

14.1 DCF and Option Valuation for a Single Cash Flow

We will now demonstrate five ways to compute the present value of the project 2 cash flows.

Compute DCF separately for the cash flow components First, we can recognize that the project 2 cash flows are created by the difference between two cash flows of differing risk, each of which should be discounted at a different rate. The present value of the difference between these cash flows is

$$V_2 = \frac{\$42.692}{1.11} - \frac{\$35}{1.06} = \$5.443$$

This is a classic DCF calculation, made simple by the fact that we split the cash flows into two components, each with a known discount rate.

Compute the forward price for the net cash flow: Method 1 A second way to calculate the present value is to use forward prices for the cash flow components to compute the forward price for the net cash flow. Specifically, we saw in discussing project 1 that the forward price for the risky cash flow is $40.769, and clearly the forward price for $35 is $35. Thus, the forward price for the net cash flow is

$$\$40.769 - \$35 = \$5.769$$

The present value of this forward price is

$$\frac{\$5.769}{1.06} = \$5.443$$

Compute the forward price for the net cash flow: Method 2 A third way to calculate the present value entails computing the forward price for the net cash flows by computing the dollar risk premium of the period 1 cash flow and subtracting this from the expected period 1 cash flow. What is the dollar risk premium of the period 1 net cash flow?

In order to compute the dollar risk premium, we need to assess the difference in dollar risk between the project 1 and project 2 cash flows. The ratio of risk between the two projects is

$$\frac{X_{2u} - X_{2d}}{X_u - X_d} = \frac{\$16.361 - (-\$3,848)}{\$51.361 - \$31.152} = 1 \qquad (14.11)$$

As you might expect, since the risky portion of the cash flows is the same in project 1 and project 2, their dollar risk is the same. Hence, the risk premium is the same, $1.923, as given by equation (14.4).

The expected cash flow is

$$E(X) = 0.571 \times \$16.361 + (1 - 0.571) \times (-\$3.848) = \$7.692$$

The forward price (certainty-equivalent cash flow) is

$$\$7.692 - \$1.923 = \$5.769$$

Thus, the value of the project is

$$\frac{\$5.769}{1.06} = \$5.443$$

Standard DCF In a standard DCF valuation we compute the value of the project 2 cash flow by discounting the expected net cash flow at a single discount rate. We can easily compute the expected cash flow; the problem is figuring out the correct discount rate. We can see that the discount rate is going to be different in project 2 than in project 1. We know from equation (14.11) that we have the same dollar risk in project 2 as in project 1, but we also know that project 2 will be worth less than project 1 because the project 2 cash flows are uniformly lower. By investing in project 2, we are bearing the same dollar risk with a smaller initial investment, hence the *percentage* risk premium will be greater for project 2.

How do we determine the risk premium for project 2? We saw in Chapter 11 that we can use the *elasticity* of an option to determine the risk premium on the option relative to the stock. We can perform a similar calculation here. The elasticity is the relative dollar risk of the two projects, given by equation (14.11), scaled by the relative value of the two projects. This scaling converts dollar risk into percentage risk. Thus, the elasticity of project 2 relative to project 1 is

$$\text{Elasticity} = \frac{X_{2u} - X_{2d}}{X_u - X_d} \frac{V_1}{V_2} = \frac{\$16.361 - (-\$3,848)}{\$51.361 - \$31.152} \times \frac{\$38.461}{\$5.443} = 7.067 \quad (14.12)$$

This calculation tells us that the risk premium of project 2 is 7.067 times greater than the risk premium of project 1. We obtain the project 2 beta by multiplying the project 1 beta by 7.067:

$$7.067 \times 1.25 = 8.833$$

The DCF calculation is therefore[4]

$$\frac{0.571 \times 16.361 + (1 - .0571) \times (-3.848)}{1 + 0.06 + 8.833 \times (0.10 - 0.06)} = 5.443 \quad (14.13)$$

Here the calculation truly is circular: We used the correct present value ($5.443) for project 2 to obtain the DCF value for project 2! You should therefore think of this example as demonstrating that DCF gives the correct answer, but there would be no point in mimicking this calculation in practice unless you simply wanted to demonstrate how to perform a DCF valuation.

---

[4] Had we simply discounted the expected cash flow at 11%, which was the appropriate rate of return for project 1, we would have obtained a present value (incorrect) of

$$\frac{0.571 \times 16.361 + (1 - .0571) \times (-3.848)}{1 + 0.06 + 1.25 \times (0.10 - 0.06)} = 6.930$$

It is important to understand that we *could* have performed a DCF calculation without already knowing the answer, but this would have entailed some algebra. We are trying to compute the present value of project 2, V_2. Here is the DCF present-value expression, including the elasticity calculation, written out in full:

$$\frac{pX_{2u} + (1-p)X_{2d}}{1 + r + \frac{X_{2u}-X_{2d}}{X_u - X_d}\frac{V_1}{V_2}\beta(r_M - r)} = V_2$$

We know everything in this expression except V_2, for which we can solve. The chapter appendix shows that when we solve for V_2, the result is a certainty-equivalent valuation.

Risk-neutral valuation The fifth approach to valuing the project 2 cash flows is to perform risk-neutral valuation. To do this, we need only recognize that the project 2 cash flows are functions of the project 1 cash flows; the only source of risk is variation in X. With this recognition, we can use the risk-neutral probability we already computed for project 1, and we obtain as the present value

$$\frac{0.476 \times 16.361 + (1 - 0.476) \times (-3.848)}{1.06} = 5.443$$

The risk-neutral probability depends on X, which is the underlying source of project risk, not on other characteristics of the project.

Project 3

Project 3 is the same as project 2 except that the firm does not operate the project if doing so results in a negative cash flow. That is, the cash flow is

$$X_3 = \max(X - \$35, 0)$$

The firm thus has an option to shut down production to avoid a negative cash flow. Because cash flows are strictly greater for project 3, its value must exceed that of project 2. The first two valuation methods that we used for project 2 do not work for project 3, because the cash flow is not a simple difference of two easy-to-value cash flows. We will consider the remaining three methods.

Compute the forward price for the net cash flow: Method 2 We compute the forward price for the project 3 cash flows by adjusting the dollar risk premium for project 1 by the relative variability of project 3 and project 1 cash flows. The dollar risk premium is

$$\frac{X_{3u} - X_{3d}}{X_u - X_d} V\beta(r_M - r) = \frac{16.361 - 0}{51.361 - 31.152} \times 1.923 = \$1.557$$

We can then compute the forward price (or certainty-equivalent cash flow) for project 3 cash flows by subtracting the dollar risk premium from the expected cash flow:

$$pX_{3u} + (1-p)X_{3d} - \frac{X_{3u} - X_{3d}}{X_u - X_d} V\beta(r_M - r)$$
$$= 0.571 \times 16.361 + (1 - 0.571) \times 0 - \$1.557 = \$7.786$$

The project present value is therefore
$$\frac{\$7.786}{1.06} = \$7.345$$

As we discussed, because we can shut down to avoid losses, the present value of cash flows is greater for project 3 than for project 2.

Standard DCF Because the cash flow has optionality, a DCF valuation using an 11% discount rate is not appropriate. While the underlying cash flow, X, has a beta of 1.25, the operating cash flow beta is greater. To calculate the beta of the project, we compute the elasticity, comparing the percentage sensitivity of the project cash flow with the operating option to that without. The elasticity is

$$\frac{16.361 - 0}{51.361 - 31.152} \times \frac{38.461}{7.345} = 4.239$$

The elasticity is lower for project 3 than for project 2 because the dollar variability of project 3 cash flows is less than the dollar variability of project 2 cash flows, and the value of project 3 is greater.

Using the elasticity, the discount rate for the project is

$$4.239 \times 1.25 \times (0.10 - 0.06) = 0.272$$

The DCF valuation is

$$\frac{0.571 \times 16.361 + (1 - 0.571) \times 0}{1 + 0.272} = 7.345$$

Risk-neutral valuation We can also value the project by computing the risk-neutral expected value of the cash flows and discounting at the risk-free rate. We obtain

$$\frac{p^* X_{3u} + (1-p^*)X_{3d}}{1+r} = \frac{0.476 \times 16.361 + (1 - 0.476) \times 0}{1.06} = \$7.345$$

Summary

What do these three simple one-period valuation examples demonstrate? There are several conclusions:

1. DCF and risk-neutral valuation give the same answer, but in a given circumstance one may be easier than the other to implement.

2. Even if we plan to perform a risk-neutral valuation, a DCF valuation may be necessary in order to obtain a forward price. If there is a forward market or present value that we can observe in the market, the DCF valuation is not necessary. (When

valuing stock options, we rely on the observed stock price, which you can think of as the result of a DCF valuation.)

3. The appropriate DCF discount rate will vary with project characteristics, whereas the risk-neutral probability remains the same as long as the economic variable determining the cash flow (X) remains the same.

In practice when we estimate beta, we might be more likely to observe comparable projects that are more like project 3 than project 1. In this case, DCF and risk-neutral valuation are equivalently simple for that project (the cash flows we observe are like project 1). However, if we wish to alter assumptions about how the project will be operated, risk-neutral valuation will generally be simpler.

14.2 MULTIPERIOD VALUATIONS

Most projects span multiple periods. A common assumption when using DCF in multiperiod valuations is that expected cash flows grow at a constant rate and are discounted over time at a constant rate. In this section we will explore this assumption as we continue our comparison of DCF and option pricing. It turns out that a constant discount rate is appropriate only under special economic conditions; essentially, it is necessary that the project be such that cash flow uncertainty resolves over time at a constant rate.[5] Analogous assumptions are typically made when performing a risk-neutral valuation, but as in the one-period project case, risk-neutral valuation is more readily adaptable to changes in project characteristics.

Table 14.2 summarizes the examples we will consider in this section. The three projects in Table 14.2 are multiperiod versions of the three projects in Table 14.1, which we discussed in the previous section. In project 1, cash flows evolve over time with constant uncertainty each period. Project 2 cash flows are project 1 cash flows less $35. Project 3 cash flows are project 2 cash flows, although the firm can halt production to avoid losses.

It will be convenient at this point to define the terms *static DCF* and *dynamic DCF*. A static DCF valuation is one where beta is constant over time and across nodes. Standard valuation examples in introductory finance with a constant beta are static valuations. A dynamic DCF valuation is one where beta varies over time, depending on project characteristics. We will see that project 1 is a static DCF valuation, while projects 2 and 3 are dynamic.

The purpose of these examples is to highlight the assumptions commonly made in performing multiperiod DCF valuations, and to show that these same assumptions also simplify the real options valuation. These examples will also illustrate the comparative

---

[5] This point has long been discussed in the discounting literature. See Fama (1977) and Myers and Turnbull (1977). A standard textbook treatment is Brealey et al. (2006, section 9.4). See also Trigeorgis (1996) for a discussion in the context of real options valuation.

TABLE 14.2

Cash flows, true probabilities, and risk-neutral probabilities from investments that pay risky cash flows for 3 years. Project 2 cash flows are project 1 cash flows less $35. Project 3 cash flows are the greater of project 2 cash flows and zero. The probabilities are the unconditional time 0 probabilities of reaching a given node, computed using either true or risk-neutral probabilities.

Project 1			Project 2			Project 3		
1	2	3	1	2	3	1	2	3
51.361	65.949	84.680	16.361	30.949	49.680	16.361	30.949	49.680
31.152	40.000	51.361	−3.848	5.000	16.361	0.000	5.000	16.361
	24.261	31.152		−10.739	−3.848		0.000	0.000
		18.895			−16.105			0.000
Expected Cash Flows (true probabilities)								
42.692	45.566	48.633	7.692	10.566	13.633	9.343	12.542	16.117
Expected Cash Flows (risk-neutral probabilities)								
40.769	41.553	42.352	5.769	6.553	7.352	7.786	9.503	11.180

True Probabilities			Risk-Neutral probabilties		
1	2	3	1	2	3
0.571	0.326	0.186	0.476	0.226	0.108
0.429	0.490	0.420	0.524	0.499	0.356
	0.184	0.315		0.275	0.392
		0.079			0.144

simplicity and power of risk-neutral valuation when making plausible assumptions about a project.

Project 1

As in the previous section, assume that cash flow forecasts are based on projections of how the project will perform, depending upon the economy's performance. If the project does well in a given period, it may do better or worse the following period. For example, if the cash flow in year 1 is 51.361, the following year it may be 65.949 (with probability 57.1%) or 40 (with probability 42.9%). The magnitude of the up and down moves is a measure of the analyst's uncertainty about subsequent cash flows. The cash flows in the table assume that cash flow increases are 128.4% of the previous period cash flows, and cash flow decreases are 77.9% of the previous period cash flows.[6] Thus, the amount of uncertainty and the rate at which it resolves is constant over time, in that each cash flow change is a constant percentage of the previous cash flow. Also, from the perspective of period 0, the risk from the project between period 1 and period 2 is the same as the risk from any node between period 2 and period 3. When the cash flow is greater in one period, all subsequent cash flows are likely to be greater as well. This is the sense in which there is constant resolution of uncertainty.

The panel labeled "True Probabilities" reports the time 0 probabilities of reaching any given node.[7] You can multiply these probabilities by the corresponding cash flow to calculate the expected cash flow in each period. Risk-neutral probabilities are also constant and the time 0 risk-neutral probabilities of reaching any node are computed in the same way.

DCF valuation How do we discount the multiperiod project 1 cash flows in Table 14.2? The key is to recognize that the proportional risk going forth from each node is the same. It is then reasonable to assume that the systematic risk (β) is the same at each node, looking ahead a period. This same level of systematic risk propagates forward. So the appropriate one-period discount rate at each node is 11%, and the appropriate discount rate for cash flows two periods away is 11% each period, and so forth. We can therefore employ traditional DCF, discounting each year's expected cash flows at 11%. We then obtain a DCF valuation of

$$\frac{\$42.692}{1.11} + \frac{\$45.566}{1.11^2} + \frac{\$48.633}{1.11^3} = \$111.00 \qquad (14.14)$$

The cash flow assumptions for project 1 may seem implausibly restrictive, but such assumptions implicitly underlie the typical traditional DCF analysis. When you use a constant β in an introductory, you are assuming an economic structure like this.

Risk-neutral valuation Just as the true probabilities of cash flow moves are constant in Table 14.2, so are the risk-neutral probabilities. The risk-neutral present value is computed by discounting expected cash flows at the risk-free rate. We obtain

$$\frac{\$40.769}{1.06} + \frac{\$41.553}{1.06^2} + \frac{\$42.352}{1.06^3} = \$111.00 \qquad (14.15)$$

---

[6] These cash flow moves imply a continuously compounded cash flow volatility of $0.5 \times \ln(51.361/31.152) = 0.25$.

[7] This calculation takes into account all possible ways of reaching a given cash flow node. For example, there are two ways to reach the $40 node in period 2: by reaching 51.361 and then 40, or by reaching 31.152 and then 40. Either has the probability of an up move and a down move in the cash flows, or $0.571 \times (1 - 0.571) = 0.245$. Since there are two ways to get to 40, each with the same probability, the probability of reaching 40 is $2 \times 0.245 = 0.490$.

Project 2

As in Table 14.1, project 2 cash flows are the result of subtracting $35 from each of the project 1 cash flows. In Section 14.1, we saw that the discount rate for the project was increased by the leverage (relative to project 1) implicit in the cash flows. The multi-period version of project 2 is even more complicated because implicit leverage changes period to period and node to node.

The easiest way to value project 2 is to compute the difference in the present value of the risky and risk-free cash flows:

$$\$111.00 - \$35 \times \left(\frac{1}{1.06} + \frac{1}{1.06^2} + \frac{1}{1.06^3}\right) = \$17.448$$

We can obtain the same answer using risk-neutral valuation and the expected cash flows in Table 14.2:

$$\frac{\$5.769}{1.06} + \frac{\$6.553}{1.06^2} + \frac{\$7.352}{1.06^3} = \$17.448 \qquad (14.16)$$

Firm behavior in this example is static in the sense that the firm never alters its production behavior. Nevertheless, it is not correct to discount the stream of net cash flows by a single discount rate. The reason is that the fixed $35 component of the cash flow is a varying percentage of the cash flow each period and at each node, so that the appropriate discount rate is always changing. Thus, even in this relatively simple case where operational decisions are static, beta evolves from one node to another because proportional risk changes from node to node on the cash flow tree.[8]

We can verify the changing discount rate by considering two nodes. First, consider the top node in period 2, where $X_2 = \$30.949$. The value at this node is $30.393 for project 2 and $63.412 for project 1. The elasticity at this node is therefore

$$\text{Elasticity} = \frac{X_{2u} - X_{2d}}{X_u - X_d} \frac{V_1}{V_2} = \frac{\$49.680 - \$16.361}{\$64.949 - \$40.000} \times \frac{\$63.412}{\$30.393} = 2.086$$

At the middle node in period 2, where $X_2 = \$40$, we have

$$\text{Elasticity} = \frac{X_{2u} - X_{2d}}{X_u - X_d} \frac{V_1}{V_2} = \frac{\$16.361 - (-\$3,848)}{\$51.361 - \$31.152} \times \frac{\$38.462}{\$5.443} = 7.067$$

This is the same elasticity we obtained for the one-period project in the last section.

The point of these calculations is to demonstrate that the appropriate discount rate for the net cash flow varies from node to node, making DCF quite complicated, and unnecessary given that we can perform risk-neutral valuation. One objection to risk-neutral valuation in the context of a corporate project is that it is unfamiliar to decision

---

[8] For a discussion of DCF when risk varies in this fashion, see Hodder et al. (2001) and McDonald (2006a, sections 11.2 and 19.1).

makers. However, someone who does not understand risk-neutral or certainty-equivalent valuation is unlikely to do DCF correctly in a case like that of project 2.

To see how much of an error we make with traditional DCF, we can compute the expected cash flows in each period and see what present value we obtain with naive DCF. Using the true expected cash flows in Table 14.2, the DCF valuation using an 11% discount rate is

$$\text{Incorrect DCF valuation} = \frac{\$7.692}{1.11} + \frac{\$10.566}{1.11^2} + \frac{\$13.633}{1.11^3} = \$25.474$$

This answer is 50% greater than the correct value of $17.488. Another way to assess the error is to note that we obtain the correct answer only if we use the single discount rate of 33.39%. Alternatively, we could use a different discount rate for each period. We have already seen (in the previous section) that a 41.3% discount rate is appropriate for the period 1 cash flow. For periods 2 and 3, a single discount rate of 34.6% and 30.2% would give the correct answers. These discount rates are simply internal rates of return. The correct approach would specify a different discount rate at each node; this would give rise to the rates we have computed.

Project 3

Project 3 is more complicated than project 2 since it cannot be valued as the difference of two simple-to-value cash flows. The cash flow beta changes from node to node. However, a valuation using the risk-neutral probability (or certainty-equivalent) is straightforward. Using the expected cash flows in Table 14.2, the present value is

$$\frac{\$7.786}{1.06} + \frac{\$9.503}{1.06^2} + \frac{\$11.180}{1.06^3} = \$25.190 \qquad (14.17)$$

The DCF calculation is complicated in exactly the same way as in project 2, because systematic risk changes node to node. Using the true expected cash flows, a discount rate of 20.79% for the stream of cash flows gives the correct answer. The single discount rates that would give the correct answer are 27.2% for period 1, 21.8% for period 2, and 19.7% for period 3.

Summary

The examples in this section have illustrated the well-established point that traditional static DCF, using a constant discount rate, is a correct discounting method only under the special assumption that risk resolves at a constant rate over time. By contrast, risk-neutral valuation automatically addresses the problem of discounting cash flows even when risk premiums are dynamically changing. A risk-neutral valuation requires strong assumptions, but in the examples we have examined, traditional DCF requires *stronger* assumptions to obtain the correct answer. In any case, however, a preliminary DCF valuation is required in order to characterize the risk of the project.

14.3 EXAMPLES OF REAL OPTIONS IN PRACTICE

As we discussed in the introduction, many real investment projects have optionlike features. For example, consider the following project characteristics:

1. The decision about when (and whether) to invest in a project
2. The ability to shut down, restart, and permanently abandon projects
3. The ability to invest in projects that may give rise to future options
4. The ability to be flexible in the future about the choice of inputs, outputs, or production technologies

Project 3 in Table 14.2 is an example of a project that can be operated when profitable and shut down when unprofitable. There are numerous option-like features in real assets.

With any valuation problem, it is necessary to analyze the specific problem. In this section, we look at three examples that use option analysis to value assets: a commodity extraction problem, peak-load electricity generation, and pharmaceutical research and development. A common feature of these examples is that it would be difficult to value the projects using simple DCF. It is necessary in each case to use a valuation technique appropriate to the project.

Commodity Extraction

The management of natural resource investments is an important application of option techniques.[9] The extraction of a resource from the ground exhibits many similarities to the exercise of a financial option. The resource has a value that can be realized by paying an extraction cost. The market for the resource is typically competitive so that the behavior of any one producer does not affect the price.

Consider the problem of extracting oil from the ground. There is an initial cost to sink a well to commence production, after which we assume we keep producing forever. Our goal in studying this example will be to understand the *economics* of this problem. The analysis is an example illustrating the costs and benefits of deferring investment. The specific formulas do not apply in every situation.

Suppose there is a plot of land that contains 1 barrel of oil. The current price of a barrel of oil is $15, the oil forward curve is such that the effective annual lease rate, δ, is 4% (constant over time and across maturities at a point in time), and the effective annual risk-free rate, r, is 5% (also constant over time). There is no uncertainty about the future price of oil. The barrel can be extracted at any time by paying $13.60, which we denote X. Finally, to make matters simple, suppose that the land is completely worthless once the oil is extracted. We want to know (a) when the oil should be extracted and (b) how much the land is worth.

---

[9] See in particular Brennan and Schwartz (1985), McDonald and Siegel (1986), and Paddock et al. (1988).

If the price of oil at time 0 is S_t, the time 0 forward price for delivery at time T is given by

$$F_{0,T} = S_0 \left(\frac{1+r}{1+\delta} \right)^T \tag{14.18}$$

Since prices are certain, the future spot price will equal the forward price; hence, the spot price of oil will grow forever at the rate $(1+r)/(1+\delta) - 1 = 1.05/1.04 - 1 = 0.9615\%$ per year.

How much would you pay for this plot of land? The obvious answer—a bid of $1.40 (= \$15 - \$13.60)$—ignores the possibility of delaying investment. *You cannot value the land without first deciding under what circumstances you will extract oil from the ground.* A bid of $1.40 is too low. The correct answer is to select T to maximize the present value of net extraction revenue,

$$\frac{S_T - x}{(1+r)^T} \tag{14.19}$$

Using equation (14.22) to model the change in the oil price over time, we can mechanically find the T that maximizes expression (14.19). However, we want to discuss the reasons for delaying investment.

Optimal extraction Consider the costs and benefits of delaying extraction. If we delay extraction, the barrel of oil in the ground appreciates at 0.9615% per year, less than the risk-free rate. We lose 4% per year—the lease rate—on the value of the barrel. However, extracting the barrel costs $13.60. By delaying extraction for 1 year we earn another year's interest on this amount.

Thinking about costs and benefits in this way suggests a simple decision rule: Delay extraction as long as the cost exceeds the benefit. The benefit in this case is constant from year to year since the extraction cost is constant, but the cost of delaying extraction—the forgone dollar lease payment—grows with the oil price.

This line of thinking leads to a back-of-the-envelope extraction rule. Since the interest rate (5%) is 25% greater than the dividend yield (4%), the dividend yield lost by not investing will equal the interest saved when $S = 1.25 \times \$13.60 = \$17$. Thus, we should expect it to be optimal to extract the oil when $S \approx \$17$.

A more precise calculation is to compare the NPV of investing today with that of investing tomorrow. At a minimum, if we are to invest, we must decide that the NPV of investing today exceeds that of waiting until tomorrow to invest. If we let r_d and δ_d represent the daily interest rate and lease rate, respectively, then we defer investing as long as the present value of producing tomorrow exceeds the value of producing today. Since tomorrow's oil price is today's oil price times $(1+r_d)/(1+\delta_d)$, we delay investing as long as

$$\frac{1}{1+r_d} \left(S \frac{1+r_d}{1+\delta_d} - X \right) > S - X$$

This expression shows that we defer investment as long as

$$\frac{S}{X} < \frac{\frac{r_d}{1+r_d}}{\frac{\delta_d}{1+\delta_d}} \qquad (14.20)$$

In this case we have $r_d = 1.05^{1/365} - 1 = 0.013368\%$, with the daily lease rate $\delta_d = 0.010746\%$. The trigger price, at which $S = X\frac{r_d}{\delta_d}\left(\frac{1+\delta_d}{1+r_d}\right)$, is \$16.918.

Note that, since daily rates are essentially the same as continuously compounded rates, we get the same answer by using continuous compounding. We invest when

$$S_t = \frac{\ln(1.05)}{\ln(1.04)} \times \$13.60 = \$16.918$$

This shows why our back-of-the-envelope answer of \$17 is not exactly right. Instead of computing the ratio of effective annual rates (5%/4%), we want to compute the ratio of continuously compounded rates ($\ln(1.05)/\ln(1.04)$).

Value and appreciation of the land We know that we will extract when oil reaches a price of \$16.918/barrel. How long will this take? The annual growth rate of the price of oil is $1.05/1.04 - 1 = 0.9615\%$. We have to find the t such that $\$15 \times (1.009615)^t = \$16.918$. Solving gives us $t = 12.575$ years. At that point the value of extraction will be \$16.918 − \$13.60. Hence, NPV today is

$$\frac{\$16.918 - \$13.60}{1.05^{12.575}} = \$1.796$$

This is what we would pay for the land today. This substantially exceeds the value of \$1.40 were we to extract the oil immediately.

At what rate does the land appreciate? The oil in the land is appreciating at 0.9615% per year; nevertheless, *the land itself appreciates at 5%*. If the land appreciated at less than 5%, no one would be willing to own it since bonds would earn a higher return. In fact, our valuation procedure ensures that the land earns 5%, since that is the rate at which we discount the future payoff. *The properly operated oil reserve, whether producing or not, must at all times pay the owner a fair return* (in this case, 5%).

Using an option pricing formula The problem of deciding when to extract the oil is equivalent to deciding when to exercise a call option. By paying the extraction cost (the strike price), we can receive oil (the stock). As with a financial call, early exercise is a trade-off between interest saved by delaying exercise and dividends forgone. Once we have possession of the oil, we can lease it; hence, oil's lease rate is the dividend yield.

We can verify the equivalence of this problem to an option pricing problem by using an option pricing formula to reach the same answer. It is possible to extract at any time, so the problem in this case is to value a perpetually lived American call option. (See Box 14.1 for a discussion of this kind of option.) Using the CallPerpetual formula, set

Box 14.1: A Formula for Perpetual Call Options

The Black-Scholes formula computes the value of a European call—such an option has a definite expiration date and can only be exercised at expiration. In general there is no simple formula for the value of an American option, with one exception: There is a formula when the option is infinitely lived. The infinite-life case is tractable since the price at which the option is exercised never changes, because the remaining life of the option (infinity) never changes. The formula for a perpetual call looks like this:

$$\text{Price of perpetual call} = \frac{K}{h-1}\left(\frac{h-1}{h}\frac{S}{K}\right)^h \quad (14.21)$$

where

$$h = \frac{1}{2} - \frac{r-\delta}{\sigma^2} + \sqrt{\left(\frac{r-\delta}{\sigma^2} - \frac{1}{2}\right)^2 + \frac{2r}{\sigma^2}}$$

This formula may not look particularly intuitive, but it is worth making several comments. First, embedded in the formula is the result that it is optimal (i.e., it maximizes the value of the call) to exercise the call when the stock price reaches a value above the strike price, given by $S^* = Kh/(h-1)$. (Because $h \geq 1$, $S^* > K$.) Second, the inputs ot the formula include S, K, σ, r, and δ. Time does not enter, because the option is infinitely lived: The time to expiration is constant (infinite). Third and finally, you can verify that if $\delta = 0$, then $h = 1$. This in turn implies that $S^* = \infty$. The option in this case is never exercised. This is the result that an option on a non-dividend-paying stock is never exercised.

The formula is implemented in the spreadsheets accompanying this book as CallPerpetual for calls and PutPerpetual for puts. The formulas are array formulas, returning both the value of the option and the price at which exercise is optimal.

$S = \$15$, $K = \$13.60$, $\sigma = 0.0001$, $r = \ln(1.05)$, and $\delta = \ln(1.04)$.[10] The CallPerpetual function reports both the value of the option and the level at which exercise is optimal. Note that we use the convenience yield as the dividend yield. We get

CallPerpetual($15, $13.60, 0.0001, ln(1.05), ln(1.04)) = {$1.796, $16.918}

The option price is $1.796 and the optimal decision is to exercise when the oil price reaches $16.918, exactly the answer we just obtained. The option formula implicitly makes the same calculations.

If volatility is positive, the option becomes more valuable and the price at which extraction is optimal also increases. For example, when oil price volatility is 15%, the trigger price is higher and the land is more valuable. Using the perpetual call formula,

---

[10] To use equation (14.21), we must convert the interest rate and dividend yield to continuously compounded rates.

we obtain $\overline{S} = 25.3388$ as the price at which extraction should occur and \$3.7856 as the value of the option:

CallPerpetual[\$15, \$13.60, 0.15, ln(1.05), ln(1.04)] = {\$3.7856, \$25.3388}

Peak-Load Electricity Generation

In Chapter 6 we explained that electricity forward prices can vary substantially over the course of a day. They also vary seasonally: In the United States, electricity forward prices are high in the summer and low in the winter. In addition to this predictable variation, electricity prices can be volatile. On extremely hot days, for example, prices can spike to 100 times their average price.

A peak-load plant, as the name suggests, produces only when it is profitable to do so, exploiting spikes in the price of electricity.[11] Such plants are designed so that they can be idled when the price of electricity is less than the cost of fuel, but they can be quickly brought online to produce power when the price of electricity is high or when the price of fuel declines. Because it is turned on only when profitable, owning a peak-load plant is like owning a strip of call options, with options maturing daily.[12] The underlying asset is electricity. The strike price is the cost of inputs required to produce a unit of electricity, including the cost of the fuel—typically natural gas—and other variable costs associated with operating the plant.[13] The **heat rate,** H, of a plant is the efficiency with which it turns gas into electricity (the number of MMBtus required to produce a megawatt hour (MWh)).[14]

For the moment, let's consider only electricity and gas prices, and assume that we can ignore distribution costs and marginal operating, maintenance, and other costs. Then, the profit of the plant is

$$\text{Profit} = \max(S_{\text{elec}} - H \times S_{\text{gas}}, 0)$$

This is the payoff to a European exchange option (see Box 13.4 on page 411). The difference between the price of electricity and the cost of generation, $S_{\text{elec}} - H \times S_{\text{gas}}$, is called the **spark spread.** There are operating costs besides gas, but the spark spread is the variable component of marginal profit.

---

[11] I thank David Moore of El Paso Corporation for helpful discussions and for providing representative data.

[12] Operators will think not only about day-to-day operations, but hour-to-hour as well, since a plant may be operated during the day and not at night.

[13] In practice, the term "strike price" is sometimes used to refer only to nongas variable costs.

[14] The definition of heat rate is the number of BTUs required to produce one kilowatt/hour of electricity. The heat rate times 1000 is the number of British Thermal Units (BTUs) to produce one MWh. For example, if the heat rate is 9000, then 9000 × 1000 = 9m BTUs is required to produce 1 megawatt/hour of electricity. If the price of natural gas is \$3/MMBtu, then the gas cost of producing one MWh of electricity is \$27.

FIGURE 14.1

Forward price (top panel) and volatility (middle panel) curves for electricity and natural gas. The bottom panel depicts the spark spread implied by the forward price curves, assuming a heat rate of 9000.

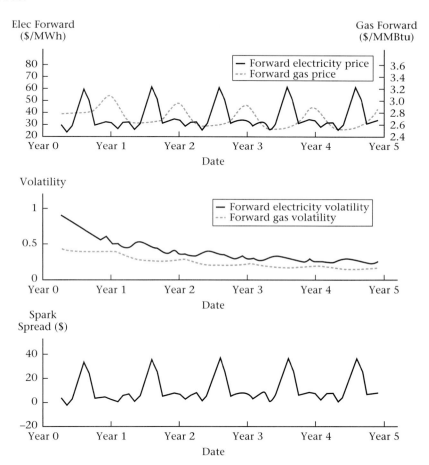

In order to value the option, we need forward prices and volatilities for electricity and gas and the correlation between the two. The top panel in Figure 14.1 shows representative forward curves for electricity and gas. The price curve for gas exhibits seasonal winter peaks. The electricity curve, by contrast, exhibits summer peaks. The bottom panel shows the spark spread implied by the prices in the first panel.

The value of a plant is the sum of the operating options it provides. Let F_{E,t_i} and F_{G,t_i} represent the time 0 forward prices for electricity and gas delivered at time t_i. If we ignore other marginal operating costs, then the value of the operating plant is[15]

$$\text{Value of plant} = \sum_{i=1}^{n} \text{BSCall}(F_{E,t_i}, H \times F_{G,t_i}, \hat{\sigma}_{t_i}, r, t_i, r) \qquad (14.22)$$

where $\hat{\sigma}_{t_i}^2 = \sigma_{E,t_i}^2 + \sigma_{G,t_i}^2 - 2\rho\sigma_{E,t_i}\sigma_{G,t_i}$. Because volatility changes with the time horizon in Figure 14.1, volatility in expression (14.22) has a time subscript. Equation (14.22) provides the value of the plant taking account of optionality. We could also value the plant assuming operation at all times; this would be a static NPV calculation. We can see how the static value relates to the true value by using put-call parity to rewrite equation (14.22):

$$\sum_{i=1}^{n} \left[e^{-rt_i}(F_{E,t_i} - H \times F_{G,t_i}) + \text{BSPut}(F_{E,t_i}, H \times F_{G,t_i}, \hat{\sigma}_{t_i}, r, t_i, r) \right]$$

$$= \underbrace{\sum_{i=1}^{n} e^{-rt_i}(F_{E,t_i} - H \times F_{G,t_i})}_{\text{Static NPV}} + \underbrace{\sum_{i=1}^{n} \text{BSPut}(F_{E,t_i}, H \times F_{G,t_i}, \hat{\sigma}_{t_i}, r, t_i, r)}_{\text{Option not to operate}} \qquad (14.23)$$

This way of writing the plant's value makes apparent the difference between a static NPV calculation and the real options valuation. The static calculation assumes operation at all times; we can value the plant by simply discounting the spark spread computed using forward prices. Equation (14.22) also makes it clear that *the value of a peak-load plant does not stem from operating when prices are high—all plants operate when prices are high—but rather from* shutting down *when prices are low*. In reality, equation (14.23) is overly simplified. There are marginal distribution, operation, and maintenance costs associated with an operating plant. Represent these costs as c. When we take these into account, marginal profit is

$$\text{Profit} = \max[S_{\text{elec}} - (H \times S_{\text{gas}} + c), 0]$$

This payoff is that of a **spread option,** since the payoff is positive if the spread $S_{\text{elec}} - H \times S_{\text{gas}}$ exceeds c. An option with this payoff cannot be valued using the Black-Scholes formula, because neither $S_{\text{elec}} - H \times S_{\text{gas}}$ nor $H \times S_{\text{gas}} + c$ is lognormally distributed. Equation (14.22) is therefore an approximation once nonfuel costs are added to the strike price.[16]

---

[15] Because the underlying asset is a forward price, the risk-free rate, r, is used as the dividend yield. This is the Black formula, equation (11.7).

[16] Haug (1998, p. 59) discusses approximations that can be used to value spread options.

Box 14.2: Peak-Load Manufacturing at Intel

Manufacturers investing in production capacity and facing uncertain demand experience the same peak-load production problem as electricity producers. Consider a manufacturer investing in production capacity and facing uncertain demand. How should the manufacturer choose plant capacity? Consider choosing the plant's capacity to meet expected demand. If demand turns out to be less than forecast, the firm will either produce at a loss or have an idle plant. If demand is greater, the firm will forgo revenue. If it is necessary to produce whether demand is high or low, then extra capacity has no option value. However, if it is possible to idle an unused plant when demand is low, then *extra production capacity is like a peak-load facility*. The extra capacity gives the firm a call option.

Intel in 1997 had to decide upon the capacity of a new plant. Semiconductor fabrication facilities ("fabs") cost about $2 billion and take 2 years to construct, 1 year for the shell—the building—and 1 year for the equipment. The shell cost was about $350 million, with the rest reflecting equipment cost.

Intel analysts proposed building a shell 1 year ahead of schedule. If demand were high, the firm would be able to install equipment a year early and earn an extra year of revenue. If demand were low, the firm would maintain the building until needed, which was relatively inexpensive.

The planners sought to persuade senior management that early construction of a shell provided benefits. Intel analysts developed a simple binomial model that illustrated the costs and benefits of early construction. They verified that the Black-Scholes formula gave approximately the same option value. Intel then built the shell 1 year early.

When we include other costs, the static NPV of a peak-load plant is typically negative. Adding the shutdown option, however, makes NPV positive. One implication is that, in equilibrium, after the optimal number of peak-load plants have been constructed, electricity prices will continue to be variable. Otherwise, the marginal peak-load plant would have negative NPV. Thus, the existence of peak-load technology will not eliminate equilibrium variability in electricity prices.

As a final point, note that the volatility curves in Figure 14.1 are declining over time. From the standpoint of year 0, a 2-year volatility is less than a 1-year volatility. This is in contrast with stocks, for which we typically assume volatility is constant over time.

Box 14.2 describes an investment problem at Intel that was similar to a peak-load problem.

FIGURE 14.2

The development process for a new drug. Probabilities are the percentage of pharmaceutical drugs proceeding from one stage to the next. For example, 74% of drugs submitted for FDA approval receive it.

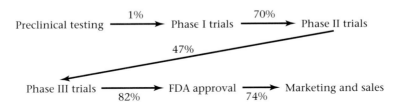

Source: Schwartz and Moon (2000).

Pharmaceutical Research and Development

Research and development is a capital expenditure like any other, in that it involves paying R&D costs today to receive cash flows later. If R&D is successful, a project using the new technology can be undertaken if its NPV is positive. This final option is a call option, just like the other projects we have analyzed. The R&D leading up to this project is therefore like an option premium: We pay R&D costs to acquire the project. R&D can be thought of as acquiring future investment options.

Drug development by pharmaceutical firms provides a particularly clear example of the options in R&D since the drug development process has clearly delineated points at which there is a decision to abandon or continue development. Figure 14.2, based on a description in Schwartz and Moon (2000), summarizes the process, along with the probabilities of progressing from one stage to the next. In practice, stages sometimes run together, but Figure 14.2 depicts a standard description of the process.

As R&D costs are paid over time, pharmaceutical firms are able to resolve uncertainties about their technical ability to produce and market the product. Specifically, they answer the questions: Will the project work, and, if it works, will anyone want it? At all times, project managers have the option to continue or stop the research. In effect, each ongoing investment purchases an option to continue development.

Figure 14.2 shows that most potential drugs are abandoned before phase I trials. As with peak-load electricity generation, value arises from what is not done. A pharmaceutical company that pursued all potential drugs, no matter how unpromising, would reap full rewards from successful drugs but would be bankrupted by the unsuccessful drugs. The put option to abandon a drug is what creates value for the firm.

How do we evaluate pharmaceutical investments? The underlying asset is the value of the drug if brought to market. How do we find the value of this asset? With the

FIGURE 14.3

An example of staged investment. The value of the project, if developed, is in the top line at each node. The value of the option to develop the project is shown below the value of the project. In each year, it is necessary to pay the amount in the Investment row to keep the project alive in the next period. The tree is generated as a forward tree assuming $S = \$100$, $\sigma = 0.50$, $r = 0.10$, and $\delta = 0.15$.

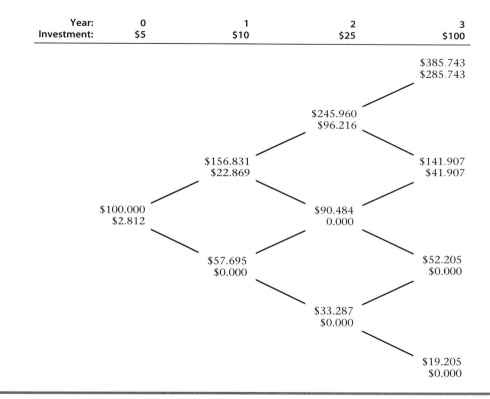

peak-load electricity plant, we have forward prices for both the input (natural gas) and the output (electricity). We can estimate volatilities from market prices. However, in pharmaceuticals, we must estimate development costs, potential revenues, volatilities, and correlations without the benefit of observing market prices. Project payoffs will vary with the state of the economy and, hence, have systematic risk, which must also be estimated.

Assuming that all of these inputs are known, we can evaluate the sequential investment as in Figure 14.3. The figure presents an example in which, in each period, it is necessary to pay an investment cost (shown in the Investment row) to keep the project alive for another period. The static NPV of the project is negative, since the initial value of the developed investment is $100, but the present value of the investment costs at a 10% rate of interest is $108.60. This static calculation ignores the staging of the investment, which permits making later-year investment costs only if the project shows promise. With staging, the value of the development option is $2.812. Schwartz and Moon (2000), building on work by Pindyck (1993a), developed a general valuation model, with staging, that is applicable to pharmaceutical R&D.

CHAPTER SUMMARY

Real options is the analysis of investment decisions taking into account the ability to revise future operating decisions. Examples of real options include timing options (the ability to choose when to make an investment), shutdown options (the ability to stop production in order to avoid losses), sequential investments where the decision to make later investments depends on the outcome of earlier investments (common in R&D), and natural resource extraction. Investment decisions in which such options are present can be analyzed using pricing tools such as the Black-Scholes model, perpetual options, and binomial trees. In some cases the optimal decision is equivalent to the problem of when to exercise an American option. In general, however, a simple option formulation is just a starting point for analysis. When properly implemented, DCF and option pricing methods are consistent and produce the same valuation.

Even when standard option pricing models are not directly applicable, understanding the economics of derivatives is helpful in understanding the economics of investment and operation decisions.

FURTHER READING

Early papers that used techniques from financial options to analyze real assets include Brennan and Schwartz (1985), and McDonald and Siegel (1985, 1986). These papers study investment timing and the option to shut down and restart. Brennan (2000) insightfully summarizes the literature since then. There are several valuable books on real options, including Dixit and Pindyck (1994) and Trigeorgis (1996).

A number of papers have applied real options to understanding the real estate market. These include Titman (1985) and Grenadier (1996, 1999).

Many firms use capital budgeting techniques more sophisticated than simple discounted cash flow. Triantis and Borison (2001) survey managers on their use of real options, identifying three categories of real options usage: as an analytical tool, as a language and framing device for investment problems, and as an organizational process. McDonald (2000) argues that the use of high hurdle rates in capital budgeting could be an approximate way to account for real options.

PROBLEMS

Use the following information to answer problems 14.1–14.8. Here is a tree of cash flows like that in Table 14.2:

1	2	3
134.9859	182.2119	245.9603
74.0818	100.0000	134.9859
	54.8812	74.0818
		40.6570

Assume that the effective annual risk-free rate is 7%, the expected return on the market is 11%, the cash flow beta is 2, and the true probability of the high cash flow in a given period is 53.2%. You can verify that the up and down moves from any given cash flow node imply the same u and d.

Project 1 cash flows are those above. Project 2 cash flows are those above less $90. Project 3 cash flows are the maximum of project 2 cash flows and zero.

14.1 Verify the following:
- The present value of the cash flow in period 1 is $92.59.
- The forward price for the period 1 cash flow is $99.07.
- Assuming the discount rate is constant across all nodes, the present value of the 3-period cash flow is $257.71.

14.2 Verify that the risk-neutral probability of an up move is 0.4104. Using the risk-neutral probability and discounting at the risk-free rate, repeat the previous problem.

14.3 Using risk-neutral valuation, what is the value of project 2 assuming that it lives only 1 period? What is the value assuming that it lives 3 periods?

14.4 Compute the forward price for project 2 cash flows in period 1 and verify that discounting your answer at the risk-free rate gives the same value as in the previous problem.

14.5 What is the elasticity of the period 1 cash flows of project 2 with respect to the project 1 cash flows? What is the appropriate discount rate for valuing the period 1 cash flows in project 2? Verify that using this elasticity, you obtain the same answer as when using risk-neutral discounting (the answer to the previous problem).

14.6 What is the elasticity of period 1 cash flows in project 3? What is the correct discount rate for these cash flows? Compute the value of the period 1 cash flows using both DCF and risk-neutral valuation.

14.7 What is the forward price for the period 1 cash flows in project 3? What project value do you obtain using this forward price?

14.8 Suppose you are standing at the top two nodes in period 2. Compute the elasticities for the project 3, period 3 cash flows, with respect to project 1 cash flows. Verify that the elasticity increases as the period 2 cash flows decrease.

14.9 The stock price of XYZ is $100. One million shares of XYZ (a negligible fraction of the shares outstanding) are buried on a tiny, otherwise worthless, plot of land in a vault that would cost $50 million to excavate. If XYZ pays a dividend, you will have to dig up the shares to collect the dividend.

   a. If you believe that XYZ will never pay a dividend, what would you pay for the land?

   b. If you believe that XYZ will pay a liquidating dividend in 10 years, and the continuously compounded risk-free rate is 5%, what would you pay for the land?

   c. Suppose that XYZ has a 1% dividend yield and a volatility of 0.3. At what price would you excavate and what would you pay for the land?

14.10 Repeat Problem 14.9, only assume that after the stock is excavated, the land has an alternative use and can be sold for $30m.

14.11 Consider the oil extraction project discussed in Section 14.3. Suppose that the land can be sold for the residual value of $R = \$1$ after the barrel of oil is extracted. How does this affect the extraction decision and what is the value of the land?

14.12 Consider the oil extraction problem when there is uncertainty. Compare the extraction rules and land value when volatility is 15% and 20%. Explain the differences. Use the CallPerpetual function to answer this question.

In the following two problems, assume that the spot price of gold is $300/oz., the effective annual lease rate is 3%, and the effective annual risk-free rate is 5%.

14.13 A mine costing $275 will produce 1 ounce of gold on the day the cost is paid. Gold volatility is zero. What is the value of the mine?

14.14 A mine costing $1000 will produce 1 ounce of gold per year forever at a marginal extraction cost of $250, with production commencing 1 year after the mine opens. Gold volatility is zero. What is the value of the mine? (*Hint:* from equation (12.9) (p. 357), the value of a perpetuity paying one ounce per year is S_0/δ, where δ is the lease rate.)

Appendix 14.A THE RELATIONSHIP BETWEEN DCF AND RISK-NEUTRAL VALUATION

This appendix shows how to perform a DCF calculation by computing the elasticity.

Denote the original (project 1) cash flows as X_u and X_d, and the project 2 cash flows as X_{2u} and X_{2d}. The present values of these cash flows are V and V_2, respectively. We wish to compute V_2.

As discussed in the text, the beta for project 2 is related to that for project 1 by the elasticity of project 2 cash flows with respect to project 1 cash flows:

$$\Omega = \frac{X_{2u} - X_{2d}}{X_u - X_d} \frac{V}{V_2}$$

The DCF equation is therefore

$$\frac{pX_{2u} + (1-p)X_{2d}}{1 + r + \Omega\beta(r_M - r)} = \frac{pX_{2u} + (1-p)X_{2d}}{1 + r + \frac{X_{2u}-X_{2d}}{X_u-X_d}\frac{V}{V_2}\beta(r_M - r)} = V_2$$

Notice that V_2 appears both on the right and left sides of this equation. We can algebraically manipulate the equation, however, to obtain

$$\frac{pX_{2u} + (1-p)X_{2d} - \{[(X_{2u} - X_{2d})/(X_u - X_d)]V\beta(r_M - r)\}}{1 + r} = V_2 \quad (14.24)$$

The term in curly braces in the numerator of this equation has a simple interpretation. The dollar value of the systematic risk in project 1 is $V\beta(r_M - r)$. The fraction of this systematic risk borne by project 2 is $(X_{2u} - X_{2d})/(X_u - X_d)$. Thus, the numerator is the expected cash flow for project 2 less the dollar value of risk in this project. The numerator is the *certainty-equivalent cash flow* for project 2, and it is discounted at the risk-free rate.

Finally, we can also see how risk-neutral probabilities can be obtained from the certainty-equivalent. Rewrite equation (14.24) to obtain

$$\frac{p^*X_{2u} + (1-p^*)X_{2d}}{1 + r} = V_2 \quad (14.25)$$

where

$$p^* = p - \frac{V\beta(r_M - r)}{X_u - X_d}$$

That is, the risk-neutral probability p^* is the true probability less the dollar risk premium $(V\beta(r_M - r))$ as a percentage of the dollar risk of the underlying asset $(X_u - X_D)$.

The Greek Alphabet

The use of Greek letters is common in writing about derivatives and mathematics in general. Important concepts in this book are option characteristics that have the names of Greek letters such as "delta" and "gamma."

Table A.1 presents the complete Greek alphabet, including both lowercase and uppercase forms. Some of the letters look like their Roman counterparts. Not all of these symbols are used in this book.

TABLE A.1 The Greek alphabet.

alpha	α	A	nu	ν	N
beta	β	B	xi	ξ	Ξ
gamma	γ	Γ	omicron	o	O
delta	δ	Δ	pi	π	Π
epsilon	ϵ	E	rho	ρ	P
zeta	ζ	Z	sigma	σ	Σ
eta	η	H	tau	τ	T
theta	θ	Θ	upsilon	υ	Υ
iota	ι	I	phi	ϕ	Φ
kappa	κ	K	chi	χ	X
lambda	λ	Λ	psi	ψ	Ψ
mu	μ	M	omega	ω	Ω

B Continuous Compounding

In this book we use both effective annual interest rates and continuously compounded interest rates. These are simply different conventions for expressing the same idea: If you invest $1 today, how much will you have after 1 year? One simple unambiguous way to answer this question is using zero-coupon bonds. If you invest $1 in zero-coupon bonds costing $P(0, T)$ for a $1 maturity payoff at time T, then at time T you will have $1/P(0, T)$ dollars. However, it is more common to answer the question using interest rates rather than zero-coupon bond prices.

Interest rates measure the rate of appreciation of an investment, but there are innumerable ways of quoting interest rates. Continuous compounding turns out to provide a particularly simple quoting convention, though it may not seem so simple at first. Since in practice option pricing formulas and other financial formulas make use of continuous compounding, it is important to be comfortable with it.

Continuous compounding might seem esoteric; an auto dealer, for example, is likely to give you a blank stare if you ask about the continuously compounded loan rate for your new car. However, continuous compounding is convenient mathematically and is widely used in derivatives. Moreover, it is not often appreciated that almost *all* interest rate quoting conventions are complicated, sometimes devilishly so. (If you doubt this, read Appendix 7.A).

B.1 THE LANGUAGE OF INTEREST RATES

We begin with definitions. There are two terms that we will use often to refer to interest rates:

- **Effective annual rate:** If r is quoted as an **effective annual rate,** this means that if you invest $1, n years later you will have $(1 + r)^n$. If you invest x_0 and earn x_n n years later, then the implied effective annual rate is $(x_n/x_0)^{1/n} - 1$.

- **Continuously compounded rate:** If r is quoted as an annualized **continuously compounded rate,** this means that if you invest $1, n years later you will have

e^{rn}. If you invest x_0 and earn x_n n years later, then the implied annual continuously compounded rate is $\ln(x_n/x_0)/n$.

Let's look at this definition in more detail.

B.2 THE LOGARITHMIC AND EXPONENTIAL FUNCTIONS

Interest rates are typically quoted as "$r\%$ per year, compounded n times per year." As every beginning finance student learns, this has the interpretation that you will earn an interest rate of r/n per period for n periods. Thus, if you invest \$1 today, in 1 year you will have

$$\left(1 + \frac{r}{n}\right)^n$$

In T years you will have

$$\left(1 + \frac{r}{n}\right)^{nT} \tag{B.1}$$

What happens if we let n get very large, that is, if interest is compounded many times a year (even daily or hourly)? If, for example, the interest rate is 10%, after 3 years we will have the following:

- $(\$1 + 0.1)^3 = \$1.331$ with annual compounding
- $(\$1 + 0.1/12)^{36} = \$1.3482$ with monthly compounding
- $(\$1 + 0.1/365)^{1095} = \$1.34980$ with daily compounding
- $(\$1 + 0.1/8760)^{26,280} = \$1.349856$ with hourly compounding

The exponential function is e^x, where e is a constant approximately equal to 2.71828....[1] If compounding is *continuous*—that is, if interest accrues every instant—then we can use the exponential function to compute future values. For example, with a 10% continuously compounded rate, after 3 years we will have a future value of

$$e^{0.1 \times 3} = \$1.349859$$

Notice that assuming continuous compounding gives us a result very close to that assuming daily compounding. In Excel, we compute continuously compounded results using the built-in exponential function, exp. The above example is computed as $\exp(0.1 \times 3)$.

Why does the exponential function play a role in interest calculations? The number e is *defined* as

---

[1] Maor (1998) is a mathematical history of e.

$$e^{rT} \equiv \lim_{n \to \infty} \left(1 + \frac{r}{n}\right)^{nT} \tag{B.2}$$

Thus, the expression defining e is the same expression used for interest compounding calculations, equation (B.1). By using e, you can compute a future value.

If you know how much you have earned from a $1 investment, you can determine the continuously compounded rate of return by using the natural logarithm, ln. Ln is the *inverse* of the exponential function, in that it takes a dollar amount and gives you a rate of return. In other words, if you apply the logarithmic function to the exponential function, you compute the original argument to the exponential function. Here is an example:

$$\ln(e^{rt}) = rt$$

Example B.1 Suppose you have a zero-coupon bond that matures in 5 years. The price today is $62.092 for a bond that pays $100. The annually compounded rate of return is

$$(\$100/\$62.092)^{1/5} - 1 = 0.10$$

The continuously compounded rate of return is

$$\frac{\ln(\$100/\$62.092)}{5} = \frac{0.47655}{5} = 0.09531$$

The continuously compounded rate of return of 9.53% corresponds to the annually compounded rate of return of 10%. To verify this, observe that

$$e^{0.0953} = 1.10$$

Finally, note that

$$\ln(1.10) = \ln(e^{0.0953}) = 0.0953$$

Changing Interest Rates

When we multiply exponentials, exponents add. So we have

$$e^x e^y = e^{x+y}$$

Suppose you can invest for 4 years, earning a continuouously compounded return of 5% the first 2 years and 6% the second 2 years. If you invest $1 today, after 4 years you will have

$$e^{2 \times 0.05} e^{2 \times 0.06} = e^{0.10 + 0.12} = \$1.2461$$

We could of course do the same calculation using effective annual rates. For the first 2 years we earn $e^{0.05} - 1 = 5.127\%$, and for the second 2 years, $e^{0.06} = 6.184\%$. The future value of $1 is

$$1.05127^2 1.06184^2 = \$1.2461$$

This calculation gives us the same answer.

What is the average annual rate earned over the 4 years? The average annual continuously compounded rate is

$$\frac{1}{4} \ln(1.24608) = 0.055$$

which is the average of 5% and 6%.

However, if we express the answer in terms of effective annual rates, we get

$$1.24608^{0.25} - 1 = 5.6541\%$$

This is *not* the average of 5.127% and 6.184%, which is 5.6554. This makes calculations with continuous compounding easier.

Symmetry for Increases and Decreases

On March 4, 1999, the NASDAQ composite index closed at 2292.89. On March 10, 2000, the index closed at 5048.62. On January 2, 2001, the index closed at 2291.86, essentially the same level as in March 1999. The percentage increase from March 1999 to March 2000 was

$$\frac{5048.62}{2292.89} - 1 = 120.19\%$$

The subsequent decrease was

$$\frac{2291.86}{5048.62} - 1 = -54.60\%$$

When computing simple rates of return, a price can have an increase exceeding 100%, but its decrease can never be greater than 100%.

We can do the same calculations using continuous compounding. The continuously compounded increase from March 1999 to March 2000 was

$$\ln(5048.62/2292.89) = 78.93\%$$

while the subsequent decrease was

$$\ln(2291.86/5048.62) = -78.97\%$$

When using continuous compounding, increases and decreases are symmetric.

Moreover, if the index dropped to 1000, the continuously compounded return from the peak would be

$$\ln(1000/5048.62) = -161.91\%$$

Continuously compounded returns can be less than −100%.

PROBLEMS

B.1 A bond costs $67,032 today and pays $100,000 in 5 years. What is its continuously compounded rate of return?

B.2 A bond costs $50 today, pays $100 at maturity, and has a continuously compounded annual return of 10%. In how many years does it mature?

B.3 An investment of $5 today pays a continuously compounded rate of 7.5%/year. How much money will you have after 7 years?

B.4 A stock selling for $100 is worth $5 one year later. What is the continuously compounded return over the year? What if the stock price is $4? $3? $2? What would the stock price after 1 year have to be in order for the continuously compounded return to be -500%?

B.5 Suppose that over 1 year a stock price increases from $100 to $200. Over the subsequent year it falls back to $100.

    a. What is the arithmetic return [i.e., $(S_{t+1} - S_t)/S_t$] over the first year? What is the continuously compounded return [i.e., $\ln(S_{t+1}/S_t)$]?

    b. What is the arithmetic return over the second year? The continuously compounded return?

    c. What do you notice when you compare the first- and second-year returns computed arithmetically and continuously?

B.6 Here are stock prices on 6 consecutive days: $100, $47, $88, $153, $212, $100. Note that the cumulative return over the 6 days is 0.

    a. What are the arithmetic returns from the first to the second day, the second to the third, and so forth?

    b. What are the continuously compounded returns from the first to the second day, the second to the third, and so forth?

    c. Suppose you want to compute the cumulative return over the 6 days. Suppose you don't know the prices but only your answers to (a) and (b). How would you compute the cumulative return (which is 0) using arithmetic returns and continuously compounded returns?

Glossary

Absolute priority A procedure for a firm in bankruptcy in which junior creditors are not paid unless more senior creditors have been fully repaid.

Accreting swap A swap where the notional amount increases over the life of the swap.

Accrued interest The prorated portion of a bond's coupon since the previous coupon date.

Alpha-porting Using a futures overlay to transfer a portfolio alpha (a measure of superior performance) from one asset class to another.

American option An option that may be exercised at any time during its life.

Amortizing swap A swap where the notional amount declines over the life of the swap.

Arbitrage A transaction generating a positive cash flow either today or in the future by simultaneously buying and selling related assets, with no net investment of funds, and with no risk.

Asian option An option in which the payoff at maturity depends upon an average of the asset prices over the life of the option.

Asian tail A reference price that is computed as an average of recent prices. For example, an equity-linked note may have a payoff based on the average daily stock price over the last 20 days (the Asian tail).

Ask price The price at which a dealer or market-maker offers to sell a security. Also called the *offer price*.

Asset swap A swap, typically involving a bond, in which fixed bond payments are swapped for payments based on a floating rate.

Asymmetric butterfly spread A butterfly spread in which the distance between strike prices is not equal.

At-the-money option An option for which the price of the underlying asset approximately equals the strike price.

Back-to-back transaction A transaction where a dealer enters into offsetting transactions with different parties, effectively serving as a go-between.

Backwardation A forward curve in which the futures prices are falling with time to expiration.

Barrier option An option that has a payoff depending upon whether, at some point during the life of the option, the price of the underlying asset has moved past a reference price (the barrier). Examples are *knock-in* and *knock-out* options.

Basis The difference between the cash price of the underlying asset and the futures price.

Basis point 1/100th of 1%, i.e., one ten-thousandth (0.0001).

Basis risk The possibility of unexpected changes in the difference between the price of an asset and the price of the contract hedging the asset.

Bear spread The sale of a call (or put) together with the purchase of an otherwise identical higher-strike call (or put).

Bermudan option An option that can only be exercised at specified times during its life.

Bid-ask spread The difference between the bid price and the ask price.

Bid price The price at which a dealer or market-maker buys a security.

461

Binary option An option that has a payoff that is a discrete amount—for example, $1 or one share. Also called a *digital option*.

Binomial tree A representation of possible asset price movements over time, in which the asset price is modeled as moving up or down by a given amount each period.

Black formula A version of the Black-Scholes formula in which the underlying asset is a futures price and the dividend yield is replaced with the risk-free rate. See equation (11.7) (p. 316).

Black-Scholes formula The formula giving the price of a European call option as a function of the stock price, strike price, time to expiration, interest rate, volatility, and dividend yield. See equation (11.1) (p. 310).

Bobl German government bond issued with a maturity of 5 years.

Bootstrapping This term has two meanings. First, it refers to the procedure where coupon bonds are used to generate the set of zero-coupon bond prices. Second, it means the use of historical returns to create an empirical probability distribution for returns.

Boundary condition The value of a derivative claim at a certain time, or at a particular price of the underlying asset. For example, a boundary condition for a zero-coupon bond is that the bond at maturity is worth its promised maturity value.

Box spread An option position in which the stock is synthetically purchased (buy call, sell put) at one price and sold (sell call, buy put) at a different price. When constructed with European options, the box spread is equivalent to a zero-coupon bond.

Bubill German government bond issued with a maturity of less than 1 year (typically 6 months).

Bull spread The purchase of a call (or put) together with the sale of an otherwise identical higher-strike call (or put).

Bund German government bond issued with a maturity of 10 or more years.

Butterfly spread A position created by buying a call, selling two calls at a higher strike price, and buying a fourth call at a still higher strike price, with an equal distance between strike prices. The butterfly spread can also be created using puts alone, or by buying a straddle and insuring it with the purchase of out-of-the-money calls and puts, or in a variety of other ways.

Calendar spread A spread position in which the bought and sold options or futures have the same underlying asset but different times to maturity.

Callable bond A bond where the issuer has the right to buy the bond back from bondholders by paying a prespecified amount.

Call option A contract giving the buyer the right, but not the obligation, to buy the underlying asset at a prespecified price.

Call protection A period during which a callable bond cannot be called.

Call schedule A contractual feature of a callable bond, specifying the price at which the company can buy the bond back from bondholders at different points in time.

Cap An options contract that serves as insurance against a high price. (See also *Interest rate cap*.)

Caplet A contract that insures a borrower against a high interest rate on a single date. A collection of caplets is an *interest rate cap*.

Capped option An option with a maximum payoff, where the option is automatically exercised if the underlying asset reaches the price at which the maximum payoff is attained.

Carry Another term for owning an asset, typically used to refer to commodities. (See also *Carry market* and *Cost of carry*).

Carry market A situation where the forward price is such that the return on a cash-and-carry is the risk-free rate.

Cash-and-carry The simultaneous spot purchase and forward sale of an asset or commodity.

Cash-and-carry arbitrage The use of a cash-and-carry to effect an arbitrage.

Cash settlement A procedure where settlement entails a cash payment from one party to the other, instead of delivery of an asset.

CDO See *Collateralized debt obligation*.

Central limit theorem One of the most important results in statistics, which states that the sum of independent and identically distributed random variables has a limiting distribution that is normal.

Cheapest to deliver When a futures contract gives the seller a choice of asset to deliver to the buyer, the asset that is most profitable for the short to deliver.

Clean price The present value of a bond's future cash flows less accrued interest.

Clearinghouse A financial organization, typically associated with one or more exchanges, that matches the buy and sell orders that take place during the day and keeps track of the obligations and payments required of the members of the clearinghouse.

Collar The purchase of a put and sale of a call at a higher strike price.

Collar width The difference between the strike prices of the two options in a collar.

Collateralized debt obligation A financial structure that consists of a pool of assets, financed by issuing financial claims that reapportion the return on the asset pool.

Commodity spread Offsetting long and short positions in closely related commodities. (See also *Crack spread* and *Crush spread*.)

Compound option An option that has an option as the underlying asset.

Concave Shaped like the cross section of an upside-down bowl.

Constructive sale A term in tax law describing the owner of an asset entering into an offsetting position that largely eliminates the risk of holding the asset.

Contango A forward curve in which futures prices are rising with time to expiration.

Contingent convertible bond A bond that becomes convertible once a contingency (for example, the share price is greater than $100 for 30 days) has occurred.

Continuation value The value of leaving an option unexercised. You make an exercise decision by comparing the continuation value to the value of immediate exercise.

Continuously compounded rate A way of quoting an interest rate such that if $1 is invested at a continuously compounded rate of r, the payoff in 1 year is e^r.

Convenience yield A nonmonetary return to ownership of an asset or commodity.

Conversion A risk-free position consisting of an asset, a purchased put, and a written call.

Convertible bond A bond which, at the option of the bondholder, can be surrendered for a specified number of shares of stock.

Convex Shaped like the cross section of a bowl.

Convexity The second derivative of a bond's price with respect to a change in the interest rate, divided by the bond price.

Cooling degree-day The greater of (i) the average daily temperature minus 65 degrees Fahrenheit and (ii) zero.

Cost of carry The interest cost of owning an asset, less lease or dividend payments received as a result of ownership; the net cash flow resulting from borrowing to buy an asset.

Covered call A long position in an asset together with a written call on the same asset.

Covered interest arbitrage A zero-investment strategy with simultaneous borrowing in one currency, lending in another, and entering into a forward contract to guarantee the exchange rate when the loans mature.

Covered write A long position in an asset coupled with sale of a call option on the same asset.

Crack spread The difference between the price of crude oil futures and that of equivalent amounts of heating oil and gasoline.

Credit derivative A claim where the payoff depends upon the credit rating or default status of a firm.

Credit-linked note A bond that has payments determined at least in part by credit events (e.g., default) at a different firm.

Credit risk Risk resulting from the possibility that a counterparty will be financially unable to meet its contractual obligations.

Credit spread The difference between the yields on a bond that can default and on an otherwise equivalent default-free bond.

Cross-hedging The use of a derivative on one underlying asset to hedge the risk of another underlying asset.

Crush spread The difference between the price of a quantity of soybeans and that of the soybean meal and oil that can be produced by those soybeans.

Cumulative distribution function A function giving the probability that a value drawn from a distribution will be less than or equal to some specified value.

Cumulative normal distribution function The cumulative distribution function for the normal distribution; $N(x)$ in the Black-Scholes equation.

Currency swap A swap in which the parties make payments based on the difference in debt payments in different currencies.

Currency-translated index An investment in an index denominated in a foreign currency, where the buyer bears both currency and asset risk.

Debenture A bond for which payments are secured only by the general credit of the issuer.

Debt capacity The maximum amount of debt that can be issued by a firm or secured by a specific asset.

Default premium The difference between the yield on a bond and that on an otherwise equivalent default-free bond.

Default swap A contract in which the swap buyer pays a regular premium; in exchange, if a default in a specified bond occurs, the swap seller pays the buyer the loss due to the default.

Deferred swap A swap with terms specified today but for which swap payments begin at a later date than for an ordinary swap.

Delivery The act of the seller (e.g., of a forward contract) supplying the underlying asset to the buyer.

Delta The change in the price of a derivative due to a change in the price of the underlying asset.

Delta-gamma approximation A formula using the delta and gamma to approximate the change in the derivative price due to a change in the price of the underlying asset.

Delta-gamma-theta approximation A formula using the delta, gamma, and theta to approximate the change in the derivative price due to a change in the price of the underlying asset and the passage of time.

Delta-hedging Hedging a derivative position using the underlying asset, with the amount of the underlying asset determined by the derivative's sensitivity (*delta*) to the price of the underlying asset.

Derivative A financial instrument that has a value determined by the price of something else.

Diff swap A swap in which payments are based on the difference in floating interest rates on a given notional amount denominated in a single currency.

Digital option Another name for a *binary option*.

Dirty price The present value of a bond's future cash flows (this implicitly includes accrued interest).

Distance to default The distance between the current firm asset value and the level at which default occurs, measured in standard deviations.

Diversifiable risk Risk that is, in the limit, eliminated by combining a large number of assets in a portfolio.

Down-and-in A knock-in option for which the barrier is less than the current price of the underlying asset.

Down-and-out A knock-out option for which the barrier is less than the current price of the underlying asset.

Drift The expected change per unit time in an asset price.

DTCC Depository Trust and Clearing Corporation. The legal entity in the United States that maintains possession of stocks and bonds on behalf of brokers and other financial institutions.

Duration Generally, the weighted average life of the bond, which also provides a measure of the bond's sensitivity to interest rate changes. Two common duration measures are *modified duration* and *Macaulay duration*.

Effective annual rate A way of quoting an interest rate such that the quoted rate is the annual percentage increase in an amount invested at this rate. If $1 is invested at an effective annual rate of r, the payoff in 1 year is $1 + r$.

Elasticity The percent change in an option price for a 1% change in the price of the underlying asset.

Equity-linked forward A forward contract (e.g., for currency) where the quantity to be bought or sold depends upon the performance of a stock or stock index.

European option An option that can only be exercised at expiration.

Exchange option An option permitting the holder to obtain one asset by giving up another. Standard calls and puts are exchange options in which one of the two assets is cash.

Exercise The exchange of the strike price (or strike asset) for the underlying asset at the terms specified in the option contract.

Exercise price Under the terms of an option contract, the amount that can be exchanged for the underlying asset.

Exercise style The circumstances under which an option holder has the right to exercise an option. "European" and "American" are exercise styles.

Exotic option A derivatives contract in which an ordinary derivative has been altered to change the characteristics of the derivative in a meaningful way. Also called a *nonstandard option*.

Expectations hypothesis A term with multiple meanings, one of which is that the expected future interest rate equals the implied forward rate.

Expiration The date beyond which an unexercised option is worthless.

Fair value Another name for the theoretical forward price: spot price plus interest less the future value of dividends.

Financial engineering Creating new financial instruments by combining other derivatives, or more generally, by using derivatives pricing techniques.

Floor An option position that guarantees a minimum price.

Forward contract An agreement that sets today the terms—including price and quantity—at which you buy or sell an asset or commodity at a specific time in the future.

Forward curve The set of forward or futures prices with different expiration dates on a given date for a given asset.

Forward premium The annualized percentage difference between the forward price and the spot price.

Forward rate agreement A forward contract for an interest rate.

Forward strip Another name for the *forward curve*.

Funded A position that is paid for in full at the outset. A prepaid forward, for example, is a funded position in a stock. See also *Unfunded*.

Futures contract An agreement that is similar to a forward contract except that the buyer and seller post margin and the contract is marked-to-market periodically. Futures are typically exchange-traded.

Futures overlay Converting an investment in asset A into the economic equivalent of an investment in asset B by entering into a short futures position on asset A and a long futures position on asset B.

Gamma The change in delta when the price of the underlying asset changes by 1 unit.

Gap option An option where the option owner has the right to exercise the option at strike K_1 if the stock price exceeds (or, depending on the option, is less than) the price K_2. For an ordinary option, $K_1 = K_2$.

Greeks A term generally referring to delta, gamma, vega, theta, and rho, all of which measure the change in the price of a derivative when there is a change in an input to the pricing formula.

Haircut The collateral, over and above the market value of the security, required by the lender when a security is borrowed.

Heating degree-day The greater of (i) 65 degrees Fahrenheit minus the average daily temperature and (ii) zero.

Heat rate A measure of the efficiency with which heat can be used to produce electricity. Specifically, it is the number of British Thermal Units required to produce 1 kilowatt/hour of electricity.

Hedge ratio In a hedging transaction, the ratio of the quantity of the forward or futures position to the quantity of the underlying asset.

Hedging An action—such as entering into a derivatives position—that reduces the risk of loss.

Implied forward rate The forward interest rate between time t_1 and time t_2 ($t_1 < t_2$) that makes an investor indifferent between, on the one hand, buying a bond maturing at t_2, and, on the other hand, buying a bond maturing at t_1 and reinvesting the proceeds at this forward interest rate.

Implied repo rate The rate of return on a cash-and-carry.

Implied volatility The volatility for which the theoretical option price (typically computed using the Black-Scholes formula) equals the observed market price of the option.

Interest rate cap A contract that periodically pays the difference between the market interest rate and a guaranteed rate, if the difference is positive.

In-the-money option An option that would have value if exercised. For an in-the-money call, the stock price exceeds the strike price. For an in-the-money put, the stock price is less than the strike price.

Investment trigger price The price of an investment project (or the price of the good to be produced) at which it is optimal to invest in the project.

Jensen's inequality If x is a random variable and $f(x)$ is convex, Jensen's inequality states that $E[f(x)] \geq f[E(x)]$. The inequality is reversed if $f(x)$ is concave.

Kappa Another name for *vega*.

Knock-in option An option in which there can only be a final payoff if, during a specified period of time, the price of the underlying asset has reached a specified level.

Knock-out option An option in which there can only be a final payoff if, during a specified period of time, the price of the underlying asset has *not* reached a specified level.

Kurtosis A measure of the peakedness of a probability distribution. For a random variable x with mean μ and standard deviation σ, kurtosis is the fourth central moment divided by the squared variance, $E(x-\mu)^4/\sigma^4$. For a normal random variable, kurtosis is 3.

Lambda Another name for *vega*.

Lattice A binomial tree in which an up move followed by a down move leads to the same price as a down move followed by an up move. Also called a *recombining tree*.

Law of one price The assertion that two portfolios generating exactly the same return must have the same price.

Lease rate The annualized payment required to borrow an asset, or, equivalently, the annualized payment received in exchange for lending an asset.

Leverage effect A rise in the stock price volatility when the stock price declines.

LIBID London Interbank Bid Rate. See *LIBOR*.

LIBOR London Interbank Offer Rate. A measure of the borrowing rate for large international banks. The British Banker's Association determines LIBOR daily for different currencies by surveying at least eight banks, asking at what rate they could borrow, dropping the top and bottom quartiles of the responses, and computing an arithmetic average of the remaining quotes. Since LIBOR is an average, there may be no actual transactions at that rate. Confusingly, LIBOR is also sometimes referred to as a lending rate. This is because a bank serving as a market-maker in the interbank market will offer to lend money at a high interest rate (LIBOR) and borrow money at a low interest rate (LIBID). (The difference between LIBOR and LIBID is the bid-ask spread in the interbank market.) A bank needing to borrow will thus pay LIBOR, and a bank with excess funds will receive LIBID.

Lognormal distribution A probability distribution in which the natural logarithm of the random variable is normally distributed.

Long A position is long with respect to a price if the position profits from an increase in that price. An owner of a stock profits from an increase in the stock price and, hence, is long the stock. An owner of an option profits from an increase in volatility and, hence, is long volatility.

Long forward The party to a forward contract who has an obligation to buy the underlying asset.

Macaulay duration The percent change in a bond's price for a given percent change in one plus the bond's yield. This calculation can be interpreted as the weighted average life of the bond, with the weights being the percentage of the bond's value due to each payment.

Maintenance margin The level of margin at which the contract holder is required to add cash or securities to the margin account.

Mandatorily convertible bond A bond that makes payments in shares instead of cash, with the number of shares paid to the bondholder typically dependent upon the share price.

Margin A deposit required for both buyers and sellers of a futures contract, which indemnifies the counterparty against the failure of the buyer or seller to meet the obligations of the contract.

Margin call The requirement that the owner of a margined position add funds to the margin account.

This can result from a loss on the position or an increase in the margin requirement.

Market corner Owning a large percentage of the available supply of an asset or commodity that is required for delivery under the terms of a derivatives contract.

Market-maker A trader in an asset, commodity, or derivative who simultaneously offers to buy at one price (the bid price) or to sell at a higher price (the offer price), thereby "making a market."

Market-timing The allocation of assets between stocks and bonds in an attempt to invest in whichever asset is going to have a higher return.

Market value Generally refers to a price determined by trades between arm's-length buyers and sellers. Stock exchanges use the term to refer to the total share value (price of a share times number of shares outstanding) of companies listed on the exchange.

Mark-to-market The procedure of revaluing a portfolio or position to reflect current market prices.

Modified duration The percent change in a bond's price for a unit change in the yield. Modified duration is also Macaulay duration divided by 1 plus the bond's yield per payment period.

Monte Carlo valuation A procedure for pricing derivative claims by discounting expected payoffs, where the expected payoff is computed using simulated prices for the underlying asset.

Naked writing Selling options without an offsetting position in the underlying asset.

Net payoff Another term for *profit*.

Nondiversifiable risk Risk that remains after a large number of assets are combined in a portfolio.

Nonrecombining tree A binomial tree describing asset price moves in which an up move followed by a down move yields a different price than a down move followed by an up move.

Nonstandard option See *Exotic option*.

Nontraded asset A cash flow stream that cannot be purchased directly in a financial market. Many corporate investment projects are nontraded because they can only be acquired by buying the entire company.

Normal distribution A bell-shaped, symmetric, continuous probability distribution that assigns positive probability to all values from $-\infty$ to $+\infty$. Sometimes called the "bell curve." (See also *Central limit theorem*.)

Notional amount The dollar amount used as a scale factor in calculating payments for a forward contract, futures contract, or swap.

Notional principal The notional amount for an interest rate swap.

Notional value See *Notional amount*.

Numeraire The units in which a payoff is denominated.

Offer price The same as the *ask price*.

Off-market forward A forward contract in which the forward price is set so that the value of the contract is not zero.

Off-the-run A government bond that is not one of the recently issued bonds.

On-the-run The most recently auctioned government bonds at the government's specific auction maturities.

Open interest The quantity of a derivatives contract that is outstanding at a point in time. (One long and one short position count as one unit outstanding.)

Open outcry A system of trading in which buyers and sellers in one physical location convey offers to buy and sell by gesturing and shouting.

Option elasticity The percent change in an option price for a 1% change in the price of the underlying asset.

Option overwriting Selling a call option against a long position in the underlying asset.

Option writer The party with a short position in the option.

Order statistics The n draws of a random variable sorted in ascending order.

Out-of-the-money option An option that would be exercised at a loss. An out-of-the-money call has the stock price less than the strike price. An out-of-the-money put has the stock price greater than the strike price.

Outperformance option An option in which the payoff is determined by the extent to which one asset price is greater than another asset price.

Over-the-counter market A term used generally to refer to transactions (e.g., purchases and sales of securities or derivatives contracts) that occur without the involvement of a regulated exchange.

Par bond A bond for which the price at issue equals the maturity value.

Par coupon The coupon rate on a *par bond*.

Partial expectation The sum (or integral) of a set of outcomes times the probability of those outcomes.

Path-dependent A derivative where the final payoff depends upon the path taken by the stock price, instead of just the final stock price.

Payer swaption A *swaption* giving the holder the right to be the fixed-rate payer in a swap.

Paylater strategy Generally used to refer to option strategies in which the position buyer makes no payments unless the option moves more into the money.

Payoff The value of a position at a point in time. The term often implicitly refers to a payoff at expiration or maturity.

Payoff diagram A graph in which the value of a derivative or other claim at a point in time is plotted against the price of the underlying asset.

Payout protected A characteristic of a derivative where a change in the dividend payout on the underlying asset does not change the value of the derivative.

Perpetual option An option that never expires.

Prediction market A kind of derivatives market in which the payoff is determined by some future event or outcome. A common contract pays $1 if a particular event occurs, zero otherwise.

Prepaid forward contract A contract calling for payment today and delivery of the asset or commodity at a time in the future.

Prepaid forward price The price the buyer pays today for a prepaid forward contract.

Prepaid swap A contract calling for payment today and delivery of the asset or commodity at multiple specified times in the future.

Price limit In futures markets, the size of a futures price move such that trading is halted temporarily.

Price participation The extent to which an equity-linked note benefits from an increase in the price of the stock or index to which it is linked.

Price value of a basis point The change in a bond price due to a 1-basis-point change in the yield of the bond. Frequently abbreviated PVBP.

Profit The payoff less the future value of the original cost to acquire the position.

Profit diagram A graph plotting the *profit* on a position against a range of prices for the underlying asset.

Proprietary trading Taking positions in an asset or derivative to express a view—for example, that a stock price will rise or that implied volatility will fall.

Psi The change in the price of a derivative due to a change in the dividend yield.

Purchased call A long position in a call.

Purchased put A long position in a put.

Put-call parity A relationship stating that the difference between the premiums of a call and a put with the same strike price and time to expiration equals the difference between the present value of the forward price and the present value of the strike price.

Put option A contract giving the buyer the right, but not the obligation, to sell the underlying asset at a prespecified price.

Puttable bond A bond that the investor can sell back to the issuer at a predetermined price schedule.

Quanto A derivatives contract with a payoff in which foreign-currency-denominated quantities are treated as if they were denominated in the domestic currency.

Quasi-arbitrage The replacement of one asset or position with another that has equivalent risk and a higher expected rate of return.

Ratings transition A change in the credit rating of a bond from one value to another.

Ratio spread Buying m of an option at one strike and selling n of an otherwise identical option at a different strike.

Real options The applications of derivatives theory to the operation and valuation of real (physical) investment projects.

Rebate option A claim that pays $1 at the time the price of the underlying asset reaches a barrier.

Receiver swaption A *swaption* giving the holder the right to receive the fixed rate in a swap.

Recombining tree A binomial tree describing asset price moves in which an up move followed by a down move yields the same price as a down move followed by an up move. Also called a *lattice*.

Recovery rate The percentage of par value received by a bondholder in a bankruptcy.

Reference price A market price or rate used to determine the payoff on a derivatives contract.

Repo Another name for a *repurchase agreement*.

Repo rate The annualized percentage difference between the original sale price and final repurchase price in a repurchase agreement.

Repricing The replacement of an out-of-the-money compensation option with an at-the-money compensation option.

Repurchase agreement The sale of a security coupled with an agreement to buy it back at a later date.

Reverse cash-and-carry The simultaneous short-sale and forward purchase of an asset or commodity.

Reverse conversion A short position in an asset coupled with a purchased call and written put, both with the same strike price and time to expiration. The position is equivalent to a short bond.

Reverse repo Another name for *reverse repurchase agreement*.

Reverse repurchase agreement The purchase of a security coupled with an agreement to sell it at a later date. The opposite of a repurchase agreement.

Rho The change in value of a derivative due to a change in the interest rate.

Risk averse A term describing an investor who prefers x to taking a risky bet with an expected value equal to x.

Risk management The active use of derivatives and other techniques to alter risk and protect profitability.

Risk neutral A term describing an investor who is indifferent between receiving x and taking a risky bet with an expected value equal to x.

Risk-neutral measure The probability distribution for an asset transformed so that the expected return on the asset is the risk-free rate.

Risk-neutral probability In the binomial model, the probability of an up move in the asset price such that the expected return on the asset is the risk-free rate.

Risk premium The difference between the expected return on an asset and the risk-free rate; the expected return differential that compensates investors for risk.

Schaetze German government bond issued with a maturity of 2 years.

Self-financing portfolio A portfolio that retains specified characteristics (e.g., it is zero-investment and risk-free) without the need for additional investments in the portfolio.

Settlement The time in a transaction at which all obligations of both the buyer and the seller are fulfilled.

Share-equivalent The position in shares that has equivalent dollar risk to a derivative. (See also *Delta*.)

Sharpe ratio For an asset, the ratio of the risk premium to the return standard deviation.

Short A position is short with respect to a price if the position profits from a decrease in that price. A short-seller of a stock profits from a decrease in the stock price and, hence, is short the stock. A seller of an option profits from a decrease in volatility and, hence, is short volatility.

Short-against-the-box The *short-sale* of a stock that the short-seller owns. The result of a short-against-the-box is that the short-seller has both a long and short position and, hence, bears no risk from the stock yet receives the value of the shares from the short-sale.

Short call A call that has been sold.

Short forward The party to a forward contract who has an obligation to sell the underlying asset.

Short put A put that has been sold.

Short rebate The rate of return paid on collateral when shares are borrowed.

Short-sale A transaction in which an investor borrows a security, sells it, and then returns it at a later date to the lender. If the security makes payments, the short-seller must make the same payments to the lender.

Skewness A measure of the symmetry of a probability distribution. For a random variable x with mean μ and standard deviation σ, skewness is the third central moment divided by the cubed standard deviation, $E(x - \mu)^3/\sigma^3$. For a normal variable, skewness is 0. (See also *Volatility skew*.)

Spark spread The difference between the price of electricity and that of the quantity of natural gas required to produce the electricity.

Spot curve The set of zero-coupon bond prices with different maturities, usually inferred from government bond prices.

Spot price The current market price of an asset.

Spread Simultaneously buying and selling closely related derivatives. A spread in options is a position in which some options are bought and some are sold, and all options in the position are calls or all are puts. (See also *Calendar spread* and *Commodity spread*.)

Spread option An option with a payoff where a spread (the difference between prices) takes the place of the underlying asset.

Stack and roll A hedging strategy in which an existing stack hedge with maturing futures contracts is replaced by a new stack hedge with longer dated futures contracts.

Stack hedge Hedging a stream of obligations by entering futures contracts with a *single* maturity, with the number of contracts selected so that changes in the *present value* of the future obligations are offset by changes in the value of this "stack" of futures contracts.

Static NPV The net present value of a project at a point in time, ignoring the possibility of postponing adoption of the project.

Stock index An average of the prices of a group of stocks. A stock index can be a simple average of stock prices, in which case it is *equally weighted*, or it can be a weighted average, with the weights proportional to market capitalization, in which case it is *value-weighted*.

Straddle The purchase of a call and a put with the same strike price and time to expiration.

Straddle rules Tax regulations controlling the circumstances in which a loss on a claim can be realized when a taxpayer continues to own related securities or derivatives.

Strangle The purchase of a put and a higher-strike call with the same time to expiration.

Strike price Another term for *exercise price*.

Strip hedge Hedging a stream of obligations by offsetting each individual obligation with a futures contract matching the maturity and quantity of the obligation.

STRIPS Acronym for "Separate Trading of Registered Interest and Principal of Securities." STRIPS are the interest and principal payments from Treasury bonds and notes traded as individual securities.

Structured note A bond that makes payments that, at least in part, are contingent on some variable such as a stock price, interest rates, or exchange rates.

Swap A contract calling for the exchange of payments over time. Often one payment is fixed in advance and the other is floating, based upon the realization of a price or interest rate.

Swap spread The difference between the fixed rate on an interest rate swap and the yield on a Treasury bond with the same maturity.

Swap tenor The lifetime of a swap.

Swap term Another name for *swap tenor*.

Swaption An option to enter into a *swap*.

Tailing A reduction in the quantity of an asset held in order to offset future income received by the asset.

Tenor Time to maturity or expiration of a contract, frequently used when referring to swaps.

Term repo A repurchase agreement lasting for a specified period of time longer than one day.

Term sheet A brief document summarizing the payments, dates, obligations, and contingencies associated with a financial transaction.

Theta The change in the value of a derivative due solely to the passage of time.

Time decay Another term for *theta*.

Total return swap A swap in which one party pays the total return (dividends plus capital gains) on a reference asset, and the other party pays a floating rate such as LIBOR.

Traded present value The value an investment project would have once the investment was made; also called *twin security*.

Twin security See *Traded present value*.

Underlying asset The asset whose price determines the profitability of a derivative. For example, the underlying asset for a purchased call is the asset that the call owner can buy by paying the strike price.

Unfunded A position that is not paid for at the outset, and for which cash inflows and outflows can later occur. A forward contract, for example, is an unfunded position in a stock. (See also *Funded*.)

Up-and-in A knock-in option for which the barrier exceeds the current price of the underlying asset.

Up-and-out A knock-out option for which the barrier exceeds the current price of the underlying asset.

Value at risk The level of loss that will be exceeded a given percentage of the time over a given horizon.

Vanilla A standard option or other derivative. For example, ordinary puts and calls are "vanilla" options.

Variance swap A forward contract that settles based on cumulative squared asset returns.

Vega The change in the price of a derivative due to a change in volatility. Also sometimes called *kappa* or *lambda*.

Vertical spread The sale of an option at one strike and purchase of an option of the same type (call or put) at a different strike, both having the same underlying asset and time to expiration.

Volatility The standard deviation of the continuously compounded return on an asset.

Volatility skew Generally, implied volatility as a function of the strike price. Volatility skew refers to a difference in premiums as reflected in differences in implied volatility. Skew is sometimes used more precisely to refer to a difference in implied volatilities between in-the-money and out-of-the-money options.

Volatility smile A volatility skew in which both in-the-money and out-of-the-money options have a higher volatility than at-the-money options (i.e., when you plot implied volatility against the strike price, the curve looks like a smile).

Volatility surface A three-dimensional graph in which volatility is plotted against strike price and time to maturity.

Volatility swap A forward contract that settles based on some measure of the standard deviation of returns on an asset.

Warrant An option issued by a firm with its own stock as the underlying asset. This term also refers more generally to an option issued in fixed supply.

Weather derivative A derivative contract with a payment based on a weather-related measurement, such as heating or cooling degree-days.

Written call option A call that has been sold; a *short call*.

Written put option A put that has been sold; a *short put*.

Written straddle The simultaneous sale of a call and sale of a put, with the same strike price and time to expiration.

Yield curve The set of yields to maturity for bonds with different times to maturity.

Yield to maturity The single discount factor for which the present value of a bond's payments is equal to the observed bond price.

Zero-cost collar The purchase of a put and sale of a call where the strikes are chosen so that the premiums of the two options are the same.

Zero-coupon bond A bond that makes only a single payment, at maturity.

Zero-coupon yield curve The set of yields to maturity for zero-coupon bonds with different times to maturity.

References

Acharya, V. V., John, K., and Sundaram, R. K., 2000, "On the Optimality of Resetting Executive Stock Options," *Journal of Financial Economics*, 57(1), 65–101.

Allayannis, G., Brown, G., and Klapper, L. F., 2003, "Capital Structure and Financial Risk: Evidence from Foreign Debt Use in East Asia," *Journal of Finance*, 58, 2667–2709.

Allayannis, G., Lel, U., and Miller, D., 2004, "Corporate Governance and the Hedging Premium Around the World," Working Paper, Darden School, University of Virginia.

Allayannis, G. and Weston, J., 2001, "The Use of Foreign Currency Derivatives and Firm Market Value," *Review of Financial Studies*, 14(1), 243–276.

Aristotle, 1948, *The Politics*, Clarendon Press, Oxford, UK, translated by Ernest Barker.

Arzac, E. R., 1997, "PERCs, DECs, and Other Mandatory Convertibles," *Journal of Applied Corporate Finance*, 10(1), 54–63.

Asquith, P., 1995, "Convertible Bonds Are Not Called Late," *Journal of Finance*, 50(4), 1275–1289.

Bartram, S. M., Brown, G. W., and Fehle, F. R., forthcoming, "International Evidence on Financial Derivatives Use," *Financial Management*.

Baubonis, C., Gastineau, G., and Purcell, D., 1993, "The Banker's Guide to Equity-Linked Certificates of Deposit," *Journal of Derivatives*, 1(2), 87–95.

Berk, J. and DeMarzo, P., 2007, *Corporate Finance*, Addison-Wesley/Pearson Education, Boston MA.

Bernstein, P. L., 1992, *Capital Ideas: The Improbable Origins of Modern Wall Street*, Free Press, New York.

Bernstein, P. L., 1996, *Against the Gods: The Remarkable Story of Risk*, John Wiley & Sons, New York.

Black, F., 1976, "The Pricing of Commodity Contracts," *Journal of Financial Economics*, 3(1/2), 167–179.

Black, F., 1989, "How We Came Up with the Option Pricing Formula," *Journal of Portfolio Management*, 15(2), 4–8.

Black, F. and Scholes, M., 1973, "The Pricing of Options and Corporate Liabilities," *Journal of Political Economy*, 81, 637–659.

Bodie, Z., Kaplan, R. S., and Merton, R. C., 2003, "For the Last Time: Stock Options Are an Expense," *Harvard Business Review*, 3–11.

Bodie, Z. and Rosansky, V. I., 1980, "In Commodity Futures," *Financial Analysts Journal*, 3–14.

Bodnar, G. M., Hayt, G. S., and Marston, R. C., 1998, "1998 Wharton Survey of Financial Risk Management by US Non-Financial Firms," *Financial Management*, 27(4), 70–91.

Brealey, R. and Myers, S., 2000, *Principles of Corporate Finance*, Irwin McGraw-Hill, Burr Ridge, IL, 6th edition.

Brealey, R., Myers, S., and Allen, F., 2006, *Principles of Corporate Finance*, Irwin McGraw-Hill, Burr Ridge, IL, 8th edition.

Brennan, M. and Schwartz, E., 1985, "Evaluating Natural Resource Investments," *Journal of Business*, 58, 135–157.

Brennan, M. J., 1991, "The Price of Convenience and the Evaluation of Commodity Contingent Claims," in D. Lund and B. Øksendal, (eds.) *Stochastic Models and Option Values: Applications to Resources, Environment and Investment Problems, Contributions to Economic Analysis*, pp. 33–71, North-Holland, Amsterdam.

Brennan, M. J., 2000, "Real Options: Development and New Contributions," in Brennan and Trigeorgis (2000), chapter 1, pp. 1–10.

Brennan, M. J. and Schwartz, E. S., 1977, "Convertible Bonds: Valuation and Optimal Strategies for Call and Conversion," *Journal of Finance*, 32(5), 1699–1715.

Brennan, M. J. and Schwartz, E. S., 1990, "Arbitrage in Stock Index Futures," *Journal of Business*, 63(1), S7–31.

Brennan, M. J. and Trigeorgis, L., (eds.) 2000, *Project Flexibility, Agency, and Competition: New Developments in the Theory and Application of Real Options*, Oxford University Press, London.

Brown, G. W., 2001, "Managing Foreign Exchange Risk with Derivatives," *Journal of Financial Economics*, 60(2–3), 401–448.

Brown, G. W., Crabb, P. R., and Haushalter, D., 2006, "Are Firms Successful at Selectively Hedging?" *Journal of Business*, 79(6), 2925–2949.

Burghardt, G. and Hoskins, W., 1995, "The Convexity Bias in Eurodollar Futures," *Risk*, 8(3), 63–70.

Carter, D., Rogers, D., and Simkins, B., 2004, "Fuel Hedging in the Airline Industry: The Case of Southwest Airlines," Unpublished, SSRN ID 578663.

Chance, D. M., Kumar, R., and Todd, R. B., 2000, "The 'Repricing' of Executive Stock Options," *Journal of Financial Economics*, 57(1), 129–154.

Chicago Board of Trade, 1998, *Commodity Trading Manual*, Chicago Board of Trade.

Chicago Board Options Exchange, 2003, *VIX: CBOE Volatility Index*, Technical report, Chicago Board Options Exchange.

Collin-Dufresne, P. and Solnik, B., 2001, "On the Term Structure of Default Premia in the Swap and LIBOR Markets," *Journal of Finance*, 56(3), 1095–1115.

Constantinides, G. M., 1984, "Warrant Exercise and Bond Conversion in Competitive Markets," *Journal of Financial Economics*, 13(3), 371–397.

Cooper, L., 2000, "Caution Reigns," *Risk*, 13(6), 12–14, South Africa Special Report.

Cornell, B. and French, K. R., 1983, "Taxes and the Pricing of Stock Index Futures," *Journal of Finance*, 38(3), 675–694.

Cornell, B. and Shapiro, A. C., 1989, "The Mispricing of US Treasury Bonds: A Case Study," *Review of Financial Studies*, 2(3), 297–310.

Cox, J. C., Ingersoll, J. E., Jr., and Ross, S. A., 1981, "The Relation Between Forward Prices and Futures Prices," *Journal of Financial Economics*, 9(4), 321–346.

Cox, J. C., Ross, S. A., and Rubinstein, M., 1979, "Option Pricing: A Simplified Approach," *Journal of Financial Economics*, 7(3), 229–263.

Cox, J. C. and Rubinstein, M., 1985, *Options Markets*, Prentice Hall, Englewood Cliffs, NJ.

Crabbe, L. E. and Argilagos, J. D., 1994, "Anatomy of the Structured Note Market," *Journal of Applied Corporate Finance*, 7(3), 85–98.

Credit Suisse Financial Products, 1997, *CreditRisk+*, Technical report, Credit Suisse First Boston, London.

Culp, C. L. and Miller, M. H., 1995, "Metallgesellschaft and the Economics of Synthetic Storage," *Journal of Applied Corporate Finance*, 7(4), 62–76.

Dixit, A. K. and Pindyck, R. S., 1994, *Investment Under Uncertainty*, Princeton University Press, Princeton, NJ.

Duffie, D., 1999, "Credit Swap Valuation," *Financial Analysts Journal*, 55(1), 73–87.

Duffie, D. and Yurday, E. C., 2004, *TRAC-X: Emergence of Default Swap Index Products*, Case F-268, Stanford Graduate School of Business.

Edwards, F. R. and Canter, M. S., 1995, "The Collapse of Metallgesellschaft: Unhedgeable Risks, Poor Hedging Strategy, or Just Bad Luck?" *Journal of Applied Corporate Finance*, 8(1), 86–105.

Edwards, F. R. and Ma, C. W., 1992, *Futures and Options*, McGraw-Hill, New York.

Emanuel, D. C., 1983, "Warrant Valuation and Exercise Strategy," *Journal of Financial Economics*, 12(2), 211–235.

Fama, E. F., 1977, "Risk-adjusted Discount Rates and Capital Budgeting Under Uncertainty," *Journal of Financial Economics*, 5(1), 3–24.

Faulkender, M., 2005, "Hedging or Market Timing? Selecting the Interest Rate Exposure of Corporate Debt," *Journal of Finance*, 60(2), 931–962.

Fleming, I., 1997, *Goldfinger*, Fine Communications, New York.

Fleming, M. J. and Garbade, K. D., 2002, "When the Back Office Moved to the Front Burner: Settlement Fails in the Treasury Market After 9/11," *FRBNY Economic Policy Review*, 8(2), 35–57.

Fleming, M. J. and Garbade, K. D., 2003, "The Repurchase Agreement Refined: GCF Repo," *Current Issues in Economics and Finance*, 9(6), 1–7.

Fleming, M. J. and Garbade, K. D., 2004, "Repurchase Agreements with Negative Interest Rates," *Current Issues in Economics and Finance*, 10(5), 1–7.

Forster, D. M., 1996, "The State of the Law After *Procter & Gamble v. Banker's Trust*," *Derivatives Quarterly*, 3(2), 8–17.

French, K. R., 1983, "A Comparison of Futures and Forward Prices," *Journal of Financial Economics*, 12(3), 311–342.

Froot, K., Scharfstein, D., and Stein, J., 1994, "A Framework for Risk Management," *Journal of Applied Corporate Finance*, 7(3), 22–32.

Fuller, K. P., 2003, "Why Some Firms Use Collar Offers in Mergers," *Financial Review*, 38(1), 127–150.

Galai, D. and Masulis, R. W., 1976, "The Option Pricing Model and the Risk Factor of Stock," *Journal of Financial Economics*, 3(1/2), 53–81.

Garman, M. B. and Kohlhagen, S. W., 1983, "Foreign Currency Option Values," *Journal of International Money and Finance*, 2(3), 231–237.

Gastineau, G. L., Smith, D. J., and Todd, R., 2001, *Risk Management, Derivatives, and Financial Analysis Under SFAS No. 133*, Research Foundation of AIMR and Blackwell Series in Finance.

Géczy, C., Minton, B. A., and Schrand, C., 1997, "Why Firms Use Currency Derivatives," *Journal of Finance*, 52(4), 1323–1354.

Goodman, L. S. and Fabozzi, F. J., 2002, *Collateralized Debt Obligations: Structures and Analysis*, Wiley, New York.

Gorton, G. and Rouwenhorst, K. G., 2004, "Facts and Fantasies About Commodity Futures," NBER Working Paper 10595.

Graham, J. R. and Rogers, D. A., 2002, "Do Firms Hedge in Response to Tax Incentives?" *Journal of Finance*, 57, 815–839.

Grenadier, S. R., 1996, "The Strategic Exercise of Options: Development Cascades and Overbuilding in Real Estate Markets," *Journal of Finance*, 51(5), 1653–1679.

Grenadier, S. R., 1999, "Information Revelation Through Option Exercise," *Review of Financial Studies*, 12(1), 95–129.

Grinblatt, M. and Longstaff, F. A., 2000, "Financial Innovation and the Role of Derivative Securities: An Empirical Analysis of the Treasury STRIPS Program," *Journal of Finance*, 55(3), 1415–1436.

Grossman, S. J. and Stiglitz, J. E., 1980, "On the Impossibility of Informationally Efficient Markets," *American Economic Review*, 70(3), 393–408.

Guay, W. and Kothari, S. P., 2003, "How Much Do Firms Hedge with Derivatives?" *Journal of Financial Economics*, 70, 423–462.

Güntay, L., Prabhala, N., and Unal, H., 2004, "Callable Bonds, Interest Rate Risk, and the Supply Side of Hedging," Working Paper, University of Maryland, Smith School of Business.

Gupta, A. and Subrahmanyam, M. G., 2000, "An Empirical Examination of the Convexity Bias in the Pricing of Interest Rate Swaps," *Journal of Financial Economics*, 55(2), 239–279.

Harris, M. and Raviv, A., 1985, "A Sequential Signalling Model of Convertible Debt Call Policy," *Journal of Finance*, 40(5), 1263–1281.

Haug, E. G., 1998, *The Complete Guide to Option Pricing Formulas*, McGraw-Hill, New York.

Haushalter, G. D., 2000, "Financing Policy, Basis Risk, and Corporate Hedging: Evidence from Oil and Gas Producers," *Journal of Finance*, 55(1), 107–152.

Hodder, J. E., Mello, A. S., and Sick, G. S., 2001, "Valuing Real Options: Can Risk-Adjusted Discounting Be Made to Work?" *Journal of Applied Corporate Finance*, 14(2), 90–101.

Horwitz, D. L., 1996, "*P&G v. Banker's Trust*: What's All the Fuss?" *Derivatives Quarterly*, 3(2), 18–23.

Hu, H. T. C. and Black, B., 2006, "Empty Voting and Hidden (Morphable) Ownership: Taxonomy, Implications, and Reforms," *Southern California Law Review*, 79(4), 811–908.

Huddart, S., 1998, "Patterns of Stock Option Exercise in the United States," in J. Carpenter and D. Yermack, (eds.) *Executive Compensation and Shareholder Value*, chapter 8, pp. 115–142, Kluwer Academic Publishers, Norwell, MA.

Ingersoll, J. E., Jr., 1977, "A Contingent-Claims Valuation of Convertible Securities," *Journal of Financial Economics*, 4(3), 289–322.

J. P. Morgan, 1997, *CreditMetrics–Technical Document*, Technical report, J. P. Morgan & Co., New York.

Jagolinzer, A. D., Matsunaga, S. R., and Yeung, E., 2007, "An Analysis of Insiders' Use of Prepaid Variable Forward Transactions," *jar*, 45(5), 1055–1079.

Jarrow, R. A. and Oldfield, G. S., 1981, "Forward Contracts and Futures Contracts," *Journal of Financial Economics*, 9(4), 373–382.

Jarrow, R. A. and Rudd, A., 1983, *Option Pricing*, Richard D. Irwin, Homewood, IL.

Johnson, S. A. and Tian, Y. S., 2000a, "Indexed Executive Stock Options," *Journal of Financial Economics*, 57(1), 35–64.

Johnson, S. A. and Tian, Y. S., 2000b, "The Value and Incentive Effects of Nontraditional Executive Stock Option Plans," *Journal of Financial Economics*, 57(1), 3–34.

Jorion, P., 1995, *Big Bets Gone Bad: Derivatives and Bankruptcy in Orange County*, Academic Press, San Diego, CA.

Kealhofer, S., 2003a, "Quantifying Credit Risk I: Default Prediction," *Financial Analysts Journal*, 59(1), 30–44.

Kealhofer, S., 2003b, "Quantifying Credit Risk II: Default Prediction," *Financial Analysts Journal*, 59(3), 78–92.

Kulatilaka, N. and Marcus, A. J., 1994, "Valuing Employee Stock Options," *Financial Analysts Journal*, 50, 46–56.

Lewis, M., 1989, *Liar's Poker*, Penguin, New York.

Litzenberger, R. H., 1992, "Swaps: Plain and Fanciful," *Journal of Finance*, 47(3), 831–850.

Lowenstein, R., 2000, *When Genius Failed: The Rise and Fall of Long-Term Capital Management*, Random House, New York.

Lucas, D. J., (ed.) forthcoming, *Measuring and Managing Federal Financial Risk*, University of Chicago Press.

Macaulay, F. R., 1938, *The Movement of Interest Rates, Bond Yields and Stock Prices in the United States Since 1856*, National Bureau of Economic Research.

Maor, E., 1998, *e: The Story of a Number*, Princeton University Press, Princeton, NJ.

McConnell, J. J. and Schwartz, E. S., 1992, "The Origin of LYONs: A Case Study in Financial Innovation," *Journal of Applied Corporate Finance*, 4(4), 40–47.

McDonald, R. L., 2000, "Real Options and Rules of Thumb in Capital Budgeting," in Brennan and Trigeorgis (2000), chapter 2, pp. 13–33.

McDonald, R. L., 2003, "Is It Optimal to Accelerate the Payment of Income Tax on Share-Based Compensation?" Unpublished, Northwestern University.

McDonald, R. L., 2004, "The Tax (Dis)Advantage of a Firm Issuing Options on Its Own Stock," *Journal of Public Economics*, 88(5), 925–955.

McDonald, R. L., 2006a, *Derivatives Markets*, Addison-Wesley, Boston, MA, 2nd edition.

McDonald, R. L., 2006b, "The Role of Real Options in Capital Budgeting: Theory and Practice," *Journal of Applied Corporate Finance*, 18(2), 28–39.

McDonald, R. L. and Siegel, D., 1986, "The Value of Waiting to Invest," *Quarterly Journal of Economics*, 101(4), 707–727.

McDonald, R. L. and Siegel, D. R., 1985, "Investment and the Valuation of Firms When There Is an Option to Shut Down," *International Economic Review*, 26(2), 331–349.

McMillan, L. G., 1992, *Options As a Strategic Investment*, New York Institute of Finance, New York, 3rd edition.

Mello, A. S. and Parsons, J. E., 1995, "Maturity Structure of a Hedge Matters: Lessons from the Metallgesellschaft Debacle," *Journal of Applied Corporate Finance*, 8(1), 106–120.

Merton, R. C., 1973a, "The Relationship Between Put and Call Option Prices: Comment," *Journal of Finance*, 28(1), 183–184.

Merton, R. C., 1973b, "Theory of Rational Option Pricing," *Bell Journal of Economics and Management Science*, 4(1), 141–183.

Merton, R. C., 1974, "On the Pricing of Corporate Debt: The Risk Structure of Interest Rates," *Journal of Finance*, 29(2), 449–470.

Merton, R. C., 1977, "On the Pricing of Contingent Claims and the Modigliani-Miller Theorem," *Journal of Financial Economics*, 5(2), 241–249.

Merton, R. C., 1999, "Finance Theory and Future Trends: The Shift to Integration," *Risk*, 11(7), 48–51.

Miller, M. H., 1986, "Financial Innovation: The Last Twenty Years and the Next," *Journal of Financial and Quantitative Analysis*, 21(4), 459–471.

Mitchell, M. and Pulvino, T., 2001, "Characteristics of Risk and Return in Risk Arbitrage," *Journal of Finance*.

Modest, D. M. and Sundaresan, M., 1983, "The Relationship Between Spot and Futures Prices in Stock Index Futures Markets: Some Preliminary Evidence," *Journal of Futures Markets*, 3(1), 15–41.

Modigliani, F. and Miller, M., 1958, "The Cost of Capital, Corporation Finance, and the Theory of Investment," *American Economic Review*, 48(3), 261–297.

Mood, A. M., Graybill, F. A., and Boes, D. C., 1974, *Introduction to the Theory of Statistics*, McGraw-Hill, New York, 3rd edition.

Myers, S. C., 1977, "Determinants of Corporate Borrowing," *Journal of Financial Economics*, 5(2), 147–175.

Myers, S. C. and Turnbull, S. M., 1977, "Capital Budgeting and the Capital Asset Pricing Model: Good News and Bad News," *Journal of Finance*, 32(2), 321–333.

Paddock, J. L., Siegel, D. R., and Smith, J. L., 1988, "Option Valuation of Claims on Real Assets: The Case of Offshore Petroleum Leases," *Quarterly Journal of Economics*, 103(3), 479–508.

Petersen, M. A. and Thiagarajan, S. R., 2000, "Risk Measurement and Hedging: With and Without Derivatives," *Financial Management*, 29(4), 5–29.

Pindyck, R. S., 1993a, "Investments of Uncertain Cost," *Journal of Financial Economics*, 34(1), 53–76.

Pindyck, R. S., 1993b, "The Present Value Model of Rational Commodity Pricing," *The Economic Journal*, 103(418), 511–530.

Pindyck, R. S., 1994, "Inventories and the Short-Run Dynamics of Commodity Prices," *Rand Journal of Economics*, 25(1), 141–159.

Reinganum, M. R., 1986, "Is Time Travel Impossible? A Financial Proof," *Journal of Portfolio Management*, 13(1), 10–12.

Rendleman, R. J., Jr. and Bartter, B. J., 1979, "Two-State Option Pricing," *Journal of Finance*, 34(5), 1093–1110.

Richard, S. F. and Sundaresan, M., 1981, "A Continuous Time Equilibrium Model of Forward Prices and Futures Prices in a Multigood Economy," *Journal of Financial Economics*, 9(4), 347–371.

Ronn, A. G. and Ronn, E. I., 1989, "The Box Spread Arbitrage Conditions: Theory, Tests, and Investment Strategies," *Review of Financial Studies*, 2(1), 91–108.

Routledge, B. R., Seppi, D. J., and Spatt, C. S., 2000, "Equilibrium Forward Curves for Commodities," *Journal of Finance*, 55(3), 1297–1338.

Saly, P. J., Jagannathan, R., and Huddart, S. J., 1999, "Valuing the Reload Features of Executive Stock Options," *Accounting Horizons*, 13(3), 219–240.

Schwartz, E. S., 1997, "The Stochastic Behavior of Commodity Prices: Implications for Valuation and Hedging," *Journal of Finance*, 52(3), 923–973.

Schwartz, E. S. and Moon, M., 2000, "Rational Valuation of Internet Companies," *Financial Analysts Journal*, 56(3), 62–75.

Sharpe, W. F., 1976, "Corporate Pension Funding Policy," *Journal of Financial Economics*, 3(3), 183–193.

Sharpe, W. F., 1978, *Investments*, Prentice Hall, Englewood Cliffs, NJ.

Shiller, R. J., 2003, *The New Financial Order: Risk in the 21st Century*, Princeton University Press, Princeton, NJ.

Siegel, D. and Siegel, D., 1990, *Futures Markets*, Dryden Press, Chicago.

Smith, C. W. and Stulz, R. M., 1985, "The Determinants of Firms' Hedging Policies," *Journal of Financial and Quantitative Analysis*, 20(4), 391–405.

Smith, D., 2002, "Two Common Textbook Misstatements About Bond Prices and Yields," Unpublished, Boston University School of Management.

Smith, D. J., 1997, "Aggressive Corporate Finance: A Close Look at the Procter & Gamble–Bankers Trust Leveraged Swap," *Journal of Derivatives*, 4(4), 67–79.

Spatt, C. S. and Sterbenz, F. P., 1988, "Warrant Exercise, Dividends, and Reinvestment Policy," *Journal of Finance*, 43(2), 493–506.

Srivastava, S., 1999, "Value at Risk Analysis of a Leveraged Swap," *Journal of Risk*, 1(2).

Stein, J. C., 1992, "Convertible Bonds As Backdoor Equity Financing," *Journal of Financial Economics*, 32(1), 3–21.

Steiner, R., 1997, *Mastering Repo Markets*, FT Market Editions, Pitman Publishing, London.

Stigum, M., 1990, *The Money Market*, McGraw-Hill, New York, 3rd edition.

Stigum, M. and Robinson, F. L., 1996, *Money Market & Bond Calculations*, Richard D. Irwin, Inc., Chicago.

Stoll, H. R., 1969, "The Relationship Between Put and Call Option Prices," *Journal of Finance*, 24(5), 801–824.

Stoll, H. R., 1973, "The Relationship Between Put and Call Option Prices: Reply," *Journal of Finance*, 28(1), 185–187.

Sundaresan, S., 2002, *Fixed Income Markets and Their Derivatives*, South-Western, Cincinnati, OH.

Tavakoli, J. M., 1998, *Credit Derivatives: A Guide to Instruments and Applications*, Wiley, New York.

Tavakoli, J. M., 2001, *Credit Derivatives & Synthetic Structures: A Guide to Instruments and Applications*, Wiley, New York, 2nd edition.

Titman, S., 1985, "Urban Land Prices Under Uncertainty," *American Economic Review*, 75(3), 505–514.

Triantis, A., 2005, "Realizing the Potential of Real Options: Does Theory Meet Practice?" *Journal of Applied Corporate Finance*, 17(2), 8–16.

Triantis, A. and Borison, A., 2001, "Real Options: State of the Practice," *Journal of Applied Corporate Finance*, 14(2), 8–24.

Trigeorgis, L., 1996, *Real Options: Managerial Flexibility and Strategy in Resource Allocation*, MIT Press, Cambridge, MA.

Tsiveriotis, K. and Fernandes, C., 1998, "Valuing Convertible Bonds with Credit Risk," *Journal of Fixed Income*, 8(2), 95–102.

Tuckman, B., 1995, *Fixed Income Securities*, Wiley, New York.

Tufano, P., 1996, "Who Manages Risk? An Empirical Analysis of Risk Management Practices in the Gold Mining Industry," *Journal of Finance*, 51(4), 1097–1138.

Tufano, P., 1998, "The Determinants of Stock Price Exposure: Financial Engineering and the Gold Mining Industry," *Journal of Finance*, 53(3), 1015–1052.

Turnbull, S. M., 1987, "Swaps: Zero Sum Game?" *Financial Management*, 16(1), 15–21.

Zwick, S. and Collins, D. P., 2004, "One Year In and the Jury Is Still Out," *Futures*, 33(1), 66.

Index

Main entries in **bold** indicate words that can be found in the Glossary. Page numbers with an 'n' refer to footnotes. Page numbers with an 'r' are found in the References section.

ABX index, 374, 378
Accreting swaps, 235
Accrued interest, 216
Acharya, V. V., 417, 473r
Acquisitions
   collars in, 412–416
   offer types, 413, 414
Adverse selection, 100
Allayannis, G., 107, 119, 473r
Allen, F., 474r
Allen, P., 364
Alpha-porting, 147
Amaranth Advisors, 172
American options, 40, 250
   on currency, 298
   early exercise of, 260, 262–264
   European options versus, 260–261
   on stock index, 296
   time to expiration, 264–265
Amortizing swaps, 235
Analogy, pricing prepaid forward by, 127
Anderson, J., 172
Apple SPARQS, 360
Arbitrage, 70
   cash-and-carry, 136
   covered interest, 159–160

   pricing prepaid forward by, 128–129
   pro forma calculation, 136n
   quasi, 137
Arbitrage CDO, 370
Argilagos, J. D., 379, 475r
Aristotle, 6, 7, 473r
Arzac, E. R., 379, 473r
Ashanti Goldfields, 366n
Asian options, 363–364
   arithmetic, 364
   participation rate, 364
   value, 363
Ask price, 17
Ask yields, 216
Asquith, P., 417, 473r
Asset allocation, 146–147
Assets
   elasticity, 388
   lease rate, 21–22
   real, 423
   underlying, 29
Asset swaps, 229
Asymmetric butterfly spreads, 267
At-the-money options, 51
   calls, 252
   time to expiration, 323

Averages
  financial markets and, 11–12
  weighted, 329

Back-to-back transactions, 224
Backwardation, 168
Balance sheet CDO, 370
Ballmer, S., 404
Bankruptcy, 104
Barrier options, 363
Barriers, 363
Bartram, S. M., 107, 118, 473r
Bartter, B. J., 278, 301, 478r
Basis points, 198
Basis risk, 114–117, 118
  examples, 114–117
  hedge, 148n
Baubonis, C., 87n, 362, 379, 473r
Bear spreads, 74
Berk, J., 105n, 473r
Bermudan options, 40
Bernstein, P. L., 23, 473r
Beta
  index futures and, 148
  specification, 427n
Bid-ask spread, 18, 22
  example, 18
  unreasonable, 18n
Bid price, 17
Binomial formula, 283
Binomial models
  alternative, 307–308
  lognormality and, 304–307
  probabilities assignment, 305
  use of, 301
Binomial option pricing, 277–308
  American options and, 294–295
  on currencies, 297
  for different numbers of binomial steps, 311
  with dividends, 283–285
  for European put option, 293
  formula, 301
  on futures contracts, 297–299
  mispriced option arbitrage, 282–283

  one-period binomial tree and, 277–288
  options on other assets, 295
  put options and, 293–294
  risk-neutral, 285
  on stock index, 295–296
Binomial trees
  constructing, 286–287
  Cox-Ross-Rubinstein, 287, 307
  European call option, 289–291, 292
  example, 287–288
  forward, 287
  forward price computation with, 285
  interpretation, 280
  Jarrow-Rudd, 308
  lattice, 290n
  lognormal distribution approximation, 304
  multiple periods, 291–292
  node option price, 299
  nonrecombining, 290
  one-period, 277–288
  option on currency, 298
  option on futures contract, 300
  option on stock index, 296
  recombining, 290
  solution, 280–282
  two periods, 288–291
  uncertainty, 286
  working backward through, 290
Black, B., 243, 476r
Black, F., 152, 309, 310, 334, 342, 383, 417, 473r
Black formula, 119n, 316–317
Black-Scholes analysis, 313
Black-Scholes formula, 42n, 48n, 96n, 309–345
  applying to assets, 314–317
  assumptions, 314
  call options, 310–313
  call price computation, 312
  cumulative normal distribution function, 311, 312
  history, 310
  inputs, 310–311, 341, 342
  introduction to, 309–314
  option prices from, 119
  options on currencies, 316
  options on futures, 316–317

options on stocks with discrete dividends, 315–316
　　in peak-load manufacturing, 445
　　perpetual call, 441
　　prepaid forward prices, 315
　　put-call parity and, 313
　　put options, 313
　　put price computation, 313n
　　in valuing bond convertible, 395
　　in valuing insurance contracts, 387
　　valuing warrants with, 394
Black-Scholes model, 277
　　adaptation, 314
　　compensation option early exercise, 408
　　implied volatility, 336–339
　　performance assessment, 337
　　in valuing payoffs, 385
　　volatility, 335–341
Black-Scholes prices, 79n, 258n, 318
Bobls, 10n
Bodie, Z., 166n, 178, 409, 473r
Bodnar, G. M., 107, 118, 474r
Boes, D. C., 478r
Bondholders, 392
Bond markets, 6
Bond price
　　change, 198
　　clean, 216
　　conventions, 215–216
　　dirty, 216
　　graph slope, 203–204
　　Macaulay duration and, 200
　　sensitivity, 199, 200
Bonds
　　accrued interest, 216
　　basics, 183–192
　　callable, 397–401
　　catastrophe, 13
　　cheapest to deliver, 204
　　commodity-linked, 355–357
　　convertible, 359, 394–397
　　convexity, 198, 202–204
　　coupon, 188–189, 351–352
　　coupon payments, 215n
　　currency-linked, 357–358

　　defaultable, 388
　　duration, 198–201
　　duration matching, 201–202
　　equity-linked, 352–355
　　fixed-rate, 229
　　floating-rate, 229, 231
　　German government, 10n
　　implied forward rates, 186–188
　　off-the-run, 185
　　on-the-run, 185
　　options on, 254–255
　　par, 188–189
　　position values comparison, 203
　　prepaid forward, 254
　　price participation, 359
　　price value of a basis point (PVBP), 198
　　pricing formulas, 216
　　pure-discount, 255
　　Treasury, 204–207
　　valuation based on stock price, 401
　　yields, 215
　　zero-coupon, 36–38, 64, 185–186, 209, 351
Bootstrapping, 289
Borison, A., 448
Box spreads, 74–75
Brealey, R., 105n, 433n, 474r
Brennan, M. J., 152, 178, 397n, 417, 438n, 448, 474r
Brown, G., 118, 119, 473r, 474r
BSCall spreadsheet function, 42n, 332n
Bubills, 10n
Bull spreads, 73–74
　　bond plus, 360
　　Greeks for, 326
　　profit diagram, 75
　　as vertical spreads, 73
Bunds, 10n
Burghardt, G., 233n, 244, 474r
Butterfly spreads, 82–84
　　creation methods, 84
　　iron, 84n
Buyers, risk management perspective, 100–103
Buying
　　methods, 18–19
　　options, 41

Buying *(continued)*
    short-selling versus, 21
    stock, alternative methods, 125–126

Callable bonds, 397–401. *See also* Bonds
    binomial valuation, 399, 400
    callability, 398
    call schedule, 398
    convertible, 400–401
    nonconvertible, 398–400
    value, 397
Call options, 39–46, 257. *See also* Options
    at-the-money, 252
    barrier, 363
    Black-Scholes formula for, 310–313
    covered, 360
    delta, 318, 319
    dollar-denominated, 258
    elasticity, 327
    European, 261
    exercising prior to dividend, 263
    gamma, 319, 320
    hedging with, 101–103
    as insurance, 56
    as insured position, 44
    on non-dividend-paying stock, 262–263
    perpetual, 440–442
    premium, 40, 254
    profit, 252
    psi, 325
    purchased, 42–44
    rho, 324
    Sharpe ratio, 329
    summary, 57
    theta, 323
    two-period European, 289–291
    vega, 321
    written, 42–44
CallPerpetual formula, 440–442
Call protection, 398
Call schedule, 398
Canter, M. S., 118, 119, 475r
Capital Asset Pricing Model (CAPM), 147, 150
Capped participation, 364

Caps, 65
Carruthers, D., 14
Carry, 161
Carter, D., 116, 119, 474r
Cash-and-carry, 135
    reverse, 136
    transactions and cash flows for, 135
Cash-and-carry arbitrage, 136
Cash flow CDO, 370
Cash flows
    for cash-and-carry, 135
    certainty equivalent, 451
    credit default swaps (CDSs), 376
    discounted, 423, 424–433
    distribution of, 104
    one-period, 424–428
    for outright stock purchase, 251
    reverse cash-and-carry, 136
    short-selling, 22
    for synthetic stock purchase, 251
    total return swaps, 242, 243
Cash interest, commodity-linked bonds, 355–356
Cash settlement, 38
Catastrophe bonds, 13
CBOE variance futures contract, 340–341
CDOs. *See* Collateralized debt obligations
CDs
    alternative structures, 363–364
    defined, 84n
    economics of, 85–86
    equity-linked, 84–87, 361–362
    graphing payoff on, 85
    as interest-bearing bank account, 84n
CDS indexes, 376–378
    ABX, 378
    CDX, 377–378
    defined, 376
    funded/unfunded, 377
    replication, 377
    TRAC-X, 377
CDSs. *See* Credit default swaps
CDX, 377–378
Certainty equivalent cash flow, 451
Chance, D. M., 417, 474r

Characteristics and Risks of Standardized Options, 57
Cheapest to deliver, 204
Chicago Board of Trade (CBT), 9, 10
Chicago Board Options Exchange (CBOE), 10, 340–341
Chicago Mercantile Exchange (CME), 6
    futures contracts, 9, 10
        housing futures index contract specifications, 176
Clean price, 216
Clearinghouses, 139
Clearing members, 140
Clearing trades, 3
Clinton, Hillary, 20
Coleman, N., 172
Collared stocks, 76
Collars, 76–79
    in acquisitions, 412–416
    cost of, 79
    fixed offer, 413
    floating offer, 413
    forward price and, 79
    420–440, 109
    purchased, 77
    understanding, 78–79
    zero-cost, 77–78, 109–112
Collar width, 76
Collateral, posting, 3n, 3
Collateralized debt obligations (**CDOs**), 370–373
    arbitrage, 370
    balance sheet, 370
    cash flow, 370
    claims, 370
    with correlated defaults, 372–373
    with independent defaults, 370–372
    managed, 370
    market value, 370
    nth to default baskets, 373
    pricing, 371, 372, 373
    static, 370
    structure, 371
    subprime crisis and, 374
    tranched, 370, 372
Collin-Dufresne, P., 233n, 474r
Collins, D. P., 141, 480r

Combined position, 62
Commitments
    binding, 247
    firm, 249
Commodities
    complexity, 178
    expected price, 166
    financial assets versus, 164
    lease rate, 166–168, 178
Commodity extraction, 438–442
    delay, 439
    land value and appreciation, 440
    optimal, 439–440
    option pricing formula, 440–442
Commodity futures, 164–168
    price formula, 166
    seasonality and storage costs, 164–166
Commodity Futures Trading Commission, 14
Commodity-linked bonds, 355–357
    cash interest, 355–356
    interest in-kind, 356
    perpetuities, 356–357
    zero-coupon, 355
Commodity swaps, 220–227
    counterparty, 223–224
    financial settlement, 221–222
    market value, 225–227
    physical settlement, 221–222
    price, 222–223
Commodity swaption, 240
Compensation options, 403–412
    company treatment, 404–405
    early exercise, 408
    exercise behavior, 408n
    exercise of, 263n
    Google and, 406, 407
    inputs, 406–409
    Level 3 Communications, 409–412
    Microsoft and, 404
    use of, 404
    valuation, 406
Connors, John, 404
Constantinides, G. M., 417, 474r
Constant maturity Treasury (CMT) rate, 236

Contango, 168
Continuous compounding, 440, 455–459
Continuous dividends, 130–131, 132–133
Continuously compounded rate, 192n, 455
   increase/decrease symmetry, 458
   of return, 457, 458
Continuously compounded yields, 191–192
Control variables, 424n
Convenience yield, 167
Conversion, 253
Conversion premium, 397
Convertible bonds, 394–397
   Black-Scholes formula and, 395
   callable, 400–401
   conversion, 395
   conversion premium, 397
   defined, 359n
   maturity payoffs, 396
   payoff, 395
   valuation of, 397
Convex, 320
Convexity, 198, 202–204
   example, 203
   formula, 202
Cooling degree-day, 174
Cooper, L., 366n
Corn, forward curve, 165
Cornell, B., 152, 208, 474r
Corporate finance theory, 402n
Correlation coefficient, 150
Cost of carry, 139
Counterparties, 101
Coupon bonds, 188–189
   engineered, 352
   infinitely-lived, 356–357
   with options, 358–359
   paying cash, 351–352
   price participation, 359
Coupon rate, 189, 190–191
Covered calls, 67–68, 360
   payoff diagram, 68
   profit diagram, 68
   selling, 71
   writing, 72

Covered interest arbitrage, 159–160
Covered puts, 68. *See also* Put options
   payoff diagram, 69
   profit diagram, 69
Covered writing, 66
Cox, J. C., 152, 260n, 271, 278, 301, 342, 474r, 475r
Cox-Ross-Rubinstein tree, 287, 307
Crabb, P. R., 474r
Crabbe, L. E., 379, 475r
Cracking, 173
Crack spread, 173
Credit default swaps (CDSs), 243, 373–376
   buyers, 373
   cash flows, 376
   premium, 387
   protection buyer, 374
   reference assist, 375
   swap writer, 374
Credit derivatives, 16
Credit guarantees
   government, 387
   valuing, 386–388
Credit risk, 38–39
Credit spread, 376
Credit structures, 369–378, 379
   CDOs, 370–373
   CDS indices, 370, 376–378
   CDSs, 370, 373–376
   types of, 370
Cross-hedging, 147–150
   with imperfect correlation, 148–150
   with perfect correlation, 147–148
Crude oil
   hedging jet fuel with, 115, 116
   NYMEX contract specifications, 172
   NYMEX listing, 170
   processing, 173
   producer price index, 8
   refinement, 173
   swap, 220–227
Culp, C. L., 118, 119, 475r
Cumulative normal distribution function, 311, 312
Currencies
   options on, 254, 297, 316

Index   487

prepaid forward price on, 316
transaction expression, 159
Currency contracts, 157–160
   covered interest arbitrage, 159–160
   forward, 159
   listings, 158
   prepaid forward, 157–158
Currency-linked bonds, 357–358. *See also* Bonds
   coupon payments discount, 358
   currency formula, 358
Currency options, 258–259
   dollar-dominated, 258
   euro-dominated, 258
Currency swaps, 235–240. *See also* Swaps
   diff, 239–240
   formulas, 238–239
   market-maker net exposure, 237
Currency swaption, 241

DAX, 7
DCF valuation, 425, 437, 532–533. *See also* Discounted cash flow
   assumptions, 437
   multi-period, 435
   risk-neutral, 427–428, 431, 432
   standard, 430–431, 432
Dealers, purchased option price, 100n
Debenture, 384n
Debt. *See also* Equity
   defaultable, 386
   delta of, 389
   elasticity, 388
   equity conflicts, 390–392
   expected return on, 388–392
   junior, 393
   multiple issues, 392–393
   option-based model, 392
   as options, 383–386
   tranches, 393
   value at maturity, 385
   value at time, 384
   yield to maturity on, 386
Debt capacity, 105
Debt Exchangeable for Common Stock (DECS), 360

Debt holders, 392
Debt-to-asset ratio, 391
Debt-to-value ratio, 386
Defaultable bonds, 388
Default-free interest rates, 184
Default swaps, 243
Deferred swaps, 232–233
Delivery, 38
Delta, 279, 318–319. *See also* Greeks
   call, 318, 319
   of debt and equity, 389
   defined, 317
   interpretation, 298n
   market-makers' use, 342
   put, 319
   puts and calls, 319
   as share-equivalent of options, 318
Delta approximation, 325
Delta-gamma approximation, 325
Delta-hedging, 330–334
   example, 331–333
   market-maker, 331
   market maker profit, interpreting, 333–334
   market-making and, 330n
   marking-to-market, 332, 333
   rebalancing portfolio, 332
DeMarzo, P., 105n, 473r
Derivatives, 2
   accounting rules, 107n
   nonfinancial firm use, 107
   perspectives, 16–17
   theory, 1
   uses, 15–16
   weather, 174–175
Derivatives markets, 6–11
   existence, 7n
   prediction, 14
   price variability and, 7
   size, 1–2
   start of, 6
Derivatives-related losses, 1n
Diff swaps, 239–240
Dirty price, 216

Discounted cash flow (DCF), 423, 424–433. *See also* DCF valuation
   calculation with elasticity computation, 451
   computing forward price for net cash flow, 429–430, 431–432
   computing separately for cash flow components, 429
   discount rate, 433
   dynamic, 433
   equation, 451
   one-period cash, 424–428
   option pricing and, 423
   standard, 430–431, 432
   static, 433
Discounted present value, 127–128
Discrete dividends, 130, 132
Disney, R., 126n, 365, 366
Distress costs, 104
Diversifiable risk, 13
Dividends
   continuous, 130–131, 132–133
   discrete, 130, 132
   exercising calls prior to, 363
   liquidating, 265n
   option value and, 406n
   payment seasonality, 130n
   present value, 132
   pricing prepaid forwards with, 129–131
   pricing with, 283–285
   of short-sold stock, 21–22
   yield, 130, 131, 178
Dixit, A. K., 448, 475r
Dollar-denominated call options, 258
Dollar/pound exchange rate, 8
Dorgan, B. L., 32
Dow Jones
   CDX, 377–378
   EAGLES, 360
   MITTS, 360
DTCC, 18
Duffie, D., 377n, 379, 475r
Duration, 198–201, 210
   Macaulay, 199–201
   matching, 201–202
   modified, 199
   as slope of bond price graph, 203–204
Dynamic DCF, 433

Early exercise, 260, 262–264
   calls on non-dividend-paying stock, 262–263
   prior to dividend, 263
   for puts, 263–264
   summary, 264
Economic observer, 16
Edwards, F. R., 39n, 118, 119, 475r
Effective annual rate, 455
Elasticity, 430, 432
   call, 327
   computing, 451
   debt, 388
   as leverage measure, 327
   option, 325–329, 388
   in percentage change computation, 326–327
   of portfolios, 329
   put, 327
   volatility and, 327
   weighted average, 329
Electricity, 168–169
   day-ahead price, 169
   forward markets, 169
   forward price, 443
   as nonstorable, 169
   peak-load generation, 442–445
   price discovery, 169
   production, 168
   volatility, 443
Embedded options, 367–369
End user perspective, 16
Energy futures, 168–173
   crude oil, 171–173
   electricity, 168–169
   natural gas, 169–171
Enron
   hidden debt, 226
   swaps, 227
Equity. *See also* Debt
   debt conflict with, 390–392
   delta of, 389

expected return on, 388–392
as options, 383–386
value at maturity, 385
value at time, 384
vega of, 390
Equity Appreciation Growth LinkEd Securities (EAGLES), 360
Equity holders, 390–391
Equity-linked bonds, 352–355. *See also* Bonds
cash coupon payments, 353–354
interest in-kind, 354–355
with options, 359–360
valuation equation, 353
zero-coupon, 352–353
Equity-linked CDs, 84–87. *See also* CDs
fees, 362
originating bank, 361
payoff at expiration, 85, 86
perspectives, 87
as pre-packaged solution, 86–87
pricing, 361–362
reverse-engineering for, 86
structuring, 362
wholesale cost, 361
Equity-linked notes
with options, 359–360
types of, 360
Eurex futures contracts, 9
Euro-denominated put options, 258
Eurodollar futures, 160–164
FRAs versus, 196–197
interest payment, 164n
LIBOR, 178
price construct, 164
price at expiration, 162
specifications, 163
uses, 163
Eurodollar strip, 161–162
European options, 40
American options versus, 260–261
call, 261
call, Black-Scholes formula, 310–313
differences in premiums, 266n, 267n
put, 261
put, binomial tree for pricing, 293
put, Black-Scholes formula, 313
time to expiration, 265
Excel
duration functions, 200n
TBILLEQ function, 218
Exchange options, 255–259, 411
Exchange ratio, 413
Exercise, 40
Exercise price, 40
Exercise style, 40
Exotic options, 113
Expectations hypothesis, 191
Expected commodity price, 166
Expiration, 29, 40
short-selling payoff and profit, 65
time to, 260, 264–265
Exponential function, 456
External financing, hedging and, 104–105

Fabozzi, F. J., 379, 476r
Fair value, 133
Fama, E. F., 433n, 475r
FASB. *See* Financial Accounting Standards Board
Faulkender, M., 119, 475r
Federal Deposit Insurance Corporation (FDIC), 387
Federal Home Loan and Mortgage Corporation (Freddie Mac), 387
Federal National Mortgage Association (Fannie Mae), 387
Fehle, F. R., 473r
Fernandes, C., 401, 480r
Financial Accounting Standards Board (FASB), 15, 404
option grants as compensation, 404
Statement of Financial Accounting Standards (SFAS) 123R, 405, 406
Financial assets
buying, 18–19
commodities versus, 164
dividend yield, 177
short-selling, 19–21
trading of, 3–4
Financial engineering, 16–17, 349

Financial markets
  averages and, 11–12
  overview, 2–11
  purposes, 13
  role of, 11–17, 22
  size and activity measures, 4–5
Financing, short-selling for, 19–20
Fishman, J., 420
Fixed collar offers, 413
Fixed stock offers, 413
Fleming, I., 119, 475r
Fleming, M. J., 210, 475r
Floating collar offers, 413
Floating interest rates, 239
Floating stock offers, 413
Floors, 61–64
Foreign exchange, forward price, 358
Forster, D. M., 236, 475r
Forward contracts, 29–39, 123, 125. *See also* Futures contracts
  binding commitment, 247
  currency, 159
  expiration date, 29
  functions, 29
  hedging with, 94–96
  long (buyer), 31
  off-market, 71
  offsetting position, 140n
  outright purchase versus, 34–36
  payoff, 31–34
  prepaid, 126
  short (seller), 31
  on stock index, 33
  as stock purchase method, 126, 132–139
  summary, 57
  swaps relationship, 219
  synthetic, 68–72, 133–136
  underlying asset, 29
  as zero-cost collars, 111–112
Forward curve
  in backwardation, 168
  in contango, 168
  corn, 165
Forward premium, 133

Forward price, 132, 426–427
  computing for net cash flow, 429, 431–432
  electricity, 169, 443
  expected commodity price and, 166
  foreign exchange, 358
  formula, 139
  in future price prediction, 137–139
  futures comparison, 145
  natural gas, 171, 443
  prepaid, 426
  present value, 429
  risk premium and, 138
Forward rate agreements (FRAs), 193–198, 209–210
  Eurodollar futures versus, 196–197
  settlement in arrears, 193
  settlement at time of borrowing, 193–194
  strip, 228
  synthetic, 194–196
Forward tree, 287, 420–440
  collar, 109, 110
FRA. *See* Forward rate agreements
Freddie Mac. *See* Federal Home Loan and Mortgage Corporation
French, K. R., 145n, 152, 474r, 475r
Froot, K., 104n, 475r
Fuller, K. P., 475r
Funded, 377
Futures contracts, 139–145, 151. *See also* Forward contracts
  Black formula, 316–317
  commodity, 164–168
  energy, 168–173
  Eurodollar, 160–164
  examples, 7, 9
  index, 145–150
  natural gas, 169–171
  Nikkei 225 index, 141
  options on, 297–299, 316–317
  prepaid forward price, 316
  S&P 500, 140–142
  single stock, 141
  stacking, 117
  Treasury-bond, 204–207, 210

Treasury-note, 204–207, 210
variance, 340–341
VIX, 340
weather and housing, 173–177
Futures markets, 32
Futures overlay, 147

Gain, 109–113
Galai, D., 417, 475r
Gamma, 319–320. *See also* Greeks
    call, 319, 320
    convex, 320
    defined, 317
    put, 319, 320
Garbade, K. D., 210, 475r
Garman, M. B., 316, 475r
Garman-Kohlhagen model, 316
Gastineau, G. L., 107n, 119, 473r, 476r
Gates, B., 256–257, 404
Géczy, C., 107, 119, 476r
General collateral repurchase agreements, 208
German government bonds, 10n
Gold
    insurance, 93–100
    prices, 111
    producer's perspective on risk management and, 93–100, 117
Gold-linked notes, 366–367
Gold-mining firms, 366
Goodman, L. S., 379, 476r
Google
    compensation options and, 406, 407
    transferable stock options (TSOs), 407
Gorton, G., 166n, 178, 476r
Government credit guarantees, 387
Graham, J. R., 107, 476r
Graphing
    payoff on CDs, 85
    payoff on forward contract, 33–34
Graybill, F. A., 478r
Greek alphabet, 453
Greeks, 317–329, 342
    for bull spread, 326
    computation, 317

definition of, 317–318
delta, 317, 318–319
gamma, 317, 319–320
as mathematical derivatives, 317n
measures for portfolios, 324–329
mnemonic device, 318
psi, 318, 322–324
rho, 318, 322
theta, 317, 322
use of, 317
vega, 317, 320–322
Grenadier, S. R., 448, 476r
Grinblatt, M., 210, 476r
Gross domestic product (GDP), 5
Grossman, S. J., 129n, 476r
Guay, W., 107, 476r
Güntay, L., 417, 476r
Gupta, A., 233n, 244, 476r
Guth, R. A., 404

Haircuts, 208
Harris, M., 417, 476r
Haug, E. G., 444n, 476r
Haushalter, G. D., 107, 474r, 476r
Hayt, G. S., 474r
Heating degree-day, 174, 175
Heat rate, 442
Hedged profit, 95
Hedge quantity, 149
Hedge ratio, 115n
Hedges
    median, 107
    stack, 116–117
    strip, 116
Hedging, 15
    bankruptcy and, 104
    with call option, 101–103
    debt capacity and, 105
    distress costs and, 104
    empirical evidence on, 107–108
    external financing and, 104–105
    with forward contract, 94–96, 101
    jet fuel with crude oil, 115
    nonfinancial risk management and, 106–107

Hedging *(continued)*
   option risk in absence of, 330
   with put option, 96–97, 98
   reasons against, 106
   reasons for, 104–107
   risk aversion and, 105
   short-selling for, 20
   strategy selection, 103, 117
   taxes and, 105
Historical volatility, 335–336
Hodder, J. E., 436n, 476r
Homeowner's insurance, as put option, 54–55
Horwitz, D. L., 236, 476r
Hoskins, W., 233n, 244, 474r
Housing futures, 175–177
   CME index contract specifications, 176
   use of, 177
Hu, H. T. C., 243, 476r
Huddart, S., 408n, 476r, 479r
Hunter, B., 172
HYDI, 377

IASB. *See* International Accounting Standard Board
IBM, 411
Implied forward rate, 186–188
Implied repo rate, 134, 136
Implied volatility, 336–339. *See also* Volatility
   computing, 337
   examination, 339
   out-of-the-money puts/in-the-money calls, 338
   for S&P 500 options, 339
   spreadsheet function, 337n
   uses, 337
   VIX index, 337, 338
Index. *See also* Stock index
   ABX, 374, 378
   CDS, 376–378
   fair value, 133
   NASDAQ, 149–150
   obligation to buy, 65n
   S&P 500, 141n, 142, 148n
   T-bond, 207
   VIX, 337, 338

Index futures, 145–150
   asset allocation, 146–147
   beta and, 148
   cross-hedging, 147–150
   reasons to use, 145
Ingersoll, J. E. Jr., 397n, 417, 474r, 476r
Inglis, M., 108
Insurance
   amount adjustment, 99–100
   call options as, 56
   cost, reducing, 99
   gold, 93–100
   minimum price with put option, 96–97
   moral hazard, 56n
   options as, 54–56
   put options as, 54–56
   selling, 66–68
   by selling calls, 97–99
   strategies, 61–68
Intel, peak-load manufacturing, 445
Intercontinental Exchange (ICE), 172
Interest
   accrued, 216
   cash, 355–356
   in-kind, 354–355, 356
   open, 5, 142
Interest rate contracts
   continuously compounded, 192n
   default-free, 184
   listing of, 162
   principles, 160
Interest rates
   changing, 457–458
   continuously compounded, 192n, 455
   effective annual, 455
   floating, 239
   language of, 455–456
   measurement, 455
   quoting, 72n
   stacks, 197–198
   strips, 197–198
Interest rate swaps, 227–235
   accreting, 234–235
   amortizing, 234–235

asset, 229
counterparty, 229–230
deferred, 232–233
simple, 227–229
swap curve, 233–234
swap rate computation, 230–232
term sheet, 230, 231
Interest rate swaption, 241
International Accounting Standard Board (IASB), 15, 404
International Swap Dealers Association (ISDA), 222
In-the-money options, 50, 323
Intrade.com, 14
Iowa Electronics Markets, 14
Iron butterfly, 84n
iTraxx index, 7–10

Jagannathan, R., 479r
Jagolinzer, A. D., 366, 477r
Jarrow, R. A., 152, 178, 477r
Jarrow-Rudd tree, 308
Jet fuel, hedging with crude oil, 115, 116
John, K., 473r
Johnson, S. A., 417, 477r
Jorion, P., 1n, 23, 477r
J. P. Morgan, 360, 377, 476r
J. P. Morgan Chase, 226, 227, 404

Kaplan, R. S., 473r
Kappa, 317n
Kealhofer, S., 379, 477r
Klapper, L. F., 473r
Kohlhagen, S. W., 316, 475r
Kothari, S. P., 107, 476r
Kulatilaka, N., 408n, 477r
Kumar, R., 474r

Lambda, 317n
Land
 appreciation, 440
 value, 440
Lattice, 290n
Law of one price, 279

Lease rate, 21–22, 139
commodity, 166–168, 178
negative, 356n
Lel, U., 473r
Lending rates, locking in, 194n
Level 3 Communications
compensation options, 409–412
multiplier, 409, 411–412
outperform stock options (OSO), 409
valuing outperformance feature, 410–411
Leverage, 125–126, 327
Levin, C., 172
Lewis, M., 23, 477r
LIBOR. See London Interbank Offer Rate
Limit orders, 19
Liquidating dividends, 265n
Litzenberger, R. H., 244, 477r
Logarithmic function, 457
Lognormal distribution
binomial tree approximation, 304
comparison, 306, 307
as probability distribution, 304
stock price, 306
Lognormality, binomial model and, 304–307
London Interbank Offer Rate (**LIBOR**), 162
as cost of funds measure, 164
Eurodollar futures contracts based on, 178
quote, 164
stock index swap, 243
swap curve, 233
swap rates, 234
Long, 31
Long forward position, 52
Long positions, 51–52, 53
floors and, 61–65
graphical, 34
payoff diagram, 63
Longstaff, F. A., 210, 476r
Long-Term Capital Management (LTCM), 209
Lowenstein, R., 477r
Low exercise price options (LEPOs), 129
Lublin, J. S., 404
Lucas, D. J., 387, 477r

Ma, C. W., 39n, 475r
Macaulay, F. R., 199n, 477r
Macaulay duration, 199–201. *See also* Duration
　constant, 203n
　examples, 200, 201
　Excel duration function, 200n
　formula, 199
　interpretation, 199
　zero-coupon bond, 200
Maintenance margin, 143
Managerial risk aversion, 105–106
Maor, E., 456n, 477r
Marcus, A. J., 408n, 477r
Margin calls, 143
Margins
　balance decline, 143
　maintenance, 143
　marking to market and, 142–144
Market corner, 207
Market depth, 20
Market-makers, 18
　as counterparty in swaps, 229
　in currency swaps, 237
　delta-hedging, 331
　delta use, 342
　derivatives perspective, 16
　hedging floating-rate payments, 231
　payment, 18
　profit, interpreting, 333–334
　speculative positions and, 330n
Market-making, 330
Market orders, 18
Markets. *See also* Financial markets
　bond, 6
　derivatives, 6–11
　futures, 32
　over-the-counter (OTC), 3, 10–11, 141
　prediction, 13, 14
　stock, 5–6
Market value, 5
Market value CDO, 370
Marking-to-market, 140
　delta-hedging, 332, 333
　margins and, 142–144
　with present value, 144
Marston, R. C., 474r
Masulis, R. W., 417, 475r
Matsunaga, S. R., 477r
McConnell, J. J., 379, 477r
McDonald, R. L., 325n, 334n, 408n, 417, 424n, 436n, 438n, 448, 477r
McMillan, L. G., 89, 477r
Mello, A. S., 118, 119, 476r, 478r
Meriwether, J., 209
Merrill Lynch, 360, 374
Merton, R. C., 1, 23, 57, 89, 209, 260n, 271, 309, 310, 342, 417, 473r, 478r
Metallgesellschaft A. G. (MG), 118
Microsoft
　compensation options and, 404
　SFAS 123 and, 407
Miller, D., 473r
Miller, M., 23, 118, 119, 236, 310, 349n, 475r, 478r
Minton, B. A., 476r
Mitchell, M., 416n, 478r
Modest, D. M., 152, 478r
Modified duration, 199. *See also* Duration
　Excel duration function, 200n
　yield change and, 203n
Modigliani, F., 349n, 478r
Modigliani-Miller theorem, 349–350, 389
Mood, A. M., 478r
Moon, M., 446, 448
Moore, D., 442n
Morgan Stanley, 360, 374, 377
Mullins, D., 209
Multi-period valuations, 433–437. *See also* Valuations
　DCF, 435
　risk-neutral, 435
Multiplier, 409, 411–412
Myers, S., 105n, 392n, 433n, 474r, 478r

Naked writing, 66
NASDAQ index, 149–150, 458
Natural gas, 169–171
　characteristics, 170–171
　forward prices, 171, 443
　volatility, 443

Net payoff, 36
Net present value (NPV), 392
    comparison, 439
    negative, 445
    positive, 445
    static, 444, 445, 448
New York Mercantile Exchange (NYMEX)
    crude oil listing, 170
    futures contracts, 9, 10
    Henry Hub natural gas contract, 170
    light, sweet crude oil contract specifications, 172
Nikkei 225 index futures contract, 141
No arbitrage, 72, 128–129
    bounds, 136–137
    with profit diagrams, 72n
Nondiversifiable risk, 13
Nonfinancial risk management, 106–107
Nonrecombining trees, 290
Northrop Grumman–TRW merger, 413–416
    regulatory approval, 415n
    risk arbitrageurs, 416
Notional amount. *See* Notional value
Notional principal, 228
Notional value, 5
Notes. *See also* Bonds
    with embedded options, 367–369
    equity-linked, 359–360
    gold-linked, 366–367
    structured, with options, 358–366
    structured, without options, 350–358

Offer price, 17
Offer structures, 413
Off-market forward, 71
Off-the-run, 185
Oldfield, G. S., 152, 178, 477r
One-period binomial trees, 277–288
On-the-run, 185
Open interest, 5, 142
Open outcry, 139
Option elasticity, 325–329, 388
Option Greeks. *See* Greeks
Option overwriting, 66

Option prices
    computing, 278–280
    effect on futures price, 298n
    minimum and maximum, 261
Options
    American-style, 40, 250, 260–261, 262–264
    Asian, 363
    at-the-money, 51
    barrier, 363
    on bonds, 254–255
    buying, 41
    call, 39–46
    compensation, 263, 403–412
    coupon bonds with, 358–359
    on currencies, 254, 297, 316
    currency, 258–259
    debt as, 383–386
    delta, 279
    dollar risk, 325–326
    embedded, 367–369
    equity as, 383–386
    equity-linked notes with, 359–360
    European, 260–261
    exchange, 255–259, 411
    to exchange stock, 256–257
    exercising, 248
    exotic, 113
    on futures, 316–317
    as insurance, 54–56
    in-the-money, 50
    mispriced, arbitraging, 282–283
    moneyness, 50
    out-of-the-money, 51
    outperformance, 411
    overpriced, 282
    percentage risk, 326–327
    premiums, 252
    put, 46–51
    put-call parity, 70–72, 87, 250–255
    real, 423–451
    risk premium, 328–329
    Sharpe ratio, 329
    spread, 444
    on stock index, 295–296

Options *(continued)*
   on stocks, 251–254
   on stocks with discrete dividends, 315–316
   strike price, 260
   structured notes with, 358–366
   synthetic, 254
   terminology, 40–41
   time to expiration, 260
   underpriced, 282–283
   volatility, 327
Option writers, 44, 46
OTC. *See* Over-the-counter markets
Out-of-the-money options, 51, 323
Outperformance options, 411
Overpriced options, 282
Over-the-counter (OTC) markets, 3, 141
   growth, 10–11
   trading value, 4

Paddock, J. L., 438n, 478r
Par bonds, 188–189
Par coupons, 188–189
Parity
   for American options, 250
   generalized, 255–259
   pure-discount bond, 255
   put-call, 70–72, 87, 250–255, 270
Parsons, J. E., 118, 119, 478r
Participation
   capped, 364
   price, 359
   rate, 364
Payer swaption, 240
Paylater strategies, 113–114
Payoff, 31–34
   combined, 62
   comparison, 35
   convertible, 395, 396
   forward and futures payoff, 145
   forward contract, 31–34
   graphing, 33–34
   net, 36
   purchased call option, 42–44
   purchased put option, 47–48
   spread option, 444
   VIX futures contract, 340
   written call option, 44–46
   written put option, 48–50
Payoff diagrams, 36
   covered call, 68
   covered put, 69
   illustrated, 37
   long position, 63
   purchased call option, 44
   short position, 66
   zero coupon bonds in, 36–38
Peak-load electricity generation, 442–445
Peak-load facility, 445
Pension Benefit Guarantee Corporation (PBGC), 387
Perpetual options, 440–442
Perpetuities, 356–357
   commodity, 357
   defined, 356
Petersen, M. A., 118, 478r
Petrie, K. N., 417, 478r
Pharmaceutical R&D, 446–448
Pindyck, R. S., 178, 448, 475r, 478r
Portfolios
   elasticity of, 329
   Greek measures for, 324–329
   rebalancing, 332
   risk premium of, 329
Prabhala, N., 476r
Prediction markets, 13, 14
   growth in, 14
   on terrorism, 32
Preferred Equity Redeemable for Common Stock (PERCS), 360
Premium Equity Participating Shares (PEPS), 360
Premiums
   call option, 40, 254
   CDS, 387
   conversion, 397
   decline, 266
   difference, 266
   forward, 133
   forward contract, 132
   option, 252

put option, 46, 254
risk, 138, 328–329, 429–430
Prepaid forward contracts (prepays), 126, 151
  bond, 254
  currency, 157–158
  pricing by analogy, 127
  pricing by arbitrage, 128–129
  pricing by discounted present value, 127–128
  pricing with dividends, 129–131
  pricing in parity relationship, 255
  on stock, 127–132
  use of, 126n
  variable, 364–366
Prepaid forward prices
  Black-Scholes formula, 315
  on currency, 316
  for futures, 316
  on stocks with discrete dividends, 315
Prepaid swaps, 220
Present value
  calculation, 427
  discounted, 127–128
  of dividends, 132
  forward price, 429
  marking to market with, 144
  stack hedges and, 116
Price discovery, 169
Price limits, 140
Price participation, 359
Prices
  ask, 17
  bid, 17
  Black-Scholes, 258
  clean, 216
  dirty, 216
  exercise, 40
  forward, 132, 137–139
  minimum, guaranteeing with call option, 101–103
  minimum, guaranteeing with put option, 96–97
  offer, 17
  spot, 31, 166
  strike, 40, 99, 260, 265–270, 442n
  swap, 222–223
  variability, 7

Price value of a basis point (PVBP), 198
Probability distribution, 96
Procter & Gamble (P&G) swap, 236
Producers, risk management perspective, 93–100, 117
Profit, 36
  call, 252
  hedged, 95
  market-maker, interpreting, 333–334
  purchased call option, 42–44
  purchased put option, 47–48
  put, 252
  short forward position, 94–95
  unhedged, 94
  written call option, 44–46
  written put option, 48–50
Profit diagrams, 36
  bull spread, 75
  butterfly spread, 83
  covered call, 68
  covered put, 69
  long and short call, 58
  long and short forward, 58
  long and short put, 58
  long positions, 53
  option writer, 46
  purchased call option, 45
  purchased collar, 77
  purchased put option, 49
  purchased straddle, 80
  short positions, 53
  written put option, 51
  zero-coupon bonds in, 36–38
Psi, 322–324. *See also* Greeks
  calls, 325
  defined, 318
Pulvino, T., 416n, 478r
Purcell, D., 473r
Purchased calls, 42–44
  payoff and profit for, 42–44
  payoff diagram, 44
  position, 52
  profit diagram, 45
Purchased puts, 47–48
  payoff and profit for, 47–48

Purchased puts *(continued)*
   position, 52
   profit diagram, 49
   in zero-cost collar, 111
Pure-discount bonds, party, 255
Put-call parity, 70–72, 87, 250–255, 270
   Black-Scholes formula and, 313
   equivalence of positions, 71–72
   no arbitrage, 72
   versions, 271
Put options, 46–51, 87, 257. *See also* Options
   American, 295
   barrier, 363
   Black-Scholes formula for, 310–313
   buyers, 47
   delta, 319
   early exercise, 263–264
   elasticity, 327
   euro-denominated, 258
   European, 261, 293
   gamma, 319, 320
   hedging with, 96–97, 98
   as insurance, 54–56
   minimum price guarantee, 96–97
   premium, 46, 254
   profit, 252
   purchased, 47–48
   sellers, 50n
   Sharpe ratio, 329
   summary, 57
   theta, 323
   written, 48–50
Put warrants, 402–403

Quasi-arbitrage, 137

Raghavan, Anita, 141
Ratio spreads, 75–76
Raviv, A., 417, 476r
Real assets, 423
Real options, 423–451
   commodity extraction, 438–442
   DCF and, 424–437
   examples, 438–448

   methodology, 424
   peak-load electricity generation, 442–445
   pharmaceutical R&D, 446–448
   valuation, 424
Receiver swaption, 240
Recombining trees, 290
Recovery rate, 370–373
Reduced transaction cost, 15
Reference assist, 375
Regulatory arbitrage, 15–16, 17
Reinganum, M. R., 152, 478r
Reinsurance market, 13
Rendleman, R. J. Jr., 278, 301, 478r
Repo rate, 208
Repos, 207–208, 210
   general collateral, 208
   haircut, 208
   reverse, 208
   special collateral, 208
   term, 207
Repurchase agreements. *See* Repos
Research and development (R&D), 446–448
Reverse cash-and-carry, 136
Reverse conversion, 253
Reverse repos, 208
Rho, 322. *See also* Greeks
   calls, 324
   defined, 318
Richard, S. F., 152, 479r
Risk
   in absence of hedging, 330
   arbitrageurs, 416
   basis, 114–117, 118
   decisions affecting, 106
   diversifiable, 13
   existence, 12–13
   housing price, 177n
   nondiversifiable, 13
Risk averse, 105
Risk-free rate, 444
Risk management, 15, 93–122
   buyer's perspective, 100–103
   nonfinancial, 106–107
   producer's perspective, 93–100, 117

reasons for, 103–108
for stock-pickers, 150
Risk-neutral pricing, 285
Risk-neutral probability, 229, 285, 427–428, 451
   computation, 428
   economic meaning, 427
   risky cash flows and, 434
Risk-neutral valuation, 431, 432–433. *See also* Valuations
   multi-period, 435
   one-period, 427–428
Risk premium, 138, 429. *See also* Premiums
   options, 328–329
   percentage, 430
   of portfolio, 329
Risk sharing, 12–13
Robinson, F. L., 210, 215, 216, 479r
Rogers, D. A., 107, 474r, 476r
Ronn, A. G., 89, 479r
Ronn, E. I., 89, 479r
Rosansky, V. I., 166n, 178, 473r
Ross, S. A., 474r, 475r
Routledge, B. R., 178, 479r
Rouwenhorst, K. G., 166n, 178, 476r
Rubinstein, M., 260n, 271, 301, 475r
Rudd, A., 477r

S&P 500 futures contract, 140–142
   as cash-settled contract, 141
   specifications, 142
S&P 500 index, 141n, 142, 148n
S&P/Case-Shiller home price index, 175
Saly, P. J., 417, 479r
Schaetze, 10n
Scharfstein, D., 475r
Schmidt, E., 256–257
Scholes, M., 209, 309, 310, 334, 342, 383, 417, 473r
Schrand, C., 476r
Schwartz, E. S., 152, 178, 379, 397n, 417, 438n, 446, 448, 474r, 477r, 479r
Seasonality, 164
Securities and Exchange Commission (SEC), 15
   corporation reporting requirements, 15
   Edgar Web site, 364n

Selling
   covered call, 71
   methods, 18–19
Separate Trading of Registered Interest and Principal of Securities. *See* STRIPS
Seppi, D. J., 479r
Settlements, 3, 38, 193–194, 207, 221–222
Shapiro, A. C., 208, 474r
Shareholders, 392
Share repurchase, 402
Sharpe, W. F., 57, 278, 479r
Sharpe ratio, 329
Shiller, R. J., 23, 479r
Shimko, D., 89n
Short, 31
Short forwards, 31
   position, 52
   profit on, 94
Short positions, 52, 53
   caps and, 65–66
   closing/covering, 21
   graphical, 34
   payoff diagram, 66
Short-sale, 19–21, 22
   cash flows, 22
   examples, 20–21
   reasons for, 19–20
Sick, G. S., 476r
Siegel, D., 152, 178, 438n, 448, 477r, 478r, 479r
Simkins, B., 474r
Simon, R., 404
Single stock futures, 141
Smith, C. W., 104n, 479r
Smith, D. J., 216n, 236, 476r, 479r
Smith, J. L., 478r
Solnik, B., 233n, 474r
Spark spread, 442
Spatt, C. S., 417, 479r
Special collateral repurchase agreements, 208
Speculation
   derivative use for, 15
   short-selling for, 19
   volatility, 79–84
Spot price, 31, 166

Spread options, 444
Spreads, 73–76
   bear, 74
   box, 74–75
   bull, 73, 326
   butterfly, 82–83
   crack, 173
   ratio, 75–76
   vertical, 73
Srivastava, S., 236, 479r
Stack and roll, 117
Stack hedges, 116–117
   interest rate, 197–198
   present value and, 116
Staged investment, 447
Standard DCF valuation, 430–431, 432
Standard deviation, 286, 287
Statement of Financial Accounting Standards (SFAS)
   123R, 405, 406
   133, 107
State variables, 424n
Static DCF, 433
Static NPV, 444, 445, 448
Stein, J., 417, 475r, 479r
Steiner, R., 207n, 479r
Sterbenz, F. P., 417, 479r
Stiglitz, J. E., 129n, 476r
Stigum, M., 210, 215, 216, 479r
Stock indexes, 30
   forward contract on, 33
   options on, 295–296
Stock markets, 5–6
Stock Participation Accreting Redemption Quarterly-pay Security (SPARQS), 360
Stock prices
   bond valuation based on, 401–402
   expected, 127
Stock Return Income Debt Securities (STRIDES), 360
Stocks
   alternative purchase methods, 125–126
   collared, 76
   exchange options, 256–257
   fair value, 133
   forward contract, 126, 132–139
   fully leveraged purchase, 125–126
   options on, 251–254
   outright purchase, 125
   prepaid forward contract, 126, 127–131
   splits and mergers, 4n
   switching to T-bills, 146
   synthetic, 253
   trading, 3
Stoll, H. R., 89, 479r
Stop-loss orders, 19
Storage, 165
Straddles, 79–82
   advantages/disadvantages, 80
   profit diagram, 80
   strangle and, 80–81
   written, 81–82
Strangle, 80–81
Strike price, 40, 442n
   appropriate, choosing, 99
   different, 265–270
   options, 260
   reducing, 99
Strip hedges, 116
   engaging in, 116
   interest rate, 197–198
STRIPS, 185
Structured notes, 350–366
   with options, 358–366
   without options, 350–358
Stulz, R. M., 104n, 479r
Subprime crisis, 374
Subrahmanyam, M. G., 233n, 244, 476r
Sundaram, R. K., 473r
Sundaresan, M., 152, 478r
Sundaresan, S., 210, 479r
Swap curve, 233–234
Swap rate
   computation, 230–232
   as coupon rate on par coupon bond, 232
   expression, 232
   LIBOR, 234
Swaps, 123, 219–246
   accreting, 235
   amortizing, 235

asset, 229
commodity, 220–227
counterparty, 223–224, 229–230
credit default, 243, 373–376
currency, 235–240
default, 243
deferred, 232–233
diff, 239–240
exchange of net payments, 244
financial settlement, 221–222
fixed price in, 244
forward contracts relationship, 219
interest rate, 227–235
market value, 225–227
net payment, 230
obligation, 225
oil, 220–227
payments, 219, 225
physical settlement, 221–222
prepaid, 220
price, 222–223
problems caused by, 226–227
Procter & Gamble (P&G), 236
total return, 241–243, 244
variance, 340–341
Swap spreads, 234
Swap tenor, 228
Swap term, 228
Swaptions, 240–241
commodity, 240
currency, 241
interest rate, 241
payer, 240
receiver, 240
Synthetic forwards, 68–72
creating, 133–135
at prices other than $420, 112–113
short positions, 134
Synthetic FRAs, 194–196
Synthetic options, 254
Synthetic stock, 253
Synthetic T-bills, 253

Tagliaferro, M., 420, 421

Tailing, 117n, 131
Tavakoli, J. M., 244, 379, 479r, 480r
Taxes, hedging and, 105
Taylor series expansion, 202n
Tenor, 240
Term repos, 207
Term sheets, 230, 231
Thales of Miletus, 6, 7
Theta, 322. *See also* Greeks
calls, 323
defined, 317
puts, 323
time decay, 322
Thiagarajan, S. R., 118, 478r
Thurm, S., 408n
Tian, Y. S., 417, 477r
Time decay, 322
Time to expiration, 260, 264–265
American options, 264–265
at-the-money options, 323
European options, 265
in-the-money options, 323
out-of-the-money options, 323
Titman, S., 448, 480r
Todd, R. B., 474r, 476r
Total return payer, 241
Total return swaps, 241–243, 244
cash flows, 242, 243
credit default, 243
default, 243
TRAC-X, 377
Trading
OTC, 3–4
volatility, 339–341
volume, 4
Tranched CDX, 378
Transaction costs, no-arbitrage bounds with, 136–137
Treasury bills
allocating from index futures to, 147
conventions, 216–218
rate change, 9
synthetic, 253
yields, 216–217

Treasury-bond futures contracts, 204–207, 210. *See also* Futures contracts
   cheapest to deliver, 204
   settlement procedures, 207
   success, 206
Treasury inflation-protection securities (TIPS), 185
Treasury-note futures contracts, 204–207, 210. *See also* Futures contracts
   cheapest to deliver, 204
   invoice price, 204
   settlement procedures, 207
   specifications, 205
   success, 206
   10-year, 204n
Triantis, A., 448, 480r
Trigeorgis, L., 433n, 448, 474r, 480r
Trottman, M., 115n
Tsiveriotis, K., 401, 480r
Tuckman, B., 210, 480r
Tufano, P., 118, 480r
Turnbull, S. M., 244, 433n, 478r, 480r
Two-period European call, 289–291. *See also* European options
   call option pricing, 290–291
   tree construction, 289–290
   tree illustration, 289

Unal, H., 476r
Underlying assets, 29
Underpriced options, 282–283
Unfunded, 377
Unhedged profit, 94

Valuations
   bonds, 401–402
   callable bonds, 399, 400
   compensation options, 406
   convertible bonds, 353
   DCF, 425, 428
   equity-linked bonds, 353
   multi-period, 433–437
   real options, 424, 428
   risk-neutral, 427–428, 431, 432
Variable prepaid forwards (VPFs), 364–366

Variance swaps, 340–341
Vega, 320–322. *See also* Greeks
   calls, 321
   defined, 317
   of equity, 390
   for long-lived options, 320n
   as option price derivative, 322n
   units, 322
Vertical spreads, 73
VIX index, 337, 338
Volatility, 335–341
   blended, 410
   butterfly spreads and, 82–84
   continuously compounded returns, 314
   elasticity and, 327
   electricity, 443
   future estimate, 336
   historical, 335–336
   implied, 336–339
   natural gas, 443
   options, 327
   skew, 337
   speculation, 79–84
   as standard deviation of continuously compounded return, 287
   straddles and, 79–82
   time horizon and, 444
   total, 315n
   trading, 339–341
   vega and, 320, 321
Volatility skew, 337, 339, 342

Warrants, 393–394
   exercise of, 394
   outstanding, 394
   put, 402–403
Weather derivatives, 174–175
Weston, J., 107, 119, 473r
White, G. L., 108
Writing
   covered, 66
   covered call, 67–68, 72
   naked, 66

Written call options, 44–46
    payoff and profit for, 44–46
    position, 52
    profit diagram, 46
Written put option, 48–50
    payoff and profit for, 48–50
    position, 52
    profit diagram, 51
Written straddles, 81–82
    profit at expiration, 82
    profit diagram, 83
Wyden, Ron, 32

Yeung, E., 477r
Yield curve, 186
Yields
    ask, 216
    bond, 215
    continuously compounded, 191–192
    convenience, 167
    dividend, 130, 131
    Treasury bill, 216–217
    U.S. government bills, notes, bonds, 184
Yield to maturity, 185–186
Yurday, E. C., 377n, 475r

Zero-cost collars, 77–78. *See also* Collars
    bootstrapping, 189
    constructing, 109–111
    forward contracts as, 111–112
    unhedged position against, 111, 112
Zero-coupon bonds, 64, 209. *See also* Bonds
    commodity-linked, 355–357
    equity-linked, 352–353
    implied forward price, 187
    Macaulay duration, 200
    paying cash, 351
    in payoff/profit diagrams, 36–38
    price, 351
    STRIPS, 185
    yield to maturity, 185–186
Zero-coupon yield curve, 186
Zwick, S., 141, 480r